About the Authors

LEN COLODNY is the bestselling coauthor of *Silent Coup: The Removal of a President*, which spent thirteen weeks on the *New York Times* bestseller list. He lives in Florida.

TOM SHACHTMAN is the author of thirty books, including *Decade of Shocks, 1963–1974*; *Absolute Zero and the Conquest of Cold*; and *Rumspringa: To Be or Not to Be Amish*. He lives in Connecticut.

The Forty Years War

ALSO BY LEN COLODNY

Silent Coup: The Removal of a President (with Robert Gettlin)

ALSO BY TOM SHACHTMAN

Airlift to America

Rumspringa: To Be or Not to Be Amish

Dead Center: Behind the Scenes at the World's Largest Medical Examiner's Offfice (with Shiya Ribowsky)

Laboratory Warriors

"I Seek My Brethren"

Absolute Zero and the Conquest of Cold

Around the Block

The Inarticulate Society

Skyscraper Dreams

Decade of Shocks, 1963–1974: Dallas to Watergate

The Phony War, 1939–1940

Edith and Woodrow

The Day America Crashed

THE FORTY YEARS WAR

The Rise and Fall of the Neocons, from Nixon to Obama

LEN COLODNY and TOM SHACHTMAN

HARPER PERENNIAL

NEW YORK • LONDON • TORONTO • SYDNEY • NEW DELHI • AUCKLAND

HARPER ● PERENNIAL

A hardcover edition of this book was published in 2009 by Harper, an imprint of HarperCollins Publishers.

THE FORTY YEARS WAR. Copyright © 2009 by Len Colodny and Tom Shachtman. All rights reserved. Printed in the United States of America. No part of this book may be used or reproduced in any manner whatsoever without written permission except in the case of brief quotations embodied in critical articles and reviews. For information address HarperCollins Publishers, 10 East 53rd Street, New York, NY 10022.

HarperCollins books may be purchased for educational, business, or sales promotional use. For information please write: Special Markets Department, HarperCollins Publishers, 10 East 53rd Street, New York, NY 10022.

FIRST HARPER PERENNIAL EDITION PUBLISHED 2010.

Designed by Renato Stanisic

Library of Congress Cataloging-in-Publication Data is available upon request.

ISBN 978-0-06-168829-4

10 11 12 13 14   OV/RRD   10 9 8 7 6 5 4 3 2 1

LEN COLODNY

To my grandchildren, Samantha Peyton Colodny and Jeremy Len Hollis, with love, and the hope that they will live in a more peaceful world. And in memoriam to Howard S. Liebengood, friend, adviser, and "great American."

TOM SHACHTMAN

To Harriet, as always, my inspiration and chief sounding board.

Quarrels would not last so long if the fault were on only one side.
—FRANÇOIS DE LA ROCHEFOUCAULD, 1613–1680

Contents

Foreword xi

Prologue: Is This the Beginning of the End of the Neocons? 1

BOOK ONE: OPPOSING NIXON
Section I: The Road to China
1 Nixon's Foreign Policy Dreams 13
2 The Anti-Nixon 23
3 Sending Signals 32
4 Young Men in a Hurry 48
5 "Actual or Feigned" 59
6 Cambodia and Echo 72
7 Crises Expose Fissures 84
8 Approaching the Zenith 96

Section II: Undermining the Presidency
9 Making Allies into Enemies 107
10 "A Federal Offense of the Highest Order" 120
11 "Three out of Three, Mr. President" 132
12 A Meeting of Mind-Sets 146
13 Actions and Reactions 158

Section III: The Haig Administration
14 Three Quick Strikes 175
15 Nullifying Nixon 193
16 Protecting the Flanks 210
17 Endgame 216

BOOK TWO: THE TRIUMPH OF THE NEOCONS
Section IV: The Post-Nixon Years
18 A Short Honeymoon 229
19 Yielding to the Right 249
20 Primary Battles 260
21 The Carter Interregnum 272

Section V: The Reagan Evolution
22 Fits and Starts 293
23 The High Tide of Anti-Communism, and After 304
24 Not Going to Baghdad 326
25 The Post–Cold War Dilemma 345

Section VI: Full Power
26 Neocons Versus Clinton 359
27 From Candidate to Bush 43 372
28 The Neocon Hour of Triumph 385
29 The Cheney Regency 406
30 Losing Power 417

Epilogue: Foreign Affairs and the Election of 2008 427

Acknowledgments 435
Notes and Bibliography 437
Index 469

Foreword

"The real war," warned Walt Whitman, "will never get in the books." He was tolling history's neglect, or evasion, of the "infernal background" and bleak "interiors" of the American Civil War. As usual, the poet was right about his countrymen. It took more than a century for what he called "surface courtesies" in the hagiography of authors North and South to yield to the revelation of more authentic, inglorious reality.

Whitman's omen obviously applied to much of our past, and nowhere more crucially than in the stunted writing about recent American foreign policy. We may read a growing literature in praise or blame for what the United States has done in the world over the past four decades, but still lethally little of the people and politics who are the essence of that history and its grim hold on the present. Getting the "infernal background" and "interiors" of policy makers into a book, *The Forty Years War* is an incomparable contribution to our recent history. Whitman would smile.

With meticulous research and dauntless investigative journalism, Len Colodny and Tom Shachtman not only rewrite much of the record since the 1970s but disclose decisive portions of it for the first time. The book opens with a masterful perspective on the fateful presidency of a Richard Nixon who still shapes our world. Continuing Colodny's groundbreaking work with Robert Gettlin in *Silent Coup*, the authors offer a further revision of what they call the "toxic mix of fact, myth, and distortions" in the conventional view of the Watergate scandal, and a stunning revelation of how much Nixon's historic fall traced to his statesmanship as well as his criminality—how this deeply flawed yet visionary president was both a casus belli and early casualty of the Forty Years War.

The further treasure in these pages is what the authors excavate of more recent history, buried until now in unreleased archives and prevailing cliché. The post-Nixon years marked the more dramatic rise, furtive and open, of the neoconservatives—known by the aptly crude abbreviation "neocons"—who are the now fearsome, now ludicrous belligerents in the book's four-decade conflict, though the often-unnamed forces behind them are no less decisive. In many respects, crucial history is probed here in depth for the first time: the lasting significance of Gerald Ford's brief but compromised, compromising presidency, the inner battles of Jimmy Carter's administration against the massive war chest and confected credentials of unprecedented reaction, the startlingly mixed record of conservative icon Ronald Reagan in the Oval Office, and the dozen locust years in the presidencies of George Herbert Walker Bush and Bill Clinton, in which Washington lost the chance to redefine post–cold war foreign policy by the best of past statesmanship, and so opened the way to neocons with the worst of it.

Colodny and Shachtman are surely right that the latter Reagan era, and the sequel of the elder George Bush, were marked by "a very Nixonian pragmatism." Yet it was moderation without vision, at a revolutionary moment when vision was indispensable. The two Clinton terms of shallow policy and characterless leadership that followed are a bleak reminder of how much the ensuing neocon triumph owed to the failure, default, and outright complicity of the neo-liberal Democratic establishment. As the authors document, the wrack and ruin of the Forty Years War—from blind collusions in the Watergate crisis to the post-9/11 enabling acts of George W. Bush by a Democratic Congress—have been a bipartisan disaster.

The ultimate gift of this book is its cast of characters. Whether these names are famous, forgotten, or simply never noticed, we live with the legacy of them all. At the heart of the drama—at the starting point of the war, at every action, and in symbolic terms at its present stage, well after his death—stands arguably the most important unknown figure in recent American history, the redoubtable Fritz G. A. Kraemer. The bureaucratic-political as well as ideological godfather of the neocons, Kraemer, with his fascinating story, must be left to the coming pages. As with so much the authors reveal, it is enough to say that it is all richly symbolic. The hold of Old World tribalism over Washington's foreign policy through the second half of the twentieth century and the start of the twenty-first is one of the great unacknowledged scandals in American governance. That the United States approached the world of 9/11, and its tumultuous aftermath, in bondage to the mentality of an expatriate European official educated in the 1920s—a bureaucrat steeped in the stereotypes of a vanished world—epitomizes our failure as a nation to conduct ourselves knowledgeably and responsibly in world affairs.

The long-neglected "interiors" of the neocon world shown in this book hardly add up to the black magic by which diffident politicians, as well as most of the media and public, seem to believe policy is made. Whitman's "infernal background" is all here—the banality, expedience, myths, relentless shallowness, the feet-of-clay fiction of a global-affairs "elite" on either side of the aisle. Their noses pressed firmly to the windows of a foreign policy establishment of suitably anticommunist Democrats and a rapidly dwindling remnant of moderate Republicans (even dilettantes have standards, after all), the neocon wannabes soon gave up. Led by touts and pamphleteers, they played shrewdly to the post-détente arms control anxiety of military-industrial giants, as well as to the old fears and felt exclusion of corporate and individual wealth, to build their own mimicking foundations, institutes, and centers through the 1970s and 1980s. These resulting think tanks—or "think pits," as author and editor Sam Smith has called them—were remarkable exercises in the sociology of knowledge without knowledge, producing for their hundreds of millions in supposedly public-interest donations a flood of Kraemeresque indoctrination and propaganda—yet not a single enduring work of scholarship about either the outside world or the history of American diplomacy.

The lushly funded faux-establishment did serve its actual purpose, however, as employment agency and welfare office. By the turn of the century, it had propagated a fiercely right-wing and anachronistic government-in-waiting of credentialed mediocrities, well prepared, as a critic once said in despair of the Ottoman Empire general staff, not to fight even the irrelevant last war but the one before. Enter peculiarly vulnerable George W. Bush, neocon avatars Dick Cheney and Don Rumsfeld, along with the variously feeble opposition of Colin Powell and Condoleezza Rice, and there was the critical mass of disaster. As *The Forty Years War* chronicles, their base self-promotion and intellectual emptiness would have been merely pathetic if it had not been paid for in a burst of blood in West Baghdad or the Helmand Valley, in hours of cemetery tears and years of hospital agony, in the squandering of national treasure from which, unlike the previous four decades of waste and plunder, there will be no escape.

What follows is both primer and indictment. It is impossible to overestimate the true cost of this history, of the wantonness of the power seeking and of the bipartisan political decadence that allowed it to flourish and succeed. Not since David Halberstam's *The Best and the Brightest* has a work so captured the culture and inner reality of our common malfeasance before the world. And, like Halberstam's classic, it is also both portent and warning.

As President Barack Obama's establishment regime takes office with its own tribal politics and mentality, its own largely unknown provenance, the war traced here goes relentlessly on—not only between the new officialdom and die-hard neocons in and out of government, but deep within the ranks of a beleaguered presidency where unseen battles shape our future much as they did over the past four decades.

Whitman knew that the lethal secrets of great struggles began to disappear from the beginning. "Think how much, and of importance, will be—how much, civic and military, has already been," he wrote well before Appomattox, "buried in the grave, in eternal darkness." With the example and inspiration of *The Forty Years War*, we can only hope that other historians will emerge with sequels to bring further light to these dark corners.

—*Roger Morris*

THE FORTY YEARS WAR

President George W. Bush, Vice President Dick Cheney, and Secretary of Defense Donald Rumsfeld, during Rumsfeld's mustering-out ceremony, December 15, 2006. *(Department of Defense)*

Prologue

Is This the Beginning of the End of the Neocons?

O n Friday, December 15, 2006, a clear, cool day in Washington, D.C., the nineteen-gun salute at the Pentagon could be heard for miles as the military began the ceremonies for the retiring secretary of defense, seventy-four-year-old Donald H. Rumsfeld. As Rumsfeld strode the grounds, inspecting the formal phalanxes of army, navy, and air force warriors in full-dress uniforms, the pomp and ritual conveyed the sense of an era coming to an end.

Since his arrival at the Defense Department in 2001, Rumsfeld and the professional military had battled continuously over the conduct of the wars in Iraq and Afghanistan and over his attempts to restructure America's armed forces. Yet the Pentagon brass had grown to appreciate him, and on this retirement day each service would award him a medal. They would even present one to his wife.

In their speeches, President George W. Bush and Vice President Richard B. Cheney would praise Rumsfeld to an audience of military and civilian Department of Defense employees, senators, a former chairman of the Joint Chiefs of Staff, former Rumsfeld associates, friends, family, and members of the press. But every adult in the crowd knew that the disastrous November midterm elections, in which Republicans had lost many seats in Congress, had cost Rumsfeld his job; two days later, Bush forced him to resign. The secretary had stayed on until the Senate confirmed his successor, Robert M. Gates, who would take over on the following Monday. A long time before, during the Ford administration, Donald Rumsfeld had been the youngest secretary of defense in history. Today he would leave as the oldest.

Rumsfeld had become a lightning rod for criticism of the Bush administration's foreign policy. Retired professional military commanders, newspaper and television commentators, dozens of Democratic senators and congressmen, and some Republican legislators had repeatedly called for his resignation. There had been a sense, reporter Thomas Ricks observed, that "as long as Donald Rumsfeld was defense secretary, it would have been difficult to reorient the U.S. effort in Iraq." The reason, Ricks suggested, was Rumsfeld's "inability to change course" after he made a mistake—what he called the secretary's "tragic flaw." Reporter Bradley Graham would later reveal that Bush had determined to fire Rumsfeld by early October 2006, a month before the election. When in November voters reversed the standing Republican majority in the Senate and increased the Democrats' majority in the House of Representatives—a result widely interpreted as a rejection of the administration's conduct of the war in Iraq—Rumsfeld became the administration's sacrificial lamb. Firing Rumsfeld ostensibly freed President Bush to pursue a new direction in Iraq.

Rumsfeld refused to go quietly. On the day before the election, sensing that the axe was coming, he completed a memo to the president designed to show he had the flexibility to solicit and champion ideas for change of direction. "Clearly, what U.S. forces are currently doing in Iraq is not working well enough or fast enough," he wrote, suggesting setting new social, political, and military benchmarks for the Iraqi and American governments, training additional Iraqi troops and police, and placing more U.S. troops on the Syrian and Iranian borders to prevent the entry of foreign terrorists. If the memo was positioned to save Rumsfeld's job, it failed; Bush fired him anyway. Some leading congressional Republicans opined that if Bush had forced Rumsfeld's resignation before the election, as they had recommended, their party would have retained control of the Senate.

At the retirement ceremony, the president lauded Rumsfeld for producing "more profound change at the Department of Defense over the past six years than at any time since the department's creation in the late 1940s. . . . These changes were not easy, but . . . this man knows how to lead, and he did, and the country is better off for it."

Vice President Cheney had fought Rumsfeld's removal, according to newspaper reports, because it signaled a retreat from the administration's war policies, but also because he and Rumsfeld had been the closest of allies since 1969. As Cheney recalled in his own speech at the ceremony, Rumsfeld had hired him, right out of graduate school, for a job in the administration of Richard Nixon. Cheney underscored his and Rumsfeld's kinship by pointing out that he had followed Rumsfeld in becoming a White House chief of staff, a secretary of defense, and a member of the House. Rumsfeld was the toughest boss he ever had, Cheney said, but one who never demanded more of his subordinates than he did of himself. "In this hour of transition," the vice president concluded, "every member of our military, and every person at the Pentagon, can be certain that America will stay on the offensive. We will stay in the fight until [the terrorists'] threat is defeated and our children and grandchildren can live in a safer world." It was a sentiment often expressed by well-known Rumsfeld subordinates former deputy secretary of defense Paul D. Wolfowitz and former undersecretary for defense policy Douglas J. Feith, both in the audience and both long associated with the foreign policy school known as "neoconservatism."

After Cheney, Rumsfeld took his turn at the podium. An awkward speaker in his early days in Washington, he had become a polished one, holding his own during more than four hundred press conferences since 2001. Though he announced that he had decided not to look backward in retirement, the most memorable line in his remarks reached back to the origins of Rumsfeld's worldview, decades in the past. "When I last departed this post in 1977," he reminded the audience, "I left cautioning that weakness is provocative, that weakness inevitably entices aggressors into acts that they would otherwise avoid." It was a posture devised for a Cold War world in which the United States was still squared off against the USSR—but even with the Cold War long over, he insisted, his message about dealing with the future needed to be the same:

> It should be clear that not only is weakness provocative, but [that] the perception of weakness on our part can be provocative, as well. A conclusion by our enemies that the United States lacks the will or the resolve to carry out missions that demand sacrifice and demand patience is every bit as dangerous as an imbalance of conventional military power.

Provocative weakness: Though some senior Pentagon officials might have recognized the phrase, few who saw clips from Rumsfeld's speech, or read the transcript, would have understood that with those words Rumsfeld was doing what the Bush administration had done since it took office in 2001: drawing on the rhetoric, and the thinking, of a little-known, now-deceased civilian intellectual at the Pentagon, Dr. Fritz G. A. Kraemer.

Although the public had no awareness of Fritz Kraemer, he had influenced generals, service secretaries, secretaries of defense, and secretaries of state since the 1940s. It was Kraemer who had coined the term "provocative weakness." That concept, which reflected his militaristic approach to foreign policy, along with other Kraemer tenets such as his rejection of diplomacy and his emphasis on morality as a guide for policy, made Kraemer the unacknowledged godfather of the George W. Bush administration's ways of relating the United States to the rest of the world—more so than the philosophies of the University of Chicago's Leo Strauss or of those Trotskyites-turned-conservatives who founded the neocon movement. "Fortunately," as Wolfowitz said in 2004, "we do have a president" [George W. Bush] who is "prepared to see [the world and the evil in it] the way Fritz Kraemer would have seen it." And the ideas they shared ranged from Kraemer's basal distrust of international organizations such as the United Nations, to his preference for elite rule, to his belief in the need for the United States to spread democracy, to his championing of Christianity.

Rumsfeld's echoing of Kraemer, first in 1977 and again in 2006, testified to the influence and longevity of ideas that Kraemer had disseminated in off-the-record tutorials with Rumsfeld, Henry Kissinger, Alexander Haig, Wolfowitz, Richard Perle, and many others from the 1940s until shortly before his death in 2003. Kissinger and Haig, his most important protégés, had each struggled during their years as presidential advisers to reconcile their loyalty to their commanders in chief with their allegiance to Kraemer's ideas. Others who had listened closely to Kraemer included James Schlesinger, another secretary of defense under Nixon and Ford; conservative Democratic senator Henry M. "Scoop" Jackson; Brigadier General Vernon A. Walters, who became acting head of the CIA; chief arms limitation negotiators General Ed Rowny and Fred Iklé; Admiral Elmo Zumwalt, chief naval officer during the Nixon years; and General Creighton Abrams, commander of U.S. forces during the war in Vietnam.

Kraemer's militaristic tenets and the geopolitical strategies based on them, and the senior officials who agreed with his ideas and used them as a basis for foreign and military policies, constituted one side, the ideologues' side, of a forty years war fought against the equally strong pragmatist side for control of U.S. foreign policy. That war began when Richard M. Nixon took office in 1969 and continued to the start of Barack H. Obama's presidency in 2009.

Richard Nixon's ascension to the presidency gave him the opportunity to make a dramatic transition in American foreign policy, a radical departure from the policies of the first quarter century of the Cold War. But confronted with an intractable shooting war in Vietnam, he became enmeshed in finding a way out, a struggle that affected all of his other foreign policy initiatives. How to extract the United States from Vietnam was the main subject of the only known meeting between Nixon and Fritz Kraemer, in the Oval Office just before the 1972 election. It was also the main subject of contention in the early phases of the forty years war between those "pragmatists" who embraced Nixon's approach to policy and those "ideologues"—later known as the neoconservatives—whose policies were dictated less by circumstance than by certain fixed principles.

The defining foreign policy of the George W. Bush administration was the preemptive war in Iraq. But while reporters and historians had noted the similarities between the long wars in Iraq and Vietnam, few had examined the links between what happened during the Richard M. Nixon administration and during the George W. Bush administration. The two were connected in many important ways, not the least of which was through the adoption of neoconservative principles by such latterly prominent men as Rumsfeld, Cheney, Wolfowitz, and Perle, who began their public careers and fashioned their hard-line views under Nixon.

In his 2006 farewell speech, Rumsfeld pointed to similarities between the challenges of the Cold War and those of the era that began on September 11, 2001, when terrorists attacked the World Trade Center in New York City and the Pentagon. The Cold War struggle against Communism, Rumsfeld said, had been long and of "uncertain duration," a war against an "ascendant" ideology and an empire that was "clearly expanding." The same, he implied, could be said for the current, ongoing war against militant Islam's ideology and expansionist empire.

The Nixonian phase of the Cold War did set the mold for Bush's "global war on terror," and not only in those ways that Rumsfeld identified. The deeper and less obvious connection between the accomplishments and failures of the Nixon administration and those of the Bush administration goes beyond the negative and positive lessons about strategies and tactics that such men as Rumsfeld, Cheney, Perle, and Wolfowitz took from their early days—lessons they would draw upon in the twenty-first century. Yet this connection has largely remained hidden—at least in part because most of what the public knows or remembers about the Nixon years has been filtered through the prism of Watergate, with its toxic mix of fact, myth, and distortions. The story of Nixon's presidency, and particularly of his fall, concerns matters well beyond the conventional story of Watergate, with its emphasis on the actions of Nixon's enemies on the left. Nixon's fall had as much to do with his triumphs, his radical alterations to the status quo ante in foreign policy—the successful opening to China, détente with the Soviet Union, and a negotiated end to the war in Vietnam—and with his enemies on the right as it did with the burglary at the Watergate complex and the cover-up that followed.

After Nixon's fall conservative enemies gained strength from having contributed to that fall and they then successfully stymied the Nixonian foreign policies of the Gerald Ford and Jimmy Carter administrations. For the ideologues, these were the years of negative accomplishment. The early Reagan era was a time of potential positive accomplishments for them, but as the Soviet Union waned, a very Nixonian pragmatism resurfaced and prevailed in the later Reagan years and during the presidency of George H. W. Bush.

The end of the Cold War presented opportunities and challenges for pragmatists and ideologues alike. After the disintegration of the Communist empire, the ideologues had to look elsewhere for a cause to unite them. The pragmatists were also left without a coherent rationale on which to base decisions on foreign policy; the result was the capricious, ad hoc approach to policy decisions that marked the presidency of Bill Clinton. During the Clinton years, a group of out-of-office ideologues opposed to Clinton came together to fashion an alternative: a simplified, neoconservative foreign policy they hoped to put into practice when Clinton left office. George W. Bush chose several members of this movement as key advisers—finally handing the neoconservatives the levers of foreign policy, a goal they had long held but never before attained.

Neocon idealism and Kraemerite militarism meshed most perfectly as the George W. Bush administration grappled with how to formulate the proper American response to the attacks of September 11. Advocates of diplomacy and pragmatism were scarce within the councils of power, and their answers to the overwhelming problems then facing the United States seemed inadequate to the situation. Ideology ruled the day; the Bush administration framed its military and other actions to counter the new terrorist threat in terms of America's strength, resolve, and moral superiority, and those actions were greeted with widespread public support.

Yet that moment of neocon triumph lasted only a year. By the time the administration invaded Iraq in early 2003, public opinion had begun to shift—and increasingly, as the occupation of Iraq dragged on and on, the American people grew less confident in the neocons' assertions of principle, and more concerned about the pragmatic costs of war.

By 2006, the balance had shifted to favor a less didactic approach to American foreign policy. When the congressionally chartered Iraq Study Group (ISG) issued its report, the *Washington Post* commented that it might as well be called "The Realist Manifesto." Citing the "diminishing" U.S. influence within Iraq, the bipartisan ISG panel recommended two pragmatic and thoroughly Nixonian measures that already had widespread public support: phased U.S. troop withdrawals from Iraq, and U.S. dialogues with Iraq's neighbors Iran and Syria. The recommendations were completely at odds with the Bush administration positions, which sought to raise the number of troops in Iraq for a "surge," and to shun Iran and Syria so long as those countries were controlled by dictatorial regimes unfriendly to the United States and openly critical of U.S. actions.

Some commentators suggested that the 2006 election results, Rumsfeld's firing, and the ISG report signaled the end of neocon influence on foreign policy, or at least the beginning of the end. Some neocons outside the administration even began to criticize Bush, Cheney, and Rumsfeld for their conduct of the war in Iraq. But they continued to assert that the United States had been correct in invading Iraq in the first place, in attempting to instill democracy there and elsewhere, and in refusing to engage in diplomatic deal making with "axis of evil" regimes. Would that stance continue to appeal to enough Americans for it to prevail?

The Bush administration held its ground, expressing its determination to "win" in Iraq despite the vote of no confidence it had received in 2006. Though the surge was regarded in many quarters as a success, having brought down sectarian violence, by the end of Bush's second term there was still no end in sight for what was now a deeply unpopular war.

The 2008 election would be the first since 1952 in which neither the incumbent president nor his vice president was a candidate, thus presenting an opportunity for new directions. As the campaign and primaries rolled on, it became clear that the leading Republican candidates, Senator John McCain and former Massachusetts governor Mitt Romney, were both being advised on foreign policy by neocons and were committed to an ideological, militarist view of foreign policy. Meanwhile, the leading candidates on the Democratic side, Senators Hillary Clinton and Barack Obama, were pragmatists, Obama calling for direct talks with Iran and an increase in troop levels in Afghanistan.

When the primaries concluded and the winners were McCain and Obama, voters in the general election were presented with an even clearer choice between two philosophies. In his saber-rattling campaign rhetoric McCain frequently echoed Fritz Kraemer, stressing the need to actively counter all threats in a hostile world. Obama, by contrast, offered a pragmatic array of policies, embracing the use of military power where necessary but in other areas advocating diplomacy to head off future problems.

Would Obama's election mean the triumph of pragmatism? Or would the neocons simply go underground, regroup, and wait for another chance to push the United States into an aggressive, military-based posture versus the rest of the world? In short, would the forty years war over foreign policy continue?

We believe the answer to that last question can be found in deciphering how and why that long war began, and how and why it was able to continue, unabated, through the course of seven presidencies.

Book One

OPPOSING NIXON

President Richard Nixon, National Security Adviser Henry Kissinger, and General Alexander Haig, discussing Vietnam at Camp David, November 13, 1972. *(Ollie Atkins, White House)*

SECTION I

The Road to China

Privates Henry Kissinger and Fritz Kraemer, Camp
Claiborne, Louisiana, 1944. *(World Security Network)*

1

Nixon's Foreign Policy Dreams

Ａll American presidents, as they enter office, have big dreams. Some approach the presidency wanting to alter the social structure of the country. Richard M. Nixon wanted to change the international alignment of nations. His blueprint for American foreign policy entailed radical changes to the status quo based on what he considered a realistic assessment of the world. He was planning to pursue détente with America's main Cold War enemy, the Soviet Union; to bring about a rapprochement with "Red China," the People's Republic of China, a country that for decades he had pushed the United States to isolate from world affairs; and to negotiate a quick settlement to the war in Vietnam, a war he had supported from the sidelines and had repeatedly urged the U.S. government to win on the battlefield. Nixon's foreign policy dreams had been in formation for a decade. They affected how he ran his campaign, how he chose personnel for his administration, and how he conducted its affairs once in office.

As Nixon was inaugurated in January 1969, the noted foreign policy historian Hans Morgenthau was just publishing A New Foreign Policy for the United States, in which he argued that American foreign policy "has lived during the last decade or so on the intellectual capital . . . accumulated in the famous fifteen weeks of the spring of 1947 when the policy of containment, the Truman Doctrine, and the Marshall Plan fashioned a new American foreign policy. . . . This capital has now been nearly exhausted."

The main reason for exhaustion was the apparent stalemate of the war in Vietnam, which the United States was fighting against an enemy backed by the main Communist powers, the Union of Soviet Socialist Republics and the People's Republic of China. Recognizing the toll the war had taken, Nixon planned to supersede the goal of containment that had informed the policies of Truman, Eisenhower, Kennedy, and Johnson, and that had mired the United States in Vietnam, with something quite different: engagement with America's Communist enemies. He envisioned this approach bringing him a string of policy triumphs and a place in history as a grand peacemaker.

During his years as a representative, senator, and vice president (1947–1961), Nixon had become the country's leading anti-communist. Though many still considered him as such, he spent much of the 1960s decoupling himself from his earlier, inflexible stance. One landmark in this transformation came on July 29, 1967, in a speech to the Bohemian Club, a private association of Republican movers and shakers, at their annual retreat near San Francisco.

In the address, Nixon argued that more changes had taken place in a single generation than ever before in human history, and the result was a "new world" in which total Soviet dominance of Communist countries had diminished, replaced by "a bitter struggle for leadership" between the USSR and China. And this internal Communist struggle opened the door for American "discussions with the Soviet leaders at all levels . . . to explore the areas where bilateral agreements would reduce tensions."

Nixon widened this opening in an article in the October 1967 issue of *Foreign Affairs*. "Asia after Vietnam" envisioned a series of new regional defense pacts to meet the challenges of future Vietnam-type wars and to counter the might of China. "The regional pact becomes a buffer separating the distant great power from the immediate threat. Only if the buffer proves insufficient does the great power become involved, and then in terms that make victory more attainable and the enterprise more palatable," Nixon ventured. Though "Red China's threat is clear, present, and insistently and repeatedly expressed," he wrote,

American policy toward Asia must come urgently to grips with the reality of China. This does not mean . . . rushing to grant recognition to [Beijing], to admit it to the United Nations and to ply it with offers of trade—all of which would serve to confirm its rulers in their present course. . . . [But] we simply cannot afford to leave China forever outside the family of nations, there to nurture its fantasies, cherish its hates and threaten its neighbors. There is no place on this small planet for a billion of its potentially most able people to live in angry isolation.

Nixon's article seems to have rung few alarm bells among his anti-Communist friends, perhaps because he emphasized the need to keep one's powder dry while talking with the enemy. But Nixon recognized that his ideas ran counter to his public image, and he offered his new rationale only to sophisticated audiences. In his 1968 campaign rhetoric, he largely maintained his posture as the strongest anti-Communist candidate in the race. Nonetheless, in his acceptance speech at the Republican convention that year, he extended a surprisingly straightforward olive branch:

> To the leaders of the Communist world, we say: After an era of confrontation, the time has come for an era of negotiation. Where the world's superpowers are concerned, there is no acceptable alternative to peaceful negotiation. . . . The years just ahead can bring a breakthrough for peace [through] intensive negotiations [and] a determined search for those areas of accommodation . . . on which a climate of mutual trust can eventually be built.

To most of his listeners, and to the country's reporters and columnists, his phrases seemed no more than rhetoric, the sort of bland pledge that politicians often utter but seldom follow up with action. Nixon would manage to complete the 1968 race without having to face serious questions that might have forced him to elaborate on his foreign policy intentions.

The American public's distaste for the war had pushed President Johnson to take himself out of the running for reelection. Nixon began the general election campaign with a lead over Johnson's vice president, Hubert H. Humphrey, mostly because of the Republican candidate's frequently repeated promise to bring the war in Vietnam to an end. But Nixon refused to say precisely how he planned to end the war, and Democrats soon began charging that his "secret plan" was merely an election-season ploy. The "secret plan" was like a mirror that reflected only the image the gazer wished to see: Nixon haters saw it as a transparent ruse, convinced there was no such plan. His centrist supporters saw it as a promise to end the war diplomatically. And his conservative partisans saw it as a vow to win the war on the battlefield.

Nixon knew he needed conservatives to win the election. Twenty years later, during the 1988 election season, he reportedly told George H. W. Bush that he'd learned that "you can't win the election with just these people. But you can't win the election without these people." To help maintain support on the right during the 1968 campaign, Nixon appointed three young conservatives as advisers on foreign affairs: Richard V. Allen, Richard Whalen, and Martin Anderson. Nixon took Allen on at the request of a

major campaign donor who was also a large supporter of the Hoover Institution, where Allen had worked, but made little use of him, sending Allen to
Korea and Japan to explain the implications of his *Foreign Affairs* article to
leaders there, and enlisting him to produce a superfluous book called *Nixon
on the Issues.*

The most notable policy intellectual angling for a position on the Nixon
campaign was Henry A. Kissinger, a Harvard professor who for years had
been advising New York's moderate Republican governor, Nelson Rockefeller. After Nixon defeated Rockefeller in the primaries, Kissinger hedged
his bets: He offered his services to both the Humphrey campaign—pledging
to share Rockefeller's secret files on Nixon—and the Nixon campaign, promising to share secret information from the Paris peace talks. Nixon took him
up on the scheme, and for the remainder of the campaign Kissinger worked
assiduously to pry information from the peace talks, reporting it to Nixon
through Allen, sometimes in phone calls conducted in German.

Kissinger, who turned forty-five in 1968, may have seemed the quintes-
sential foreign policy wunderkind, but his ascendancy had been anything
but preordained. Born Jewish in Fürth, Germany, in 1923, he had arrived
in New York at the age of fifteen, five years after the Nazis had taken power
and made life intolerable for German Jews. He was headed for a relatively
ordinary life—attending night classes in accounting—when he was drafted
into the U.S. Army in 1943. After a year in the army, he landed at Camp
Claiborne, the Louisiana training facilities for the 84th Infantry, where he
met Fritz Kraemer.

The encounter would change Kissinger's life. "My role was not discovering Kissinger," Kraemer later recalled: "My role was getting Kissinger to
discover himself. [At age twenty-one] Kissinger knew nothing but understood everything." To the younger refugee, Kraemer, a self-assured private,
fifteen years older, with two doctorates and a rapier of an intellect, was an
alluring leader. "I was in awe of Kraemer," Kissinger later recalled. Kraemer
helped Kissinger obtain assignments and promotions in the army and urged
him to set his sights beyond accountancy. Kraemer steered him to Harvard
and later helped Kissinger choose the subjects of his master's and doctoral
theses. In 1957 Kissinger came to prominence in foreign policy circles when
he turned a Council on Foreign Relations Study Group's deliberations into
a 450-page book under his own name, *Nuclear Weapons and Foreign Policy,*
which improbably became a bestseller. A Harvard professor, he was also a
consultant on military and missile planning to Presidents Eisenhower, Kennedy, and Johnson.

Nixon's need to know about the Paris deliberations in 1968 derived from
his greatest fear during the campaign—that Johnson would con the public

into believing the war in Vietnam was about to end, which would tilt the electorate to Humphrey. To deter that scenario, Nixon circumvented the law by secretly sending messages to President Nguyen Van Thieu of South Vietnam, using as intermediary Anna Chennault, the Chinese-born widow of a celebrated and controversial American general. Thieu, a career military officer, had been part of a military junta that had overthrown the postcolonial leader; elected president with a slim plurality, he had constructed a regime that was nearly as corrupt as its predecessor and more than willing to let U.S. forces bear the brunt of the heavy fighting.

As Nixon had feared, at the end of the summer of 1968 his lead in the polls vanished overnight when Humphrey began advocating a halt to the bombing, effectively distancing himself from Johnson. Hearing rumors of a peace settlement, Nixon used the Chennault channel to warn Thieu not to sign any peace agreement before the election, promising that South Vietnam would get a better deal from a Nixon presidency.

Nixon's messages were intercepted and made their way to Johnson, who characterized them to Senator Everett Dirksen as "treason." Johnson also told Humphrey, who recognized that revealing them would hurt Nixon at the polls, yet decided against releasing the information; there was no proof that Nixon had personally ordered the attempts to sway Thieu, and the revelation would raise questions as to how the information had been obtained.

Trying to manage the situation, Johnson made a conference call to all three candidates (the third was former Alabama governor George Wallace). He warned Nixon obliquely not to further interfere in the negotiations, and Nixon told the president he would stop. But he did not—partly because he feared that Johnson would launch an "October surprise" designed to throw the election at the last moment. And on the weekend before the election Johnson delivered that surprise, announcing a bombing halt and a breakthrough in the peace talks.

On Election Day the race was too close to call. Not until mid-morning of the next day was the final tally counted. Nixon garnered 301 Electoral College votes, thirty more than he needed. In the popular vote, he won by a half-million out of 73 million votes cast—a margin of two-thirds of 1 percent.

The narrow margin is generally attributed to Wallace's presence in the race: If Wallace had not siphoned conservative support away from Nixon and taken five Deep South states, the argument goes, Nixon would have won more easily. But there is evidence to the contrary—that conservative voters actually provided Nixon's margin of victory. The Wallace spoiler argument does hold when the example is Texas, since Humphrey only carried the state by 1.5 percent while Wallace received 19 percent. But it falters when measured against figures from other states where conservative voters were a more significant factor and Wallace voters a less significant one, such as in five states that Nixon won narrowly: California (3 percent), Illinois (2.9 percent), Ohio (2.2 percent), New Jersey (2.1 percent), and Missouri (1.1 percent). Had the first four—states that frequently voted Democratic—gone for Humphrey, the Electoral College tally would have been tipped in the Democrat's favor. Equally significant, the turnout in all five close-call states was more than 80 percent, and more than 87 percent in New Jersey and Ohio. By contrast, the turnout in states won by Humphrey was in the 60–70 percent range, and in those won by Wallace, in the 50 percent range. Nixon also won in states where Wallace had been leading prior to the election: Florida, Tennessee, North Carolina, and South Carolina; intervention by Senators Strom Thurmond and John Tower, arguing that a vote for Wallace was a vote for Humphrey, helped put those states in the Nixon column on Election Day.

Most conservatives who backed Nixon had no idea how radically he planned to change American foreign policy. Indeed, judging by later reactions from the right, if he had been more forthcoming about his ideas before the election, they might well have stayed home and not voted at all.

During the presidential transition period, Nixon began setting into motion his plan to end the Vietnam War—the so-called secret plan which did exist but would have surprised many of those who voted him into office, had they known its character. The plan entailed neither accepting defeat nor pushing for all-out military victory; rather, the Nixon administration would play the USSR and China against each other to force them to persuade their client state, North Vietnam, to negotiate an end to the war on terms favorable to the United States and to South Vietnam.

This approach had its roots in lessons Nixon had taken away from the last major war in which the United States had been involved—the Korean War. In 1953, shortly after Dwight Eisenhower was elected, he had threatened both Communist China and the USSR, and Nixon believed that these threats had resulted in the quick conclusion of the war. On a post-election trip to Florida, Nixon stopped at Walter Reed Hospital in Washington to see the dying Eisenhower; he may have told him, as he did other intimates, that he would bring an end to the war in Vietnam within ninety or a hundred days of taking office.

A most important concomitant of Nixon's plans entailed appointing a national security adviser more in tune with his ideas than the three young conservative Turks he had enlisted during the campaign. Richard Allen, convinced that he himself was too young, and definitely too conservative, to serve as national security adviser, recommended Henry Kissinger for the post. But the leaders of the American Enterprise Institute and the Hoover Institution urged Allen to join the administration in some capacity—"We need you in there," they pleaded, as a counterbalance to Kissinger—and Allen accepted the post of deputy national security adviser.

Before Nixon agreed to appoint Kissinger, he chatted with the professor for three hours at the Pierre Hotel in New York City, the president-elect's post-election headquarters. Nixon was already determined to cut the State Department, the CIA, and the Department of Defense out of the foreign policy loop—to run the show himself, with an appointed national security adviser and a reinvigorated National Security Council. For Nixon, one benefit of this approach was that White House employees were not subject to Senate confirmation and could not be required to testify by any congressional committees. Kissinger, whose disdain for the Washington bureaucracies had deepened during a decade of close contact with them, enthusiastically agreed with Nixon's scheme.

After accepting the post in secret, he called Fritz Kraemer to let him know about the offer. "You are not going to be able to make foreign policy," Kraemer warned. "You will not be the engineer but at best the brakeman on the train. The right will call you the Jew who lost us Southeast Asia; the left will call you a traitor." If it were a purely personal question, Kraemer said, he would urge him not to take the job—but he advised Henry to accept for the country's sake, because he was the best-qualified man in America for the position.

Kraemer was puzzled that his protégé Kissinger would accept a post in which he would take orders from Nixon, a man Kissinger had previously and quite openly disliked. Kraemer later said that he felt Kissinger's willingness to do so devolved from the "damage to his soul" inflicted by the Nazis, which forever made Kissinger "seek order, hunger for acceptance [and] try to please those he considered his intellectual inferiors."

Three linked bureaucratic challenges awaited Nixon and Kissinger. The first was to bring the foreign policy bureaucracy to heel—to ready it to accept orders from the White House. The second was to fill out the top policy posts with men who would not contradict the president's wishes. The third was to counter the Johnson administration's attempts to hamstring the incoming administration. All presidents, as they prepare to leave Washington, try to get their successors to commit to continuing their policies. Johnson's attempt at inveigling took the form of a memo to Nixon outlining the current negotiating posture on arms negotiations and stressing that the Soviets felt it was "important to move promptly" on this because "the clock is ticking against you as well as against me. . . . We must move on the missile talks, if we can, to create an environment in the world which will make it easier for Japan, Germany, Israel, and India to put the [Nuclear Non-Proliferation Treaty] through their parliaments." Johnson wished to hold a summit with the Russians and wanted Nixon to attend. Nixon's reaction was to send word to the Soviets through Kissinger that "the President-elect meant it when he said that this was to be an era of negotiation not confrontation," but that if a summit was held before he took office, then "the Nixon Administration will be forced to find some way to make it clear that we will not be boxed in." The interim summit died.

The key to controlling the bureaucracy, Nixon and Kissinger agreed, was to reconfigure the National Security Council (NSC). To assist in making that transition Nixon called an old friend—General Andrew Goodpaster, mainstay of the Eisenhower NSC—back from Vietnam. Goodpaster and Kissinger's former Harvard colleague Morton Halperin, then deputy assistant secretary of defense, would create the new NSC. When Kissinger and Halperin drafted a plan for the reorganization, Goodpaster was perturbed that it would exclude the State Department from giving advice or executing policy—which was just what Nixon wanted. "If the Department of State has had a new idea in the past 25 years, it is not known to me," Nixon would later say. "I refuse to be confronted with a bureaucratic consensus that leaves me no options but acceptance or rejection," Nixon explained.

But Kissinger knew the bureaucracy would need a distraction, and he had just the man to concoct one: Daniel Ellsberg, a former student of his at Harvard who had spent years at the Pentagon and then had returned to work at the RAND Corporation, the venerable Cold War classified-research think tank in California. Ellsberg was currently compiling for the Pentagon a multivolume compendium of actions in past administrations relating to the war in Vietnam. At the Pierre's coffee shop, Kissinger met with Ellsberg to design questionnaires for Defense, State, and CIA on all aspects of foreign policy—questionnaires whose main purpose was to occupy the bureaucrats while Nixon and Kissinger consolidated power.

On December 27, Ellsberg delivered to Kissinger a twenty-seven-page document. It was terrific, Kissinger said, but had two problems. One, it put forth the option of total unilateral withdrawal of American troops; that was unacceptable to Kissinger and was deleted from the draft. Two, it had no plan for battlefield victory by the United States. Ellsberg had excluded that option because he thought it would only "recreate the illusion that we could somehow win this war." Kissinger, student of Kraemer, disagreed.

Nixon hated the CIA, believing it had misled him in 1960 about the "missile gap," allowing John F. Kennedy to outflank him on that issue and win the election. So he reappointed the current CIA director, Richard Helms, but permitted Kissinger to stop the CIA from its previous practice of directly passing to the president the President's Daily Briefing book. Kissinger and Nixon wanted such materials read first by a senior Nixon staffer. Like the professor he was, Kissinger attacked the character of the current PDBs—and by implication the agency that compiled them—as poorly written, badly organized, and lacking necessary detail. The Agency redid its homework, thereafter preparing for Kissinger and Nixon a much longer PDB than they had prepared for the Johnson inner circle. To meet Kissinger's "insatiable" demand on other issues, CIA experts worked overtime to draft papers on Korea, China, France, and the like, in support of each item in the expanded PDB. And Kissinger challenged the Agency's role as sole provider of intelligence on security matters, inviting the Joint Chiefs of Staff to present at an intelligence briefing on the U.S.-Soviet strategic balance. By the end of the transition, Kissinger, at Nixon's behest, had thoroughly shaken up the CIA.

To round out his senior foreign policy team, Nixon needed a secretary of defense and a secretary of state. His first choice for Defense was a Democrat, Senator Henry M. "Scoop" Jackson, a staunch anti-Soviet and an expert on military hardware. Jackson had chaired the Democratic National Committee in 1960, but he felt that his party had run away from him to the left in the years that followed, especially on defense. Since Nixon would be the first president elected since 1840 without his party also winning at least one house of Congress, Jackson could help him with the Democrats. Jackson accepted the Defense post privately but then reneged, telling Nixon that he could do the administration more good by remaining in Congress. Nixon then offered the post to Melvin Laird, a smart, military-minded Republican congressman from Wisconsin, a long-term colleague whom Nixon thought he could control. For State, Nixon chose William P. Rogers, a social and professional friend since the Eisenhower years, when he had been Eisenhower's second-term attorney general. Rogers confessed himself ignorant of foreign affairs. "Nixon considered Rogers' unfamiliarity with the subject an asset," Kissinger later wrote, "because it guaranteed that policy direction would remain in the White House."

Rogers and Kissinger would become rivals—as Nixon may have intended, since he reveled in their clashes. "Rogers felt that Kissinger was Machiavellian, deceitful, egotistical, arrogant, and insulting," Nixon wrote in his autobiography. "Kissinger felt Rogers was vain, uninformed, unable to keep a secret, and hopelessly dominated by the state department bureaucracy."

Nixon's law partner and campaign manager John Mitchell, who was to be attorney general, would not have as large a hand in foreign affairs as President Kennedy had given his attorney general, his brother Robert. H. R. "Bob" Haldeman, whom Nixon chose as White House chief of staff, would be involved in foreign policy, but only as a sounding board and enabler for the president.

Nixon considered his Cabinet officials as a façade behind which he and his aides would operate, especially in foreign policy. After presenting the nominees to the public in one group press conference, Nixon lost interest in the hiring process, leaving it to those aides.

For the new National Security Council, Kissinger retained a few hold-overs from the Johnson years, including Morton Halperin; Sven Kraemer, a former student and the son of Fritz Kraemer; and Helmut "Hal" Sonnen-feldt, a longtime friend, fellow German refugee, and friend of Kraemer's. For the critical position of military assistant, Kissinger received nominations from many quarters. One name was common to the lists compiled by Good-paster, former secretary of defense Robert McNamara, and former assistant secretary of defense Joseph Califano: Colonel Alexander M Haig, Jr.

A West Point graduate, Haig had begun his career on the staff of General Douglas MacArthur. In between fighting in Korea and commanding a battalion in Vietnam, he had worked at the Pentagon with Califano, and was currently deputy commandant of cadets at West Point. Haig had an impressive bio and good recommendations; he also came with a personal note from Fritz Kraemer. "Above all he is a man of strong character besides being intelligent," Kraemer wrote, "and gifted with an innate understanding of political and psychological imponderabilities."

Kraemer's word clinched the deal: Kissinger hired Haig.

2

The Anti-Nixon

On a frigid day in April 1929, the future management guru Peter Drucker, then twenty-one, stood on a bridge over the Main River in Frankfurt. There, in a kayak amid stray ice floes, he was astounded to see "a cadaverous man, naked except for the scantiest of black bathing trunks and a monocle on a wide black ribbon . . . furiously paddling upstream. And the stern of the fragile craft flew the black, white, and red battle pennant of the defunct German Imperial Navy." Its captain was Fritz Gustav Anton Kraemer—a fellow international law student, Drucker soon discovered, and an eccentric one, who on land favored knee-length riding boots and riding breeches rather than the tweed jackets of the other students. Kraemer looked like "a cross between a greyhound and a timberwolf," Drucker thought, but the two taught a seminar together, and Drucker was impressed with his colleague's formidable intellect.

Drucker would later aver that Kraemer's attitudes had been fully formed by the age of twenty-one. Yet Kraemer's view of the world—at least as it manifested itself in the years he spent as mentor, confidant, and adviser to Kissinger and Haig—was hugely affected by World War II and the Cold War.

Though Fritz Kraemer was only ten in 1918, when the Great War ended, he later told his son Sven that he came to understand that that war had "destroyed all foundations—lives, institutions, values, and faiths." When Drucker met Fritz Kraemer in 1929, as the liberal Weimar Republic of the 1920s had passed its height and was starting to disintegrate, Fritz was already a throwback, maintaining not only the clothing but also the mental stance of a Prussian monarchist of the Great War era. (He even sent an annual birthday telegram to the deposed kaiser.) Kraemer's father was director of public prosecutions in Düsseldorf; his mother ran a boarding facility for "difficult children," some of them Jews. Fritz had spent his youth in Swiss and German boarding schools, absorbing a classical education, and had taken a year at the London School of Economics. By 1929, runaway inflation had all but completely eroded the Kraemer family fortune. Sven would later assert that during the 1920s and early 1930s his father had disdained Germany's most influential intellectuals—Marx, Freud, and Nietzsche—as "destructive nihilists," and judged "Berlin's Brechtian cabarets and the Weimar Republic's babbling politicians as the works of a decadent bourgeoisie lacking higher values and unable to understand the coming Nazi revolution, a revolution of nihilism."

A practicing Lutheran with a deep belief in God, morality, and the importance of honor—attributes Kraemer associated with the Prussian militarist model—he considered liberals too sentimental and soft to withstand the forces of evil, and too naïve to hold and use power. The young Drucker and Kraemer frequently argued the subject; Kraemer opposed not only liberals but also the Nazis as they prepared to seize power. In later years, Drucker would liken Kraemer's "old-fashioned Prussian conservative" stance to that of the aristocrats who in 1944 almost succeeded in killing Hitler.

In a series of one-on-one policy debates—some of which lasted until dawn—Kraemer and Drucker disagreed on three basic points, all of which would have relevance in the war over foreign policy that erupted in the Nixon administration forty years later.

First, Kraemer contended that foreign policy must have primacy over domestic policy to assure a nation's survival. Second, he insisted that the essence of foreign affairs was "political strength and ultimately military might." Drucker insisted on the importance of economic power, but Kraemer believed economic matters could not substitute for or trump military strength. And that gave rise to point three, that "the only foreign policy worth pursuing was the balance of great powers."

Kraemer and Drucker also disagreed on a fourth point: Kraemer thought that no nation could succeed at changing the alignment of nations in its favor without a "genius foreign minister" at the helm. Drucker argued that Kraemer's favorite shining examples belied this: The tenures of Richelieu, Metternich, and Bismarck, he pointed out, had produced chaos and defeat. Kraemer said he had no desire to be a general or foreign secretary, a Bismarck or Metternich; rather, he aspired to the position of political adviser to the chief of the general staff of the army, and eventually, political mentor to a great foreign secretary. Kraemer told Drucker that he didn't like the limelight—that he was a "thinker and not a doer."

After completing his law degree in 1930, Kraemer married Britta Bjork-ander, a Swede he had met in Geneva when they were both teenagers. As soon as the Nazis announced restrictions on Jews, the couple moved to Italy. (Drucker writes that Kraemer left Germany because it was a point of honor with him not to be associated with a German regime that demonized and punished Jews.) Within the year, Kraemer took a job teaching at the University of Rome—in Italian, no less—while taking a second doctorate there, this time in political science. Shortly thereafter he began to write for the League of Nations the first of eight scholarly tomes on international law and economic issues. On the Tiber, in his kayak that flew the imperial flag, he had a run-in with a Nazi officer who demanded that he take the flag down; he fought in court for his right to fly it and won the case. Sven later proudly told stories of his father's regular brawls with Communists and Nazis alike, in which he received scars from both extremist groups.

In 1937, when Mussolini formally became Hitler's ally, Kraemer's friends advised him to leave Italy. Parking Britta and infant son Sven with his mother in her Wiesbaden boarding school, Kraemer decamped first to Great Britain and then to the United States, with the aid of Drucker and through a program that had already brought a few thousand German Jews to teach in the States and Great Britain. When World War II began, it trapped Britta, Sven, and Kraemer's mother behind enemy lines.

Unable to secure a university position in America, Kraemer worked on a Maine potato farm, then as a researcher at the Library of Congress and at other odd jobs before being drafted in 1943. The army brass quickly noted his talents and gave him the task of lecturing and preparing officers to go into Germany after D-Day. It was during this assignment that he and Kissinger found one another.

Sent overseas, Kraemer served with distinction in Europe in 1944–45. He also brought Kissinger over. "Somewhat incongruously, a few miles from the front, Kraemer would lecture me . . . on his view of history and current events during long evenings at various combat headquarters and on walks through the shells of conquered towns," Kissinger later wrote. "Kraemer was as learned as he was dramatic, as dedicated as he was eloquent."

After the Battle of the Bulge, Kraemer was captured by German forces. But he convinced the garrison that seized him to surrender without a shot being fired—a feat for which the United States awarded him a Bronze Star and a battlefield commission. He helped debrief German scientists so they could be brought to the States and served as librarian for the documents amassed in support of the Nuremberg trials. One day, on a break, he walked up to a home in a village, where he found a seven-year-old boy standing outside. "Is Frau Kraemer at home?" he asked. Suspicious, the boy asked who he was. "I am your father," Kraemer said. What followed was a joyous reunion with his wife, son, and mother, who had survived the war despite repeated harassment and interrogation by the Gestapo.

Kraemer's philosophy gained specificity from what he saw as the central event leading to World War II—the refusal of Great Britain and France to stop Hitler when he believed they still could have, at Munich in 1938. This appeasement was the original case in point of what Kraemer called "provocative weakness": the Allies' unwillingness to go to war, signaling Hitler that any move to seize Czechoslovakia and Poland would likely go unopposed. In the ashes of World War II, Kraemer applied this theory to a new enemy, Communism, whose ideology, proletarianism, and tyrannical suppression of its people he considered the evil equal of Hitler's National Socialism. To Kraemer, the West's yielding to Soviet expansionism was equivalent to the Allies' appeasement at Munich.

In 1948, at the age of forty, Fritz Kraemer accomplished one of his life's aims, becoming an official adviser to the U.S. Army chief of staff. Mustered out of the service as a lieutenant colonel, he entered the Pentagon as a civilian. Visiting Kraemer there in the early 1960s, Peter Drucker was stunned to see the army chief of staff pop into Kraemer's office every ten minutes to get advice and to invite "Dr. Kraemer"—who by now habitually also carried a swagger stick to complement his monocle—to attend a meeting of the Joint Chiefs of Staff (JCS).

Kraemer had some influence at Defense as an adviser, but in 1956 he complained to Kissinger in a letter that both he and Kissinger knew that "history is not really made by pens or printers' ink," and that they must remain "mercilessly aware . . . that, in truth, men will adopt the bold and imaginative policies we want them to adopt, not because their brains are convinced by conclusive arguments, but because their hearts are moved."

Kraemer was one of a trio of fervent anti-Communists in Washington. He was friendly with the other two: James Jesus Angleton, the legendary CIA spymaster who ruled a large part of the Agency's operations in the 1950s and 1960s, and Jay Lovestone, the former head of the Communist Party of the U.S.A. in the 1920s, who had since become a leading public anti-Communist as well as head of the AFL-CIO's European operations and close adviser to George Meany. Lovestone and, to a lesser extent, Angleton, would trade information from their sources with Kraemer, always on an unofficial basis.

Kraemer's philosophy was not unique. Plenty of philosophers and strategists on the right, including Leo Strauss and Albert Wohlstetter, said and wrote similar things. But Kraemer's influence stemmed from his expressing his ideas simply and powerfully—and from giving them a more overtly military turn than many of his colleagues on the right. Kraemer's advice to those he counseled, both officially and informally, was "both inspiring and very tough," as Sven later put it. Haig found most impressive Kraemer's "strong convictions and his great love of free world ideals and principles." He considered Kraemer's "insights on global events nothing short of remarkable."

Kraemer's advice was almost always delivered in person rather than in writing: Though Kraemer read and spoke English very well, it took him a long time to master written English, so he tended to pass on his insights in one-on-one sessions with Pentagon officials and governmental insiders. Once a month, he also gathered some of the Pentagon beat reporters, such as Nick Thimmesch of the *Baltimore Sun* and William Beecher of the *New York Times*, for a regular, though off-the-record, session, briefing them on the state of affairs in various parts of the world as he viewed it.

Kraemer often said that his virtues did not include humility and patience. He did not pursue sustained dialogues with those who substantially disagreed with him. When lecturing, he seldom permitted dissenters or negative questioners more than one thrust. He was unusual among Pentagon staffers in that he refused promotions and upgrades in civil service scale. He brushed aside offers to elevate his title above that of adviser and declined awards and citations. In the decades he worked at the Pentagon, he filled his cramped office with piles of yellowing, musty newspapers in several languages, which he clipped and underlined in red, blue, and yellow, and with copies of the hundreds of military and diplomatic cables he read daily. He had an ascetic lifestyle—keeping no TV at his home, staying fit through exercise—because he believed that rejecting the trappings of power and the emoluments of money reinforced the purity and force of his arguments.

Ed Rowny, in 1957 an army officer assigned as an aide to the chairman of the JCS, met Kraemer when he asked Fritz to look at a letter he had drafted for the chairman. Rowny at that point held two master's degrees from Yale, read and spoke Russian, and was also a West Point graduate who had helped MacArthur formulate plans for the Inchon landing in Korea—all credentials Kraemer admired. After reading Rowny's letter aloud, however, he pronounced it "too long," "too bourgeois," and lacking in unity, coherence, and emphasis. Two years later Rowny and Kraemer were thrown together again, as fellow students at the army's War College. At the War College course, which lasted many months, they became friends—two men of formidable intellect and compatible philosophy.

At the conclusion of the course, Kraemer and Rowny tied for the prize for best essay. After winning a toss to determine who would deliver his paper first, Rowny later recalled, Kraemer dumbfounded everyone by presenting

his paper "in his stentorian voice" as a monologue by French general Ferdinand Foch, German foreign minister Joachim von Ribbentrop, and Benito
Mussolini—each in his native language. "He had his baton for the German
swagger stick, a beret for speaking in French, and to dip into Italian he
waved his hands a lot," Rowny remembered.

Kraemer's other lifelong friends included Vernon "Dick" Walters, an
army intelligence officer who spoke seven languages and had done simultaneous translation for Eisenhower, Truman, and Vice President Richard
Nixon. Walters later said that Kraemer's "ability to look above the horizon
and recognize before most others the signs of coming events" made his
advice "invaluable." Kraemer, Rowny, and Walters shared many things:
a military background, a tough assessment of the world, patriotic pride, a
belief in elites, a faith in the idea that military force should be the primary
tool in the conduct of U.S. foreign affairs, and a fundamental distrust of
Communism and of all dictatorial regimes.

The 1950s and early 1960s produced many examples of what Kraemer
labeled as provocative weakness: the Suez Canal crisis, a Hungarian revolution that was viciously put down by the USSR, the Cuban Missile Crisis.
In each case, he advocated immediate U.S. and NATO military responses,
and saw the moves made by Egypt and the USSR as having been emboldened by the Western democracies' refusal to respond firmly. When President Kennedy faced down the Soviets in 1962, Kraemer applauded: The
action upheld his notion that only prompt, full, military-based responses
could successfully deter aggression. But he bridled at Kennedy's concurrent
willingness to remove U.S. missiles from Turkey in an ultimate trade with
the USSR for removal of its missiles from Cuba. And he was upset when
President Lyndon Johnson would not unleash the military to attempt to win
in the burgeoning war in South Vietnam.

Kraemer's views were consonant with sentiments widely held among the
professional military and, to a lesser extent, by traditional anti-Communist
conservatives such as William F. Buckley, Jr. But the Buckley school differed from Kraemer in that they held out hope for diplomacy. Kraemer fundamentally distrusted diplomacy that lacked military power to back it up.
He dismissed those he considered overeducated and underexperienced as
"brilliant fools," and feared that a "bourgeois society"—which he believed
that the Western democracies had become—would never understand the
"devastating effect of provocative weakness on totalitarian dictatorships like
the USSR," which repeatedly took Western weakness as license to expand
their empire. "We [the United States of America] are a rich country," he
said in one seminar; "we are comfortable, and it's hard for us to get a grip
on revolutionary tenacity." Assessing the history of the decades since the

Russian Revolution of 1917, he declared that diplomacy in dealing with the Soviets had almost always failed to protect the West.

To counter totalitarian dictatorships, Kraemer thought it necessary for the United States and Europe to adhere to certain fixed moral values. He considered himself "a missionary of and for absolute values and for a cause." That cause was liberty and democracy as they existed in opposition to totalitarian enterprises. He saw his mission as "fighting the triumph of the expedient over the principled." "Modern technicians in high places," he wrote, "do not grasp the reality that never has anything been presented to nations on a silver platter and that great and difficult goals have never been attained without passion and a flame of true conviction." Diplomacy, he declared, was a cardinal example of that basest sin, moral relativism: "Intellectuals have always preached that everything is relative and that there are no absolute values. The result is spiritual emptiness. Everything is possible and therefore nothing is. The worst thing about a loss of faith is not the fact that someone has stopped believing but that they are ready to believe anything," he wrote.

The debate over moral relativism versus moral absolutism has raged since the days of David Hume in the late eighteenth century. Fritz Kraemer, a staunch absolutist, embraced the notion that there are fixed moral values, and that any individual, or government, must be judged by the strength of its adherence to them. Modern diplomats fell into the relativistic trap, Kraemer charged, by becoming captives of the countries to which they were posted, or about which they developed areas of expertise. This "clientitis" prevented diplomats from having the best interests of the United States at heart when they made policy recommendations. "Fanatical men from the left or right—or, perhaps, nations hating each other—who are on the verge of throwing the match into the powder keg are most unlikely to listen to reason and desist because we beseech them with mere words," he told a friendly interviewer. "They can, however, be made to listen if you are able actually to bear down on them, not brutally but forcefully."

Nothing is possible without power, Kraemer was fond of saying. Diplomacy without the threat of armed force is toothless. And economics is no substitute for military force. The one way to prevent war was to develop military might and to make sure that other countries understood your willingness to use it.

BY THE EARLY 1960s, Fritz Kraemer had given up his youthful fascination with the ideal of the "genius foreign minister." Instead he began to worry about the dangers of such an adviser having too much power. In a 1966 book, Henry Kissinger echoed Kraemer's concerns, writing, "The statesman is suspicious of those who personalize foreign policy, for history teaches him the fragility of structures dependent upon individuals."

When Peter Drucker visited Kraemer around that time, Fritz talked on and on about Kissinger. But Kraemer had also begun to focus on a younger generation of protégés—chief among them Alexander Haig.

Haig was at the Pentagon when they met, working on NATO and Berlin. The two men regularly discussed the continual crises in those two arenas, as well as the larger struggle with the Soviet Union. Kraemer considered West Point the most positive example of elitism in action, and Haig was a West Pointer; he also shared Kraemer's admiration for Douglas MacArthur, his former commander. Both men were devout Christians, although Haig was a Catholic and Kraemer was a Protestant. Haig found in Kraemer a "spell-binder" who combined "logic, factual knowledge and conceptual depth with a spirited and inspirational personal demeanor," as Haig remembered in a 1975 letter to Thimmesch; from the day he and Kraemer met, he said, they were "close, both personally and professionally."

In 1961, Kraemer recommended Haig for a higher-level job with Assistant Secretary of Defense Joseph Califano. Haig did well at that job and verified Kraemer's faith in him by standing up to Secretary Robert McNamara, contradicting the secretary in a meeting—a risky move for a junior officer. And so, when the opportunity arose to recommend a military assistant to Kissinger, Kraemer had passed over candidates such as his good friend Ed Rowny and chose Haig—a younger man, more political, less scholarly, and accustomed to dealing with the powerful. Years later, when Rowny found out that Kraemer had recommended Haig over him, Rowny was saddened but came to understand the move.

In such decisions, Kraemer was guided by his belief in the need to seed the elite with those of superior intellect and savvy, pledged to high ideals and trained in his way of thinking. He envisioned moving his protégés into the highest positions in the country, from which they could govern and assure America's dominance in the world. He recognized that such notions didn't exactly jibe with the concept of egalitarian democracy, but he had come to despise the bourgeois attitude. "We don't want people to be exceptional, to tower above others, we want mediocre—and with time increasingly mediocre—people that don't differ from each other." Citing the Founding Fathers as a prime example, Kraemer asserted that in every era "astoundingly small groups [had] caused new beginnings," and that these groups always consist of "a few personalities of substance who by competence and character are able and determined to serve a cause with energy and devotion." In the past century, he pointed out, "small, heroic groups" had saved civilization by a combination of "strength, will, and power." Power was not a privilege, he avowed, but an obligation of the governing elite. And such an elite was urgently needed if the Western democracies were ever to "emerge from a period of degeneration."

Kraemer's acolytes and admirers treated his entwined principles, values, and personality as they would a religion. And he treated them as an ordained clergy who had earned the right to rule—so long as they did so by his principles.

By 1969, IT was as obvious to Fritz Kraemer as it was to Nixon and Morgenthau that the strategy of Communist containment had outlived its usefulness. Actively opposing the Communists had worked, to a degree, in Europe and on the Korean peninsula, but now Communism was on the move elsewhere. Whereas Richard Nixon felt the way to halt Communist expansion was to engage the enemies in dialogue and thereby reduce the threat to the United States and the West, Kraemer believed that dialogue would likely be futile. Only steel, he felt, could stop Communist expansion. While the American public was clamoring for an end to the war in Vietnam, Kraemer wished to expand it, prosecute it vigorously, and win it on the battlefield and at any peace talks. And it was crucial, he felt, that the incoming Nixon administration had an NSC director (Kissinger), an NSC chief military aide (Haig), and at least two staffers (Sven and Sonnenfeldt), who were willing to listen closely to him.

"Kraemer's values were absolute," Kissinger would later say in a eulogy. "Like the ancient prophets, he made no concessions to human frailty or to historic evolution; he treated intermediate solutions as derogation from eternal principle." Kissinger called Kraemer "a lighthouse . . . a beacon that amidst the turmoil of the moment guides us to the transcendental." Sonnenfeldt considered him "a fixed point." Haig and others saw him as a polestar to follow when the path ahead was obscured.

As the Nixon administration began in January 1969, that path ahead was anything but clear.

3

Sending Signals

During the early months of any new president's administration, the public, the press, the country's foreign allies and enemies, and all other groups look for signs of what the newcomers will do. The early days of Richard M. Nixon's administration were particularly crowded with such signals, but not all that Nixon and his team sent were intentional, and some were not received in the way that the senders had hoped. The misperceptions, in large part, were the consequence of Nixon's obsession with secrecy. The new president risked compromising his pragmatic policies by not permitting people to see them, to evaluate their logic and thus to appreciate their appropriateness before they were put into effect. By concealing the policies while they were being developed, he created an atmosphere of subterfuge and obfuscation—and, in doing so, sowed serious doubts about his administration in the minds of the American ideologues who would become his detractors.

ON ENTERING THE White House, Nixon hung a portrait of Woodrow Wilson in a place of honor, a tribute to Wilson's internationalist outlook, though he disagreed fundamentally with the concept of "open covenants, openly arrived at," which Wilson had espoused in his Fourteen Points. Richard Nixon's surface actions often concealed what he really felt. Considering himself extremely well prepared to be president, he had little interest in the ideas of others. His ability to work a room as well as any senator or representative, readily memorizing names and details of the families of those he needed on his side so he could make polite inquiries, masked his acute discomfort with small talk. Straitlaced and moralistic, he collected information on the sexual misconduct of his political allies and enemies alike, and his private conversation was laced with ethnic slurs. He chose his subordinates for loyalty, not for brilliance.

He was also a man of single-minded determination. At fifty-five, he owed his good health to a rigorous diet he had followed for several years, in which he ate only half of anything served to him on a plate. He believed that the key to having a successful presidency was to maintain a similarly tight control over the White House and the executive branch. He had a low regard for academics and a high regard for men who had run for and won public office; among foreign leaders he particularly admired de Gaulle and the more overt autocrats—Marcos of the Philippines, Somoza of Nicaragua, Shah Pahlavi of Iran, Suharto of Indonesia. He had grand dreams, especially in foreign affairs, and a belief that accomplishing them would require him and his associates to work almost totally in secret. As he would tell his aides at the moment of his greatest triumph, "Without secrecy there would have been no invitation or acceptance to visit China. Without secrecy there is no chance of success in it." He took the same approach to détente with the USSR and negotiations with North Vietnam. If outsiders should learn his intentions, he believed, naysayers would kill the initiatives before they could take hold as policy.

"The greatest title history can bestow is the title of peacemaker," Nixon said in his first inaugural address.

> This honor now beckons America—the chance to help lead the world at last out of the valley of turmoil and onto that high ground of peace that man has dreamed of since the dawn of civilization. . . . After a period of confrontation, we are entering an era of negotiation. Let all nations know that during this administration our lines of communication will be open.

Yet the offer went only so far: When Soviet ambassador Anatoly Dobrynin pressed for an early appointment, Nixon put him off, not wanting to seem too eager to make a deal.

The administration's most insistent foreign policy problem was the war in Vietnam. It had been almost a year since the Communists' Tet Offensive of 1968, the event that tilted the majority of the American public to a negative stance on continued U.S. participation in the war. The number of American troops in South Vietnam was cresting, nearing its all-time high of more than half a million. General Creighton Abrams, who had taken over from William Westmoreland as chief commander just after Tet, was one of several generals who had learned from Kraemer. In less than a year, Abrams's new "clear-and-hold" strategy, which replaced Westmoreland's ineffective "search-and-destroy" policy, had reversed the Communists' gains. Saigon had regained control of large portions of land; more villagers were deserting the Viet Cong for the Saigon government, and fewer missiles were being lobbed at the capital city. Abrams, known as "Abe," and his deputy, Goodpaster, believed they were finally in position to win the war.

The question was whether Nixon would let them do so. For years the Joint Chiefs of Staff had railed that Lyndon Johnson's rules of engagement had seriously hampered pursuit of the enemy on the ground and limited the choice of air and sea targets. The chiefs now wished to chase the enemy into its sanctuaries in Laos and Cambodia, to bomb North Vietnam's cities, and to mine its harbors—to wage total war to force the enemy to sue for peace.

Nixon believed that unleashing U.S. forces to wage a broader war in Vietnam would not only prolong the conflict, it would also enrage the Soviets and the Chinese, who supplied the North Vietnamese—a turn of events that could scuttle his grand plans to transform the world order. But Nixon was keeping those plans secret from the Joint Chiefs, so for the moment he had to accede to their wishes in Vietnam. And so he said yes to Operation Dewey Canyon, a Marine sweep into the A Shau valley on the Laos border designed to interdict the flow of North Vietnamese soldiers and supplies. From Military Assistance Command, Vietnam (MACV) in Saigon to the Joint Chiefs of Staff in the Pentagon, the American military command sighed in relief; perhaps, they thought, Nixon would actually permit them to win the war.

Just how wrong they might be was brought home at an intimate luncheon that defense secretary Melvin Laird hosted for Nixon and Kissinger at the Pentagon on January 27, 1969. The affable Laird was an astute politician—he had served in the House for many years, and was closely allied with Minority Leader Gerald Ford and the various appropriations committee chairmen and ranking Republican members—and he could be a ruthless player behind the scenes. He planned to make himself invaluable to Nixon in pushing military matters through Congress, but also to consolidate a base of power from which to challenge Nixon when they disagreed. As Kissinger later wrote, "Laird would think nothing of coming to a White House meeting with the Joint Chiefs of Staff, supporting their position, then indicating his reservations privately to the President and me, only to work out a third approach later with his friend [House Appropriations Committee Chairman George] Mahon."

At the time, the chairman of the Joint Chiefs was General Earle "Bus" Wheeler. Nixon and Kissinger thought Wheeler was too closely associated with Johnson to be trusted. But Wheeler believed he knew what Nixon wanted, and for the luncheon he prepared a list of "potential military actions which might jar the North Vietnamese into being more forthcoming at the Paris peace talks." The list never made it out of his pocket. Instead Nixon and Kissinger requested a menu of "actual or feigned" actions, with emphasis on the latter—deceptions meant to *suggest* a serious threat, rather than an actual offensive.

The president's express preference for deception over real actions should have been a clear sign that the military would not be allowed to win the war on the battlefield. Yet within a few weeks Nixon sent the brass a conflicting signal, granting a long-standing JCS request to bomb the North Vietnamese sanctuaries in Cambodia. The purpose, Nixon later wrote, was not only to interdict the North Vietnamese but also to let them know that aggressive actions such as Tet would not go unpunished.

The bombing effectively disrupted North Vietnam's supply lines, but Nixon undercut its impact by insisting that it be done secretly, and that Wheeler conceal the purpose even from most of the U.S. military hierarchy, including the service secretaries and vice chiefs of staff, by creating an extensive double set of books.

In Paris, at secret talks with Kissinger, North Vietnamese chief negotiator Le Duc Tho scoffed at the A Shau valley offensive and the Cambodian bombings. North Vietnam refused to budge from the cease-fire conditions issued during the Johnson years: 1) American troops must leave Vietnam; 2) the Saigon government must yield to a new one, to be selected from slates that included North Vietnamese candidates; and 3) the Viet Cong, who were allied with North Vietnam, would not relinquish positions already held inside South Vietnam. (At that time the North did not acknowledge that any of its own troops were in the South.) When these conditions had been presented to Johnson in 1968, Nixon had called them unacceptable, so this early in his presidency he could hardly accept them as the elements of a "peace with honor."

Lieutenant General Vernon Walters, an attaché in Paris who had facilitated the talks (and helped to keep them quiet), updated Fritz Kraemer on the talks, and on Kissinger's frustration. Kraemer was an avid consumer of such insider information, which helped him maintain the upper hand with friends and protégés while also giving him trading stock for his dealings with anti-Communist colleagues such as Lovestone and Angleton.

After Kissinger settled in Washington, he and Kraemer established a pattern: They would phone each other's office and speak, guardedly, using code words, sometimes reporting on recent events but more often simply arranging Kissinger's late-night visits to Kraemer's home on the northwest edge of Washington. Their office conversations—recorded for posterity along with thousands of other Kissinger office "telcons"—have the tone of teacher-pupil consultations, with Kraemer often giving instructions and Kissinger replying obediently. Kissinger agreed to head off press inquiries, to phone a Kraemer acquaintance who needed encouragement or was looking for a promotion. Their unrecorded nighttime dialogues, according to friends, were usually devoted to policy; before presenting his ideas to Nixon, Kissinger would often try them out on Kraemer, confident that his mentor would discover the holes in his logic and by doing so force him to make the argument stronger. Kissinger also sent Haig to brief Kraemer, expecting Kraemer's comments in return. In these exchanges Kraemer insisted that Kissinger must stick to his principles in the conduct of military and foreign affairs.

ON FEBRUARY 17, nearly a month after taking office, Nixon finally received Anatoly Dobrynin, the Soviet ambassador. Dobrynin had been in the United States since 1962; he spoke English well and liked the States far better than his superiors in the Kremlin did. As recently released records show, he was also more transparent and honest in reporting to his superiors about the Kissinger meetings than Kissinger was in reporting to Nixon.

At this first meeting, Dobrynin tried to raise the topic of the Strategic Arms Limitation Talks (SALT), which had been on hold. Nixon conditioned the arms limitation talks to "linkage" on other issues; he would agree to restarting SALT only if the Soviets showed a willingness to move toward Nixon's positions on adjusting the balance in the Middle East, or on slowing down Soviet military supply of North Vietnam. And he told Dobrynin to discuss such matters with Kissinger on a back-channel basis—a secret arrangement designed to cut through diplomatic folderol and, not incidentally, to allow Nixon to advocate one position in public while pursuing another in private.

At the first back-channel meeting, held four days later, Kissinger told the ambassador some reassuring and some startling things. Kissinger announced Nixon's willingness to acknowledge that the Soviet border states belonged to the USSR's sphere of influence, implying that America would not come to the rescue if another Czechoslovakia should try to break away—a drastic reversal of decades of U.S. policy. Conservatives would have howled in anger and betrayal had this become public. But, as Dobrynin's reports reveal, Kissinger had even more startling news for the Soviets: The United States, Kissinger said, would no longer look for a "military solution" in Vietnam; they "would have no objection if, after [a Vietnam peace] agreement is reached, events in Vietnam were to take their own 'purely Vietnamese' course and thereafter develop 'in keeping with the historical traditions and experience of the Vietnamese people.'" Dobrynin took that phrasing to mean that U.S. forces would not intervene if, after hostilities ended, South Vietnam should go Communist.

It was extraordinary: Here was Richard Nixon, just a month after taking office, informing the USSR that he was now willing to accept an outcome in Vietnam that was tantamount to defeat for the United States. This would certainly have been unwelcome news to the Joint Chiefs, to Abrams and Goodpaster in Saigon, and to the more than 500,000 troops who believed they were in Vietnam to win complete independence for that country. Shortly thereafter, Secretary of Defense Laird and Secretary of State Rogers would also declare in behind-the-scenes meetings their desire to get U.S. troops out of Vietnam and relinquish any thought of winning the war. Six weeks in, the Nixon administration's four top foreign policy officials were acknowledging that the Vietnam War was irrevocably lost.

Kissinger's message to Dobrynin about U.S. intentions in Vietnam was meant as a signal of potential rapprochement with the Soviet Union. But the USSR, knowing that the Nixon administration was no longer looking for a "military solution" in Vietnam, had no incentive to stop supplying North Vietnam. If anything, they now had reason to step up their efforts—in hopes of ending the war sooner, on their own terms.

BUREAUCRACIES ARE BY nature cumbersome beasts, but when aroused, they can exert considerable force. When State, Defense, and the CIA realized that Nixon intended to conceive and conduct foreign policy solely through Kissinger and the NSC—that is, without them—they began to push back. Leakers from their bureaucracies made pessimistic answers to the Kissinger-Ellsberg questionnaires and then fed those answers to the press. And Secretaries Laird and Rogers compounded matters around this time by sending up signals of independence from the administration's stated policies.

Secretary of State Rogers implied to Dobrynin that U.S. support for Thieu wasn't unshakable—which suggested, without saying so directly, that it could be negotiated away. Rogers's gaffe soon meshed in Nixon's mind with State's refusal to facilitate his initial attempts to make an approach to China. Today the opening to China is considered Nixon's grandest accomplishment, but in 1969, when Nixon broached the idea to Kissinger, the national security adviser confided to Haig, "Our Leader has taken leave of reality. . . . He thinks this is the moment to establish normal relations with

China [and] ordered me to make this flight of fancy come true." Nixon directed Kissinger to have the State Department reach out to the Chinese through intermediaries, but when State dragged its collective feet, a frustrated Nixon ordered the NSC to investigate options for a China opening "without any notice to people who might leak," meaning the State Department and its secretary.

Defense secretary Laird's signal of independence was more significant, more deliberate, and less easily countered. Testifying before Congress, he announced that the Sentinel antiballistic missile (ABM) defense program had been delayed indefinitely—before Nixon had agreed to the decision. Since the 1962 Cuban Missile Crisis, the Soviets had been building missiles at a breakneck pace, and by 1969 they had almost reached parity in terms of numbers of missiles, if not in warhead tonnage or in their ability to hit numerous targets. The United States knew that the Soviets were testing an ABM system known as Galosh that would be used to form a defensive ring around Moscow; that was one reason the U.S. military had begun to develop a similar system, called Sentinel.

People with knowledge of ABMs, such as Deputy Secretary of Defense David Packard—a founder of Hewlett-Packard—were against Sentinel, convinced that no ABM system could adequately protect a major American city. Even the chief U.S. arms negotiator, Gerard Smith of the State Department's Arms Control and Disarmament Agency (ACDA), disliked Sentinel because he couldn't figure out how to deal with it through the SALT talks framework. Yet other conservatives inside and outside the administration continued to advocate publicly for a new ABM system, and as the fight persisted, it threatened to derail Nixon's larger plans.

Realizing that his dream of making deals with the Soviets could be thwarted if his right flank forced him to build more missiles, Nixon soon turned over the leadership of the fight for an American ABM to Scoop Jackson and his friends.

BEFORE THE ABM battle began in earnest, Nixon had his first clear conflict with the right. It involved a long-running feud over U.S. intelligence estimates of Soviet power. For years, the experts at the RAND Corporation, working for the Pentagon, had issued high estimates of the number and strength of Soviet missiles, characterizing them as a major threat to U.S. national security. In contrast, experts from the CIA and State Department offered much lower estimates, painting a far less forbidding picture of the Soviet missile threat. The low-ballers believed that the Soviets would stop production of new missiles once the USSR had caught up to the United

States in numbers of missiles; the highballers believed the Soviets would continue building missiles until the strategic balance tipped in their favor.

During the Johnson years, Kissinger and Kraemer had agreed with the high-estimators, charging that the CIA's less alarmist advice refused to take into account "Soviet objectives and strategies." This was an ideological argument, contending that the facts and figures presented by the CIA estimators were not enough, by themselves, to evaluate the true nature of the Soviet threat. At a press conference, Nixon confounded the high-estimators. Asked whether the United States would seek parity or superiority in nuclear arms, Nixon responded that he would pursue "sufficiency," a vague term he neither defined nor quantified. Kissinger soon fell in line with that sentiment.

His reversing a prior stand on an important issue was a sign of how quickly Henry Kissinger arrived at the understanding that he could amass substantial power only if Nixon trusted and relied on him. This meant furthering Nixon's goals however he could, even if he disagreed with them. Idealism is difficult to maintain when an ambitious man is close enough to power to feel its thrill, and harder still when the fount of that power is an ultra-pragmatist.

In his memoirs, Kissinger describes himself in his early months in the Nixon administration as "naïve" regarding some aspects of his role as national security adviser, and "ignorant of the ways of Washington." Despite his decade of consulting to the executive branch, Kissinger was not entirely comfortable as a manager of bureaucrats. For help he turned to Kraemer's other protégé, Al Haig. At forty-four, Haig was only a year younger than Kissinger; though a dutiful aide-de-camp, he considered himself more Kissinger's peer than his subordinate, and well beyond Kissinger in bureaucratic know-how. (The same was true in the treacherous world of Washington society: For one early formal dinner, Haig even helped Kissinger put on his tuxedo and bow tie.)

The complicated interplay between these two Kraemer protégés, Kissinger and Haig, would continue throughout the Nixon years. Caught between their idealistic tutor and their pragmatic boss, they were constantly readjusting the balance of their loyalties—to Nixon, to Kraemer and his philosophy, and to one another.

Haig was eager to position himself as Kissinger's deputy, and he steadily elbowed his competition, particularly such relative liberals as Halperin, out of the running. Haig's hard-line ally at the NSC was Sven Kraemer. A foreign policy conservative in his father's mold—though their relationship was not always easy—Sven was brilliant in his own right, writing what a later historian characterized as the one 1969 memo about Vietnam that merited serious consideration by Kissinger, Nixon, and the Department of Defense (DoD).

As Kissinger warmed to the prospect of wielding the president's power as his own, Haig—not yet as close to Nixon—hewed closer to Kraemerite hawkishness. This dynamic played out in the six-month saga of the "actual or feigned" actions memo that Nixon and Kissinger had requested of Wheeler in their January meeting. The memo consisted of recommendations by Wheeler's staff that had been given to Laird, who sent them to Kissinger to forward to Nixon. Haig, an army colonel with no stars on his shoulders, saw the memo before Kissinger, and recommended to the national security adviser that the memo be bucked back to the four-star general for more work, because the suggestions were poor. The largest "feigned" action relied on staged events including a "technical escalation of war" by nuclear means, which meant putting America's forces on DEFCON 3, or worldwide high alert. That was an excess, and it was clear to Haig that Laird and Wheeler had included it only because they thought Kissinger or Nixon wanted it. (The DoD appended a note warning that if the enemy saw through any such deception—a very real possibility, in their view—"subsequent indications of serious US intent would lose their credibility.") Kissinger agreed, and directed Haig to write to the JCS, over Kissinger's signature, asking them to propose "less elaborate actions which . . . might be undertaken with reduced risks of news media recognition or domestic turbulence."

EARLY IN MARCH 1969, at Nixon's request, Wheeler and Laird flew into Saigon to assess progress there. The United States and South Vietnam were effectively countering a second Tet offensive: The visitors could see that there was much less rocket damage to Saigon than during Tet 1968. But while Wheeler was willing to judge such signs as positive, Laird was only interested in asking Abrams and Goodpaster how soon the South Vietnamese could take over the bulk of the fighting and how many American troops Nixon could promise to bring home that year. Abrams told Laird, quite directly, that the South Vietnamese were not ready to assume the lead on the battlefield. Nonetheless, Laird insisted that the fighting had to be turned over to them "before the time given the new Administration runs out."

After Laird and Wheeler left to return home, Abrams remarked to his staff that the secretary of defense "certainly had not come to Saigon to help us win the war."

When he returned, Laird reported to Nixon that the continuing huge American military presence in Vietnam was sapping the initiative of Saigon's forces and their willingness to defend themselves. Insisting that antiwar sentiment could capsize the administration if Nixon didn't end the war quickly, Laird recommended withdrawing 50,000 to 70,000 U.S. troops by year's end. Nixon leaped at the idea; it was exactly the way to quickly reduce American casualties and bring U.S. involvement in the war to a close. To discuss the plan's feasibility, Nixon had Goodpaster flown to Washington for a March 28 NSC meeting (while there, he would also attend Eisenhower's funeral). Sensing that the die was already cast, Goodpaster reported—contrary to what he and Abrams had said just weeks earlier—that the South's forces were substantially improved, allowing "de-Americanization" to proceed apace. Objecting to the term *de-Americanization*, Laird substituted his own: *Vietnamization*.

Vietnamization and the new Safeguard anti-missile system, in the view of many on the right, amounted to a backpedaling from confrontation with the Communists. Similar initiatives had long been advocated by the left. But while Nixon was perfectly willing to steal the left's thunder, he was wary of being perceived by the right as drifting into leftist softness. So when, with Kissinger's help, he laid out his big-picture thoughts in an April 14 memo to his top foreign policy team, he couched them in standard anti-Communist rhetoric. He began by citing a study by the Institute for Strategic Studies in London that said the Russians had reached parity in nuclear weapons and were about to surpass the United States in land-based intercontinental ballistic missiles (ICBMs). To Nixon, the key point of the report was its prediction that this Soviet achievement would diminish American resolve and lead to a period in which the United States would no longer dominate the world because of a loss of U.S. will.

"The great fundamental issue," Nixon's memo warned, "is very simply whether we will allow the Soviet Union to pass the United States in overall nuclear capability and leave us in a second-rate position." The correct response, he argued, was to hold off negotiation with the Soviets until the United States had deployed the Safeguard missile defense system. But the "problem" of Vietnam must also be solved, he asserted, by Vietnamizing the ground war while mounting new bombing campaigns and air support of South Vietnamese operations, with an end goal of driving the North Vietnamese to the peace table. As a matter of course, Vietnamization would entail bringing home significant numbers of U.S. ground troops over the next several years.

This internal memo would have alarmed Nixon's critics on the right, with its vision of progressive U.S. withdrawal from its commitment to an independent South Vietnam. And they would have been more angered by a second memo, from Kissinger (though over Nixon's signature), on "Vietnamizing of the war," which proceeded from the startling assumption that American withdrawals of troops would not be matched by the North Vietnamese. While running for office, Nixon had insisted that U.S. withdrawals must not be unilateral. Now he washed away that line in the sand: In another Kissinger policy about-face, he agreed. Though Nixon's dovish plan to pull out American troops ran counter to everything Kraemer had taught Kissinger, the man Bob Haldeman had already dubbed the "hawk of hawks" was quick to embrace Nixon's troop withdrawal plan.

One reason was that Nixon convinced Kissinger that the best way to deal with the USSR was to clear away the "problem" of Vietnam—even if it meant conceding sway over the entire area to the Communists—so that the two superpowers could get down to bargaining on larger and more intractable issues including nuclear arms control, force reductions in Europe, and peace and balance in the Middle East.

The idea fit well with Kissinger's predilections for big-power bargaining, and with his ongoing evolution from Kraemerite ideologue to Nixonian pragmatist. As Stanley Hoffmann, an Austrian-born historian and longtime colleague of Kissinger's at Harvard, observed in a review of Kissinger's book *American Foreign Policy* that April, Kissinger was in the process of distancing himself from his youthful insistence that geopolitical problems could be solved only by military force. On one hand, Hoffmann wrote, Kissinger's writings were marked by "the brooding melancholy of a man who has experienced tragedy as a child and an adolescent, studied and reflected on history—especially that of revolutionary ages—and realized how tenuous civilization and legitimacy are. He has a nostalgia for aristocratic ages, with their concern for quality and detachment from the yoke of bureaucracy or the cult of success." On the other hand, Hoffmann noted a distinction between Kissinger's "tough-mindedness" and pure hawkishness, "for a hawk judges the Soviets on their presumed evil intent, and overestimates the potency of America's might." In Kissinger's earlier study of Metternich, Hoffmann pointed out, he had drawn a sharp contrast between the "statesman" who "manipulates reality" and who has a "wary" view of human nature, and the prophet who—in Hoffmann's words—"wants to create reality, believes in man's perfectability, and represents exaltation." Kissinger, Hoffmann concluded, wanted to be a statesman but recognized the pull of the "visionary side" of man and the need for that vision as part of the statesman's motivation.

By the time Hoffmann's review appeared, Kissinger was so busy dealing with a realistic crisis that he had no time to think in terms of being a visionary—or even a statesman.

AT 7:20 A.M. on the morning of April 15, 1969, Kissinger awakened President Nixon by phone with bad news: A few minutes earlier, forty-eight miles east of the Korean peninsula, North Korean MiGs had shot down an unarmed and unescorted U.S. Navy EC-121 reconnaissance plane. All thirty-one men aboard were missing, presumed dead.

The EC-121 incident was the administration's first foreign policy crisis. "We were being tested," Nixon wrote in his memoir. Kissinger, in his, suggests that Nixon thought the strike by a Communist power was a signal meant for him personally, a test of his resolve akin to that posed by Khrushchev to Kennedy in 1961 over Berlin—a challenge that Nixon felt Kennedy had failed. In a similar incident in 1968, when the North Koreans captured the USS *Pueblo*, Nixon, then a presidential candidate, had derided President Johnson for refusing to take aggressive action. "Force must be met by force," Nixon wrote of his initial reaction to the EC-121 crisis, and it was out of this impulse, even before the facts were known, that he asked to review his options for retaliation.

Kissinger assigned the task of detailing the military options to Haig, Halperin, and Lawrence Eagleburger, and he also consulted Fritz Kraemer. Haig may also have talked to Kraemer about the matter, as he did frequently in those days. Both protégés were mindful of the relevance of Kraemer's belief in the importance of acting decisively and quickly in such crises; they knew Kraemer's view that an absence of immediate and forceful action would amount to an American display of provocative weakness.

Yet the American ability to act quickly was hampered because U.S. officials lacked the facts to make a conclusive analysis of the incident, from which they could fashion a response. Had the shootdown been an accident or a deliberate act? A coordinated Communist powers' reaction to something outside Korea, such as the bombing of the Cambodian sanctuaries? Evidence from an intercept suggested that the Soviet navy was surprised by the strike. But Pyongyang had issued a communiqué two hours after the event—the sort of message that usually took them much longer to concoct. As the CIA noted, April 15 was North Korean leader Kim Il-Sung's fifty-seventh birthday; the shootdown could have been a tribute. (Later, U.S. analysts concluded that the EC-121 incident had most likely been instigated by an internal power struggle within North Korea; the losing faction may have shot down the plane to demonstrate its belligerence and so keep their jobs and their heads.)

The first reaction from the JCS was to alert army units in South Korea, to prepare a number of jet fighter units to fly in, and to ready several large ships from Vietnam and the Philippines to travel westward. But in reviewing their options Kissinger and Nixon were chagrined to discover that the only ready-to-use U.S. plans for action in Korea concerned the repelling of an invasion of South Korea from the North. The brass had not completed construction on a new array of troop bomb shelters, or the amassing of appropriate stockpiles of weapons, which steps had been decreed after the *Pueblo* incident.

Haig's group presented the president with ten military options, ranging from seizing a North Korean ship at sea to a blockade of North Korean ports, a shore bombardment of a portion of North Korea, and an air strike against the base from which the MiGs were presumed to have flown. Of these, Kissinger and Nixon favored an aggressive but proportional military response—the raid against the MiG base. According to Nixon, Kissinger argued that "a strong reaction from the United States would be a signal that for the first time in years the United States was sure of itself. It would shore up the morale of our allies and give pause to our enemies." Fritz Kraemer would not have phrased this argument any differently. And Nixon agreed.

A dose of realism punctured that balloon. U. Alexis Johnson, an assistant secretary of state, pointed out (and later recalled in his autobiography) that "when [North Korean] radar picked up our planes coming in for the attack, the North Koreans might easily conclude that we had launched a general attack and consequently put into motion all their well-prepared plans for attacking the south. That would unleash a much larger war, for which we were not prepared."

Kissinger was undeterred by this warning. If things got nasty and the North Koreans did attack, he insisted, the United States could always bomb them into submission. Kissinger told the NSC meeting that he would be willing to use nuclear weapons for that purpose. No one else at the table was.

Nixon hesitated. With the prospect of the EC-121 event escalating into World War III looming before them, Secretary of State Rogers recommended that Nixon do little in response. "The weak can be rash; the powerful must be restrained," Rogers said.

Rogers's formulation was the direct opposite of Kissinger's Kraemerite proposal. Kissinger's belligerence was further deflated when the State, Defense, and CIA bureaucracies weighed in with reports on the crisis—one of which said there was little justification in international law for a retaliatory strike, that such strikes were only permissible while the incident was in progress. Outnumbered and outranked in this bureaucratic fight, Kissinger yielded. And so did Nixon. Dragging its feet, the military failed to act on Nixon's order to dispatch ships to the site until April 19; they would not arrive on station in the Sea of Japan until, at the earliest, April 21.

At a press conference on the morning of April 19, Nixon conveyed a more bellicose stance than the one he had actually adopted. He told the media that he had dispatched ships to the Sea of Japan, hoping to create the impression in the American public's mind—and perhaps in the North Korean mind—that he was contemplating a carrier-based strike, although he had already ruled out that option.

The EC-121 incident faded from the headlines without any significant

American response to it. Within the administration, the incident and the tepid U.S. reaction left all sides unhappy. In a lessons-learned memo to Nixon, Kissinger elided over their shared responsibility for the response, slamming military procedures as "generally unresponsive, pedantic and slow." In his memoirs, Kissinger flagellated the decision-making process surrounding the EC-121 incident: "We set the crisis machinery into motion with great deliberation," he recalled, "watching ourselves with rapt attention at each step to make sure we were not shooting from the hip"—yet he "never had the impression that Nixon had his heart in a retaliatory attack." In his own autobiography, Nixon claimed precisely the opposite—that he had wanted to launch a decisive military strike but had yielded to caution, afraid of jeopardizing his other recent foreign policy initiatives.

The Nixon administration's handling of the EC-121 incident sent the very message to America's enemies, as well as to anti-Communists in the United States, that Kraemer and his protégés feared: that under Nixon the United States would speak loudly but leave its big stick on its shoulder, even when deliberately provoked. Kraemer was so upset that he sent a three-page memo to Kissinger on June 13 that was both a post-action report on the EC-121 crisis and a broad indictment of where Nixon and Kissinger were heading with their foreign policy. Jumping out at him from his reading of classified cables and innumerable newspapers from all over the world, Kraemer wrote, was a single "global impression: that we, the United States, simply 'want out.'"

Kraemer worried that the United States and its allies had in recent years been displaying what amounted to provocative weakness on many fronts— citing their inadequate reactions to

> the invasion of Czechoslovakia, the capture of the *Pueblo*, the shooting down of the EC-121, the shelling of our fishing boats by Peru, the unfriendliness of other Latin American nations in connection with the Rockefeller trip. . . . In each of these cases it may have been statesman-like and prudent not to retaliate by anything but words. In sum total, however, the image of the United States as a paper tiger is coming dangerously close to being universally accepted.

He underlined his conclusion: "This all-pervasive feeling that the United States—at least for some time to come—does not want to become actively 'involved' in any confrontation, constitutes an almost irrepressible temptation for any wild-eyed elements to use for action the broad leeway we appear willing to concede to them." Kraemer's partial solution: if the United States was unwilling to confront others in a tough manner, "we must at least make a better pretense of such willingness."

. . . .

IN AN ARTICLE on the front page of the May 9, 1969, *New York Times*, military correspondent William Beecher partially revealed the secret bombing of the Cambodian sanctuaries of the North Vietnamese. Beecher was pro-military, as were many of the Pentagon beat reporters, and extremely well versed in military affairs. Fritz Kraemer trusted Beecher not to reveal secret information that he had picked up that might be detrimental to U.S. interests.

The White House reacted sharply to the Beecher report, even though it was incomplete and did not mention deception. Nixon was in the final stages of preparing a major address that would lay out his peace plan for Vietnam. He was not planning to reveal that while his administration was talking peace it was currently bombing in North Vietnam, South Vietnam, Laos, and Cambodia. Should that bombing become widely known, Nixon's peace plan, with its call for mutual withdrawal, would sound considerably less credible. Such news would reinvigorate antiwar forces, awaken Congress from its slumber, and convince the Soviets that they had little incentive to respond to Nixon's overtures. Nixon's honeymoon would come to an abrupt end.

Who was the leaker? One candidate was Morton Halperin, who had been Beecher's roommate at Harvard and remained a close friend. On the day the *Times* story ran, Kissinger cut off Halperin's access to classified material and discussed with FBI director J. Edgar Hoover a wiretap on Halperin's home telephone. Hoover said he would only arrange the tap if Attorney General Mitchell authorized it, and Mitchell soon complied. According to a Hoover memo, Kissinger also wanted the tap for a more personal reason: to "destroy whoever did this . . . no matter where he is." Taps were also placed on two other NSC staffers and on Laird's chief military aide, Colonel Robert Pursley, whose frequent questioning of Kissinger's demands (as conveyed by Haig) had made him a thorn in the sides of both White House aides.

In the annals of Nixon administration history, these wiretaps are usually identified as opening the Pandora's box that led to Watergate. But they served another function: They enmeshed Kissinger and Haig in activities that they would work hard to conceal for the remainder of their careers, and that would affect the way they made decisions during the entire course of the Nixon administration.

As the taps stayed in place—turning up nothing of value—agents compiled logs of them, creating a paper trail. Haig and Kissinger both read the logs, at one point perusing them in the presence of a senior FBI official. ("It is clear that I don't have anybody in [my NSC] office I can trust except Colonel

Haig here," Kissinger told the official.) Kissinger, Haig, and the FBI soon had to conclude that the leaker could not have been Halperin, because the classified leaks continued after closing off his access. Once these additional leaks emerged, Nixon raged at Haldeman that there were to be no more NSC meetings, because they produced papers that would then circulate through the bureaucracy and leak. From here on, Haldeman noted in his diary, Nixon would "make decisions privately, with K." Kissinger insisted that the NSC meetings continue, or else their absence would give fodder to the press and alarm America's enemies. The meetings resumed, but now they were mainly for show: By mid-June 1969, Nixon and Kissinger alone were making all decisions on national security and foreign policy.

Even so, Kissinger, with input from Haig, had the FBI place wiretaps on a growing list of targets in the media, the Pentagon, and the NSC. One Kissinger aide was forced to resign, ostensibly because he was heard speaking to a reporter, though the aide was never indicted. Kissinger liked to contend that toughness on presumed leakers kept the NSC, DoD, State, and CIA on notice that no one would be permitted to interfere with administration policies—or to attempt to counter those policies by exposing them to the public.

But that was not the only message transmitted by the White House's frantic reaction to the Beecher leak. The North Vietnamese already knew their Cambodian sanctuaries were being bombed, but hints of the White House's efforts to stop the leaks about the Cambodian bombings confirmed their sense that Nixon was afraid of reigniting antiwar activity on the home front. Furthermore, since the United States did not send in ground troops after the bombings to clean out the sanctuaries, the entire Cambodian bombing campaign—and the effort to conceal it—constituted a spectacular display of American weakness.

Fritz Kraemer's predictions were coming to pass. After conferring with their Chinese counselors, North Vietnam's leaders reaffirmed their determination to stay the course: They would endure the bombs and decline to negotiate with the United States, in the expectation that sooner or later mounting domestic and international pressure would force the Nixon administration to withdraw its troops from the battlefield—handing the North Vietnamese the ultimate victory in the long war.

By the late spring of 1969, the boast that Richard Nixon and Henry Kissinger had made privately to themselves and others—that they would end the war in Vietnam within a hundred days of taking office—was dust. Trying to project strength, Nixon and Kissinger had instead made exactly the mistake that Fritz Kraemer had warned them against: They had displayed a provocative weakness.

4

Young Men in a Hurry

The Nixon administration's assumption of power was a changing-of-the-guard moment. The generation of leaders who had fought in World War II, and who had led the country through the Eisenhower, Kennedy, and Johnson years and had been appointed to the senior positions under Nixon, began to admit to their councils and to positions of minor power the generation born around the time of that war. Slowly, through 1969 and early 1970, thousands of young men, and some young women, came to Washington or took new jobs there in the various executive branch agencies or in congressional offices. A handful of them, then of only minor importance, would later become significant actors in this story of the long struggle to control American foreign policy.

FOR TWO OF these young men, Richard Perle and Paul Wolfowitz, Nixon's inability to bring the war in Vietnam to a quick close presented an opportunity for advancement. As resurgent antiwar sentiment compromised other areas of the administration's foreign policy, the White House began to realize that it lacked enough votes in the Senate to pass the authorization for the Safeguard anti-ballistic missile system. Nixon would later call the battle over the Safeguard ABM "the biggest congressional battle of the first term." But at the time he let others fight it for him.

Authorization for previous missile systems funding had sailed through Congress with hardly a comment. In 1969, however, there were new questions to be posed. Had the Soviets reached nuclear parity? Could they launch a first strike that would leave the United States unable to respond? Did the difference between a MIRV (Multiple Independently Targetable Reentry Vehicle) and a MRV (Multiple Reentry Vehicle) ensure the safety and security of our country? Not enough hard intelligence was available to answer these questions properly—which meant that the answers provided by one side or the other tended to be political rather than solely factual.

Nixon was unwilling to commit many White House resources to the Safeguard appropriations battle, believing (with Gerard Smith and Kissinger) that once Safeguard was begun at any level of funding it would be negotiated away at the next round of talks. So he gladly ceded leadership of the Safeguard fight to a man who did care about ABMs, Scoop Jackson.

Often called "the senator from Boeing" for his championing of the defense contractor in his home state of Washington, Jackson had made himself an expert on national defense and missile defense in particular. He was friends with Fritz Kraemer and Ed Rowny, and the three agreed on national defense matters. Jackson scorned fellow Democratic senators such as George McGovern, Eugene McCarthy, and Mike Mansfield as lost causes when it came to national security; to his mind, they were not just antiwar but also antimilitary and anti–national defense. But he was determined to sway other Democratic colleagues to vote for Safeguard. To help make his case he needed "independent" experts to testify to the need for the missile defense system; to provide them he turned to a couple of old Cold Warriors, Dean Acheson, a former secretary of state, and Paul Nitze, a former secretary of the navy and arms control expert who had been advising presidents since World War II. Nitze, in turn, hired three graduate students as interns for the summer. Two of these were Perle and Wolfowitz.

Nitze actively disliked the president, whom he had known since Nixon was a senator. Back then, Nitze had been asked to tutor Nixon, but he threw up his hands when Nixon seemed incapable of listening for more than five minutes without interrupting and going off on a tangent, usually about himself. Nitze also held no brief for Kissinger, whose bestseller he had eviscerated in a magazine review so scathing that Kissinger had threatened to sue the publisher. Still, Nitze saw the opposition to Safeguard much as Nixon might have—as a "misguided child" of antiwar sentiment, seated in "the desire of many to wish away the problems of national security." To help promote the system, Nitze formed a small group with a grand name, the Committee to Maintain a Prudent Defense Policy, backed by Acheson and the man he expected to be the prime witness before Jackson in the Senate: Albert Wohlstetter.

A RAND mathematician then teaching at the University of Chicago, Wohlstetter was already a legend as a defense guru who had introduced such

terms and concepts as "first strike" and fail-safe," which had guided Cold
War nuclear policy. Wohlstetter suggested hiring two of his current graduate students, Wolfowitz and Peter Wilson, and a former protégé, Perle, then
in a Princeton graduate program. These three would create the background
memos, props, and charts for Wohlstetter's testimony.

Perle had been in the mathematician's orbit since his high school days in
California, when he was a classmate of Wohlstetter's daughter. As Kraemer
had with Kissinger, Wohlstetter had highly influenced Perle's choices from
then on, steering his talents into economics at the University of Southern
California and the London School of Economics, and convincing Perle to
adopt his conservative, militarist view of the world. During the Vietnam
War, Perle avoided military service by pursuing graduate degrees; he had
completed a master's and had been preparing his doctoral dissertation when
he was summoned to Washington in 1969.

Wolfowitz, a son of a Cornell mathematician, "probably would have
ended up a very unhappy biochemist," he later said, had he not encountered
Wohlstetter and other conservative luminaries at the University of Chicago.
Now he was firmly on the road to pursuing an academic career as an international political scientist, whose conservative bent matched that of his new
friend Perle. Both young men were Democrats, and like Jackson and Nitze
they had no thought of transferring their loyalty to the Republican Party.
Jackson became their model. As Perle later recalled, "Paul and I were both
enormously impressed with Jackson." Perle was not, however, "a fan of Richard Nixon, and never became a fan of his, although I came to regard him as
pretty shrewd and intelligent."

Nitze and Wohlstetter were heavy on experience and specific knowledge
about missile defense but light on cash. The White House's congressional
liaison, a former Nitze deputy, put him in touch with William Casey, a
former World War II intelligence officer who had made millions on Wall
Street. Casey also favored the ABM and had established a committee of
Republican conservatives outside the government; they lacked technical
expertise on the subject but had plenty of money. The Casey and Nitze
groups joined in the effort to foment public interest in Safeguard, as a way
to pressure recalcitrant senators. Two southern Democratic senators, Strom
Thurmond and John Stennis, also worked toward that goal; Nixon considered them friends, and they usually voted with him.

Thurmond's main assistant that summer in the ABM fight was J. Fred
Buzhardt, a friend of Al Haig's from their days at West Point. After serving in
the Army Air Corps he attended law school, then went to work for Thurmond.
From 1956 to 1966 he was the South Carolina senator's assistant on defense
matters, writing pseudonymous articles highly critical of Secretary of Defense

McNamara. Thurmond's wife considered Buzhardt a ruthless ideologue; on her deathbed she cautioned Thurmond never to be alone in a room with him, since Buzhardt was more interested in the cause than the man, and therefore, she implied, might betray Strom. In 1968, Buzhardt's cause had been helping Nixon win the election. In 1969 it was the Safeguard ABM.

This fight had everything—pure favor-trading politics, the twisting of intelligence information, and testimony so complicated and contradictory that it later spawned an entire book. Jackson's logic and persuasive tactics convinced a few fence-sitters to give him the benefit of the doubt and vote with him. When Stennis threatened to return to Mississippi and not take part in the floor vote on Safeguard unless Nixon delayed desegregation in Mississippi, the administration did so. And when the most recent National Intelligence Estimate labeled a new Soviet missile about which the intelligence community had scant information an MRV instead of a MIRV—a designation that would make it less of a threat to the United States, one that might not require a Safeguard system to counter it—Kissinger, Laird, and the Joint Chiefs collectively lobbied CIA director Richard Helms to change the designation to "probably" a MIRV. The switch convinced enough senators to tie the floor vote on the $490 million Safeguard appropriation bill at 50-50, and Vice President Spiro Agnew cast the deciding vote in favor of Safeguard.

Perle and Wolfowitz took away from the ABM fight a sense of satisfaction at having helped operate the fulcrum of power, experience in moving the White House in the direction they wanted it to go, and a reaffirmation of their anti-Communist principles at a time when most of their generation had forsaken Cold War ideology. Wolfowitz returned to his graduate studies. Jackson offered Perle a job, with the promise that in his spare time he could write his dissertation. He never did, but in Jackson he found something more, a surrogate father. Jackson, he recalled, "would counsel me on the things fathers counsel kids about. And because he was not my father, I was probably more willing to take his advice." Fred Buzhardt was rewarded by the administration with a plum job as associate counsel to the Department of Defense. Buzhardt was overjoyed at the job, he told his family, because it would allow him to combine his three passions: the law, the military, and government service.

ALTHOUGH NIXON HAD campaigned as a law-and-order man, once in office he was prepared to compromise with the heavily Democratic Congress. His actions in the social sphere would eventually do more to further Lyndon Johnson's liberal agenda than Johnson himself had done—making greater progress on school integration, assistance to the poor, welfare reform, broadening of Medicare and Medicaid, health-care reform, and environmental conservation. One program he could not abide, however, was Johnson's "war on poverty," administered in large part by the Office of Economic Opportunity (OEO). In the spring of 1969, Nixon cajoled four-term Illinois congressman Donald Rumsfeld, who had campaigned heartily for him, to resign his House seat and direct the office.

Rumsfeld was a thirty-seven-year-old Princeton graduate who had just won reelection to Congress. A former navy fighter pilot (though he had never seen combat), he was slightly dovish on the war—he wanted the troops brought home quickly—and was a supporter of an all-volunteer military, an idea Nixon championed. Rumsfeld had been instrumental in Gerald Ford's upset win for minority leader of the House, but the party hierarchy had not rewarded him with a leadership post. When Nixon offered him the job at OEO, however, Rumsfeld played the reluctant bride. He protested that he had actually voted against establishing OEO in the first place and had voted for a bill to restrict its reach. "That is exactly why we want you," Nixon said. Rumsfeld relented, accepting on the condition that the director's post bear the title of aide to the president, with Cabinet rank, and fought for those perks with a campaign in the newspapers until Nixon granted them.

Friends and critics alike described Rumsfeld as he entered the executive branch as a bantam cock. At Princeton he had played on the 150-pound-and-under football team and wrestled as a welterweight. Now, as OEO head, he exhibited the same characteristics in mental matters; a reporter summed him up as "agile, imaginative, and pragmatic." Though Rumsfeld had had a decade-long friendship with a very liberal New York congressman—they had wrestled together for fun, and planned to publish a newspaper together—in the next election Rumsfeld endorsed his friend's conservative opponent.

Rumsfeld's Washington peers considered him diligent but square, and in his OEO post he earned the nickname "the Undertaker." It was an apt moniker: His brief from Nixon was to rein in OEO, to return its operations from local to federal control, and ultimately to dismantle it. His first action was to lateral its most successful program, Head Start, to the Department of Health, Education, and Welfare (HEW). Under Rumsfeld's command, the antipoverty agency was steadily gutted, almost without anyone noticing. "Rumsfeld has not licked his enemies," a critic said, "but he has very coolly led them into a bog of confusion." Rumsfeld told the wife of an assistant attorney general that he regularly gave in "a little" to the demands of conservatives in order to get them off his back. "He's a great actor [in] a campy little skit," one reporter concluded after listening to Rumsfeld explain an action he was about to take at OEO. As a high-ranking member of the executive branch, he cherished his opportunities to dine occasionally with President Nixon and was intimately involved in the political maneuvering that suffused White House day-to-day operations. Before long, he was mimicking Nixon's habit of putting his feet on his desk when relaxing in his office.

Soon after beginning work at OEO, Rumsfeld received a blueprint for bureaucratic change sent in by a former colleague, Congressman Bill Steiger, and authored by Steiger's twenty-eight-year-old aide, Richard Cheney. Beyond its actual content, the memo served as an updated résumé for Cheney: A year earlier, he had sought a job with Rumsfeld but flunked the interview.

As a Wyoming scholarship student at Yale, Cheney had come under the influence of a professor who was an expert on the CIA, H. Bradford Westerfield, who stressed in his course the important work of "valiant cold warriors" holding back the advances of the Communists. "I was at the peak of my hawkishness," Westerfield later recalled of that era. Cheney did not stay long at Yale; the university yanked his scholarship because his grades were too low. He moved back home, got a job putting in power lines, and resumed his education, soon obtaining his bachelor's degree. He went on to graduate work at the University of Wisconsin, where he maintained his draft deferment, first as a student and then as a married man and expectant father. He later said that he had avoided the draft because he "had other priorities." While at Wisconsin he won a fellowship to work in Washington and applied to work in Congressman Rumsfeld's office; when that didn't happen he applied for the job with Steiger.

In May 1969, Steiger took Cheney along to a meeting of the Students for a Democratic Society on the Madison campus of the University of Wisconsin. But while Steiger was impressed by the conference and the radical students, Cheney was aghast. When he read on Steiger's desk a note from Rumsfeld looking for help at OEO, Cheney crafted the memo on how to overhaul a federal bureaucracy, betting that Steiger would pass it on to Rumsfeld. Shortly thereafter, Cheney received a phone call from Rumsfeld offering him an assistant's position. Within months, Cheney had become so valuable that Rumsfeld asked him to forgo returning to graduate school and to remain as his top assistant at OEO. They worked extremely well together, Rumsfeld the flamboyant chief and Cheney the self-effacing but steely aide. "Cheney is quiet, almost to the point of bashfulness," a reporter would later observe, "a description no one would suggest for the more abrasive Rumsfeld."

Ken Adelman, then a young OEO staffer who became close to both Rumsfeld and Cheney, remembers Cheney in 1969 as "very conservative." Another friend from that era later recalled that "Dick said what [his colleagues] all thought but didn't say aloud" regarding money, race, partisanship, and scorn for antiwar protesters. "Reactionaries," a White House staffer later called the pair. Cheney soon became indispensable to his boss as they struggled with liberal colleagues at OEO and attempted to return power from the periphery—actions that sharpened their belief in the need for ideological rigor in directing the actions of a government agency.

NIXON'S ATTEMPTS AT communicating secretly with the leaders of Moscow, Beijing, and Hanoi required Kissinger to ask the U.S. military to provide secure communications channels to handle these messages. Admiral Thomas Moorer, the chief of naval operations (CNO), designated channel SR-1 for Kissinger's uses. Throughout Nixon's first term, many secret military and diplomatic messages were sent and received over this channel.

Housekeeping and monitoring of this SR-1 channel, and others, were among the tasks assigned to a young naval lieutenant when he began at the Pentagon on August 1, 1969. Robert U. Woodward had been in the navy's ROTC program at Yale and was in the process of completing his obligatory service years. After he did sea duty off the shores of Vietnam, two former skippers, Francis J. Fitzpatrick and Robert Welander, recommended him for a Pentagon job, where they preceded him.

Woodward worked in the Pentagon communications center, but his most important job was as a briefer, a junior officer who collected and presented information to the most senior officers on a daily basis. The job of briefer was a prize, a challenge given to those whom the navy considered potential future leaders, including Richard Lugar, who would become the long-serving senator from Indiana, and Bobby Ray Inman, who would rise to be CNI (chief of naval intelligence), then director of the National Security Agency and deputy director of the CIA.

For Woodward, the job as briefer was "kind of a high-ranking position for a guy who has four years active duty and an NROTC background," according to Admiral Eugene Carroll, a deputy chief of personnel of the navy in that era. Carroll characterized Woodward's rise from lieutenant junior grade to full lieutenant in the previous thirty-nine months as "awfully, awfully, awfully fast. I don't remember any program which resulted in anybody making lieutenant in less than four years."

Each morning, a team of briefers presented the daily briefing in a hundred-seat theater on the fourth floor of the Pentagon's D ring, to an audience of two or three dozen navy flag officers, brass from other services, and civilians from the office of the secretary of defense. A 1975 briefer recalled that the level of information they had to convey was often so high that at times during the briefing "we'd have to ask certain people to leave the room, since they weren't cleared for the information we'd present." Later in the day, briefers routinely presented information from the morning briefing to cleared individuals in congressional or executive branch offices. Admiral Moorer later recalled that as CNO he frequently sent Woodward to the White House to brief Alexander Haig in his basement office.

Haig and Woodward would both later deny this relationship. But several other people—among them an NSC member at the time, and an assistant secretary of defense for public information, as well as Secretary of Defense Laird—confirmed Moorer's recollections. Recently, Woodward has said that he was in the White House, waiting for an appointment with someone, when he met W. Mark Felt, whom he finally identified in 2005 as "Deep Throat," his most important source on the Watergate story. Felt, a high-ranking FBI official, was at the White House during that period to meet with Al Haig regarding the wiretaps on newsmen and NSC staffers.

Woodward remained at the Pentagon for only a year, but it was a year during which the upper brass in the navy, to whom he reported, became increasingly dissatisfied with Nixon, Kissinger, and their foreign policy initiatives. And they did not keep their dissatisfaction to themselves, openly discussing it with colleagues.

That Woodward was a junior colleague in good favor with the top brass is underscored by the timing and means of his exit from the Pentagon. In April 1970, several months before he was due to leave his military billet, Woodward applied for a job with the *Washington Post*. On July 3, he separated from the navy—but did so after serving only five years of a six-year commitment. To leave without completing that sixth year in 1970, while the country was at war, was highly unusual, according to Admiral Eugene LaRocque, who had been at the Pentagon in that era: "Officers can resign about any time except on their commitment and then they've got to fulfill their commitment unless something very—somebody's really working for them. Now Admiral Moorer could've called over [to the personnel bureau] and gotten that taken care of in a minute." Admiral Carroll, who served in the personnel bureau in the 1970s, agreed: "That [the resignation] I don't understand without Moorer telling somebody to accept the resignation."

Woodward won entry to Harvard Law School but attended for only two weeks before taking a trial position at the *Washington Post*. Editor Harry Rosenfeld recalled that Woodward had "come to us on very high recommendations from someone in the White House." That person has never been identified. Rosenfeld conceded in an interview that to hire someone with no clips (prior newspaper articles bearing his byline) was unusual but said that "we gave him a tryout because he was so highly recommended" and had been "an intelligence officer in the Navy."

Yet Woodward's first days at the *Post* did not go easily. None of his copy made it into the paper, and eventually his supervisors advised him to seek seasoning elsewhere. He applied to the suburban *Montgomery County Sentinel*. Roger Farquhar, who hired Woodward for the *Sentinel*, later remembered three reasons for doing so: a "fantastic" recommendation from "Naval intelligence" attesting to Woodward's very "strong work ethic"; his Yale degree; and something the young reporter said at the end of his interview. Standing in the doorway, Woodward told Farquhar, "I want to work here so bad that I can taste it."

Asked whether there had been any recommendation from the *Washington Post*, Farquhar said no, it was strictly navy, all the way.

ONE OF FRED Buzhardt's first assignments at the Pentagon, in 1969–70, found him trying to contain a burgeoning scandal involving PX depots in Vietnam. A conspiracy of suppliers, contractors, and supply office personnel had colluded to skim small fortunes from the depots, until Don Stewart, a DoD investigator and former FBI field agent with decades of experience, launched an inquiry. Stewart soon discovered that Buzhardt was trying to impede his investigation, telling him it was all right for him "to 'go out and ask a couple of questions, but don't get into this,' you know," because the scandal would be detrimental to the army. In addition to asking Stewart to go easy, Buzhardt later bragged to Bill Gulley, chief of the military office in the Nixon White House, that in order to handle the PX scandal, "I created a dummy audit board and put it in my desk drawer. A couple of months would pass and when someone would ask me how things were progressing with the audit, I'd make up a little progress report from the audit board that never existed and show it to them."

In 1970, Buzhardt was promoted to general counsel of DoD.

WILLIAM SAFIRE, THEN a speechwriter for Nixon and later a *New York Times* columnist, noticed one striking similarity among Nixon, Haldeman, Kissinger, and Haig: All were "loners, in a superficially gregarious way." White House colleagues came to hold two very different views of Alexander Haig. To some, a reporter wrote, he was "brilliant, diplomatic, and an organization wizard," while others saw him as "manipulative and ruthless." All agreed, however, that Haig was "ambitious, hard-working, and loyal."

Whatever fealty Haig professed to hold for Nixon and Kissinger, however, he remained an army officer whose loyalties were to the U.S. Army. Among his closest NSC colleagues was Captain Rembrandt Robinson, head of the military liaison office with the JCS. When Haig met with other NSC members, colleagues observed, he never closed his office door, but when he met alone with Robinson it was always closed. In this and other ways, NSC colleagues later said, Haig conveyed that he was passing to Robinson information from Kissinger or Nixon that Haig's bosses had wanted to keep from the Pentagon. Robinson would later be a central figure in an espionage ring that stole documents from Kissinger and sent them to nonauthorized recipients in the offices of the Joint Chiefs of Staff. Welander, Woodward's former skipper, would also be part of the ring.

In the spring of 1969, Kissinger decreed that the State Department's negotiations with Spain to renew leases on bases should be kept from the Pentagon. NSC member and longtime Kissinger confidant Hal Sonnenfeldt, acting as liaison to State on the matter, "exploded" when the content of his eyes-only memo to Kissinger on the bases was brought up at an interagency meeting by a military participant, a colleague remembered, and Sonnenfeldt blamed the leak on Haig. A second leak involved the secret Kissinger-Dobrynin lunches at secluded locations outside of Washington: Kissinger-Sonnenfeldt memos on these sessions also found their way back to the JCS, and the only logical candidate to have sent them was Haig.

Accounts by former NSC colleagues suggest that Haig tended to endure Kissinger's verbal gibes in group meetings but was capable of intimidating him physically one-on-one. Several NSC members believed that Kissinger feared Haig might attack him physically if they got into a heated argument. But Haig and Kissinger were also very close, especially in their work on the wiretaps, which other NSC members did not know about. After Halperin faded as a rival, Haig's power increased; Haig also successfully distanced himself from Tony Lake, a former foreign service officer in Vietnam who had become more liberal as the war in Vietnam dragged on, and who was therefore increasingly out of step with Kissinger.

Haig's most important personal goal was making sure he came to Nixon's attention, often sidestepping Kissinger's efforts to insulate the president from him and others on the NSC. According to military office head Bill Gulley, Haig used two techniques to curry favor with Nixon. The first was by passing "little, intimate bits of gossip about Kissinger" through Haldeman to Nixon, knowing that Nixon assiduously collected dirt on employees, enemies, and potential enemies. The second derived from Haig's position as military decoder of messages: When Kissinger was away, Haig received his coded messages for the president, decoded them for Nixon, then encoded

Nixon's responses to Kissinger. According to Gulley, Haig would not simply encode or decode what he was given: "[He] did a little editing here and a little rephrasing there, making a suggestion that this or that point might fall in line better with the President's view . . . rather than [with] Kissinger's. The result would be messages sent back . . . with little changes, from Nixon, changes which in fact had been suggested by Haig [who] was manipulating both players."

Kissinger installed a "dead-key" system in his NSC office, a phone line on which a second person—sometimes a secretary, sometimes Haig—could monitor both sides of a conversation but could not join the conversation. Haig frequently listened in on Kissinger's phone calls with the president, Cabinet secretaries, ambassadors, reporters, and others. White House counselor Chuck Colson wandered into Haig's office on several occasions and saw him monitoring a Kissinger conversation on the dead key. During one such session, Haig whispered to Colson, "He's selling us out on Vietnam!" Later, after Kissinger had left the office, Haig cursed him in absentia for "selling us out" and told Colson, "I['ve] got to get hold of Kraemer." Shortly thereafter, according to Colson, "Kraemer would come to the White House to talk to Henry," to rekindle his fire for the kind of aggressive, give-no-quarter solutions to problems that Kraemer—and Haig—desired.

5

"Actual or Feigned"

Nixon's grand plans for altering the geopolitical balance of the world were threatened by the continuing virulence of the war in Vietnam. As 1969 wore on, the Nixon administration attempted both to resolve the Vietnam War and to launch its plan to transform America's relationship with the USSR. At first the public was unaware of the linkage between these goals. But knowledgeable insiders soon realized that Nixon was pulling troops out of Vietnam even as he was trying to make risky deals with the Soviets. This angered and emboldened those who disagreed with Nixon's actions. Their reactions would take many forms, some of which would require quite a bit of time to develop before they posed a serious threat to Nixon's policies and even his hold on his office. But they began that spring.

ON MAY 14, as he prepared the speech in which he would offer a mutual-withdrawal peace plan, Nixon had Kissinger bring Ambassador Dobrynin to the Lincoln Bedroom—where no one could overhear their remarks—to assure Moscow that he did not seek a "military solution to the Vietnam problem," as Dobrynin put it in his notes. Kissinger repeated that the United States sought "a fairly reasonable interval between conclusion of a [peace] agreement" and the establishing of a nondemocratic governmental system in South Vietnam.

As a new "Hamburger Hill" battle and its casualties offered fresh evidence that the Vietnam War was not going away, antiwar sentiment surged.

In response, Nixon became even more determined to withdraw from the war through Vietnamization. After securing President Thieu's agreement to allow him to withdraw 25,000 troops, he announced the move in June. Nixon was "jubilant," Kissinger recalled, considering the troop withdrawal "a political triumph [that] would buy him the time necessary for developing our strategy." That was a realistic assessment. Haig would later say that he had been ideologically opposed to Vietnamization, labeling it in hindsight "as phony as a two-dollar bill," but at the time he raised few objections.

The American public cared little whether Vietnamization was a political triumph; voters were simply happy to have some troops removed from harm's way. Most conservatives went along, perhaps hoping the withdrawal of 5 percent of the in-country troops was merely a symbolic cut. Then a former Johnson administration secretary of defense upped the ante. Clark Clifford proposed in an article that the United States withdraw 100,000 troops by year's end and 200,000 by the close of 1970. Nixon took Clifford's numbers as a challenge to draw down on an even faster schedule. In a meeting with liberal Republican senators, he forecast near-complete withdrawal in time to positively influence the 1970 midterm elections—prediction the senators immediately passed on to the press. Conservatives protested that the timetable was too hasty. Kissinger later conceded their point, writing that the accelerated timetable had done "serious damage" to the American position versus the North Vietnamese in the secret Paris talks because it "drained of virtually any plausibility" Nixon's previous insistence that both sides mutually withdraw troops. The North Vietnamese had been demanding unilateral withdrawal of American troops for years; in July 1969 that became U.S. policy.

The notion that Vietnamization could end American involvement in the war gave Nixon another idea, which he introduced at a press conference on Guam after welcoming the Apollo crew back from the first manned landing on the moon. In a question-and-answer session, Nixon first dismissed the dovish notion that the United States should withdraw from Asia entirely, saying that we should continue to play "a significant role" and would keep our treaty commitments to the various countries of the region. But he added that "we must avoid that kind of policy that will make countries in Asia so dependent upon us that we are dragged into conflicts such as . . . Vietnam."

Did this mean, a reporter asked, that the United States would not be involved in future Vietnam-type conflicts?

"We are going to handle each country on a case-by-case basis," Nixon responded, explaining that he was "attempting to avoid that creeping involvement which eventually simply submerges you. . . . I want to be sure that our policies in the future . . . reduce American involvement. [Our role will be] one of assistance . . . in helping them solve their own problems, but not going in and just doing the job ourselves."

The president had not intended these remarks as a big policy shift. But when news media started referring to them as the "Nixon Doctrine," he warmed to the idea. Over the next year he refined it, with Kissinger's help, and made it into a centerpiece of American policy. But while the Monroe Doctrine in 1823 and the Truman Doctrine in 1947 had broadened the sphere of national interest, Nixon's doctrine redefined America's national interest downward and made it conditional: "The United States will participate in the defense of allies and friends but . . . cannot—and will not—conceive all the plans, design all the programs, and undertake all the defense of the free nations."

This highly pragmatic approach to foreign policy led the United States to increase its backing of surrogate defenders, especially the authoritarian anti-Communist regimes to which Nixon had always been partial. For instance, the United States accelerated sales of military equipment to Shah Pahlavi so that Iran could act as a bulwark against the USSR in the upper Persian Gulf.

The doctrine set the United States firmly on a path toward the "de-militarization of foreign policy," a decoupling of U.S. foreign policy and American military might. Economic power, sales of military equipment, and diplomatic trade-offs would steadily become more important in our overseas relationships. Demilitarization of foreign policy combined with drastic reductions in the number, posture, and composition of the U.S. armed forces. In the 1970s, the American military would be transformed from one peopled largely by millions of draftees to a new, "all-volunteer" military consisting of a much lower number of paid professionals.

Old-style American anti-Communists saw Nixon's doctrine as a shocking retreat from John F. Kennedy's inaugural vow: "We shall pay any price, bear any burden, meet any hardship, support any friend, oppose any foe, in order to assure the survival and the success of liberty." In their view, Nixon was asserting that the United States would not go just anywhere to fight—that it would pick its battles, and that the burdens we chose to bear would depend on the moment and the circumstances. Patrick Buchanan, the White House speechwriter and in-house conservative, warned Nixon of "widespread confusion" in the press about the doctrine. Alarmed, Nixon asked Kissinger to assess the damage; Kissinger reported that Buchanan had overstated the case, citing two conservative columnists who praised it. Nixon was relieved.

To Fritz Kraemer, however, the doctrine was anathema. The essence of its failure was its "moral relativism"—its stated goal of weighing political and other pragmatic consequences before using military force to address the ills of the world. Kraemer believed that America's moral core values, which he identified as freedom, democracy, honor, and resistance to totalitarianism, were integral to its leadership of the world—more important than the raw power and superiority of its military—and that any foreign policy that trimmed the need to adhere to these values was an abomination. As the Nixon Doctrine began to take shape, and as Kissinger emerged as its main elucidator, Kraemer watched in chagrin as his protégé seemed to cast aside the principles they once shared.

NIXON AND KISSINGER had already begun to pin their hopes for ending the war in Vietnam on turning the Chinese and the Russians against one another—a strategy that must have seemed increasingly reasonable as Soviet-Chinese border tensions broke out into open warfare in March 1969 at the Ussuri River, China's northeastern border. Although American hardliners had long dismissed the relevance of the Sino-Soviet split, insisting that Communism was monolithic and indivisible, that notion was now contradicted by direct battles between Soviet and Chinese troops that took the lives of hundreds, perhaps thousands. It became clearer that the only thing keeping the two Communist giants in harness was the need to back North Vietnam in its war with the United States.

A paper by Sinologist Allen Whiting, suggesting that China now needed the United States as a counterweight to Soviet moves against its sovereignty, spurred Kissinger to reconsider his previous objections to Nixon's pet project, an opening to China. The continually rising Sino-Soviet border tensions were on the minds of Nixon and Kissinger during their conversations aboard the presidential yacht *Sequoia* in early July as they debated how to accelerate the end of the war in Vietnam. Nixon was determined to "go for broke," to end the war "one way or the other—either by negotiated agreement or by increased use of force." He wrote to Ho Chi Minh urging peace talks on the basis of his proposals and instructed the intermediary who would hand Ho the letter to say that if no breakthrough had been achieved by November first, "I [Nixon] would regretfully find myself obliged to have recourse to measures of great consequence and force."

The Hanoi Politburo responded to Nixon by authorizing an attack on a big U.S. base and a hundred additional sorties against towns in the South. These attacks quickly forced Nixon to delay further American troop withdrawals and to give serious consideration to aggressive new U.S. military action. At Nixon's request, an elated Kissinger directed an NSC team to design a "savage blow" that would force North Vietnam to the bargaining table to sue for peace. The team consisted of Haig, Rem Robinson,

Tony Lake, and another Russian expert, Roger Morris. Haig and Robinson jumped into the plan, which became known as "Duck Hook." Morris recalls viewing contingency plans that included tactical use of nuclear weapons. He and Lake rejected Robinson's first draft as too timid, too much like the nibbling approach of the Johnson era. Robinson soon submitted a plan with larger and sharper teeth.

Kissinger liked the Duck Hook plan. Nixon, uncertain about using such a drastic military push to end the war, wondered if he should just accelerate Vietnamization and troop withdrawals. Dismayed by the president's hesitation, Kissinger sent Nixon a memo that was important in its day and that Kissinger still considered relevant in 2006, when he unearthed a copy to use to stiffen the spine of Vice President Cheney in regard to keeping troops in Iraq: "Withdrawal of American troops will become like salted peanuts to the American public: The more U.S. troops come home, the more will be demanded."

Kissinger's ardent plea for more warlike action also featured strong political recommendations drawn from a Sven Kraemer memo on the governance of South Vietnam. Because Thieu's government provided no "bridge to neutralist figures who could play a role in a future settlement," Kissinger wrote, "there is not enough of a prospect of progress in [Saigon] to persuade Hanoi to make concessions." The North would continue its "protracted warfare," a "low-cost" strategy aimed at "producing a psychological, rather than military, defeat for the U.S." Therefore, strong U.S. military action was needed now.

The arguments worked; Nixon swung back in line. "To achieve maximum political, military, and psychological shock," Duck Hook would begin with four days of all-out attacks, bombings, and harbor minings. Originally scheduled to begin November 1, the plan was moved forward two weeks by Nixon so that it would begin before the October 15 antiwar march on Washington.

Part of the plan was to use the threatened attack to pressure the Soviets to help the United States at the negotiating table. On September 27, as Kissinger met with Dobrynin to give him advance word of Duck Hook, the president interrupted their meeting with a prearranged phone call whose message Kissinger then conveyed to the ambassador: "The train had just left the station and . . . headed down the track." Dobrynin replied to Kissinger that he hoped it wasn't a train but an airplane, so that it could still change course.

Nixon's timing in making an appeal to the USSR was poor. Just a few days earlier, Soviet premier Alexei Kosygin had met at the Beijing airport with his Chinese counterpart Zhou En-Lai during the Soviet's return journey from

Hanoi after attending the funeral of Ho Chi Minh, and in four hours the two men had settled many of their border dispute issues.

The planning of Duck Hook had been kept from Laird and Rogers, but eventually they had to be informed so they could execute details and apprise foreign partners. When they finally got the word, the two Cabinet officers threatened to resign if Duck Hook was triggered, arguing that the United States could not publicly pursue Vietnamization and peace talks while simultaneously escalating on the battlefield.

Nixon thought otherwise; he was fond of simultaneously taking two seemingly antithetical actions. But he could not dispel the potential negative political effect of two Cabinet resignations. He and Kissinger went to Key Biscayne, Florida, to figure out what to do. Nixon had two options, Kissinger said pithily: "to bug out or to accelerate." His choice: "We must escalate or [the] president is lost."

Nixon retorted that the presidency could be lost anyway if Duck Hook failed, and that it might well fail.

Nixon's decisions frequently hinged on how much public criticism he could bear. The combination of the potential fallout from resignations by Rogers and Laird, and from the antiwar "moratorium" rally scheduled for mid-October, convinced Nixon not to begin Duck Hook; instead, he would pursue another way to push North Vietnam. Rather than mount an actual attack, he decreed, the United States would produce a *feigned* one—similar to those that Wheeler's staff had dreamed up in early 1969. Nixon wanted precisely the option that Haig, Kissinger, and the Joint Chiefs had previously criticized as the most ludicrous and dangerous of all the feigned options—an alert that looked like a prelude to nuclear war. "It was important that the Communists not mistake as weakness the lack of dramatic action on my part in carrying out the [November 1] ultimatum," he later wrote. Anxious to prevent a perception of weakness, Nixon instructed Laird to prepare an unprecedented show of force, an exercise that mimicked a high DEFCON level, for October 13–14.

This was not easily accomplished. Haig and Kissinger were furious when Defense seemed not to understand how close to an actual alert the elevated-DEFCON exercise would have to be in order to raise a genuine alarm among the Soviets. Secretary Laird's military aide, Colonel Robert Pursley, had "shouting matches" with Haig over the matter.

At this important moment, the army threw a curveball at Al Haig. An internal army memo appeared on which Haig's name had been added to the list of invitees to attend Harvard's Executive Management course—right away. The assignment would take him out of the White House but would punch his ticket for higher management in the army, something Haig wanted. When Kraemer saw the internal memo, he phoned Kissinger and pleaded with him to squelch the transfer. Kissinger agreed. To lose Haig just then was "absolutely out of the question," he told Kraemer. "I need him where he is." Kraemer said he would convey the message to the army brass, and implied that if Kissinger really did need Haig that badly, the White House should recommend Haig for a promotion.

In the weeks that followed, Haig advanced from his assistant's role to a position in which he was able to directly plan military actions. The vehicle for the promotion was the feigned alert, a plan on which Haig was able to work directly with Nixon and Kissinger.

The trio needed Laird's help to effect the alert, so Nixon called him in, and to persuade him reminded the defense secretary of President Eisenhower's use of feigned military activity to pressure the Communists to end the Korean War. But as Nixon's chief aide, Haldeman, would later reveal, Nixon was also borrowing another, riskier notion of Eisenhower's: that the president of the United States must never be totally predictable to the country's enemies. Nixon believed he could achieve his objectives by making the Soviets and the North Vietnamese fear he was slightly mad, mad enough that he might trigger a nuclear war at any time. The prospect of an unhinged president with access to the nuclear button, he felt, should scare America's enemies to the bargaining table.

In the run-up to the high-DEFCON alert, Haig personally pushed the JCS on one element he knew about from his participation in the Cuban Missile Crisis: He demanded a higher-level ground forces alert ratio than the plan proposed. The demand went up the chain of command, signed off by everyone until it reached JCS chairman Wheeler, who personally vetoed it. That it went so far was a testament to Haig's growing power.

The high-DEFCON alert was to be an elaborate ruse. It would include strategic stand-downs of the sort that the enemy knew would precede an actual nuclear strike, as well as increased naval activity and surveillance of Soviet shipping, and nuclear-armed B-52s circling Alaska. It had to be completed before November 1, for on that date Hanoi and Moscow would realize that Duck Hook had been canceled, and would also conclude that the alert had been a bluff.

On October 15, the antiwar moratorium march was held. Hundreds of thousands of marchers nearly overwhelmed Washington. Watching them from inside the White House, Nixon instructed himself, "Don't get rattled—don't waver—don't react." He was writing a speech that he hoped would put Vietnam behind him. The feigned DEFCON alert was another part of that hope.

"K has all sorts of signal-type activity going on around the world to try to jar Soviets + NVN," Haldeman noted in his diary on October 17. "Appears to be working because Dobrynin has asked for early mtng, which we have set for Monday. K thinks this is good chance of being the big break—but that it will come in stages. P[resident] is more skeptical." Before the Dobrynin meeting, Kissinger told Nixon in a memo, "Your basic purpose will be to keep the Soviets concerned about what we might do around November 1." Should Dobrynin bring up the raised military alert activity, Nixon should say it was routine—which would suggest, perversely, that it was anything but.

As Nixon prepared to greet Dobrynin, Kissinger told Nelson Rockefeller he felt the ploy had about a 30 percent chance of success. However, the Soviet ambassador seemed to have understood what game was afoot; in his October 20 meeting with Nixon, Dobrynin never mentioned the upgraded U.S. military activity, though Moscow had made him aware of it. Nixon was reduced to asking again for help with Vietnam, warning the ambassador, "The Soviet Union is going to be stuck with me for the next three years and three months, and during all that time I will keep in mind what is being done right now, today. If the Soviet Union will not help to get peace, then we will have to pursue our own methods for bringing the war to an end."

After that meeting, Kissinger told Kraemer he felt the plan's chances for success had dropped to only 10 percent. The plan "has no business succeeding," he said, "but it may."

In this moment, when—despite the best efforts of the Nixon-Kissinger plan, and despite the mobilization of the Strategic Air Command bombers and all other signals—Dobrynin ignored the threat from the "madman" in the White House, the Nixon strategy to push the Soviets to pressure the North Vietnamese collapsed.

A few days later, Dobrynin told another U.S. official that such attempts to pressure the USSR—including Nixon's visit to Romania during the summer and his coy public statements regarding the Sino-Soviet border clashes; Dobrynin did not specifically mention the nuclear alert—would never succeed in persuading the USSR to help the United States end the Vietnam War. "The reaction in the Kremlin to tactics of this kind would always be the opposite of what [Washington] desired."

EVEN BEFORE THE scrubbing of Duck Hook and the feigned alert, on September 22, Kraemer felt he could no longer remain silent. His unease spurred him to write a five-thousand-word memo to Kissinger, a passionate and detailed dissection of the direction that the Nixon administration was taking. In its alarm, it echoed the concerns of Kissinger's near-contemporaneous "salted peanuts" memo to Nixon, but it went much further, drawing implications from the troop withdrawals that Kissinger had only hinted at.

Kissinger was so impressed with Kraemer's paper that he passed it on to Nixon—without Kraemer's name on it. His cover note said, "Although I do not agree with its every last word, it does define the problem we face—the generally deteriorating strategic position of the United States during the past decade." Nixon read the document carefully and made numerous notes on its margins, for instance, saying of a cogent paragraph on the relationship between the USSR, China, and the United States, "Good analysis." The president then directed Kissinger to send copies to Rogers, Laird, and Helms for comment, though without naming Kraemer as its source. Few documents that came to Kissinger in this fashion were treated with this much respect and concern by the administration.

Kraemer's paper was an expansion of the themes of his June memo. A *tour d'horizon* in the grand manner, it insisted that advances in communications and transportation had condensed the world and at the same time made it interconnected in ways unknown previously in human history. Therefore, in Kraemer's view, the modern world must be accepted and dealt with as "a single, strategic theater" rather than as a series of far-flung situations and crises, which was how bureaucrats had been working with it. "The man who daily struggles with the agonizing problem of Vietnam can hardly be expected to pay special attention to the latest coup in Libya, and the person concerned with US aid to Latin America has little time or inclination to consider recent political developments in Czechoslovakia."

But his job was to be a generalist, Kraemer wrote, and upon weighing the cables and dispatches from everywhere, and reading all those newspapers in many languages, he discerned some immediate adverse results of the still-forming Nixon Doctrine. He cited specific examples of unease in Japan, Indonesia, Singapore, and elsewhere in Asia: the Philippine Foreign Office, he pointed out, had changed its prior references in cables from "Chinese mainland" to "People's Republic of China" and in other ways was being more accommodating to the Mao regime. Such signals would indicate to any "objective analyst, be he in [Beijing] or Bonn," that the United States was heading for "an ultimate pull-out, a radical reduction of military commitments . . . not simply in hotly contested Vietnam but on a worldwide basis."

Jumping to South America, he told stories of juntas in Ecuador, Peru, and Bolivia expropriating American military and American oil company properties as they took over their countries. Casting his eye on the Middle East, he boldly predicted that American withdrawals and refusals to act would result in the loss of more Arab states to radical regimes. They would also force India to become closer to the USSR to offset Chinese influence. The West Germans, he noted, were edging toward the USSR, in reaction to having been twice rebuffed in Washington in recent months, and of now being convinced that the United States would shortly remove its troops from their country.

What did it all mean? Trouble for the United States down the road, he predicted.

"The policy on which we seem embarked is very obviously dictated by a conviction that 'public opinion' demands it and that, accordingly, the government is essentially helpless to act otherwise," Kraemer summed up, and concluded with the warning, "Anyone with a sense of history will grasp the tragic elements in this situation."

ON THE EVENING of November 3, 1969, a year after his election, Nixon gave his most important speech on the Vietnam War. He did not tell the American public of the feigned DEFCON alert, which had had no positive effect, or about his cancellation of the Duck Hook attacks. Instead, to an audience estimated at 70 million Americans, he forthrightly rejected the idea of ending the war so that Johnson's war did not become Nixon's war. He had an "obligation," he said, to think beyond the war's possible effect on "the next election." Hitting his stride, Nixon asked rhetorically, "How can we win America's peace?" and answered that it must be won, because "our defeat and humiliation in South Vietnam . . . would promote recklessness in the councils of those great powers who have not yet abandoned their goals of world conquest. This would spark violence wherever our commitments help maintain the peace—in the Middle East, in Berlin, eventually even in the Western Hemisphere."

Nixon's declaration echoed Kraemer's warnings about provocative weakness and may have been formulated, in part, as a response to the challenges posed by Kraemer in his "Single Strategic Theater" memo. The United States must win in Vietnam, Nixon argued, because to lose would unleash our enemies. Nixon cited the positive results of American troop withdrawals and South Vietnamese military development, including a reduction in U.S. casualties and in the enemy's infiltration rate. But he cautioned that "an announcement of a fixed timetable for our withdrawal would completely remove any incentive for the enemy to negotiate an agreement. They would simply wait until our forces had withdrawn and then move in." The key point in achieving peace, he stated, was that the American people be unified behind his program. He castigated the "vocal minority" that was telling him to declare the war lost; should they "prevail," he said, "this nation has no future as a free society." He asked for the support of the "silent majority" who agreed with his plan for a just peace. "The more support I can have from the American people, the sooner that pledge can be redeemed; for the more divided we are at home, the less likely the enemy is to negotiate at Paris. Let us be united for peace. Let us also be united against defeat. Because let us understand: North Vietnam cannot defeat or humiliate the United States. Only Americans can do that."

It was, Nixon later judged, his most successful speech as president. It was met by a grand outpouring of support for his plan to end the war—support that was evident at the November 15 "moratorium." While hundreds of thousands of protesters marched against the continuation of the war, the "silent majority" mounted a number of smaller counter-marches, among them a 15,000-person demonstration by the Young Americans for Freedom. YAF's national director told a reporter that Nixon "would not be unhappy to see his options on the war expanded by right-wing pressure—and we aim to please." Demonstrations by "hard-hats" in New York, San Francisco, and other big cities expressed the desire for a "win" in Vietnam, preferably a military one.

Nixon's poll ratings soared. The House of Representatives passed a resolution—the first regarding the war since the enabling Gulf of Tonkin resolution in 1964—endorsing by a 334–55 vote Nixon's efforts to achieve "peace with justice."

Some conservatives argued publicly that Nixon's success in mobilizing the "silent majority" gave him an opening to take more aggressive military action to push North Vietnam to the bargaining table. Had these conservatives known what had gone on behind the scenes with the run-up to, and then away from, Duck Hook, and with the feigned high alert they would have been apoplectic. They did not know, and so continued to support Nixon's approach.

AFTER A YEAR in office the tenor of a presidency, and the character of the president, have usually become obvious. But Nixon, that most guarded of men in public, was still an enigma to most Americans. However, after his first year certain things about Nixon and his foreign policies had become quite clear to several critical audiences.

Although the American public did not know about the fake DEFCON alert, North Vietnam, the USSR, and China did, and had likely deduced that the threatened Duck Hook had been canceled. Now able to see through

Nixon's anti-Communist rhetoric, these countries could conclude that he was a maker of empty threats, intent on drawing down American troops, ordering ineffectual bombing, and propping up an inadequate South Vietnamese army—tactics that could only accelerate the Communists' victory in Vietnam.

The Joint Chiefs of Staff, in particular Admiral Thomas Moorer, who was being considered to replace Wheeler, were alarmed by Nixon's approach toward American foreign policy. They recognized Nixon's eagerness to go around them at the drop of a hat and his willingness to deceive them on matters ranging from troop levels to negotiations with the Soviets. And as a result they became determined to keep abreast of what Nixon and Kissinger were planning, to help them prepare to counter any moves they might disagree with. The Joint Chiefs began their program of resistance through small measures—stalling on orders to withdraw troops from South Korea, the Philippines, and Japan, and to reduce the size of the military by a million men. They also seized an opportunity on SALT, the Strategic Arms Limitation Talks, by letting senators know that they hated the administration's current proposals: The Senate was unlikely to ratify any agreement that the military felt would adversely affect security.

Kissinger now fully understood that Nixon's pattern of actions and nonactions offered an opportunity for him to rise in the president's confidence and to exercise presidential power as his own. He had also learned that the only way to ensure his access to that power was to shelve Kraemer's absolutist notions and further Nixon's realist compromises. After the "salted peanuts" memo, Kissinger never again deeply questioned the direction of the president's policies.

Kraemer's other protégé, Al Haig, newly elevated to brigadier general, saw his own route to power as an adroit cheerleader for Nixon's need to voice bellicose thoughts. Haig would never be able to best Kissinger at his own game, but he could develop ways to go around him and to act as a counterweight to Kissinger in Nixon's mind. As one fellow NSC member would later recall, when Nixon was angry at Kissinger he would not permit Kissinger to present the daily briefing that day and instead would call in Haig for that purpose. Such freeze-outs could last for days until Kissinger had been properly chastised.

At the turn of 1970, Nixon expressed his new confidence in Haig by sending him to Saigon as the leader of an NSC delegation that included Sven Kraemer. Haig came back with a report that purported to be a realistic assessment but was tinged with his own ideology that favored an aggressive continuation of the war on the battlefield. Haig told the president that he saw "hopeful signs" on the ground, citing statistics showing that the Saigon government now controlled four-fifths of the land area of the South. But he dismissed reports of successful Vietnamization as "phony": Haig reported that the front lines of the ARVN, the South's army, were staffed only by poorly trained draftees, since Saigon allowed volunteers to stay behind the lines in relative safety. The main threat to South Vietnam, Haig told Nixon, was coming from the Cambodian sanctuaries, which the bombing had not sufficiently destroyed. Sooner or later, the United States, rather than just South Vietnam, would have to take aggressive military action to clean the North Vietnamese out of the area. In Haig's report were the justifications for the calamitous "incursion" into Cambodia in the spring of 1970.

6

Cambodia and Echo

Despite Nixon's continuing support from the so-called silent majority, by early 1970 his approval ratings had begun to slide, although congressional and departmental leaders were still willing to work with him. Potential opponents of his foreign policies looked for opportunities to counter those Nixon initiatives they believed to be bad for the country—including his management of the war in Vietnam and his direct negotiations with the USSR on arms control. Nixon's difficulties were exacerbated by a series of missteps involving leading officials at the Pentagon and the State Department. Nixon himself often seemed to have no idea of the character and philosophies of the men who were moving into high positions of power in his administration, and no appreciation for how they might use the levers of the bureaucratic process to counter his policy initiatives.

Though Nixon had read Kraemer's September 22, 1969, memo, he had little knowledge of Kraemer's continuing influence. A sense of it is captured in a memo Haig sent Kraemer on January 9, 1970, in response to a note in which Kraemer asked Kissinger whether Henry was even reading the cables he had so carefully culled and marked for his attention, since a batch of them had been returned to him within twenty-four hours. Haig apologized at some length, explaining that this lapse had occurred because he had taken a few days off while Kissinger had been with the president at his home in San Clemente, California, and so an underling had returned the cables. This was not, Haig assured Kraemer, "the normal procedure. As I have told you on numerous occasions, I read each and every cable which you send over and find them invaluable. In Henry's case, the score is less consistent but nevertheless well above the eighty percent mark." Haig reported that he also took it upon himself to reinforce the cables by specially marking the ones of greatest significance, and he told Kraemer that "in at least a half dozen cases these cables and an analysis of them have been forwarded to the President."

THE PENTAGON EXPECTED the ailing "Bus" Wheeler to retire as chairman of the Joint Chiefs on July 1, 1970, and to be replaced by Admiral Tom Moorer, whom Nixon considered a staunch ally. What Nixon did not know was just how seriously Moorer disagreed with his policies on the USSR, China, and Vietnam.

If Moorer got the job, he would need to be replaced as chief of naval operations, and one candidate for that position came with many recommendations: Admiral Elmo Zumwalt, who had impressed Laird and Nixon with his efforts to further Vietnamization by reinvigorating Vietnam's brown-water fleet (the gunboats that plied its many rivers). Zumwalt was young for his rank, and for him to become CNO he would have to be jumped over older colleagues; Nixon had no problem signing off on that; he may have known that Zumwalt was close to Paul Nitze, but was sorely unaware of how close Zumwalt was philosophically and personally to Scoop Jackson and Kraemer.

Around the same time, Nixon made an enemy out of an old friend by an inept attempt to recruit Lieutenant General Vernon Walters to take on a thankless task. A fast and accurate translator, well versed in the ways of army intelligence, Dick Walters had helped Kissinger during the secret peace talks in Paris, hiding him in cars and in friends' apartments. (Nixon didn't know that Walters had also been keeping Fritz Kraemer updated on the talks.) Haldeman summoned Walters to the White House to say that Nixon was having problems obtaining good notes from his meetings with officials and foreign dignitaries, and wanted Walters, with his linguistic abilities and legendary memory, to sit in on all presidential meetings and take notes. Walters stood up, drew himself up to his full height, and told Haldeman, "A general commands troops. He is not a secretary." He returned to his Paris post, disillusioned about his long-term friendship with Nixon.

The SALT talks were poised to resume in the spring of 1970, and Paul Nitze was surprised when, after the ABM battle, the administration offered him a post on the negotiating team. Nitze was a bona fide arms control expert—in the early 1960s he and Zumwalt, then his military assistant, had coauthored a paper on nuclear arms limitation. But he understood that it was his being a Democrat that made him useful to the administration politically. Nitze had picked up enough information about the ongoing talks to disapprove of their direction, and later wrote that he took the job mainly to be in a position to derail the talks if that proved necessary. He immediately prevailed upon old pals at State to generate a "Red Team Report." As he expected, it warned that the Soviets would not negotiate in good faith at SALT, and for that reason U.S. negotiators should make no concessions.

Nixon and Kissinger offended some people by simply failing to address important issues. Ray Garthoff of State, the executive secretary of the SALT delegation, later wrote that the team was disturbed by a White House instruction not to discuss MIRVs—the most formidable weaponry in the superpowers' pipelines. The Soviets, behind in the MIRV race, were delighted to have the topic off the table; the longer MIRVs went undiscussed, the more time the Soviets had to catch up to the United States in their own MIRV development and testing efforts. Chief U.S. negotiator Gerard Smith later labeled the unwillingness to discuss a ban on MIRV testing as the "leading lost opportunity" of the talks, one that negatively affected the security of the world for decades to come—and that soured the U.S. SALT team on the Nixon administration.

IN THE USUAL annals of the Nixon administration, the extension of the Vietnam War into Cambodia in the spring of 1970, which triggered massive protests, is understood as a watershed for the left. But the decision to go into Cambodia in a severely constrained way was also a watershed for the administration's internal opponents of the president's foreign policies. It solidified their determination to take more active measures to counter those policies.

The war in Vietnam was not ending, two of Nixon's nominees for the Supreme Court had been rejected, and desegregation was not going well. Nixon believed that undertaking new military action could increase his public approval, as it had always raised the American public's estimation of prior presidents. He saw an opportunity in the North Vietnamese "sanctuaries" inside the neighboring country of Cambodia.

Prince Norodom Sihanouk ruled Cambodia, but beneath him a military cabal had recently formed, led by the ambitious Lon Nol. Each year, Sihanouk spent time in France, ostensibly to restore his health but really to get away from his responsibilities. In 1970 his burden was particularly onerous: North Vietnamese forces, which had been operating inside his borders for some time, had expanded their sway, to the point that Sihanouk had to complain about them to Moscow and Beijing.

Nixon reasoned that eliminating these North Vietnamese sanctuaries in Cambodia would force North Vietnam to settle at the peace table. But at first he resisted the notion of having U.S. troops do the job; rather, he wanted Cambodia to invite or permit South Vietnamese troops in for that purpose. Recently, when North Vietnamese invaders had similarly threatened to topple the pro-American government of Laos, Thailand had offered troops to fight them, provided that American pilots could join in and give them air cover. The state and defense departments had objected, but Kissinger and Haig enthusiastically supported the idea, and Nixon had acceded to Thai and Laotian requests for American pilots; the joint forces repelled the North Vietnamese well enough to secure Laos for at least the coming year. Nixon, Kissinger, and Haig wanted to do the same for Cambodia, as a test of Vietnamization and of the Nixon Doctrine. When Sihanouk refused to decide on letting in South Vietnamese troops—and then headed off on another restorative trip to France—Lon Nol, with tacit agreement from the United States, staged a coup.

Nixon urged the NSC to find ways to back Lon Nol and to send in the South Vietnamese. Now was the time to strike! But introducing American forces into Cambodia—even as advisers to the South Vietnamese—would mean widening the war. The National Security Council divided on the issue.

At a private meeting at Kissinger's home, NSC staffers William Watts, Roger Morris, Tony Lake, Larry Lynn, and Winston Lord all voiced fears that an incursion into Cambodia by widening the war would ignite a firestorm of protest in the United States and throughout the world. Kissinger disparaged these concerns, coming as they did from the advisers he considered his "bleeding heart" liberal "house doves." Kissinger wanted the incursion. This was a moment that called for Kraemer-like military aggression, and for once Nixon was willing to authorize real, not feigned, action.

Nixon would shortly announce that 150,000 more U.S. troops would come home from the Vietnam theater of operations in the next twelve months. Thus it was all the more imperative to complete the eradication of the Cambodian sanctuaries. Nixon and Kissinger asked Abrams by phone whether the South Vietnamese could be "100 percent successful" in handling such an "incursion." Abrams could not promise that, and so Nixon reluctantly concluded that U.S. forces must be used, and in more than an advisory capacity: They would have to carry the fight into the Cambodian battlefields.

The incursion into Cambodia was Nixon's most important strategic decision on the war, and one he made without any direct input from his secretary of defense, because Nixon knew that Melvin Laird would not want to use U.S. troops to accomplish the mission. Eventually, of course, Laird had to be brought into the loop—but Haig demanded that the Pentagon keep the plan secret from the State Department. Secretary Rogers found out anyway, and he, Laird, and Assistant Secretary of State Alex Johnson objected at an NSC principals meeting. Johnson painted the whole mission as unrealistic, citing as an example its objective of destroying "COSVN," the North's supposed field operational headquarters, which was believed to be in the area of the proposed invasion. How could the invading troops find a target that some sources said was mobile, with elements dispersed over 110 square kilometers of jungle?

The hard-liners—the Joint Chiefs (represented by Moorer), Haig, and Agnew—had no answer for that question. They simply argued that South Vietnamese troops alone might not accomplish the objectives; only U.S. troops could guarantee success.

Nixon and Kissinger were both excited by the prospect of the Cambodian action. On April 20, Haldeman noted in his diary that Nixon had taken over "responsibility for war in Cambodia" and plunged himself into the details. "Kissinger's really having fun today, he's playing Bismarck," Nixon confided to Haldeman. And Nixon told the NSC that it was important for "Suharto and the Indonesians, as well as for the Thai and the Lao, to know that we were standing firm." In such pronouncements, Nixon sounded very much like Fritz Kraemer.

Nixon watched the recently released movie *Patton* three times in as many days before issuing the final order to invade. Yet because he was afraid of criticism for being too warlike, his order included a severe limitation: U.S. ground forces were not to advance more than thirty kilometers inside the Cambodian border, a limitation that hampered the military to the point of preventing a victory.

As the moment of the incursion approached, Watts declared the whole thing wrong. "Your views represent the cowardice of the Eastern Establishment," Kissinger snarled. When Watts moved toward Kissinger, Haig barked, "You've just had an order from your Commander-in-Chief and you can't refuse," Watts retorted, "Fuck you, Al. I just have and I resigned." Lake, Morris, and Lynn also quit. "We have often heard courage equated with a standing up to criticism," they wrote to Kissinger in a letter, "but it is not enough to dismiss the critics for their motives or manliness, nor to ridicule them with the catch phrases of the Right."

The liberal exodus from the NSC had no effect on the president's plans, which he announced to the nation on April 30. "This is not an invasion of Cambodia," he claimed, explaining that the areas to be attacked in the "incursion" were wholly under the control of the North Vietnamese. "We take this action not for the purpose of expanding the war into Cambodia but for the purpose of ending the war in Vietnam and winning the just peace we all desire."

Had Nixon justified the incursion to the public as a straightforward, militarily necessary extension of prior attempts to clean out the North Vietnamese sanctuaries, the "silent majority" could readily have supported it. But Nixon escalated his rhetoric:

> If, when the chips are down, the world's most powerful nation, the United States of America, acts like a pitiful, helpless giant, the forces of totalitarianism and anarchy will threaten free nations. . . . It is not our power but our will and character that is being tested tonight.

With such phrases Nixon positioned the incursion as a titanic test of wills. That overstatement, coupled with his attempt to depict the invasion as not an invasion, produced a firestorm of reaction. Protesters shut down two hundred American colleges and universities—the most numerous, widespread, and violent protests the nation had ever seen, culminating in the shooting deaths of four youths at Kent State University in Ohio. Nixon had anticipated some protests, but nothing as large as this. The stock market dived. "It's isn't 1970 anymore," the *Wall Street Journal* warned; "it's 1928 and seven-eighths."

The protests were equally vocal within the halls of official Washington. Two hundred and fifty State Department employees signed a protest. Nixon ordered Alex Johnson to fire them all, but he never carried out the order. Cabinet secretaries Walter Hickel and George Romney went public with their dissent. Rogers and Laird told journalists that they had opposed the incursion. When Vice President Agnew started giving speeches castigating the media for playing up the protests, labor secretary George P. Shultz declared that it was time to muzzle him.

Great Britain, France, and West Germany expressed embarrassment at not having been consulted before the invasion and did not rally to support Nixon's move. North Vietnam canceled Paris peace-talk sessions. The Chinese drew back from American approaches, and Soviet Premier Kosygin called the first Kremlin press conference in a decade to ask, "What is the value of international agreements, which the United States is or intends to be a party to, if it so unceremoniously violates its obligations?" SALT talks halted. A U.S.-Soviet summit meeting scheduled for the fall was put off indefinitely.

The Senate readied an amendment, drawn up by Republican senator John Sherman Cooper and Democratic senator Frank Church, that would cut off all funding for operations in Cambodia after July 1. On May 8, to head off passage of Cooper-Church—which would seriously impact the executive branch's ability to wage war—Nixon did precisely what he'd vowed on April 30 not to do: He gave in to public pressure and announced that all American troops would be out of Cambodia by June 30.

Fritz Kraemer, the military, and others on the right all reacted to Nixon's retreats by concluding that Nixon had failed them. By constraining the troops in the field, hyping the incursion into a test of wills with the Communist world, and then backing down almost immediately when public opinion turned against him, Nixon, they felt, had taken a sound military venture and undercut its chances of success at every step of the way. John Lehman, a young NSC staffer who would become Ronald Reagan's secretary of the navy, wrote that the impact of Nixon's pledge to get troops out of Cambodia on a deadline set by Congress—and not to send them in ever again— "actually ran much deeper" than a simple agreement not to return to battle. It hampered the military and "narrowed the parameters of future options to be considered. Everyone was aware that ground had been yielded."

THE DEMONSTRATIONS OVER Cambodia that Al Haig watched from his basement office in the White House were, he later wrote, "a combination of demonic ceremony, class picnic, collective tantrum, and mating ritual." At one point, a disheveled Nixon appeared before his cubicle, managed a rare smile, and tried to reassure Haig, knowing that his aide had been "deeply disturbed by the decision to limit the duration and depth of the operation."

Perhaps as restitution, Nixon soon sent Haig on his first solo mission, to meet with Lon Nol in Cambodia, while U.S. troops were still in country. As the new brigadier general prepared to go, Kissinger brushed the star on Haig's uniform and teased that if he behaved properly, Kissinger would get him a second star. Haig brought the Cambodian leader bad news: that American troops would soon be pulled out. Lon Nol wept. Haig put an arm around his shoulder and told him that Nixon would give him a great deal of help. The promise exceeded both his instructions and the parameters of Nixon's deal with the Senate on Cooper-Church.

In this tense atmosphere, leaks revealing intramural dissent over Cambodia infuriated the White House. (One military source told the New York Times that the invasion had been "oversold because of political considerations and is being undercut because of political considerations.") To combat such stories, and new leaks to Beecher of the Times, Kissinger and Haig requested four additional wiretaps. The tapping program soon escalated toward one of the Nixon administration's worst potential excesses: the formation of a high-level intelligence community committee led by White House aide Tom Charles Huston. A rigidly conservative young lawyer and YAF stalwart, Huston had a disdainful view of the Bill of Rights. His committee set about trying to find ways for all of the military and civilian intelligence agencies to obtain more information on domestic protesters. William Sullivan of the FBI and Richard Helms of the CIA saw an opportunity to force the retirement of FBI director J. Edgar Hoover and obtain White House blessing for activities previously considered illegal. Under the Huston Plan, as the committee's product would later be known, the CIA and FBI would be permitted to open Americans' international mail, listen in on their international phone calls, obtain copies of their telexes, perform electronic surveillance on protesters and college students, and break into the homes and offices of dissenters. Nixon approved the Huston Plan, but when Attorney General John Mitchell found out about it he summoned Hoover, who then raised objections to its legality (though he had raised no such concerns during the committee's meetings). Mitchell added his own objections and pushed Nixon to rescind the order. Four days later, the president did so. The affair left the CIA, FBI, and National Security Agency angry at Nixon, blaming him for tantalizing them and not delivering.

ON JULY 1, 1970, Admiral Thomas Moorer officially took over as chairman of the Joint Chiefs of Staff. Moorer's southern homespun personality and drawl masked a considerable intellect: He had been valedictorian of his high school at such a young age that he had had to wait a year before entering the U.S. Naval Academy. A pilot, he served with distinction in World War II and since then had commanded every important theater of naval operations. He was also known as a capable political infighter.

Moorer's replacement as chief of naval operations, Bud Zumwalt, was a battleship officer in the tradition of most previous CNOs. Unashamedly intellectual, he had a large vocabulary and liked to use it. His most recent post had been in Vietnam—to which Moorer had sent him, Zumwalt believed, to keep him from undue influence in Washington. But the top two navy men agreed on the dangers facing the U.S. military from abroad and from the White House. At Zumwalt's first JCS meeting, Moorer noted that this would be the third fiscal year in a row of budget cuts, and worried that "we may already be at a condition of having inadequate forces," making it more likely that "the Soviets could blackmail us and we could have a Cuba in reverse. We're just fortunate we have not [yet] had a confrontation." Zumwalt agreed.

While the Chiefs understood that Nixon was constrained on the budgetary front by the temper of the times and were therefore willing to go along with the cuts that he requested, they bristled at one of his diplomatic salvos. After no progress had been made in the round of arms negotiations in Helsinki at the turn of the year, the United States had developed four new proposals dealing with MIRVed weapons. As a matter of course, Kissinger ran the four options by JCS, which had said it could live with them. But in early July, JCS learned—to their dismay—that not only had the Soviets rejected all four of the options, but that Kissinger had recently presented a fifth, without consulting the Chiefs, State, or the SALT negotiators. This was known as Option E, and the Chiefs dubbed it "E for Echo" because it so closely resembled Soviet proposals. Echo would decrease the number of U.S. bombers without demanding an equivalent cut in Russian ballistic missiles—precisely the sort of bad trade-off that Nitze and Zumwalt had warned against in their 1963 article. The Chiefs guessed that Nixon was so anxious over Vietnam that he was offering the USSR anything he could think of in return for their help in ending the war.

The larger problem surfaced when the SALT talks resumed. "Having already made substantial concessions" to the Soviets in Option E, Nitze later wrote, "we had little left with which to bargain. It was a costly mistake from which we were never fully able to recover." The U.S. negotiators' unwillingness to force a ban on MIRVs, another expert has judged, was a "fateful decision that changed strategic relations . . . to the detriment of U.S. security."

The Chiefs received another negative indication three weeks later. When the commander of the Strategic Air Command briefed them on a study of a potential nuclear exchange with the Soviets, Zumwalt later wrote, it became clear "that the weapons then available to the US in a second strike . . . could not inflict anything like the casualties on Russia that Russia already had inflicted upon us [in a first strike], bringing into question the whole concept of 'assured destruction' on which our national deterrent strategy then rested." The Chiefs sent Nixon a copy of the study. But Kissinger, discussing it at an NSC meeting with Zumwalt and Moorer, stated that "it was very clear that the Soviets were aiming at nuclear superiority, through SALT if possible, without SALT if necessary." Zumwalt and Moorer were astonished to realize that Kissinger thought there was nothing the United States could or should do to counter this Soviet thrust toward nuclear arms superiority.

This was a significant shift for Kissinger, one that ran counter to most of his writings before he became Nixon's adviser, and to Kraemer's insistence on never yielding to totalitarianism in any way. Kissinger's shift deeply troubled Kraemer. He importuned Kissinger to meet with fervent anti-Communist Jay Lovestone—"I see him once a week and he is a man of gold." Kraemer hoped that Lovestone would dissuade Kissinger from softening the American stance toward the USSR, but Kissinger was unresponsive. Kraemer felt certain that Kissinger's adherence to Nixon's line was fueled by his need for fame and public celebration, a goal Kraemer himself abhorred.

For Moorer and Zumwalt, the frightening thing about Kissinger was his pessimism about the United States' ability to maintain its edge over the USSR, as expressed in the E for Echo fiasco and in Kissinger's despair over the SAC study. It was shortly after those events that Moorer mounted the first concerted effort to undercut the leftward drift of the Nixon administration from within: He ordered the military liaison office, operating in the basement of the White House, to spy on Kissinger, the NSC, and the president. The principal thief would be a young clerk, Yeoman Charles Radford.

The Moorer-Radford espionage affair, buried for many years and still largely unknown to the public, merits much closer attention. Though the scheme itself lasted only a year and a half, its results—and the reverberations of its exposure—continued through the end of Nixon's presidency and beyond.

The plan originated with Moorer. At his direction, the military staffers who worked at the liaison office at the White House, but reported to him at the Pentagon, stole a substantial number of sensitive documents from Kissinger and the NSC and therefore from the president. Moorer, who had sworn when accepting his office as chairman to observe the Espionage Act, was the main receiver of the stolen goods. The intermediary was the newly elevated Rear Admiral Rem Robinson, chief of the military liaison office, and Radford did the stealing.

A timid young man brought up in foster homes, now a Mormon with a wife and small children, Radford had served in India as a military aide. Intensely loyal to his superiors, he did what he was told without question. After he arrived in the basement of the White House to replace a civilian secretary, a trickle of petty thefts—which had been already ongoing on an intermittent and opportunistic basis—grew into a flood of efficiently executed grand larceny. To further his reach, Radford later said, he ingratiated himself with "people in the reproduction center, and in the burn center, and in the bookkeeping center. You know, I was everywhere. Always constantly moving and talking." He rifled burn bags, swiped documents off desks, and copied them before their recipients returned, passing five thousand such documents to Robinson. "We're talking about a library," Radford later confessed. Robinson then sent some of the purloined material on to Moorer and Zumwalt.

The motive behind this criminal enterprise—as Admiral Robert Welander, who later replaced Robinson as liaison officer and continued the spy ring with Radford and others, later explained—stemmed from JCS concerns about the drift of U.S. foreign policy and being cut out of the loop. "The Chiefs' viewpoint was being disregarded," he said. "We wondered who the hell is the son of a bitch who is coming up with the information" to justify such things as the rapid drawdown of troops in Vietnam, which the Chiefs thought were endangering security. The documents Radford stole helped the Chiefs understand how those decisions were being made—and gave them a way to slow the steamroller.

In his autobiography, Zumwalt offered a more cerebral take on the reasoning behind all such anti-administration actions. They were mandated, he wrote, by the

> deliberate, systematic, and unfortunately very successful efforts [by] the President [and] Kissinger . . . to conceal, sometimes by simple silence, more often by articulate deceit, their real policies about the most critical matters of national security. . . . Their concealment and deceit was practiced against . . . officials within the executive branch who had a statutory responsibility to provide advice about matters of national security. . . . Conscientious officials, when they find that the direct channels through which they are accustomed to transact their business have been blocked, inevitably and properly seek other, circuitous ones that make it possible for them to meet their responsibilities.

BY LATE 1970, Nixon was removing more than ten thousand troops each month from the war zone, immunizing him against further protests from the left. When doves tried to pass an amendment that would pull out all U.S. forces by the end of 1970, it failed: Nixon's pace was fast enough for the majority of Congress. But the very actions by Nixon that mollified the center and the left alarmed the right.

Scoop Jackson began to move steadily away from Nixon, having learned from Nitze and Zumwalt about the administration's giveaways in the SALT negotiations. Jackson was running for reelection, and Nixon sought to appease him by approving a decision not to use Republican Party funds to support his opponent. But that free pass wasn't enough to dissuade Jackson from corralling thirty Democratic and Republican senators, hawks as well as doves, to call for an "internationally supervised standstill cease-fire throughout Vietnam." Nixon obligingly had Kissinger float the idea in Paris. The North Vietnamese rejected it.

While the public did not know the details of Nixon and Kissinger's SALT negotiations, many on the right did know these details from the private reports of Nitze, Jackson, and others, and they were worried. Their concerns fed into a general conservative fear that Nixon was giving away the store to the Soviets, that détente was a one-way street. "As the possibility emerges for new agreements with the Soviet Union, plus a Nixon-Kosygin meeting at the UN in October, converging with the congressional election campaign, the Administration is watching [its] right flank," the *Washington Post* reported on September 1, 1970.

The *Post* made that characterization in the wake of Nixon's performance at a California press conference, where he tried to assuage conservative fears that the United States would succumb to Soviet nuclear blackmail, and that cuts in U.S. military appropriations budgets would jeopardize our ability to "win a war" with the Soviet Union.

Nixon answered media questions on this subject rather directly. Nonconfrontation with the USSR was essential, the president explained, because in a nuclear war there would be no winners. It was a good time to bargain, Nixon went on, to take advantage of the USSR having "a great potential enemy on the East," Red China. The *Post* noted the significance of this statement: Nixon was now publicly breaking from the old Republican line and conceding that Communism was not monolithic—"the equivalent of heresy"— shredding the long-held conservative "security blanket" idea that Communism was indivisible and had to be fought everywhere and at every opportunity. The *Post* article concluded, with a sigh, "The education of right wings about the real world is a continuing process for most Presidents."

No sooner were these words in print, however, than the Nixon administration was confronted with an onslaught of new crises. This next period would test not only the mettle of Nixon and Kissinger in dealing with them, but also the patience of Kraemer and others on the right in assessing whether to remain loyal to Nixon—or to actively oppose him, as the Chiefs had already begun to do.

7

Crises Expose Fissures

Nixon and Kissinger agreed that the crises confronting them in the fall of 1970—events from Southeast Asia to the Middle East to the Caribbean—were tests of the administration posed by international Communism. Fritz Kraemer and others on the right shared that interpretation and eagerly petitioned the administration to use military force against the Communist enemy and his surrogates. But while Kraemer-inspired, ideologically based rationales for military action suffused Kissinger's and Haig's recommendations during this period, Nixon took the opposite tack. He did everything he could to defuse the crises by any means other than military confrontation so that he could advance his long-term goals. By refusing more active confrontation, however, Nixon provided fodder to those who had begun to oppose his policies—and to those who would attempt to reverse those policies during the presidencies of Gerald Ford, Jimmy Carter, Ronald Reagan, George H. W. Bush, Bill Clinton, and George W. Bush. That long sweep of history was defined by this fundamental clash between ideologues and pragmatists, opposing philosophies that emerged sharply in the crises of 1970–71.

ONE DAY, IN the late summer of 1970, Henry Kissinger walked into Bob Haldeman's office and slammed a file of photos onto his desk. The pictures, he explained, were taken from a spy plane high above the southern coast of Cuba; they showed the areas near a submarine support base being built at Cienfuegos. Kissinger pointed at photos showing open spaces—which he identified as soccer fields—and said, "Those soccer fields could mean war, Bob." After all, Kissinger said, Cubans don't play soccer; Russians do. Kissinger and the CIA's analysts—who seldom agreed on the interpretation of any intelligence—were certain that the Cienfuegos base was being readied for "double nuclears": nuclear-powered Soviet submarines designed to carry nuclear missiles. To Kissinger, the CIA, and the JCS, it had the makings of a new Cuban missile crisis. Recently, the USSR had asked the United States to reaffirm the arrangement made during the 1962 crisis, that it would not invade Cuba if the Soviets agreed not to place offensive missiles there. This smelled of danger to Kissinger, to the CIA, and to the JCS. Kissinger and Moorer wanted military action, an air strike that would take out the Cienfuegos base altogether. The JCS also wanted to call up the reserves. Kissinger directed Haig and Rem Robinson to write up potential courses of presidential action, with emphasis on military options.

When Kissinger told Nixon about the building of the base and the proposed military response, Nixon deflected Kissinger's rush to action, responding in a memo, "I want a report on a crash basis on: (1) What CIA can do to support any kind of action which will irritate Castro; (2) What actions can we take which have not yet been taken to boycott nations dealing with Castro; (3) Most important, what actions can we take, covert or overt, to put missiles in Turkey—or a sub base in the Black Sea—anything which will give us some trading stock."

This was a remarkable refusal to rise to the bait. Nixon was well known for wanting to best President Kennedy in every way, and here was an opportunity to confront the Soviets even more directly over Cuba than Kennedy had in October 1962. But Nixon's longer-term goal of détente with the USSR led him to try to de-escalate this crisis. Mindful that the 1962 public showdown had embarrassed Khrushchev and contributed to the Soviet leader's downfall, Nixon did not want to embarrass the current Soviet leaders. And he was anxious to prevent anyone else from doing so, warning against the possibility of "some clown senator demanding a blockade," and trying to distract Kissinger so that he couldn't talk to the press, sensing that his national security adviser might try to rally public opinion around a dramatic and aggressive move.

But Nixon was too late to stop Kissinger, who had fumed to C. L. Sulzberger of the *New York Times* that the Soviets were "horsing around in Cuba." When Sulzberger's article was printed, the Pentagon quickly confirmed the existence of the nuclear sub base at Cienfuegos, in an "inadvertent" admission.

Now alarmed, the right called for military action to take out the base. Nixon instructed Kissinger to calm the waters by speaking to a clutch of reporters on background and to go over the problem quietly with Dobrynin. Kissinger obeyed. The results were some soothing news stories but no word from Dobrynin on Cienfuegos before Nixon and Kissinger left Washington for a short overseas trip. Haig was instructed to reconnect with Dobrynin on the matter.

"Either you take those weapons out and dismantle the base in Cienfuegos, or we will do it for you," Haig says he told Dobrynin. According to Haig's account, the ambassador flushed angrily and called Haig's threat "intolerable." When Kissinger got word of the confrontation he called Haig from Air Force One and railed at him: "You can't talk to the Russians that way. You may have started a war." A few days later, though, Dobrynin gave Kissinger a note reaffirming the 1962 agreement and stating that the USSR would not build a base to service nuclear-powered submarines.

In later years, neocons would construe this crisis as Haig did, contending that tough words and the threat of military action had won the day. Yet the Soviets did not dismantle the Cienfuegos base. Aerial photographs in *Time* in December 1970 showed a more complete base, with an anti-sub mesh offshore, anti-aircraft guns, and a facility for off-loading spent nuclear fuel. By 1972 the base had been further enlarged. The only subs the Soviets did not bring to Cienfuegos were the "double nuclears."

Another Communist-tinged crisis in the Americas that fall was in Chile, where Salvador Allende, an avowed socialist and a friend of Cuban leader Fidel Castro, had been elected by a narrow plurality over two candidates to his right and was about to take office and assume power. Brigadier General Vernon Walters waxed apoplectic about the need for the United States to prevent that from happening, thundering in a memo to Kissinger, "We are engaged in a mortal struggle to determine the future shape of the world." Kissinger passed the memo to Nixon, who made approving comments on it. The president, Kissinger, Walters's bosses at the Pentagon, and Walters's friend Fritz Kraemer all agreed on the need to prevent Chile from going Communist. But the Joint Chiefs did not want the U.S. military involved in the internal political affairs of a sovereign country, and Nixon was not inclined not push the brass on it. Rather, he assigned the task to the CIA, in the expectation that it would be done secretly, if at all. But Allende took office, quickly nationalized several large industries, and began redistributing the country's wealth.

The Nixon administration chose to oppose Allende's leftist rule through economic pressure, and the CIA worked against him and searched to find a leader for a coup that would topple him. Allende's continuation in office despite such actions gave conservatives a reason to call for increased U.S. intervention in South American affairs through the remainder of the 1970s, and to push covert action in Central and South America during Ronald Reagan's presidency in the 1980s.

During the same week as the Cienfuegos base crisis, a more serious and much more complex crisis overtook the Middle East. During the Nixon administration's first eighteen months, Nixon and Kissinger had mostly ignored the region, ceding sway over it to Rogers, and hardly paying attention until the various countries were at the brink of war. Egypt and Syria, both backed by the USSR, were poised to attempt to take back territory seized by Israel during the 1967 war, and also to strike Jordan, which was on friendlier terms with Israel and was similarly considered to be in the orbit of the United States.

An unexpected event ignited the crisis. The Palestine Liberation Organization (PLO) hijacked four Western planes, three of which were then flown to Amman, Jordan. Many of the hostages were Americans. The hijackings occurred while King Hussein of Jordan was deciding whether to ask the U.S. government for military assistance against a possible invasion by Syria, whose tanks, with Soviet advisers on board, were massed on the Jordanian border.

By this time Nixon and Kissinger were routinely cutting the JCS out of the decision-making process, so Chairman Moorer did not learn of the Jordanian request for military assistance until Al Haig placed a call to Kissinger, tracking him down at a dinner honoring Laird. Moorer was there, too, and as the two flew back to the White House by helicopter, Kissinger filled him in. There was more to the impending crisis than the PLO, Jordan, and Syria: At the Suez Canal, Soviet airmen were operating Egyptian aircraft and missile batteries, preparing to recover the canal and seize territory in Gaza that was now controlled by Israel.

Israel's prime minister, Golda Meir, apprised Nixon of the seriousness of the situation. She told him that Israel was prepared not only to resist the Egyptians at Suez but also to send forces to assist King Hussein in defending the integrity of Jordan. Nixon asked Meir not to send Israeli forces into Jordan without consulting him first, and she agreed.

Kissinger proposed a U.S. military mission to shore up the Jordan regime. The JCS opposed it and threatened to go public if overruled. "We've been burned in Vietnam, and before we get out there on the sand [of the Middle East] we want a much more detailed foreign policy scenario than we have now," one unidentified JCS member reportedly complained. Another wondered, "How could we have got out of there in any possible way with good results?"

In terms that still resonate today, with the present wars in Iraq and Afghanistan, the Chiefs argued to Nixon and Kissinger that anything the

United States might gain from helping Jordan would be offset by the new enmity that other Arab entities would be sure to feel at the prospect of American forces fighting on the soil of Muslim countries.

Nixon opted first for a show of force rather than the use of it, telling Kissinger, "I want you to push through the bureaucracy my feelings, having a landing team ready for evacuation [of American citizens]. As far as their going in and fighting, that is another thing." He also instructed, "We want the Sixth fleet stuff in the open. . . . I want everything that can be done to be done in the open," so the Soviets would be sure to notice. Air units were placed on alert. Haig later asserted that the president would have been derelict in his duty had he neglected to perform these prudent moves. Haig claims to have assisted Nixon in making sure that they were done openly, so that "the Soviets and their collaborators would quickly know from their own intelligence what we were doing and draw the accurate conclusion that we were determined to prevent the fall of [King] Hussein and his government."

The Syrian tanks crossed the border into Jordan and then quickly returned. The American fleet maneuvers became known, Kissinger delivered a tough note to the Soviets, and Rogers made a statement calling on the Syrians to withdraw, but that was not the end of the action. Two days later the Syrian tanks crossed back over the border and this time engaged in battle with Jordanian tanks. King Hussein now sent a frantic telegram asking the United States to intervene, but Nixon still had another card to play: He approved an Israeli request to make air strikes in support of the Jordanians. When matters worsened, the Israelis requested permission for a ground attack. Nixon hesitated.

At this important juncture, Haig took action on his own:

> I had no authority to encourage the Israelis to mobilize, but, inasmuch as we had promised to discourage the Soviets, I ordered a COB aircraft . . . to fly a command planning team from one of the U.S. carriers to Tel Aviv, informing Kissinger of my action after the fact. This was designed to create the impression in Moscow, which monitored Sixth Fleet radio traffic, that joint U.S.-Israeli operations in Jordan might be imminent.

Haig's action was in defiance of Nixon's express wishes and of the Chiefs' reluctance to directly involve the U.S. military. Had the COB plane been shot down, the United States might have become embroiled in war. Haig also directed the Israelis to bomb the Syrian columns inside Jordan, arguing that Nixon had already authorized them to help Hussein—although the assistance envisioned by the president had not been spelled out.

The Soviets now urged the Syrians to withdraw completely and suggested that the United States do the same with the Israelis. They did, and further crisis was averted. Yet there would be repercussions aplenty; the problems would fester until they erupted more violently in the October 1973 Middle East war.

Once again, it was not the facts of the crisis but their interpretation that shaped how neocons later understood the standoff. In his memoir, Haig asserts that Kissinger's "tough note" and Haig's own signals prevented a Moscow-conceived takeover of Jordan, thereby demonstrating that "America's moral and military strength was irresistible when involved in the right cause," a notion that by the time he wrote the memoir had become a neoconservative tenet. Most historians have not shared Haig's view. Many believe, as the JCS did at the time, that in these Egyptian and Jordanian mini-wars the United States did not defeat the Soviets, but rather managed a narrow escape from military commitments it might not have been able to keep.

In another fall 1970 crisis, the North Vietnamese refused to yield at the bargaining table in the secret Paris talks, which absorbed a large proportion of Kissinger's energy. The North Vietnamese had no reason to retreat. When they heard Nixon tell U.S. voters on October 7, 1970, that 100,000 troops would be withdrawn from Southeast Asia over the next twelve months, they knew they could sit tight. In his speech Nixon also outlined a new five-point peace plan—one that eliminated, for the very first time, the demand that North Vietnam withdraw from the South as a precondition for a cease-fire. Nixon was accepting the once-heretical idea that North Vietnam's troops would remain in South Vietnam even after the United States went home.

The November midterm election results left the makeup of the Senate and House largely unchanged; commentators said the results showed that Americans, tired of the war in Vietnam, agreed with Nixon's way of ending it, including bringing home the troops at a rapid pace. Around this time, Nixon suggested to Kissinger and others that he might remove virtually all of America's troops from Vietnam by the end of 1971. Kissinger advised against it, arguing that if all U.S troops came home, the North might overrun South Vietnam before the 1972 presidential election season, when Nixon would be seeking a second term. Kissinger's suggestion: Wait to pull all the troops out, "so that if any bad results follow they will be too late to affect the election."

Nixon agreed. He would keep pulling out troops, but not too quickly.

Kissinger reinforced the same message in a back-channel meeting with Dobrynin in early 1971, telling the Soviet ambassador that if North Vietnam did not interfere while the U.S. withdrew all of its troops, respected a cease-fire during that extraction, and did not act precipitously for "a certain period of time, not too long, after the U.S. withdrawal . . . [and] war breaks out again between North and South Vietnam, that conflict will no longer be an American affair."

The Chiefs, not privy to such back-channel exchanges, knew nothing about this new abandonment of an American military commitment. After the various crises of the fall of 1970, however, they had seen enough of Nixon's policies to be dismayed by the administration's waning commitment to oppose Communist expansion. Their anxiety on this front was heightened by a conversation between Zumwalt and Kissinger on a train ride to the U.S. Military Academy of West Point, New York, in November. Zumwalt had recently spoken with Nixon about the negative public opinion of the war, and Nixon had assured him that public opinion could be turned around by a combination of good diplomacy and battlefield success. On the train ride, when Kissinger heard that from Zumwalt, he made a surprising rejoinder, recorded in Zumwalt's contemporaneous notes:

> K does not agree with the P that the American people can be turned around. He states strongly that the P misjudges the people. K feels that US has passed its historic high point like so many earlier civilizations. He believes US is on downhill and cannot be roused by political challenge. He states that his job is to persuade the Russians to give us the best deal we can get, recognizing that the historical forces favor them.

Kissinger further explained that Americans had "neither the stamina nor the will to do the hard things they would have to do to prevent [this downhill slide] from happening; that the duty of policymakers, therefore, is at all costs to conceal from the people their probable fate and proceed as cleverly and as rapidly as may be to make the best possible deal with the Soviet Union while there is still time to make any deal."

Kissinger may have seen this position as the ultimate in realism. But to many people, and especially to the military, it seemed like rank defeatism. The administration's eagerness to give in to the Soviets convinced Zumwalt and Moorer that the Nixon-Kissinger policies presaged disaster for the United States—and that they must be reversed.

IN LATE 1970, the Democratic-controlled Congress, determined to hold Nixon to his commitments on Cambodia, made a supplemental appropriations bill for the continuation of the war in Southeast Asia contingent upon Nixon's honoring his pledge not to send any American ground troops into Cambodia.

Cambodia was sliding toward complete chaos, and the United States had to take some action or risk losing Cambodia as well as Vietnam. To keep his political head above water, Nixon wanted enough fighting taking place in Southeast Asia to prevent a Communist victory in Vietnam until after his re-election. This was no easy task. As he often did in difficult situations, Nixon looked for someone to blame; increasingly, he targeted the military brass.

In one late-night conversation with Kissinger, Nixon lambasted the JCS for not doing more to provide intelligence and air support in Cambodia. The air force, Nixon charged, neutralized only "one or two trucks a day" out of eight hundred sorties, but sought "fifteen hundred air medals" for their work. "Get ahold of Moorer tonight," Nixon instructed; "I want a plan where every goddamn thing that can fly goes into Cambodia and hits every target that is open." But he also directed that even South Vietnamese troops airlifted in were to be categorized as support personnel, because "unless we make an absolute commitment [to Congress] that no American ground forces are going to be used in Cambodia, you'll never get the supplemental." The supplemental military appropriations bill contained the money to allow the U.S. armed forces to continue fighting in South Vietnam, plus aid for Cambodia disguised under a $500 million request for support of Israel.

After the call, Kissinger chuckled with Haig over the president's unreasonable demands. They did call Moorer but made certain that Nixon's orders were not carried out.

The next day, after the White House offered assurances to Congress that no American ground troops would go to Cambodia, the House passed the supplemental budget by a vote of 344 to 21. Senate Democratic leaders objected to it, though, and in the days that followed Secretary of State Rogers brokered a compromise that was actually a defeat for Nixon. The full Congress passed the supplemental, but it also finally passed a slightly altered version of Cooper-Church that permitted American air missions in Cambodia only if aimed at the North Vietnamese and forbade American ground troops from entering Cambodia.

During the Reagan years, and even more frequently in the George W. Bush era, neoconservatives would charge that during the Nixon era the heavily Democratic Congress cut off funds for prosecution of the Vietnam War and therefore was responsible for the loss of Vietnam to the Communists. Fritz Kraemer had predicted this argument in 1969, citing a World War I concept he knew well from his youth, one that was known in German as *dolchstosslegende*. In a memo, Kraemer defined the concept as "the propaganda tale of the stab in the back" of the fighting troops, done by the politicians. "Unfortunately," Kraemer wrote in the memo, this excuse "can be invented in any country and at any time."

The facts of the Vietnam War situation in late 1970 belie the contention, made years later, that liberal politicians prevented the war from being won by cutting off its funding. Before Congress acted, Nixon had reduced U.S. fighting forces in South Vietnam from 543,000 to 344,000 and pledged to bring home another 100,000 by the end of 1971. As a result, the Chiefs judged that they didn't have enough U.S. troops left in Vietnam to win a war. This conclusion was reached well in advance of the first successful congressional cutoff of funds. The appropriations commitment to the support of Cambodia, for instance, would continue through two more budget cycles before being restrained. In 1969–72, Congress did not prevent the United States from "winning" the war; if anyone did, it was Nixon—by withdrawing so many troops so quickly; by continuing the Johnson administration's operating restraints on the military; by reducing military budgets so that they provided significantly less money than was required to train and equip South Vietnam's forces to take over on the battlefield; and, last but not least, by conceding that North Vietnamese troops could remain in South Vietnam after any cease-fire.

NIXON'S NEED TO demonstrate some progress in the war to the American public led to the military campaign known as Lam Son 719, an ARVN thrust into southeastern Laos to clean out North Vietnamese sanctuaries. Because this campaign was eventually judged as disastrous, no one later claimed credit for instigating it.

Evidence suggests that the campaign did not originate in the Pentagon. Nixon did not dream it up, though he agreed to it—primarily because American troops would be involved only as communications providers and suppliers of airpower—and Kissinger did not push for it very hard, either, since he was desperately trying to move the separate talks with the Russians and the Chinese off dead center. In 1992, Al Haig wrote that, "prodded remorselessly by Nixon and Kissinger, the Pentagon finally devised a plan" for the Laos incursion. But Creighton Abrams biographer Lewis Sorley and diplomatic historian William Bundy, among others, assert that the impetus came principally from Haig, while military historian General Bruce Palmer concludes that the culprits were Thieu and Ambassador Ellsworth Bunker in Saigon. In any event, after Lam Son 719, Haig knew where to lay the blame: "Those of us involved in the planning," he later wrote, "were appalled by the Defense Department's handling of the operation which resulted in the serious mauling of an ARVN which had been recently rejuvenated."

If this reasoning sounds familiar, it is: The same rationale would be trotted out by politicians in the 1970s, 1980s, 1990s, and in the twenty-first century, each and every time some military action planned by the White House went awry in its execution.

Haig also asserted that the plan for Lam Son 719 was always that if the South Vietnamese troops got into trouble in Laos, U.S. ground troops would be sent in, "despite congressional restrictions." "Haig could not accept, apparently, that Congress, through its constitutional power of the purse, could set conditions for military operations," Bundy observes. "That a senior military officer might be so wrong on a central constitutional point is striking (and disturbing)." Haig's championing of the Lam Son 719 operation, which flew in the face of opposition by the Joint Chiefs, Rogers, Laird, and eventually even Helms and Kissinger, suggests that he was going his own way on this—likely with encouragement from Fritz Kraemer, for this was a plan that relied on faith and on the inherent value of aggressive military action.

Nixon green-lighted Lam Son 719 because he now trusted Haig more on military matters than he did the commanders in the field, the Joint Chiefs, or Kissinger. Military historian Palmer, who at the time was working at the Pentagon with Laird—and was also being advised by Kraemer—later wrote: "Incredibly, [Haig's] military assessments of the situation in Vietnam were given more weight than the judgments of General Abrams, other responsible commanders in the field, and the Joint Chiefs of Staff."

However, Haig failed to convey to Nixon information that might have aborted Lam Son 719 before it began, such as Abrams's contention to Haig that the proposed incursion would run smack into the bulk of the North's concealed troops in Laos and would likely be trapped there. After visiting Southeast Asia, Haig returned to the White House and gave a readiness report that finessed both objections, selling Lam Son 719 energetically to Nixon.

Beyond its relevance to the planned Laos incursion, Haig's trip also became the occasion for a new front in the Moorer-Radford espionage campaign. Haig was accompanied on the journey by a new personal aide, Yeoman Radford; Haig had specifically asked Robinson for him. During the journey Radford stole and copied an enormous amount of material; the volume and quality were so high that later investigators suspected that Haig must have encouraged the theft. "I thought that [Haig] was placing quite a bit of trust in somebody that he didn't know that well," Radford later said. Admiral Robert Welander, who would soon replace Robinson in the liaison office, confessed in 1971, "Were I in the same case [as Haig] and having borrowed a yeoman, I think I would have concluded that most of the things the yeoman might have been exposed to would in turn be exposed to the guy he normally works for." Welander added, "I think Haig knew that Radford was observing things. It was stuff that Haig expected me to . . . make available to the chairman."

The documents Radford stole on this trip revealed to Moorer and Zumwalt, for the first time, how Nixon was obtaining the data on which to base troop withdrawals, as well as some information on the secret negotiations with North Vietnam and the USSR, and a hint of the talks with China. None of those morsels involved good news for the military. They redoubled the espionage, anxious to learn more about other ways in which Nixon and Kissinger might be compromising the safety and security of the United States.

Delayed by rains, Lam Son 719 was steadily dogged by vicious anti-aircraft fire that eventually destroyed one hundred American helicopters and damaged six hundred more, with substantial losses of aircrews. Enemy fire soon pinned down and battered the South Vietnamese. Receiving the news of these continuing reverses in Washington, Nixon directed Haig to return to Saigon and relieve Abrams. Haig was willing—and, he thought, able—to take over, but he counseled patience. Nixon soon thought better of removing his most successful commander and changed Haig's mission to fact-finding.

Despite Haig's visit, and to Nixon's chagrin, South Vietnamese leader Thieu pulled his troops out of Laos almost a month ahead of schedule.

Although North Vietnamese casualties from Lam Son 719 were high, and huge quantities of their arms and materiel were destroyed, the South lost 8,000 of the 22,000 troops in what observers described as a rout. But on April 7, Nixon claimed victory, arguing that the ARVN had demonstrated that "without American advisors they could fight effectively against the very best troops North Vietnam could put in the field. . . . Vietnamization has succeeded," he announced. "Our goal is a total American withdrawal. . . . We can and we will reach that goal through our program of Vietnamization."

But it was clear to most that Lam Son 719 had been no victory, and Vietnamization anything but a success—and this only heightened the right's anxieties about Nixon. Masses of troops had come back from Vietnam; the president had given in on Cooper-Church, on future military budgets, on opposing Allende, and on permitting Soviet influence in the Middle East. There were rumors about potential giveaways at the SALT talks. Having finally reached the White House, this lifelong opponent of Communism seemed to be giving away the store.

The first open revolt on the right came from the young. In the spring of 1971, the Young Americans for Freedom, the college-age conservative vanguard, held their annual meeting with their elders, the editors of *National Review*. The youngsters informed the graybeards that YAF would shortly announce that they were withholding support from the administration, and might even look for an alternative candidate to back in 1972. The *National Review* editors were not yet willing to agree, but they listened.

By the spring of 1971—that is, well before any hint of the adventures that would culminate in the Watergate scandal had even appeared—the crises of the previous six months had exposed deep schisms inside the administration and in Nixon's supporters on the outside. Even as he approached the high point of his presidency, that split was intensifying, as was its potential for harming Richard Nixon.

8

Approaching the Zenith

In a long and arduous campaign, the moment of greatest vulnerability is when the goal is in sight, for that is when each setback seems inordinately hard to overcome. In 1971, just as the Cambodia incursion had done a year earlier, the Lam Son 719 invasion of Laos retarded the Nixon administration's efforts to reach new ground with the USSR and China. To break through the impasses, Nixon and Kissinger used each Communist power's antipathy to the other. Great strides were made toward Nixon's goals of détente with the Soviets and rapprochement with the Chinese. But there was a cost to these accomplishments, in terms of what the United States had to yield to those Communist powers, and that cost became increasingly unacceptable to Nixon's detractors on the right.

ACCORDING TO THE administration's early 1971 annual report on foreign policy, the Nixon Doctrine was working. South Korea, Thailand, Taiwan, the Philippines, and Japan, knowing that the United States would be less likely to fight future battles for them, became more self-reliant, beefing up their armed forces, aided by U.S. grants. Thailand, Malaysia, and the Philippines also sought military aid from the USSR in addition to the States. Australia and New Zealand became more active in the defense of their region. The report also codified some pragmatic changes in policy, such as acknowledging the USSR as a superpower with legitimate interests in the Middle East and a "vital strategic desire to secure herself and her territories against

China." As *Time* reported, the theme of the policy review was "acceptance of the facts of international life."

Kissinger had long since embraced Nixon's pragmatic perspective, but he continued to lambaste the CIA from an ideological point of view. The latest National Intelligence Estimate (NIE) was slightly better than the previous year's—but not by much, in Kissinger's estimation, because it still ignored "Soviet doctrinal and strategic writings, economic information, analysis of Soviet institutions [that are] fundamental to understanding present Soviet programs and estimating future ones." For years Kraemer and Wohlstetter had pointed to these lacunae in their criticism of NIE estimates. To evaluate the threat potential of America's enemies independently of the CIA, Kissinger allowed his longtime rival, economist James Schlesinger, to bring into the NSC a former RAND colleague, Andrew Marshall, to set up an Office of Net Assessment (ONA) for that purpose. Later, ONA would move to the Pentagon, where Marshall and his operation would serve as a complement to Kraemer.

That spring, though Kraemer and Kissinger agreed on such matters as the inadequacy of the NIEs, they disagreed on many others. Kraemer felt forced to tell his protégé two things he knew Kissinger didn't want to hear: that there were limits to personal diplomacy, and that Kissinger must not underestimate the deviousness of the Soviets. Kraemer felt Kissinger was moving too quickly to reach an agreement with the Soviets and that his haste would allow the Soviets to take advantage of the United States.

In making these comments, Kraemer was likely referring to a matter Kissinger had discussed with Dobrynin: "a freeze on offensive deployments—specifically, land-based missiles—in return for a formal ABM agreement," as a Kissinger memo put it. Kraemer and others were concerned by a loophole in this freeze to which Kissinger had already agreed: Because submarine-launched ballistic missiles (SLBMs) were not specifically named in the freeze list, it appeared that the Soviets would be free to continue to build and deploy them. Kraemer's dismay on this point echoed the objections of chief negotiator Gerard Smith, Senators Jackson and Stennis, and Chairman Moorer, who all insisted on limits on Soviet SLBMs. When faced with such united opposition, Nixon almost always backed down; he sent Kissinger to the Soviets to insist on the adjustments.

Leonid Brezhnev, the Soviet leader, did not object too strenuously to the revised arrangement on SLBMs; he needed a deal with the United States in order to reduce tensions on the USSR's western flank and prevent the United States from becoming too close to China. An engineer and manager of technical production facilities, Brezhnev had been in political administration in the USSR since the start of World War II; during Khrushchev's time he had been an anti-Stalinist, but after overthrowing Khrushchev in 1964 and becoming first secretary of the Communist Party, Brezhnev reversed direction, rehabilitated Stalin, and violently suppressed the 1968 uprising in Czechoslovakia. That intervention became the defining instance of the "Brezhnev Doctrine," which arrogated to the USSR the right to interfere in the internal affairs of its satellite countries.

In early 1971, however, what Brezhnev wanted and needed was a deal with the United States. He was hoping that Nixon would grant the USSR "Most Favored Nation" (MFN) trade status and lift its embargo on wheat sales. To obtain these concessions, Brezhnev helped Nixon with Congress. Senate Majority Leader Mansfield had introduced a plan to pull all of America's troops out of Europe as a way of pressuring the administration to end the war in Vietnam. To counter Mansfield, Brezhnev announced on May 14 that the USSR was ready to enter into negotiations for mutual force reductions in Europe. This convinced enough senators to switch sides and vote against Mansfield's plan, defeating it, to Nixon's relief.

The May 20 exchange of letters between Nixon and Brezhnev was only a first step in the direction of full détente—more a promise than a treaty, outlining only an "interim" agreement to work out two separate treaties in the near future, one regarding ABM and the other a potential freeze on offensive weapons.

Not good enough, critics such as Kraemer and Jackson complained. These were only interim agreements; they would take years to resolve, years during which the Soviets would be able to keep building and deploying strategic arms without fear of retaliation. Nixon's support in conservative quarters was fading fast, and he would need both Republican and Democratic conservatives in order to pass treaties with the Soviets.

THROUGHOUT MOST OF the spring of 1971, Zhou En-Lai had refused to answer Kissinger's letters—a pressure tactic from a master tactician. Born at the end of the nineteenth century and educated partly in Europe, Zhou had been China's premier and its most senior diplomat since 1949. Second in command to Mao Ze-Dong, he was considered much more open-minded; while Mao had pushed the Cultural Revolution, Zhou had resisted its worst effects. He understood that Nixon and Kissinger needed the opening to China as much as China did.

Nixon kept pressing. China could be the capstone of his plan to reorganize the diplomatic alignment map of the world. He kept offering carrots, and in early April 1971 he finally got a bite. In response to a U.S. promise of relaxing an embargo, the Chinese table tennis team, at a championship in Japan, invited the American team for a visit. Nixon immediately issued an executive order that lessened the impact of the old embargo against U.S. firms trading with China, which would allow more dollar-denominated currency to flow into China's coffers. On April 27, the Pakistani ambassador to Washington delivered a note from Zhou saying that Beijing would receive a special envoy from the United States: Henry Kissinger, Secretary Rogers, "or even the President."

It was extraordinary news, the breakthrough that Nixon had long been awaiting; Nixon and Kissinger toasted Zhou's invitation with champagne. Rapprochement with China would force the Soviet Union to yield more to the United States, lest the U.S. and China join hands against the USSR. Flush with his triumph, Nixon toyed with Kissinger, suggesting that Rogers or another emissary should now go to China. But to dispatch anyone but Kissinger would widen the circle of those who knew the secret, so after a day Nixon relented.

The news was so top-secret that only a handful of people in the government knew about it. But Kissinger told Fritz Kraemer. "Well," Kraemer responded, "I suppose when you have two Bolshevik regimes as your enemy, it makes a certain amount of sense to collaborate with the weaker of the two and drive a wedge. But Kissinger—*no* concessions on Taiwan!"

Kraemer was on target: Taiwan was Beijing's sore point. For nearly a quarter century the United States had been championing Taiwan, and that posture—coupled with America's refusal to allow China into the United Nations—had served to keep China isolated. Every president since Eisenhower thought this posture was absurd, but the strength of the pro-Taiwan lobby in the United States had prevented every administration from resolving it. Eisenhower had tried for "dual recognition," which would acknowledge the sovereignty of both China and Taiwan, but he confessed to his NSC that he could not even propose such a thing because "so many members of Congress want to crucify anyone who argues in favor of permitting any kind of trade between the free nations and Communist China." John Kennedy and Lyndon Johnson had also favored dual recognition, to no avail. During his 1960 campaign for president, Nixon had pledged that if elected he would order the U.S. ambassador to the United Nations to veto any attempt to have China replace Taiwan at the UN. Would he feel the same way in 1971? Zhou was counting on Nixon to reverse that stand.

Two ancillary matters threatened to derail the meeting of Kissinger and Zhou. Arrangements between Washington and Beijing were being handled through a third party, Pakistan's leader, Yahya Khan—and then, as the negotiations were under way, long-simmering disputes between Pakistan and

India came to the surface, spurred by Pakistani mistreatment of East Pakistan's Bangladeshis. Nixon was anxious not to upset Yahya, a dictator whom
he considered a friend. "We should just stay out" of the Bangladeshi problem, he said. "What the hell can we do?"

Of course there were things Nixon's administration could have done:
The United States could have acted as a mediator or facilitator of dialogue
between India and Pakistan on this issue. But Nixon felt sure that doing so
would upset Yahya and potentially threaten Nixon's planned rapprochement
with China. His decisions in this looming conflict alarmed the embassy staff
in Islamabad, who sent a message of protest to the president. He dismissed it,
and on the cover of a policy memo regarding Pakistan, wrote out an instruction to " all hands. Don't squeeze Yahya at this time." The recommendation
and wording may have originated with Haig or Kissinger.

The second matter threatening to spoil the China opening was a bombshell that burst on June 13, 1971, when the *New York Times* published excerpts from "The Pentagon Papers," a compilation of documents regarding
the conflict from 1945 to 1968, some of them still classified as secret. Compiled by a handful of RAND and Pentagon civilian insiders, and meant as
an internal review for the government, the Pentagon Papers had been kept
under a cloak of secrecy; very few printed copies existed. The Papers made
for daunting reading, but for those who could bear to plow through, they
offered an eye-opening chronicle of how the United States became involved
in Vietnam; of how the conflict and U.S. troop commitments had steadily
escalated; and of the many mistakes Truman, Eisenhower, Kennedy, and
Johnson had made in prosecuting the war. To antiwar readers, they constituted a damning indictment of U.S. policy, lies, and blundering. To proponents of the war, they contributed little to continued support of the fight for
the independence of South Vietnam.

As Fritz Kraemer later stated, the Pentagon Papers revealed such a long
and detailed record of indecision and ineptitude that an enemy such as
North Vietnam could only conclude that the United States was, indeed, a
"helpless giant."

Nixon had not even read the *Times* article when he spoke with Haig
in what Nixon had expected to be a routine call. When Nixon asked about
matters in the news, Haig exploded: "Goddamn *New York Times* exposé . . .
devastating security breach . . . greatest magnitude of anything I've ever seen."

When Nixon learned of the contents of the Papers, he saw no immediate
reason for anger; after all, they referred only to actions taken prior to his election. But Kissinger was afraid that the Papers could harm him, because he
was already certain that Halperin or Ellsberg had given them to the *Times*.
He tried to prod Nixon into action by saying that the release of the Papers

threatened the negotiations with China. When that hot-button argument failed to move Nixon, Kissinger (according to Haldeman's diary) took a riskier approach: If Nixon issued no strong reaction to this publication, he said, it would suggest "that you're a weakling, Mr. President."

By the end of the day, Nixon was fired up about the leaks, ready to prosecute the leaker and the *Times*. "People've gotta be put to the torch for this," he told Haldeman. "We're up against an enemy, a conspiracy. . . . They're using any means, we are going to use any means. Is that clear?" Attorney General Mitchell won a court order enjoining the *Times* from further publication; the *Washington Post* immediately picked up where the *Times* had left off, printing more of it and enmeshing the administration in an enormous, headline-grabbing controversy.

Nixon decided that the plague of leaks must stop and that the leakers must be pursued. He dismissed the ongoing investigations by DoD and the FBI as inadequate: Hoover, a friend of Ellsberg's father-in-law, wasn't chasing down leads properly, and Nixon presumed that Laird and his DoD people weren't inclined to support him. There was evidence on the latter point: When an assistant attorney general conveyed the president's wish for quick action on the Pentagon Papers leak, Fred Buzhardt, the DoD counsel, refused point-blank to cooperate. Don Stewart later said that Buzhardt "ran the Ellsberg case for politics"—in this instance, to protect Laird—and "impeded the investigation." Because Defense was also recalcitrant, the White House conceived a separate investigative unit. "If a conspiracy existed, I wanted to know," Nixon later wrote. "I wanted the full resources of the government brought to bear to find out. If the FBI was not going to pursue the case, then we would have to do it ourselves." To conduct such an investigation would be to step into quicksand, so in-house conservatives Pat Buchanan and Dick Allen declined the honor of leading the unit. The task fell to the lower-ranked David Young, Kissinger's appointments secretary, who had since moved to the Domestic Council, and to an assistant to Nixon top aide John Ehrlichman, Egil "Bud" Krogh, a lawyer with a CIA background.

Meanwhile, final preparations were being made for Kissinger's trip to Asia. Haig decided to send Yeoman Radford of the liaison office along with Kissinger as a valet, secretary, and factotum. At the time, Nixon had ordered all information about Kissinger's trip to China to be kept from most White House aides, the Cabinet, the NSC, the Joint Chiefs, Congress, and foreign countries. Haig, who knew about the trip, asked the new liaison officer, Admiral Robert Welander, to handle the arrangements. Welander had joined the office only a few weeks earlier, after Rem Robinson finally received the seagoing commission he had long sought. Radford was not happy about the change in bosses; he found Welander to be more cautious about the espionage activities than Robinson, and less willing to filter the material before passing it to the JCS. As Radford prepared to leave for China with Kissinger in early July 1971, Welander gave the yeoman simple instructions about his espionage mission: "Be careful and don't get caught."

In the previous ten months, papers that Radford and others had stolen from Kissinger and the NSC had revealed to the Chiefs their systematic exclusion from the Kissinger-Dobrynin negotiations and from the content of the Paris peace talks. But they had not realized how thoroughly they had been bypassed until Radford and Kissinger arrived in California after their round-the-world trip on July 13, two days before the opening to China was announced. During that trip, Radford accumulated so much material that he had had to ship some of it home by diplomatic pouch. Although he remained in Pakistan on July 9–10, while Kissinger traveled to Beijing, he did accompany Kissinger afterward to Paris, and it was during that long flight that Kissinger's aides compiled some memos on the Beijing trip. Radford was able to make notes on these, and when the Kissinger party landed at the El Toro Naval Air Station near Nixon's home in San Clemente, Radford took his last batch of purloined papers and notes and brought them directly to the visiting officers' quarters, where Welander and Moorer were staying. In a bedroom he went over these with Welander, who passed some to Moorer in the living room as Moorer prepared to meet with Nixon and Kissinger. The prizes included material on Kissinger's talks with Zhou En-Lai, recorded in such documents as the hastily dictated memos of the July 9 and 10 meetings, and Radford's notes on Kissinger's summary, addressed to the president, TOP SECRET/SENSITIVE/EXCLUSIVELY EYES ONLY.

For Moorer, the unpleasant surprise that Kissinger had met with Zhou was exacerbated by the gushing tone of Kissinger's summary, in which he said that Zhou "ranks with DeGaulle as the most impressive foreign statesmen I have met" and labeled his discussions with the Chinese as "the most searching, sweeping, and significant . . . I have ever had in government." Moreover, any U.S. military officer's attention would have been seized by the list of topics Kissinger had discussed with Zhou: "Taiwan, Indochina, relations with . . . Japan and the Soviet Union, South Asia . . . arms control." Kissinger told Zhou that U.S. forces would be removed from Taiwan in two stages: When the war in Vietnam ended, the United States would send home the forces that had been based on Taiwan for the war effort. After that, the United States would withdraw those stationed there principally for the defense of Taiwan. This would have been news to anyone in the U.S. military. When Zhou expressed a fear that the United States, the USSR, and a remilitarized Japan would collude against China, Kissinger assured him that would not happen. The Chinese even warned Kissinger that they would stand by Pakistan in the war now brewing over Bangladesh, so the United States should not back India.

To Moorer, every word of this was an outrage. Was U.S. policy now to be dictated by China? He was equally struck by Kissinger's pledge that the United States would inform China "in advance of major decisions we have with other major powers that might affect you," and by his promise to explain to the Chinese, before negotiations with the USSR, "our approach to SALT."

On the subject of Vietnam, Kissinger told Zhou that the United States could not "participate in the overthrow of people with whom we have been allied." However, if fighting should restart after a Vietnam peace agreement was in place and American troops had withdrawn, "we will not intervene. . . . What we require is a transition period between the military withdrawal and the political evolution. . . . If [then] the Indochinese people change their government, the US will not interfere." This was the message Kissinger had repeated secretly to Dobrynin for two years, now stated plainly in the stolen documents Moorer held: "We are ready to withdraw all of our forces by a fixed date and let objective realities shape the political future."

For Tom Moorer, the meaning of these confidential memos was clear: Nixon and Kissinger had bought their "opening to China" with secret concessions to the PRC that might well compromise the security of the United States of America around the world.

IN THE LATE afternoon of July 15, 1971, several helicopters lifted off from the El Toro Naval Air Station. Bearing the president and an entourage of aides and reporters, the choppers winged their way north to Burbank and the NBC studio where the sketch comedy show *Laugh-In* was usually taped. There the president made the startling announcement, live on national television, that the United States was pursuing an "opening to China." Nixon revealed that the Chinese had invited him to visit Beijing, that he had accepted, and that to prepare for his visit Henry Kissinger had already made an advance trip to Beijing and had held preliminary talks with Zhou En-Lai.

Nixon's announcement was brief, only ninety seconds, but it would stun the world, and Nixon knew it. Once the red light on the Burbank studio's television cameras went off, the exuberant president wanted to relax, to have dinner in Los Angeles before returning home. Someone suggested that a Chinese restaurant would be an appropriate place to go. But Nixon had a favorite place in mind—Perino's, an Italian restaurant—and soon he was ushering Kissinger, Haldeman, Ehrlichman, and a few other aides there, along with a handful of reporters. After lecturing everyone on fine wines, Nixon ordered a magnum of Lafite Rothschild 1961, at a cost of $250.

Section II

Undermining the Presidency

Fritz Kraemer meeting with Nixon and Kissinger in the Oval Office, October 24, 1972. *(Ollie Atkins, White House)*

9

Making Allies into Enemies

Nixon knew that the opening to China would be his largest achievement in foreign policy, the one for which he would be remembered. He suspected that this unexpected alteration of the status quo would attract vilification from those on the right. What he did not expect—as a realist who accepted the ramifications of an already-changed world and refused to cling to tenets he felt were outmoded—was that his reversal of decades of U.S. policy toward China would spur some on the right to do more than complain. Decisively alienated by the China opening, they would work from this day forward to reverse his foreign policies of détente, rapprochement, and discontinuing the fight in Vietnam; in the process they would undermine his presidency.

In nature, two streams on either side of a mountain may appear to be coursing in different directions until the point at which they meet and form a single, powerful river. The underground, almost invisible stream of the right's undermining of Nixon for foreign policy reasons, and the better-recognized stream that is known as the Watergate Affair had been running in parallel since the first wiretap had been placed in the spring of 1969. Two years later, in the spring of 1971, the streams began to intersect continually.

As President Nixon approached the mountain's highest points, the two streams became so intimately related that the tale of one cannot be fully understood without knowing that of the other.

NIXON'S ANNOUNCEMENT OF the opening to China produced worldwide repercussions. Told of the impending announcement, Alex Johnson of State, a former ambassador to Japan, immediately thought of the "Asaki Night-mare," a famous dream recounted by a former Japanese ambassador to the United States that one day U.S. officials would reverse their China policy without alerting Japan and thereby cause the downfall of the Japanese government. No such fall occurred after Nixon's announcement, but, as Johnson later wrote, "After this 'Nixon shokku' . . . there has never again been the same trust and confidence between our two governments."

Heeding Zhou's warning, Henry Kissinger told India's ambassador that if China intervened in the brewing India-Pakistan war, the United States would not defend India. Within weeks India and the USSR signed a mutual defense treaty, an alliance that greatly disturbed the NSC because it raised the prospect of U.S. forces being drawn into a military conflict between a Soviet-backed India and a China-backed Pakistan.

"No one was more surprised and confused than the Kremlin when it received the news" of the China opening, Anatoly Dobrynin later wrote. Kissinger insisted to Dobrynin that Nixon's forthcoming meeting with the Chinese "had no bearing whatsoever on American-Soviet relations." But of course it did, and the Soviets recognized this four days after the announcement, when they suddenly agreed to restart SALT negotiations. Kissinger thought he saw similar positive movement from the North Vietnamese in Paris, reporting to Nixon that in his next meeting "their whole tone . . . is completely different. . . . They are wavering. . . . I was absolutely brutal [with them] at the end."

Kissinger worried that if the North Vietnamese agreed to a negotiated settlement too soon, Nixon might want to throw Thieu overboard, and he wanted to prevent that. Kraemer agreed, warning in a memo about the dangerous consequences of getting out of Vietnam too soon. Kissinger passed Kraemer's memo on to Nixon, though without Kraemer's name attached. Even so, Nixon recognized the memo's authorship—"I could tell from his style"—and was struck by Kraemer's "rather gloomy picture. . . . Here we are all over Asia, pulling out and getting out and so forth. But it does show you, doesn't it Henry, the real dangers we're playing with here." Kissinger tried to placate Nixon, confiding that Kraemer could be "a bit apocalyptic" and asserting that the opening to China would moot all the critics' fears, right as well as left. Nixon could not take that chance; eager to placate American conservatives, he ordered them stroked.

As Nixon made his brief announcement on July 15, the phone rang in the California governor's mansion in Sacramento, where Governor Ronald Reagan, Senator James Buckley of New York, and his brother William F. Buckley, Jr., editor of the *National Review*, were watching the broadcast. The trio had long been among Taiwan's most ardent supporters and had frequently charged that the Democrats had "lost" China in the 1940s and

1950s by failing to prevent the ouster of the Nationalists. Nixon had said the same things for years prior to his election as president. Now here he was, the fellow anti-Communist whom the trio had helped elect, promising to "open the door for more normal relations with China" while pledging that "our action in seeking a new relationship with the People's Republic of China will not be at the expense of our old friends."

The call, which Reagan took, was from Henry Kissinger. As Bill Buckley later revealed, Kissinger tried to assure the three conservative leaders that "the strategic intentions of the President were in total harmony with the concerns of the conservative community." None of the three believed Kissinger, although the governor did agree to applaud the China move in public.

"F.D.R. would have hesitated to go to Berlin to wine and dine with Adolf Hitler—but we are about to do that, and all the liberals who can't stand the Greek colonels are jumping for joy," Buckley would soon write. His brother Jim told a reporter that the China move would "inevitably strengthen the hand of those [in the United States] seeking accommodation with the Communists at almost any price," and that "the grand scale of this overture to Beijing will be anything but reassuring to those [in Asia] who have to live with the aggressive reality of mainland China."

Nixon's foreign policy thunderclap, and the secrecy that had shrouded it from debate, also evoked anger from bureaucrats at Defense, State, and the CIA who had spent their entire adult lives fighting Communism. Nixon seemed to be waving the white flag of surrender, and they wondered if he and Kissinger had other betrayals in mind.

Bill Buckley would soon sum up all these fears in a *New York Times Magazine* article headlined "Say It Isn't So, Mr. President." "Is he one of us?" Buckley asked, going on to pillory Nixon's foreign policy initiatives as first cousins to the liberal stances of the hated internationalist senator J. William Fulbright. Buckley wondered whether Nixon had been

> taken in by the other side's reveries . . . based on the notion that the leadership of the Communist world suddenly stepped forward, as after a speech by Billy Graham, to submit to prefrontal lobotomies, after which they returned to duty at Helsinki, and other pressure points in the world, to push SALT through to international peace and harmony, to tranquilize their legions in Vietnam, Egypt, Chile, West Germany, and Madagascar, whose name I mention simply to meet the anapestic challenge.

Later in July, at the suggestion of his mentor, James Burnham, Buckley convened in his Manhattan apartment a dozen conservative leaders to discuss their future stance toward the Nixon administration. Earlier that spring they had stopped short of withholding further support of Nixon (as the YAF had done), but in the intervening months Nixon had first signed the May 20 letters with Brezhnev, which they viewed as giveaways to the USSR, and had now turned his back on Taiwan and embraced China. A former Communist, since the late 1930s Burnham had been Communism's most consistently thoughtful critic, the intellectual force behind the *National Review*. The "Manhattan Twelve" had an obligation to the conservative movement, he argued, to publicly suspend support for the administration. The conferees agreed.

News of this incipient revolt soon reached the White House, producing an invitation to the twelve to meet with Kissinger and Haig in Washington. Jeffrey Bell of the American Conservative Union recalled the "patronizing" atmosphere of that White House meeting:

> Kissinger sat there and told us, "Some of ze tings dat I am going to dell you you must not even dell your vives." . . . We laughed about it afterwards. We had certain information from good sources about what they were saying. We knew, for example, that they were willing to compromise with the Soviets on missile accuracy. They were willing to compromise away hard-target capability. Kissinger and Haig just sat there and denied that was true.

Soon the Manhattan Twelve would hand White House counselor Chuck Colson a six-page list of demands to be met in exchange for their support of Nixon in 1972. These demands included an agreement that the administration would accept no SALT treaty that ceded to the Soviets leadership in land- and sea-based missile launchers; a "demonstration by action" that American foreign policy was not committed to the "illusion of détente"; an overt statement that the United States would continue its defense of Taiwan; and vigorous prosecution by the U.S. military of the war in Vietnam.

None of these matters was dismissible as outmoded. Taiwan certainly needed defending, the war in Vietnam was not being prosecuted very well, and détente could easily prove to be worse than an illusion if the Soviets surpassed the U.S. military in SLBMs or other such armaments. Conservatives had legitimate worries about the basic safety and security of the United States as the country continued to face foreign powers that most Americans still believed to be steadfastly inimical to the United States.

To prevent the spark of the Manhattan Twelve from igniting a larger conflagration, Nixon invited three highly conservative Republican senators to the White House for an intimate cocktail party. Senators John Tower of Texas, Bob Dole of Kansas, and Paul Fannin of Arizona had all been staunch Nixon supporters on foreign policy, so to the press Nixon couched his party for the trio as a thank-you to "early birds" who had helped him during his years out of office. After the event, the three senators did refrain from publicly criticizing the China opening, but one told a reporter, "I've had to grit my teeth and swallow hard to remain a loyalist."

One who had already learned that lesson the hard way was Don Rumsfeld. Back in May, Rumsfeld had made a cardinal mistake. Seeking a way out of the Office of Economic Opportunity, he had sent Nixon a memo outlining a mission for a "high-level Presidential aide" to oversee Southeast Asia as hostilities wound down and to fashion a Nixonian version of the Marshall Plan to reconstruct it. Rumsfeld, of course, would be glad to serve as that high-level aide. No one at the White House leapt at the idea, and so during a staff meeting Rumsfeld questioned Kissinger about the war, asking why it wasn't being ended more quickly. Affronted by the younger man's impertinence, Kissinger complained to Nixon, and the president, though busy preparing that evening's speech about Lam Son 719, took time out to discuss Rumsfeld with Haldeman. "Let's dump him right after this," Nixon suggested. Haldeman reminded him that he had already arranged for Rumsfeld to accompany HEW secretary Robert Finch to Europe. Nixon welcomed the opportunity to send Rumsfeld away for a time, telling Haldeman he was "disappointed" in his young acolyte. "We have given him, time and time again, opportunities to step up, and he will not step up and kick the ball."

"I used to think he was a presidential contender," Haldeman said, "but he isn't."

"He's like Finch. They both have the charisma for national office but neither has got the backbone," Nixon opined.

When Rumsfeld returned from Europe, after the China announcement, he sought an audience with Nixon. On a personal level, the president still retained a fondness for Rumsfeld, whom he identified to Haldeman as "a ruthless little bastard." In midsummer of 1971, during Rumsfeld's few moments with Nixon, he offered no further prescriptions for the war.

"When we get down to it, the war will be over one way or another, next year at this time," Nixon said. "[The Democrats] got us in, we got us out."

"Exactly, that's right," Rumsfeld responded.

Nixon said he would consider Rumsfeld for the post of ambassador to NATO, and that he would be a Cabinet officer some day—although the one post for which Rumsfeld would be unsuitable, Nixon ventured, was secretary of defense. He then asked Rumsfeld to take on a thankless task, chairman of the president's council on wage and price controls. Rumsfeld and Cheney moved to that office shortly thereafter. But Rumsfeld remained opposed to Nixon on foreign policy—though he had learned to keep his opinions to himself.

REAGAN AND THE Buckleys weren't the only conservatives Nixon was worried about losing. Kissinger was dispatched to sell Scoop Jackson on the opening to China, framing it as an anti-Soviet move. Although the relationship between Jackson and Kissinger had not yet yielded to open warfare— they still occasionally had dinner together at Jackson's home—it was "not a warm and cordial one," as Richard Perle would later put it. But Jackson was receptive, observing that "playing the China card" had "deeply tactical as well as broader strategic objectives" that meshed with his wish to contain the USSR by every means. He did, however, suggest some caveats. As Perle later recalled, Jackson considered the China of 1971 a weak political player,

> incapable of extending itself, even in its own region, much less globally. It . . . had such immense internal problems and demands that he did not believe that they posed a significant threat. . . . The Soviet Union, on the other hand, was . . . a clear threat to Western Europe. . . . So it was a geo-political judgment as to where the danger lay and in Scoop's view it lay with a strong and robust Soviet Union, and a weak China could not be an effective balancing element.

What Jackson sought to do next was ensure that, after the China opening, Nixon did not lose sight of the importance of tough negotiation with the USSR. Shortly thereafter, Jackson would use a well-timed leak to force the issue.

The publication of the Pentagon Papers had only heightened Nixon's obsession with leaks. In his July 19 chat with the White House staff he had made clear the connection between policy and leaking: "Why does it hurt to say . . . '[the China opening] will drive the Soviets up the wall,' 'it will help us in Vietnam,' and so forth? The answer is that [the way] to make sure [those things] don't happen is to speculate that they will." Therefore, Nixon insisted, he did not want the staff to give the press any more information about the China opening.

Some staffers in the Roosevelt Room guessed that Nixon was referring obliquely to a new investigative entity he had set up in the executive branch, one that would be led by Bud Krogh and David Young and would become known, because of its assignment to stop leaks, as the Plumbers.

A lawyer who had worked for Nelson Rockefeller on foreign policy before becoming Kissinger's appointments secretary, Young was considered by most of the White House staff an intelligent man who had become uncomfortable in the Haig-dominated NSC and unwilling to continue under Kissinger's thumb. Krogh, also a lawyer, had worked for Ehrlichman's firm in Seattle before joining the White House, but he had previously been involved with the CIA in Vietnam. Krogh bragged to Ehrlichman that he had hand-carried gold for the CIA to Vietnam; Ehrlichman and Haldeman later came to believe that Krogh maintained ties to the Agency even during his time at the White House. Neither allegation was ever proven. Speechwriter William Safire thought of Krogh and Young as a pair of "straight arrows."

Their first order of business in the new office was not the investigation of the Pentagon Papers leak, but of a new policy leak that hit the front page of the *New York Times* on July 23. For the previous four days, since the USSR agreed to renew the SALT talks, the president and his inner circle had discussed options for those talks. So Nixon, Kissinger, and Haig were stunned when Bill Beecher's *Times* story revealed the fallback negotiating position they had just developed—which was to settle for controls on submarine-launched ballistic missiles if the USSR would not agree to other options. The effect of the leak was not only to compromise the U.S. negotiating position but also to harden it. Now Kissinger could no longer refuse to seek such controls, or else congressional critics would lambaste him. That certainty made any agreement with the Soviets on the SLBM issue more difficult to achieve.

Because the leak compromised security by revealing secret information to an enemy power, it was tantamount to treason. Don Stewart, chief investigator for the Pentagon, thought the Beecher leak the most important of his nearly twenty years at DoD. Nixon wanted the source found and punished. He also wanted to prevent future leaks and demanded that "polygraphs" be given to everyone at DoD and State who had access to the documents underlying the leak. Haig objected vociferously to such widespread testing, predicting that it would lower morale and cause resignations. Haig also insisted that the testing was unnecessary because the Pentagon had already identified a prime suspect—William Van Cleave, a consultant and former NSC staffer who had recently been seen talking to Beecher. Van Cleave was brought in and grilled.

The identification of Van Cleave as prime suspect was unusual. Other national security leaks had been immediately attributed to people on the left, such as Halperin and Ellsberg. But the effect of this July 23, 1971, leak was to push Nixon and Kissinger to the right, and so a conservative became the focal point of suspicion. Nixon wasn't convinced that Van Cleave was the leaker. "Little people do not leak," he said. He guessed that the leak had more likely come from someone higher up and had been made for a specific political purpose.

A few hours later, Haig reported to Nixon that more than two hundred individuals at Defense and State could have seen the SALT negotiating positions material. And some of that material had been sent by State to legislators such as Scoop Jackson. Stewart was then easily able to confirm that the leaker must have been Jackson's young alter ego, Richard Perle. Perle did very little without his boss's approval, so blame for the leak arguably belonged with Jackson himself, attempting to force the administration to take a harder line on SALT. When Nixon was informed of the leaker's identity, he closed the inquiry. He would do nothing to upset what he thought of as his good working relationship with Jackson—even if that meant not punishing anyone for leaking top-secret information involving the future safety of the United States.

IN ITS PRELIMINARY damage assessment on the release of the Pentagon Papers, the CIA worried that the leak might prove "only an opening salvo in a campaign of selective major leaks." The White House agreed and sought the Agency's help in assisting the Plumbers. Director Helms seized the opportunity. Although a loyal public servant who tried to please whatever president he served, Helms disliked Nixon. The president treated Helms with contempt at principals' meetings, refused to see Helms alone, and rebuffed him or bucked him down to subordinates when Helms pleaded for an audience. Helms disagreed with what he considered Nixon's cozying up to the Communist powers and refusal to vigorously continue the fight in Vietnam—a shift he felt made a mockery of the work the CIA, and Helms personally, had done in that country.

The stories of the Plumbers and of the right's efforts to undermine Nixon would intersect at many important junctures. When the White House made requests of the CIA, for example, they would go through General Robert Cushman, a high Agency official who had been a military aide to Nixon during his vice presidency. Cushman was one of those military lifers, like Haig and Dick Walters, whom Nixon helped to advance in their military careers. In 1973, at a critical moment, Cushman would testify to several congressional committees in a way that damaged Nixon's hopes of continuing in office.

Cushman had once shared an office at the CIA with E. Howard Hunt, a legendary officer who had briefly been Bill Buckley's boss at the Agency. Helms had Hunt's espionage novels prominently displayed in his office and occasionally gave them as gifts to visitors. Hunt had recently retired from

CIA to work for Mullen and Company, a well-known CIA front. For two years Hunt had been pestering fellow Brown University alumnus Chuck Colson, a high-level Nixon aide, for a job at the White House. In the wake of the Pentagon Papers leak, one opened up. Hunt was hired.

Once installed at the White House, Hunt sent regular reports and packages to CIA headquarters in Langley, Virginia, and visited there to seek assistance from Cushman and others on various Plumbers tasks. James McCord, another former CIA agent with a background in technological devices—and with a conspiratorial mind that he expressed in various right-wing writings—also later joined the Plumbers, as did former FBI agent, prosecutor, and Treasury official G. Gordon Liddy. "The intensity of the national security concern expressed by the President fired up and overshadowed every aspect of [our] unit's work," Bud Krogh later wrote. Nixon acknowledged to his aides that the FBI and Justice Department inquiries into Ellsberg's actions would gather evidence that would stand up in court, but he expected the Plumbers to amass information that could be used to influence the court of public opinion. He wanted to discredit Ellsberg in the press the same way he had discredited Alger Hiss almost twenty years earlier. Kissinger contributed to that goal by telling reporters, on background, that Ellsberg was a wild man who had shot at Vietnamese peasants from helicopters, took hallucinogenic drugs, and had unusual sexual habits.

It soon emerged that Ellsberg had been overheard talking on the phone with Halperin. This was not good news for the White House: In a court proceeding Ellsberg's defense lawyer could demand that the government turn over all evidence, including any records of conversations—and that action would reveal the still-secret wiretaps. So Nixon ordered the logs and summaries of the tapes destroyed; the instruction went through Haig to the FBI. This attempted destruction of potential evidence in a criminal trial would remain hidden for a crucial two years.

To further discredit Ellsberg, Hunt pushed the Plumbers unit to ask the CIA for a psychological profile of Ellsberg and wrote a memo recommending that the White House "obtain Ellsberg's files from his psychiatric analyst," Dr. Lewis J. Fielding. The CIA did send over a profile, but Hunt, Young, and Krogh found it inadequate, boilerplate stuff. As Krogh later recalled, Hunt then "basically sold Young and me on the idea that . . . we can find out whether [Ellsberg] has been quote 'turned' or not. . . . Was he, you know, turned in Cambridge? Was he working for the other side? Is there material that can be used to discredit him so that he would not become the kind of anti-war spokesperson that other people rallied to? All that originated with Hunt."

Krogh and Young sent Ehrlichman a formal proposal to remove the

Ellsberg files from Fielding's office surreptitiously, a proposal whose language disguised the intent to break in. Ehrlichman signed off on it, appending a handwritten note, "If done under [the] assurance that it is not traceable."

The Plumbers broke into Fielding's office twice. First Hunt and Liddy did the job themselves, to case the joint; then a group of Cuban émigrés, CIA contract employees Hunt had worked with over the past decade, were sent in to take the files. The story that later gained wide acceptance was that the bumblers Hunt and Liddy had failed, obtaining no material they could use to discredit Ellsberg. The notion that the CIA gained nothing from the Fielding office break-ins, combined with the Agency's assertion that the Cubans were no longer on its payroll at the time of these break-ins (or, later, at the time of the burglary at the Democratic National Committee headquarters in the Watergate complex) served to distance the CIA from any involvement in Watergate.

The real story is more complicated. During the second break-in, the Cubans went inside the Fielding office while Hunt and Liddy remained on guard; when they emerged, the Cubans told Liddy they had found nothing of value and had overturned things to make it look like a drug addict had ransacked the office. Strangely, though, the Cubans then went back to the hotel and drank champagne. Liddy was puzzled: What were they celebrating? Black-bag professionals like the Cuban-émigré team usually photographed targeted materials and returned them carefully so as to leave no trace of any intrusion. But in this instance the Cubans had made a deliberate mess. Eugenio Martinez, one of the burglars, would tell Senator Howard Baker that he had participated in three hundred to four hundred similar CIA operations, and that the one at the Fielding office "was clearly a 'cover' operation with no intention of finding anything."

Soon after the Fielding office break-in, Cushman informed Ehrlichman that the Agency would no longer furnish assistance to Hunt. The CIA had no further interest in cooperating with the administration's out-of-bounds escapades. By November 1, Krogh and Young had also become disillusioned. They wrote to Ehrlichman that the entire pursuit of Ellsberg was off the mark; after all, they and the intelligence community had decided, Ellsberg had merely given the Papers to the press, "not to a foreign power." Moreover, the whole issue seemed moot: After the *Times* and the *Post* published the papers, "DoD published virtually the same material." "There has been no apparent damage as a result of Ellsberg's disclosures," Young and Krogh concluded. Two years later, a grand jury in Los Angeles verified their assessment by handing down an indictment of Ellsberg that included no charge of espionage. In November 1971, Krogh and Young, at their own requests, moved on to other assignments.

KISSINGER HAD TOLD Beijing that the United States would no longer stand in the way of China's desire to replace Taiwan as the sole representative of the Chinese peoples at the United Nations. But Nixon could not afford the political cost of publicly abandoning Taiwan, whose support was a bedrock tenet of the right. So he gulled some of his most steadfast conservative allies, including Senator James Buckley, into leading a doomed charge for "dual recognition," for the UN General Assembly to seat both Taiwan and the People's Republic of China.

Kissinger never conceded that this was a ruse—not even to Fritz Kraemer, who expended his energies and used his overseas contacts to lobby small countries to vote with the United States on a two-Chinas resolution. When the overwhelming majority of the 130 General Assembly members voted to oust Taiwan and seat Beijing, Kraemer called Kissinger to commiserate, saying, "We tried."

"By that time it was too late," Kissinger lied. "You can't tell me there were four or five [countries] that couldn't have been switched. . . . We could have gotten Ecuador and Guiana." Kissinger sent Haig the next day to brief Kraemer on the administration's valiant efforts to prevent the unseating of Taiwan.

Kissinger was now using Kraemer in various ways, among them to provide Nixon with a controlled critique from the right. One such instance was recorded in a November 1971 Oval Office tape. During a foreign affairs roundup, Nixon and Kissinger were filling in Attorney General Mitchell about the recent concluding of a four-party agreement on access to Berlin, a pact Nixon characterized as "pretty good."

> KISSINGER: The agreement now is—I have this friend, this right-wing friend in the Pentagon, I've shown you some memos of his—Kraemer . . .
> NIXON: Kraemer, yeah.
> KISSINGER: Who, when he was—
> NIXON: He always is the one you send in, who gives us the analyses—
> Kissinger: Yeah.
> NIXON: I like him.
> KISSINGER: Well, he was—
> NIXON: I should meet him sometime.
> KISSINGER: Well, I'll bring him in.

NIXON: All right, go ahead. Tell him that I do read his stuff though.
KISSINGER: Yeah. All right, I will tell him that. . . . Well, he had said
that Berlin was lost all along.
NIXON: I know.
KISSINGER: And I, in fact, showed you memos of his. Well, he has now
studied the text of the agreement that [we have] signed and he says it's
unbelievable. It's, you know—He says the basic situation is lousy, which
we know. But the agreement is such that it's unbelievably good. So
there we came out all right.

In the immediate wake of the General Assembly vote, the Senate passed
a nonbinding, Buckley-sponsored resolution calling on Nixon to cut American underwriting from a third to a quarter of the UN's budget. Jim Buckley's
brother Bill accused the Maoists of executing between 10 million and 50
million Chinese and pledged his undying support to a democratic Taiwan.
Reagan sent a telegram to Taiwan's leader, Chiang Kai-Shek, charging that
the UN had been "reduced to the level of a kangaroo court."

Continuing the long-standing U.S. commitment to defend Taiwan had
been one of the Manhattan Twelve's conditions for Nixon if he wanted their
support in 1972. His refusal to save Taiwan's status at the UN moved the
Twelve to consider backing a presidential run by a Republican conservative,
Ohio representative John Ashbrook. This was a serious matter for Nixon, because polls showed him running even with Democratic front-runner Senator Edmund Muskie. Should Ashbrook enter the lists, especially on a third-
party line, he might siphon votes from the right and cause Nixon to lose in
1972. To prevent that scenario, Nixon tried to mend fences with Reagan,
John Tower, and the Buckleys.

Fritz Kraemer, still smarting from the abandonment of Taiwan, turned
his anger on his newly famous protégé. Asked by a journalist in the fall of
1971 for his judgment of Kissinger's future, Kraemer told Bernard Collier
that he hoped Kissinger would retire to a Greek isle, "write serious books
on power and politics in the world," and be remembered as an insightful de
Tocqueville—since, Kraemer implied, Kissinger was no longer on the path
to being a modern Metternich.

In a cardinal example of how to alienate friends and create enemies,
Nixon fumbled when he tried to head off a presidential run by Scoop Jackson. The flurry of interest in Jackson for the Democratic nomination in 1972
came at a moment when one of the issues of the day was the reluctance of
the Thieu regime in South Vietnam to hold free elections. This bothered
congressional critics, and so in a private September 15, 1971, letter to the

president, Jackson urged Nixon to push Thieu to hold those elections to prevent further erosion of U.S. congressional support for the war effort.

When he was asked about the Saigon elections at a press conference, Nixon cited Jackson's letter—and misrepresented it, saying that Jackson advocated that the United States use pressure to topple Thieu in the same way that Kennedy had used pressure to topple Prime Minister Diem in 1963. Furious, Jackson responded by releasing the letter to the press. Its details gave the lie to what Nixon had said, diminishing Nixon's credibility. The incident turned Jackson from a sometime supporter into an outright enemy, who would go on to lead the fight against Nixon and his foreign policies in the halls of Congress.

By the fall of 1971, Nixon's handling of China, and his overreactions to leaks, had cost him the support of many such allies—from Jackson and the Manhattan Twelve to other congressional conservatives, top CIA officials, and some of his White House staff.

He understood, at least partially, that he had alienated these former supporters, but he thought that things were going well enough that he no longer needed them as much he had.

10

"A Federal Offense of the Highest Order"

The Moorer-Radford spy ring operated from the early fall of 1970 to late December 1971. In the story of how and why it operated and ended, and some of the immediate consequences of its discovery and of the ways President Nixon chose to deal with it, information is the key: who had it and who did not, who knew what and when they knew it. Nixon and his top aides made some decisions about the spy ring based on incomplete information and made others in the absence of information that had been deliberately withheld from them. The results would come back to haunt Nixon during his second term.

MODERN PAKISTAN, CREATED after World War II, was awkwardly divided, spiritually as well as physically. East Pakistan contained Muslims and Bangladeshis who resembled the neighboring peoples of India. West Pakistan, separated from the East by part of India, was peopled by Punjabs, Pashtuns, and Mohajir, who had more in common with Afghans than they did with their countrymen in the east. Yahya Khan, ruler of Pakistan, had imposed martial law in 1969 and was regularly accused by opponents of being, in the words of one writer, "ruthless, uncompromising, insensitive, and grossly inept." When the East Pakistan Bangladeshis moved for independence, encouraged by India, Yahya Khan quashed their rebellion, killing or jailing tens of thousands. India played up the plight of the Bangladeshis at Yahya's hands to the world's media, and by the fall of 1971 open warfare between India and Pakistan loomed.

The United States professed neutrality in this matter but was far from neutral behind the scenes. In addition to feeling obligated to Yahya for the opening to China, Nixon disliked the Indian people, in particular Prime Minister Indira Gandhi; he was uncomfortable around powerful women such as her and Golda Meir, and he felt that India had repeatedly tried to play the United States off against the USSR to gain assistance.

In early November 1971, Indians called on their government to take military action to protect fellow religionists in the Bangladeshi area. In response, Nixon ordered Kissinger to encourage China to express its support for West Pakistan. "Threaten to move forces or move them, Henry, that's what [the Chinese] must do now," Nixon instructed. He also told Kissinger to warn the USSR to stay out of the picture and not to threaten to intervene on India's side. Kissinger conveyed these messages. In the one to Beijing, he reiterated his pledge to Zhou in July—that if coming to the aid of Pakistan brought China into conflict with the USSR, the United States would aid China.

The Chinese had no intention of becoming that involved and did not move their troops toward the Pakistan-India border. The situation in East Pakistan continued to deteriorate in the direction of all-out strife. The Washington Special Actions Group (WSAG), a council of top military intelligence and foreign policy officials that Kissinger had organized to handle such incidents after the EC-121 crisis, met to discuss Pakistan every few days. Even so, Zumwalt later recalled, "We were always behind events and our responses were as ineffectual as they were tardy." David Packard, the hard-line assistant secretary of defense, was adamant in the WSAG meetings that if the United States could not do anything effective on the Indian subcontinent or in its adjoining waters, it should do nothing at all. Zumwalt and Moorer agreed.

Up to this point, the Moorer-Radford spy ring had mainly been stealing classified materials from the NSC and Kissinger so that the Chiefs could understand the White House's secret decisions and how they might be affecting the safety and security of the country. But in late November 1971, worried over the potential consequences of the Indian subcontinent crisis, Moorer went further. Before this he and Zumwalt had been technically guilty of improper possession of classified materials—the same crime of which Ellsberg stood accused. Now, in response to the Indian crisis, Moorer and Zumwalt would step further over the legal line by committing more serious violations of the espionage statutes.

War between India and Pakistan began on December 3, 1971. Pakistan launched a preemptive airborne attack on six Indian airfields, in the hope of disabling India's air force and winning a quick victory. Yahya and his associates knew that if Pakistan did not win in the first flush of the war, India's much larger armed forces were likely to prevail. But the Pakistani blow was not a knockout, and India began to fight back.

"The President very definitely wants to tilt the present situation toward the Paks," Kissinger told the WSAG after learning that hostilities had commenced. Zumwalt vociferously objected to the idea of "tilting" toward Pakistan, since

> it would help the Soviets cement their position in India. That [argument] infuriated Henry. In a White House corridor . . . I went after him again . . . and he berated me severely and shrilly. A favorite gambit of his . . . is to challenge his adversary to take his case to the President. I said I would be glad if he would arrange such a meeting. That was the last I heard of that.

Nixon had UN ambassador George H. W. Bush introduce a cease-fire resolution in the Security Council; as Nixon and Kissinger expected, the USSR vetoed it twice. By then a few days had elapsed and the tide of the war had turned. India was poised to do more than free East Pakistan. It was apparent to observers on the scene, and to Washington through intelligence reports from a spy in the Indian cabinet, that India could easily roll on and effectively crush West Pakistan. To prevent Yahya's complete defeat, Nixon ordered a carrier group, Task Force 74, to sail into the Bay of Bengal. This, he believed, would warn the Soviets not to let their ally India destroy Pakistan.

Zumwalt, Moorer, and Laird opposed sending Task Force 74 unless it had a much more specific mission. If it simply showed up in the area where the Soviet navy was already in force, they argued, that would increase the chances of U.S. naval forces becoming dangerously involved in a confrontation with the Soviets. Nixon overrode their objections and ordered the task force dispatched.

The brass and Laird succeeded in delaying Task Force 74 in Singapore for two days and further neutralized Nixon's orders by sending the force to a part of the Indian Ocean where it would have the least chance of bumping up against the Soviet naval forces, rather than the best chance, as Nixon had wanted. When the Soviets sent in a second group of ships, apparently reacting to the appearance of TF 74 in the Indian Ocean, Laird, Zumwalt, and Moorer felt justified in their caution.

At this critical juncture, in the middle of a war in which the superpowers might become involved, syndicated columnist Jack Anderson charged in his column that the United States, despite its profession of neutrality, was in a "tilt" toward Pakistan, and that a U.S. naval task force was heading into the Indian Ocean.

The White House flew into an uproar: This twelfth recent leak to Anderson divulged a secret policy and exposed as a sham America's claims of neutrality in an ongoing war. It had all the hallmarks of a deliberate leak by Nixon's opponents, now shifting their tactics from behind-the-scenes actions to public actions.

The leakers were too late to change the tilt policy: By December 14, when Anderson's column appeared, the actual war on the Indian subcontinent was almost finished. India's forces overwhelmed West Pakistan's so completely that the Pakistanis surrendered two days after the article's publication.

Before that surrender, however, Admiral Welander read the Anderson article.

Welander's first thought, he later said, was that the leak might have come from Yeoman Radford, because he knew that Radford and Anderson were social acquaintances. He conveyed this information to Haig. Rather than passing the news up the chain of command to Kissinger, his own superior, Haig alerted Ehrlichman, whose bailiwick included supervision of the Plumbers. Haig's refusal to inform Kissinger is curious; considering what happened in the weeks that followed, it raises the question of how deeply Haig was involved in matters concerning Yeoman Radford.

Ehrlichman assigned the Plumbers to follow up on the "tilt to Pakistan" leak. Although David Young and Bud Krogh had already asked to be relieved of their duties as Plumbers, this had not yet been completed, so David Young took on the task of learning who might have leaked to Anderson. The column in question had included certain details that convinced Young that the leak must have come from someone with intimate knowledge of the WSAG deliberations.

Don Stewart in the Pentagon also worked on the leak, and within days he and a polygraph expert questioned everyone in the White House military liaison office, including Welander, who refused to say anything without his lawyer present, and Radford. In the first part of Radford's polygraphed interrogation by Stewart, late in the afternoon of December 16, the yeoman refused to admit leaking to Anderson.

The columnist, in a much later interview on a related subject, echoed Nixon's contention that leaks of this import seldom came from a "salute and 'click his heels' type enlisted man." But Anderson said they did come, regularly, from "generals and admirals," and for the express purpose of altering policy. The latter, he implied, was what happened in the "tilt-to-Pakistan" leak—a column for which Anderson would shortly receive the Pulitzer Prize.

After Radford denied to Stewart that he was the source of the column, Stewart asked him a routine question frequently put to suspects in polygraph tests, whether he had done anything else out of bounds. Almost immediately

Radford confessed to having purloined a "library" of documents from the briefcases of Kissinger and Haig and from various NSC offices.

That revelation, which came late on Thursday, December 16, shocked both Stewart and Young, to whom Stewart conveyed the information. Separately, over the next few days, Young and Stewart worked on the ramifications of the disclosure. Stewart reduced the interrogation to a written report, part of which mentioned Haig, whose name Radford had invoked. When Stewart submitted that report to his superiors, they refused to send it over to the White House before he excised certain portions of it. He did so, but he also made certain that Young received the unexpurgated version.

By the evening of December 21, Young had amassed quite a bit of information on Radford, Welander, and the operation of the spy ring. Because he was handling this for Ehrlichman, Young did not say anything about it to Kissinger or Haig. Neither Stewart nor Young yet had the complete story of the spy ring's operation. Stewart's attempt to talk to Welander had been short-circuited, and Young had not spoken to Welander. Still, Young had enough information to give Ehrlichman a stunning report of a spy ring that the military had been operating in the White House.

At that moment, President Nixon, who had been vacationing in Key Biscayne over a long weekend, returned to Washington. He was aware of the ongoing leak investigation but knew little beyond that. Ehrlichman had briefed Haldeman and Attorney General Mitchell about it, and on Nixon's return home he found these three senior advisers, all grim-faced, needing to speak with him in the Oval Office.

The main actor was Ehrlichman. The press referred to Ehrlichman and Haldeman as "the Berlin Wall" for their Teutonic names, their crew cuts, and their vigilance in protecting the president from people he did not wish to see. Friends since college and fellow Christian Scientists, they had worked with Nixon since his run for governor of California in 1962. Haldeman had been an advertising executive with a large company, Ehrlichman a zoning and real estate lawyer in Seattle. Loyal, efficient, and seemingly tireless, they were invaluable to Nixon. Ehrlichman knew how to present matters cogently, quickly, and without overtly indicating his bias on the material.

In this meeting, which was captured and recorded by hidden microphones, Ehrlichman told Nixon that the various secret documents used by Anderson in the "tilt" column could only have come from the "one place in the federal government where all these documents were available": the military liaison office of the White House.

"Jesus Christ," Nixon said.

When Ehrlichman explained that Yeoman Radford had confessed to having stolen large numbers of documents, Nixon then asked, "How in the name of God do we have a yeoman having access to documents of that kind?"

Ehrlichman added details: Radford had also been pilfering from Haig and Kissinger on their trips abroad, and the documents had all been given to Radford's superiors, first Robinson and then Welander, who had forwarded them to the Joint Chiefs.

"Don't expect anything out of those crackers," Nixon retorted, then immediately asked, "Is Henry aware of this?"

"I'm sure not," Ehrlichman said.

"Is Haig aware of this?"

"I don't know," Ehrlichman said, cautious because he knew that Haig was a favorite of Nixon's, and as yet no interviewee had really implicated Haig. Welander had not yet been intensively interviewed by anyone familiar with the full range of what Radford had already said. "I suspect Haig may be aware, by some kind of backchannel basis. Because after this [Radford polygraph] came out and it was reduced to writing by the interrogator, Young was advised by the interrogator that he was having some trouble with his superiors, and that he was going to have to excise his report to leave that material out." Ehrlichman laid out his reasoning for Nixon, suggesting that if Stewart's "superior"—Fred Buzhardt—knew of the report, then it was logical and likely that other men who knew the workings of the Pentagon, such as Haig, would also have found out. After a digressing question from Nixon about the name and function of this interrogator, which Ehrlichman provided, the aide returned to the question of whether Haig was "aware." "I don't know," Ehrlichman repeated, "but if this thing runs true to form, undoubtedly his radar has picked this up by now."

Ehrlichman then read a list of the types of documents Radford had admitted stealing.

"I'll be damned," Nixon responded. Then, believing he had grasped enough of the gist of the story to now make a decision, Nixon opined, "Prosecuting is a possibility for the Joint Chiefs."

"I agree with you," Attorney General Mitchell jumped in, "but we have to take it from there as to what this would lead to if you pursued it by way of prosecuting Moorer. Even a public confrontation, you against the Joint Chiefs aligned on that side directly against you. And the—what has been done has been done. I think that the important thing is to paper this thing over."

Nixon did not immediately back down on his desire to prosecute, and Mitchell, who knew the president as well as any man alive, suggested a number of half measures with which Nixon would be more comfortable.

The brass would move the liaison office from the White House back to the Pentagon and reassign Welander out of Washington. A new security officer would ride herd on Kissinger and the NSC. Mitchell would sit down with Moorer and "point out [that] it's the end of the road."

Nixon asked if the other Chiefs were involved. Zumwalt, he was informed. When Ehrlichman revealed that Welander and Rem Robinson had known that Radford was a social friend of Anderson's, Haldeman jumped into the conversation, observing, "It's almost as though they meant to do something."

Recalling the Chiefs' recent objection to sending the TF-74 carrier group into the Indian Ocean, Mitchell agreed. But Mitchell did not want to prosecute anyone, not even Anderson, because if Radford testified under immunity, "Lord knows where this is going to lead to."

Nixon's resolve to prosecute was melting. He told the group he understood that this mess shot his relationship with the Joint Chiefs "right out of the roof of the Pentagon." Then he went back to Haig. "I am sure that Haig must have known about this operation." After all, Haig had served as Nixon's direct channel to the Joint Chiefs. Ehrlichman demurred again. (Later, Ehrlichman said he had done so because he had not yet asked Welander about Haig.) Ehrlichman said that he had "lost sleep" over what to do with Moorer before deciding "You can't touch him." He was convinced that Nixon couldn't remove the chairman without permanently damaging Nixon's relationship to the JCS.

"I agree," Nixon said at last. "I'd like to be present when you talk to Moorer," he told Mitchell.

"No," Mitchell said abruptly, explaining that the conversation with Moorer would be "a confrontation."

This produced immediate acquiescence from Nixon, who could not stand confronting anyone directly. He protested mildly that the Joint Chiefs should have shut down the pilfering operation the moment they saw materials that must have come from Kissinger's briefcase. But he also ventured that what the Chiefs had done was "a federal offense of the highest order." In his view, in spying on the president and his chief aides, purloining top-secret papers, and deliberately leaking secret documents to the press, they had committed treason. From this moment on, Nixon could have no doubts that the Chiefs had been undermining his presidency and attempting to reverse his policies.

EHRLICHMAN WAS DETAILED to interview Welander. David Young had amassed a mountain of background material, including a written confession he prepared for Welander's signature. Young would be in the room with Welander and Ehrlichman, and so would a tape recorder.

Ehrlichman, a brilliant tactician, got Welander to confess in this interview by refusing to be prosecutorial or to come on strong. When Welander refused to sign the written confession, Ehrlichman did not insist on it. Rather, he led Welander gently through the establishment and operation of the military liaison office, and then on into the espionage. From time to time Welander would pick up the unsigned confession, read from it, and agree with various sentences or paragraphs that Young had written, sometimes adding previously unknown details.

Welander added, for instance, that among the papers stolen by Radford was "a full recount of our involvement in Cambodia from Day One which would make the Pentagon Papers pale by comparison." These were the sort of documents to which "the Chairman had not been privy" before the espionage scheme began.

Since Haig's briefcase had been rifled on his trip to East Asia in January 1971, Ehrlichman asked if Haig had understood that Radford would steal from him on his trips.

"Al Haig has cut me in on what we've been thinking about on the most recent thing and given me a copy of game plans and so on," Welander responded. In advance of Haig's trip to Vietnam, Welander had informed Haig of what he (on behalf of Moorer) would be interested in, such as the rate of troop withdrawals; Radford then purloined documents on those subjects. "I had complete copies of memcons [memos of conversations] from Al's recent trip," Welander boasted. One contained "an indication of a meeting Henry was to have had in Paris . . . the first indication we have that this avenue was open." Welander strongly implied that Radford's stealing gave Haig cover, so that Haig would not have to send things to Moorer secretly in defiance of direct orders from Nixon and Kissinger.

After the interview, Young told Ehrlichman he believed "that Al Haig had probably planted Radford to help the military spy on Henry."

A source close to the investigation, on learning what Welander had confessed about Haig, had a revelation: What he had observed for two years in the basement of the White House, and thought of as vaguely suspicious behavior by Haig, had been Haig in the process of working with the Moorer-Radford ring.

Ehrlichman did not act on what Welander told him about Haig in the taped confession. Years later, trying to make sense of his failure to follow the lead, he guessed that he had "heard what Welander was saying [about Haig], but I didn't fully realize the implications in terms of Haig's role as an agent of the Joint Chiefs." Had he done so, Ehrlichman asserted, he would have recommended that Haig be severed from the White House for being just as involved as Radford, Welander, Robinson, and Moorer.

Secretary Laird obtained a copy of the Welander confession tape. Years later, he recalled that "Haig was drawn in through the back door" during the conversation, and that after hearing the tape he was convinced that Haig had known about the collecting of material by Radford, Welander, and Robinson. Whether Haig had promoted the espionage or merely knew of it, Laird would not or could not say; either way, though, he believed that for Haig not to have revealed the theft was not "fair to the president," that Haig should have told Nixon about it. Then again, when Laird realized that Haig had known about the stealing, he too neglected to share this conclusion with Nixon.

The evening after Ehrlichman interviewed Welander, Kissinger telephoned Ehrlichman at home, and Haig phoned Young. Both Kissinger and Haig said they wanted to hear the tape of Welander. Young then called Ehrlichman to report Haig's call—Haig had berated him for going after Welander—and to argue that Haig should be kept away from the Welander tape. Ehrlichman could not do that. The next day, Kissinger and Haig listened to the Welander confession tape. After doing so, they told Haldeman that Welander and Moorer should be fired.

The president instead telephoned the chairman to wish him a happy holiday season. Moorer understood that the call was the president's steely way of letting the chairman know the jig was up, but that the president was not going to fire him—at least not right now. For Nixon's part, he could rest assured that from then on Moorer would be what Ehrlichman termed "a pre-shrunk admiral," doing Nixon's bidding without question. In 1972, Nixon reappointed Moorer for a second term as chairman.

Nixon never listened to the Welander tape. He thought he had no need to. But in choosing not to listen to it, he deprived himself of any real understanding of Haig's involvement in Moorer-Radford. That lack of knowledge was obvious in Nixon's next conversation with Haig, alone, in which the president did his best to allay what he presumed to be Haig's greatest fear—telling him that "the worst thing we could do now is hurt the military."

Attorney General Mitchell did have a brief sit-down with Moorer. It was not recorded, but after the meeting Mitchell spoke to Ehrlichman, who conveyed the gist of it to the president: Moorer "admits that he saw stuff, but [explained] that he operated on the assumption that his liaison man was working this all out with Henry. I [Ehrlichman] said [to Mitchell], 'Well, did you get a plea of guilty or a not guilty?' And he says, 'I got a *nolo contendere.*'" Moorer, in other words, admitted no guilt but would not contest the charges.

Years later, Moorer would make another confession: Instead of keeping the stolen papers in his own files after looking at them—as he would have if he'd obtained them legitimately—he routinely gave them back to Welander for return to the White House through Al Haig. This was as close an acknowledgment of the criminal nature of the spy ring as would ever be obtained from its instigator.

The president focused his ire on Radford and Kissinger. Nixon had been told that Charles Radford and Jack Anderson might have been having a homosexual relationship. Actually, the one social connection the two men shared was as fellow Mormons; there was no indication that either man was gay. Nonetheless, Nixon directed Ehrlichman to uncover and expose such a relationship, and instructed Laird to have Radford come in and submit to another polygraph test on his sexual proclivities. Laird told Ehrlichman that if Radford went to the press about such an attempt, the fallout could be worse. So Radford was never asked about that; instead he was exiled to the Naval Reserve Center in Oregon, where his phone was tapped.

As for Kissinger, Nixon had told Ehrlichman, "Don't let K blame Haig," as Ehrlichman put it in his diary. This instruction had nothing to do with Haig's culpability; rather, it reflected Nixon's belief that Kissinger would blame Haig as a way of deflecting responsibility from his own laxity in running the NSC.

Kissinger's fame had skyrocketed since the China opening; Nixon's veiled warning was his way of holding him at bay.

As ADMIRAL WELANDER prepared to leave town for his new post, Laird ordered him to turn over the materials in his safe. Rather than do so, Welander called Haig. Shortly thereafter, Ehrlichman told Welander to bring the materials to him. Instead Welander gave the documents to Haig. An Ehrlichman aide soon placed a packet of documents in Ehrlichman's safe, but Ehrlichman did not look at them and never learned whether Haig had deleted anything from those documents that would have reflected badly on him.

On January 7, 1972, Fred Buzhardt, Haig's old friend at DoD, summoned chief investigator Don Stewart from a vacation that had begun days before the Ehrlichman-Welander interview. Buzhardt told Stewart that they had to interview Welander. Because Stewart had been out of town, he was unaware that Ehrlichman and Young had interviewed Welander, and thus had no knowledge that anyone had hinted at Haig's involvement in the spy ring. Buzhardt told Stewart that the interview of Welander was "for the president," and Stewart had no reason to disbelieve him, since he didn't know that Ehrlichman had already done such an interrogation Welander for Nixon. By now, Nixon and his senior staff had gone to the West Coast. Laird later asserted that Buzhardt made the decision to interview Welander without Laird's knowledge.

Comparing the transcripts of the two Welander interviews, the Ehrlich-man-Young conversation and the Buzhardt-Stewart re-interview, reveals two major differences. In the Buzhardt-Stewart re-interview, Welander lays the blame for the spy ring more clearly on Moorer and on Radford and claims to have done nothing wrong himself, to have acted as an innocent conduit. Just as important, in this second interview Welander absolves Haig from involvement in the ring; instead he portrays Haig as a victim of the thievery.

Stewart labeled this Pentagon interview of Welander a "re-interview" be-cause he had briefly spoken to Welander on the subject right after Radford had confessed. At that time, the admiral had objected to being questioned without a lawyer present, and Stewart had stopped the interview. Stewart recalled that incident to Buzhardt in January 1972 as they prepared for the "re-interview," and he suggested that they not read Welander his rights, as a gambit to see how far Welander was willing to go without a lawyer. Buz-hardt agreed. To Stewart's amazement, Welander made no objection to going through this "re-interview" without a lawyer. At the time, that fact gave Stewart little pause; years later, he concluded that it suggested We-lander must have known he would create the opportunity to conceal certain things when questioned.

Stewart later came to believe that the reason for the "re-interview"—indeed, its sole purpose—was to protect Haig by generating a document that could substitute for the Ehrlichman-Young interview if any outside entity should ever look into the matter. In creating this document, Buzhardt followed the pattern he had described earlier to Bill Gulley of the White House's military office in regard to the PX scandal investigation: writing a phony but apparently authoritative document that could be produced at the request of an outside investigator.

The Welander "re-interview" was neither recorded nor transcribed, but during it Stewart took notes and afterward Stewart dictated from those notes of the proceedings to a secretary, who typed up a report. There were to be no copies; the original was to go to Buzhardt. But the unusual procedural aspects had aroused Stewart's suspicions. Telling the secretary that he had to proofread the report of the Welander re-interview, Stewart—unbeknownst to Buzhardt—made a copy for himself.

SEVERAL WEEKS LATER, Fritz Kraemer telephoned Henry Kissinger to urge that Haig be given command of a division. Although Kraemer did not say so, Haig was looking for a way out of the White House after Moorer-Radford was settled and the details hidden.

Kissinger already had such a thing in the works for Haig, he replied, but these things took time. "I know that your protégé sometimes gets impatient with me," he teased.

"Ah, when you are not there he defends you like a lion," Kraemer said.

"I have until the end of March and I will get it done before the end of March. I first wanted the promotion completely established and then I made the request."

Kraemer expressed his fear that "the Princeton Ph.D."—General Andrew Goodpaster, then in charge of NATO's troops—might object: Kraemer and Goodpaster did not like one another, and that feud might spill over to spoil Haig's chances to advance. Kissinger assured Kraemer that he would not let that happen.

NIXON'S DECISION TO paper over the Moorer-Radford espionage was, in effect, a cover-up. As cover-ups often do, it inspired further cover-ups by others to conceal the first and the bad deeds that underlay it. Buzhardt's "re-interview" of Welander was only the opening action in this cascade. Soon, Young's voluminous record of his investigation would vanish from the White House files. The tape of Welander's confession, which implicated Haig, would disappear beyond the reach of even Ehrlichman, who had been the main interrogator. That tape would be the most well-concealed secret of the White House. Those who kept it hidden were motivated by the desire to preserve their positions of power. But their conduct in office was also motivated by disgust at Nixon's foreign policies. And together these two motives fueled their ongoing efforts to undermine the Nixon presidency.

11

"Three out of Three, Mr. President"

In a 236-page "State of the World" document, issued in early 1972, Nixon claimed that he had already brought about the radical shift in foreign policy that he had promised on assuming the presidency. "Our alliances are no longer addressed primarily to the containment of the Soviet Union and China behind an American shield," the document declared. "They are instead addressed to the creation with those powers of a stable world peace."

That was the theme that Nixon expected to define 1972, his fourth year in office, and one that he expected to culminate in his reelection by a landslide. He carefully arranged the timing of a series of foreign policy triumphs to occur at regular intervals throughout the year, carrying him through to an easy reelection and a strong second-term mandate. He would visit Beijing in February, sign SALT and ABM treaties with the Soviet Union in May, and sign a peace accord for Vietnam shortly before or after the election.

What he did not expect was that these steps toward realizing his foreign policy dreams would galvanize the opposition that had already begun to mobilize against him.

ON JANUARY 25, 1972, Nixon ordered even more troops home from Southeast Asia; by May 1, only 69,000 would remain in South Vietnam. In a speech on January 27, Nixon said that the United States was prepared to withdraw all American forces within six months of the signing of a cease-fire and peace treaty, so long as the North Vietnamese returned American prisoners currently in their hands. If the agreement specified new elections, he added, the current Saigon government would step down before they occurred. Such a cease-fire should cover the whole of Southeast Asia, and he promised that after the war the United States would reconstruct all of Indochina, including North Vietnam. The January 27 speech was as complete a statement as could be imagined of American disengagement from the war, and of Nixon's eagerness to settle that war on almost any terms. Nixon's proposal went beyond what even the liberals of the Senate had called for.

Surprisingly, the usually vocal right wing said hardly a word against it. In later years the neoconservatives would rail that the United States had abandoned South Vietnam instead of "staying the course" and winning the war, but the conservatives of the time raised little objection about Nixon's new posture toward Vietnam—certainly not enough to deter even slightly Nixon's reelection express. Perhaps they reasoned that a Republican victory in the fall was more important than any disagreement with Nixon over the conduct of the war, since the domestic and foreign policy positions of that year's Democratic presidential contenders were anathema to Republican conservatives.

Most polls in early 1972 showed Nixon ahead of any challenger. But he was harried on the right by George Wallace, who was running again, this time as a Democrat. Muskie led the Democratic pack, followed by George McGovern and Scoop Jackson. If Jackson gained any traction as a Democratic standard-bearer, it would mean problems for Nixon, for he bridged party lines on Nixon's wedge issues: Jackson was against busing but sent his children to an integrated public school, he was an environmentalist but not a left-winger, and he had better support than Nixon from organized labor. Nixon believed his ideal opponent was McGovern, who would draw the antiwar crowd's support just as the war was winding down, and could be painted (in Jackson's phrase) as the candidate of "acid, amnesty, and abortion."

To assure McGovern's nomination, Nixon supporters went after Jackson and Muskie. Muskie took a first blow when a spurious letter surfaced during the New Hampshire primary season charging that he had made racist remarks about "Canucks," a derogatory term for the French-Canadian minority in Maine. When a series of slurs about the candidate's wife followed, the candidate reacted by breaking down and crying during a public appearance in New Hampshire; he barely prevailed in the primary, which he was expected to win handily, and his candidacy was mortally wounded.

The prominence of the Muskie sob story obscured a challenge to Nixon in New Hampshire from John Ashbrook, a Republican congressman from Ohio. With the backing of some (though not all) of the Manhattan Twelve,

Ashbrook charged that Nixon's conduct was opening the door for China to fill the power vacuum in Southeast Asia caused by the U.S. troop withdrawal and warned that the president would give away too much to the USSR at the forthcoming SALT talks. Ashbrook maintained that Nixon had abandoned every pledge he had ever made—chief among them "that Communism was the deadly enemy of freedom, and that America must never betray the allies who stood with her in opposition to its advance." Nixon won the New Hampshire primary with 67 percent of the vote; Ashbrook came in a distant third, well behind peace candidate Pete McCloskey. But Vice President Spiro Agnew, a favorite of the right for his bellicosity and militarist tendencies, gathered an unprecedented 45,000 write-in votes—a tally that was judged to be a protest against Nixon. Combined with Ashbrook's appeal on foreign affairs, it suggested that future Republicans who ran against Nixon's foreign policies could score big at the polls.

WHEN NIXON STEPPED off the plane in Beijing, he stuck out his hand for Zhou En-Lai to shake. This symbolic gesture was meant to supersede the memory of John Foster Dulles refusing to shake Zhou's hand in 1954. In this and in many other ways, the Nixon-Mao-Zhou meetings in late February produced a great show for the world's media. Yet the substance of the meeting had less impact on world affairs than the opening-to-China announcement had: As the principals understood, the fact of their meeting in Beijing was as important as anything actually decided there.

As conservatives had feared, while Nixon was smiling for the camera, Kissinger was conveying secrets to the Chinese, sharing U.S. intelligence about Soviet armaments and nuclear strike capabilities. "Nobody in our government except for the President and [his accompanying staff] know that we have given you this information," Kissinger told them. He and Nixon also reiterated to Zhou, privately, that they opposed independence for Taiwan and would actively discourage Japanese expansion in East Asia and Korea. To the Chinese rulers, Nixon gave a guarantee: "US would oppose any attempt by the Soviet Union to engage in aggressive action against China."

Alexander Haig read the notes of such meetings each day, and while working on the leaders' final statement (known as the Shanghai Communiqué), he grumbled repeatedly to Haldeman aide Dwight Chapin that Nixon and Kissinger "are selling us out to the Communists!" At that time, Chapin thought Haig was simply expressing his frustration at being overworked; later he realized that Haig's anger was far more deep-seated.

Others shared Haig's sentiments, and Nixon knew it. Aware that many people might reject the secret pledges he was making to China, Nixon concealed those promises from the top foreign policy officials—Laird, Rogers, and Helms—and from the Joint Chiefs of Staff. He hid precisely those matters that would most upset conservatives such as arms negotiator Paul Nitze, and Scoop Jackson, Bob Dole, and other senators. Nixon was willing to commit the United States to these actions, yet he was unwilling to tell people he'd done so. The problem for Nixon's radical new policy toward China was in the follow-through. In order to move the two countries toward full diplomatic recognition and becoming each other's most important trading partner, thousands of details had to be arranged by the bureaucracies of State, Defense, CIA, and other agencies; without their cooperation, little could be accomplished. But since Nixon and Kissinger were keeping some important matters from the bureaucrats, and many bureaucrats were uncomfortable with the policy, very little actually happened. While Nixon succeeded in making the opening to China, opposition to his policies prevented the fruits of the new accommodation between the United States and China from being reaped during his remaining years in office.

Nixon was also unwilling to share the details of the new Chinese relationship with the American electorate. Had the public learned, for instance, that he'd discussed the abandoning of Taiwan with China, and that his team had passed state secrets to an ally of the Soviet Union, it might have produced an uproar and cost him deeply in the fall election.

Jackson in particular would have made hay out of the information; he badly needed such an issue to invigorate his campaign. After his poor finish in New Hampshire, in order to remain viable Jackson would have to perform well in the next primary state, Florida. In that primary Nixon secretly backed Wallace, to the tune of $600,000, hoping that Wallace would knock off Jackson and slow the campaigns of the other mainstream Democratic candidates. Donald Segretti, employed by Nixon associates, sent out a letter on fake Muskie stationery that accused Jackson of homosexuality—and, absurdly, also alleged that Jackson had fathered an out-of-wedlock child with a seventeen-year-old girl. The letter had some effect: Jackson finished third and left the race shortly thereafter. Segretti later pled to criminal distribution of the letter and served several months in jail.

After the Florida primary, Jackson's rising antipathy toward Nixon moved him to agree to chair the effort to elect enough Democrats to make the next Congress veto-proof.

Wallace exceeded Nixon's expectations by winning every Florida county; he now became a more serious threat to Nixon, whether he won the Democratic nomination or ran in the fall on the American Independent Party line. Through the next two months Wallace continued to win Democratic primaries; McGovern ran right behind him, picking up strength and delegates.

. . . .

IN THE SPRING of 1972, E. Howard Hunt, G. Gordon Liddy, James McCord, and the Miami Cuban émigrés—the team that had burglarized the office of Daniel Ellsberg's psychiatrist—moved their base from the White House to the Committee to Re-Elect the President. From that base of operations, they engaged in activities that would culminate in the June 17 attempted burglary at Democratic National Committee headquarters in the Watergate office complex.

Although today popular history connects Richard Nixon with the planning of that break-in, and with the other illegal actions performed that spring, the weight of evidence reveals the opposite: that Nixon knew little to nothing about those preparations. White House tapes and a myriad of documents show Nixon, Kissinger, and the NSC staff occupied that spring with the details of the May summit with Brezhnev; with the continuing SALT talks, which were expected to produce a document for Brezhnev and Nixon to sign at that summit; and with Vietnam, where the largest battle of the war was shaping up.

General Creighton Abrams, the commander of U.S. forces in Vietnam, had expected North Vietnam to launch yet another Tet offensive in 1972, and tried to delay it by bombing the North and its supply lines. Nixon also gave direct orders to attack the enemy on the ground before this year's Tet, and when the order wasn't carried out he railed against Abrams. The decision to hold back the troops wasn't Abrams's fault: Unbeknownst to the president, Laird had countered his orders. Nonetheless, when the North Vietnamese began their offensive a week before Easter Sunday and made steady initial progress, Nixon became irate and blamed everyone but himself. But he was the true culprit. If there was one reason for the inadequate U.S. and South Vietnamese response at the outset of the Easter Offensive, it was that Nixon had reduced American strength in country to a level that could not sustain the war. When Nixon figured out that Laird was countermanding orders, he called Admiral Moorer on the carpet, saying, "I am the commander in chief, and not the secretary of defense—is that clear?" Nixon would brook no further excuses from Moorer: it was to be full speed ahead.

Moorer tugged his forelock. He was enthusiastic about the aggressive actions Nixon was finally willing to take—increased bombing of the North and of the demilitarized zone (DMZ). After serious discussions with Haig, Nixon authorized the heaviest bombing of the war. The operation known as "Linebacker" targeted the North Vietnamese troops and oil storage depots near Haiphong and Hanoi, though not the cities themselves—Nixon and

Kissinger had specifically promised the Soviets to spare the cities, in the hope that the USSR would reciprocate by pressuring North Vietnam to end the war at the peace table. In conjunction with the bombing, the United States mined North Vietnam's ports (other than Haiphong), elating Moorer, who had been urging that measure for eight years. According to military historians, Linebacker did exactly what Nixon, Moorer, and Haig desired: It "ruined North Vietnam's economy, paralyzed its transportation system, reduced imports by 80 percent, and exhausted its air defenses."

Nonetheless, ARVN units continued to fall back. The North Vietnamese captured several large cities. Abrams cabled that the situation was no longer looking good.

Once again, at an important juncture in a battle, Nixon sent Haig to Saigon. And once again Haig returned and told the president that the South Vietnamese forces had "not been outclassed or outfought as in the past," that Abrams was only being "alarmist." Yet in retrospect the opposite seems true: While the South Vietnamese forces, aided by American power, had successfully fended off the largest attacks of the war, the net effect of the Easter Offensive was that the South lost more troops than it could replace, and the North overran a sizable portion of South Vietnam that it never again relinquished.

In the Reagan years, it became an article of conservative faith that the "success" of repelling the Easter Offensive could have led to a "win" in South Vietnam. This belief was coupled with a second assertion, that the United States had not been able to capitalize on the success because of a "cut and run" policy that had been enacted into law by a liberal Democratic Congress. Yet the facts contradict this misreading: Some 475,000 U.S. troops had already been brought home before Easter 1972, and among the remaining forces seasoned veterans had largely been replaced by younger and greener recruits. Those factors compromised any potential U.S.-led ground invasion of North Vietnam and any chance of the United States "winning" the war after repelling the Easter Offensive and the successful Linebacker bombing campaign.

THE MOST NIXONIAN of foreign policy moments occurred during that Easter Offensive, as Nixon enjoyed his capacity to drink toasts with the Soviet leaders in Moscow and sign historic agreements to limit nuclear weapons even as his regular-ordnance bombs destroyed the Soviets' ally North Vietnam. He had left detailed orders with Haig to ensure no "letting up" of the bombing during his visit, to prevent any newspaper from writing that "we made a deal with the Russians to cool it in Vietnam while trying to negotiate agreements with them in Moscow"—even though Nixon had agreed to spare the cities of Hanoi and Haiphong for precisely that purpose.

Moorer and his fellow Chiefs, however, judged the conjunction of bombing and treaty signing as incongruous at best, and at worst as bordering on treason—a fraternizing with the ultimate enemy while engaged in the largest battle of a long war.

For months before the summit, the Chiefs had been alarmed by reports from SALT negotiators that Kissinger was prepared to allow the Soviets to keep building SLBMs despite the United States having canceled its own new ones. This had produced what a SALT historian called an "open revolt" in which "Moorer, Laird, and Jackson . . . agreed with conservatives" that for the Soviets détente was simply a diplomatic cover permitting the continuation of the expansionist Brezhnev Doctrine. Now, while Nixon and Kissinger negotiated in Moscow, back in Washington Al Haig took up the cudgels on SLBM. As Haig recalled in 2000, one evening during that 1972 summit, "disturbed" by the SLBM decision, he roused Nixon and Kissinger "out of bed at midnight and made them renegotiate on the submarine issue for four hours, because they had made a profound mistake and the Chiefs wouldn't agree to it. Nor would I." He added that Fritz Kraemer had become "profoundly disappointed" with Kissinger over the details of the SALT agreement.

"It is no comfort that the liberals will praise the agreement," Nixon warned Haig upon his return, thinking about the chances of Senate ratification. "But let us remember that the liberals will never support us—the hawks are our hard core, and we must do everything we can to keep them from jumping ship after getting their enthusiasm restored as a result of our [bombing] operation in the North." Nixon was right: The most effective public opponent of the Nixon policies became Scoop Jackson, who regularly coordinated his actions with the Chiefs, Nitze, other hard-liners—and with Haig. Philip Odeen, an NSC staffer on arms control, later recalled that the White House took "a lot of pressure . . . from Scoop Jackson and people who shared his views, a lot of it coming through Al Haig."

The conservative hawks had new allies in the fight to derail the Moscow accords: the Russian dissident Andrei Sakharov and the exiled novelist Aleksandr Solzhenitsyn, who expressed sentiments similar to the longtime warnings from Kraemer, Burnham, and the Buckleys not to trust the Soviets. In particular, Sakharov and Solzhenitsyn echoed Kraemer's objections to any pact on the grounds of moral relativism, as exemplified by the Nixon administration's willingness to ignore the Soviets' massive human rights violations in an unseemly rush to sign treaties with Moscow that would appeal to the American public. Moreover, Jackson added, in pursuit of the agreement the administration was continuing to trade with the Soviets, bolstering their economy rather than wrecking it, and thereby hastening the fall of the Soviet empire.

Jackson objected to many specifics of the ABM and SALT agreements, charging that they were either significantly flawed, to the detriment of the United States, or dangerously ambiguous. The Soviets refused, for instance, to specify the "throw weight" of their missiles or to give precise definitions to the terms "light" and "heavy" missiles. Though Jackson lacked the votes to defeat the ABM and SALT agreements, he managed to delay them by voicing such objections, forcing the administration to go on record with responses that would limit its later parameters for negotiation. As Odeen recalled, "What the issues and goals were going to be for SALT II in part came out of a group on the Hill, Richard Perle [and others who] had a lot of clout with the White House political types."

On May 15, George Wallace was shot and nearly killed while campaigning in Maryland. The news of Wallace's fate—he would survive but be permanently paralyzed—did not make Nixon unhappy. The timing also allowed him to exert greater control over the investigation: J. Edgar Hoover had died less than two weeks before, and the FBI's new acting head, Nixon appointee L. Patrick Gray III, was easily able to wrest supervision of the case (and of the shooter, Arthur Bremer) away from local and state police.

From his hospital bed, Wallace continued to win primaries—Maryland, Michigan, Tennessee, and North Carolina. Nixon believed that the Democrats would never nominate Wallace but feared that he might run on an independent line, and so Nixon importuned the Reverend Billy Graham to try to persuade him to drop out entirely. Ultimately, however, the matter was decided at the polls: As the primaries moved into northern states, George McGovern gained ground, and by early June the South Dakotan had outdistanced Wallace and all but wrapped up the nomination.

As most people know, late on the night of June 17, 1972, police caught burglars inside the Watergate office building headquarters of the Democratic National Committee—burglars later found to have been in the pay of the Committee to Re-elect the President (CRP). But many aspects of that burglary have escaped attention. For instance, during the preparations for the burglary, the burglars—a group of Cuban ex-CIA operatives—ran into instances of such poor planning that they later told interviewers that they thought it unworthy of their CIA-veteran leaders, Hunt and McCord.

Those leaders had taken the burglars' IDs from them and had issued them easily traceable hotel keys and new hundred-dollar bills, which were found upon their arrest. The currency led investigators down a clear money trail, and to serious trouble for the White House. The burglars also had an additional mysterious item seized by the police—a key that fit only one lock in the DNC offices. It opened the desk of a DNC secretary who did not work directly with Chairman Larry O'Brien or other top officials in the office—a fact that belied later claims that the burglary was aimed at O'Brien or those other officials.

Bob Woodward, recently hired at the *Washington Post*, began his investigations into Watergate when he attended the burglars' arraignment on June 18. The presence of the Cubans and McCord at the arraignment startled Woodward. When McCord told the judge he'd recently retired from the CIA, the reporter muttered, "Holy shit! The CIA." But he didn't pursue the angle, though *Post* managing editor Ben Bradlee was a longtime friend of CIA director Helms and a brother-in-law to Cord Meyer, the Agency's assistant director for plans.

Bob Bennett, today a senator from Utah, was then head of Mullen and Company, a public relations firm and CIA front that employed Hunt. Later, a CIA memo from agent Martin Lukoskie described Bennett as boasting of feeding stories to Woodward to steer him away from the CIA's hand in the Watergate affair. Precisely which stories has never been documented, but after making his own inquiries White House counselor Chuck Colson came to believe that Bennett had pointed various reporters toward him in the period just after the break-in. Later, when the Senate Watergate Committee tried to get the CIA to confirm or deny whether Woodward had ever worked for or been associated with the Agency, the committee did not receive a satisfactory answer; a few hours after Senator Howard Baker sent a memo to the director about this, Woodward called Baker to complain—an action that does nothing to dispel the notion of a possible working conduit between the CIA and the *Washington Post*.

WHEN NIXON LEARNED of the attempted burglary at the Watergate, according to everyone he interacted with on that day, he was incredulous. Since he was not in Washington when the news came, his immediate reaction was not preserved on tape, but it likely resembled the surprise he displayed on learning of the Pentagon Papers leak in the spring of 1971, and after hearing about the extent of the Moorer-Radford spy ring that December. To Nixon, it made no sense politically for anyone to have targeted the Washington DNC headquarters: After all, the party's chief officials were in Miami, the

Democratic nomination was wrapped up, and of all his potential rivals the Democrats had chosen McGovern, the easiest candidate for him to defeat.

Nixon did not publicly acknowledge, then or ever, that the climate he had created in the White House (and, by extension, in the CRP) had emboldened others to conceive the break-in. Nor did he insist on finding and exposing those who might have ordered the break-in. Rather, because of his inaction, his employees immediately began a cover-up of White House involvement in that planning. They presumed that he wanted this cover-up, and he gave them no reason to think otherwise.

By June 23, six days after the break-in, this cover-up was already threatening to unravel. In a meeting that day, White House officials told the CIA to try to block the FBI's efforts to investigate the matter. A tape of a conversation between Nixon and Haldeman recounting that order later became known as the "smoking gun"; when revealed in transcript form in late July 1974, it led directly to Nixon's resignation.

John Wesley Dean III, the White House counsel, was at the center of these cover-up activities. Dean, who had roomed with Barry Goldwater, Jr., at Staunton Military Academy and was close to Senator Goldwater, had entered the administration after working as chief minority counsel to Republican members of the House Judiciary Committee and on a National Commission on the Reform of Federal Criminal Law. An associate deputy attorney general under John Mitchell in the Department of Justice for a time, he had then been brought over to the White House. In July 1970, when White House counsel John Ehrlichman moved up a notch, Dean was given his position.

On June 21, 1972, four days after the Watergate break-in, Ehrlichman had phoned the FBI to let Pat Gray know that Dean would be handling the matter for the White House; Dean then met with Gray and informed him that he would sit in on all FBI interviews of White House personnel. According to Gray's memoir, Dean learned late on June 22, from a visit to Gray at FBI headquarters, that the FBI had traced the money carried by the burglars, and that the top men at the FBI, in trying to figure out the complicated money trail, had raised the possibility that they might have stumbled on a CIA operation because the trail led into Mexico. According to Gray, he also told Dean he'd already spoken that afternoon with CIA director Helms, who denied any connection between the CIA and the break-in. "There is no CIA involvement," read a note Gray penned during his conversation with Helms, time-dated at 5:37 P.M. Gray writes that he also reiterated to Dean on June 23 that, although the FBI had not entirely ruled out some CIA connection, in regard specifically to the money trail, "Dick Helms has told me the Agency has no involvement in this."

At 8:15 A.M. on June 23, 1972, Dean telephoned Haldeman to say that the FBI was "out of control." The Bureau had traced the hundred-dollar bills, and later that very day, Dean warned, the Bureau would learn why a check from a Nixon reelection campaign contributor, written on a Mexican bank, had been deposited in the bank account of one of the burglars. "Our problem now is to stop the FBI from opening up a whole lot of other things," Dean said, according to Haldeman's contemporaneous notes. Dean added that Mitchell and CRP finance chairman Maurice Stans wanted the Mexican bank inquiry stopped because they were worried that the FBI would uncover and reveal the names of CRP contributors who had been guaranteed anonymity. Dean further told Haldeman that the FBI believed that the people behind the burglary were CIA, and that Mitchell had suggested that Haldeman have Dick Walters—the Agency's new deputy director—call Gray, "and maybe the CIA can turn off the FBI down there in Mexico."

Mitchell's logs show no conversations between Mitchell and Dean on June 22 or on the morning of June 23, but Dean's invocation of Mitchell's name carried weight with Haldeman, as it did with Nixon when Haldeman repeated Dean's message to the president. Haldeman said that Dean "analyzed very carefully last night and concludes, concurs with Mitchell's recommendation that the only way to solve this" was to have the CIA block the FBI. Nixon adopted the blocking idea. He instructed Haldeman to speak to Walters and get it done. Nixon also suggested that pressure could be put on Helms by mentioning that Hunt's long involvement with the Cubans would "open up whole, the whole Bay of Pigs thing."

Walters had been appointed deputy director at Nixon's request. Nixon's long association with Walters gave him reason to expect the deputy director to be responsive when he and Agency director Helms came to the White House to meet with Haldeman and Ehrlichman. In that meeting, Helms was compliant, especially after Haldeman mentioned the Bay of Pigs— which, as Nixon expected, infuriated and cowed Helms. The CIA director later testified that he agreed to have Walters call Gray because it was possible the president knew about a Mexico CIA operation that even Helms himself was unaware of.

According to Gray's memoir, Walters came to see him and said, "If the investigation gets pushed further south of the border, it could trespass onto some of our covert projects. Since you've got five men under arrest, it will be best to taper the matter off here." Walters then referred to an interagency agreement under which the FBI and CIA agreed not to expose the other's sources. Gray agreed that the investigation would be handled "in a manner that would not hamper the CIA."

In several phone calls and meetings between June 23 and 28, according to Walters, Dean pressured him unsuccessfully to have the CIA put up bail and otherwise pay for the burglars. On the twenty-eighth, Walters—who usually relied on his phenomenal memory—took the uncharacteristic step of recording in several memcons his June 23 White House visit, his conversations with Gray, and his subsequent interchanges with Dean. These memoranda effectively enmeshed the White House in having the CIA obstruct the FBI. The Walters memcons would become among the most important documents in the history of Watergate. They would also be critical to the right's campaign to undermine Nixon.

IN AUGUST, WHEN the Senate took up a resolution to ratify the SALT treaty with the USSR, Scoop Jackson introduced an amendment that would change the parameters of future agreements. It had been cooked up by Perle and another, uncredited contributor, Fred Charles Iklé. The author of an important historical study on how modern wars ended, Iklé had been a strategist at RAND for some years. Reliably anti-Communist and suspicious of arms control efforts, he had been hired by the Arms Control and Disarmament Agency (ACDA), the State Department division responsible for directly negotiating with the Soviets on arms control.

The amendment required that the United States would not be limited to a lower level of strategic forces than that of the Soviet Union. Nixon did not like it, but he worried that the ABM and SALT agreements might fail if Jackson withheld his support. Dismissing that possibility, Kissinger recommended rejecting the amendment. Nixon overruled him and accepted it. Jackson then supported the SALT I treaty, which passed by an 88–2 margin.

This overwhelming vote—in a Senate still deeply divided into hawks and doves on the Vietnam War, and during an election year in which Democrats wanted to accentuate their differences from Republicans—was a significant triumph for the White House. Nixon had completed a far-reaching agreement with America's principal Cold War enemy, and on terms so mainstream that even the seriously polarized Senate had united to support it.

But this was the high point for détente in the Nixon years. Although the superpowers agreed to limit ABM sites to two apiece, and to freeze the number of offensive missile launchers, there was no agreement on stopping either side from developing MIRVs to replace MRVs, and in other ways the SALT I treaty reflected its name: it was an "Interim Agreement" that covered only "Certain Measures." Substantial further work would be required in order to make meaningful inroads in halting the nuclear arms race and in achieving true cooperation between the superpowers. Because of opposition from Jackson, the Joint Chiefs, the CIA, and those who agreed with their hard-line anti-Soviet positions, almost no further progress was made during the Nixon years.

Richard Perle, Jackson's assistant, had become more polished and more hard-line since 1969. According to Douglas Feith, who later worked as a summer intern for Jackson, Perle "helped make Jackson more effective than Jackson otherwise would have been." This effectiveness was not limited to opposing SALT I. Perle also helped generate another amendment, this one to a U.S.-Soviet trade bill that took Jackson's fight against Nixon's policies to a new level. Eventually known as the Jackson-Vanik Amendment for its initial sponsors in the Senate and House, it penalized the USSR on trade unless Russian Jews were permitted freer emigration. Kissinger hated this amendment because it constrained his ability to maneuver. Nixon also publicly disagreed with Jackson-Vanik, but he was dogged by polls showing that his stance was costing him electoral support from American Jews.

As a result of this impasse, on September 30, 1972, Nixon invited Senator Jackson for a stroll in the Rose Garden. During their walk—beyond the reach of aides or microphones—they made a deal. Jackson agreed to withdraw Jackson-Vanik and to lobby against fellow Democrats' attempts to make Jewish emigration an election issue. In exchange Nixon agreed to fire twelve members of ACDA whom Jackson disliked, plus chairman Gerard Smith, and to allow Jackson to choose their replacements.

Nixon seems not to have recognized that, in allowing Jackson to choose the administration's arms control negotiators with the USSR, he was handing the SALT talks to men whose predilections were directly contrary to his own and Kissinger's. The president doubtless thought that he and Kissinger would be able to use their back channels and personal diplomacy to override the bureaucrats on arms control. But that notion did not take into account the makeup of Jackson's revamped ACDA—including Iklé as the new director; Paul Nitze; and a new member, Jackson's longtime friend General Edward Rowny, a Kraemer pal and a hard-line anti-Communist. Iklé would soon hire Paul Wolfowitz, whose doctoral thesis had been on nuclear proliferation, to join the group. The formidable combination that resulted—Iklé, Rowny, Nitze, Wolfowitz, Moorer, Zumwalt, Jackson, and Perle—would mount serious challenges to Nixon's policies toward the USSR, and all but knock the détente express off the rails.

"IT LOOKS LIKE we've got three out of three, Mr. President," Kissinger said on returning from Paris in early October. Nixon had achieved a détente treaty with the Soviets, rapprochement with China, and, now, apparently, agreement with the North Vietnamese on a peace accord to end the

Vietnam War. At the celebratory dinner—steaks, a Chateau Lafite Roth-schild—Nixon noted in his diary that Haig "seemed rather subdued."

By late October 1972, during the closing weeks of the presidential campaign, Nixon's lead in the polls was so enormous, and the electorate's apparent distaste for McGovern was so strong, that liberal Democrats such as former senator Eugene McCarthy assured Kissinger that they weren't lifting a finger on behalf of their party's nominee. Nixon's reelection seemed assured.

Although peace in Vietnam was the goal most fervently desired by the American public, the other two accomplishments—bringing Red China into the family of nations, and achieving some measure of détente with the Soviet Union—would have longer-lasting implications, leading eventually to the end of the Cold War. But few people saw the forthcoming peace in Vietnam—not yet assured, despite Kissinger's jubilation—as a victory. For those on the left, peace in Vietnam came too late and at too great a cost in American lives. For those on the right, it was not a peace but a surrender, a decision to walk away from a true confrontation with the forces of evil.

At this significant moment, Nixon invited to the White House a man who had been sending him strategy memos for years, and who had at last been publicly identified as Kissinger's mentor: Dr. Fritz Kraemer.

12

A Meeting of Mind-Sets

T he only known meeting between President Richard Nixon and Fritz Kraemer took place on October 24, 1972, in the Oval Office. Many of the Nixon tapes have been transcribed; most of the transcriptions concentrate on "abuse of power" and related matters. The October 24 conversation, which we have transcribed for this book, has another subject: It captures a fascinating encounter between the defining—though heretofore secret—voice of the right wing of American foreign policy in the Cold War era and the two men, Nixon and Kissinger, who were in the midst of a radical attempt to transform that policy. It offers a glimpse into the minds of all these: of Nixon at his most intelligent and charming; of an expansive Kissinger, on the verge of the triumphant Paris peace agreement of January 1973, which would earn him the Nobel Peace Prize; and of a bold and prescient Fritz Kraemer, predicting the adverse consequences that would follow a flawed peace accord.

IN THE FALL of 1972, the president's relationship with Kissinger and Haig changed, as Haig's rank in the army was significantly raised. On Nixon's express orders, and after some campaigning by Kraemer, the army awarded Haig two more stars, jumping him over 240 ranking officers to make him eligible for the post Nixon wanted him to have: vice chief of staff of the U.S. Army.

After Haig's elevation was announced, White House staffers noticed, he began acting more defiantly toward Kissinger. Haig believed he was back on a path to becoming chairman of the Joint Chiefs, and no one could disagree with his reasoning.

The main reason Haig might have expected to achieve that goal in the near term was Nixon's high opinion of him. Haig had become a valued adviser, a counterweight to his nominal boss, especially when Kissinger was out of reach or out of favor. General Bruce Palmer, who was working at the offices of defense secretary Laird and army secretary Robert Froehlke, recalled that Nixon and Kissinger had submitted annual letters about Haig, in lieu of reports from his army superiors, that "raised our eyebrows (and blood pressure) more than a little, for they portrayed Haig as the most outstanding officer serving on active duty in any service, including the service chiefs."

There was a deal in the works: Creighton Abrams, who had returned from Vietnam, would replace the retiring Westmoreland as army chief of staff, and Haig would become vice chief. Nixon had wanted to make Haig chief of staff, but Laird and the entire army hierarchy resisted, since Haig had had no previous upper chain-of-command experience. Nixon didn't like Creighton Abrams; according to Abrams's biographer, he refused to accept Abrams as chief until Laird reminded Nixon that he'd promised to let Laird make all important personnel decisions. Haig's appointment as vice chief sweetened the deal for Nixon. According to General Palmer, Abrams disliked the idea of Haig as vice chief but realized he had no choice. Haig, for his part, agreed to remain at the White House until a peace treaty had been signed; after that he would make his triumphal return to the Pentagon, having risen from colonel to four-star general in three and a half years at the White House.

In mid-October 1972, Henry Kissinger was in Saigon, trying to sell Thieu on the peace terms he'd worked out in Paris with North Vietnam. While Kissinger was out of town, Haig brought the departing army chief of staff, William Westmoreland, to meet with Nixon.

Westmoreland came to the Oval Office to decry the peace terms obtained by Kissinger. Though the JCS had nominally agreed to Kissinger's terms, Westmoreland's objections signaled discontent among the Chiefs. After the visit, Nixon and Haig jointly cabled Kissinger in Saigon, instructing him to obtain Thieu's "wholehearted" approval. If he couldn't, Haig suggested in an additional cable to Kissinger, he should be prepared to "denounce" Hanoi's terms and walk away from an agreement.

Thieu's approval wouldn't be easy to obtain. In the summer of 1972, Kissinger had lied to the South Vietnamese leader, telling him that the United States would play conciliator toward North Vietnam during the negotiations so that Nixon would look like a peacemaker for the American electorate, but that after the election the United States would return to the battlefield with vigor. In October, when Kissinger brought Thieu the terms of the proposed agreement, Thieu realized that the U.S. government had no intentions of continuing the fight. He refused to go along with the agreement.

During this period, Haig showed Nixon reams of intelligence predicting that a "bloodbath" would follow an accord based on current terms. He pleaded for delay until better terms could be obtained from North Vietnam, possibly through renewed bombing and harbor mining.

Kissinger learned about Haig's end run while in Saigon. It was a bitter pill: After all, Haig had been with Kissinger in Paris, and had supported the agreement then. "Many wars have been lost by untoward timidity," Kissinger cabled back to Haig, "but enormous tragedies have also been produced by the inability of military people to recognize when the time for a settlement has arrived."

This was a rebuke aimed not only at Haig, but also at their common mentor, Fritz Kraemer, who had been advising Haig actively in recent weeks. According to General Palmer, Kraemer felt Kissinger "was often immersed in a state of deep depression, almost despair, over the course and direction of the negotiations on the Vietnam War," and Kraemer had been trying to assuage his protégé emotionally on this subject. Haig told Palmer similar things about Kissinger's fragile emotional state.

In early October, Nixon read an article by one of his favorite reporters, Nick Thimmesch, portraying Kraemer as the man who had discovered Kissinger. Thimmesch and Nixon had been friendly since the 1950s; the reporter had written sympathetically about Nixon's family and was one of the few who had toured the world with Nixon when he was out of office. Most recently Thimmesch had accompanied Nixon to the summit and written a complimentary article for which Nixon had sent him a handwritten note of thanks. Nixon had not known the details of the Kraemer-Kissinger relationship and was intrigued, remembering (as he put it in a later letter to Thimmesch) that "Henry would send [Kraemer's] memoranda in to me, even when Henry disagreed with him, because he felt that I ought to be exposed to views so ably expressed by a true scholar." So that October, with Kissinger in Saigon, Nixon asked Haig to summon Kraemer to the Oval Office.

Kraemer had come to the White House many times before to speak privately with Kissinger or Haig, but had never had a session, formal or informal, with the president. He accepted the invitation.

Haig made the arrangements, which included obtaining a memo from Sven on how Nixon should talk to his father. "You will find Dr. Kraemer an exceptionally knowledgeable and intense student of history," Sven wrote, adding, "He will be fully prepared to discuss a broad range of strategic and psychological issues with you." Sven added in a note to Haig that he was certain that "my father and Dr. Kissinger would agree (perhaps for different reasons)" that there should be no publicity about the meeting. Haig expected to be the third person in the room when Nixon and Kraemer met. By the time the meeting came around on October 24, however, Kissinger had returned from his travels and insisted on supplanting Haig. Before the meeting, Kissinger warned Nixon by memo that Kraemer would likely disagree with some of his policies. He also warned Kraemer not to lecture the president.

Nixon had little inkling that his guest that day was the foremost champion of foreign policy principles that ran directly counter to his own—or that those ideas had percolated through several groups that were actively trying to reverse or block administration policies. He may not even have been aware of Kraemer's profound influence on Haig.

EVEN AS THE White House photographer snapped a photo of Kraemer with his protégé and his president, the three began to chat. Nixon was considerate and flattering, saying he was intrigued by Thimmesch's description of Kraemer's long path to the United States and to his position in the Pentagon. Kraemer countered with a story of how "kind" the FBI had been when they had interviewed him in this country, given that with his background he could have been an enemy agent. "I admire your rhetoric and strength," he told Nixon.

The president spoke of the "enormous changes" going on in the world; surely mindful of Kraemer's well-known critique of totalitarian regimes as untrustworthy diplomatic partners, he got down to business with an unusual opening statement: "I have no illusions about the so-called good intentions of the leaders of our enemies."

Kraemer responded as though he and Nixon were equals, with a demonstration of his tough-minded analysis. Brezhnev, he observed, was constrained by always having to refer to his ruling clique before making decisions. His actions were further hampered, Kraemer said, by "uncontrollable forces." To illustrate, he pointed to the "handful of young Egyptian officers" (a group that included Anwar Sadat) who had effectively forced the Soviet military out of Egypt in 1970 after many years of Soviet training and control of the Egyptian armed forces. Once the Soviets were ousted from the country, Egypt refused even to buy further arms from the USSR.

"Now, China is entirely different," Kraemer opined, "because [its leaders] are very great men." Mentioning that he had undertaken an in-depth analysis of Mao in 1965, he said he felt he knew the Chinese leader well—although, he observed, no one knew great men well enough.

"Great men are the least dangerous," Kissinger chortled.

As the conversation flowed, Kraemer did precisely what Kissinger had warned him against: He mounted his soapbox to lecture the president. The timing of the cease-fire, he warned, must be imposed the instant Nixon announced it, to prevent the enemy using the "gap" between announcement and imposition to "jump forward" with their troops. Moreover, to keep it honest, it must be supervised by an international force.

Kraemer then segued into a survey of his geostrategic views on the post-armistice elections in Vietnam. Kissinger deflected the conversation to tactics, interrupting with a description of how he had pressed the North Vietnamese to settle before the U.S. election. He had used the election as a deadline, Kissinger said, "not in order to support the president but in order to not have the other side use the occasion to make changes." The North Vietnamese, like the Soviets, habitually made changes as a deadline approached, but in this instance "we have a deadline that they cannot change."

"We're not going to let them dictate the timing," Nixon put in. It was as though the president and Kissinger were rationalizing what they had done, looking for Kraemer's approval.

"They will not understand your psychology," Kraemer warned. "Right up until the election they'll think they have a terrible tiger by the tail." The reason to hold a tiger by its tail, legend has it, is to stay close enough to avoid its claws and fangs. Kraemer's point was that the North Vietnamese were holding close to the Americans, giving in on minor matters, but not stomping away from the negotiating table, so that they could wrest an agreement from Nixon before the election that he would be bound to observe thereafter.

Nixon tried to agree with Kraemer, saying that this was why he was going to "let 'em guess" what he would do with his new mandate after the election.

Kissinger revealed that the problem with the North Vietnamese was not that they were recalcitrant negotiators, but rather that they'd met every recent demand within twenty-four hours:

KISSINGER: For example, we've made the proposal that their prisoners would have to stay in South Vietnamese jails . . .

NIXON: Forty thousand political prisoners!

KISSINGER: . . . political prisoners stay in South Vietnamese jails, which we thought was unacceptable—but they have accepted. Now you know that this is not an easy thing, for them to sign a document saying that they have to release South Vietnamese military prisoners but *their* political prisoners have to stay in jail.

KRAEMER: But, you know, this cease-fire in place gives such an advantage to them that it can do great harm . . .

NIXON: But I think that is [offset] by other things. . . . They have
taken hell. I mean the bombing has hurt, mining has hurt. . . . And
I agree that the cease-fire will only be temporary and give them an
advantage . . . but I think they had reached a point [of hurting]. . . .
They've read Mao: he was always willing to retreat. . . .
KISSINGER: We may have been too successful with our threats. We've
told them, for example, that all communications will be cut off on
November seventh, because the president would have to . . . reorganize
the government . . .

Kissinger confided that, until October 8, the U.S. strategy had been to
"waste as much time as possible." On that date, however, the North Vietnamese began making concessions, and it became "almost impossible to
slow them down. For example, we asked for a cease-fire in Cambodia, and
they accepted within thirty-six hours."

To Kraemer, this was all evidence that the enemy would say anything
in order to ensure the fate of a basically flawed agreement—one that would
allow them to claim victory and then do as they pleased. He was dubious
that a cease-fire in Cambodia could be enforced, because of Chinese influence there. And in Laos, he said, the United States would have to contend
with the now-ineffectual but still demanding Prince Souvanna Phouma,
whom Kraemer began to quote in French.

This was too esoteric for the president. He changed the subject—to who
was supporting him on the war and on the peace negotiations, and who was
not. Nixon pointed out that "so-called" journalists, commentators, professors, and clerics all criticized him routinely; he wondered why he had so
little support from intellectuals but said he was pleased to enjoy the backing of "the workers, the ethnics, the farmers, the Southerners. The further
you get away from Washington, the more support." His point, he said, was
that the nation had endured a long war, and out of concern for the 55,000
Americans who had died,

we will not now—cannot now—will not now—do something based
on an election. Beyond that, we cannot give to American foreign
policy a blow, a failure—stab in the heart—that will echo around
the world . . . so we're doing everything we can to get it right, and
it's very difficult. Seeing as we want the right kind of a settlement
for Vietnam, we have to make a determination as well, because we
cannot allow [Thieu] to be the sole judge of that. . . . This will be a
factor for years to come. . . .

Here was the opening Kraemer had been waiting for. "May I formulate one or two things about that?" he asked Nixon. With the president's assent, he launched into an inventory of the likely adverse effects of a bad Vietnam settlement on U.S. foreign relations, his comments echoing those he had penned three years earlier in his agonized but finely argued "Single Strategic Theater" paper. The primary audience for the settlement of the war in Vietnam, he insisted, was not Vietnam, North or South, but other nations, especially our enemies, the Soviet Union and China:

> If it should prove that we, the United States, are not able to guarantee to keep South Vietnam viable, as a moral commitment, then the question [that] will arise—for friend, foe, and our other interests—is, Who can the United States ever be successful in defending . . . in a relatively short war? . . . Everyone from Rio de Janeiro to Copenhagen, Hanoi to Moscow, and so on will say that enormous American power could not deal with a small nation of thirty-one million people. Therefore, as a lawyer, I would say that [the United States] *cannot* be trusted.

Though Kraemer never uttered the phrase "provocative weakness," the concept informed his warnings about the need for strength in diplomacy.

"The foreign policy of the United States is on the line," Nixon acknowledged. That was why he and Kissinger had to "squeeze every ounce out of this [settlement]," he said, "because the war in Vietnam isn't about Vietnam . . . it's about Southeast Asia, it's about the world."

But Kraemer refused to be distracted. The settlement, he insisted, would put Thieu in a "difficult" position and make it hard for South Vietnam to defend itself.

Nixon tried to close the conversation, telling Kraemer, "I value your advice," especially with regard to the Russians (the subject of several Kraemer memos), even though that advice sometimes subjected his policies to "the third degree." More important, Nixon said, was that "you and Henry, from impressive intellectual backgrounds," supported those policies. Nixon disparaged the overemphasis at Harvard and Yale on "I.Q.," intellectual quotient, when what really counted—and counted with him—was "C.Q., character quotient." Kraemer nodded in agreement; in later years, he would actually adopt Nixon's formulation as his own.

It was time for Kraemer to leave, but before he did he made a point of telling the president that he considered Al Haig "brilliant"—a word he told the president he didn't use loosely—and that Haig's promotion "has been accepted with *elation* by all the field grade officers." Nixon was gratified, and returned the compliment by mentioning Kraemer's " remarkable son." ("Sven," Kissinger stepped in with the name when it wasn't on the tip of Nixon's tongue.) The president presented Kraemer with a pair of presidential seal cufflinks and the conversation was concluded.

After they left the Oval Office, Kraemer later told a friend, Kissinger was furious with him. "You've just ruined all my policies," Kissinger said, shocked that Nixon seemed to favor Kraemer's predictions about the forthcoming settlement over his. Back in the Oval Office later that day, Nixon asked Kissinger what "that fella Kraemer" thought about his idea of stopping the bombing while continuing to negotiate on the peace accord. "He's against any settlement," Kissinger grumbled. "Much as I admire him, he's basically—"

Nixon interrupted to say, "He wants to kill them all." He added that Kraemer was entitled to his views, but on this subject, "we have to do what is right."

Kraemer later told his friend that Kissinger's outburst was just further proof that his pupil had become "too flexible," commingling "what is good for my country with what is good for my career." When the precise terms of the settlement with North Vietnam became known, Kraemer, according to the same sources, warned Kissinger, "If you sign that treaty I shall never speak to you again."

ON THE SAME day Kraemer met with Nixon, Nguyen Van Thieu made a fiery speech rejecting the proposed treaty. In response, North Vietnam published the draft agreement. And in response to that, at an October 26 press conference, Kissinger summarized its key provisions and announced, memorably, "Peace is at hand."

Those on the left immediately decried the announcement as a ploy to swing voters in the upcoming presidential election, now less than two weeks away. But the news played only a small part in what would be the largest landslide victory in American presidential history. On November 7, Richard Nixon was reelected by an astonishing margin, winning 47 million votes and 49 states to McGovern's 1 state (and the District of Columbia) and 29 million votes. It was a victory for the president, not his party: Nixon had very short coattails. Although the 1972 election brought North Carolina's Jesse Helms into the Senate, replacing a retiring Democrat, it was otherwise a Democratic onslaught. The Democrats increased their numbers in the House and Senate; Scoop Jackson, who directed the Democratic Party's congressional campaign, had helped produce a nearly veto-proof majority in both houses of Congress.

The day after the election, Nixon sent Haig to Saigon to talk to Thieu, military man to military man, and convince him to accept a peace agreement that neither liked.

The terms, anathema to South Vietnam, were substantially the same as the ten-point program proposed by Hanoi in 1969. For instance, the 1972 agreement codified the Communist tenet that Vietnam was one country and not two, thus justifying the prospect that North Vietnamese troops—no longer considered "foreign"—would remain in the South after the cease-fire. (U.S. troops, on the other hand, would be withdrawn completely.) The agreement would be enforced by a four-country board, with two of the countries appointed by the Communists, ensuring a stalemate on important questions, including any future truce violations. The proposed agreement, in short, offered the United States a clear path to get out of the war, but did little to assure the continuation of a non-Communist South Vietnam.

On his first visit to Saigon after Nixon's reelection, Haig hand-carried a letter from the president insisting that the United States would use its might to enforce the treaty, promising to "react very strongly and rapidly to any violation of the agreement." Nixon mentioned only one condition for that commitment: that South Vietnam "does not emerg[e] as the obstacle to a peace which American public opinion now universally desires."

Haig's meeting with Thieu was strained. "If Russia invaded the U.S.," Thieu asked, "would you accept an agreement where they got to stay and then say that it was a peace?" Haig did not respond; Thieu later claimed this was because Haig "knew I was right." Thieu also knew that Nixon's letter did not bind the United States to a course of action: Congress would have to ratify such a document for it to be binding. Thieu then handed Haig a list of sixty-nine proposed amendments to the accord—amendments that all but reversed the intent of the current terms.

"I WANTED TO discuss two things with you," Kissinger told Kraemer by phone as he arranged to visit his mentor on the evening of November 27, 1972. "One, really to explain to you in some greater detail than I had a chance to the first time exactly where we stand on Vietnam. And the second, I will have to make some decisions about what I am going to do."

"You as a person?" Kraemer responded.

"I mean in relation to the administration. And I wanted to get your judgment on that also."

"Yes, and that has to be certainly—shall I say, persistently—looked into. But anyway nothing rushed should be done I think."

"I can't do anything anyway until these negotiations go one way or the other."

Shortly after his evening conversation with Kraemer, Kissinger headed back to Paris. There, as he and everyone else expected, North Vietnam rejected Thieu's sixty-nine proposed amendments and broke off the peace talks.

When Kissinger returned, Haig met him at the airport. The only option left, he told Kissinger, was the harshest one: to launch a massive round of B-52 raids on North Vietnamese cities. Kissinger assented. Later, to Kraemer, he poured out his despair over the breakdown of the peace talks. Kraemer told him not to lose heart, and to go ahead and bomb.

Nixon readily agreed to the bombing campaign, which was dubbed "Linebacker II." The large phalanxes of B-52s and their payloads that flew over North Vietnam starting on December 18 overwhelmed the country's 1,200 SAM missiles. In the midst of the campaign, Haig flew back to Saigon to tell Thieu that the bombing was designed to show North Vietnam how the United States would punish any treaty infractions. "Should Hanoi violate the agreement, then the legal, psychological, and patriotic basis will exist for brutal U.S. retaliation," Haig later wrote that he told Thieu. "Unless the U.S. finds an entirely new basis to justify the sacrifices that the American people have been asked to bear, there is no hope that the American Congress will be willing to do so." Haig repeated the same message to Lon Nol in Cambodia and to the Thai leaders: The United States would station forces in Southeast Asia "for hair-trigger response to violations" and would aid their countries in the post-settlement era. Therefore, they must hold on.

Linebacker II was enormously devastating. Using laser-guided ordnance, the U.S. Air Force disabled virtually all railroads in Haiphong and Hanoi. The bombs shattered nine major storage and repair areas for trucks, nine port supply areas, ten airfields, the nation's electric grid, four large power plants, and radio and television facilities. After a one-day hiatus for Christmas, the bombing resumed; it would continue until December 29, when North Vietnam agreed to accept the October settlement. At the peace table, North Vietnam acceded to a few small, almost meaningless changes in the agreement and declared itself ready to sign if the other parties did. As diplomatic historian William Bundy concluded, "The Christmas bombing extracted no significant concession from Hanoi."

In later years, conservatives would assert quite the opposite—that the bombing forced North Vietnam to sign a peace accord, lest the bombing continue indefinitely. But the terms of the 1973 peace agreement belie that contention. The wording was everything Kraemer had feared. Moreover, it codified what Nixon and Kissinger had already conveyed to Dobrynin and

Zhou: that the accord would provide only a "decent interval" between its signing and an "evolution" to a Communist-controlled government.

In any event, the ones who actually needed convincing to sign the accord were the South Vietnamese—as Haig's visit to Thieu in the midst of the bombing demonstrated. In addition to the letter Haig carried to Thieu on that trip, Nixon wrote twenty others to Thieu between December 31, 1972, and late January 1973, all offering variations on the same arguments. On January 5, Nixon wrote, "Should you decide, as I hope you will, to go with us [and sign the peace accord], you have my assurance of continued assistance in the post-settlement period, and that we will respond with full force should the settlement be violated by North Vietnam." Thieu underlined that passage and showed the letter to his cabinet. When pleading did not work, Nixon sent Haig on a third visit to Saigon to warn Thieu that the United States would sign an accord with the North regardless of whether South Vietnam chose to participate. After this, Thieu told his staff, "If Kissinger had the power to bomb the Independence Palace to force me to sign the agreement, he would not hesitate to do so."

The threats finally succeeded where the Christmas bombing had not.

Convinced that the agreement was the best he could get, Kissinger tried to convince Kraemer. "I can't of course say a great deal on the telephone," he told his mentor on January 18, "but on the agreement itself, we do have the DMZ now in a very satisfactory [configuration]—and we have the word 'administrative structure' removed. That means the three countries of Vietnam."

"And is of course absolutely decisive."

"And I have in there in a way which you as a lawyer will understand, but I don't want anyone to say until it's published, there are four different references to the sovereignty of South Vietnam."

"My gosh, that's more than I expected." Kraemer had sent Kissinger memos about the importance of putting in legal restrictions on the North Vietnamese, so that in case of violations of the accord, South Vietnam, and its ally, the United States, would have the right to take military action against the North.

Kissinger also conveyed that they had done "really well" on the international groups of soldiers who would monitor the demilitarized zone, and that the North Vietnamese contingent would be stationed "away from centers of population."

Kraemer was unhappy at the prospect of only a few thousand international soldiers patrolling such a large area, and of having the North Vietnamese anywhere in the mix. But he was pleased that Kissinger had negotiated positively on some of the things Kraemer thought important. He told Kissinger that when he went out the next day to fulfill a lecture commitment, he would be "a happier man now."

Yet Kraemer's assurances masked the concerns he had earlier voiced to Nixon: that the agreement would never hold, that South Vietnam's future would slowly slip away, and that the United States would do nothing to prevent it.

Those concerns were lost on Henry Kissinger, who was already looking ahead to Paris. In that city, on January 27, 1973, he would sign the agreement to end American participation in the war in Vietnam.

13

Actions and Reactions

The idea that for every action there is a reaction is true not only in physics. As Fritz Kraemer understood, the same causality plays out in politics and diplomacy. "History is not a dotted line," he was fond of saying, "it's a straight line. Everything that happens in world affairs is related in some way to a series of prior events."

Kraemer worried about adverse world reaction to what he believed was America's too-hasty exit from the battlefields of Vietnam, as codified in the Paris Peace Accord of January 1973. In Richard Nixon's second term, that and many additional reactions occurred in response to actions he had initiated during his first term. These domestic reactions would cripple his foreign policies and his ability to stay in power. The most damaging of them would wreak their havoc in a stunningly short period of time: By April 1973, a president who had been elected by the largest electoral margin in history just six months earlier was reduced to taking desperate measures in his attempt to survive in office.

This was also the period, Henry Kissinger noted a quarter century later, that saw the birth of the neoconservative movement. In *Years of Renewal*, published in 1999, Kissinger writes that things began to change in the summer of 1972, and that throughout Nixon's remaining years in office his foreign policies were opposed by two groups: traditional conservatives—Kissinger characterized their disagreement with Nixon as "in the nature of a family quarrel"—and those liberals-turned-conservatives who would become known as the neocons. "What drove conservative disquiet into outright opposition was the emergence of the so-called neoconservatives. . . .

Once they had changed sides, their anti-Communism was intense, often eloquent." But while they brought "intellectual rigor and energy to the debate" on foreign policy, Kissinger thought that their "single-mindedness" had a downside. "When the neoconservatives moved to the radical right, they packed in their bags their visceral dislike of Nixon even though technically they were now on the same side."

Kissinger's description is affected by hindsight; in 1972–73, there were no neoconservatives per se, but there were groups of right-leaning Republicans and of right-leaning Democrats. They came from different starting points on the political spectrum, and their agreement was at this time limited to only one subject: their intense and deep opposition to the Nixon-Kissinger foreign policies.

One important subset of these like-minded conservatives began to coalesce in late 1972. "Moderate" Democrats (as the *New York Times* called them) who were associated with Scoop Jackson and Hubert Humphrey formed a new alliance they called the Coalition for a Democratic Majority, which they hoped to use to reclaim their party from the McGovernites. This segment of the party was less concerned about social policy than about foreign policy; they had wanted the war effort in Vietnam to continue, had objected to détente, and were wary of U.S. coziness with the Chinese. Convened by Ben Wattenberg, coauthor of the recent influential book *The Real Majority*, and Richard Perle, the group's founders included prominent former Trotskyites who had long since renounced Communism, migrating to the Democratic Party and thence to its right edge: Norman Podhoretz, editor of *Commentary*; his wife, author Midge Decter; and Irving Kristol, cofounder of *The Public Interest* and a professor at New York University. The Coalition also attracted Jeane Kirkpatrick, an international affairs professor at Georgetown; arms expert Max Kampelman, a consultant to Hubert Humphrey; and a bevy of Dixiecrats among its seventy initial signatories. "The belief that the security of the United States depends upon a stable and progressive world community has been challenged by the idea that the United States must withdraw from its international responsibilities and effect a serious diminution of its own power," the group said in its founding statement—a shot aimed not only at the McGovernites but also at Nixon and Kissinger. The Coalition wanted to champion candidates who embraced their beliefs; without such candidates, Decter later wrote, a group of believers was only "a lot of hot air."

Many in the Coalition assumed that candidate would be Scoop Jackson. As soon as Congress reconvened in early 1973, Jackson reintroduced his Jackson-Vanik bill and accumulated enough cosponsors in the Senate to override a veto. From this position of strength he began to pressure Nixon not to put the USSR on the list of Most Favored Nations, which would make it eligible for support and trade concessions. Jackson's position was so unassailable that Kissinger had to lobby the USSR to remove the "exit tax" on Jews emigrating to Israel and the West. In mid-March, the USSR agreed; that only spurred Jackson to demand more—a continual monitoring of Soviet emigration practices and a higher number of Soviet exit visas for Jews and other minorities. The USSR's Most Favored Nation status hung fire as each new concession was demanded and granted.

Admiral Moorer also came under pressure from Jackson, in his case to name Lieutenant General Edward L. Rowny as the Chiefs' representative to the SALT talks. Rowny was a veteran of World War II, had served (with Haig) on MacArthur's staff in Korea, and had commanded troops in Vietnam; a Russian speaker, he was NATO's expert on Mutual and Balanced Force Reduction. But Moorer didn't want him, largely because he thought Rowny was being foisted on him by Kissinger. "Over my dead body will you be my representative," Moorer told Rowny at their interview. Shortly thereafter, however, he learned that Rowny was Scoop Jackson's choice as well. The next day, he called Rowny back and told him, "I'm dead." If Rowny was good enough for Jackson, he was good enough for the JCS.

During the remaining eighteen months of the Nixon administration, Moorer would find that Rowny, Iklé, Nitze, and the other Jackson-supported new members of the arms-control negotiating team were more in tune with him and the Joint Chiefs than the old ones had been, and more willing to push back against what they all saw as Nixon and Kissinger excesses and giveaways to the Soviets.

Rowny had heard plenty about Kissinger from his old friend Fritz Kraemer. "To Kraemer, Kissinger was Machiavelli (because of his love of intrigue), Talleyrand (because of his passion for negotiation), and Rasputin (because of his hold on the lives of others) all rolled into one." But while Kraemer was willing to forgive his protégé his lapses from the hard line, Rowny had no such need. Shortly, at the SALT II talks, Rowny proved his bona fides to Moorer by helping him expose Kissinger's back-channel attempt to promote a "Basic Principles" agreement that in Rowny and Moorer's view favored the Soviets. When the press got wind of Kissinger's proposal, he was forced to move toward the Chiefs' harder stance.

Another counterweight to Kissinger—and to softer dealings with the USSR—came into power when Nixon elevated James Schlesinger. Schlesinger and Kissinger had been academic rivals at Harvard, and their rivalry continued while Schlesinger was at RAND, where he had become close to the Wohlstetters. Nixon had initially given Schlesinger a post at the Office of Management and Budget; when he did well there, Nixon rewarded him with the thankless task of reforming the Atomic Energy Commission. After nine months as its chief, Schlesinger had cleaned up the stodgy old agency, so in early 1973 Nixon appointed him director of the CIA, banishing Helms to Iran as an ambassador. When Schlesinger arrived at Langley on February 2, his first words were "I'm here to make sure you don't screw Richard Nixon." He used his new broom to get rid of fourteen hundred employees.

Shortly after Schlesinger's arrival at the CIA, an event occurred, out of the public eye, that would have a large impact on the Nixon presidency: Dick Walters, the CIA's deputy director, informed Schlesinger about the June 23, 1972, White House meeting in which Haldeman and Ehrlichman had told Helms to block the FBI's investigation into the Watergate burglars' money trail, and about Walters's own exchanges with Dean in the ensuing days. All of these conversations, he told Schlesinger, were covered in memcons he had written.

Among the younger figures in the Nixon administration, one who managed to avoid being ensnared in the Watergate matter was Donald Rumsfeld, who was named ambassador to NATO and decamped with his family for Brussels in February 1973. In later years, friendly biographer Midge Decter would conclude that at least part of Rumsfeld's motive for accepting the NATO post was a belief that "political operatives in the White House, and perhaps even the president himself, had ultimately been responsible for Watergate, and that it would be the better part of wisdom to find himself a spot somewhere out of town."

Rumsfeld did not bring Cheney along to Brussels; his young aide returned to the private sector. But in Brussels Rumsfeld did come under the influence of two foreign policy hard-liners: Paul Nitze, the arms negotiator, and General Andrew Goodpaster, the Supreme Allied Commander–Europe (SACEUR), chief of all American forces in Europe and of NATO.

Alexander Haig, meanwhile, finally took his post at the Pentagon as vice chief of staff of the army. On his first call to Haig there, Nixon discovered that they were not communicating on a secure line; neither Laird nor the chairman of the Joint Chiefs had such a line to the White House in their offices. Nixon had one installed for Haig.

THROUGHOUT THE SUMMER of 1972, the national media had treated Watergate as an inside-the-Beltway story. Only a few newspapers—principally the less than 5 percent that supported McGovern—ran stories that competed with or tracked the investigations of Bob Woodward and Carl Bernstein of the *Washington Post*. Congress largely ignored all the revelations, doing little in the way of investigation. Then, in September 1972, the *Post* duo discovered an unreported Nixon campaign slush fund: $350,000 in cash, used for politi-cal purposes. In October, they reported that the fund had been controlled by Haldeman, which put the scandal inside the White House. The *Post* scoop became the heart of a two-part report on the *CBS Evening News with Walter Cronkite.* After it aired, *Post* publisher Kay Graham said that the network had finally succeeded in turning a local story into a national one. It was too late to have any effect on the November election, but afterward the story's growing visibility translated into pressure the new Congress could not ignore.

In January–February 1973, the Senate, seeking a way to look into the $350,000 slush fund, formed a committee to examine campaign irregulari-ties, putting it under the chairmanship of Sam Ervin, a Democrat from North Carolina. Although the leaders packed the committee with right-leaning Democratic and Republican senators—including some fierce parti-sans of the president and some Democrats who had consistently voted with the administration—intense public scrutiny forced the members to examine many, though not all, of the issues surrounding Watergate. As they began, Nixon had a 68 percent favorable rating in the Gallup Poll, his highest ever. Polls also showed that the public had no appetite for continuing the war: 59 percent did not want to send further military aid to South Vietnam, and 71 percent did not want the United States to resume bombing if the North resumed hostilities. The public's main concern about Vietnam was the swift return of American POWs.

Those two matters—the return of the POWs and the bombing of the North for treaty violations—soon became intertwined. Well before the ex-piration of the time allotted for the United States to remove its troops, the North began committing gross violations of the peace accord. When Hun-gary and Poland, two members of the peace accord's four-power supervisory committee, refused to certify these as violations, Nixon, Kissinger, Haig, Abrams, and the Joint Chiefs planned to restart the bombing in late Febru-ary. The plan was held up by a glitch in the repatriation of POWs; Nixon expected to green-light the bombing after mid-March, when Hanoi was due to release the prisoners.

It was a bad time for delay: Watergate was about to explode. Judge John Sirica threatened the convicted burglars with extended sentences if they refused to reveal who had ordered them into the DNC headquarters. Hunt, who could reveal such information, demanded hush money to maintain silence, as he had done at intervals since days after the break-in. McCord let it be known that he was thinking of sending Sirica a letter fingering his "superiors."

It was in this climate that confirmation hearings began on March 1 for

L. Patrick Gray III, hearings both Gray and the White House expected to be "bloody." Under pressure, Gray admitted that he'd discussed the FBI's investigation of Watergate with Dean, the president's counsel. At the same time, *Time* magazine published a report that the FBI had been involved in wiretapping newsmen. Gray testified that he had found "no record of any such business" in FBI or Department of Justice (DoJ) files. On March 6, Haldeman told Nixon that Dean thought Gray was doing poorly in the hearings, was "letting out too much" about White House business. Nixon decided not to push for confirmation—to let Gray "twist slowly, slowly in the wind," as Ehrlichman memorably put it. Senators clamored to hear from Dean about discussions he had had with Gray about the FBI's Watergate investigation, and about Dean's own investigation, which the White House insisted Dean had conducted in the summer of 1972.

At a press conference, reporters asked Nixon for documentary proof of Dean's investigation. None was provided. Soon the pressure was mounting on Nixon to allow subordinates such as Dean to testify. On March 12, Nixon yielded a bit, saying that normally his staff would "decline a [congressional] request for a formal appearance" but that in this instance "executive privilege will not be used as a shield to prevent embarrassing information from being made available." The Ervin Committee (which had not been involved in the Gray confirmation hearings) now unanimously invited Dean to testify.

IN LATER YEARS, conservatives would argue that if Richard Nixon had resumed bombing North Vietnam when it flagrantly violated the peace accord in the spring of 1973, Vietnam could have been saved from eventual Communist rule—and that it was Watergate that kept Nixon from doing so. This is untrue. To understand why, it's crucial to explore an area of Watergate history that has also become tangled and misperceived: the time leading up to John Dean's March 21 "cancer upon the presidency" confession. For decades, historians have taken their road map for those eight days from the tape of the last day, March 21, the moment when many believe the president first learned of the cover-up. But Dean and Nixon met or spoke on the telephone almost daily between March 13 and March 20, and the records of these interchanges are a better guide to what Nixon knew, and did, and when. Moreover, information revealed during those meetings would become crucial to how the White House, under Alexander Haig, would prepare for and react to Dean's Senate testimony in May and June 1973. The tapes were available to Nixon to review, and he did review some of them on June 4, 1973, but most of them were not later transcribed and did not become public. In 1995, the full set of tapes were obtained from the government in a private lawsuit, and it is from that set that the excerpts below have been taken—some of them newly transcribed for this book.

On March 13, John Dean's name came up during the Gray hearings. One senator insisted that, regardless of what Nixon had said recently, Dean would have to testify or Gray would not be confirmed. Later that day, Dean advised Nixon, "the committee have an executive session this afternoon to invite me to testify."

> PRESIDENT: Would you respond under oath?
> DEAN: I think I would be willing to, yes.
> PRESIDENT: That's what I'd say because that's what I am preparing in the press [memo]. I'll say you'll respond under oath in a letter; you will not appear in a formal session.

Dean and Nixon thought that would take care of the problem of the Gray hearings. But grand jury problems remained. Dean laid out for the president precisely who from the White House would have problems testifying, and why. Nixon's concern grew as Dean's tale wound closer to Haldeman and Ehrlichman; Nixon believed that the Ervin Committee was out to get Haldeman. He wondered if Haldeman might have a "problem" in regard to Watergate because of his appointments secretary, Dwight Chapin, whose name had been mentioned in connection with trickster Donald Segretti. But the conversation quickly came around to another Haldeman aide, Gordon Strachan:

> DEAN: Well, Chapin didn't know anything about the Watergate, and—
> PRESIDENT: You don't think so?
> DEAN: No. Absolutely not.
> PRESIDENT: Did Strachan?
> DEAN: Yes.
> PRESIDENT: He knew?
> DEAN: Yes.
> PRESIDENT: About the Watergate?
> DEAN: Yes.
> PRESIDENT: Well, then, Bob knew. He probably told Bob, then. He may not have. He may not have.

Dean then assured Nixon that Strachan would not give up Haldeman if Strachan had to testify under oath, but Nixon was still incredulous:

PRESIDENT: But he knew? He knew about Watergate? Strachan did?
DEAN: Uh-huh.
PRESIDENT: I'll be damned. Well, that's the problem in Bob's case, isn't
it? It's not Chapin then, but Strachan. 'Cause Strachan worked for him.

In admitting that Strachan knew about the break-in before it happened,
Dean had finally told the president something that Dean had known for
nine months. In *Blind Ambition*, Dean's autobiography, he wrote that a
few days after the break-in, when Liddy mentioned Strachan as possibly involved, "I felt queasy. I really didn't want to know more because I had to
assume that if Strachan knew, Haldeman knew, and if Haldeman knew,
the president knew. It made sickening sense." Decades later, in a deposition for the 1995 lawsuit, Dean acknowledged that in June 1972, when he
received the information from Liddy about Strachan, he had withheld it
from his boss, Ehrlichman, because "I didn't feel that it was my job to tell
Ehrlichman things I assumed he already knew or to be telling tales on one
senior staff member and his staff versus another senior staff member and
his." Despite these feelings—and despite Dean's direct contact with Nixon
at intervals during the ensuing nine months—he had not told Nixon about
Strachan until March 13, 1973.

Nixon understood the implications of Strachan's early involvement: that
all the statements made by the White House since the burglary, insisting
that no one there had had advance knowledge of the break-in, had been lies.

Ehrlichman had recently advised Nixon to get all the facts out, fire whoever was responsible, and move on. Dean had opposed that approach, which
would have meant revealing such matters as the six "overt acts" to which he
would later plead guilty, such as having coached Jeb Magruder, a former
deputy to Mitchell at CRP, in preparing perjured testimony. Nixon had
been leaning toward the approach until March 13, but after learning about
Strachan he changed his mind and began, for the first time, to participate
actively in the cover-up.

On March 16, reporters asked again for documentation of Dean's internal White House investigation of Watergate. Later that day, Nixon made a
suggestion to Dean:

> What could be helpful, if it could be worked out, is just something
> that, where, ah, in the most general terms, the description, saying—
> what I might even say in answer to a press conference question but in
> more general terms—that "the investigation has been conducted and
> we find this, that, and the other thing"—and whack! Just like that. You
> see what I mean?

Drafting such a report was "going to be tough," Dean replied. Even so, Nixon wanted a report to "find out what our vulnerabilities are." Dean immediately promised: "Maybe there will be some time when I should possibly report a little fuller than I really have, so you can appreciate in full some of the vulnerable points and where they lead to." Nixon wanted a paper "so that my reiterated statements from time to time that, well, 'no one in the White House is involved,' have some basis"—in other words, a Dean Report that would serve as the authoritative statement of his findings.

Dean demonstrated his understanding of the goal by articulating what Nixon should be able to say in response to a press query: "A lot of my conclusions were based on the fact that there was not a scintilla of evidence in the investigation that led anywhere in the White House. . . . There's nothing in the FBI files that indicates anybody in the White House was involved. . . . Nothing in what's been presented before the Grand Jury indicating White House involvement."

Nixon agreed: That was exactly what he wanted. Dean ended the conversation with the salutation "We will win," signaling his belief that he and the president were a team on the issue of keeping Watergate from tainting the White House.

Some historians believe that in a Senate trial Nixon might have successfully refuted the charge of obstruction of justice in regard to his June 23, 1972, instruction to the CIA to impede the FBI's investigation, because the order had some grounds in national security. But this reasoning does not apply to the March 16 conversation, with its revelation that Nixon had joined the cover-up and was now beginning to orchestrate it.

The March 16 tape also highlights Nixon's craftiness. If Dean produced a "Dean Report," Nixon could say he relied on it. If that report raised more questions than it answered, Nixon could blame Dean for conducting a bad investigation and waiting too long to write it up. If Dean failed to produce a report, Nixon could just as readily blame Dean for an investigation gone awry.

Dean continued to drop bombshells. On March 17 he told Nixon that there were more individuals in the White House, beyond Strachan, who were "vulnerable" because of the roles they had played in the cover-up. He quickly named Haldeman, Ehrlichman, Colson, and Mitchell, and even added himself to the list. He also revealed that Hunt and Liddy had burglarized the offices of Dr. Lewis Fielding, Ellsberg's psychiatrist. Nixon was aghast but thought the matter wouldn't come up in Senate hearings.

On March 20, Nixon met with Dean and Richard A. Moore, an aide, in the Oval Office. Moore had been working with Dean on a statement for the press. Dean advised against putting out a new statement that would cover potential grand jury testimony and whom the president would permit to appear before Congress. When he showed an earlier version of such a statement to press secretary Ron Ziegler, Dean said, Ziegler predicted how a typical newsman would respond: "'Your document right here, while it is responsive as far as we're concerned, it's gonna raise as many questions as it answers. And can you answer all those questions?' And, of course, once you answer one, it opens up a whole other set of questions."

Moore and Nixon disagreed with Dean. They wanted a new statement, and they set up a typewriter in the Oval Office to use in drafting it. (Moore, who can be heard on tape typing during the meeting, did not know the extent of Dean's involvement in the cover-up, or what Nixon knew.) Nixon read a paragraph from the draft statement, which said that in the course of an interview with Dean, Liddy had discussed establishing an intelligence operation. "I'd be inclined just to knock that out," Nixon ruled. "I'd just say there were limited problems involving campaign law compliance. And . . . then I would say never at any time were there any discussions that had anything to do with intelligence gathering operations."

Dean had further objections.

DEAN: Now, uh, they'd ask, "Did I meet with Segretti also?" And yes, I did meet with Segretti. "How did I meet with him?" Uh, he called me. "Who put him in touch with me?" Gordon Strachan. "Why did Gordon Strachan put him in touch with you?" Because Gordon Strachan had been called by him to tell him he was being interviewed by the FBI and wanted to know what it was all about it. "What did you tell Mr. Segretti when you met with him?" I told him that when he went before the Grand Jury, to tell the truth. He was concerned that he had to give up the names—Strachan, Chapin, and Kalmbach. I told him if that came back, he had to do that.

NIXON: I would summarize that in one sentence and say, "My . . . my contact [with] Mr. Segretti was when he called my office to uh, in regards to his appearance before the Grand Jury. And I directed him, as I directed all who made such inquiries." Very general.

And so it went, paragraph after paragraph, with Moore occasionally pausing to point out questions raised by the statement, saying "we have to do something about this line." Nixon and Dean tried to make the statement read as though no one in the White House had known anything about the break-in, and that activities such as Segretti's had gone on at a level far below Nixon. In rewriting and editing this fraudulent document, Nixon was taking full charge of the cover-up.

That evening, Hunt threatened to reveal the names of his sponsors in the White House unless Dean paid him an additional million dollars. It was this demand, Dean later wrote, that spurred him to ask for a meeting with the president on March 21 to lay everything out. Hunt's threat was aimed directly at Dean, who, according to later testimony, had acted as Hunt's superior in the days after the Watergate break-in. As Colson would attest in the 1995 civil suit, two days after the break-in Dean ordered Hunt out of the country. Testimony in the 1970s from Nixon's personal attorney Herbert Kalmbach and private detective Tony Ulasewicz revealed that, between the June 1972 break-in and mid-March 1973, Hunt had been receiving money at Dean's request, by a complicated route: Directed by Dean, Kalmbach had given it to Ulasewicz for delivery to Hunt's lawyers and (before her death) to Hunt's wife.

In his March 21 meeting with Nixon, when Dean opened the floodgates by telling Nixon there was a "cancer upon the presidency," he negated statements he had made earlier that week. On March 16, Dean had claimed there was "not a scintilla of evidence" of White House involvement in Watergate; now he emphasized to Nixon what he had first broached on March 17, that *everyone* had been involved in the planning or cover-up, including Haldeman, Ehrlichman, and himself. Dean laid out his major points of concern: "One, we are being blackmailed; Two, people are going to start perjuring themselves very quickly that had not had to perjure themselves to protect other people in the line." Magruder, he alleged, had already perjured himself. Haldeman, Ehrlichman, Mitchell, and Dean himself were involved in the cover-up, "and that is an obstruction of justice."

Nixon did consider obtaining the million dollars to buy Hunt's silence, although he did not instruct anyone to find or convey the money. He also considered firing everyone or insisting that all testify before the grand jury without immunity—an idea seconded by Haldeman and Ehrlichman. Nixon was willing to take some losses to bring Watergate to a close. "Delaying is the great danger," he mused. But he still pinned some hopes on a Dean Report—a document he could give to Ervin—and soon Dean was on his way to Camp David to write it.

WITH DEAN MOMENTARILY out of the way, Nixon could return to the prospect of new bombing in North Vietnam. The repatriation of the POWs had been pushed back even further, and Nixon had accordingly postponed the bombing—until someone leaked to the press about the possibility. This rumor rekindled the fires of antiwar protest and raised the question of whether Nixon possessed the legal authority to order bombing after all

American soldiers had left Vietnam, as they were supposed to do by April 1. An increasingly vocal contingent in Congress argued that he did not.

With Congress and public opinion sharply opposed to renewed bombing, Nixon gave up the idea. The condemnation he had suffered for the Christmas bombings still reverberated in Washington and among America's allies; if Nixon began bombing again—and followed up by sending new ground troops into Vietnam—he would certainly rekindle this anger. Only a leader committed on principle to winning the battle in Southeast Asia would take such a risk—and Richard Nixon felt no such commitment. In this, as in so many other things, Nixon was a pragmatist, not an ideologue. Soon he had Ziegler issue a categorical statement: "The United States government has no intentions, no plans, and no desire to reintroduce American ground forces into Southeast Asia." At the end of the day, it was not Watergate that forced Nixon to renege on his promise to bomb North Vietnam for peace treaty violations; it was a fear of widespread backlash that stayed his hand.

On March 29, the day after the last group of POWs came home, the president proclaimed that the final item in "peace with honor" had been achieved. His "mission accomplished" statement provoked an immediate reaction: Congressmen pointed out that since 1970, the only authority the president had possessed to bomb in Indochina was to preserve the safety of American soldiers; now that the soldiers had returned, Nixon had no further authority to bomb. The following week, the Senate voted 88–3 that no funds could be used for the reconstruction of North Vietnam—promised in the Paris peace agreement—without specific approval from Congress. "These demonstrations of a much more assertive attitude on Capitol Hill," historian William Bundy observes, "were bipartisan, and came before Watergate revelations had major public impact."

On April 7, as the military situation in Cambodia and South Vietnam continued to deteriorate, Al Haig and a few NSC staff members, including Sven Kraemer, left for the Southeast Asian capitals. Although the administration insisted it was no longer bombing in Cambodia, in fact it continued to bomb extensively there, and occasionally in Laos, and to fly into Phnom Penh C-130s loaded with military equipment. Haig, Sven and Fritz Kraemer, and other like-minded people believed that the Southeast Asian dominoes should not be permitted to fall and that North Vietnam would certainly take over South Vietnam, Cambodia, and Laos unless U.S. bombing and military assistance returned to earlier high levels. When Haig arrived in Saigon, there were only 220 American soldiers left in the country, most of them serving as embassy guards. Bombing was indeed the only available recourse for retaliation.

By then, however, Nixon was no longer willing or able to pull the "hair-trigger" and make the military response Haig had promised back in January to Thieu, Lon Nol, and the Laotian leaders. By April, after the last POWs had returned, it had become obvious to those leaders—and to Haig—that Nixon had no desire to fight Congress for the right to back up his pledges with action.

And there were other signs that Nixon was retreating from any pretense of toughness, including reports that the United States was appeasing the USSR at SALT II, and was also reluctant to take a hard line on human rights and minority emigration in its talks with the USSR.

ON MARCH 30, the Ervin Committee released to the public James Mc-Cord's letter to Judge Sirica, charging that the trial had contained perjured testimony, and implicating (without explicitly naming) higher-ups in the decision to burglarize the DNC headquarters.

John Dean returned from Camp David with no Dean Report; instead, on April 2 he began discussions with prosecutors on what he might offer in exchange for immunity. The prosecutors expressed interest after hearing just a bit of what Dean had to say.

The president, Haldeman, and Ehrlichman soon learned that Dean was negotiating for a deal. On April 14, Nixon asked Ehrlichman what secret, national security–related activities Dean might expose. Ehrlichman cited the 1969–71 wiretaps, the break-in at the office of Ellsberg's psychiatrist, and the Moorer-Radford espionage. Nixon thought he could invoke national security as grounds to refuse to provide details on all three matters—but he worried nonetheless. He decided to fire Dean, though at first he did not demand his resignation. Rather, he had Dean cut off from as many White House activities and sources of information as possible.

The wiretaps and Fielding office break-in were likely to be revealed in Ellsberg's trial for violating the espionage statute by copying and releasing the Pentagon Papers. Ellsberg had been tried the previous year, but Judge Matthew Byrne had declared a mistrial after he was unable to force the administration to give defense attorneys all the evidence in government documents relating to Ellsberg. The administration had provided nothing of substance on that front during the remainder of 1972, and only in late April 1973 were four reports of interviews about Ellsberg "found" in Fred Buzhardt's office. By then the four men had testified in the new trial.

The transcripts of the men's earlier interviews revealed serious discrepancies in their respective testimonies. Judge Byrne threatened to suspend the trial over this. He had already dismissed the most serious count against Ellsberg because the government had withheld DoD analyses dismissing an intimate relationship between the Pentagon Papers and the national defense. Another potential bombshell from the government's files was still hidden but would soon surface: the logs of the 1969–71 wiretaps on which Ellsberg had been heard talking to Morton Halperin.

To refute all these matters, the government called as a rebuttal witness General Haig, who took the stand in full-dress uniform. Newspaper reports noted that Haig's glittering stars and chest full of medals impressed the jurors. On the stand, Haig attacked the credibility of defense witnesses Halperin and Allen Whiting, who had testified that disclosure of the Pentagon Papers could not have damaged U.S. national defense or aided a foreign enemy. Haig's testimony was brief and nasty, especially regarding Halperin, his early rival to become Kissinger's deputy; Haig said that neither Halperin or Whiting knew enough, or were high up enough in the national security hierarchy, to make such judgments. The defense, caught unawares by Haig's sudden appearance, did not have enough information at hand to dispute Haig's false statements. They could have pointed out that Halperin had been in the NSC and at DoD, and that Kissinger had thought well enough of Whiting to accept his analysis on matters regarding China before 1971. "For those few who knew the inner workings of the NSC staff," wrote Roger Morris (once on that staff), "Haig's testimony on the two men amounted to virtual perjury."

Haig was also asked a routine question—whether he knew of any evidence material to the proceedings but not yet presented—and he answered in the negative. That assertion was closer to actual perjury, since Haig did know, in great detail, about the 1969–71 wiretaps. He was one of the few who had read the logs and who knew that Ellsberg had been overheard on the Halperin tap. It had been because Ellsberg had been overheard on the taps that Nixon, in the summer of 1971, had ordered those logs and other evidence of the taps removed from the FBI, to prevent that evidence being presented at the expected trial of Ellsberg. The defense had demanded them in 1972 but the prosecution had not produced them. Now the defense demanded them again.

Attorney General Richard Kleindienst threatened to resign unless he was permitted to send Judge Byrne a memo exposing what the government knew about the Fielding break-in. On April 27, after receiving the document, Byrne read it aloud in open court, spurring a large outcry—and a renewed demand for the wiretap evidence held by the administration. By April 30, Nixon recognized that the 1969–71 wiretaps would soon be revealed to the public, and that these wiretaps and the prior attempts to hide their evidence would further implicate Haldeman and Ehrlichman in the sorts of illegal activities Dean was prepared to tell the world about. Nixon realized he would have to fire Haldeman and Ehrlichman, and they agreed.

On the evening of April 30, Nixon took to the airwaves to accept the resignations of Haldeman, Ehrlichman, and Dean, whom he had kept around
since April 16. He announced that he was replacing Kleindienst with Elliot
Richardson—not because Kleindienst had done anything wrong, but because he had been close to Mitchell. The new attorney general would be
empowered to appoint a special prosecutor for Watergate-related matters.
Before closing, Nixon reminded his audience that he had momentous matters to deal with in foreign affairs, including important meetings on the
future of Europe and the "potentially explosive Middle East."

The White House tapes and logs of the period just after the departure
of Haldeman and Ehrlichman, his two closest associates, convey the sense
of a president precariously afloat on an enormous sea, battered by gale-force
winds—chief among them Dean's accusations, but also the revelations of
the 1969–71 wiretaps and the Plumbers' activities, then surfacing at the Ellsberg trial. Haldeman knew that someone would have to replace him as Nixon's gatekeeper and protector, and he knew the characteristics such a person
must have. It must be someone who had the president's trust, who knew how
the White House worked, and who knew how to get things done—ruthlessly
if necessary. Haldeman could think of only one man who fit this bill: General Alexander Haig. Chuck Colson agreed.

Henry Kissinger objected. For the previous four years, he had technically
reported to Nixon through Haldeman; he had no wish to do so through
Haig, his former subordinate, and would only agree not to oppose Haig publicly in exchange for unfettered future access to Nixon. Haldeman assured
Kissinger that Haig would not stand between him and Nixon.

Joe Califano, legal adviser to the DNC and the *Washington Post*, was one
of Haig's former bosses and a close friend. He told Haig not to take the position at the White House. According to Haig's memoir, Califano saw Nixon
as a marked man: "Don't you know we have this guy?" he says Califano
asked him at the time. ("We've got both of 'em," he continued: Vice President Agnew was then suspected of taking bribes, though the investigation
had not yet been made public.) Haig told Califano he was signing on as
Nixon's chief of staff because as a military officer it was his duty to "take that
hill" even if he died doing it.

On May 3, the general met with the president for five minutes. He began
his job the next day, while Nixon went to Key Biscayne and the Bahamas for
a long weekend.

At this crisis point, a man deeply opposed to Richard Nixon's foreign
policies, and who had his own secret to conceal, ascended to a position of
enormous power in the Nixon White House.

The Haig Administration

Haig in the White House on his first day as White House
Chief of Staff, May 4, 1973. *(UPI Photo, Corbis)*

14

Three Quick Strikes

Alexander Haig entered the White House in early May 1973 with a secret to conceal and an agenda to pursue. The secret was his participation in the Moorer-Radford spy ring. The agenda was his Kraemerite opposition to the Nixon-Kissinger foreign policies. Haig's new position was ideal for achieving these goals, and he furthered them by taking advantage of unexpected opportunities.

In the first months of Haig's tenure as White House chief of staff, Nixon suffered three crippling blows. Previous histories have credited only the revelation of the White House taping system as crucial to Nixon's undoing. But two other, earlier events also contributed to his downfall: the decision to drop the use of executive privilege as a shield to prevent disclosures, and the White House's failure to adequately confront and rebut the testimony of John Dean.

WHEN HAIG TOOK over, Nixon's political situation was bad but was not considered fatal. Of the seventeen former White House and CRP associates under investigation or indictment, only Dean was pointing a finger at Nixon, and he had not yet testified. Polls continued to show that 48 percent approved of Nixon's handling of the presidency; and although 50 percent did think he had a hand in the cover-up of Watergate, a far lower percentage wanted him out of office.

Nixon was drinking more than in past years, according to people in the White House at that time; his secretary, Rose Mary Woods, counted his pills to ensure that he took only his allotted doses of Dilantin, an anti-epileptic medicine known to interact badly with alcohol and to heighten disorientation, and of tulenol, a sleeping draught. In the evenings the mix of liquor and medicine exacerbated Nixon's paranoid tendencies and wish for isolation, and diminished his capacity for reasoned thought. Because Nixon now spent two of every three days out of the White House—at Key Biscayne, San Clemente, or Camp David—Haig's power within the government soon became almost absolute. "Al controlled everything, everybody and everything," Larry Higby recalled. Colonel Jack Brennan, Nixon's military aide, remembered Haig saying, "I'm the hero and I'm saving this guy [who] doesn't know what the hell he's doing." With Kissinger abroad, trying to settle the war in Cambodia and the future of Berlin, Haig became the de facto national security adviser.

Nixon later wrote that he acquiesced in Haig's being "a more rigid administrator," tougher on the Cabinet and other attention-seekers than Haldeman had been:

> Haig purposefully set out to structure this kind of White House operation because he felt that during the first term we had made our big mistakes over little things. Watergate was the most obvious case in point: if it had been handled effectively at the outset, it would never have reached this point. Haig was determined not to let this kind of mistake happen again. To prevent it, he drew more and more authority and responsibility to himself.

Haig advised Nixon to hire legal counsel for Watergate. At first he proffered the highly regarded criminal defense attorney Edward Bennett Williams, although Williams was then representing the *Washington Post*. When Nixon objected, Haig reports in his autobiography, he suggested Califano. When Nixon rejected Califano, Haig "without enthusiasm" nominated his friend J. Fred Buzhardt, who had little criminal trial experience. Buzhardt would retain his post as counsel to DoD while serving as Nixon's in-house lawyer.

Wearing these two hats entailed an enormous conflict of interest. Although Democratic senators soon demanded that Haig resign from the army to fill the civilian post of White House chief of staff (Haig complied), no one objected to having Buzhardt fill the role of defense attorney for the president of the United States while he was still acting as general counsel to the Department of Defense, and his salary was being paid by Defense. As a government lawyer, not a privately paid defense attorney, Buzhardt was required to turn over to the other side any evidence he found of official wrongdoing. He never did.

Buzhardt later said that he was hired on May 4 and came to the White House the following day to confirm that. Yet White House logs show that the president was in Key Biscayne on May 5, so he could not have met Buzhardt that day; they also show that Buzhardt had his first meeting with Nixon at 5:30 P.M. on May 9. This difference is significant because between May 5 and 9 Nixon's ability to remain in office was negatively affected by several matters. The first among these was Haig's learning of the White House taping system. Alexander Butterfield, former Haldeman aide and currently chief of the Federal Aviation Administration, later testified that he told Haig about the system within Haig's first few days as chief of staff, and that Haig responded, "I know about that." Steve Bull, a White House aide who was then in charge of the taping system, also recalls filling in Haig during those first days. Kissinger remembered that Haig informed him of the taping system in May 1973. Haig's knowledge that the tapes existed, and his access to those tapes, would be crucial to the events of that summer.

Another important matter in the May 5–9 period involved the testimony to Congress of General Robert Cushman, the Marine Corps chief and former deputy director of the CIA. In 1971, Cushman had been in charge of the Agency's efforts to assist E. Howard Hunt, including providing Ellsberg's psychological profile and materials for the Fielding office break-ins. In late April 1973, when Hunt told the FBI about the Fielding break-in and the CIA's involvement in it, the road soon led to Cushman. Around May 1 the FBI asked Cushman what he knew, and Cushman admitted to FBI agents that the CIA had helped Hunt. That story broke in the press on May 6.

Cushman, then in Amsterdam, wanted to address the matter at a press conference, but the Pentagon instructed him to say nothing and to return home to make an affidavit about the CIA's assistance to Hunt. The reason for Cushman's abrupt silencing was never given, but Buzhardt, the DoD counsel, likely had a hand in it. This was an early instance of Buzhardt's conflict of interest: What Cushman could testify to, and the materials he could provide as documentation, concerned matters that were very clearly detrimental to the welfare of Buzhardt's new client, President Nixon.

Neither Buzhardt nor Haig informed Nixon that Cushman's testimony could hurt him; nor did they do anything to prevent that testimony. And so, when Cushman testified to three different committees on a single day, May 10, 1973, he established precedent in three ways: by testifying at all, by submitting an affidavit, and by surrendering CIA documents to the legislative branch. Each of these could arguably have been prevented by a presidential claim of executive privilege.

The third matter that arose May 5–9 concerned a series of Cabinet shifts that were announced by the White House on May 10. Though these changes would later be dismissed as a shuffling of deck chairs aboard the *Titanic*, the shifts actually had a specific and decided effect: They brought into positions of power people who were ideologically aligned with Al Haig. Ever since Nixon announced he was sending Richardson to Justice on April 30, for instance, Beltway oddsmakers considered David Packard, longtime assistant secretary of defense, the favorite for the top job, but on May 10 the new nominee was Jim Schlesinger, a consistent opponent of Kissinger and (like Haig and Kraemer) an open skeptic of the administration's position on SALT II. William Colby, a long-serving CIA operative and an old acquaintance of Haig's, was tapped to head the Agency; until Colby's confirmation, Kraemer's and Haig's friend Dick Walters would serve as acting director.

Similarly, Haig influenced a series of White House decisions to bring in from the cold a few former officials and confidants. One was Melvin Laird, who had retired as secretary of defense in January 1973, but now agreed to return as a domestic policy adviser. Laird later said he accepted the offer only after Buzhardt assured him that Nixon was not guilty of the Watergate offenses; he soon learned he wouldn't be allowed to see Nixon privately and was shut out of most policy decisions. Nixon had also asked repeatedly for the return of John Connally, the former secretary of the treasury, whose advice he considered savvy; Connally got a White House office, but Haig closed him off from Nixon as well, and Connally soon returned to Texas.

Haig also muscled to the sidelines Nixon's official counsel, Leonard Garment. Garment's prior legal advice to Nixon had been largely appropriate and sage: In mid-April, for instance, he advised Nixon that because of Dean's revelations, "you are in possession of knowledge that you cannot be in possession of without acting on"—namely, that Haldeman and Ehrlichman had taken part in the cover-up—and that Nixon must therefore fire them in order to protect the presidency. Though Garment retained his job after Haig and Buzhardt took over, he seldom thereafter saw Nixon in person—because, he said, "Haig trusted Buzhardt and not me."

Nixon suffered other blows around this time. On May 10, a grand jury indicted two of his former Cabinet members, Mitchell and Stans, and the House voted for the first time to cut off funding for a Southeast Asian war-related activity, the bombing in Cambodia. Now that the POWs had come home, centrist and conservative Democrats who had previously sided with Nixon on the war had no further reason to do so. Their votes made it possible for the House to pass the bill that cut off funding for bombing in Cambodia. Senate Majority Leader Mansfield then announced that he would insert similar bans into every new appropriations bill until Nixon agreed to halt American participation in all Southeast Asian wars; he did so with the support of Stennis, who had previously backed Nixon on almost every vote.

Stennis said he changed his vote this time because he was incensed that Haig had promised Lon Nol that there would be renewed bombing, and had done so without consulting Congress.

Finally, it was also on May 10 that Judge Byrne suspended the Ellsberg trial over the revelations of the 1969–71 wiretaps—and the revelation of an improper approach by Ehrlichman, who had asked Byrne if he was interested in becoming the new FBI director. On May 11, Byrne declared a mistrial, freeing Ellsberg and his codefendant. "The totality of the circumstances of this case . . . offend a sense of justice," Byrne told the court.

As JAMES SCHLESINGER headed out the CIA door in May 1973 to become secretary of defense, he issued a far-reaching edict: "Any CIA employee who believes that he has received instructions which in any way appear inconsistent with the CIA legislative charter shall inform the Director of Central Intelligence immediately." This demand led directly to the release of the most damaging information about Richard Nixon: Haldeman's June 23, 1972, instruction to the CIA to "block" the FBI's investigation.

That order surfaced as a result of Schlesinger summoning Dick Walters home from Taiwan to prepare materials on the CIA's involvement in Watergate, as requested by the Senate Armed Services Committee. Schlesinger was so eager for this information that he sent a helicopter to meet Walters when his plane landed and fly him directly to Langley to get to work. As Schlesinger knew—because Walters had told him so in February—the deputy director had in his safe eight memcons about meetings and phone calls in June–July 1972 covering the effort to have the CIA block the FBI's investigation of the burglars' money trail and detailing Dean's attempts to have the CIA pay bail and stipends for the burglars.

On May 10, Walters retrieved the memcons from his safe and made an affidavit based on them. Curiously, he then took the affidavit to an outside notary to be certified as authentic. On May 11, at Haig's request, Walters arrived at the White House, handed Haig copies of the eight memcons, and showed him the notarized affidavit. He told Haig he was to testify on Monday and, according to Walters' autobiography, brought up the matter of executive privilege, saying that he recognized that Nixon could forbid him to testify on those grounds. In saying this, perhaps Walters felt he was discharging his duty to Nixon as an old friend, even though Nixon had treated him cavalierly in the recent past.

Haig immediately gave the memcon copies to Buzhardt and sent Walters back to the CIA with instructions to sit tight until Haig met with Nixon on the matter at midday. In that meeting, recorded by the White House taping system, Haig rang the alarm bell. He bluntly told Nixon that Walters had a new incoming missile that he and Buzhardt judged as "quite damaging" and briefly laid out the dangerous information about the June 23 meeting—though he stressed, as he said Walters had, Dean's subsequent role in pushing the CIA to take responsibility for and pay for the burglars.

Haig's emphasis on Dean's role, rather than on the explosive revelation that Haldeman and Ehrlichman had told the CIA to block the FBI's investigation into Watergate, distracted Nixon by feeding into his focus on Dean, his chief accuser. Haig pointed out that Walters said he and the CIA had resisted Dean's pleas; Nixon was happy to hear it. Haig further reported that Walters had come to the White House because Schlesinger had instructed him to deliver copies of the memcons there and to the attorney general, but "we sent [Walters] back to the agency, told him not to take any telephone calls, [and] return here immediately with every copy [of the memcons]. And these are vital national security matters and cannot go anywhere." Haig had also warned Schlesinger that the White House was "reviewing the memcons for—for executive privilege due to the whole broad character of it."

Nixon expressed relief: The news was bad, but he took sustenance from Haig's assurance that Walters and Schlesinger would protect the president. Even so, later in the conversation with Haig, Nixon was adamant about what should be done: "Walters' memcons should not get out," and executive privilege should be invoked to cover the memcons and to prevent Walters from testifying. Just as he wouldn't allow Haldeman or Ehrlichman to give Congress any papers they had compiled while in the White House—those papers rested in a White House safe—Nixon insisted he wouldn't allow Walters to give Congress the memcons or to testify.

In the end, of course, none of these decisions in regard to Walters held. The White House did not invoke executive privilege. Dick Walters did testify. And his memcons did "get out," causing immense damage by revealing Nixon's attempt, six days after the Watergate burglary, to have the CIA block the FBI.

Nixon's chief concern on May 11 was with Walters's documents. He understood that Walters would testify to the Senate Armed Services Committee on Monday, May 14, about CIA involvement in Watergate, but he was too preoccupied with the potentially damaging ramifications of the memcons to recognize the danger of Walters actually testifying. The White House tapes contain no evidence that Haig even mentioned to Nixon that Walters was apparently willing to be barred from testifying. Haig knew that Nixon avoided unpleasant truths, so after giving Nixon the bad news about the memcons he stressed the good: that if Haldeman and Ehrlichman would say that their directive on June 23, 1972, had been made in a legitimate context, Walters's testimony and memcons would help Nixon rather than harm him.

Nixon grasped at the straw Haig offered. He summoned Haldeman, who arrived in ten minutes. When Haldeman learned of the Walters memcons he recognized that they could mean trouble, even though he was not allowed to view the documents themselves. The former chief of staff was adamant that executive privilege be invoked, to cover not only what the president had said to him (on June 23 and at any other time) but also all documents. His lawyers had told him, and he repeated for Nixon, that "executive privilege is an objective and selective judgment on the part of the President. . . . And it can be made case-by-case, totally selectively. It can be made paper-by-paper. Obviously you weaken your case every time you let the bar down at all. You make it harder to keep it up for the next one."

Haldeman recalled that Nixon and he had wanted the CIA to *limit*, not to block, the FBI, because the FBI was wandering too far off the trail of the burglars and effectively inserting itself into a political matter it had no business investigating. This recollection clashed seriously with the account of the June 23 event in the Walters memcon, but, as Haldeman later emphasized, he did not see the memcon on May 11. Nor did Haig ask Haldeman for further details (from his memory or notes) that might have challenged Walters's account. Rather, after Haldeman left the Oval Office, Haig returned to tell Nixon that, upon further review of the memcons, Buzhardt now believed they were "very damaging to John and Bob." Buzhardt, Haig reported, now saw Ehrlichman and Haldeman as "guilty." This shocked Nixon, who considered Buzhardt a hardheaded analyst. To protect Haldeman and Ehrlichman, the president now suggested that Walters make up "a sanitized version, with all the national security stuff out." It is unclear whether Nixon expected Walters simply to delete "national security" matters from his memo, or to write a wholly new, shorter, "sanitized" summary of it. In any case, Haig immediately demurred. "I don't trust Walters to do that," Haig said; the memcons were "so detailed, so precise" that a cut-down version would be suspect.

Nixon fled to Camp David. That Saturday, Haig phoned to tell him that Cushman had testified to three congressional committees and had given them CIA memoranda on Hunt—actions that set precedent for further such cooperation. "We're just going to have to take the heat, Mr. President," Haig told Nixon. They must instruct Walters to testify and to turn over his papers. They had no choice.

It was a highly questionable recommendation. As Haldeman had told Nixon, executive privilege could be invoked selectively, on a case-by-case basis. Although any specific invocation of the privilege could be challenged by Congress, they were powerless to gainsay it. Yet Haig now insisted that Nixon must allow Walters to testify and to release the memcons. To ease the pain, Haig told Nixon that the memcons were "very helpful and very clean" because they pinned the blame on Dean for his attempts to make the CIA bear responsibility for the burglars. "Why are [the memcons] helpful?" Nixon asked once more.

"Helpful in the context that here was the real bad guy [Dean] that was putting the wrong kind of twist into it, and the fact that he couldn't ever— you see, if he had had presidential authority . . . when he got continually stymied—God, he would have used [that authority] ten times over," Haig said.

Haig's "real bad guy" dust blinded Nixon. By seven o'clock Saturday evening, Nixon had accepted that Walters must testify and was reduced to pleading that the deputy director not tell the committee, "Look, they called us in and tried to ask [us] to fix the case and I, we wouldn't do it." Haig assured Nixon that Walters was trustworthy and loyal, bolstering his case by pointing out that he and Walters had collaborated on a few secret things and had never told Nixon. As Haig correctly figured, the president was comforted by the idea that his soldiers had been protecting him even behind his back.

The following day, Haig offered Nixon two new reasons to release the memcons. First, like any diary, they were likely to be considered self-serving and thus suspect. Second, he pointed out, "You did furnish Cushman's memcons to both the committee and the grand jury."

"You really wonder, though," Nixon said, "how you can justify giving them Cushman's and not giving them Walters'."

To this, Haig said, Buzhardt had an answer: They could be withheld under a "broad statement that they contain national security."

The national security rationale resonated with Nixon, and he decided to withhold the memcons. But Haig and Buzhardt did not advise Nixon that allowing Walters to testify to the *contents* of the memcons, and on the basis of a sworn affidavit detailing that content, would let the cat out of the bag, and moot the withholding of the actual papers.

On Monday, May 14, Walters appeared before the Senate Armed Services Committee. In his testimony, he elevated the alleged crimes committed by Haldeman and Ehrlichman from complicity in a mild cover-up of a failed burglary to a high-level obstruction of justice—directing the CIA to impede the FBI's investigation of criminal wrongdoing. Although Walters's appearance was held behind closed doors, the following day Senator Stuart Symington released to the press a long statement detailing what Walters had said. The immediate uproar about an obstruction of justice badly injured Nixon.

But the Walters testimony had another disastrous though previously hidden consequence for Nixon: It pointed Haig and Buzhardt to the White House tapes for June 23, 1972—tapes that would likely confirm Walters's memories of his meeting with Haldeman, Ehrlichman, and Helms. In those tapes, far more than in the March 21 "cancer upon the presidency" tape Nixon was worried about, lay critical proof that Nixon had ordered an obstruction of justice—an impeachable offense.

THE PROSPECT OF John Dean poised to testify to the Senate and to the nation, on live television, convinced Nixon that he needed to issue a preemptive statement regarding what Dean could be expected to say. He also needed to provide an explanation for the Huston Plan, a copy of which Dean had managed to take with him, and to explain other matters being bruited about in public, including the Fielding office break-in, the 1969–71 wiretaps, the Plumbers' other activities, and the Walters memcons. Nixon was also convinced that he needed to issue definitive denials that he had known in advance of the Watergate burglary or ever discussed paying hush money to the burglars.

Between May 15 and May 22, Buzhardt and Haig worked on this all-in-one statement with Ziegler and two speechwriters. They touched base with dozens of other people to compile Nixon's answers to questions that had been asked before and that they presumed would be asked now.

Haig was distracted from his work that week by his need to defend himself and Kissinger. Learning that Seymour Hersh of the *New York Times* was about to publish a story attributing the 1969–71 wiretaps to Kissinger's instigation, Haig tried to dissuade the reporter from publishing on the grounds that both Hersh and Kissinger were Jewish. "Do you honestly believe that Henry Kissinger, a Jewish refugee from Germany who lost thirteen members of his family to the Nazis, could engage in such police-state tactics as [to] wiretap his own aides?" Hersh did not yield to the pressure, and the *Times* printed the story.

Sven Kraemer later commented that in this period Haig repeatedly protected Kissinger for reasons that defied logic and past mutual acrimony. But in protecting Kissinger, Haig was also protecting himself. He did so, in part, by having Nixon take the blame—persuading Nixon to assert in the forthcoming statement that "I authorized the entire program" of wiretapping, for instance, which took the heat off Kissinger and Haig, even though Nixon privately told Ziegler that "Henry ordered the whole goddamn thing." Kissinger had devoured the wiretap logs, Nixon insisted. "He reveled in it, he groveled in it, he wallowed in it!" he shouted.

The statement Haig and Buzhardt were preparing became even more important on the morning of May 16, when the *Washington Post* printed a lengthy Bernstein and Woodward story about various "Watergate" activities—including the 1969–71 wiretaps—under a banner headline running across the entire front page: "Vast GOP Undercover Operation Origins." From the early morning of that day, Nixon met for hours with Buzhardt, Haig, and Ziegler on how to respond—before deciding, ultimately, to do so only in the May 22 statement.

On that evening of May 16, according to *All the President's Men*, the source Woodward called Deep Throat told him about the statement preparation meetings and the vulnerabilities the writers had discussed with Nixon, most of them pertaining to the March 21 Dean meeting: the raising of executive clemency, Dean's dealings with Liddy, and Hunt's attempts to obtain hush money. The next day, Woodward contacted his lifelong friend Scott Armstrong, one of the Senate Watergate Committee's investigators (hired on his recommendation), and urged the committee to call Alexander Butterfield as a witness.

By May 1973 Butterfield had become the FAA administrator. Before that he had been a White House assistant to Haldeman, unknown to the public. The committee had little ostensible reason to call him. We believe that Woodward urged them to do so because he knew that Butterfield could reveal the White House taping system. The fact that the committee initially ignored Woodward's pleas suggests that the senators and investigators had no idea what Butterfield's testimony might disclose.

On May 22, the White House issued Nixon's four-thousand-word statement. "Already, on the basis of second- and third-hand hearsay testimony by persons either convicted or themselves under investigation in the case, I have found myself accused of involvement in activities I never heard of until I read about them in news accounts," it began. The statement covered a wide array of subjects, from alleged payoffs to the Watergate burglars to wiretapping, the Huston Plan, and the Plumbers. Most of the paragraphs dealt with matters that Nixon said involved "national security." On the wiretapping of reporters and others, Nixon stated, "a special program of wiretaps was initiated in mid-1969 and terminated in February 1971. . . . I authorized this entire program." Nixon also asserted that these wiretaps "were legal at the time." He admitted that many details of the Huston Plan that had been aired in public were true, saying, "The options initially approved had included authorization for surreptitious entry—breaking and entering, in effect—on specified categories of targets in specified situations related to national security." He revealed that he had authorized the Plumbers the week after the publication of the Pentagon Papers, and that their "principal purpose was to stop security leaks and to investigate other sensitive security matters."

Many of the statement's assertions painted Nixon into corners. One, noted above, was his claim of sole responsibility for the 1969–71 wiretaps. A second concerned the subject of the Walters 1972 memcons. In the statement, Nixon lumped the Walters matter together with quite different subjects: Because of "the scale of national priorities with which I had to deal," Nixon said, he had to ensure "that neither the covert operations of the CIA nor the operations of the [Plumbers] should be compromised. It was certainly not my intent, nor my wish, that the investigation of Watergate be impeded in any way." That assertion raised more questions than it answered. A third corner: "Executive privilege will not be invoked as to any testimony concerning possible criminal conduct in the matters presently under investigation, including the Watergate affair and the alleged cover-up." This unequivocal stance precluded Nixon from later arguing against the release of the White House tapes, or against insiders divulging knowledge of the tapes.

Even as the press and the public were parsing this May 22 statement, the next day Buzhardt issued new restrictions on Haldeman's and Ehrlichman's access to their papers that were still in White House hands. Until then, the two former aides had been permitted to take notes as they reviewed papers and to make occasional copies; henceforth they were forbidden to make any copies or even to take notes while in the room with their papers. This would hamper their ability to defend themselves in court.

In the wake of the May 22 statement, Nixon faced a hailstorm of criticism. At one o'clock on the morning of May 25, Nixon phoned Haig to ask, "Wouldn't it be better to just check out?" Nixon probably meant he should just resign. When Haig demurred, Nixon said, "No, no, seriously; because, you see, I'm not at my best. I've got to be at my best and that means fighting this damned battle, fighting it all out." But soon the president thrust the thought aside in preparation for two climactic events: Leonid Brezhnev's impending visit, and John Dean's expected Senate testimony.

When the May 22 statement failed to alleviate the pressure on Nixon, Buzhardt and Haig prodded Nixon to listen to the tapes so that he could respond even more directly and in detail to Dean. This request took on special urgency after a lengthy Bernstein and Woodward article on June 3, 1973, recounting in great detail what John Dean was prepared to testify to: some thirty-five meetings with the president.

On June 4, 1973, Nixon spent all of his office hours listening to the tapes. During the morning he took extensive notes as he listened; then, near lunchtime, according to an account in Woodward and Bernstein's *The*

Final Days, he called in Buzhardt to review the notes with him. Then, alone again, he plunged back into the tapes. Late that day, Nixon recounted to Buzhardt his own versions of what had been said on twenty tapes. According to Woodward and Bernstein, as the president spoke Buzhardt began taking notes. These included Nixon saying that Dean had told him about Strachan on March 13, and quoting the March 16 line "not a scintilla of evidence." Buzhardt's notes did not become extensive until Nixon began to read from his own notes about the March 21 recording, at which point Buzhardt, in the recounting of the scene by Woodward and Bernstein, felt "waves of uneasiness [and] saw the intrinsic contradictions. . . . The more Nixon read, the more Buzhardt realized that John Dean had a case."

No competent defense attorney would have accepted at face value his client's account of such key pieces of potential evidence. Any such attorney would have insisted on listening to every Nixon-Dean tape himself, since that was where evidence impugning the accuracy and self-serving nature of Dean's expected Senate testimony could likely be found. But Buzhardt did not do that. Nor did he suggest destroying the tapes, which had not yet been requested as evidence and were the president's property and thus within his legal right to destroy—even though such an action would have protected Buzhardt's client from later being hoist on their petard.

Late in the day on June 4, Nixon phoned Haldeman to say that he had listened to the tapes and that "the only thing he [Dean] has in there, which he did hit about the seventeenth, or maybe the fourteenth, was that Strachan might be involved in terms of getting material"—that is, that Strachan might have received the fruits of the burglaries or wiretaps. "That was a 'might,'" Haldeman echoed, "and there's still doubt about that."

This Nixon-Haldeman conversation is revelatory about the president's unwillingness to understand his own predicament. He has listened to a tape of Dean admitting Strachan's involvement, among other matters, and has misperceived it rather completely. He has also listened to other tapes that contain material quite detrimental to him, and missed their importance and potential impact, should they ever be released. And now he was attempting to embed these misperceptions in the mind of his former chief confidant.

On June 6 and 11, Buzhardt met with the Senate committee minority counsel, Fred Thompson, to prep him to question Dean before the committee. An affidavit written by Thompson suggests that some details of Buzhardt's account differed from what Nixon had told him. For instance, the reference to Strachan definitely having early knowledge of the break-in was altered. Buzhardt apparently used the phrase "could be" to characterize that knowledge. Buzhardt also made no mention of the "not a scintilla of evidence" claim.

Before Dean could appear, however, Senate Majority Leader Mike Mansfield agreed to postpone his testimony for eight days, so that the president could meet Soviet premier Leonid Brezhnev without the distraction of ongoing Senate hearings.

SIX MONTHS EARLIER, Nixon had set high goals for this summit. But between the efforts of Scoop Jackson and his handpicked U.S. contingent of SALT negotiators to slow the progress of détente, and the far-reaching agreement Brezhnev had recently signed with West Germany, the results of the summit were destined to be limited. The heads of state signed minor pacts— on air transport, agriculture, and joint scientific study of the oceans—but the agreement-to-agree to SALT gave the Russians another year to finish testing their MIRVs before they had to sign a limiting pledge. Brezhnev visited the Senate but ran up against obdurate opposition from Jackson, who succeeded in quashing the trade deal Brezhnev wanted and in holding Russia's MFN status hostage to better conditions for Jewish and other ethnic emigration and to better "human rights" treatment.

For these sorts of roadblocks, Kissinger blamed Jackson's adviser Richard Perle. Kissinger later credited Perle with "one of ablest geopolitical minds I have ever encountered," and with being "the chief designer of Jackson's confrontation with Nixon."

Far too intelligent not to have realized that some of the charges he was making were more cynical than substantive, Perle [aimed] to stymie the administration's arms control policies by submerging them in technical controversies, to block trade with the Soviet Union by making it dependent on changes in Soviet emigration policies, and to isolate the administration by accusing it of indifference to human rights. . . . Jackson and his neoconservative supporters spawned the myth that Nixon was sacrificing American military security on the altar of arms control theory.

The day after Brezhnev left the United States, John Dean began his Senate testimony. For six hours he read from a prepared statement, and what he had to say, then and during the four days of questioning that followed, electrified the senators and a public that was riveted by the nationally televised coverage. Buzhardt had been alerted to what Dean would say by Thompson, who briefed him on Dean's testimony in camera of June 16, but Buzhardt failed to gave Thompson the ammunition he needed to skewer Dean's public testimony. This allowed Dean to conceal that he had known that some White House staffers had advance knowledge of the Watergate break-in for nine months before he told Nixon about it in March 1973. Had the senators and the public understood this fact, it would have seriously diminished Dean's credibility.

The White House got a second chance at Dean, via a memo Buzhardt provided to the Senate committee that supposedly took into account what Dean had already testified to and tried to impugn it. Signed by Buzhardt, but prepared largely by Garment, it became known as the "Golden Boy memo" because it presented the fair-haired Dean, whom the White House had viewed as a young man of great promise, as involved in planning the break-in and even masterminding the cover-up.

As *Time* magazine reported, however, the questions "failed to rattle the accuser. Contradicting point after point in quick response, Dean easily handled the attack." Dean could deflect the Golden Boy memo because it failed to make use of the information in Buzhardt's possession. The questioners made no reference to whether Dean had told Nixon about Strachan on March 13; nor did they demand that Dean respond to the Walters memcons. Portions of the memcons had been leaked to the *New York Times*, which printed excerpts, but Buzhardt had the complete documents, and their details could have provided serious ammunition for a sharp questioning of Dean's motives and actions. Without that ammunition, the committee could not effectively counter Dean's denial that he had suggested using the CIA to block the FBI, or refute his characterization of the June 23–28 Walters contacts, which he said had been at Walters's instigation, not his.

As Dean neared the end of his testimony, Buzhardt stopped Laird in the halls of the White House to say that he had previously "misled" his former boss. "I was wrong," Buzhardt now said, as Laird later recalled it. "The President did have knowledge, and I've just got to level with you."

Later, Buzhardt would contend that Nixon never let anyone listen to the tapes, and that he, Buzhardt, had chosen not to listen to them on principle, because as an officer of the court he would then have had to disclose information of the sort that he referred to as "a smoking pistol." But over the summer of 1973, when Nixon was in California and wanted to hear one particular tape, a courier to take it to him could not be arranged, so Nixon asked Buzhardt to listen and tell him what it said.

After Dean's testimony, polls continued to show that it was still only his word against the president's, and that if Dean's allegations could not be proved by anything other than his say-so, most people still gave Nixon the benefit of the doubt. Nine months earlier, Nixon had been reelected by the largest electoral landslide in American history; few people had an appetite for overturning that mandate.

Then, suddenly, it became possible to prove or disprove Dean's allegations. On July 5, Senate Watergate Committee staff spoke with Larry Higby, formerly Haldeman's closest assistant, who had continued on in the White House after Haig had replaced Haldeman. Higby had known about the taping system since its inception. He was one of those who informed Haig about it early in Haig's tenure as chief of staff.

Haldeman had told Higby that if the Senate committee staff brought up the taping system, he must claim executive privilege. But on July 5, Higby finessed the staffers' questions and escaped without mentioning the taping system or needing to claim executive privilege. Higby later recalled that the staffers had not shown him the affidavit Thompson had prepared based on his talks with Buzhardt.

On July 6, Higby told Haig about the committee's questions and speculated that the committee would eventually unearth the taping system. Haig acted surprised to learn that such a taping system existed, and told Higby, "I'll get back to you." Haig's surprise was feigned. Several accounts, including Higby's own, confirm that Haig had learned of the taping system early. The absolute latest he could have known about it was June 4, the day Nixon spent listening to tapes.

On July 7, Haig told Higby that if he were asked about the taping system, he should "tell the truth"—a directive that shocked Higby, who had expected Haig, like Haldeman, to tell him not to say anything because the taping system was covered by executive privilege.

As it happened, Higby was not summoned to testify. Instead, Woodward brought to the committee's attention, for a second time, the name of Alexander Butterfield. On Friday, July 13—a day Nixon spent at Bethesda Naval Hospital with viral pneumonia—investigators Scott Armstrong and Don Sanders interrogated Butterfield.

While Nixon, despite his illness, was conducting business in his hospital room—he saw Haig and Ziegler, and had substantive phone conversations with Kissinger and treasury secretary Shultz—the two Senate committee staffers questioned Butterfield. They had in hand the month-old Thompson affidavit, with its very detailed recounting of some Nixon-Dean conversations, which had ostensibly been given to Thompson to impugn Dean. But Armstrong, Woodward's friend, used it on July 13 for precisely the opposite purpose: After having Butterfield read the memo, he had Sanders ask how the president could have had such a detailed recollection of events. Since the question did not specifically mention a taping system, Butterfield ducked it. Later, after several hours of grilling on other subjects, Sanders asked a more direct query: Would Dean have had reason to believe that a particular conversation with Nixon was taped? Is it possible that "conversations in the

President's office are recorded"? Butterfield immediately confirmed the existence of the taping system.

On a flight to New Hampshire for an FAA event the next day, Saturday, Butterfield compiled thirty-one handwritten pages of notes on what he would say if he had to testify. But he later asserted that he did not phone the White House to advise that he might be called, or to seek guidance on whether his testimony might be blocked by executive privilege.

Sam Ervin and Howard Baker, the committee's leaders, planned to call Butterfield to testify on Monday; fearing a leak, they did not alert the other committee members. Yet somehow Haig learned on Saturday that the taping system might be revealed, and on Sunday Thompson phoned Buzhardt to alert him that the committee was aware that "every conversation in the White House is on tape," and to instruct him to ready those tapes to be turned over. Scott Armstrong later recalled his outrage that Thompson had tipped off Buzhardt: "When the prosecutor discovers the smoking gun, he's going to be shocked to find that the deputy prosecutor [has] called the defendant and said, 'You'd better get rid of that gun.'"

Woodward also learned of the taping system on Saturday, in a call from the committee staff (though he has denied that it came from Armstrong). Woodward then informed Bernstein that a taping system existed, but at first the duo did not write about it. Concerned "about a White House set-up," as they put it in *All the President's Men*, they "decided not to pursue the story for the moment." When they informed Ben Bradlee of the impending testimony about the taping system, he rated the story a "B+" and decided not to print it.

On Monday, when the taping system was revealed, the news was labeled "the story of the century," so the *Post*'s stated rationale for not publishing it Sunday or Monday—that it wasn't a good enough story—is hard to believe. But not printing it did serve to keep the impending revelation secret, thus avoiding the possibility that Nixon might try to stop Butterfield or anyone else who knew of the system from testifying. Later Buzhardt and Haig asserted that they hadn't told Nixon that the taping system was about to be revealed because he was too ill to be disturbed. But Nixon had been well enough to see visitors, conduct official business, and talk on the phone with Haig several times on Sunday. Moreover, a cardinal rule in politics is to never let bad news surprise the boss, and the revelation of the taping system was bad news indeed.

When Butterfield returned to Washington on Sunday, the committee told him to be ready to testify the following day. Howard Baker suggested that Butterfield call the White House. In a later interview, Butterfield said that he didn't phone Haig, his close friend; instead he left a message for

Garment, who knew very little of the matter. After checking with Haig, Garment returned Butterfield's call. In that conversation, both Butterfield and Garment later separately recalled, Garment gave Butterfield no instructions forbidding him to testify or if forced to testify, to refuse to answer questions about the taping system by saying that the subject was covered by executive privilege. And even after the Butterfield-Garment calls, no one in the White House told Nixon that the taping system was about to be revealed.

What would the president have done if he had been alerted of Butterfield's impending testimony before the fact? He would almost certainly have moved to block the testimony on the grounds of executive privilege. As Nixon later wrote, he was shocked when he learned—too late to prevent it—of Butterfield's testimony: "I thought that at least executive privilege would have been raised by any staff member before verifying [the taping system's] existence." Once the taping system did surface, after all, Nixon ordered Shultz to shield it on exactly those grounds. Shultz soon issued a letter saying that no Secret Service agent could testify about things learned in the course of his duties at the White House.

Shultz's shielding letter arrived at the committee as Ervin and Baker were preparing to question a Secret Service agent, who thereafter refused to testify. But the moment that Butterfield completed his testimony, another letter to Ervin arrived—from Buzhardt, confirming that a presidential taping system had been active since 1971.

Nixon could still have destroyed the tapes, claiming that considerations of executive privilege, national security, and privacy demanded such an action. Joe Califano, for one, later asserted that Nixon would have been able to weather the storm such a bonfire would have caused. After the tapes were revealed in public, however, Garment opined that they were now sought-after evidence in criminal trials and Senate hearings and therefore it would be criminal to destroy them.

According to Haig's autobiography, Buzhardt was concerned that the tapes likely contained material—"offhand remarks"—that would be "misunderstood and misconstrued, and . . . very damaging if exposed in raw form to the world." This was reason enough for the tapes to be destroyed, he argued. But Nixon later recalled Haig warning that destroying them would "forever seal an impression of guilt in the public mind." Nixon agreed with him, and the tapes were spared. Haig would still later call the failure to destroy the tapes Nixon's "big mistake," but according to Nixon's memory, Haig himself was among those who argued for preserving them. (Nixon himself soon regretted the decision: On July 19 he wrote on his bedside pad, "Should have destroyed the tapes after April 30, 1973.")

Nixon's approval ratings plummeted after the taping system was revealed.

The press and the public clamored for Nixon to release the tapes of conversations between himself and Dean. The special prosecutor, Archibald Cox, and the Senate Watergate Committee both called for the release of those tapes. If the White House refused to release them, Sam Ervin told reporters, "I would inform the President that the committee was going to hold him guilty," presumably of withholding evidence of criminal conduct.

Most people did not yet think the president guilty of a crime; they continued to believe, as *Time* put it, that the tapes when released would be subject to "semantic shadings, conversational contexts, and inconclusive interpretations of what the participants in presidential dialogues really meant." But most people now believed that Nixon no longer had a valid legal justification to hold back the tapes.

In 1971, HAIG, pursuing Kraemerite goals in an attempt to block Nixon's foreign policy advances, had undermined the president by taking part in the Moorer-Radford espionage ring. Haig had been relatively junior then. In the early summer of 1973, as White House chief of staff, Haig once again stepped in at a critical moment in the Nixon administration and altered the course of events—this time far more seriously, and with disastrous results for the president. As the fall of 1973 approached, it seemed as though only one question remained for Haig: Would his goals be better served if the weakened president remained in office or if he were forced out?

15

Nullifying Nixon

During the summer and fall of 1973, men associated with the theories of Fritz Kraemer—especially Alexander Haig, but also James Schlesinger and others—used their new positions of responsibility to bring Nixon's foreign policies to a halt. While they did not instigate the key events themselves, they seized on them to weaken Nixon at every turn.

FRITZ KRAEMER TURNED sixty-five on July 3, 1973, just as John Dean wrapped up his Senate testimony. At a birthday party that General Walters helped organize, Kraemer was presented with a Wilkinson sword encased in a cane and inscribed with the words "Strategist, Scholar, Counselor, Patriot." Ed Rowny played Kraemer's favorite songs on a harmonica; Kissinger and Haig sent telegrams from San Clemente. "Your integrity and selflessness have inspired all those whose lives you touched," Kissinger wrote. "Those of us who have known you are indeed fortunate." Nuclear strategist Herman Kahn's tribute was typical: "If there is anyone in the Pentagon who has stood for the good and true, in terms that we simply no longer use as much as we should, it is Fritz Kraemer." Kraemer held back tears, telling his friends, "A man doesn't cry on a night like this."

Kraemer was still very active, a popular lecturer at the war colleges and service colleges; in later years he let the steel in the sword-cane show, to command his audience's attention. As one colleague recalled, he also became a bit garrulous as he aged: "When it came time for him to leave my office I had literally to push him out the door, still talking and wildly gesticulating."

A few days after the party, Kissinger phoned Kraemer and asked to see him that evening to discuss "where the country is in foreign policy—I mean what can realistically be done—and what I should do now."

"You know my answer beforehand," Kraemer put in.

"I know that I can't leave now . . . but still, one has to discuss how one can—let's talk about it tonight." The prospect that Kissinger might be elevated to secretary of state had been broached, but given Nixon's increasingly shaky fortunes, Kissinger was uncertain as to whether he should push for this prize.

Kraemer evidently took this uncertainty as an occasion to step up his production of strategy papers for Kissinger. Ten days later they discussed two of these—one on dealing with the Soviets and a second on how to counter attempts that certain Cambodian factions were making to "cash in on our present weakness," as Kraemer put it—that is, the weakness caused by America's withdrawal from Southeast Asia. "They know very well that on a given date we must stop" the bombing in Cambodia, Kraemer explained to Kissinger. "They said to themselves, 'The U.S. is in a bind, we are in a bind, but we just by being iron-hard can get something.'"

"Okay, I now understand," Kissinger allowed. Kraemer urged him to reread his papers just to be sure.

If Kissinger no longer listened quite as closely to Kraemer, there was another who did: Secretary of Defense James Schlesinger. Kraemer had previously enjoyed some influence over individual service secretaries, but he had clashed repeatedly with Schlesinger's predecessors as secretary of defense, McNamara and Laird. Schlesinger and Kraemer shared a mutual friend, Scoop Jackson, and similar passions. They liked military music, they attended Lutheran churches—Schlesinger, born a Jew, had converted in his twenties—they were firmly anti-Soviet, and they were both intellectuals who characterized themselves as anti-intellectuals; Schlesinger's belief that the concept of an intelligentsia sprang from Marxist theory brought a smile to Kraemer. Shortly after Schlesinger's installation at the Pentagon, he likened détente to a velvet glove encasing a mailed fist, an analogy Kraemer admired. More important, Kraemer and Schlesinger agreed that the United States could trust neither the Soviets nor the Chinese in critical matters. As Kissinger would later write, "Schlesinger persuaded Kraemer that he was in sympathy with his approach." Schlesinger must also have recognized that Kraemer's word carried weight with Haig—and by that point getting something done by the White House meant persuading Haig.

At this moment it had also become clear to most American politicians and foreign governments that if Kissinger weren't promoted soon to secretary of state he would leave the administration, a departure that would doubtless hasten its collapse. For Fritz Kraemer, Kissinger's elevation would mean he was finally achieving his dream of being adviser to a foreign secretary. Yet it would come at a moment when Kraemer's aversion to Kissinger's personal conduct and approaches to dealing with America's enemies was reaching full strength. Kraemer had always warned of the dangers of a foreign secretary amassing too much personal power—and, as it became clear that Kissinger was likely to retain his post as national security adviser while becoming secretary of state, that was exactly what was about to happen.

Kissinger viewed his new dual responsibilities as two halves of the same foreign policy task. More fundamentally, though, he rejected Kraemer's reasoning on principle, arguing Kraemer could only cling to such rigid theories of ministerial propriety because he had no actual policy responsibilities. Kissinger, on the other hand, had nearly total responsibility for making and administering U.S. foreign policy. He had to maneuver in a real world far too complex to be explained by Kraemer's categorizations, a world that required subtle calibration of America's positions based on the country's military, economic, and political realities and aspirations. He could not chop these problems down to size until they fit on the Procrustean bed of Kraemer's principles. "Kraemer's values were absolute," Kissinger would later say in his eulogy, "he treated intermediate solutions as derogations from principle. And therein lay the source of our . . . estrangement. . . . For the prophet, there can be no gap between conception and implementation; the policymaker must build the necessary from the possible. . . . Kraemer could not accept this distinction." As a result, Kissinger suggested, "We began to see less of one another, largely because I found the gap between [Kraemer's] expectations and what I could deliver increasingly painful."

Within two years, Kraemer and Kissinger would break off relations. They would not speak again for thirty years. And in the summer of 1973, as that chasm was beginning to widen, Fritz Kraemer shifted his attentions to Schlesinger.

Another reason for Kraemer's enthusiasm for Schlesinger was that the new defense secretary had brought Andrew Marshall and his Office of Net Assessment from the NSC into the Pentagon. For Schlesinger, Marshall and Kraemer became complementary voices. Fritz was strategy, Andy was tactics; Fritz was interested in geopolitical theory, Andy in future weapons systems. And on the major challenges of the moment—not trusting the Soviets or Chinese, preventing provocative weakness, and assuring that the United States remained the dominant power in the world—Kraemer, Marshall, Schlesinger, Jackson, and Haig all agreed.

In this period they combined forces to block Nixon's foreign policies, usually by countering Kissinger. When Kissinger made a SALT proposal that seemed to favor the Soviets, Haig helped Ed Rowny and Paul Nitze table it. When Kissinger testified before Congress, especially on aspects of détente, his questioners were often able to cite leaked CIA or DoD documents to impugn or refute his positions. Even as popular enthusiasm mounted for Kissinger becoming secretary of state, Haig and other powerful Kraemerites were using their positions to halt the administration's progress on concluding new treaties and slowing the arms race.

In later years, the Arms Control and Disarmament Agency would come to be known as one of the two birthplaces of the neocons; the other was Scoop Jackson's Senate office. In the Jackson office, the group included Perle, Douglas Feith, and Elliott Abrams. The ACDA office—thanks to Jackson's intervention—now featured Iklé, Rowny, Nitze, and new hire Paul Wolfowitz. Sven Kraemer, the NSC's arms control expert, befriended Wolfowitz and brought him to meet his father, and soon Wolfowitz became an admirer of Fritz Kraemer, frequently amazed, he later wrote, at the perspicacity of Kraemer's predictions about world events.

President Nixon was beginning to comprehend the full force of one of those predictions. During their October 1972 meeting, Kraemer had outlined what he thought would be the inevitable consequences of ending the war in Vietnam on improper terms. One such result now devolved from Nixon's ongoing clash with Senate Majority Leader Mike Mansfield, who had threatened to shut down the federal government by holding up appropriations bills unless Nixon agreed not to initiate any further military action in Southeast Asia after August 15, 1973, without express permission from Congress. Afraid that a governmental shutdown at this point would cost him even more congressional support, Nixon accepted Mansfield's strictures, although warning Mansfield and House Speaker Carl Albert in a public letter of "dangerous potential consequences" in stopping the bombing in Cambodia, because "this abandonment of a friend will have a profound impact in other countries."

Nixon's letter to Mansfield and Albert threatened retaliation if the North Vietnamese should violate the peace agreement, but the Communist powers had little fear that Nixon would make good on the threat. Dobrynin, the Soviet ambassador, needled Kissinger on the subject after a series of North Vietnamese violations of a cease-fire in Cambodia. Kissinger should have expected as much, Dobrynin said; after all, by agreeing to cut off further bombing, the United States had given up all leverage against Hanoi.

. . . .

THE LATE SUMMER and fall of 1973 brought a parade of challenges: the forced resignation of Spiro Agnew as vice president, the Middle East war, and the Saturday Night Massacre, in which Nixon's attempts to fire Special Prosecutor Archibald Cox resulted in the resignations of the attorney general and his first deputy, bringing on a firestorm of criticism and the introduction of a first bill of impeachment in the House of Representatives. The public for the most part did not recognize that these events involved actions by those who opposed Nixon's foreign policies, who used the various crises as occasions to further undermine the policies and to hasten Nixon's departure from the presidency. Kissinger would later write, "In the supercharged atmosphere of 1973–74, the attacks on Nixon's foreign policy—especially on détente—began to merge with Watergate. Nixon lost his leverage in Congress and thereby the carrots and sticks without which there was no sustaining any serious Soviet policy." That succinct summary concealed a myriad of behind-the-scenes maneuvers by the opponents of détente.

THAT SUMMER, HAIG and Buzhardt became involved in Vice President Spiro Agnew's legal difficulties. Agnew was under investigation for bribery and might have to resign; he was alleged to have taken money from construction contractors when governor of Maryland, and to have continued to attempt to extort money from them after becoming vice president. The charges against Agnew would include income tax evasion and money laundering. Constitutional scholar Robert Bork, who had recently been appointed solicitor general, became convinced after reading the Agnew file that the vice president must be indicted. When Bork met with Haig and Buzhardt, however, it became clear that "the White House staff had been set up to stop this idea of indicting Agnew." Haig and Buzhardt may have wanted to retain Agnew because the vice president's conservative views matched their own, but Nixon wanted to keep him in office because he feared that if a vice president could be indicted, so could a president. Haig agreed to let Attorney General Richardson and Bork lay out the case for the president.

Bork lowered Nixon's anxiety about precedent by reasoning that the Constitution's separation-of-powers clause protected a president from indictment because the president was integral to the day-to-day functioning of the government, but that a vice president, whose responsibilities were limited, enjoyed no such protection. "Buzhardt and I had a lengthy debate," Bork recalled. "Nixon leaned back in his chair with his feet on his desk and . . .

finally said, 'I guess you're right. You have to indict him.' Fred Buzhardt and Al Haig nearly fell off their chairs because that was not what they expected at all."

Soon Haig asked Bork to resign as solicitor general and take on Nixon's legal defense, because "all kinds of crazy things were going on and [Haig] wanted to get things back under control," as Bork later put it. Among those "crazy" things, Bork learned, was a "military penetration" of the White House. Bork was mystified by Haig's use of the term "military penetration," since he had no knowledge of the Moorer-Radford affair, and he did not ask for clarification, perhaps because his main objective in this conversation with Haig was to avoid having to take on Nixon's defense. To escape the assignment, he made conditions he was certain Haig and Nixon could not accept:

> I told Haig that I had to hear the tapes. . . . I explained that I couldn't put on a case without listening to the evidence. I also made a point of asking who was going to pay me. Nixon? And I was told, no, that I'd be on the government payroll. I said, "A government attorney is sworn to uphold the Constitution. If I come across evidence that is bad for the president, I'll have to turn it over. I won't be able to sit on it like a private defense attorney." After a few observations of that sort, it was decided that I was not the man for the job.

Of course, the same conditions—including having legal responsibility for turning over "evidence that is bad for the president"—also applied to Buzhardt, who was also on the government payroll. But no one said so at the time, and Buzhardt consistently avoided living up to that requirement.

In the weeks after Dean's testimony, the president increasingly spent his workday hours out of the White House, often on the presidential yacht. When he was in residence, his schedule featured protocol visits from foreign dignitaries. Various U.S. government officials who tried to see Nixon were deterred by Haig, who insisted that they first bring their questions to him; Haig would provide them with answers, and only sometimes claim he had consulted Nixon. OMB director Roy Ash, working on the federal budget for the next fiscal year, flew to California to confer with Nixon; though he stayed several days, he admitted to the *Wall Street Journal* that he dealt only with Haig.

After similar rebuffs, members of a presidential advisory board headquartered in the Executive Office Building finally decided to show up at Nixon's door and demand to see the president on an urgent matter. "I am the president," Haig told them, according to one member of the board, before sending them away.

. . . .

IN LATE AUGUST 1973, Judge Sirica ruled that Nixon must surrender the tapes. Accepting the president's need to shield certain parts of the conversations, Sirica said that he would review the tapes and turn over to the grand jury only the portions that were not covered by executive privilege. Both sides appealed, and a ruling from the Appeals Court was expected by October.

While the public waited for the outcome of this drama, it had no inkling of another that was unfolding behind the scenes. Haig and Buzhardt were busy fending off a matter that could disinter the Moorer-Radford espionage affair and thus threaten Haig. Don Stewart had been the Pentagon's chief investigator on Moorer-Radford; by mid-1973, he was desperate for a new job. Calling the White House for help, he asked for David Young, his contact there for Moorer-Radford. But Young had long since left the White House, so Stewart's call was routed to Richard Tufaro, an aide to Garment. After listening to Stewart—who, among other things, complained about Buzhardt—Tufaro wrote Garment a memo: "Stewart clearly is in a position to damage the Administration because of his direct involvement in White House investigations of national security leaks," Tufaro said. He reiterated to Garment his earlier warning about "the risk of putting Buzhardt in such a sensitive position" in the White House because of Buzhardt's prior activities.

Garment apprised Buzhardt of Stewart's inquiry. In reaction, Buzhardt—who still retained his position as Defense Department counsel—immediately ordered all of Stewart's files seized and the investigator put on desk duty.

When Stewart heard nothing from Tufaro, he wrote to White House aide Bill Baroody (a former aide to Laird), saying that if he had to take a job on Capitol Hill, that during his job interviews he might be forced to divulge details about the Ellsberg case and the Jack Anderson case—that is, the leak that had led to the exposure of the Moorer-Radford spy ring. Furthermore, he said, he would be justified in doing so because these matters concerned not national security but politics, as exemplified (to Stewart) by the hampering role Buzhardt played in each case.

Baroody promptly showed this Stewart letter to Buzhardt and Garment, who considered it tantamount to blackmail. "Fred believed that it would be calamitous for the country to have [Moorer-Radford] come out. Haig also felt this way," Garment later said. A phone call to Attorney General Richardson, accompanied by the Baroody and Tufaro memos, triggered an investigation, but Henry Peterson, head of the DoJ's criminal division, judged that the materials did not "warrant a criminal investigation." Richardson would try twice more, through other Justice officials, but they agreed with Peterson.

Stewart was never indicted. During this period, Jack Anderson added to the already boiling pot by publishing a self-congratulatory article recalling his India-Pakistan war "tilt" column and mentioning the precise room in the Pentagon where Stewart had interrogated Welander. This brought the entire matter to the attention of the Watergate Committee investigators.

Called in for a Senate committee interview, Stewart outlined the Moorer-Radford espionage in a way that went beyond what Howard Baker and others had previously understood. Baker now tried to investigate further, but ran into a wall: a Buzhardt letter that forbade Ehrlichman and Haldeman from talking about "the 1971 matter" on grounds of national security. David Young also told Baker, "That is the one thing that the president told me not to discuss at all," and pleaded with the senator to speak directly to Nixon about it. Yet Baker was unable to get in to see Nixon, and Haig refused Baker's request for the Pentagon's report on Moorer-Radford.

THE WEAKER THE man in office, the more damage he does to the institution. Opponents of Nixon on the right worried that the longer he remained in office, the more he would do to weaken the powers of the presidency. They believed he had already injured the ability of future presidents to control foreign policy—ceding authority to Congress, for instance, by allowing them to dictate where he could send forces. They were further alarmed at the diminution from Congress's overriding Nixon's veto to pass the War Powers Act, which mandated that any president must clear with Congress military actions lasting more than thirty days. The Joint Chiefs believed that the War Powers Act unduly hampered the military's ability to maneuver and to respond to attacks against the United States. (During the George W. Bush administration, Dick Cheney, Donald Rumsfeld, and their allies would cite the constraints of the War Powers Act as forcing the Bush White House to exert an iron-handed control of foreign policy in a way that excluded true consultation with Congress.)

The question of whether Nixon should remain in office clearly divided Kraemer's protégés Kissinger and Haig, now approaching the pinnacle of their influence. For Haig, whose control over White House business was growing daily, Nixon's conduct of foreign policy—and his increasingly scandal-plagued administration—threatened to cripple the presidency, and he wanted Nixon out. Kissinger, on the other hand, preferred that the weakened Nixon remain in office, as that would increase Kissinger's power and his ability to run foreign affairs without Nixon's interference. Though they differed on the timing of Nixon's exit, during the summer and fall of 1973, Haig took vigorous measures to protect Kissinger. The matter of the 1969–71 wiretaps threatened to hold up Kissinger's confirmation as secretary of state; a full investigation of the tapes, of course, would have hurt not just Kissinger but also Haig, who had worked on the taps and provided the names of some of the "targets." There was one solution that would shield both Haig and Kissinger: a letter from Nixon accepting full and sole responsibility for the taps. Ten days before Kissinger's confirmation hearings began, such a letter was on the desk of Senator William J. Fulbright, chair of the Foreign Relations Committee.

When the matter of the taps came up at the hearings anyway, Kissinger blamed them on Nixon, Mitchell, and the now-dead J. Edgar Hoover. "I had been in the government only four months, and it didn't occur to me to question the judgment of these individuals." He minimized his role (and Haig's) in choosing the targets and said that he had not really read the logs. Even so, the committee refused to confirm Kissinger unless the DoJ provided a once-secret FBI summary report on the tapping program. On direct instructions from the president—as relayed by Haig—Justice refused to release it. Unwilling to have a showdown, the committee agreed to a compromise: Two senators were allowed to view the report and make notes on it, and in a page-long memo to the committee they concluded that Kissinger's involvement in the taps was "not such as to bar him from confirmation."

Henry Kissinger was sworn in as secretary of state on September 22, 1973. The ceremony was attended by Fritz Kraemer, along with Kissinger's parents, though Kraemer later told reporter Nick Thimmesch that he was so angry with Kissinger over this aggrandizement of personal power that he almost stayed home.

Kissinger moved his day-to-day operations to the State Department headquarters at Foggy Bottom. Although Kissinger retained the title of national security adviser, he put his deputy, air force general and Columbia Ph.D. Brent Scowcroft, in charge of the White House national security assistant's office. Kissinger's departure from Pennsylvania Avenue may have marked his ascent to the peak of his power—but *it* left Al Haig even more firmly in charge at the White House.

IN EARLY OCTOBER 1973, an array of domestic and foreign affairs crises converged on President Nixon, culminating in the event known as the Saturday Night Massacre, which occurred during the Yom Kippur War in the Middle East and during the crisis over Vice President Agnew's resignation and the search for his successor. These crises provided opportunities to Kissinger and Haig; Kissinger used them to seize control of foreign policy for himself; Haig used them to diminish Nixon's control of his presidency.

The war commenced on October 6, 1973, the Jewish high holy day of Yom Kippur, when Egyptian troops crossed the Suez Canal and the Syrians launched a simultaneous attack on Israel's Golan Heights. U.S. and Soviet leaders had been trying to work together to head off such a confrontation since the preceding spring, but to no avail. While the superpowers may have seen such a war coming, the United States was caught off guard by its timing—and by the 70 percent hike in oil prices, agreed to by Arab oil ministers on the war's first day. It was a signal that the oil producers were going to carry out a threatened boycott of the United States and European countries for backing Israel.

Nixon first learned of the attacks while at Key Biscayne. He wanted to return to the capital immediately, but Haig and Kissinger conspired to discourage that so that Kissinger could deal with Brezhnev and Dobrynin, mostly without involving Nixon, for the first several days of the war.

"The best thing that could happen for us is for the Israelis to come out ahead but get bloodied in the process," Kissinger told Schlesinger, because that would demonstrate that a U.S.-backed country would prevail over a Soviet-backed country.

But Schlesinger, Moorer, Zumwalt, and other DoD officials feared that Israel might actually lose the war, especially after the Soviet-backed Egyptians and Syrians made serious headway against Israel in the first few days, in part because Israel lacked adequate military supplies. The Chiefs sought to remedy that, but Kissinger blocked the resupply while attempting to blame the delay on Schlesinger, the supposed Arabist and convert from Judaism.

This action, more than any other by Kissinger, incensed future neocons such as Richard Perle and Paul Wolfowitz and alienated them forever from the Nixon-Kissinger approach to policy. For them, a principle—the defense of America's only true ally in the Middle East—was at stake, yet Kissinger was trying to exploit the crisis to score points with the Soviets. Perle, who had stationed himself at the Israeli embassy in Washington, overheard what he characterized as Kissinger lying to the ambassador repeatedly about whether American supplies were en route. Kissinger also blocked Israeli prime minister Golda Meir from an emergency meeting with Nixon, knowing that she would plead for resupply. Haig demonstrated his distance from Kissinger by moving to circumvent him, allowing Israel's ambassador in to see Nixon. The ambassador did exactly what Kissinger had feared Meir would do and that Haig expected—he won an agreement from Nixon to ramp up the resupply at once. Elmo Zumwalt then facilitated it, as he later wrote, by doing what "I would not have done if I had been sure that Richard Nixon, and not the unelected, unaccountable Henry Kissinger, was making national policy about the war. I told Scoop Jackson that I was quite sure that it was the

White House . . . that was delaying the resupply [and that] Israel was going to lose if the United States did not get its equipment aloft at once." Jackson now sprang into action. Most NATO member countries refused to permit American planes to land at their air bases and refuel while taking supplies to Israel, lest they anger the Arab countries on whom they depended for oil. Portugal offered the Azores for a landing and refueling site, but only if Congress dropped a resolution censuring Portugal for actions in Africa. Haig got Jackson in to see Nixon, and he extracted from the president an order to speed the resupply to Israel in exchange for Jackson's pledge to kill the Portugal-censuring resolution.

During this crisis, Haig also had to handle urgent domestic matters—the deal for Agnew's *nolo contendere* plea and the behind-the-scenes work to secure approval for his replacement. Agnew's resignation, which became effective when it was announced on October 10, not only created a vacancy in the vice presidency, it also removed the most logical conservative heir to Nixon for 1976 and would shortly lead to a campaign to draft Ronald Reagan for that position. Foreign policy conservatives did not view Minority Leader Gerald Ford, chosen by Nixon because he would easily win confirmation as vice president, as hawkish enough in foreign affairs.

Two days later, with the war virtually at its height—and on the same day Nixon presented Gerald Ford as his choice for vice president—the federal appeals court handed down its decision: Nixon must surrender the Oval Office tapes to Sirica and the Senate. His only alternative was to file an appeal with the Supreme Court within the week. Buzhardt suggested a compromise: Enlist Senator John Stennis, a long-serving Mississippi Democrat, to listen to the tapes and authenticate the transcripts.

In the lore of Watergate, it was Cox and Richardson's refusal to accept this "Stennis compromise" that triggered the Saturday Night Massacre. But this oversimplification glosses over actions by Haig and Buzhardt that exacerbated the crisis. In several meetings that week, Haig and Buzhardt pushed Attorney General Richardson to fire Archibald Cox, as Nixon demanded. When Richardson refused, they put forth the Stennis plan. Stennis was friendly to Buzhardt, Haig, and Nixon; he also had a history of rigging committee hearings by stacking witnesses and testimony, which was why they all expected his reading of the tapes to be advantageous to Nixon. (It didn't hurt that Stennis was also hard of hearing.) Richardson agreed to accept the Stennis authentication idea but would not yield on Cox's right to demand other tapes. He advised separating the issues, assenting now to the Stennis authentication and dealing later with Cox's need for more tapes—and he warned Haig that he would resign if he were forced to fire Cox.

Critically, though, Archibald Cox refused to accept the idea of Stennis authenticating someone else's transcripts. According to Nixon's later account, which largely agrees with those of Richardson and Cox, Haig never told him of Cox's refusal. Rather, Nixon later wrote, Haig told him only of "Richardson's assurance that if Cox refused to accept the Stennis compromise, Richardson would support me in the controversy that was bound to come." On that basis, Nixon signed a letter to Richardson, which Haig read over the phone to the attorney general, agreeing to allow the Stennis plan, a "limited breach of Presidential confidentiality" that Ervin and Baker had also accepted, but that Richardson was to direct Cox "to make no further attempts . . . to obtain tapes."

By misleading all parties, in short, Haig turned a potential compromise—one that Richardson could have signed and forced on Cox—into a confrontation that could only hurt Nixon.

The next morning, Haig suggested that Richardson fire Cox and then resign if he felt he needed to. Richardson refused, and came to the White House. In the Oval Office, Nixon reminded Richardson that the Middle East war was at a crisis point and asked him to hold the resignation until the crisis passed. Richardson was unable to agree, and resigned. Thereafter, William Ruckelshaus, the deputy attorney general, was asked to fire Cox; he also refused and resigned. That left the job to Solicitor General Robert Bork. Convinced that there would be governmental chaos if he too resigned—and that Nixon had a right to fire any executive branch employee—he proceeded to fire Cox.

The resignations and firing, dubbed the "Saturday Night Massacre" by the press, left little doubt in the public mind that the tapes contradicted Nixon's claims of innocence. On October 24, in the immediate aftermath of the massacre, the House Judiciary Committee began to consider impeachment proceedings against the president.

ON THAT SAME day, a new development threatened to change the dynamic of the evolving Middle East war: a potential Soviet decision to intervene.

By then, the Arab states' oil embargo had exacerbated tensions between the United States and its NATO allies, as well as causing shortages at gas pumps in America and Europe. Newly resupplied, Israeli forces had pushed Egypt and Syria to the brink of defeat—and reduced them to begging the USSR for help. A UN cease-fire had been agreed to, but it was being ignored by both sides. Early on the evening of October 24, Dobrynin informed Kissinger that the USSR would support a resolution, put forth by some neutral nations at the UN, to use U.S. and Soviet forces as peacekeepers for the conflict. Kissinger replied that the United States would veto such a resolution.

After 10:00 P.M., Dobrynin called Kissinger again and read him a new letter from Brezhnev to Nixon: "If you find it impossible to act with us jointly in this matter [i.e., sending troops to enforce the cease-fire] we should be faced with the necessity urgently to consider the question of taking appropriate steps unilaterally."

An alarmed Kissinger immediately convened a meeting of the Washington Special Action Group (WSAG), the multi-agency advisory group set up after the EC-121 crisis. This meeting, which began after Nixon had retired for the night, was attended by Kissinger, Haig, Schlesinger, Moorer, and others. The group decided that the best response to Brezhnev's threat was a combination of two actions: a soft letter of response from Nixon to Brezhnev, which Kissinger wrote and sent over Nixon's signature without consulting Nixon, and an American threat, a DEFCON 3–level nuclear alert.

This extraordinary decision—to put U.S. nuclear armed forces on the highest peacetime alert—was made without notifying Nixon, who was asleep by the time the alert was initiated shortly before midnight. Later reports from participants such as Lawrence Eagleburger allege that Nixon had drunk so much that he could not have been awakened. Other reports suggest that Kissinger and Haig had tried to rouse Nixon earlier in the evening but gave up. Whatever the case, the decision to let the president sleep, while putting the country and the world on a nuclear alert not seen since the Cuban Missile Crisis of 1962, was Haig's. More than any other adviser, the chief of staff had the authority in the White House to insist that Nixon must be alerted and given the opportunity to authorize or reject the decision. But Haig did not insist, and so a highly dangerous nuclear alert was triggered in the president's name and without his permission.

In the morning, Nixon did retroactively ratify the decision, since it had already had the desired effect of backing the Soviets away. But if Nixon had been consulted in advance, he might not have agreed to a DEFCON 3: During the Cienfuegos base crisis, after all, Nixon had refused to take actions that would embarrass Soviet leadership, as evidence suggests that this October 25 DEFCON-3 alert did. That evening, after Nixon made some intemperate remarks at a dinner about how the U.S. action had forced the USSR to back down, Haig called to placate Anatoly Dobrynin. "I told [the president] that his remarks tonight were . . . very much overdrawn and would be interpreted improperly," Haig said.

Dobrynin told Haig that Moscow was indeed "upset" and "very angry" over the remarks. "They consider that you created all these things [nuclear alerts and threats] by reasons we don't know—we don't want to discuss it—but [it was an] artificial crisis. Why?" Dobrynin insisted that it would have been just as effective, and simpler, for Kissinger to have called him. "Then

I will be in touch with Moscow; Brezhnev will answer; and then it's natural." Dobrynin pressed further: "You were really not concerned [with going through channels], so it was the easiest way to make up an air raid without telling me. . . . Why you make it without telling us? If it was really war, I am sure you will try to prevent the war." The public nature of the alert, Dobrynin said, had "put us in a very difficult position domestically."

Haig made no attempt to disagree.

ONE OF KISSINGER's stated motivations during the Yom Kippur War—one that would have pleased Kraemer—was to decrease the USSR's influence in the region. After the shooting stopped, when Egypt and Syria did not soon settle things with Israel, Kissinger pushed this anti-Soviet agenda by first refusing to allow American and Soviet troops to serve as peace guarantors, and then by maneuvering around Soviet attempts at brokering peace. During the last months of 1973 Kissinger effectively cut the USSR out of any role in the Middle East except as an occasional supplier of arms. When Israel, Syria, and Egypt finally agreed to new borders and the oil embargo ended, it was a triumph for Kissinger—more worthy of the Nobel Prize than the Paris peace accord for which he and Le Duc Tho had actually been awarded it. Moreover, the Middle East maneuver was a victory whose anti-Soviet element paid homage to Kissinger's Kraemerite roots.

While Kissinger conducted his latest round of shuttle diplomacy, Schlesinger was preparing to issue a document announcing a major shift in American nuclear defense strategy, one that mandated a new weapons program that both Kissinger and Nixon had been trying to oppose. Early in the administration, Nixon and Kissinger had agreed that the old nuclear strategy of mutually assured destruction (MAD) was both unconscionable and inadequate to defend the United States from nuclear attack. The MAD theory presumed that if each side knew the other could destroy its cities and populations, regardless of who struck first, neither would be foolish enough to launch a first strike. In contrast, this new nuclear targeting strategy— which would soon be dubbed the Schlesinger Doctrine—proceeded from the notion that a nuclear war could be fought and won if it targeted the enemy's missiles and airfields rather than its civilian population centers. William W. Kauffman, a civilian strategist at Defense, had been advocating the theory for decades, while pushing for a "counterforce" capability—a new class of sophisticated MIRVed missiles, positioned close to the USSR, that would deter the USSR from launching a strike. Schlesinger's new doctrine embraced the need for a counterforce—even though Kissinger no longer wanted the missiles because they complicated his negotiations.

The argument for counterforce missiles presumed, as Kraemer, many Soviet dissidents, and American archconservatives all believed, that the USSR did not want real arms control, and that when it came to arms control their word could not be trusted.

Once this new approach to nuclear strategy was out of the bureaucratic bottle, Schlesinger realized, it could not be stuffed back in. It also provided an opportunity to ask Congress for additional appropriations for counter-force weaponry, and to insist on reconfiguring the negotiating strategy for SALT II. After the announcement, the *New York Times* reported that both Kissinger and Schlesinger saw the counterforce weapons as SALT bargain-ing chips, weapons that they would "prefer not to deploy . . . if Moscow would agree to comparable restraints"—but that Schlesinger was much more inclined than Kissinger "to proceed with all the programs now."

Jack Anderson reported that the two secretaries were "collid[ing] head-to-head over concessions" to be made at SALT. In this collision, most knowledgeable observers agreed, the loser was Kissinger. The winners were Schlesinger, the Chiefs, and the anti-Soviet bunch at ACDA, Iklé, Nitze, and Rowny. Meanwhile, by introducing yet another missile system, the Kraemerites had advanced the remilitarization of American foreign policy.

IN THE CONVENTIONAL telling of the Watergate story, the selection of Leon Jaworski, a former head of the American Bar Association, as special pros-ecutor led inexorably to that office's successful pursuit of the tapes and to Nixon's resignation.

Wrinkles in the relationship between Haig and Jaworski complicate that simplistic myth. When Haig told Bork about Jaworski's selection, Bork later recalled, Haig greeted it warmly: "Now we're going to get a real profes-sional." Bork wondered to himself, "Why do you want a real professional? That's the last thing Nixon needs."

Veterans of the special prosecutor's office would later write that back-room deals in the Haig-Jaworski relationship made them scratch their heads in wonder. In exchange for selecting Jaworski as special prosecutor, Haig evidently extracted a promise from Jaworski not to pursue certain national security matters. The only such matter that hadn't already surfaced was the Moorer-Radford affair, in which Haig's role might be revealed. When Ja-worski agreed to this provision he had not yet been apprised of the various prosecutions; in particular, he did not understand the implications of a Bud Krogh petition that his lawyers would present to the court the next day, seek-ing the right to obtain tapes of conversations "in December, 1971 and Janu-ary through February, 1972, in which the work of the Special Investigations

Unit was discussed, and the India-Pakistan leaks were discussed, and/or instructions were given on the necessity for absolute secrecy" regarding the Plumbers' operations. The ramifications of this request would play out over the next six months.

Events in the fall of 1973 continued to go against Nixon. During a meeting in Judge Sirica's chambers on October 30, Fred Buzhardt announced that two of the subpoenaed tapes did not exist. By Saturday, November 3, when Nixon was in Florida for the weekend, the *New York Times*, the *Detroit News*, and *Time* had run editorials suggesting that the president resign. "That weekend in Florida was a new low point for me personally," Nixon later wrote.

That weekend also became the setting for the opening scene of *The Final Days*, Woodward and Bernstein's second book. In the scene, Len Garment and Fred Buzhardt fly to Miami to urge Nixon to resign for the good of the country. When the duo arrives at Key Biscayne, however, Al Haig refuses them access to the president. What Woodward and Bernstein did not mention was that Buzhardt had likely come at Haig's request, and that the effect of the visit was to further dismay Nixon by showing him that even his lawyers thought he should go.

This message was reinforced by another seismic event, the revelation of the "eighteen-and-a-half-minute" gap in one of the subpoenaed tapes. Once again, as with Butterfield's divulging of the taping system, the event featured an internal White House revelation that could have come only from the Haig-Buzhardt group, and reporting by Woodward. On November 7, deputy presidential assistant John Bennett, whom Haig had given charge of the tapes after the taping system was revealed, testified to Sirica that Rose Mary Woods had reported a "gap" in a tape she had reviewed. On November 8, the front page of the *Washington Post* featured an article by Bernstein and Woodward, citing unnamed sources who were worried about "gaps" and "periods of silence" in the tapes. The reporters alleged "serious concern among the President's aides . . . that the latest problems regarding the tapes will further strain the credibility of the White House," and that a "high-ranked adviser" believed people would say, '"They've doctored the tapes.'"

Four of the five "sources who confirmed the difficulties," Bernstein and Woodward wrote, had dismissed them as technical glitches, but the fifth—later identified by Woodward as Deep Throat—was quoted as saying the problems were "of a suspicious nature" and "could lead someone to conclude that the tapes have been tampered with."

Only a handful of people had access to the tapes and knew of the problems with them: Nixon, Rose Mary Woods, Steve Bull, John Bennett, Haig, and Buzhardt. (The FBI did not know of the problems, and Mark Felt, later identified by Woodward as Deep Throat, had been out of the Bureau for six months.) Nixon and Woods did not talk to reporters, Bennett did not have full access, and Bull was intensely loyal to Nixon and an unlikely source. That left only Buzhardt and Haig—and Haig would later say he knew Buzhardt had been a Woodward source.

An outsider, consultant Sam Powers, discovered the "big gap" on November 14, when he began work on a tape from June 20, 1972. Woods had noted a gap in that tape; Buzhardt told Powers to expect a four- to five-minute blank. Powers found that it was much longer and appeared to have been caused by recording over what had been on the tape. Powers insisted that the gap came squarely in the middle of a subpoenaed conversation, although Buzhardt contended that this conversation was not on the list.

That June 20 conversation took place at a moment when Haldeman and Nixon had both been fairly ignorant about the burglary of the Watergate and about who in the White House and CRP had or had not been involved in it. There was likely nothing in the "gap" that incriminated Nixon in the Watergate matter. But its exposure in the fall of 1973 further embarrassed Nixon and multiplied the calls for his resignation.

As NIXON WAS distracted by the fight for his political life, Al Haig, Henry Kissinger, James Schlesinger, and other Kraemerites were wresting control of foreign policy away from him. Haig and his ally, Fred Buzhardt, took other measures to undercut Nixon's ability to remain in office. But in the next two months Haig and Buzhardt would have to temporarily set aside these efforts as the Moorer-Radford affair threatened to resurface and the pair scrambled to keep it from harming them.

16

Protecting the Flanks

The Moorer-Radford espionage story finally became public at just the moment when the nation had focused its attention on Nixon's guilt or innocence in regard to Watergate. As a result, few people paid much attention to the scandal of the Joint Chiefs' spying on the White House. But the two matters are inextricably linked. While the public believed that Haig and Buzhardt were dedicated to defending the president in his moment of crisis, they were actually engaged in protecting their own flanks, struggling mightily to deflect the congressional inquiry into Moorer-Radford. If Haig was to retain his position of power, and of influence over the administration's foreign policy, he and Buzhardt would first have to save themselves.

BY MID-NOVEMBER 1973, Haig and Buzhardt knew that two reporters for rival Chicago papers, James Squires of the *Chicago Tribune* and Dan Thomasson of the *Chicago Sun-Times*, working together, had uncovered some aspects of the "military spy ring" puzzle. The reporters' understanding was hardly complete—they did not yet have Radford's name—but they were gathering more information each day.

In the two months since Leon Jaworski's appointment as special prosecutor, Jaworski and Haig had become closer than Jaworski's subordinates thought was warranted. At one meeting, Haig readily handed Jaworski materials that the White House had previously withheld on national security grounds—materials that would allow the special prosecutor to secure indictments for Ehrlichman and Colson on the Fielding office break-in. In the same meeting, however, Haig refused to turn over to Jaworski materials relating to Moorer-Radford—materials Krogh had requested and the prosecutor wanted to see. Krogh wanted to cite Moorer-Radford as one of the matters he worked on that were covered by national security, a claim that would relieve him of responsibility for actions now alleged to have been criminal. Without seeing the actual materials, however, Jaworski could not agree to Krogh's request and had to oppose it. The judge soon denied Krogh's discovery motion, and Krogh was forced to accept a plea deal. As a result, the Moorer-Radford materials stayed in the vaults of the White House.

On December 21, 1973, Jaworski came to Haig's office to discuss the March 21 "cancer upon the presidency" tape, which Sirica had recently given to him—a tape that Jaworski said was very incriminating of the president. When Haig responded that the White House lawyers had concluded just the opposite, Jaworski said, "I think you should get the finest criminal lawyer you can find—someone not connected with the White House in any way—and let him study the tapes." Haig now agreed, and hired James St. Clair, a seasoned criminal defense attorney, to start at the White House after the turn of the year.

That timing allowed Buzhardt to be promoted to counsel to the president on January 4, 1974. (He also resigned as DoD counsel on that day, ostensibly because of his new White House duties.) During the next few months, despite Buzhardt's new title and responsibilities, he attended very few meetings of the president's legal team. Instead he spent his time defending himself and Haig on Moorer-Radford.

The Chicago reporters' first articles on the espionage ring, on January 11, 1974, named Moorer but not Radford or Welander. They included Haig's denial that the affair had occurred, and his threat to bring "lawsuits" against their papers if their allegations against the military could not be proven.

Now Woodward got into the act. Six months earlier, during the height of Haig's and Buzhardt's attempt to have Don Stewart prosecuted, Woodward had learned enough about Moorer-Radford to have requested a meeting with his former skipper, Welander. During that meeting, Woodward asked Welander for more information; Welander refused, and Woodward published nothing further about the matter. But the day after the Chicago papers published, Woodward and Bernstein published an article in the *Washington Post* filling in two facts that the Chicago reporters did not yet have—the names of Radford and Welander. The article contained one clue about who may have divulged those names, a reference to a Pentagon investigation "directed by J. Fred Buzhardt." The article made no mention of the Ehrlichman-Welander interview or of Young's probe. Rather, it took the

Haig-Buzhardt-Moorer line—that the espionage had done no harm and that the whole thing was Radford's fault. Nor did the article disclose Woodward's prior relationship to Welander, an omission that constituted a violation of professional ethics.

Another article that day, in the *New York Times*, offered a stark contrast to Woodward's. The article, by reporter Seymour Hersh, highlighted Young's investigation, reported that the Nixon White House had considered the spy scandal an extremely serious matter, and cited as evidence the fact that the stolen materials had included top-secret memos on Kissinger's talks with China before the July 1971 announcement.

In the following days, Don Stewart's name was mentioned in a news story, though mainly as the man who had tried to "blackmail" the White House the previous summer. Stewart responded with ringing denials of any attempted blackmail and with a statement that he was happy to testify to Congress. In light of all this, Schlesinger started his own inquiry. Fred Buzhardt refused to give Schlesinger the Ehrlichman-Young tape of the Welander "confession," which was physically in the White House—a tape that implicated Haig. Buzhardt later testified that he did not obey this direct order because technically Schlesinger was no longer his boss. (The expectation that he might eventually have to duck such a request from Schlesinger may have been behind Buzhardt's decision to resign from the DoD in January, despite having held simultaneous positions at the White House and at DoD for the previous eight months.) After a four-day investigation in which he was unable to obtain these materials, Schlesinger concluded that the espionage episode had been "blown out of proportion," as the *Post* contended.

The looming Moorer-Radford scandal threw further gasoline on the flames licking at the administration. The secretary of the SALT delegation, Ray Garthoff, later recalled that his team could only wonder at the implications: "Had Moorer been blackmailed and tamed by the president into agreeing to support SALT in return for being permitted to remain unsullied and kept on in his position? The very fact that the question was being asked reflected the deteriorating confidence in the national leadership." Garthoff worried about the effect the story could have on negotiations with the USSR.

Senator Stennis, the chairman of the Armed Services Committee, met individually on the matter with Moorer, Welander, Haig, Kissinger, and Schlesinger. He chose not to meet with Young, Stewart, or Ehrlichman, the very people Senator Baker had wanted most to testify under oath. Stennis then announced that he would handle the matter in a one-day, closed-door hearing. Fifteen members of his committee objected. When hearings began on February 6, Stennis was in full command of who did and did not testify, and what materials did and did not enter the official record. Almost no mention was made of the Ehrlichman-Welander interview, and scant mention of the Buzhardt-Stewart re-interview of Welander. Laird offered the latter but Stennis turned it down, because (as Laird later recalled) Stennis thought a complete investigation "would serve no useful purpose." The senator also decided not to require Haig to testify.

During this period, evidence suggests that Woodward was in close contact with Haig, Buzhardt, and Stennis. In a call to Don Stewart, for instance, Woodward mentioned the date of a Radford–Jack Anderson dinner. That surprised Stewart because (he wrote in contemporaneous notes) "this particular date had to come from the file," meaning the file he had amassed during his investigation, which Buzhardt had taken from him in May 1973. "This and the general questioning Woodward put to me makes me believe that he, too, is being provided info from the White House."

Radford did testify before the committee, informing them that his superiors had ordered his thievery, and proclaiming that he was willing to be court-martialed so that he could face his accusers in open court. He was whisked off the stand. Moorer and Welander also testified; they contended that the whole affair was the yeoman's fault.

The Ehrlichman-Welander-Young taped interview, of course, could have countered Moorer's and Welander's accounts and supported Radford's claims. But Stennis told the press he had heard enough and on March 7 called his final witness: J. Fred Buzhardt.

The ubiquitous counsel dismissed the importance of several key elements of the case: of Don Stewart, who had been prevented from testifying; of David Young's voluminous investigative record, which could not be found; and of Ehrlichman's interview of Welander, which Stennis refused to allow into the record. Buzhardt said that there was "no material substantive difference" between his re-interview of Welander and the previous one by Ehrlichman. When some senators on the committee asked to see the Young and Ehrlichman materials, Stennis blocked them from doing so.

Buzhardt then proceeded to shred the cloak of national security that Nixon had thrown over Moorer-Radford, and which Buzhardt and Haig had used repeatedly to conceal Haig's involvement. "I do not believe [my report] contains material which would . . . endanger the national security if released," Buzhardt said. If that was so, the recalcitrant senators clamored, then the report should be released. This Buzhardt refused to do, he said, because it contained private correspondence between Laird, other DoD officials, and the White House, as well as the results of polygraph exams that Radford in court might charge were "libelous." Stennis agreed and told Buzhardt to hold his re-interview. "Take it back," Stennis said. "I don't want to see a line of it."

With that, Stennis closed the hearings. Haig had once again escaped being connected to Moorer-Radford.

In speaking with the press after his Senate testimony, Buzhardt dropped another bomb. During the Pentagon Papers mess, he revealed, Defense had at his urging recommended against prosecuting Daniel Ellsberg, not because national security would be compromised in a trial but rather because the case was "too complex" to be adequately prosecuted and won. He added that there had been no real "national security" issues in either the Ellsberg case or in certain unspecified others.

Later in the spring of 1974, as he prepared for his trial, John Ehrlichman petitioned the court for the right to review evidence held in the White House that might exonerate or exculpate him. He specifically asked for the Welander interview tape and other notes that he believed would show the "national security" reasons behind the Plumbers' activities, the Fielding office break-in, and Moorer-Radford. Back in October 1973, when Krogh had asked for these materials, Buzhardt and Haig had successfully argued that they were covered by national security and could not be provided. But after Buzhardt said that none of these matters touched on national security, Ehrlichman demanded the materials. Buzhardt then switched rationales once more, claiming that the materials would be withheld on grounds of executive privilege. Ehrlichman moved to have the case dismissed because he was being denied access to materials that he needed to prepare a proper defense.

Judge Gerhard Gesell agreed, threatening to dismiss the case unless the White House complied. Ehrlichman had also subpoenaed Haig and Buzhardt as custodians of those materials. The two submitted affidavits denying that they had "custody or control of any document or object" subpoenaed, even though the materials, as they and Ehrlichman knew, were inside the White House. Gesell ordered the White House to provide Ehrlichman and his attorneys access to the materials.

As Ehrlichman later recalled, he went to the White House to review his files but was directed to remain outside Buzhardt's office, where he could hear Buzhardt reviewing (at high volume) Ehrlichman's interview with Welander—the very object of the subpoena, something Buzhardt had sworn in an affidavit that he didn't have. Ehrlichman considered this a deliberate slap in the face. Buzhardt also defied the judge's orders by refusing to grant Ehrlichman or his attorneys access to that subpoenaed tape and to the Young investigative files. Gesell threatened again to dismiss the case, and Ehrlichman's attorneys submitted an even more specific request for his notes of his December 21, 1971, discussion with Nixon about Moorer-Radford, a conversation in which, the lawyers said, Nixon had said that "any testimony" on the Plumbers' activities was "affected by national security and these activities were not to be disclosed." In response, Buzhardt—as he shortly told the court—reviewed Ehrlichman's files and submitted an affidavit saying that there was nothing in them "which bears on the issue of guilt or innocence" of Ehrlichman—in other words, attesting that Nixon had *not* thrown the blanket of national security over various Plumbers' activities. This ensured that Ehrlichman would not be able to use national security as a defense in his trial.

Shortly thereafter, Gesell allowed Ehrlichman's trial to go forward. Without the tape he had requested, Ehrlichman was unable to defend his claim that his actions were taken at the request of the president for reasons of national security, and he was convicted.

IN ANOTHER CURIOUS incident whose only purpose seems to have been Haig self-protection, at some point in early 1974 a memo in the White House files was altered.

The original memo, from Butterfield to Magruder, bore the date of January 8, 1970. Its genesis was the tap on Morton Halperin, which had turned up the news that an unknown individual who had met with Kissinger on a specific day in December was going to feed information to Clark Clifford for an anti-administration article. If Magruder wanted to identify the person, Butterfield told him, "You should go—first of all—to Al Haig" for information and also because "Al Haig can get you squared away" on ways to deal with Clifford.

This memo, and Magruder's response, might have pointed investigators to proof of Haig's involvement in the 1969–71 wiretaps. But in early 1974 the 1970 Butterfield memo was taken out of the files and a poor fake inserted— we know it was a fake because a copy of the true memo was eventually found, allowing comparison of the two versions. The date of the fake memo had been altered to January 8, 1969—that is, *before* the administration had begun. The more significant change was the deletion of most mentions of Haig's name. Also absent from the fake memo was an introductory phrase by Butterfield, "in response to your query"; the deletion made the fake memo seem like just a crazy idea of Butterfield's. In the spring of 1974, Haig gave the faked memo to the special prosecutor's office, along with many other requested documents.

HAVING DECIMATED THE ranks of Nixon defenders and having protected his own flanks, Haig could now fully devote himself to the task of forcing Nixon out of office.

17

Endgame

The conventional narrative of Watergate is that Richard Nixon was overthrown by his traditional enemies on the left. But as president, Nixon was always more concerned with the attacks coming from his traditional friends on the right, because he needed their support in order to survive. The steady drip of resentment over his radical alterations to U.S. foreign policy, particularly with regard to his overtures to the Soviet Union and China, accumulated until it leached away many former supporters on the right. As he weakened, his foreign policy opponents' attacks grew bolder, taking away more support. Attacks from within the executive branch added to the erosion. Eventually, with no conservative friends left, Nixon opted to resign.

As Nixon weakened, conservative critiques of détente were more openly and frequently voiced by those who had been the president's supporters. Nixon had elevated Daniel Patrick Moynihan, a onetime White House counselor and lifelong Democrat, by naming him ambassador to India; Moynihan briefly returned to Washington from his post to make a speech assailing Kissinger and his ilk as "men who know too much to believe anything in particular and opt instead for accommodations of reasonableness and urbanity that drain our world position of moral purpose." This was Fritz Kraemer's complaint about his protégé. What Moynihan wanted, instead of Kissinger's pessimism and pursuit of détente, was "for the United States deliberately and consistently to bring its influence to bear on behalf of those regimes which promise the larger degree of personal and national liberty."

On March 19, 1974, when Senator James Buckley issued an influential public call for Nixon to resign, he chose not to include his bedrock opposition to détente with the USSR and rapprochement with China among the factors influencing his decision—even though he would later cite both these concerns in his autobiography. Rather, he claimed that Nixon had already been "stripped of the ability to fulfill the mandate" given him in the 1972 election and should therefore remove himself before the presidency was "irrevocably weakened" in ways that would negatively affect the ability of future presidents to govern. "A cumulative loss of faith . . . has eroded [along with Nixon's] credibility and moral authority, a loss that, in my judgment, is beyond repair."

"What Buckley has done," Howard Phillips told *Time*, "is pull a plug on the President's most important reservoir," the conservative senators Nixon had been counting on to help him survive an impeachment trial. The Democratic-led House of Representatives could pass a bill of impeachment against him at any time, Nixon knew, but two-thirds of the Senate would have to vote to convict him—and that could only happen if his conservative friends on both sides of the aisle allowed it. Recognizing in the spring of 1974 the depth of the conservatives' problems with him, Nixon worked desperately to ameliorate them. When the American Conservative Union forwarded to him a statement by thirty-five representatives and senators protesting the size and content of the fiscal 1975 budget, Nixon agreed to pare it down to accommodate their misgivings. When Secretary of Defense Schlesinger wanted to have Paul Nitze nominated as assistant secretary of defense, Nixon scuttled the idea because Goldwater objected to it. The most significant alteration that Nixon agreed to came in the arena of foreign policy, and it was a stunning victory for those who had consistently opposed the Nixon-Kissinger policies: the president decided to overrule Kissinger and push ahead Senator Buckley's pet project, the new missiles at the heart of the counterforce strategy, which Buckley had been advocating for three years.

Nixon had spent the past five years working to lessen tensions with the USSR by scaling back nuclear weapons; now he was agreeing to build new ones that would upset the Soviets. The magnitude of this turnabout smacked of desperation, and reinforced the belief of many Beltway insiders that it was only a matter of time before Ford would be president. The April publication of Woodward and Bernstein's *All the President's Men* only boosted the sense that Nixon's removal was inevitable. Reporters swapped stories of Kissinger and Schlesinger separately telephoning Laird, now an executive at *Reader's Digest*, to ask Ford's opinion of them. Ford had publicly criticized Schlesinger's bristling performance at a congressional hearing, but Laird reported back to Schlesinger that Ford admired the way Schlesinger was going about his other duties. He gave similar reassurances to Kissinger.

. . . .

IN MID-APRIL 1974, the House Judiciary Committee and the special prosecutor demanded dozens of additional tapes from the White House. Nixon
did not understand how Jaworski had identified these particular tapes. In
fact, the prosecutor's demands were based on the road map of the "tape
of tapes," one of the recordings Haig had allowed Jaworski to hear. Nixon
insisted that he would not turn over these or any further tapes; instead, on
April 29, he released thirteen hundred pages of edited transcripts that Rose
Mary Woods had made of the forty-two tapes subpoenaed by the Judiciary
Committee. These, Nixon said in a televised address, provided everything
necessary "to get Watergate behind us."

Releasing these transcripts—whose nasty language and manipulative
content were bound to upset the public—was a gamble. Nixon later wrote
that it was "good strategy to the extent that it proved conclusively that Dean
had not told the truth about everything, and to the extent that it showed that
in the areas where [Dean] had told the truth, my actions and omissions,
while regrettable and possibly indefensible, were not impeachable." But the
strategy backfired. Public outrage over the foul language and mendacity
revealed in the transcripts outweighed anything Nixon might have gained
from countering Dean's accusations. The calls for impeachment or resignation grew deafening; key members of the House and Senate changed their
positions from unquestioning support of Nixon to a willingness to impeach.

The House Judiciary Committee and Jaworski rejected the transcripts as
legally inadequate and demanded the tapes themselves. On May 5, as Jaworski pressed Haig for release of the tapes, he revealed that the grand jury had
designated Nixon as an "unindicted co-conspirator." He also offered to keep
that fact secret and drop his demand for all sixty-four tapes if Nixon would
turn over eighteen of them, including conversations between himself and
Haldeman on June 23, 1972.

Haig advised Nixon to listen to the eighteen tapes before making his decision. Nixon immediately began to do so, and on May 6, 1974, he reached
the June 23, 1972, tape. He was abashed. He and Haldeman had remembered national security as a rationale for their actions that day, he wrote, but
"there was no doubt now that we had been talking about political implications." Even though he still did not recognize one of the conversations as the
"smoking gun" it would become, he decided not to release the tapes but to
force the courts to settle the matter.

Haig and Buzhardt had known about this June 23, 1972, tape for more
than a year, ever since Dick Walters had walked into the White House with
his memcons. But they had not given Nixon those memcons in 1973; if they

had, the president might well have destroyed the June 23 tape before it was subpoenaed.

A few days later, John Connally called Nixon to pass along a comment from fellow Texan Jaworski: "The President has no friends in the White House." Nixon still refused to believe it.

Sirica ruled that Jaworski could have the sixty-four new tapes he had demanded from the White House. When Nixon appealed, Jaworski opted not to wait for the Appeals Court and took the case right to the Supreme Court, which on May 31 agreed to hear it.

It seemed certain that the Supreme Court would order Nixon to turn over the tapes and that this would force him from office. This, in turn, gave his opponents an opening to further their own agendas.

Scoop Jackson seized the moment to ram through the long-simmering Jackson-Vanik Amendment, which pushed the Soviets to open wider the gates of Jewish emigration. In later years, neocons would cite the success of Jackson-Vanik as demonstrating that it was possible to be tough with the Soviets and hold them to our moral standards. Jackson went even further, introducing a measure to severely limit U.S. loans to the USSR (to purchase American wheat), which would constrain Nixon's negotiating room at the scheduled June summit with Brezhnev. Using information from Rowny, Nitze, and Iklé, Jackson made a speech severely criticizing détente and SALT. Schlesinger followed up by writing Jackson a letter—which he also released to the press—that essentially validated Jackson's critique. Kissinger would later write that with the publication of Schlesinger's letter, "serious prospects for SALT in the Nixon Presidency ended."

The hoped-for demise of the Nixon-Kissinger approach to the USSR formed the backdrop of a formal dinner held at the home of Albert and Roberta Wohlstetter in Santa Monica, California, on June 4, 1974. A group of self-described "strategic thinkers and worriers," including Paul Nitze, columnist Joseph Kraft, and Robert Bartley, the editor of the *Wall Street Journal*'s editorial page, dined on détente and declared it inedible. What the diners sought, Anne Hessing Cahn later wrote, was "the remilitarization of American foreign policy [to] contain the expansion" of the Soviet Union. A two-day conference that began the next morning reinforced their conclusions. Its message: The United States must construct a counterforce capability to continue to properly limit the Soviets.

Days after the Santa Monica dinner, on the eve of the 1974 Moscow summit, Nitze publicly resigned from the SALT team. At an NSC meeting, the Chiefs echoed Nitze and the Santa Monica group: Any agreement with the Soviets must ensure an overwhelming American advantage in strategic armaments, they insisted, or they too would go public with their disapproval.

Nixon's foreign-policy opponents were feeling so sure of themselves that at a principals' meeting, when Schlesinger introduced a new proposal to further limit Soviet nuclear arms, and Nixon said that the Soviets would reject it out of hand, Schlesinger insulted him. "But, Mr. President," Schlesinger said, "everyone knows how impressed Khrushchev was with your forensic ability in the kitchen debate [of 1959]. I'm sure that if you applied your skills to it you could get them to accept this proposal." Those in the room recognized this as a deliberate slap at Nixon.

"Many of the Defense people don't want any agreement because they want to go ahead willy-nilly with all the defense programs they possibly can and they do not want constraints," Nixon wrote in his diary that evening. Years later, the moment's bitterness seeped through in his memoir: "The military establishment and its many friends [were] up in arms over the prospect that Summit III might actually succeed in producing a breakthrough on limiting offensive nuclear weapons or a limited nuclear test ban."

After a trip to the Middle East, where he was wildly cheered, Nixon went to Moscow to meet Brezhnev. During the president's visit to the USSR, Jackson let the press know that he had deferred his own visit to Beijing so as not to embarrass Nixon. At the same time, *Foreign Policy* printed the first of two articles by Albert Wohlstetter, which charged that the National Intelligence Estimates were continuing to underestimate Soviet missile strength and deployments.

"If détente unravels in America, the hawks will take over, not the doves," Nixon warned Brezhnev. The Soviet leader wanted détente, and more. At nearly the last moment of the conference, he cornered Nixon in a grotto for three hours to beg him to sign a nonaggression pact that would require each country to come to the aid of the other if a third country—meaning China—should attack. The ploy went nowhere.

At this summit, a very frustrated Kissinger battled with Haig over who would have the room in the Kremlin closest to Nixon. Haig won. Then, at a press conference, Kissinger was asked what would happen if there were no SALT agreement before 1977. His response was astonishing. He began by saying there would be "an explosion of technology and an explosion of numbers [of missiles] at the end of which we'll be lucky if we have the present stability." Having frightened himself, he went on: "One of the questions which we have to ask ourselves as a country is: *What in the name of God is strategic superiority?* What is the significance of it, politically, militarily, operationally, at these levels of numbers? What do you do with it?" That Kissinger could question whether the United States needed to maintain strategic superiority was anathema to the inflexibly anti-Soviet crowd and only deepened their scorn for him.

Nothing of substance was achieved at Summit III, a fact that was met with relief by SALT negotiators Rowny and Iklé, ACDA assistant Wolfowitz, the JCS, Secretary Schlesinger, Scoop Jackson (who was on his way to Beijing), Richard Perle, ex-negotiator Nitze, Fritz Kraemer, Wohlstetter and his RAND colleagues, and the editorial board of the *Wall Street Journal.* "The goal of détente has not been achieved in any sense of the term Americans can accept," the foreign policy task force of the Coalition for a Democratic Majority crowed in a report issued a short time later. Nixon and Kissinger, they charged, had created a "myth of détente" to cover their failure to warn the American people about the strength of the threat posed by the USSR.

Kissinger would later write that, in these closing days of the administration, neither he nor Nixon "understood the depth of the neoconservative challenge," and that it would take him more than a decade to comprehend. At bottom, he wrote in retrospect, it was a "philosophic difference"—not over the nature of Communism, "on which we [and the neocons] were very close . . . but over the relationship of moral values to the conduct of international politics." Kissinger thought moral values were important, "even decisive," in giving negotiators the fortitude to "navigate a series of difficult choices." The neoconservatives took matters a step further: They "believed that values could be translated directly into operating programs," a conviction the pragmatic Kissinger did not share.

As NIXON RETURNED from the summit, on July 3, Butterfield testified to the House Judiciary Committee. By this time he had found the true version of his 1970 memo, discussed earlier, and was able to help the committee see that the one Haig had turned over to them was a clumsy fake, an apparent attempt by Haig to conceal his role in the 1969–71 wiretapping. The Judiciary Committee acknowledged the fakery but did nothing about it. They ceded action on that point to the Senate Foreign Relations Committee, which instructed Haig to be ready to testify about the wiretaps and the memos on July 30.

In the interim, on July 24, the Supreme Court ruled 8–0 that Nixon must turn over the tapes. Three days later, the House Judiciary Committee approved a first article of impeachment, for obstruction of justice—in precisely the matters covered by the Walters memcons and the tapes of June 23, 1972. Then the committee approved a second article, charging the president with abuse of power and violations of citizens' constitutional rights, among the violations being the 1969–71 wiretaps.

The Judiciary Committee voted on three more articles of impeachment, and the votes have relevance to the story of the post-Nixon years.

The committee narrowly approved Article III but rejected IV and V. With each vote, the tally against the articles rose, due primarily to the reluctance of conservatives to impugn such presidential actions as the incursion into Cambodia, which they saw as a reasonable prerogative of the commander in chief that should be preserved for future presidents. The House scheduled a full vote on the bill of impeachment for August 19, with a Senate trial to follow.

Nixon still thought he might survive a Senate trial, but the idea of such a trial was anathema to Haig, for it opened the possibility that Nixon might bring up the same things Ehrlichman had sought to raise in his defense—national security issues such as Moorer-Radford and the 1969–71 wiretaps. Full discussion of such matters would inevitably expose Haig's complicity and culpability.

While James St. Clair scrambled to assemble tapes to deliver in response to the Supreme Court ruling, Buzhardt—who according to court filings was in charge of the tapes for the White House—was absent, though apparently not due to the heart attack he had recently suffered. Rather, Buzhardt was helping Haig prepare to testify to the Foreign Relations Committee. On July 30, when Haig addressed a closed-door committee session on the wiretaps, Buzhardt was at his side. "I never would have submitted a name [to be tapped] that I did not get from Kissinger, or from the president with Dr. Kissinger's knowledge," Haig said, contradicting what Kissinger had told the committee recently and in his confirmation hearings.

By then, however, few cared about the wiretaps, because the evidence that would convict Nixon in the court of public opinion was finally about to come out. The next morning, the transcript of the June 23, 1972, tape was ready for internal dissemination in the White House. According to Nixon's memoir, Haig read it, told the president it was the smoking gun, and said, "I just don't see how we can survive this one." Late that day, Haig called Ford's chief assistant, Robert Hartmann, and asked to see Ford the next morning. Hartmann also attended that meeting, which made Haig uncomfortable. Haig claimed to Ford that he had not seen the June 23 transcript but that others had told him it contained a smoking gun. Ford wanted to see the evidence.

Later that day, Nixon asked Haig to tell Ford that he would likely resign but not to say when. Haig now insisted on a second meeting with Ford, this time without Hartmann. At that meeting, Ford later testified, Haig laid out Nixon's options: to resign; endure a Senate trial; or pardon himself and his former aides. Haig also raised the possibility that Nixon's successor could pardon him in exchange for Nixon's commitment to leave immediately. Ford responded that it would be improper for him to make any recommendation.

(Haig would later testify that he never raised the possibility of Nixon re-signing in exchange for a Ford pardon.) After hearing Ford's report of the Haig meeting, Hartmann recommended that Ford phone Haig with himself, Betty Ford, adviser Bryce Harlow, and others in the room. He did so on August 2, reading to Haig a statement that said, "I have no intention of recommending what the President should do about resigning or not resigning, and . . . nothing we talked about yesterday afternoon should be given any consideration" in the president's decision.

Over the weekend, Al Haig, Fred Buzhardt, James St. Clair, and Pat Buchanan all told Nixon he must resign. He resisted, deciding instead to put out the transcript of the June 23 tape and gauge the reaction. Then, if necessary, he could resign; until then, he would fight.

On Monday morning, before the White House released the "smoking gun" transcript, Haig and St. Clair told Jaworski that they had not known the contents of the June 23 tape, and that St. Clair was threatening to quit if Nixon did not resign. Buzhardt had gone around town showing copies of the transcript to selected congressmen—principal among them House Minority Leader John Rhodes. After seeing the evidence, Rhodes canceled a previously scheduled statement that he would vote against the articles of impeachment in a floor vote. Nixon was still undecided about whether to fight on through impeachment. By underlining the importance of the June 23 tape to such key supporters as Rhodes, Haig and Buzhardt did their best to persuade Nixon to resign.

After a grim-faced Cabinet meeting, Kissinger assured Nixon that resignation was the best route for the country. If Nixon stayed and slogged through a lengthy Senate trial, he warned, "the foreign policy of the nation might not be able to survive."

The public reaction to the June 23 transcript was enormous, and entirely negative. The television networks denounced Nixon. The eleven Republican House members who had voted against impeachment, including John Rhodes, all told the press that they would now change their votes if possible. These defections finally convinced the president that resignation was inevitable. Haig urged him to do it quickly. Nixon agreed.

On the eve of the resignation, Nixon later wrote, Fred Buzhardt came in with a page that he said Bob Haldeman had asked that Nixon consider inserting into his speech. In this new text, Nixon not only pardoned Haldeman, but also issued a blanket amnesty for those who had fled the Vietnam War draft. To Nixon, the prospect of pardoning those involved in Watergate, or draft dodgers, was "unthinkable." He rejected the plea.

Haldeman's last-ditch request for a pardon had been in Haig's hands for several days, in the form of a letter from Haldeman's lawyer. Haig had construed it as a threat from Haldeman to sell Nixon down the river in his testimony if the pardon was not issued, and had sent the Secret Service to Haldeman's lawyer's office to investigate. Both Haldeman and his lawyer, Frank Strickler, later denied that any such threat was implied by the letter. More curious, both men insisted that they had never linked the pardon request to any plea for draft-dodger amnesty. Yet combining Haldeman's plea with a grant of amnesty for draft dodgers ensured that Nixon would reject the idea, and that is what happened.

Late on the afternoon of August 7, Republican senators Barry Goldwater and Hugh Scott and House minority leader John Rhodes met with Nixon. Scott said that Nixon could count on no more than fifteen votes against impeachment in the Senate, and that Stennis, Goldwater, and Scott would not be among them. "I don't have many alternatives, do I?" Nixon responded.

On the morning of August 8, while Nixon was gathering himself for the difficult public resignation he would announce the next day, Haig secretly went to Leon Jaworski's suburban home and told the prosecutor that Nixon would take his tapes and documents with him to San Clemente. Jaworski agreed, with the condition that Nixon must give the special prosecutor's office access to any documents they needed.

Haig did not reveal to Jaworski that the voluminous records Nixon would transfer to California would contain such materials as the Ehrlichman-Welander tape and the tape of the December 21, 1971, Oval Office conference in which Nixon agreed not to prosecute anyone for Moorer-Radford—both items potentially devastating to Haig.

During the final hours of Nixon's presidency, a leak to the press, attributed at the time to Schlesinger, had an unnamed official instructing the military not to obey orders from Nixon without first getting approval from the secretary of defense. The ostensible reason for such an order was to prevent Nixon from using troops to block his ouster; the leak heightened public fears that Nixon might find a way to stay on. (Schlesinger later denied he had ordered anything of the sort.)

On August 8, Nixon also spoke with Ford in the Oval Office for an hour. Nixon urged his successor to continue his foreign policies, which Ford strongly endorsed. Toward that end, Nixon recommended that Ford retain Henry Kissinger as secretary of state, and—at least through a transition period—Al Haig as chief of staff because Haig, he noted, "was always loyal to the commander he served."

Book Two

THE TRIUMPH OF
THE NEOCONS

President George W. Bush on the deck of the USS *Abraham Lincoln*, May 1, 2003. *(Photographer's Mate 3rd Class Tyler J. Clements, U.S. Navy)*

SECTION IV

The Post-Nixon Years

President Gerald Ford with Chief of Staff Donald Rumsfeld and Assistant Chief of Staff Richard Cheney, April 28, 1975. *(David Hume Kennerly, Courtesy of Gerald R. Ford Presidential Library)*

18

A Short Honeymoon

The events of the era commonly referred to in America as the Sixties, the tumultuous period from the assassination of President Kennedy in November 1963 to the resignation of President Nixon in August 1974, and the arguments over the meaning of those events, particularly of the war in Vietnam, had progressively widened and deepened the chasm dividing liberals from conservatives. The civil war over foreign policy was part of that schism. During the Nixon years it had been fought mostly in the shadows: Opponents of Nixon's policies of détente with the USSR, rapprochement with China, and a negotiated end to the Vietnam War did all they could to undermine those policies, and eventually, Nixon. Now those "antis" would bring their fight further out into the open—against first Gerald Ford and then Jimmy Carter, who both attempted to continue the Nixon foreign policy agenda.

During the Ford and Carter presidencies, the "antis" began to coalesce as a group that would become known as the neoconservatives. Emboldened by their success in hastening Nixon's exit, they sabotaged the policies of an unelected president with few ideas of his own, and then of an elected president who lacked a clear foreign policy vision. Even as their philosophical guide, Fritz Kraemer, headed into retirement, they forged an identity and an agenda that drew on his ideas and sharpened them as rationales for opposition.

VICE PRESIDENTS WHO succeed presidents usually do so under difficult circumstances, and tend to keep on key personnel. That was the pattern set by Teddy Roosevelt, Harry Truman, and Lyndon Johnson. While Gerald Ford had greater reason than those men to jettison his predecessor's Cabinet-level associates, he chose not to. Among those he decided to keep on were three men who had also been close to Fritz Kraemer: Henry Kissinger: Alexander Haig, and James Schlesinger. As he entered office they also shared one additional thing in common: they all thought the new president needed them more than they needed him. It would take differing amounts of time for Ford to disabuse them of this notion.

The earliest to capitulate was Kissinger. When Ford asked Kissinger early on to convene an NSC meeting, Kissinger tried to delay, saying that the move might alarm the Soviets, but Ford insisted and Kissinger yielded. Kissinger soon realized that his long-term future would depend on whether Ford won election in his own right in 1976. Ford had pledged not to run for president but Kissinger urged him to reconsider, on the grounds such a pledge would make Ford a lame duck and have a negative impact on the effectiveness of U.S. foreign policy.

On his first day in office, Ford received an anonymous but transparent memorandum. "At this time, do not commit yourself to dealing directly with anyone but Al Haig" was its message. Ford disregarded it; he preferred to listen to varied and often contradictory advice before making a decision. He did, however, take Nixon's advice and ask Haig to remain as interim chief of staff. Though he had no desire for a Nixonian gatekeeper, Ford wanted Haig to help smooth the transition. Haig claimed he wanted to return to the army in a top post, but by staying on at the White House for a while, he maintained his power to protect himself and Buzhardt. He attempted to do so by evading a direct order from Ford. The president, advised by his friend and informal counsel Phil Buchen, had decided, at least for the moment, to maintain control of all 950 hours of tapes and 46 million pieces of paper from the Nixon years, so that both prosecutors and the new administration would have access to them. Haig, skilled at bullying subordinates, ordered a military aide to load many boxes of files addressed to Nixon onto a truck in the White House parking lot. When attorney Benton Becker, who had helped Ford through his vice presidential confirmation hearings and was now in the White House, learned about this attempted shipment, he confronted Haig and managed to stop it. Haig was able to extricate his own files from the batch and send them out anyway, but Becker discovered this, too, and forced Haig to have them returned to the White House.

The leader of Ford's transition team was Donald Rumsfeld, on temporary leave from his post as ambassador to NATO. The two had been close since 1965, when Rumsfeld had helped Ford in his campaign to become minority leader of the House. Rumsfeld would go on to play leading and very public roles in the new administration, serving as Ford's chief of staff and then as

his secretary of defense. During the Ford administration he would also un-
shackle his conservative foreign policy views and put them into practice—at
times in opposition to the wishes of his president.

Rumsfeld identified the major task facing Ford as restoring the legitimacy
and power of the presidency, which had eroded steadily throughout Nixon's
disastrous second term. That restoration could not be accomplished in the
single month Rumsfeld and the transition team had in which to perform
their work, but he established it as their goal. As his assistant he brought in
Dick Cheney, who had been working in private industry during Rumsfeld's
eighteen months in Europe. Cheney too would come to the fore in the Ford
administration: When Rumsfeld became White House chief of staff Cheney
signed on as his assistant, and when Rumsfeld became secretary of defense
Cheney took over as chief of staff—the youngest in White House history.

In later years, Rumsfeld and Cheney resisted being called neocons,
pointing out that they had always been Republicans and conservatives—as
opposed to the former Democrats, such as Perle and Wolfowitz, who had
become foreign policy hawks while maintaining certain relatively liberal domestic and economic views. But Rumsfeld, Cheney, and the neocons shared
one defining characteristic: They all subscribed to the aggressive, militarist,
antidiplomacy principles and strategies of Fritz Kraemer.

ANOTHER MAN WHO embraced Kraemerite stances, Scoop Jackson, threw
a monkey wrench into an early Ford attempt to go beyond the negatively
charged atmosphere of the Nixon White House by talking with all interested parties and fostering compromises wherever possible. It involved a
deal that Ford tried to make with Soviet ambassador Anatoly Dobrynin
within days of taking office.

On his first visit to the new president, Dobrynin offered to commit the
USSR to the annual emigration of 55,000 Soviet Jews—20,000 more than
in the previous year—on the condition that the commitment remained
only verbal. In return, the ambassador renewed his long-standing demand
for Most Favored Nation trade status for the Soviet Union, asked that his
country be granted access to credits to buy grain from the United States,
and made other such requests—all of which Scoop Jackson had blocked in
Congress for years. Dobrynin did not want to put his offer on paper, fearing that if it was made public Jackson would use the raised number of exit
visas for his own political purposes—Jackson was already the front-runner
for the 1976 Democratic nomination and had become a demon in the eyes
of the Soviet press. Responding to Dobrynin's offer, Ford did something
Nixon had never done: He invited Jackson, Kissinger, and two liberal Jewish

senators—Jacob Javits, a Republican, and Abraham Ribicoff, a Democrat—
to his office to work out a solution.

Kissinger, Javits, and Ribicoff—three of the most prominent Jewish
Americans—were willing to accept Dobrynin's number and respect his
refusal to put it on paper, but Jackson was not. He forced Ford to have
Kissinger draft a memo recapitulating the Dobrynin proposal. Ford then
used his maneuvering skills to negotiate with other congressmen to free
the trade bill so that Jackson couldn't use it as a club to affect U.S.-Soviet
relations.

Ford recognized Jackson as a foreign policy enemy, but he was unaware of
how many other such opponents were in place in his own executive branch.
These included holdovers James Schlesinger, CIA deputy director Vernon
Walters, and ACDA director Fred Iklé, as well as the new chief SALT negotiator, Alex Johnson, and Assistant Secretary of Defense William Clements.
These and other like-minded figures were fixtures at NSC meetings during
the Ford administration; at one such session, Kissinger was the only foreign
policy liberal among ten men around the table.

Kissinger understood this imbalance better than Ford but proved increasingly unable to counter it. When Schlesinger exasperated Kissinger by repeatedly rebutting his ideas in the NSC meetings, Kissinger responded by
unilaterally issuing a series of directives meant to guide SALT negotiations.
His move was stymied by Ford, who disliked Schlesinger's aloof and arrogant manner but still sought his guidance. Early on, Schlesinger told Ford
that Nixon had not heeded his warnings about the Soviets:

> Over the next seven years, the Soviets will be leading in all areas
> [of nuclear delivery systems]. They will increase substantially their
> missile throw weight, over double the present. The bomber gap will
> be narrowed, and they will reach warhead parity unless we can con-
> strain the development of MIRVs. . . . By most criteria, the U.S. would
> be perceived as having less capable forces.

Ford encountered similar views in a pair of articles Albert Wohlstetter
published in successive issues of *Foreign Affairs*. In the articles, Wohlstetter
revived the specter that the National Intelligence Estimates were underes-
timating Soviet strength—a clear rationale to reject additional attempts at
détente with the Soviets. Wohlstetter's and Schlesinger's admonitions were
buttressed by a secret CIA report to the White House, which labeled Soviet
ICBM development plans as "unprecedented in scope" and warned that
new Soviet efforts to MIRV and modernize their missiles would allow the
USSR to surpass the United States in firepower by 1980.

The anti-Communist arguments of these foreign policy conservatives were publicized by a number of leaks to the press, which put additional pressure on Ford to address them. The leaks, most of which came from Jackson, Perle, and Schlesinger, were published by sympathetic syndicated newspaper columnists Rowland Evans and Robert Novak, Joseph Kraft, Jack Anderson, and on the editorial page of the *Wall Street Journal.* Their columns warned Ford repeatedly not to give anything away to the Soviets. This theme was echoed in an admiring profile of Schlesinger, "Professor in the Pentagon," by Nick Thimmesch, which appeared in the *Washington Post* and other big-city newspapers. Thimmesch's notes show that he consulted Fritz Kraemer for the article, and Kraemer's influence was evident throughout the piece—as in Thimmesch's observation that Ford's inner circle considered Schlesinger "a worthy opponent [for] Kissinger, who must be contained, lest his Grand Canyon–sized ego make life miserable for all in the new administration." Schlesinger's "mission," Thimmesch wrote, was "a redirection of [America's] nuclear strength."

It wasn't long before Ford got the idea. "Not just any [SALT II] agreement is acceptable," he told one NSC meeting. "The terms might not be acceptable." Hard-liners cheered: They were getting through to the president.

But two weeks after taking office, Ford incensed conservatives by nominating former New York governor Nelson A. Rockefeller as his vice president. Although Melvin Laird, a close friend of Ford's since their days in Congress, championed the liberal Rockefeller as an ideal running mate for Ford in 1976—one who would unite the wings of the Republican Party and take votes from the Democrats—conservatives viewed Rockefeller as so liberal that he might as well be a Democrat, and as the patron of Kissinger, who supported foreign policies that cozied up to the Communist powers. The American Conservative Union responded to the Rockefeller nomination by breaking formally with the administration; fund-raiser Richard Viguerie, who had worked for Goldwater in 1964 and Wallace in 1968 and 1972, started mining Wallace donor lists for potential supporters of an insurgent third-party candidacy for 1976, which he hoped would attract California governor Ronald Reagan.

Ford alienated still more conservatives with his bold announcement, at a Veterans of Foreign Wars convention, that he would extend "conditional amnesty" to Vietnam War resisters who had fled to Canada to avoid the draft—the conditions including statements of contrition and periods of alternative service in social help programs. While polls showed that most Americans agreed with the proposal, Schlesinger, the Joint Chiefs, and other militarists viewed it as a sign that their dreams of trying once more to win the war in Vietnam were not to be realized.

. . . .

WITHIN A COUPLE of weeks of taking office, Ford was able to answer one question that had hung over his administration from its outset: who would get custody of Nixon's voluminous papers. The fundamental question of their ownership would reverberate for years to come, influencing the argument over the powers of the presidency relative to those of the other branches of government. Every previous president had assumed ownership of his papers after leaving office, and in late August 1974 Ford's counsels advised him that that precedent should extend to Nixon. They also, however, concluded that Ford should retain control of the Nixon materials until the special prosecutor's office determined which of them merited examination, at which point those could be separated out and the remainder sent on to Nixon. Ford agreed with the recommendation and ordered that it be followed.

Fred Buzhardt, who had remained on as White House counsel, now attempted to act on the decision's first part and to ignore the second. But as he tried to ship more documents to Nixon without Ford's knowledge, Ford's informal counsel, Phil Buchen, blocked him as he had Haig. Ford became so angered by Buzhardt's end run that he ordered Buchen to take over the counsel job, removing Buzhardt from that position and from any contact with the White House tapes. For good measure, Ford directed Haig to cease his contacts with Nixon.

"I've lost the battle," Haig told his former assistant Jerry Jones, who was still at the White House, "but I'll stay long enough to get Nixon the pardon."

The key to that pardon was the papers and tapes.

On August 30, Ford discussed the possibility of a pardon with his counsels and Kissinger and Haig. Leon Jaworski, the special prosecutor, believed it might take two years before Nixon could get a fair trial, and Ford feared that such a long wait and the ugly prospect of the trial itself would only distract the White House—and the country—from more immediate challenges. Ford would later write that he had no intention of conditioning a pardon on Nixon's "making an agreement on the papers and tapes," but that is precisely what happened. On August 30, Haig argued to Ford that Nixon should be granted an unconditional pardon and that the former president's papers should be sent to California forthwith. On the other hand, Benton Becker, who was also in the room for that meeting, told the president, as he later put it, "that if he allowed the papers and tapes to be removed from the White House, history would record this as being the final act in the Watergate cover-up." Haig did not contest the point in front of Ford, but in an unauthorized back-channel negotiation he and former Nixon press secretary Ron Ziegler, who had accompanied Nixon to San Clemente, tried to force a deal: Nixon would accept a pardon in exchange for Ford's agreement to send the papers and tapes to San Clemente.

At Ford's request, Becker flew to California and worked out with Nixon's attorney and Ziegler a deed of trust that transferred ownership of the papers and tapes to the General Services Administration. Nixon would receive copies (not the originals) of all the documents—and be granted the right to veto the release of portions of them to preserve privacy or national security. In exchange, Nixon agreed to sign a statement accepting the pardon and conceding that he had been "wrong in not acting more decisively and more forthrightly in dealing with Watergate, particularly when it reached the stage of judicial proceedings." This was not an outright admission of guilt, Becker noted to Ford, but he also pointed out a 1921 Supreme Court ruling holding that the accepting of a pardon constituted an admission of guilt. For the rest of Ford's life, he carried a card in his wallet outlining that 1921 case and its conclusions.

Nixon's right to withhold certain materials had the effect of burying the Ehrlichman-Welander confession tape and David Young's investigative report on Moorer-Radford. In future years, all attempts to obtain these materials were blocked. In December 2008, when the National Archives opened Buzhardt's papers to the public, the list of materials ostensibly available included the David Young report—but researchers looking for it were told it had been redacted.

On September 8, 1974, Ford issued a "full, free, and absolute pardon" to Nixon.

The firestorm of criticism that followed pushed Ford's approval rating from 70 to 48 percent.

IN THE WAKE of the pardon, Ford decided it was an opportune time to get rid of Haig. Ford's former press secretary, Jerry terHorst, after resigning in protest of the pardon, complained in a newspaper column that Ford had been "spending an inordinate amount of time . . . placating the sensitive feelings of General Haig." During Nixon's final year in office, terHorst wrote, Haig had been "the acting President of the United States," and after Nixon's departure Haig had had difficulty relinquishing that level of command, which was why, terHorst concluded, Haig had proved unable to work deferentially with Ford.

There was another position Haig wanted. When Creighton Abrams died on September 4, Haig set his sights on taking over as U.S. Army chief of staff. Haig, of course, was no longer even a member of the military, having been forced to retire after becoming Nixon's chief of staff. Ford felt certain that if he were to nominate Haig for the position, the confirmation hearings would undoubtedly dredge up old problems and might even end in a rejection. Instead he suggested that Haig take the dual positions of chief of the NATO forces and Supreme Allied Commander–Europe (SACEUR), presiding over the 300,000 American forces then in Europe. Haig had never commanded anything larger than a brigade of 3,000 to 4,500 men, but Ford believed that Haig's diplomatic and management experience qualified him for the posts. Moreover, neither European post required Senate confirmation.

When Kissinger objected, Haig marched into his office. Within hearing distance of the staff, Haig threatened to expose the various secrets they shared. Kissinger withdrew his objections but expressed his anger to columnist Joseph Kraft, who wrote that the Haig nomination "poses serious problems" because "circumstantial evidence connects Haig with a mountain of dirty work." The country needed answers, Kraft wrote, about what role Haig had played in the 1969–71 wiretapping, the "Pentagon spy ring," the Saturday Night Massacre, the Plumbers, the eighteen-minute tape gap, and the "doctored" Butterfield memo. All these, Kraft wrote, should be investigated by Congress. Reporter Walter Pincus picked up the thread, warning that senators questioning Haig would have to bone up on the facts, because

> three Haig appearances—before the Senate Foreign Relations Committee on the so-called "national security" wiretaps, before Judge John Sirica's inquiry into the missing and erased White House tapes, and at the trial of Daniel Ellsberg—show that Haig has a highly selective . . . memory and is adroit at devising a version of events that, in these instances, neatly served the Nixon Administration by providing less than the truth.

Fritz Kraemer was saddened and angered by Kissinger's opposition to Haig; the move pushed the two men closer to the full break that would come within a year. Kraemer was delighted at the prospect of Haig becoming SACEUR; he disliked the current holder of the post, General Andrew Goodpaster, whom Haig would be replacing, and relished the idea of his protégé returning to NATO, the turf where the two men had begun their relationship fifteen years earlier.

Before Haig could take the posts, however, he faced one last obstacle: Ford's testimony to the House on the pardon. When Buzhardt read a draft of Ford's opening remarks, prepared by Buchen and others, he was alarmed to see that Ford planned to reveal that Haig had begged Ford to pardon Nixon in exchange for Ford's elevation to the presidency. According to Haig's autobiography, Buzhardt called him and said, "These boys have prepared sworn

testimony for the President that could very well result in your indictment."
Haig hastened to the White House; when Buchen refused to let him see
Ford, he threatened to call an immediate press conference and reveal various aspects of "a secret effort by Ford people to hurry Nixon out of the presidency behind Jerry Ford's back." He was let in. Haig convinced Ford to tone
down his testimony, but when he appeared before Congress Ford said clearly
that before Nixon resigned Haig had suggested that Ford could pardon his
predecessor. This admission could have earned Haig a summons to testify,
but none came.

Goodpaster, the current SACEUR, was incensed by Ford's decision to replace him. At fifty-nine, he had had no intention of retiring and could have
returned to the Pentagon in a high position, or taken another important
post; in later years the army considered Goodpaster so valuable that they
asked him out of retirement to take on several difficult tasks. But now, in
1974, Goodpaster chose to retire in protest over Haig's elevation; he refused
even to attend the turnover-of-command ceremony at NATO, an act that
made Fritz Kraemer dislike Goodpaster even more.

The anger at Haig's usurpation extended deep into the army hierarchy.
It would surface in the coming months in the form of leaks exposing several Haig excesses—the transporting of his dog in an official vehicle, the
shipping of his whiskey on army transports—and forcing Haig to repay the
government for the expenses involved.

HAIG'S DEPARTURE FROM the White House occasioned the permanent
return of Donald Rumsfeld, hired as "staff coordinator," a title that replaced
the Nixon-era title of chief of staff.

Rumsfeld, who was once considered a liberal—though only because he
had advocated ending the war in Vietnam quickly—returned to the United
States with newly hawkish opinions on international affairs. He now characterized himself to the *Washington Post* as a foreign policy "traditionalist"
who emphasized the importance of America's ties with allies in Europe and
who worried more about a potential Communist takeover of Portugal than
about falling dominoes in Asia.

He entered the White House with dreams of self-advancement, envi-
sioning himself as a future cabinet minister, Ford's running mate in 1976,
and his successor in 1980. To achieve those goals, he seemed to believe, he
would have to banish all taint of liberalism from his record. He would also
have to train someone to replace him as Ford's gatekeeper so that he could
more easily move on and up. He asked Cheney to join him as deputy staff
coordinator.

"The understanding when I took the job," Cheney later told biographer Stephen Hayes, "was that I would get access to the president and that I would be Rumsfeld's surrogate," acting for Rumsfeld in his absence, and alternating with Rumsfeld in traveling with Ford—an arrangement that would make for an easy transition if Rumsfeld should later be promoted. The duo functioned as Ford loyalists, though they later admitted to being disheartened by Ford's decision to testify before a congressional committee and other such actions that to them smacked of presidential weakness.

This concern over presidential power and prerogatives would raise its head at several critical points during the Ford administration, involving such matters as the Freedom of Information Act, congressional oversight of the CIA, and the Foreign Intelligence Surveillance Act. The most notable issue involved the ownership of Nixon's papers. In that fight, Rumsfeld and Cheney linked up with Antonin Scalia, then an assistant attorney general. When congressional opposition to the Ford-Nixon deal that granted Nixon ownership of his papers crystallized in a lawsuit that aimed to keep those papers in the public domain, Rumsfeld, Cheney, and Scalia found themselves in the odd position of defending Nixon—whom none of them liked—in order to establish a principle that would enhance the power of future presidents. Cheney later lamented "the extent to which we have restrained presidential authority," calling it a "fundamental problem" rooted in the Nixon era. "Consumed with the trauma of Watergate and Vietnam, we have tampered with the relationship between the executive branch and the Congress in ways designed primarily to avoid future abuses of power." Fighting to have a president control his papers was one way to restore presidential power. After Rumsfeld became secretary of defense, Cheney took up the cudgels of the Nixon papers case; it would not be decided by the Supreme Court until 1977.

The dispute over ownership of presidential papers eventually gave rise to the "unitary executive theory," which argued for consolidating the power of the executive branch and for establishing the executive's primacy over the legislative and judiciary branches, whose power would therefore diminish. In the early 1980s the unitary executive theory would be a founding tenet of the Federalist Society; Scalia helped to establish one of the first chapters of that organization.

DURING RUMSFELD'S THIRTEEN months as staff coordinator, he and Cheney also acted as the implacable foes of the remaining proponents of the Nixon policies inside the Ford administration: Kissinger and Rockefeller.

Rumsfeld began by allying himself with Schlesinger in the latest version of the "battle of the estimates" over the extent of Soviet power and potential. In that era, the figures on which conclusions could be based were subject to interpretation and to manipulation, according to William Hyland, a Kissinger deputy who later became editor of *Foreign Affairs*. While CIA estimates of Soviet power were admittedly "too low," Hyland would write, the Pentagon's were "wildly wrong" on the high side. Ford sensed that both camps were guessing and was reluctant to accept either low or high estimates as his basis for action. But he was open to funding individual weapons programs, so Schlesinger concentrated on these, with assistance from Andy Marshall and his Office of Net Assessment, and with the backing of Rumsfeld in the White House councils. Schlesinger commissioned Marshall to do a report on the subject; the report agreed with Wohlstetter's high estimates of Soviet strength and recommended accelerated development of the MX missile, Trident submarine, and B-1 bomber. Rumsfeld pushed these in interdepartmental meetings; he later claimed that these particular programs survived because of his stewardship.

In November 1974, American voters' still-smoldering anger at Nixon and his pardon by Ford, in combination with the shocks from OPEC's quadrupling of oil prices and from sharply rising inflation, turned the midterm elections into a rout. Democrats took forty-nine seats in the House, increasing their majority there to more than two-thirds. In the Senate, the Democrats reached sixty seats—a nearly veto-proof Congress.

A disaster for Ford, the election was an enabling action for many conservatives. In reaction, Senator Jesse Helms of North Carolina formed a political action committee to help elect officials who agreed with his ultra-conservative stances. His work would result in the election of four such Republican senators in 1976. Meanwhile, the people around Ronald Reagan, the soon-to-be-retired governor of California, used the 1974 election results, the Nixon pardon, and Ford's continuation of the Nixon foreign policies to attack the president and establish Reagan as the leading alternative Republican candidate for 1976.

The loss also strengthened Donald Rumsfeld's resolve—and his hand—in the quest to become Ford's running mate in 1976. Rumsfeld came to believe that his best strategy to take the slot would be to embrace a more conservative, anti-Communist foreign policy line than he had in the past—and to counter Henry Kissinger whenever possible.

The United States and the USSR had scheduled a summit in Vladivostok that November. By the time Kissinger left for Moscow for a presummit discussion in October, however, there was evidence that his opponents had already won on a major point. In an NSC meeting, Kissinger agreed that the first option to be presented to the Soviets would incorporate a concept that Scoop Jackson (backed by the JCS) had forced through Congress, known as "equal aggregates of nuclear delivery systems." Kissinger thought the concept was too simplistic and favored something more complex, a carrots-and-sticks approach that he told the NSC meeting would "provide an increase in stability" by forcing the Soviets to make their armaments "more like ours—smaller missiles, lighter warheads, more bombers and submarines." Kissinger acknowledged that his more complex approach would be a difficult sale to the Soviets. To his surprise, however, when Kissinger presented Brezhnev with a choice—between the equal-aggregates plan or another in which the Soviets were permitted to retain more "strategic delivery systems" in exchange for the United States being able to deploy more MIRVed missiles—the Soviet leader told Kissinger that either would be acceptable.

As the summit at Vladivostok neared, the Ford-Kissinger bargaining strategy was assailed from the right from an unusual quarter: General Daniel Graham, the head of the Defense Intelligence Agency. Graham's attack was a sign that nothing Ford brought home from the summit would likely satisfy the ultraconservatives. At Vladivostok, the Soviets did agree to the Jackson-JCS "equal aggregates" concept; beyond that, the superpowers agreed to cap their nuclear delivery arsenals and the number of MIRVed weapons and to ban the construction of new ICBM land-based platforms. The Soviets also stopped pushing the United States to include forward-based systems (FBS) in its numbers. "I think we came away with a good agreement," Ford told the NSC after they returned. "The minimum, median, and maximum [numbers from the intelligence estimates] were all higher than the limit we negotiated."

Ford and Kissinger viewed the Vladivostok agreement as a triumph, but those on the right felt otherwise. Rumsfeld, who attended the summit, raised no objection at the time, but in later years he would tout his disapproval of it.

Rumsfeld was certainly aware, in early 1975, that the Vladivostok results irked conservatives. One of them, writing in the *Washington Post*, wondered what could have induced the Soviets to reverse years of policy and cave in to the Ford-Kissinger demands, and concluded, "It looks as if the Vladivostok agreement is based on a tacit understanding between the White House and the Kremlin to keep Jackson at bay and help re-elect Ford."

Even Jackson opposed the Vladivostok accords, objecting strongly to what he considered the too-high limits agreed, and arguing that Ford and Kissinger had accepted a permanent three-to-one Soviet advantage in delivery systems. Jackson's opposition hobbled any chance of ratifying a treaty based on the Vladivostok accords.

William Hyland, who was also at the summit, was shocked by the Jackson camp's "hostile" reaction to what Ford had brought home. "The Vladivostok agreement should have been a turning point," he later wrote, "because Ford and Kissinger had, after all, salvaged a framework for an arms control agreement." Kissinger complained to Hyland on the phone on February 22, 1975, "There is no doubt that what Jackson did after Vladivostok was a bad blow. . . . The damage these bastards have done here is incredible. . . . This is the most depressing period in our foreign policy, and totally unnecessary."

Conservatives also objected in public to the fact that Kissinger allowed the Soviets, in calculating their missile delivery systems, to exclude their Backfire bombers, which research studies commissioned by Schlesinger had shown were capable of intercontinental flight. The omission was actually a mistake about which Kissinger had failed to inform Ford properly, and Ford was angry when he discovered it.

According to many leading conservatives, though, Kissinger made a far more serious mistake when he agreed to a Soviet demand that would effectively have killed the new Tomahawk air-launched cruise missile program. Still in development, this new warhead delivery system was potentially one of the most effective new weapons in the U.S. arsenal. James Schlesinger, Ed Rowny, young arms-control staffers such as Paul Wolfowitz and John Lehman, and NSC members such as a new recruit from the CIA, Soviet expert Robert Gates, all fought hard, and in public, to prevent Kissinger from killing the missile.

Before long, critics were citing such Kissinger omissions as evidence that Ford had given in to Brezhnev at Vladivostok just as Chamberlain had done to Hitler at Munich in 1938—an analogy that would be trotted out repeatedly in the next two decades, whenever an American president fell short of the right's expectations in dealing with the Soviets or other perceived enemies.

Both sides had expected the Vladivostok summit to lead to a SALT II agreement to be finalized in 1975, one that would aim for serious reductions in nuclear arsenals right through the 1980s. After Vladivostok, however, Jackson wanted SALT II scrapped or radically changed, and he threatened to refuse to go along with Most Favored Nation status for the USSR and to insist on Jackson-Vanik sanctions on the USSR if Ford and Kissinger would not accommodate his objections on the nuclear arms negotiations. "It was an absurd situation," Hyland recalled. "We were withdrawing one of the carrots that tempted the Soviets—the prospect of trade and credits—and substituting a threat against their internal order; at the same time we were being urged to discard one of the supposed benefits—restraint on Soviet nuclear forces—by abandoning the SALT negotiations."

This was all too much for Brezhnev, who was embarrassed by his inability to force Ford to quash Jackson-Vanik. The Soviet premier refused to accept the Kissinger-Jackson exchange on Soviet emigration and withdrew the USSR's application for Most Favored Nation status—actions that seriously hurt the cause of détente.

In the next few years, the Soviets cut back Jewish emigration far below the levels Dobrynin and Brezhnev had been willing to accept, and forged trade relationships with Europe and Asia to replace the one they had been planning with the United States. This led to what Peter Rodman, a Kissinger aide at the time, labeled a "breakdown of America's Soviet policy," a "tragedy [that] postponed the day when the Kremlin leaders would learn to accommodate themselves to the international system."

IN THE EARLY days of 1975, Scoop Jackson and Donald Rumsfeld got more press than almost any other Washington official. At the time they seemed far apart in philosophy—the Democratic senator a thorn in the administration's side, the former Republican congressman, now Ford chief of staff supposedly working hard to further its goals. But they were close in their positions on foreign affairs, increasingly so as the year went on. And both were grandstanding for future runs at the presidency. Jackson made the cover of *Time*; he was profiled in the major East Coast newspapers, touted for championing liberal economic programs that appealed to the Democratic base and foreign policy stances that appealed to independent and conservative voters. Articles recounted his battles with Kissinger and his closeness to Schlesinger.

"Keep an eye on 'Rummy,'" James Reston wrote in the *New York Times*, calling Rumsfeld a "tough and efficient administrator" during the Nixon years who now "could turn out to be in the right place with the right credentials for much larger things in his party"—including the vice presidential slot in 1976 and a presidential run in 1980 as Ford's successor. To make all this happen, however, Reston and other commentators noted that Rumsfeld would need Cabinet experience. "The State, Treasury, and Defense Departments have been mentioned," the *Post* informed its readers in a three-part series on Rumsfeld.

To obtain one of those Cabinet posts, Rumsfeld needed to oust its current occupant. His first target was Secretary of the Treasury William Simon. Articles soon appeared suggesting that Ford was losing confidence in Simon. When Ford told a reporter directly that he had no interest in firing Simon, the reporter easily traced the negative Simon stories to Cheney, acting for Rumsfeld. The reporter confronted Rumsfeld, saying that he would expose his backstabbing unless Rumsfeld telephoned Simon to say that Ford had full confidence in him, and to arrange for a photo op of Ford and Simon together. Rumsfeld did as directed. The photo of Ford and Simon soon ran in many newspapers.

Kissinger was a tougher target for Rumsfeld, but in the spring and summer of 1975 Rumsfeld and Cheney acted as snipers, injuring Kissinger by hyping the misunderstanding over the Backfire bombers in the SALT II numbers and by feeding information to the media that faulted Kissinger for one-man diplomacy. "It is not America's credibility that will be questioned now as a result of the debacle in Southeast Asia, it is Kissinger's," one newspaper wrote. A Democratic adviser to several presidents—likely Paul Nitze—was quoted as saying, "When you personalize foreign policy to the extent [Kissinger] has, you must be prepared to rise with success and descend with failure. You live by the sword and you die by the sword."

Kissinger did not know that Rumsfeld was the source of these snipings; he thought they came from Schlesinger. The two secretaries had been breakfasting weekly; now each found excuses to cancel their standing date.

Rumsfeld's third target was Schlesinger, the man whose policy positions were the closest match to his own. Given the animosity between Kissinger and Schlesinger, Rumsfeld did not have to do much to undermine the secretary of defense. But he did have to establish his own belligerency and shrewdness in regard to defense matters, and as 1975 progressed his voice in NSC meetings was heard more frequently.

Polls continued to show that 25 percent of registered Republicans would not vote for the 1976 ticket if Rockefeller was on it. But Rockefeller had Ford's confidence, and if Rumsfeld wanted to be the vice presidential candidate, he would have to undercut Rockefeller. Rumsfeld's weapon in this fight was his control of the White House bureaucracy. Although Ford had given Rockefeller the leadership of the Domestic Council, Rumsfeld and Cheney refused to expedite the bureaucratic steps that would officially install Rockefeller's men in key positions there. Rumsfeld and Cheney also worked the bureaucratic levers to kill one of Rockefeller's best ideas, a plan to reduce American dependence on foreign oil by developing alternative fuel sources. Ford liked the notion but Rumsfeld and Cheney sent it for evaluation to several executive branch committees, where—as they expected—it languished and eventually expired.

LATE IN DECEMBER 1974, on the front page of the *New York Times,* Seymour Hersh published a story detailing a "Huge CIA Effort in U.S. Against Anti-War Forces . . . in Nixon Years." Within forty-eight hours, the CIA produced a memo refuting Hersh's allegations. Congressional subcommittees were immediately convened, the Senate's led by Frank Church. Throughout the early months of 1975, Ford and his advisers spent a great deal of time and energy trying to prevent all the top-secret work of the CIA from being exposed in the Church hearings.

In an NSC meeting, Rumsfeld and Cheney urged the FBI to search Hersh's premises to find the secret material on which his charges were based, and to prosecute Hersh. When senior officials said this approach would not solve the problem, the idea was dropped. Even so, Rumsfeld, Cheney, and the Justice Department continued to argue for refusing to divulge information to Congress that would compromise CIA activities, while also working to rein in the CIA's independence and make it more subject to White House control.

In later years, conservatives would contend that the Ford administration failed to prevent Congress from damaging the CIA's ability to gather information vital to the nation's security. In 1975 there was little Ford could do to stop Congress in that regard. Given the excesses that had been revealed—including illegal domestic surveillance ordered by the Johnson and Nixon administrations—Congress had legitimate concern that only increased oversight would prevent such practices in the future.

Ford also lost ground with conservatives by attempting a rapprochement with Cuba. Envoys had been making considerable progress toward normalizing relations with Castro's regime until 1975, when a civil war exploded in Angola after that country achieved independence from Portugal, and Cuban troops were prominent in the fighting. When Congress learned that the CIA was backing a different faction in Angola—embroiling the United States in another proxy war against Communism abroad—the antiwar majority passed a bill forbidding the use of U.S. troops or resources in Angola. Its passage killed any immediate hope of improving relations with Cuba. Ford issued an angry statement that Congress was intruding on foreign policy turf that constitutionally belonged to the executive branch, but he could do nothing to change the situation.

"President Ford pushed some buttons recently, and nothing happened," the New York Times reported. "He tried to provide covert military aid to favored Angolan factions and was blocked by Congress. He invoked executive privilege so that . . . Kissinger would not have to turn over information on intelligence activities . . . but Congress was able to extract the information anyway." The Times concluded that the presidency had lost considerable power—and Ford, in a response, asserted that while the presidency had not lost any "basic" power, there had been a swing of "the historic pendulum" toward Congress, one that was unfortunately "disruptive" to his ability to govern.

. . . .

IN MARCH 1975, the *Los Angeles Times* and other newspapers ran the longest article about Fritz Kraemer ever published, written by Nick Thimmesch after dozens of interviews with Kraemer, his son Sven, Henry Kissinger, James Schlesinger, Hal Sonnenfeldt, Dick Walters, and others. (Haig was in Europe and did not see a letter from Thimmesch seeking comment in time to add his voice to the article.) In the article, headlined "The Iron Mentor of the Pentagon," Schlesinger is quoted as saying that "Kraemer is a seminal influence. He makes people think at a time when many people don't want to." Thimmesch also quoted an intelligence community official, anonymous in the article but identifiable as Walters in Thimmesch's unpublished notes, which were consulted by the authors after the death of both men. "The intelligent have listened to [Kraemer]; the stupid haven't," Walters said. Kissinger labeled Kraemer "one of the most significant and profound influences on me" and vowed that "Kraemer and I are always going to be friends."

"Henry does not come to me for advice—he comes for *absolution*," Kraemer told Thimmesch. "Kraemer is abstractly idealistic," Kissinger responded in the article. "He leaves little room for options. There are times when we see more of each other, and that is usually when he is convinced I have been acting less than perfect. I listen to him, knowing that if I can only accomplish 20 percent of what should be done, I am fortunate."

The article did note that the bond between the two German émigrés had become strained since 1973. A "friend" of both men described their relationship: "Kraemer is a patriot who believes in God. Kissinger is an opportunist who is an agnostic, maybe an atheist. Kraemer knows Kissinger is out of control now, but because Kraemer believes in metaphysics, a moral order, he still has hopes for Kissinger."

In the article, Thimmesch traced Kraemer's growing disillusion with Kissinger to the latter's role in what Kraemer saw as the abandonment of U.S. commitments throughout the world—an issue he had been raising with his protégé since early 1969.

At the moment the article appeared, the final act in the Vietnam drama was playing out. For two years, the United States had been anticipating pushes by the North Vietnamese to take over all of Cambodia and South Vietnam. In later years, conservatives would charge that Ford, like Nixon in his last years in office, did nothing to prevent the loss of South Vietnam and other Southeast Asian nations to Communism. But in 1974 and 1975, the notably conservative principals at Ford's national security table produced few suggestions of aggressive actions for the United States to take in Cambodia and South Vietnam, despite evidence that the Communists' final push was about to occur. In Cambodia, that final offensive began on New Year's Day 1975, and would not conclude for several years, during which hundreds of thousands of Cambodians would die. But in 1975 Cambodia was of far less interest to Americans than South Vietnam, where a final assault was also gathering. The Ford NSC fretted about it, but no plans were made to counteract it. The only high official pleading with Ford to send in troops and air support was NATO commander Alexander Haig. In 2000, Haig recalled in an interview that he had also urged Ford to "roll up his sleeves and put the monkey where it belonged, in the Congress. Say [to the public], 'Okay, this is what's happening, and it's the Congress' fault. We've got legislative anarchy in this country, and I need the support of the American people.'"

Ford knew that Haig's accusations about Congress were false and that shifting the blame to the legislative bodies—which Kissinger also wanted to do—was inappropriate. He authorized an evacuation of South Vietnamese that eventually involved 100,000 people and began a humanitarian relief and resettlement program in California. Kissinger warned the USSR that the United States would hold it responsible if North Vietnam tried to bring down the evacuation planes; Moscow replied that the evacuation would be "unhindered." But the airlift was virtually the only action the United States took in the final weeks. American aid to South Vietnam had been cut in half since 1973, and the South Vietnamese forces were low on equipment and ammunition. The South's precarious position was exacerbated in March and April when Thieu and his generals withdrew from strategic positions, allowing the North to pour in troops and supplies for a final assault. When Ford dispatched the army chief of staff to Saigon, he returned with a request for $1 billion in immediate aid, plus renewed air and naval support. But Congress pared down the hasty request to less than $100 million, a figure that would make no difference in the outcome of the war.

Historians would later argue that Ford and especially Kissinger, by having earlier refused to expend political capital to shore up the South Vietnamese defenses, essentially denied that country the ability to repel the North's attacks. Others charged that the president and secretary of state also avoided responsibility for the final debacle by not hastening to broker an end to South Vietnamese independence that would have prevented the slaughter of tens of thousands of people during the 1975 offensive and in the reprisals made after the North took over the South.

In late April 1975, as the North Vietnamese neared Saigon, Ford told a Tulane University audience, "America can regain the sense of pride that existed before Vietnam. But it cannot be achieved by refighting a war that is finished as far as America is concerned." He was roundly cheered by the students, but once back in the capital Ford was chastised by a furious Kissinger, whom he had deliberately not consulted about the speech's reference to a "war that is finished." Some on the right never forgave Ford for what they saw as waving the white flag before the battle had been completed.

Less than two weeks after the fall of Saigon, in mid-May 1975, what CIA director William Colby described as "Khmer Communists" on the Cambodian coast went into international waters to seize a U.S. flag freighter, the *Mayaguez*, with thirty-nine crew members.

Within hours, Ford, Colby, Schlesinger, Kissinger, Rockefeller, Scowcroft, the acting chairman of the Joint Chiefs, and Rumsfeld gathered for an NSC meeting. All felt keenly the need to assuage the ghosts of the Vietnam War and the recent withdrawal from Saigon. It was a moment that seemed to demand military action.

"What are our options?" Ford asked the group.

"We can have a passive stance or we can be active," Schlesinger said. "We can do such things as seizing Cambodian assets. We can assemble [our] forces. We can seize a small island as a hostage. We might also consider a blockade." All such actions, Schlesinger warned, "would have to be scrutinized by Congress" under the War Powers Act. Moreover, there was concern that under the terms of Cooper-Church, Congress might forbid any military actions in Southeast Asia. Schlesinger also pointed out that two previous freighters, a Panamanian and a Philippine, had been seized and then released by the same group of Khmer Communists.

Kissinger countered by insisting that the most important problem was not the return of the *Mayaguez* but rather "how the U.S. appears at this time," and that even if negotiations should eventually result in the return of the *Mayaguez* and its crew unharmed, that was "not to our advantage." Therefore Kissinger advocated a "strong [diplomatic] statement and a show of force." Ford agreed. Rockefeller, whom conservatives decried as a liberal, raised the ante by rejecting as an insufficient reaction the idea of "getting out a message and getting [military] people ready." He wanted "a violent response. . . . The world should know that we will act and that we will act quickly." All now jumped on this bandwagon. Rumsfeld added a crafty notion: Rather than warning the Cambodians of impending military action, the United States should act without warning. "To the extent we want to be forceful, we do not need to make it public."

"We may wish to point out that they released other ships. This gives them a way out," Colby suggested.

"Let them figure their own way out," Rumsfeld retorted.

Ford and Rockefeller then agreed with Rumsfeld: strong action would be taken but not announced in advance. "I can assure you," Ford summed up, "that, irrespective of [having to report to] the Congress, we will move."

The next day, with big American warships on the way but with key factual issues still unresolved—the exact location of the *Mayaguez* crew, and whose control they were under—Kissinger hammered home a Kraemerite point in an NSC meeting: "It is not enough to get the ship's release. Using one aircraft carrier, one destroyer, and 1,000 Marines to get the ship out [amounts to] not much. I think we should seize the island, seize the ship, hit the mainland. I am thinking not of Cambodia but of Korea and of the Soviet Union and others. . . . We have to use the opportunity to [signal] others they will be worse off if they tackle us."

Ford assumed that "Americans were taken from the island and that some were killed." This was later shown to be untrue, but at that moment he used the assumption as reason to employ deadly force. He triggered the rescue effort.

Militarily, it was a disaster. "Virtually everything that could go wrong, did," a military history later concluded. The helicopters swooped toward the target too late—after the Cambodians had released the crew unharmed. It was revealed that the United States had known, moments before unleashing the helicopter assault, that the crew was free, but that Kissinger decreed that the attack should go forward anyway. Between accidental deaths in a preparatory exercise and the attack itself, more than three dozen servicemen died.

Ford painted the *Mayaguez* operation as a success, a demonstration that the United States was still the most powerful nation in the world, one that would not hesitate to use military power when provoked. The American news media and Congress applauded the effort and its intent, equally anxious to get beyond Vietnam.

Most Americans wanted to believe in the goodness and efficacy of the military, and to do so without reference to Vietnam. The *Mayaguez* crisis gave Americans an excuse to feel good about a military mission—and, in doing so, became the first step toward restoring a military-based U.S. foreign policy.

19

Yielding to the Right

Successful presidential candidates from Harry Truman in 1948 forward to Richard Nixon in 1972 had easily rejected pressure from the left but had found themselves needing to move to the right to counter its criticisms. Once conservatives realized that Ford's adherence to Nixon's foreign policies was not absolute, they seized every opportunity to push, pull, and trap Ford in their direction. As the 1976 election grew closer and Ford became more concerned about his chances of staying in office, the right's power to influence his stances on foreign affairs increased.

In July 1975, when exiled Russian novelist and Nobel Prize–winner Aleksandr Solzhenitsyn came to Washington to be honored at a dinner given by the AFL-CIO, Kissinger pleaded with the president not to attend or invite Solzhenitsyn to the White House, to prevent offending the Soviet leaders. Ford acquiesced, and in Ford's name Kissinger forbade Cabinet members to attend the dinner.

This was an error: Solzhenitsyn was viewed by many, not only those on the right, as a hero for his impassioned dissent to the Soviet system. Cheney sent a memo to Rumsfeld, who forwarded it to Ford, suggesting that the president meet with Solzhenitsyn as a "counter-balance," so that "we not contribute any more to the illusion that all of a sudden we're bosom-buddies with the Russians." Kissinger's attempt to keep the Cabinet from attending the dinner backfired. Someone leaked the order, and Kissinger was publicly castigated as unduly propitiating the Soviets. Secretary of Defense Schlesinger and UN ambassador Daniel Patrick Moynihan, two staunch anti-Communists, attended the dinner without repercussions. Brezhnev later needled Ford and Kissinger about Solzhenitsyn, saying that his former problem had become their problem.

On the day of the dinner, Kissinger made certain he was out of town in Minneapolis, where he gave an important speech on "The Moral Foundations of Foreign Policy." This was Kraemer's usual turf but Kissinger wanted to capture it for himself—and for Nixonian pragmatisim. In a world where "power remains the ultimate arbiter," he argued, the existence and prevalence of nuclear weapons forced the United States to "seek a more productive and stable relationship [to the USSR] despite the basic antagonism of our values." Kissinger noted that Solzhenitsyn's message was that "the U.S. should pursue an aggressive policy to overthrow the Soviet system. But I believe that if his views became the national policy of the U.S., we would be confronted with considerable threat of military conflict [and] the consequences of his views would not be acceptable to the American people or to the world." Kissinger insisted that the United States "must be true to its own beliefs or it will lose its bearings in the world. But at the same time it must survive in a world of sovereign nations and competing wills." By insisting that pragmatism in foreign policy must and should trump fixed values, Kissinger seemed to be addressing Kraemer as much as he was tweaking Solzhenitsyn.

In the eyes of the anti-Communists, Ford and Kissinger could do nothing right—even when, during this period, the State Department helped prevent a Communist takeover in Portugal and tried to fight one in Portugal's former colony, Angola. In Portugal, an infusion of American aid helped effect a transition from an autocratic regime to a more democratic, pro-NATO government. In Angola, U.S.-backed entities actively fought Soviet-backed ones until Congress pulled the plug on CIA assistance. These aggressive promotions of democracy and blocking of Soviet expansionism would later be cited as exemplars by neocons, who made the championing of democracy a centerpiece of their philosophy. As they occurred in 1975, however, the nascent neocons were distracted by another worry: an upcoming conference in Helsinki, where they feared that Ford and Kissinger would further diminish the United States in relation to the USSR.

The conference was an unusual one, bringing some thirty-five nations together to resolve unfinished business from World War II. Ford had not wanted to attend, but he was scheduled to meet Brezhnev there in a sort of side summit. Moreover, the leaders of Yugoslavia, Romania, and Hungary wanted Ford to attend in support of conference provisions that would commit signatories (including the USSR) to uphold certain human rights, particularly freedom of religion and free movement of people and ideas, which could loosen the satellites' ties to Moscow. For Ford and the United

States, the downside of the conference was that it would also affirm all extant international borders—which the Soviets would trumpet as validating their domination of Eastern Europe.

In a preconference phone call to William F. Buckley, Jr., Kissinger acknowledged that "a lot of conservatives are screaming that the Security Conference is sanctifying the Soviet presence in Europe." However, he explained,

> The Conference wasn't our idea. It isn't something I'm proud of. Our instructions to our men were to stay a half step behind the Europeans. Insofar as anything of substance at the conference is concerned, it should be looked at as a provision for peaceful change. The territorial integrity issue is something they have gone over for years. The French, British, and Germans had already made their bilateral agreements. It is more in the direction of change than sanctification.

Buckley was unconvinced. But at Helsinki, the two Germanys refused to accept the wording of the borders statement. A stalemate developed, and the statement became so hedged with codicils that it could be interpreted as giving credence to either the Soviet or the anti-Soviet position. The matter that Kissinger (and Buckley) had so casually dismissed—the human rights declarations—turned out to be the conference's most revolutionary aspect, offering the satellites ways to increase their independence that within a generation would lead to the collapse of their Communist governments and to the implosion of the USSR. These events, in turn, would fuel the neocons' belief in the transformative power of democracy promotion.

The Brezhnev-Ford summit at Helsinki was also supposed to lead to some moderate progress on SALT II. But this too stalled, entangled by the side issues of the Backfire bomber and cruise missiles.

The right's pressure on Ford continued to mount. Bob Gates, the CIA Soviet specialist who had moved to the NSC in 1974, railed at the administration for what he considered yielding to the Soviets at Vladivostok and Helsinki, complaining that it would be impossible to verify the Soviets' compliance with missile limitations. Congressional Republicans pointed out that a plank of their party's platform since 1948 had been the annual celebration of Captive Nations Week, reaffirming a U.S. commitment to the future freedom of Lithuania, Latvia, and Estonia; by signing the Helsinki accords, they said, Ford had accepted that these three nations were part of the USSR.

In his memoir of the Ford years, Kissinger chastises the neoconservative opponents of the Nixon-Ford policies as "oblivious to the context in which their prescriptions [for a crusade against Communism] had to be carried out. . . . With a non-elected president [the United States] was not in a position to conduct a crusade; in fact, the attempt to do so would have torn the country apart even further. By depicting the diplomatic strategy of the Nixon and Ford Administrations as a form of appeasement . . . the neoconservatives undercut the real foreign policy debate"—which, in Kissinger's view, was about how to find ways for the United States and USSR to coexist in a world where power was becoming dispersed more widely among a larger number of nations.

Soon, the neoconservatives would have a candidate: Ronald Reagan. At the YAF annual convention, when John Sears, the former Nixon aide who was now campaign manager for Reagan, told the young conservatives that Reagan would not run as a third-party candidate, the YAF endorsed Reagan for 1976; many members signed on to work for him. When Reagan left the governorship, YAF paid for his weekly radio addresses, which reached 20–30 million people.

Another right-wing rallying point in these months was the proposed "return" of the Panama Canal to the government of Panama. In a Ford-led NSC meeting to discuss revising the decades-old treaty with Panama, Schlesinger made the case for keeping the canal, and every public official who spoke confirmed that his mail was running 100 percent against "giving away" the canal. As others at the meeting noted, however, the United States was bound by a long-established treaty to return the canal. Moreover, South American countries were warning that they would send troops to aid Panama if the United States should attempt to renege on its treaty promise. Over Schlesinger's objections, Ford decided to continue the process that would lead to Panamanian control. Ford had determined that to have the best chance at winning in 1976 he must wherever possible embrace rightist notions, but he could not in good conscience do so in regard to the Panama Canal.

He did, however, decide to abandon détente. That subject came up in an unusual way. Arms control expert Ed Rowny was convinced that, in accords like Helsinki, "détente was playing into Soviet hands." He suggested to Schlesinger that *détente* was "a code word for a policy of unwarranted accommodation [and] a constraint only upon the policies of the United States," and needed to be dropped from the diplomatic vocabulary.

Schlesinger agreed. But he cautioned Rowny that détente was "one of Henry's sacred cows. He believes he invented the concept and will never give it up." Rowny and Schlesinger developed a presentation for Schlesinger to give to the president on the subject of dropping the word. To Schlesinger's surprise, Ford accepted the idea. The president soon instructed Kissinger that the administration would no longer follow a policy of détente, and that U.S.

officials were not to use the term but to substitute "peace through strength," a phrase Barry Goldwater had used in 1964. Kissinger was furious, but he had no choice but to follow his president's wishes.

Replacing *détente* with "peace through strength" was more than a rhetorical substitution. As an expression of how the United States should deal with the world, "peace through strength" owed much to Kraemer's notion that a nation must prevent displays of provocative weakness—that peace could only be enforced by displays of military might. The change was a serious attempt to shift away from the Nixon-Kissinger program of working with rather than endlessly confronting America's enemies.

Ford's friend Mel Laird threw another spear against détente. In the July issue of *Reader's Digest*, Laird charged that the Soviets were routinely violating their agreements with the United States, making a shambles of détente. Kissinger rebutted the article in an eight-page memo for Ford, who then used it to argue with Laird. Among the points Kissinger made was that even tough critics such as Schlesinger admitted that there was no evidence of meaningful Soviet violations of the ABM and SALT agreements. Still, the accusation about the alleged violations kept being repeated—for example, in the next issue of *Reader's Digest*, where columnist Joseph Alsop reiterated Laird's charges: "The Soviets have forged ahead with fearful rapidity. . . . If we continue to stay stock-still . . . the Soviet edge will turn into a significant Soviet strategic superiority." Conservatives were increasingly convinced that the U.S. decision to abandon South Vietnam, coupled with increases in Soviet military spending, was emboldening the USSR's attempts to install Communist-leaning regimes and undercut American global supremacy. The conservative think tanks identified the countries in potential danger: Angola, Mozambique, Ethiopia, South Yemen, Afghanistan, Nicaragua, and El Salvador.

As THE FALL of 1975 approached, former governor Ronald Reagan continued to attack the administration on many fronts, including its foreign policies and its increasing inability to control inflation and the effects of the OPEC oil price increases. To meet the Reagan threat, Ford press secretary Ron Nessen later explained, "various strategies were tried to discourage Reagan from entering the race," including selecting a southern conservative, Secretary of the Army Hollis "Bo" Callaway, as Ford's campaign manager; allowing Callaway to suggest—without objection from Ford—that Nelson Rockefeller would be a drag on Ford's nomination, thereby undercutting Rockefeller as Ford's 1976 running mate; and shifting Ford's policies "further to the right."

Rumsfeld and Cheney argued that Ford must take Reagan's issues from him—principal among them the presence of Rockefeller on the 1976 ticket and Ford's retention of Nixon holdovers on his cabinet, which reminded voters of the new administration's ties to the disgraced old one. Reagan, they suggested, would attack Kissinger's continued prominence in directing U.S. foreign policy, and Ford's apparent unwillingness to resist Congress's attempts to rein in the CIA. In reaction, Ford agreed that CIA director Colby must go—not just because Colby was a focal point of anger at the CIA, but also because he had too willingly agreed to congressional oversight.

In the fall of 1975, James Schlesinger irritated Ford once too often. In testimony before the House Appropriations Committee, the secretary of defense had some testy exchanges about the next Pentagon budget with committee chairman George Mahon, a close friend of Ford; he then gave a press conference in which he blasted the committee, and Mahon by name, for wanting "deep, savage, and arbitrary cuts." Ford now decided that Schlesinger must go.

He also determined to cut back Kissinger's power by stripping him of the national security adviser post. He settled upon Rumsfeld as the replacement for Schlesinger. Rumsfeld consulted Paul Nitze before deciding to accept the appointment; Nitze was enthusiastic, believing that Rumsfeld would be able to do a better job as secretary of defense than his predecessor because of his close relationship with Ford.

On November 1, 1975, the White House announced the high-level changes, including the substitution of Rumsfeld for Schlesinger as secretary of defense, calling George H. W. Bush home from his post as envoy to Beijing to replace Colby as director of the CIA, and elevating Kissinger's former deputy, Brent Scowcroft, to the national security adviser position. Cheney took over from Rumsfeld as White House chief of staff. In a press release, the White House said that Rockefeller was "voluntarily" taking himself off the ticket for 1976. The press instantly dubbed the firings and replacements as "the Halloween Massacre." Ford was convinced that he had made the right personnel decisions for the Cabinet and staff, but was later angry at himself "for showing cowardice in not saying to the ultra-conservatives: It's going to be Ford and Rockefeller, whatever the consequences."

Bush did not want to head the CIA. He had been hoping for a position at Commerce or Treasury when he returned from China—a position that would give him the necessary experience to become a viable vice presidential candidate. He attributed the CIA nod to the influence of Rumsfeld, pointing out to Ford that Rumsfeld was positioning himself for the VP slot. During Bush's confirmation hearings, Scoop Jackson—who had gotten along well with both Colby and Schlesinger—derided Bush and Rumsfeld as poor substitutes. Then Jackson raised a point that Bush came to believe Rumsfeld had planted with the senator: "It seems to me that President Ford should assure this Committee that Ambassador Bush will not be on the ticket." To save Bush's nomination, Ford was forced to send a letter to the committee vowing that if Bush was confirmed as CIA director, "I will not consider him as my Vice Presidential running mate in 1976."

On the morning after the firings, according to recently released transcripts of Kissinger's phone calls, Kissinger called Schlesinger to say that he regretted what had happened and that "I hope you know it wasn't my idea."

Schlesinger acknowledged that, but observed that Kissinger's "suspiciousness" had added to the difficulties of their rivalry. "I think you and I could have held this thing together," Kissinger offered, adding "maybe *only* you and I." Schlesinger said there was "an awful lot of unfair stuff" about Kissinger going around, but that on philosophic grounds, especially in regards to the Soviets, "you and I are reasonably close." "It never occurred to me that this could happen," Kissinger said, "and I did my best to prevent it."

Later the same day, Kissinger insisted to *New York Times* columnist James Reston that Schlesinger had been considerably milder toward him in NSC meetings and other councils than in his "extremely ruthless and irritating" remarks to the press. He charged that Schlesinger sniped away at administration positions but "never presented what the real alternatives were for America." Kissinger told Reston that he expected that kind of sniping from a Scoop Jackson, but not from a secretary of defense.

"The guy that cut me up inside this building isn't going to cut me up any less in Defense," Kissinger next confided over the telephone to treasury secretary William Simon. In his own conversations with the press, Simon tried to assure them that Kissinger had not engineered Schlesinger's ouster, arguing that Kissinger would not have removed himself as national security adviser even to evict his rival Schlesinger from Defense.

Despite myriad public hints that Rumsfeld was behind these personnel changes, the public, the Congress, and Fritz Kraemer still believed that Kissinger had a hand in Schlesinger's firing.

To explain the situation, Kissinger asked Kraemer to come to his office at Foggy Bottom. Kraemer entered as he often did, via the private elevator reserved for the secretary and for foreign dignitaries who did not wish to be seen consulting the secretary. According to a friend, Kraemer found Kissinger less interested in talking about Schlesinger than in agonizing over whether to resign as secretary of state. But as Kissinger spoke endlessly about whether his "role in history" would be better served by a resignation now rather than by remaining until the end of Ford's term, Kraemer became convinced that Kissinger had fatally overreached himself. In Kraemer's view,

Kissinger was no longer concerned with what was best for the country, only what was best for him—and that, Kraemer could not tolerate.

For this perceived offense, Kraemer now saw no choice but to break decisively with Kissinger. He told Kissinger he would no longer speak with him.

Kissinger was deeply wounded by his mentor's decision. Weeks later, when it became apparent that Kraemer was serious about keeping his distance, Kissinger's wife appealed to Sven to mediate, but made no headway. Some time later, Kraemer told Kissinger biographer Walter Isaacson his reasons for shutting Kissinger out of his life: "As a human being, you have to stand for political values. People must know that I do not approve of him. This is a political-ethical stance." Kraemer would not speak to Kissinger for the next thirty years. "Kraemer took Schlesinger's dismissal as a personal insult instigated by me and resolved never to speak to me again," Kissinger later wrote. "The loss of that friendship became the most painful and permanent wound of my service in high office."

As the Kissinger-Kraemer break was occurring, Thimmesch visited Richard Nixon at San Clemente. It is not known whether the two men discussed the Kissinger-Kraemer break, of which Thimmesch was certainly aware. But shortly afterward, the reporter received a "Dear Nick" letter that contained a startling request:

> The next time you see Dr. Fritz Kraemer I would appreciate it if you would ask him on a totally confidential basis to write me, for my eyes only, a memorandum . . . setting forth his views about détente and the world situation generally. He is one of the most courageous and able foreign policy observers in the nation today.

It was a moment of high irony: At the very moment when Nixon seemed to be ratifying Fritz Kraemer's status as a thinker on a par with himself, Henry Kissinger—the man who had done the most to help imagine and carry out Nixon's foreign policies—was being disavowed by his mentor.

IN LATE 1975, the shah of Iran signed a peace agreement with the Baathists who ruled Iraq. As part of that agreement, he prevailed upon the Ford administration to stop a small program of assistance to the Kurds of northern Iraq that Nixon had initiated in 1972 at the shah's suggestion. This squelching of an independence movement—in favor of balance-of-power pragmatism—came to be considered a seminal moment in the sequence of events that led to the fall of the shah in 1979, the Gulf War of 1990, and the war in Iraq that began in 2003. At the time, however, it went unnoticed by both the press and the right-wing leaders such as the not-yet-declared presidential candidate Ronald Reagan.

Interviewed by *Time*, Reagan focused on the Halloween Massacre. He said he was "not appeased" by Rockefeller's disappearance from the ticket. "If the reason [for Schlesinger's firing] is that the President wants a different approach to defense, I don't like it. It disturbs me." Reagan did not think Kissinger had lost any authority—rather that Kissinger would require a "new Nixon . . . to keep him from giving away the store." Reagan pronounced himself "against détente as a one-way street. It annoys me the way we tiptoe around. We're so self-conscious of our own strength. I'm for decreasing confrontation but not with us doing all the leaning over backward." With the campaign season right around the corner, Reagan asked, "What's going to happen if someone beats an incumbent President in these primaries?"

On James Schlesinger's last day as secretary of defense, the armed services gave him a tribute at the Pentagon. After reviewing the troops arrayed on the grounds, he addressed an audience of several thousand military and civilian employees in distinctly Kraemerite terms. "The contribution of the United States to worldwide military balance remains indispensable to all other foreign policies," Schlesinger said. "Détente rests upon an underlying equilibrium of force, the maintenance of a military balance. Only the United States can serve as a counterweight to the Soviet Union." He warned that the USSR had been increasing its military investments and that "a continuation of this trend will inevitably bring a drastic and unwelcome alteration to the preferred way of life in the United States and among our allies." He deplored the "national mood of skepticism," calling upon Americans to "sharpen our sense of values [and] rekindle an historical feel for that which defines this nation."

As a coda, Lieutenant General Daniel Graham, calling himself "a Schlesinger man," resigned as chief of the Defense Intelligence Agency. Graham, who had publicly opposed the Vladivostok and Helsinki accords, began to advise Reagan on defense, intelligence, and foreign policy—as did Schlesinger.

The Pentagon brass was wary of their new secretary, Donald Rumsfeld, although they recognized his ideological similarity to Schlesinger. The military chiefs hoped that Rumsfeld's closeness to Ford would help the military establishment, yet they doubted Rumsfeld could be the capable and forceful counterweight to Kissinger that Schlesinger had been.

Rumsfeld soon became a more successful opponent of Kissinger within the administration than Schlesinger had been, more attuned to the philosophies of the emerging neocons than Schlesinger, and more able to push a rightist agenda because of Ford's willingness to give weight to his advice.

For Rumsfeld, the Pentagon was an ideal base; from it, he could exercise his belligerence, his elitism, and his distrust for the Kissingerian brand of diplomacy. It was no wonder then that when Fritz Kraemer introduced himself to the new secretary, they hit it off and began a series of colloquies. These were as important for Kraemer as they were for Rumsfeld, because they ensured that Kraemer's influence would continue in the thoughts of a new generation of leaders. Soon Rumsfeld was parroting lines and ideas of Kraemer's. In an interview shortly after taking office, he warned that "you can be provocative by being belligerent. You could also be provocative by being too weak and thereby enticing others into adventures they would otherwise avoid." Rumsfeld also became interested in the work of Andy Marshall, who stayed on as head of the Office of Net Assessment. Over the next year, Rumsfeld would increasingly listen to the advice of Kraemer and Marshall; he repeated some of their ideas during a series of White House briefings for selected congressmen on "the growing Soviet threat."

Scowcroft, whose job it was to assess that threat, thought that Rumsfeld's staged briefings were inadequately grounded in the facts; he viewed Rumsfeld's increasingly belligerent postures in NSC meetings as "a tactical shift to the right . . . merely a matter of political convenience." But by January 1976, *Aviation Week*, a respected defense industry publication, was writing of "a marked change in congressional attitude toward the U.S. defense posture and the Soviet strategic surge," and columnists Evans and Novak—not longtime Rumsfeld fans—were crediting him with holding back Kissinger on SALT II.

That was something Rumsfeld accomplished in NSC meetings, together with the JCS and the rightists at the ACDA—Lehman, Wolfowitz, Iklé, and Rowny. Kissinger complained directly to Iklé about their opposition: "I don't understand how the Arms Control Agency can put itself to the right of the secretary of state on issue after issue," especially since ACDA was part of State. The rightists were abetted in this task by an influential Evans and Novak column charging that the draft SALT II proposals, which Kissinger was about to travel to Russia to lock in, were "major concessions to Moscow" made to salvage an agreement at any cost, and thus ensure Ford's election, rather than to bolster the security of the United States. Other reporters traced the column's origin to a "cabal" of Perle, Lehman, and Rowny.

Rumsfeld then proceeded to sabotage Kissinger's trip to Moscow. On January 21, 1976, while Kissinger was at the Kremlin, and without his knowledge, Rumsfeld convened a meeting of the NSC. That was not unusual; what *was* unusual was that Rumsfeld too was out of town. (Officials who convened an NSC meeting for a particular purpose were usually expected to lead the discussion.) At the meeting, the Joint Chiefs withdrew their support for the positions on Backfire and cruise missiles on which Kissinger was basing his negotiation. When he heard that, Ford was "angrier than I have ever seen him," Scowcroft later said. "He ranted about the total inconsistency with the previous Defense positions." Scowcroft cabled Kissinger that the situation was "surreal," but the damage to Kissinger's bargaining had been done. The SALT II treaty would stay dormant for the remainder of the Ford administration.

Rumsfeld next submitted to Congress a new military budget whose $9 billion increase exceeded what Schlesinger had recommended. The budget was premised on the notion that the increasing Soviet military buildup was causing "a gradual shift in the [world's] power balance" that would continue unchecked "unless U.S. defense outlays are increased in real terms." It did not, however, contain an authorization for the conservatives' prior favored program, the Safeguard ABM. Less than three months after Rumsfeld became secretary of defense, he all but shut down the system that Jackson, Nitze, Wohlstetter, Wolfowitz, and Perle had fought for in 1969 but that had since become a target for conservative ire, so reduced in scope that they considered it meaningless.

A LOOSE AGGREGATION of Democrat and Republican conservatives, inside and out of the administration, had succeeded in preventing Ford from continuing Nixon's foreign policy agenda. Still split between the two parties, these foreign policy conservatives did not yet have a candidate to carry the flag for the transformation of U.S. foreign policy they hoped to achieve.

In the primary season of 1976, they would find one.

20

Primary Battles

The quiet war over the direction of U.S. foreign policy erupted into open hostilities during the 1976 primary season. It was fought principally among the Republicans, for in the Democratic contests, Jimmy Carter quickly outdistanced the conservative Scoop Jackson before foreign policy could become a real issue between them. But among the Republicans, according to chronicler of the campaign Craig Shirley, the primary contests became "a *götterdammerung* for the GOP. One side or another would prevail, and the losing side would either change their ways, their ideology, or leave the party for good."

While Reagan, an outsider, led a front-and-center assault on Ford's Nixonian foreign policy, insiders fought skirmishes within the executive branch over such matters as how best to officially state the extent of the threat to the United States from the Soviet Union, how to determine the size and configuration of the defense budget, and how to best assert the inherent powers of the executive branch in relation to the legislative.

Moderate Republicans had long charged that Reagan wasn't really a Republican, that he was too far to the right of the mainstream to win a national election. In June 1975 Reagan addressed these issues before a small audience of influential conservatives at a private dinner at Washington's Madison Hotel. The attendees were beer magnate Joseph Coors; direct-mail specialist Richard Viguerie; Paul Weyrich, founder of the Committee for the Survival of a Free Congress; syndicated columnists Kevin Phillips and Pat Buchanan; Conservative Caucus chairman Howard Phillips; and two George Wallace representatives. All lobbied Reagan to mount a third-party campaign and take Wallace as his running mate. Reagan demurred. In his view, *he* was the true Republican. And he would fight for his party's nomination as the only proper way to win the presidency.

Gathering steam from his opposition to the foreign policies begun by Richard Nixon and continued by Gerald Ford, in the next eighteen months he almost succeeded in seizing the nomination from the incumbent president.

IN THE SPRING of 1975, polls put Ford ahead of Reagan by two to one. But the events of the summer and fall of 1975 changed perceptions of Ford so severely that by November 30, when Reagan officially announced his candidacy, Ford's lead in the polls had largely evaporated. Ford White House aide Jerry Jones, who attended the Reagan announcement conference, reported to Dick Cheney that Reagan "handled the questioners with a sense of candor, humor, and calm" that belied his reputation as a "lightweight." "We are in for a real battle," Jones concluded. In January 1976, the polls showed Reagan and Ford each commanding 45 percent support levels among likely primary voters nationwide.

At that early point, Reagan's regular thirty-five-minute stump speech mentioned foreign policy only once, for about thirty seconds. Yet that thirty seconds—in which Reagan lambasted détente as a "one-way street" benefiting only the USSR—usually stimulated the largest round of applause, Evans and Novak noted in a January column. As the columnists reported, Reagan's advisers believed that to win the nomination he must "shift attention to what may be the most vulnerable policy and personality in the Ford Administration, détente and Henry Kissinger." Reagan finally did so in a speech at Phillips Exeter Academy, an elite boarding school in New Hampshire: "Our foreign policy in recent years seems to be a matter of placating potential adversaries. Does our government fear that the American people lack willpower? . . . The Soviet Union has now forged ahead in producing nuclear and conventional weapons. We can afford to be second to no one in military strength, not because we seek war but because we want to ensure peace."

This seemingly mild statement rang alarm bells from Washington to Moscow. The Reagan camp did not immediately follow up on the advantage, and an outside foreign policy event—the unexpected announcement that former president Nixon had been invited to Beijing—momentarily crowded Reagan out of the spotlight. In New Hampshire, the first primary of the season, Ford eked out a narrow victory. The same happened in Massachusetts and Vermont—two states in which Republican voters as well as Democratic ones were considered relatively liberal.

Reagan's moment of truth came backstage at an event in Tallahassee, Florida. Reagan had been reluctant to hit Ford hard, adhering to what he had dubbed the Eleventh Commandment: "Thou shalt not speak ill of another Republican." Before the Tallahassee event, however, Reagan asked his southern states coordinator, David Keene, what to do. "Well, Governor," Keene said, "you can go out there and follow the Eleventh Commandment and lose your ass, or you can kick the shit out of Jerry Ford and win this thing." Reagan attacked Ford and Kissinger, charging Ford with secretly agreeing to turn the Panama Canal over to Panama, then run by Omar Torrijos, who was close to Castro. Reagan also ripped Ford and Kissinger because

> the Soviet Union, using Castro's mercenaries, intervened decisively in the Angola Civil War and routed the pro-Western forces. Yet Messrs. Ford and Kissinger continue to tell us that we must not let this interfere with détente. . . . At Dr. Kissinger's insistence, Mr. Ford snubbed Alexander Solzhenitsyn, one of the great moral leaders of our time. . . . Kissinger's stewardship of United States foreign policy has coincided precisely with the loss of United States military supremacy [and Ford] has shown neither the vision nor the leadership necessary to halt and reverse the diplomatic and military decline of the United States.

With such phrases and reasoning, Reagan came very close to what Fritz Kraemer, Rowny, Walters, and Haig had been advocating for years. Many of Reagan's foreign and military policy advisers (including Schlesinger and Graham) were closely aligned with Kraemerite views; Reagan's strong stands on military and foreign policy were the main reason they admired him so fervently and were willing to join him in campaigning against a sitting Republican president.

In many ways, Reagan fit what soon emerged as the neoconservative profile. He was a former Democrat who had been "mugged by reality" (as the neocons put it) and reacted by becoming a leading anti-Communist and small-government advocate. As a candidate in 1976, he took hard-line views, eschewed diplomacy as mostly useless, and advocated not only a remilitarized foreign policy but also a vast rebuilding of the U.S. military apparatus. He would retain these views, virtually unchanged, when he ran again in 1980.

In 1976, Reagan went beyond even Fritz Kraemer in the bellicosity of his rhetoric. For instance, he told his audiences what he would tell Omar Torrijos about the canal: "We built it, we paid for it, we're going to keep it."

Evans and Novak characterized Reagan's solution for the canal as "strident and inaccurate [and] demagogic." But they also noted that Ford's "botched" responses to Reagan's charges on the canal created the impression that the United States was "negotiating a new Canal treaty out of fear."

During the campaign, Ford's position on Panama was undercut by a series of leaked State and NSC memos on the negotiations, and by the revelation that Schlesinger had been advocating a tougher negotiating position before being replaced at Defense. Ford fought back, stating that if the United States attempted to keep the canal now, after negotiations that dated to the Johnson era, there would be "riots, more bloodshed, [and] enmity" from Latin American countries. Still, the canal was an issue in the Florida, North Carolina, and Texas primaries.

The anti-Ford foreign policy movement was further stirred by a leak to Evans and Novak concerning a secret briefing Hal Sonnenfeldt of the State Department had given in London the previous December regarding the Helsinki accords. Sonnenfeldt, a German refugee, was known to have been close to Kissinger since the 1940s; it was widely assumed that views he expressed matched Kissinger's. In the London speech, Sonnenfeldt appeared to retreat from the longtime American position that the satellite countries of Eastern Europe were "captives" of the Soviet Union: "The Soviets' inability to acquire loyalty in Eastern Europe is an unfortunate historical failure, because Eastern Europe is within their scope and area of national interest. . . . So it must be our policy to strive for an evolution that makes the relationship between Eastern Europeans and the Soviet Union an organic one."

Evans and Novak framed Sonnenfeldt's statement as a window into the secret "underpinnings of détente," and as a validation of conservative fears about Kissinger's diplomatic aims. Even the *New York Times* and *Washington Post* agreed that Sonnenfeldt had issued "an invitation to the Soviet Union to assert fuller control of Eastern Europe." Senator Buckley demanded a letter of explanation from Kissinger, and upon its receipt pronounced it unsatisfactory. Reagan made the Sonnenfeldt gaffe a target for ridicule. Ford was forced to declare that he had no secret arrangements with the USSR for the domination of Eastern Europe. In a follow-up article, Evans and Novak opined that the question of what détente really meant was at the heart of the "struggle for the soul of the Republican Party."

Other reporters jumped into the fray, seizing upon foreign policy as a fulcrum for the campaigns. Donald Rumsfeld, they wrote, had reportedly been making the case at private meetings on Capitol Hill that the United States could live without a SALT II agreement in 1976—arguing that the deadline was only Kissinger's, not the country's. "Rummy is a dummy as a SALT scholastic. But he's politically savvy as hell," an unnamed Ford "insider" worried to a reporter. In February, sixteen conservative senators, Democrats and Republicans alike, demanded that Ford "instruct [Kissinger] that negotiations should continue without regard to ill-advised demands for an immediate agreement. Hurried diplomacy creates vulnerability and distrust, not arms control and understanding."

Ford responded by reasserting his backing of Kissinger, but he did allow the bureaucrats to slow down the SALT II negotiations. Kissinger embarked on a journey to nearly two dozen world capitals before the Republican convention in August, keeping him out of the limelight and away from Republican ire. But Ford also implicitly repudiated Kissinger by announcing on March 5, 1976, what he'd decided the previous fall: that "we are going to forget the use of the word détente" in favor of "peace through strength."

Al Haig chimed in from his post at NATO, telling a radio interviewer that détente was the product of the West's combined strength, but that it could "never be a substitute for that strength." Now that Haig no longer needed to pretend he and Kissinger agreed on foreign policy—and now that Kraemer no longer reflexively lauded whatever Kissinger did—Haig could let his true Kraemerite colors show.

LEO CHERNE, A conservative economist, was Ford's choice to chair the President's Foreign Intelligence Advisory Board, known as PFIAB. In early 1976, Cherne told Congress that a reevaluation of the Soviet threat was needed. The new CIA director, George Bush, sent Cherne a congratulatory note on the subject—and with that, a seminal project of the fledgling neocons took a leap forward, with what would become the "Plan B" exercise.

The idea that the Soviet threat was growing, and that the administration wasn't doing enough about it—a notion Haig echoed in that radio interview—also spurred the resurrection of an old group, the Committee on the Present Danger, in March 1976. Buoyed by start-up money from former undersecretary of defense David Packard, the new committee included members of the Jackson-Humphrey Coalition for a Democratic Majority; Paul Nitze and several associates; Reagan advisers George Shultz and Dick Allen; academics such as Jeane Kirkpatrick; and militarists such as Elmo Zumwalt, then running for senator.

The Committee on the Present Danger (CPD) differed from the Coalition for a Democratic Majority (CDM), from whose offices it operated, in that it included Republicans as well as Democrats, and that it was more clearly aimed at changing foreign policy. What brought the partisans of CPD together was their firm anti-Soviet—and therefore anti-détente—stance. In a series of newspaper advertisements, the CPD announced that its purpose was to alert the public to "the ominous Soviet military build-up" and to the "unfavorable trends in the U.S.-Soviet military balance." Paul Nitze and other members penned articles in support of the mission. In *Foreign Affairs*, the negotiator wrote that if, as he expected, the Soviets achieved "nuclear superiority," he predicted that they would use it to undermine détente, "with results that could only resurrect the danger of nuclear confrontation or, alternatively, increase the prospect of Soviet expansion through other means of pressure." Jeane Kirkpatrick later said that she and other CPD members were worried not only that the Soviets were manufacturing strategic arms unchecked but also that they were making gains on three continents: in Southeast Asia, Africa, and Latin America.

In its repudiation of the Nixon-Ford, pragmatic approach to foreign policy, the CPD became a hothouse for neoconservative thought. And together with PFIAB—whose hawkishness had become even more pronounced under Cherne than in former years—the committee now produced its first flower. The two groups called on George Bush to agree to commission an "independent" CIA estimate of Soviet capabilities. There would be several panels, each dealing with various aspects of intelligence about the Soviets, all having as their task a reevaluation of the Soviet threat.

One such subgroup was the committee's Strategic Objectives panel. It would become known to history as Team B because it was made up of outsiders—in contrast to Team A, the in-house CIA team. Ford and Bush signed off on the establishment of the panels without much review; Ford did not realize that the members of Team B all disagreed with his foreign policies and with low estimates of Soviet strength, capabilities, and dangerousness. Bush deliberately refused to have any input to the composition of Team B, but he did write to Cherne, "I am advised that the composition . . . will conform closely to the [PFIAB] Board members' suggestions."

Team B featured Andy Marshall, Paul Nitze, Paul Wolfowitz, William Van Cleave—the former NSC member and Pentagon consultant—and Daniel Graham, the former DIA chief who had openly opposed the Vladivostok and Helsinki accords. Half a dozen other Team B members, recommended by Perle and Wohlstetter, were of the same anti-Nixon-and-Kissinger stripe. Seymour Weiss, for instance, had been exiled to Bermuda as an ambassador for consistently opposing Kissinger on détente. Richard Pipes, a well-known refugee from Communism, Russian historian at Harvard, and hawkish consultant to Scoop Jackson, led Team B. Historian Anne Hessing Cahn later wrote that an "incestuous closeness" characterized the members of the Team B panel: The panel even discussed sending drafts of their reports to Wohlstetter for vetting. As a CIA stalwart later put it, Team B was "dedicated to proving that the Russians are twenty feet tall."

. . . .

"UNDER KISSINGER AND Ford, this nation has become Number Two in a world where it is dangerous—if not fatal—to be second best," Reagan declared in his spring 1976 stump speeches.

"We are conducting our foreign policy with our eyes open, our guard up, and our powder dry," Ford responded, reminding audiences that his administration had asked Congress for a large increase in defense spending. That request was undercut by stories that Rumsfeld was not disbursing $16 billion that had already been authorized. "Now either there is a conscious effort to withhold funds in order to have a slump before the election so you won't get elected," Rockefeller warned Ford, "or it is just total stupidity and gross incompetence by Mr. Rumsfeld."

Still, Ford won his fourth and fifth consecutive primaries, in Florida and Illinois, by increasing margins; he seemed well on his way to locking up the nomination. Reagan limped into North Carolina, his staff either laid off or working for no pay. If he couldn't win in North Carolina, his campaign would be over. The American Conservative Union jumped in to help with volunteers and money, paying to air his radio commercials more than eight hundred times in the campaign's last few days. Even greater assistance was rendered by Jesse Helms, who joined Reagan in lambasting Ford's foreign policy and separately added a race-baiting note that resonated with certain North Carolina voters. Helms's organization also used its power to turn out the vote, augmenting the efforts of Reagan's southern states coordinator, David Keene.

Reagan won the North Carolina primary—the first time in American history that a sitting president had been defeated in a primary in which he had actively stumped for votes. The victory reinvigorated Reagan's campaign and certified that its most potent issue was the conservative rejection of current American foreign policy. In later years, Reagan and his 1976 campaign manager, Senator Paul Laxalt of Arizona, would credit Helms and the 1976 North Carolina primary for turning around Reagan's campaign and putting him on the path to winning the presidency in 1980.

The day after Ford's 1976 North Carolina defeat, he met in the Rose Garden with a hundred Texas Republicans—Texas was the next big primary—and promised that the United States would remain "Number One" militarily as long as he was in charge. But he refrained from attacking Reagan personally, because, as an aide explained to a reporter, he needed to pave the way for the Reagan delegates to eventually join the Ford bandwagon. Infighting was soon hampering the Ford campaign, some of it directed against Cheney, who was making day-to-day decisions as the top campaign officials passed through the revolving door.

The release of the movie of *All the President's Men* in April, and the simultaneous publication of Woodward and Bernstein's *The Final Days*, featuring an unflattering portrait of Ford, did not help Ford's cause. Such depictions of Nixon-era wrongdoing only dredged up unpleasant memories in the public mind and raised anew the question of whether Ford should have pardoned Nixon.

In southern, midwestern, and western states, Reagan flagellated the Nixon-Ford-Kissinger foreign policy, adding to his litany the charge that "weak" presidents and a liberal Congress had abandoned the war in Vietnam when the military had almost had it won. Similar opposition was coming from within the administration—from Rumsfeld; from Rowny, Wolfowitz, and Iklé; from the Jackson camp, even after Jackson was knocked out of the 1976 Democratic primaries by Jimmy Carter; and from Republican senators who shared Jackson's negative views of the administration.

Fritz Kraemer had predicted it. Seven years earlier, when he had first become alarmed at the Nixon-Kissinger policies, he had told Kissinger that one day there would be a revolt—not from the left, as the Communists had always prophesied, but from the right—and that it would be generated by anger at the diminution of the American military, the backing away from commitments around the globe, and the refusal to confront our enemies, which had become the engine of U.S. foreign policy. He had a "truly frightening suspicion" that those who "today do not even care very much about foreign affairs" would be "the first ones to yell for retribution and stampede forward over our bodies, howling that we have betrayed them . . . when it becomes clear that our well meant policy . . . will have led to defeat." In 1976, that revolt took shape in Reagan's primary campaign.

As Reagan continued to win primaries—Alabama, Georgia, Indiana, Nebraska—Ford suddenly backed out of a previously scheduled test-ban treaty signing ceremony. "Where Has All the Power Gone?" *Time* magazine wondered, citing the abrupt cancellation and a number of domestic policy decisions in which Ford had seemed to cave in to congressional demands. The magazine labeled Ford's White House "rudderless" and noted that Ford appeared "weak, uncertain, vacillating."

Ford continued to lose power to Congress. The legislative branch was poised to pass bills to redress past excesses in the espionage field,. To head off congressional action, Attorney General Edward Levi drafted a bill to establish a special court to oversee warrants for wiretapping and mail surveillance for the purpose of securing intelligence about foreign influences. The court was to be called the FISA court, after the Foreign Intelligence Surveillance Act. The bill allowed the government to surveil someone for up to a year without court oversight, unless the person was a U.S. citizen or in contact with a suspect foreign national; if a U.S. citizen was involved, the government needed to get authority from the court within seventy-two hours after the surveillance had begun.

The FISA authority would become a bone of contention a quarter century later, during the George W. Bush administration; in 1976, those who lobbied against it included Rumsfeld, Kissinger, Scowcroft, and CIA director George H. W. Bush. Their reason for doing so, as a Department of Justice brief put it, was that "the bill unnecessarily derogates from the inherent Constitutional authority of the President," in particular his authority "to conduct warrantless electronic surveillance for foreign intelligence purposes." Ford agreed with their reasoning, but he had an election to win and needed no further battles with Congress, so he decided to sign the legislation if it reached his desk. Learning this, Rumsfeld and the other internal opponents of the bill sidetracked it, arguing that it was not essential to deal with it before the election. Like SALT II, it stayed in limbo for the remainder of the administration.

WHILE IN AFRICA, Kissinger announced that the United States would back the black majority over the remnants of the colonial whites in Rhodesia. This did not play well in some parts of the United States, where Reagan sympathizers fed rumors that Ford had taken the stance on Rhodesia to cater to American blacks. Rhodesia also came up in the California primary; when asked hypothetically whether he would send U.S. troops to Rhodesia to supervise a transition to a black majority government, Reagan said yes. The Ford campaign jumped on this, suggesting that a trigger-happy Reagan would start a new Vietnam-style war in Africa. The Ford partisans' vehemence in going after Reagan, according to Evans and Novak, "inflame[d] bitter animosity within the California Republican Party and end[ed] any chances of a unified party for the fall campaign against the Democrats."

In Texas, despite help from James Baker and other Texans, Ford lost every delegate to Reagan. The insurgent candidate went on to carry many more primaries in the West and Southwest. By the close of the primary season, Ford had only a slight edge in delegates and was twenty-eight shy of nomination. The states Reagan won in 1976 would form the core of the "red-state" bloc that would provide the Republican margin of victory in 1980, 1984, 1988, 2000, and 2004.

As one member of the 1976 Republican platform committee recalled, every vote at the convention was contentious, with one side or the other winning by a small margin—a surprising development in a party that had historically been united on many issues. One of the disputed planks was a Jesse Helms "morality-in-foreign-policy" plank that roundly condemned détente, SALT, Kissinger, the Panama Canal negotiations, Ford's poor treatment of Solzhenitsyn, Helsinki, and trade with Communist countries, while affirming unwavering support for Taiwan. It was defeated by a slim margin, but Reagan stalwarts succeeded in having the committee recommend a plank stating, "Ours will be a foreign policy which recognizes that in international negotiations we must make no undue concessions; that in pursuing détente we must not grant unilateral favors with only the hope of getting future favors in return."

This was so clearly a refutation of détente, of all the Nixon policies Ford had adopted, and of Kissinger, that the secretary of state pleaded with Ford to fight to remove it. Dick Cheney later recalled that this plank "did everything but strip Henry bare of every piece of clothing on his body." Cheney would soon adopt the plank's assertions as his own, but at that point he was still a Ford loyalist and the de facto director of the campaign. He argued to Ford that this was "not the time" to have a fight over the platform, for it would play into the Reaganites' plan to disrupt the convention and make it a dangerous referendum on Ford. Kissinger threatened to quit then and there. "Well, Henry, if you're going to quit, do it now. We need the votes," one White House aide responded. Desperate to preserve the support of the right, Ford yielded to Cheney's reasoning and acquiesced to the plank. And Kissinger did not resign.

Rockefeller had warned Ford that, if Rumsfeld showed up at the convention in Kansas City, he might release New York's delegation to vote however they pleased. Ford understood that northeastern delegates—known still as Rockefeller Republicans—were the key to his victory in Kansas City, so he asked Rumsfeld to stay away. Rumsfeld complied.

At the last moment, however, Reagan made a blunder that crippled his chances. He announced that his vice presidential candidate would be Pennsylvania governor Richard Schweiker, a man whom many Reagan delegates and independent considered insufficiently conservative. Some delegates drifted away, and enough of them were captured by Ford to put him narrowly over the top.

A few people on Ford's staff had tried to persuade him that Reagan would be his best vice presidential candidate, and a few in Reagan's orbit had broached the subject with the governor. But both Reagan and Ford felt they were too far apart to be on the same ticket. Then, too, the infighting of the primaries and at the convention had sharpened the differences between their supporters, making it all but impossible for Reagan and Ford to collaborate. Instead Ford picked Bob Dole, a fairly conservative senator, whose selection Ford hoped would appease the right wing.

In accepting the nomination, Ford gave what many labeled the speech of his life. But the convention wanted to hear from Reagan. It was somewhat unprecedented for the defeated candidate to speak after the victorious one, but the clamor for Reagan was great even among Ford's closest supporters, who knew they would need Reagan's help to win in the fall. And so Reagan was permitted to give what his backers would soon refer to as "the speech," the one that propelled him toward the 1980 nomination.

In that speech, Reagan barely mentioned Ford or the need to back the president in November. Rather, he painted a word-picture of the Republican Party he imagined for the future, a party that would be strong and animated by moral clarity. "We may be fewer in number than we've ever been, but we carry the message [the American people] have been waiting for." Reagan's partisans, he implied, could wait to fight for that vision—until 1980, when he would lead the party.

The speech was a clear signal to the faithful not to work for Ford in the general election. Between the date of the convention and the November balloting, Reagan reinforced that signal by doing little to assist Ford. The president's narrow win at the convention could not hide the ideological split in the Republican Party or the clear lesson learned by the conservative forces, that even if they had been beaten this time, they would soon take over the party. Reagan and most other conservatives reasoned that their future victory would be hastened, not hindered, if Ford lost in November.

Foreign policy played a part in the general election. In his second debate with Carter, Ford claimed that Poland and the rest of Eastern Europe was not under Soviet domination—a gaffe that echoed the Sonnenfeldt Doctrine mess and that gave Carter an opening to score some points at Ford's expense. But Carter chose not to harp on Ford's foreign policies as a major issue, since he had more in common with the president on foreign affairs than Reagan had. Carter's mild stance on foreign policy obviated the need for Ford to move further to the right on those issues, which probably cost him some conservative votes.

Carter did make Richard Nixon, and Nixon's domestic legacy, his signature issue. He tied the Nixon and Ford administrations to all the ills of the country, especially the deepening problems with the nation's economy. Despite his efforts to mobilize voters, however, by October polls showed little excitement for either Carter or Ford.

As many observers predicted, turnout was the key to victory. The majority of registered voters were Democrats; though Ford won a majority of the states on Election Day, he lost to Carter in the popular vote and in the Electoral College. In the states where Ford lost narrowly, his margin of defeat was traced to low Republican turnout, attributable to Reagan partisans who did little to help get out the vote.

After the elections, those Reagan supporters immediately set to work trying to take over the Republican Party and dictate its agenda for the 1980 election. In the meantime, they would also do whatever they could to wreck Jimmy Carter's foreign policy.

21

The Carter Interregnum

M any foreign policy conservatives, both Democrats and Republicans, viewed Jimmy Carter's term in office as an interregnum during which they could function as a shadow foreign policy apparatus, work to hasten Carter's political demise, and promote the arrival of a future administration that would act on their plans to regain what they thought had been lost, America's preeminent place in the world. Scoop Jackson's defeat in 1976 released many of them from their allegiance to the Democratic Party; after losing all hope of molding that party in their image, they shifted their attention to the GOP and spent Carter's time in office working to take over that party almost completely.

Joshua Muravchik, a neoconservative himself, wrote in 2007 that the Carter years were when the neocon movement coalesced around four core beliefs that would unite them for the following thirty years. First and foremost, they were "moralists" who despised not just Communism but also all tyrants and dictators, and who championed the spread of American virtues "out of the recognition that America had gone farther in the realization of liberal values than any other nation in history." Second, neocons were "internationalists" in the Churchillian sense, who "believed that depredations tolerated in one place were likely to be repeated elsewhere. . . . Since America's security could be affected by events far from home, it was wiser to confront troubles early even if afar than to wait for them to ripen and grow nearer." Third, neocons "trusted in the efficacy of military force [and] doubted that economic sanctions or UN intervention or diplomacy, per se, constituted meaningful alternatives for confronting evil or any determined adversary."

Fourth, neocons believed in "democracy both at home and abroad." Neoconservatism, Muravchik conceded, might be "idealistic in its internationalism and its faith in democracy and freedom, but it is hardheaded, not to say jaundiced, in its image of our adversaries and its assessment of international organizations."

These beliefs had animated neoconservatism from the mid-1970s forward, Muravchik said.

The four beliefs were precisely those that Fritz Kraemer had been trumpeting for decades. Their complete congruence with neoconservative tenets was why Kraemer's influence was able to continue long after he retired from the Pentagon in 1978.

As THE FORD administration prepared to disband in early 1977, those of its members who would later become neocons, or work closely with them, scattered in various directions. Secretary of Defense Rumsfeld prepared to leave for private industry, but before doing so he threw a few monkey wrenches into incoming President Carter's plans. He proposed a 1978 military budget that included a very large increase for defense spending. The budget had no chance of being ratified by Carter and a Democratic-controlled Congress, but it was useful in buttressing Rumsfeld's points about needing to counter the growing Soviet threat. He also authorized production on two cruise missile programs, an action that incoming officials commented would complicate negotiations with the Soviets on strategic arms. And, in a valedictory speech at his mustering-out ceremony on the grounds of the Pentagon a few hours before Ford turned over the government to Carter, Rumsfeld lashed out at the principles that had guided U.S. foreign policy since the early Nixon years. He dismissed the idea that the United States had "sufficient" nuclear weaponry to counter the Soviet threat—reaching back to the concept Nixon had established in 1969 to describe the goal of U.S. nuclear weapons policy. "Continuing on down the path we have been going for years would, I'm convinced, damage terribly the capabilities that will be available to our country in the years ahead," Rumsfeld told his audience. He warned that a "domino effect" would occur if the Soviets continued to produce more weapons, and newer weapons, than the United States had—a trend he predicted would topple the United States from its dominant military position. To keep abreast of the Soviets, he warned, the U.S. military must develop the cruise missiles, B-1 bomber, and Trident submarine. He ended his speech by expressing the point that clearly underlay his spurious budget, and that was pure Fritz Kraemer: that the United States could only enjoy good relations with Communist powers when dealing with them from a position of military superiority. To do anything else would be a "provoca-tive" display of "weakness."

In an op-ed in the *Washington Post* a few days later, Rumsfeld also had some advice for the next secretary of defense: "Don't play President—you're not. The Constitution provides for only one President. Don't forget it and don't be seen by others as not understanding that fact. . . . Don't take the job, or stay in it, unless you have an understanding with the President that you are free to tell him what you think, on any subject, 'with the bark off,' and have the freedom—in practice—to do it."

Dick Cheney, the departing White House chief of staff, went home to Wyoming and prepared to run for the state's lone seat in the House. (His election was all but assured when the incumbent representative, a Demo-crat, soon announced he would not stand for reelection.) Cheney's views on military spending and SALT echoed those of Rumsfeld, not of Ford, the president who had elevated him to prominence.

Paul Wolfowitz, a Democrat, was on a "hit list" that Tony Lake, Carter's chief policy planning adviser, intended to use to clean house after Carter took office. But Wolfowitz managed to stay in government by moving to the Pentagon as deputy assistant secretary for regional programs. For him it was an ideal spot, allowing him to concentrate on long-range planning on issues such as the relationship between the defense of Israel and American inter-ests in the Middle East. The incoming secretary of defense, Harold Brown, wanted to generate future plans that went beyond simple measures of weap-onry, and asked Wolfowitz to look into threats the United States would face outside of Europe, with special emphasis on the Persian Gulf.

John Lehman became chief officer of a lobbying firm, the Abington Cor-poration, that served as a temporary home for many hard-liners who were able to use their DoD connections on behalf of corporate clients. Within two years Richard Perle would join Lehman there, bringing along some Israeli arms makers as clients.

Alexander Haig remained as head of the NATO forces and as SACEUR; Haig's position was not considered political, and Carter was willing to keep him on. Two years earlier, when Haig arrived in Brussels, he had found the American forces in Europe "drained of manpower, morale, and materiel" and in a state of readiness "below acceptable standards," as he later wrote. According to contemporary news accounts, he had repaired these problems and had won staunch allies in West Germany, Portugal, Spain, and Great Britain. In his public statements, Haig toed the Kraemer-Rumsfeld line, tell-ing one reporter that the United States was facing "what is clearly a new age of Soviet military power," and another that the USSR's military had been upgraded to be "capable of supporting an imperialistic phase in their foreign policy." Unless the trend were reversed, Haig said, NATO forces "will come under increasing strain, and could collapse." This was the ultimate expression of Rumsfeld's new "domino-effect" notion.

Kissinger vigorously opposed this conclusion. "I do not believe that the Soviet Union is achieving military superiority over the United States," he said just before leaving office, citing American superiority in the quality of its missiles and forces, if not in tanks and number of troops. But the military columnist for the *New York Times*, Drew Middleton, noted that the anti-Kissinger crowd found ready reason to dismiss the ex-secretary's argument: Kissinger was "not an objective witness because he was the architect of a policy that presumed nuclear parity, not superiority. To admit Soviet superiority would be an admission that he had been hoodwinked by the Russians."

THIS DEBATE CARRIED over into the Carter administration's decisions on foreign policy. As a candidate, Carter had signaled his general acceptance of the Nixon-Ford policies of negotiating with the USSR on arms reduction and trade, and increasing interchanges with China. He and his national security adviser, Zbigniew Brzezinski, augmented those by positioning the United States to resolve North-South rather than East-West conflicts. They viewed the current and future conflict in the world not as a battle between Communist Russia and democratic Europe and the United States, but as a battle between the "have" nations of the Northern Hemisphere, including the Soviet Union as well as the United States and Europe, and the "have-not" nations of Southern Asia, the Indian subcontinent, Africa, and South America. This formulation accepted détente and went beyond it.

The shadow government's first assault on the Nixon-Ford policies was the Team B report. The Team B panel—including Wolfowitz, Marshall, Van Cleave, Graham, and others who had consistently opposed the Nixon-Ford policies toward the Soviet Union—used the occasion of its report to attack those policies. The report assailed the integrity and acumen of the CIA, accusing past NIEs of undervaluing the "intensity, scope, and implicit threat" of the USSR because they relied on evidence of Soviet military capabilities "rather than [on the enemy's] intentions, his weapons rather than his ideas, motives and aspirations." This language reflected contentions both Kraemer and Albert Wohlstetter had been making for years.

According to historian Anne Hessing Cahn, the Team B report made several assumptions that it stated as fact. It declared that the Soviets were offensively oriented, not defensively oriented; it judged the Soviet Backfire bomber as better than the American FB-111; and it asserted that Soviet SAM missiles could be combined into a better ABM system. Cahn charges that when Team B found no evidence of a nonacoustic antisubmarine system, they wrote that this meant the Soviets had such a system and were hiding it. Team B's overall reasoning was animated by the notion that the Soviets were aiming for nuclear superiority, and that the approaches followed by the CIA's Team A, to quote the B report, "ignore the possibility that the Russians seriously believe that if, for whatever reason, deterrence were to fail, they could resort to the use of nuclear weapons to fight and win a war." Wolfowitz later explained that this language referred to the possibility of the Soviets using nuclear weapons in such conflicts as Angola or Afghanistan.

The Team B report was designed to scare the United States into higher defense spending and more assertive negotiating postures, and to force CIA analysts to focus more on Soviet intentions and not rely exclusively on data about military capabilities. The report did succeed in influencing the CIA; in its subsequent NIEs, the Agency suggested a heightened Soviet threat.

As the Team B report was being issued, several of its panelists became members of the reborn Committee on the Present Danger. The committee insisted that the United States had only a relatively brief "window of vulnerability" in which to counter the disastrous Soviet uptrend in military spending. It characterized the turmoil in postcolonial Africa, Central and South America, the Middle East, and Southern Asia as caused by or backed by the Soviet Union, and insisted that the United States must not remain neutral in those conflicts. CPD had plenty of money to spread its message, and its knowledgeable tone was persuasively presented in newspaper and radio ads and by media appearances of quotable experts such as Paul Nitze. For the moment, CPD continued to operate from the offices of the Committee for a Democratic Majority.

The CPD also reached beyond advice and commentary, attempting to prevent Carter from appointing Paul Warnke as chief arms negotiator. The fight was led by Nitze, Warnke's former superior and friend. At the request of Brzezinski, Carter had met with Nitze during the campaign, but found him arrogant and inflexible, and ignored pleas to include him in the administration. Nitze castigated Warnke for contending that even U.S. nuclear superiority would not be a "decisive factor in any political confrontation" with the USSR, and that the extended SALT negotiations had themselves been a spur to weapons development. Jackson and Perle led the political opposition to Warnke, though initially Perle concealed his sponsorship of a memo circulating on Capitol Hill that pilloried Warnke.

Columnist James Reston wrote about this battle over Warnke in the *New York Times*, seeing in it a deeper fight between those with a "gloomy" view of the human race and those who took a "slightly less pessimistic view of mankind." The gloomy ones, Reston wrote, found it "not reasonable to talk of reason: only power and fear of destruction deter the spirit of domination that stains all human character and marks particularly the conduct of the Soviet Government." *Times* columnist Anthony Lewis added, "The intensity of feeling of the opposition side signals a policy disagreement so fundamental that any imaginable arms limitation agreement with the Soviet Union will face powerful resistance," and denotes "the rise of a new militant 'coalition' on national security issues."

That coalition included the forty "nay" votes that Scoop Jackson rustled up to oppose Warnke's nomination. Though this proved insufficient to scuttle it, the votes did demonstrate to Carter, Secretary of State Cyrus Vance, and Warnke that it wouldn't be easy for the administration to corral the two-thirds of the Senate required to ratify any treaties they brought home.

Out of public view, Carter invited Jackson and Perle to fashion the administration's first salvo to the Soviets on SALT. He also agreed to what Jackson had long advocated: a proposal for mutual, radical, deep cuts in weapons programs as an initial step to nuclear disarmament. This position bothered the Chiefs, but Secretary of Defense Harold Brown, the former head of a bomb development laboratory, agreed to it, as did Schlesinger, now secretary of the Department of Energy.

The Soviets rejected the radical proposal. After spending decades catching up, they saw no reason to cut back now. But Carter got credit for trying Jackson's approach; Jackson got proof that the Soviets were uninterested in disarmament, and more reason to continue opposing proposals for compromise.

In California, as all this was happening, Dick Allen and Ronald Reagan had a long discussion about foreign policy. Reagan, Allen later wrote, "believed that America was stronger and better than the Soviets, more flexible, imaginative and just, [and] could integrate its economic, technological, capital and moral resources to emerge the victor [in the Cold War]. This was heady stuff, and very radical." Allen went to work crafting a new set of policy strategies for Reagan so that his administration could hit the ground running if he should win in 1980.

On the day after Carter took office in 1977, he caused some consternation among the Joint Chiefs of Staff when he signed a more extensive amnesty for Vietnam War draft evaders than Ford had been willing to do. Coming from a U.S. Naval Academy graduate and former officer on nuclear submarines, the Chiefs found this inexplicable. But on many other matters Carter courted the Joint Chiefs, adopting their position on the significance and threat of Russia's newest heavy missiles. The Chiefs were concerned that the largest Soviet missiles could reach the United States and destroy ours in a first strike. Nixon, Kissinger, and Ford had downplayed this threat, but Carter, Brzezinski, and Brown agreed with the Chiefs' assessment of the threat inherent in the large Soviet missiles and felt it should be beaten back, if possible, in the SALT II negotiations. Carter and Brown retained the development of the MX cruise missile and of the Pershing IIs. But Carter cut several other defense programs, sidetracking the B-1 bomber and delaying construction of aircraft carriers.

Carter's alliance with the Chiefs left Paul Warnke feeling increasingly hampered from within the administration as well as by conservatives in Congress and on the CPD. Eventually his opposition to deployment of cruise missiles in Europe put him at odds with both the conservatives and Carter himself, and he resigned before the end of 1978.

THE JOINT CHIEFS who served under Jimmy Carter had not been old enough to fight in World War II. They also differed from the former generation of warriors in their areas of experience: One even had a doctorate in nuclear physics. This new generation of military chieftains worked well with defense secretary Harold Brown, a scientist and career administrator. Fritz Kraemer, on the other hand, found himself increasingly out of step in their Pentagon. In 1978, when he reached the mandatory retirement age of seventy, he decided not to fight to stay.

Still quite vigorous, Kraemer transferred his advisory work to his home, remaining an avid gatherer of information and a disseminator of ideas. According to Ed Rowny, Kraemer enjoyed regular visits from many of those he had influenced, including Walters, Haig, Jackson, Perle, Wolfowitz, and even Rumsfeld. The visitors gave Fritz information and took away advice on current matters. A younger group of activists, including Sven Kraemer, continued championing his ideas as congressional staffers—the brains of the shadow government. Rather than be fired by Tony Lake, Sven left the National Security Council to become national security adviser to Senator John Tower, chairman of the Senate Republican Policy Committee—and thus to a group of a dozen conservative Republicans who were the mainstays of that committee.

Other legislative aides who worked closely with Sven Kraemer during the Carter years included John Carbaugh, Quentin Crommelin, Michael Pillsbury, and Perle. Carbaugh, who was Jesse Helms's national security staffer, traveled regularly to foreign hot spots to offer the senator's support to right-wing heads of state and to those who sought to depose left-wing rulers. Crommelin replaced Carbaugh on Strom Thurmond's staff. Pillsbury was the national security staffer for the Senate Steering Committee. Perle had become Jackson's leading aide.

In a June 1977 *Washington Post* profile of Perle, friends and enemies alike described him as running a "détente-wrecking operation." Perle was also one of Washington's most prolific leakers, particularly generous in feeding columnists Evans and Novak. Perle acknowledged to the *Post* that he had extensive contacts with reporters. He also admitted that he often used the media to influence the executive branch on behalf of "people who can't get a hearing" from their superiors. One of those who was having a hard time being heard was a midlevel CIA employee, David S. Sullivan, who gave Perle a copy of a cable from a Soviet who had been turned by the CIA. Sullivan leaked this cable because, it was later reported, the CIA did not want to support his complaint that the USSR was cheating on the SALT limits. The cable was quoted in a newspaper article and the source was traced to Sullivan. The CIA fired him, but the coterie of congressional aides helped him to secure a position as an aide to another right-wing senator, Gordon Humphrey of New Hampshire.

By the end of 1977, however, Perle's incessant leaking and publicity seeking had earned him the displeasure of senators, staffers, and administration officials, which resulted in a flurry of unfavorable news articles. "I really resent being depicted as some sort of dark mystic or some demonic power," Perle told the *New York Times*. One official told the paper that while Perle was generally two or three steps more hawkish than Jackson, Perle "may have gone four steps ahead" in criticizing the new agreement then being hammered out between the United States and the Soviet Union, and may have done Jackson more harm than good. Perle left Jackson's employ shortly thereafter, joining John Lehman at the Abington Corporation.

Another reason Fritz Kraemer retired was that the new Pentagon team seemed less interested in his own field of geostrategy and more interested in new technology, which was Andy Marshall's fiefdom. Perhaps because of Marshall's close ties to his former RAND associates Harold Brown and James Schlesinger, Marshall kept his post at the DoD's Office of Net Assessment. As Carter cut the military budget, Marshall became prominent in arguing for new technologies, new weapons systems, and the further transformation of the all-volunteer armed forces. According to military technology reporter Ken Silverstein, Marshall was "one of the most effective pork-seeking missiles ever deployed by the military brass," providing the Chiefs and service secretaries with a constant parade of reasons to scrap older hardware in favor of new systems, primarily missiles. According to military affairs historian Fred Kaplan, Marshall was a key contributor to the newest nuclear targeting policy review, PD-59, which argued that Soviet rearmament and the rash of localized wars made it imperative for the United States to have nuclear weaponry available for use in a tactical strike. He was joined in this recommendation by Wohlstetter and Herman Kahn. As a result, Kaplan writes, during the Carter administration, "options for nuclear war-fighting were set in policy more firmly than ever before."

Such concepts, based on the Schlesinger Doctrine, undercut the Carter administration's attempts to revive détente and pursue mutual disarmament with the USSR.

CARTER DEMONSTRATED HIS agreement with the Nixon-Ford policies by continuing the process of peacefully ceding ownership of the Panama Canal while maintaining U.S. access to it. No one expected the handover to be completed until the 1990s, but the diplomatic mechanisms for doing so had to be settled well before then. Carter submitted two treaties on the subject for ratification by the Senate. Many of the senators who had opposed SALT, full recognition of China, and Paul Warnke's nomination also opposed "giving back" the canal, but in 1978 the transfer treaties were narrowly ratified. The opponents then shifted their aim to the ways the handover was to be implemented and U.S. interests safeguarded, raising questions that kept the canal in the headlines and alive as a neocon issue.

In 1976, Rumsfeld and Cheney had managed to bury the Foreign Intelligence Surveillance Act even though Ford had agreed to sign it if Congress passed it. In 1978 Carter resurrected it and Congress passed the measure. FISA allowed the government to undertake some surveillance, including wiretapping, without recourse to the usual courts for warrants, as long as the activities being surveilled related to foreign threats to the United States, and as long as a special FISA court, operating behind closed doors, judged the wiretaps necessary. During the Carter years, the executive branch made no attempt to get around any of the FISA restrictions.

One issue on which Carter reversed Ford's stance—earning the ire of conservatives—was his attempt to defer further development of the neutron bomb, the low-explosive, high-radiation device that was designed to wipe out populations without creating massive damage to infrastructure. Al Haig jumped into this controversy, telling reporters that European leaders were "enthusiastic" about giving NATO access to such a weapon, as it would deter the possibilities of a Soviet nuclear attack. While the decision was hanging fire, Bernard Weinraub of the New York Times reported that Haig had threatened to resign over the issue (and over the fact that Carter had not consulted him on other NATO-related defense issues). According to Weinraub's story, Haig had told friends he was "tired of surprises" and of being left out of the conversation; only a plea from Secretary of State Vance had convinced him to remain at his post. According to other press reports, Haig was also angry that he hadn't been informed in advance that State would be telling NATO that cruise missiles wouldn't be raised in the next round of disarmament talks with the USSR; Haig knew from secret dispatches that they would.

Kissinger and other pragmatists decried Haig's warnings that the USSR and the Warsaw Pact countries would try to invade Europe, arguing that the USSR had little interest in expanding in Europe while it was trying to quell the Islamic-based revolts flaring up in its southwestern republics and border countries.

Brzezinski had developed the theory that a "green belt" of Muslim countries was the best bulwark against Soviet expansion. This was a marked change from the Nixon-Kissinger posture that dictators and strongmen in the Middle East would suffice to hold back the USSR. After the death of Afghan leader Daoud Khan and a coup by a pro-Communist group in 1978, Carter authorized secret help to the Afghan rebels fighting that new pro-Soviet government. He also agreed to have the CIA smuggle into the neighboring southernmost Soviet republics thousands of Korans to stir up religious-based opposition to the Moscow overlords. Covert action programs soon followed. The Soviets countered in Afghanistan by shoring up the regime and overreacting when the rebels struck. Tribesmen killed two hundred Soviet military "advisors" of the government's troops; in response, the Soviets bombed a city, killing 24,000 people. Virtually every province in Afghanistan came under rebel pressure.

If the neocons liked the Carter administration's actions in Afghanistan, they hated that he pushed Israel to make concessions to Arab states and to the Palestine Liberation Organization. The Egyptian prime minister, Anwar Sadat, had eased tensions somewhat by visiting Israel in 1977; when that initiative stalled, Carter invited Sadat and Prime Minister Menachem Begin to Camp David in the fall of 1978. In thirteen days the trio produced a "framework for peace" that led to the restoration of relations between Egypt and Israel and the return to Egypt of most of the Sinai Peninsula. The fostering of peace was applauded by the neocons—though warily, for Carter was also breaking precedent at the same time by selling advanced fighter jets to Saudi Arabia, a country that was anti-Soviet but also quite anti-Israel.

The public paid less notice, at least initially, to Carter's decision to desert an old American ally, Shah Reza Pahlavi of Iran, in favor of the exiled Iranian Muslim religious leader Ayatollah Khomeini. When the shah visited the White House and was picketed by four thousand Khomeini supporters, Carter used the occasion to pressure Pahlavi to liberalize his government to increase religious tolerance and to permit Khomeini to return from exile.

On another foreign affairs front, Carter pursued improved relations with China. Since 1971–72, few concrete steps toward full diplomatic interchanges had been taken. The stumbling block was Taiwan, still the seat of the Nationalists. The internal administration debate pitted Brzezinski, who wanted better relations with China as an anti-Soviet maneuver—the old Kissinger argument, which even Haig agreed with—against Vance, who felt the days of playing China and the USSR against one another were over. At first Carter sided with Vance, but by 1978 Brzezinski had convinced him, and the president allowed his national security adviser to make a Kissinger-like visit to Beijing.

What the Chinese wanted, in addition to U.S. disengagement from Taiwan, was arms. Congress would not approve selling China weapons directly, but Brzezinski pledged to help arrange purchases through European allies. After that, the administration began trying to convince conservative senators that full recognition of China would be helpful in pushing the Soviets back in Southwest Asia and on SALT. When enough senators agreed, the administration announced that, as of January 1, 1979, the United States would officially recognize Beijing as the only legitimate government of China, close our consulate in Taipei, and sever official relations with Taiwan. Immediate repercussions followed: As Vance had predicted, the Soviets were unhappy with the move; the announcement undermined Vance's scheduled meeting with Gromyko on SALT and led directly to the postponement of a Carter-Brezhnev summit. For their part, conservatives in Congress responded by fashioning a generous and far-reaching bill to extend military and trade support to Taiwan. The bill passed both houses easily; recognizing that a veto would be overridden, Carter signed it into law.

IN THE 1978 midterm elections, conservative Republicans picked up three Senate seats and sent fifteen new Republicans to the House—Dick Cheney among them. Although Democrats retained large majorities in both houses, the trend was away from liberalism. Recognizing this, Al Haig resigned from NATO and retired from the army in the spring of 1979; most observers presumed that he would explore a run for the presidency in 1980.

Haig's record at NATO was decidedly mixed. While he had shored up U.S. forces in Europe, he had not been able to do much to improve the military contingents of Germany, Great Britain, and other NATO countries. Reports by the House Armed Services Committee and the Congressional Budget Office painted what a reporter called a "gloomy picture" of those armies' readiness to fight a war that would last longer than a couple of weeks. In the north German plain, the CBO report said, the NATO forces were "most vulnerable" to a Warsaw Pact countries' ground attack. The congressional reports did not directly fault Haig, or even the United States, for these deficiencies. Asked about NATO's prospects as he prepared to leave his post, Haig sounded a Kraemerite note: "The drift of the West at large, and the U.S. in particular, the loss of prestige, reliability, and the way the U.S. is more tightly circumscribed than at any time it became a superpower, has unleashed a number of historically unstable forces."

The leading candidates for the 1980 Republican nomination were Ronald Reagan, Al Haig, and Bob Dole, all conservatives. Carter responded the same way Ford had in 1976: by moving to the right. The president now approved a program Haig had long advocated, the siting of Pershing II missiles in Europe within striking distance of targets inside the USSR. (Later, when Reagan sent the actual missiles to Europe, neocons applauded; the placing of the Pershing IIs was considered the capstone of Reagan's moves to stymie the "Evil Empire." The fact that Carter authorized the move was forgotten.)

Haig could not easily criticize the Pershing II deal but he did become a vocal opponent of the SALT II treaty. So did other Nixon-policy opponents, including Ed Rowny. The Joint Chiefs had agreed to support the president in public, but behind the scenes they tried to block the treaty. As the administration readied SALT II for signature in the late spring of 1979, the Chiefs summoned Rowny back from Leningrad to meet with Vance and Brzezinski to protest Vance's last-minute concessions to the Soviets. Vance withdrew them, but when Carter and Brezhnev signed the treaty in June, Rowny chose to retire rather than attend the ceremony. He then joined his neocon allies in the CPD, which set to work to prevent ratification of SALT II—and became the eldest member of the Madison Group, a new collection of conservative staffers that would help set the course of neocon policy for the next several years.

Named for its practice of meeting for lunch in a private upstairs room at Washington's Madison Hotel every other Friday, the Madison Group was a bunch of mostly young neocons convened by John Carbaugh. It might as well have been known as the Fritz Kraemer Society. They were a small group, doggedly militarist and anti-Communist, who eschewed diplomacy and considered themselves members of an elite working to promote high American ideals. According to Rowny, Sven Kraemer was the group's "chief guru," the most knowledgeable of the younger members in terms of total national security background.

Three of the group's members, Quentin Crommelin, Michael Pillsbury, and Richard Perle, had been networking together informally since Ford left office. They had joined forces to push the senators they worked for to hold up Carter's appointments to crucial posts at State and Defense, and to make certain that hard-line views were aired in the news media. Margo Carlisle, the Madison Group's only woman, was an aide to conservative senator James

McClure of Idaho. Initially a Goldwater Republican, Carlisle had worked on congressional staffs since the early days of the Nixon administration and had become the executive director of the Senate Steering Committee, a Republican group chaired by McClure; she also had close ties to the conservative Heritage Foundation and to the Department of Defense. Another Madison member—a relative outsider in the sense that he was not a Senate staffer—was Charles Kupperman, a CPD staff policy adviser whose presence solidified the relationship between the committee and the Capitol Hill staffers.

The Madison Group set itself the task of positioning its members and their neocon friends to take positions at the foreign policy levers of the next administration, which—eighteen months before the 1980 election—they presumed would be Ronald Reagan's. Their more immediate focal points were to raise defense appropriations and to defeat the SALT II treaty. For the latter purpose, Rowny was invaluable.

The fight to kill SALT II in 1979–80 mirrored the fight to save the American ABM in 1969; it even involved some of the same personnel. This time Perle joined Sven Kraemer and Ed Rowny among the experts, but once more the funders and publicists of the effort were led by Bill Casey. Casey, in turn, tied the effort to Reagan's foreign policy advisers and backers, which helped bring the Madison Groupers closer to Reagan and to potential posts in his administration. In the fight against SALT II, Rowny acted on behalf of CPD, Madison, and Casey's group of Reagan advisers, meeting with sixty-two senators and turning enough of them on the issue that the treaty's ratification was soon in doubt. After counting noses, the Carter administration asked its friends in the Senate to hold off on the vote.

In the meantime, Fred Iklé—who was already working with Reagan's foreign policy advisers—was warning friends and former subordinates, including Paul Wolfowitz, that Carter was a dead duck and they should switch their party allegiance or at least resign from his administration if they wanted to be eligible for a job in the next one. Wolfowitz did not change his party affiliation but did resign from government, becoming a professor at Johns Hopkins. In a move that established his bona fides for the Reagan crowd, Wolfowitz leaked the contents of a "Limited Contingency Report" he had been working on, a report that Secretary of Defense Brown had wanted to keep under wraps—largely because of its conclusion that the United States was inadequately prepared to intervene if a fast-moving emergency should erupt in the Middle East. That conclusion buttressed the impression that the Carter administration was inept, if not downright incompetent.

Wolfowitz's study, written with future Clinton emissary Dennis Ross, downplayed the possibility that the Soviet Union might take over the Middle

East oil fields, but did suggest that Iraq, with its Soviet arms, "may in the future use her military forces against such states as Kuwait." "The whole thrust of the study," Ross later recalled, "was to say that we had a big problem, that it would take us a long time to get any significant military force into the [Persian Gulf] area."

In October 1979, the situation in the Persian Gulf went from bad to much worse. For the previous year, to support Khomeini's attempts to "reform" Iran, Carter had refused to allow the shah of Iran into the United States. Now Pahlavi was quite ill, and Carter allowed him in to be treated in a New York hospital. With the shah out of pocket, Khomeini's revolutionaries seized power in Iran. Carter was not displeased; he sent Brzezinski to meet in Morocco with Khomeini's foreign minister and to invite Iran to enter a strategic partnership with the United States. But just days later, in November 1979, a group of Iranians took over the U.S. embassy in Tehran, seized dozens of American hostages, and precipitated the crisis that consumed Carter's final year in office.

The Madison Group members joined their counterparts in Reagan's inner foreign policy circle to trumpet the importance of that crisis to the American public—and to decry Carter's hapless attempts to resolve it.

IN THE OPINION of Ronald Reagan and his principal foreign policy advisers—Van Cleave, Allen, Iklé, Moorer, and Rowny—and of their younger colleagues in the Madison Group, Carter had done almost everything wrong during his three years in office. But the accusations they lobbed at the Carter administration had lacked a philosophic dimension. Jeane Kirkpatrick provided that in her seminal article, "Dictatorships and Double Standards," published in the November 1979 issue of *Commentary*, a pro-Israel, neocon-inflected journal edited by Norman Podhoretz. Kirkpatrick, a Democrat and a Georgetown University professor, analyzed the Carter administration's failures in a way that bolstered the arguments of the Madison Group, the CPD, and Reagan's foreign policy advisers. Carter, she charged, led by double standard: His administration took action against dictators on the right they didn't like but looked away when confronted by dictators on the left. This posture, she asserted, had accelerated the ascension of the USSR and the decline of the United States:

> Since [Carter's] inauguration . . . there has occurred a dramatic
> Soviet military buildup, matched by the stagnation of American
> armed forces, and a dramatic extension of Soviet influence in the
> Horn of Africa, Afghanistan, Southern Africa, and the Caribbean,

matched by a declining American position in all these areas. . . . In the current year the United States has suffered two other major blows—in Iran and Nicaragua—of large and strategic significance. In each country, the Carter administration not only failed to prevent the undesired outcome, it actively collaborated in the replacement of moderate autocrats friendly to American interests with less friendly autocrats of extremist persuasion.

Kirkpatrick added an observation, quite Kissingerian in its pragmatism, that the neocons initially embraced but would later be at pains to refute:

The belief that it is possible to democratize governments, anytime, anywhere, under any circumstances . . . is belied by an enormous body of evidence based on the experience of dozens of countries. . . . Vietnam presumably taught us that the United States could not serve as the world's policeman; it should also have taught us the dangers of trying to be the world's midwife to democracy when the birth is scheduled to take place under conditions of guerrilla war.

Dick Allen gave Kirkpatrick's article to Reagan—an avid reader on foreign affairs. Impressed by Kirkpatrick's acumen, Reagan asked Allen who "he" was. Upon learning Kirkpatrick's gender and background, he marked her down as a candidate for an important post in his administration and began courting her with phone calls. He disagreed with Kirkpatrick's warnings about promoting democracy to help a country stave off Communist influence but agreed with her other points. He admired her moral clarity and force.

Muravchik, the neoconservative historian, later recalled the issues that motivated him and other foreign policy neocons during the Carter years:

Contrary to Carter and the antiwar Left, neoconservatives believed that Communism was very much to be feared, to be detested, and to be opposed. They saw the Soviet Union as, in the words of Ronald Reagan, an "evil empire," unspeakably cruel to its own subjects and relentlessly predatory toward those not yet in its grasp. They took the point of George Orwell's 1984—a book that (as the Irish scholars James McNamara and Dennis J. O'Keeffe have written) resurrected the idea of evil "as a political category." And they absorbed the cautionary warning of the Russian novelist and dissident Aleksandr Solzhenitsyn against yielding ground to the Communists in the vain hope "that perhaps at some point the wolf will have eaten enough."

Late in 1979, a former Rumsfeld deputy now at Harvard, W. Scott Thompson, lit into Carter's foreign policy in the *New York Times*. Carter's "new elite," Thompson charged, "believes that we were too pre-occupied with Communism when our real priorities should have been in the third world; that we were preoccupied with military force when in fact we were too powerful." Thompson charged that Carter was expending too much energy catering to leftist revolutionaries and worrying over the "resurgence of the right" in American politics. He celebrated that right's "new realism," which, according to an unnamed "very senior" U.S. official in Europe, was now countering the Carter administration's inclination toward "betraying our European allies" by negotiating behind their backs. "Centrist" senators, Thompson wrote, were calling for Carter to "rebuild American forces to meet the Soviet threat." Moreover, he argued, the "average American gets the point"—that the SALT II treaty would give the Soviets a five-to-one advantage "in the capacity to destroy our best-protected military targets" and must therefore be rejected. Scoop Jackson convinced the Senate Armed Services Committee to issue a formal statement that SALT II was "not in the national interests of the United States," even though the committee was not involved in ratification of the treaty.

A few days later, an event occurred that validated all suspicions about the Soviets' bad intentions and mooted the argument over SALT II: On Christmas Day 1979, the USSR invaded Afghanistan. Evidently figuring that the hostage situation in Iran had sufficiently distracted the United States, the Kremlin decided that it must invade the mountainous country to prevent it from being submerged in the Muslim tide. The action succeeded in toppling the Kabul government and installing a puppet regime, but soon a rebellion had swelled up to counter the Soviets—one that would have repercussions for decades of U.S. foreign policy.

The invasion of Afghanistan was condemned by most non-Communist nations. It also gave Carter reason to withdraw the SALT II treaty from Senate consideration, preventing it from rejection by senators angry over the Soviet move.

For the neocons, the defeat of SALT II was a signal victory, not just over Carter but also over the Nixonian foreign policies that had been in place for a decade. Now they had those policies on the run; they also had a presidential candidate, Ronald Reagan, who had pledged to throw out Nixon's policies and to institute theirs instead.

IN HIS 1980 State of the Union address, the president elucidated what became known as the Carter Doctrine: "An attempt by any outside force to gain control of the Persian Gulf region will be regarded as an assault on the vital interests of the United States of America, and such an assault will be repelled by any means necessary, including military force." It was the kind of stout stance the neocons might have applauded in theory, yet they attacked it on the grounds that the administration was unwilling to back it up with adequate military muscle. Fred Iklé led off the election-year assaults with an op-ed in the *New York Times* chastising the administration for its new $158 billion military budget. That was far too low, Iklé charged; the military needed at least $1 trillion in order to

> acquire the capability to achieve such an increase rapidly when and if all-out mobilization should be demanded. . . . According to Defense Secretary Harold Brown, the Russians are continuing their military buildup and may even acquire enough forces to fight three wars at once, while we "never acquired all the readiness and mobility" to fight one large and one small war. Thus, if push came to shove, we would lack the forces to "repel" an attempt "to gain control of the Persian Gulf region" as the President, in his message to Congress, said. we would.

"Does the United States have the military capacity to 'project power' into the Persian Gulf in the event of a Soviet thrust at Iran or the Arab oilfields?" columnist William Safire chimed in. That question, he pointed out, was at the heart of the hotly debated Wolfowitz Report, a copy of which had been leaked to the *Times*. The current thinking in the Carter administration, Safire wrote, was that wiping out a "floating garrison" of as little as 1,800 troops aboard an aircraft carrier in the Gulf, or a similar garrison in Berlin, would trigger World War III—so therefore such a floating garrison should suffice to deter the Soviets from attacking. According to Safire (and Wolfowitz), "the Russians know we are bluffing": Such "tripwire" garrisons were just as symbolic and unrealistic a threat as Carter's decision to withdraw from the Moscow Olympics. "Genuine hawks," Safire wrote, know that "geopolitical power does not come out of the end of a mouth." Carter, they felt, was making commitments "that his Pentagon is too weak to keep." Safire's conclusion mirrored Fritz Kraemer's playbook: "Tough talk from weak positions invites rather than deters aggression."

The Team B veterans, most of them now part of candidate Reagan's foreign policy team, testified before sympathetic congressional panels. "The United States' failure to keep pace with the Soviet effort is . . . a direct consequence of SALT and of SALT expectations, which have clearly not borne fruit," William Van Cleave told one. In another, Dick Allen answered a question by promising that Reagan's foreign policy would be based on a "redefinition of our national interest." That redefinition was based on the idea that peace could only come through increased American military strength.

That need was bitterly underscored by the abject failure of Carter's small-bore attempt to rescue the Tehran hostages. On April 24, 1980, a secret mission dubbed Operation Eagle Claw was launched to seize the hostages and bring them to safety. But the helicopters used in the mission malfunctioned in the sandy air; five airmen and three marines died, and the hostages were not rescued. As military historian Andrew Bacevich notes, however, the more damaging repercussion of the mission was that it created "a seismic impact . . . on a nation's collective psyche," persuading the public that "the answer to whatever crisis affected the United States was not to be found in conservation or reduced expectations . . . it was to be found in the restoration of U.S. military might."

Despite this apparent hunger for a military revival, Al Haig found little support for his plans to run for president—even among his allies on the right. He had been out of the country for too long and lacked the base of support Reagan enjoyed. He chose instead to remain in private industry, where he was making more money than he had in his long military career.

Kissinger, born in Germany, was ineligible to run for president, but he wanted to return to government—despite the fact that he too was quickly becoming wealthy through his consulting firm, Kissinger Associates, whose advice was sought by governments around the world. Haig and Kissinger, of course, had long since diverged in their beliefs about foreign policy; the exception was America's embrace of China, which both continued to champion even as Kraemer lamented the abandonment of Taiwan.

By the Iowa caucuses of 1980, the first political tests of the season, Haig had faded as a candidate. In a surprise victory, however, George H. W. Bush took the state, threatening to slow the Reagan juggernaut. Like Ford four years earlier, he won primaries in five relatively liberal states, but thereafter Reagan won virtually all the delegates, and by late spring had wrapped up the Republican nomination. On the Democratic side President Carter faced interesting early challenges from Senators Edward Kennedy and Edmund Muskie, but neither took enough votes in primaries to prevent Carter's renomination.

At the Republican convention, Kissinger made a last stab at regaining power when he became the principal champion of the idea of nominating Gerald Ford as Reagan's running mate. Kissinger negotiated with Reagan's aides on Ford's behalf but insisted that he himself must also be granted a high-level post in Reagan's administration. Reagan and his aides rejected both ideas: As hard-liners, they were unwilling to saddle their ticket with the hint of returning to détente or the other foreign policies of the Nixon-Ford years. A leak eventually traced to Perle and Sullivan helped Jesse Helms prevent Kissinger from even addressing the convention.

According to Edwin Meese, Reagan personally chose George Bush as his vice presidential candidate, even though during the campaign Bush had memorably dismissed Reagan's supply-side theories as "voodoo economics." One of Bush's first assignments as Reagan's running mate was to visit Beijing. "Who better than Bush," biographer Herbert Parmet later asked rhetorically, "the man who had fought the battle at the UN over the two-China seating plan and had headed the U.S. liaison office at Beijing, to go to China to ease Communist apprehensions about a possible Reagan presidency?" Bush's centrist stances assisted the ticket, allowing moderate Republicans momentarily tempted by independent candidate John Anderson to return to the fold.

When Reagan swept the Electoral College in November, however, his victory was largely the product of his economic and moralistic appeal to blue-collar workers, whom he persuaded to abandon the Democratic Party they had long supported. Reagan's stern warnings on foreign policy contributed to his appeal, but they were not the deciding factor. Nonetheless, his election ushered in a completely new era in the country's foreign affairs, one in which neocon views of the world—and of how to assert American power—would be embraced, at least for a while, by the highest levels of government.

SECTION V

The Reagan Evolution

President Ronald Reagan at the Reykjavik Summit, with *(left to right)* Paul Nitze, Donald Regan, George Shultz, John Poindexter, Kenneth Adelman, Richard Perle, and Max Kampelman, October 12, 1986. *(Pete Souza, White House. Courtesy of Ronald Reagan Presidential Library)*

22

Fits and Starts

W hen Ronald Reagan assumed the presidency in January 1981,
he initiated a series of seminal changes in the direction of the
United States, both in its domestic affairs and in its relationships with other countries. Reagan's ideas on the role the U.S. government
should (and should not) play in the lives of American citizens, and in ending
the Cold War, produced a revolution with many lasting effects, carrying
beyond the administration of his successor, the first President Bush, and
heavily influencing the presidencies of Bill Clinton and George W. Bush, all
of whom governed in his shadow.

In foreign affairs, however, the Reagan Revolution was also an evolution.
Over the course of his time in office, Reagan became steadily less rigid in
his stances—a shift that deeply upset the neocons and other adherents to the
Kraemerite, militarist philosophy that they believed was the only valid basis
for America's relationships with other countries.

"If the next president is a hard-liner attuned to the Soviet threat," *New
York Times* columnist William Safire predicted in 1979, "he would have five
people in positions of heavy responsibility." These were Richard Allen, John
Lehman, Team B leader Richard Pipes, CIA deputy director Frank Carlucci,
and strategist Edward Luttwak. Safire predicted that Perle, Van Cleave,
Sven Kraemer, and neocons Ken Adelman and Michael Ledeen would find
homes in or near the NSC, which would again become "an exciting place
to be." Of these men, only Luttwak did not enter the Reagan administration

in early 1981, preferring to stay in academia. "When Reagan was elected," Anne Hessing Cahn wrote, "Team B became, in essence, the A Team," the chief advisers on the Soviet threat to the new administration. As did nearly the entire Team B membership, thirty-three members of the Committee on the Present Danger, including honorary member Reagan, found high-level positions in the Reagan executive branch.

Allen headed the NSC, Pipes became its Eastern European and Soviet specialist, and Sven Kraemer its arms control expert. Perle, Pillsbury, Carlucci, and Carlisle took posts at Defense. Lehman became secretary of the navy. Wolfowitz, Ledeen, and Adelman found positions at State. Iklé, Nitze, Kampelman, and Weiss became arms negotiators. Jeane Kirkpatrick was appointed ambassador to the United Nations.

Reagan surprised many by nominating Al Haig as secretary of state. In the half-dozen years since Haig had held a White House post he had separated his views from those of Kissinger, had become more enamored of military power, and was an advocate of a remilitarized foreign policy, but his old Nixon-Kissinger ties still made many neocons wary. Bill Casey and Caspar Weinberger, each of whom had expected to become secretary of state, also opposed Haig's nomination. When Scoop Jackson turned down an offer to be secretary of defense, Weinberger accepted that post. A strong letter of support from Nixon to Reagan helped tip the scales for Haig at State.

Reagan's inner circle also shut out of high positions some neocons who had directly advised Reagan in the campaign. Weinberger vetoed Team B member and Reagan campaign adviser William Van Cleave as undersecretary of defense in favor of the more moderate Frank Carlucci. As a consolation prize, Van Cleave was given the leadership of an advisory board to the ACDA. Ed Rowny, who had wanted to lead the ACDA, was passed over for that post in favor of Democrat Eugene Rostow.

Bill Casey didn't travel in neocon circles, but his strong anti-Communist bent gave them no reason to object to his nomination to head the CIA. However, intelligence community professionals were uncomfortable with Casey, who had not come from their ranks; Reagan eased their fears by appointing as Casey's second in command Admiral Bobby Ray Inman, the former director of naval intelligence and NSA chief.

With the Senate in Republican hands, there was small chance that Haig wouldn't be confirmed. But many senators were concerned about unresolved questions from his role in the Nixon-era wiretapping and in Ford's pardon of Nixon. There was plenty on the Nixon White House tapes that could hang Haig, so he worked hard to prevent them from being heard. In this, Haig got an unusual assist from a man few people would have expected to champion him: Bob Woodward. In an op-ed in the *Washington Post*,

Woodward argued that the Senate should "forget about obtaining any of the Nixon tapes" and "abandon" subpoenas for the logs of Nixon-Haig meetings. Such a search, Woodward wrote, was "unfair" and "quite possibly illegal." Even if Haig made incriminating statements on the Nixon tapes, Woodward ventured, Haig had not meant them and had uttered them only to "console Nixon." If Haig was to be held accountable, Woodward concluded, "let it happen without the tapes." No fellow reporters dared question in print the spectacle of Bob Woodward urging the Senate *not* to examine available—taped—evidence of the past actions of Nixon's last chief of staff.

Haig's memories of Kissinger's success in transferring the locus of power from the State Department to the NSC in 1969 colored a memo he wrote Reagan on January 6, 1981. Haig proposed a reversal of Kissinger's move—a transfer of power from the NSC to State that would make him the chief decision maker, what he called the "vicar for the community" that set foreign policy. Haig presented the plan to Reagan in person, but the president-elect never signed the memo, and thereafter Reagan's aides banned Haig from seeing Reagan except in the presence of a member of Reagan's inner circle—Ed Meese, Mike Deaver, or Jim Baker.

Nine weeks into the administration, a deranged assassin shot Reagan as he left the Washington Hilton Hotel after a speech, wounding him and several others. Vice President Bush was out of town. When the press asked assistant press spokesman Larry Speakes—whose boss, Jim Brady, was among the wounded—who was in charge of the government, Speakes said he was unable to answer. Hearing the exchange, Secretary Haig scrambled to the press room and gave the press his answer:

> Constitutionally, gentlemen, you have the president, the vice president and the secretary of state, in that order, and should the president decide he wants to transfer the helm to the vice president, he will do so. As for now, I'm in control here, in the White House, pending the return of the vice president and in close touch with him.

Haig was entirely wrong: The Constitution mandated that succession went through two congressional officers before devolving on the secretary of state. This telling misunderstanding highlighted both Haig's shaky grasp of constitutional democratic governance and his willingness to assume powers beyond his station.

The Reagan administration showed its true militarist colors from its earliest days. It began a huge military buildup; navy secretary Lehman commissioned many more new ships, and Weinberger dramatically accelerated the development of cruise missiles, the B-1 bomber, and other armaments.

The Pentagon's budget almost doubled during the Reagan years; as military historian Andrew Bacevich writes, the massive increases "contribute[d] mightily to lifting the armed services out of their Vietnam-induced doldrums." Troop readiness, modernization, recruitment, and retention rates soared. Beefing up the military also assisted the remilitarization of foreign policy, an objective further advanced by the success of Van Cleave and Daniel Graham in convincing Reagan to begin work on the Strategic Defense Initiative (SDI), a new system for destroying incoming missiles in midair. (SDI would become better known as "Star Wars" after it was introduced in 1983.) As Luttwak told a Heritage Foundation seminar at the time, "The real payoff of an American SDI would be its stimulation of Soviet spending on similar defenses, thereby soaking up rubles that would otherwise go for more dangerous purposes."

The Heritage Foundation generated several similar notions about how to oppose the expanding Soviet empire. The think tank's scholars conceived a schematic of the Soviet empire with Moscow at its center, surrounded by an inner ring of satellite countries, and an outer ring of countries the USSR was trying to take over, such as Afghanistan, or where it was fomenting Communist revolutions, as in Nicaragua. The Heritage scholars and Reagan wanted a "rollback" of this empire from its ragged edges toward its center.

In pursuit of this goal, Reagan outdid Carter in such matters as supporting the mujahideen in Afghanistan. Where Carter had committed $30 million to the Muslim guerrillas, Reagan furnished more than $600 million; he gave similar CIA and arms-supply assistance to anti-Communists in Angola, Cambodia, Ethiopia, Iran, Laos, Nicaragua, Poland, and Vietnam. In Central and South America, this spilled over into covert action; according to Gates, who returned to the CIA under Reagan, Casey was "obsessed" with covert action in Central America.

Casey was just setting such operations in motion when a scandal erupted at the CIA. He had appointed a millionaire business friend, Max Hugel, as the Agency's deputy director for operations. But a group of long-term intelligence operatives and managers, led by deputy director Inman, wanted to oust Hugel and set out to discredit him. Before long, transcripts of tape recordings of Hugel's business conversations, in which he was alleged to have engaged in illegal activities to boost his company's stock price, ended up in the hands of *Washington Post* reporters Patrick E. Tyler and Bob Woodward, the latter a longtime friend of Inman, who had been a high-ranked naval intelligence official in Vietnam during Woodward's time offshore. In later years, when Inman visited Washington, he sometimes stayed overnight in Woodward's apartment.

The day after the appearance of the Tyler/Woodward articles on Hugel and his business transactions, complete with transcript excerpts, Hugel resigned. Casey's hold on the CIA directorship was weakened.

For Woodward, the Hugel story was a journalistic triumph and a return to the military-based sources that had won him fame. It came at an opportune time: He had broken little news since the spring of 1977, when he published two stories about a Pentagon-run espionage operation that was being shut down after a dozen-year run. Even that story, which also involved Inman, had been controversial at best. Back in 1965, Admiral Tom Moorer had begun Task Force 157, which used military and commercial resources to spy on Soviet naval activities. But the initiative had been a headache to successive directors of naval intelligence, the DIA, and the CIA. Inman, the former director of naval intelligence who had become director of the NSA, was a longtime Moorer foe, and once Inman was in power he pushed to close TF-157 down. Woodward's stories helped.

When Moorer read Woodward's stories on the task force, he was apoplectic. He telephoned Woodward, giving him what Moorer later referred to in an interview as a "tongue-lashing" for what amounted to disclosing classified information Woodward had been privy to while in the navy. In a second interview, Moorer went even further with his criticism: "I mean every once in a while you get people that are not adverse [sic] to giving the information that they just have passing through their particular area of assignment, and passing it on to unauthorized people. Woodward was one of them."

After these military-sourced stories, Woodward wrote little of significance about national security during the rest of the Carter years. One reason is that his most important sources were gone. Fred Buzhardt, a major source for his books about the Nixon years, died in 1978. Al Haig, serving as SACEUR in Europe, was out of the D.C. loop. And others in the military appeared to have had little to convey to Woodward. The reporter's next book, written with his longtime friend Scott Armstrong, was 1979's *The Brethren: Inside the Supreme Court.* That year, Woodward was appointed metro editor of the *Washington Post*; he was generally considered on track to replace Ben Bradlee as managing editor when Bradlee retired.

During his short term as metro editor, however, Woodward was involved in two matters that embarrassed the *Post.* The first concerned a 1979 story about the president of Mobil Oil, written by Patrick Tyler at Woodward's urging. A later court summary laid out the charges:

> William Tavoulareas and his son Peter brought suit for injury to reputation after *The Washington Post* published a story that said, among other things, that Tavoulareas had used his influence as president of

Mobil Corporation to "set up" Peter as a partner in a shipping firm whose business included a multi-million dollar management services contract with Mobil.

The jury found in favor of the plaintiffs, granting the Tavoulareas family $1.8 million in punitive damages. The result was overturned in 1987 by a higher court, but in the short term it tarnished Tyler's and Woodward's reputations.

The second, and more high-profile incident, concerned Woodward's supervision of a young *Post* reporter, Janet Cooke. Woodward pushed Cooke to come up with the kinds of spectacular scoops he called "holy shit" stories. "The downside of holy shit stories," *Salon* editor at large Jack Shafer later observed, "is that they can turn out to be wholly bullshit." As the *Post*'s William Green described in a later ombudsman article, Woodward egged Cooke on until she wrote "Jimmy's World," a 1980 story about an eight-year-old boy named Jimmy who was addicted to heroin. The tale alarmed the city, which then spent money and time on a search for the boy on whom Cooke claimed to have based the article. Though Woodward was apprised of doubts about the story by fellow editor David Maraniss, Woodward reportedly observed, "In for a dime, in for a dollar," and agreed to allow the story to be nominated for a Pulitzer Prize. The article won the Pulitzer for feature writing. Almost as soon as it did, however, reports of falsehoods in Cooke's résumé began to surface. Questioned by Woodward and Maraniss, Cooke confessed that both her résumé and "Jimmy's World" were fiction. The *Post* was forced to return the Pulitzer. Woodward said,

> I believed it, we published it. Official questions had been raised, but we stood by the story and her. . . . I think that the decision to nominate the story for a Pulitzer is of minimal consequence. I also think that it won is of little consequence. It is a brilliant story—fake and fraud that it is.

Woodward's responsibilities at the paper were soon shifted away from management. His next book, published in 1985, was about the life and death of comedian John Belushi.

DURING THE 1980 campaign, Reagan had promised to hold on to the Panama Canal. Once he entered office, however, he discovered that such a stand was impractical at best and might even provoke an uprising of Central American countries against the United States. Reagan opted to return the canal on schedule. Reagan reversed another campaign promise when his administration continued Carter's policy of favoring China over Taiwan, despite Reagan's own affection for Taiwan. He also chose to continue negotiating arms reduction with the Soviets. Soon newspaper articles were labeling Reagan's alliance with the neocons as "uneasy." *Commentary*'s Norman Podhoretz was "not happy" about the "pattern" that was emerging in the administration's conduct of foreign affairs, including a weaker posture toward the Soviet Union and a favoring of domestic priorities over "rebuilding American defenses and trying to get ground troops into the Persian Gulf."

The neocons did cheer Reagan's first overt military action, a strike against an enemy on August 20, 1981. As the Sixth Fleet conducted exercises in the Gulf of Sidra—a part of the Mediterranean claimed by Libya— dictator Moammar Qaddafi's planes fired on two American fighters about sixty miles offshore. Following earlier orders from Reagan, the F-14s shot down the Libyans. Libya made no immediate military response; many assumed—wrongly, it later emerged—that Qaddafi had been cowed by the attacks.

While Reagan was getting his bearings in foreign affairs, he had yielded the foreign policy bully pulpit to Haig, who in a September speech in Berlin accused the USSR of using lethal chemical weapons, of supplying poisonous compounds synthesized by fungi—"yellow rain"—to its allies in Laos and Vietnam since 1975, and of continuing the practice in Afghanistan. Haig's claims were based on flimsy evidence, but he was scheduled to meet Soviet foreign minister Andrei Gromyko in two weeks, in the first high-level sit-down with the USSR since Reagan's inauguration, and his accusations underscored the administration's confrontational tone.

Haig was a strong proponent of increasing contact between the United States and China, to build China's importance as a counterweight to Soviet power. Kraemer disagreed with Haig on this strategy—as he had earlier with Kissinger—and he made his mistrust known in several lectures. Kraemer's argument would soon influence a Wolfowitz report for Defense on the "triangular relationship" of the United States, the Soviet Union, and China. Wolfowitz and his associates reached the same conclusion as Kraemer: that China had been overemphasized under Nixon, Ford, and Carter, principally because China was so crucial to Kissinger's reputation. Wolfowitz asserted that working closely with China would have only a negligible impact on America's larger task of properly countering the USSR. From the early days of the administration, when Wolfowitz's report was still in rough draft,

Reagan's inner circle used it to answer Haig's calls for increased interchanges with China. George Shultz, who would later become Reagan's second secretary of state, cited the report as the rationale for expanding America's relationship with Japan and for decreasing the emphasis on China.

Haig was giving the administration plenty of reasons for alarm. He testified to Congress that the United States had a contingency plan to explode a nuclear device if the USSR should invade Western Europe. Haig was intentionally vague in his remarks, but nonetheless the next day Weinberger had to deny that there was any such plan for nuclear retaliation against the USSR in the event of a ground forces invasion. When Egyptian president Anwar Sadat was assassinated, Haig told the press, "Our entire foreign policy depends on Reagan attending the funeral." After a rebuke by the White House, Haig summoned the reporters again and said, "Our entire foreign policy depends on Reagan staying home." White House insiders were not amused by Haig's egotistical protest at being overruled. "What we're getting [from Haig's State Department] is warmed-over Scoop Jackson and Kissinger ideas. That means no new ideas and no agreement," one anonymous White House source told reporters.

The battle lines emerging in the administration pitted Haig and Lawrence Eagleburger at State against Cap Weinberger and Richard Perle at Defense. The two secretaries had to get along in public, but Perle and Eagleburger accused each other of championing policy stances toward the USSR that would sell out the United States, which led to a complete stalemate on generating policy.

The CIA director, Bill Casey, was focused on making sure the administration countered the Soviets wherever and whenever possible. After a swing through Tunisia, Somalia, and Pakistan, he wrote Reagan a memo warning that the Soviets were underwriting programs to bring Middle Eastern dissidents to South Yemen for training, then send them back to Libya, Ethiopia, Syria, and Afghanistan to "organize, propagandize, or practice terrorism against the government." Casey noted that the Soviet-targeted countries "almost completely surround our friends Egypt and Israel and the oil fields."

Casey also enthusiastically supported a secret plan, created within the CIA, to support the Nicaraguan rebels known as Contras. Reagan signed a presidential finding agreeing to it in November 1981. The true purpose of the plan, hidden behind the objective of assisting the Contras, was to kill Cuban forces in Central America that the CIA believed were aiding the Sandinistas, who currently governed Nicaragua, as well as Salvadoran and Honduran leftists.

While the CIA pursued Cubans in Central America, Reagan tried to make some progress on arms limitation. At an NSC meeting on the subject, the president chose an opening gambit that would treat short- and long-range missiles differently and would aim for an eventual total elimination of long-range nuclear missiles. Although this plan would benefit the United States at the expense of the Soviets, Haig did not like it—perhaps because he did not generate it—and soon undercut it (and the president) by telling the press that the United States expected to compromise once it received a Soviet counterproposal. Haig's maneuver enraged Perle, the author of the gambit, who was already worried about what Paul Nitze, now the chief arms limitation negotiator, might give away to the Soviets. As Sven Kraemer said after seeing cables from the negotiator, "Once Paul gets hungry for a deal, all the instructions in the world won't keep him from trying to make any goddamn deal he thinks he can cut." Perle had once learned at Nitze's knee, but that was long ago; now Perle was the missile expert and Nitze, at least in Perle's and Sven Kraemer's eyes, was a problematic loose cannon. Any concessions to the Soviets on missile defense, Perle told the Senate, would be tantamount to Chamberlain yielding to Hitler at Munich.

Nitze kept negotiating, though, and the neocons took a step back. They took an even larger one after Reagan's national security adviser, Dick Allen, was eased out. In December 1981, Allen came under fire on a flimsy charge that he had accepted a bribe in exchange for arranging an interview for a Japanese reporter with Mrs. Reagan. The accusation was disproved by the FBI, but Allen, besmirched, was forced to submit his resignation. Judge William Clark, a longtime Reagan friend who had been keeping an eye on Haig at State, became the new national security adviser. The neocons were upset at Allen's departure, but Clark was another hard-liner, so they were mollified.

As national security adviser, Clark weakened Haig's voice and strengthened that of the Reagan insiders, whom Haig dismissed as nonprofessionals in strategy and diplomacy. Admiral Inman, who shared Haig's view of the Reagan appointees, resigned as the CIA's deputy director, but Haig tried to fight the insiders, using Inman's old practice of leaking to Bob Woodward. In mid-February 1982, Woodward was given the notes from a Haig staff meeting in which the secretary of state trashed current administration policy on the continuing negotiations in the Middle East, including stances he had publicly taken. According to these notes, Haig also made several undiplomatic remarks about America's allies during the meeting, labeling the British foreign secretary, Lord Carrington, a staunchly conservative friend of British prime minister Margaret Thatcher, "a duplicitous bastard," and calling America's European allies "cowardly." The notes also had Haig taking repeated swings at Reagan and his inner circle, complaining that "we are being snookered by the White House" and claiming that he'd had to ask for presidential speeches to be rewritten to "drive out the arrogant, belligerent tone."

Haig followed this mess by publicly sparring with UN ambassador Jeane Kirkpatrick over how to head off a coming war over the Falkland Islands between Great Britain and Argentina. Kirkpatrick, who had written her doctoral thesis on Argentina, had been working to restore ties with the country. She wanted the United States to remain neutral if war should break out; Haig disagreed and called for her resignation. Reagan temporarily resolved their dispute. Haig made a series of shuttle-diplomacy trips, trying to defuse the war—at a moment when Reagan was determined to have the United States totally support Thatcher, Reagan's conservative soulmate. In mid-May, after Argentina's invasion of the Falklands led Britain to declare war, Lord Carrington resigned over his failure to foresee the invasion. One White House staffer wrote a fake headline about it: "Duplicitous Bastard Resigns on Principle: A Model."

In early June, as the Falklands War continued, Israel invaded Lebanon and approached Beirut. Lebanon had made earlier provocations, including an attempt to assassinate the Israeli ambassador to Great Britain, but in this conflict Israel was perceived as the aggressor. The UN Security Council passed a unanimous resolution, with U.S. support, demanding that Israel withdraw from Lebanon, that all parties agree to a cease-fire, and that a multinational force should patrol the area.

At last, Reagan's inner circle succeeded in persuading one of its own—George Shultz—to step in as a replacement for Haig. Perhaps having gotten wind of this, Haig told Reagan that he was dissatisfied with his job, charging that too many voices in the administration were claiming to speak for its foreign policy, and complaining that there were too many policy differences between himself and Reagan. "What policy differences?" Reagan responded. There were few and they were small, both men knew. Haig had never succeeded in becoming Reagan's policy "vicar," primarily because Reagan insisted on having his secretary of state report to him rather than let Haig order him around.

So Haig resigned. The news sent shock waves around the globe. "The unease," *Time* said, "centered on the fact that the most knowledgeable and experienced foreign policy hand in an Administration not noted for diplomatic expertise had quit at a moment when the U.S. was trying to cope with a host of challenging global troubles."

During Reagan's first eighteen months in office, despite the large number of hard-liners and ideologues in his administration, he had continued many of the policies begun by Nixon, Ford, and Carter, while advancing the rebuilding of the U.S. military and occasionally flexing its strength. Now, having thrown his would-be "vicar" overboard, he was ready to steer the ship of state in a direction of his own choosing.

23

The High Tide of
Anti-Communism, and After

As when a cork is taken out of a bottle, the removal of Haig from the Reagan administration enabled the rise of the anti-Soviet policy wonks Richard Perle, Paul Wolfowitz, Sven Kraemer, and Fred Iklé, while enhancing the clout of the equally anti-Soviet CIA director, Bill Casey, and Reagan's secretary of defense, Cap Weinberger. Until Secretary of State Shultz got his bearings, the hard-liners and their recommendations went almost unopposed in councils.

They were aided in their efforts by Admiral John Poindexter, the new deputy national security adviser, and Marine Colonel Oliver North, the NSC's deputy director for political affairs. Poindexter and North itched to put policy into action and had ties to outside organizations led by ex-military men who were willing to take those actions. Former generals John Singlaub and Daniel Graham, and former CIA and military intelligence officers Richard Secord, Theodore Shackley, and Thomas Clines—all veterans of the wars in Southeast Asia—were still bitter about the U.S. losses there. They also all subscribed to the Kraemeresque belief that military action was more effective than diplomacy in obtaining desired results, and that a self-selected elite should make decisions on the use of force unilaterally, without consulting Congress. In association with State officials Elliott Abrams and Michael Ledeen, North, Poindexter, and these outside groups made official and unofficial alliances with right-leaning regimes in Taiwan, South Africa, South Korea, Saudi Arabia, Israel, and in Central America. These actions would lead to the policy disaster known as Iran-Contra.

. . . .

THE CENTERPIECE OF the president's June 1982 proposal to the Soviets for a new round of SALT talks was an idea, generated by Perle, that both sides reduce their overall warhead count to 5,000 each, of which only 2,500 could be ICBMs, and no more than 850 very heavy ones. "Under Reagan's ceilings," *Time* noted,

> the U.S. would have to make considerably less of an adjustment in its strategic forces than would the Soviet Union. That feature of the proposal will almost certainly prompt the Soviets to charge that it is unfair and one-sided. No doubt some American arms-control advocates will agree, accusing the Administration of making the Kremlin an offer it cannot possibly accept—a deceptively equal-looking, deliberately nonnegotiable proposal that is part of what some suspect is the hardliners' secret agenda of sabotaging disarmament so that the U.S. can get on with the business of rearmament.

Another hard-line administration move—viewed as a way to counter Soviet influence—was its decision to send in eight hundred marines to support a UN mandate for a multinational force (MNF) of peacekeepers in Lebanon. The force was supposed to remain in Lebanon for only thirty days, but after the Lebanese president was assassinated in mid-September— and hundreds of Palestinians in two camps were massacred by Lebanese forces while Israeli guards were stationed nearby—Reagan agreed to maintain a larger U.S. force in the region, together with troops from France and Italy, for an extended period. The stated aims of this multinational force were to enable the safe withdrawal of Israeli and PLO fighters and to restore sovereignty to Lebanon's government; at a deeper level, the MNF was also intended to counter Soviet influence on Palestinian extremists. This was very much in line with the ideological assumptions of George Shultz, the new secretary of state.

Back in the fall of 1970, when Nixon and Kissinger had dealt with a series of crises (Vietnam, the Middle East, Cuba, Chile), they treated each of them as a Cold War confrontation between the United States and the Soviet Union. As later events showed, this approach to the problems discounted important local, ethnic, and religious elements that were at least as responsible for the crises as the clash of superpowers. But by 1982 those lessons had faded; the Reagan administration treated Moscow as the prime villain behind all the problems facing the U.S., and the underlying reason for sending the marines to Lebanon.

No one cheered the marines going to Lebanon more loudly than Fritz Kraemer. Rapid military response to provocations had always been one of his tenets, and he applauded the Reagan administration's willingness to put its military muscle toward restoring peace in Lebanon and countering Soviet influence there. He had always seen the battle with the Soviet Union as involving will as well as strength, arguing that when our society "is so weak of will that it accepts no risks and wants to intervene with real force only when no sacrifices can be expected, it becomes outwardly powerless." To Kraemer, taking direct action in Lebanon—and less direct but still forceful actions in Afghanistan and other hot spots around the world—constituted proper U.S. behavior. Even after Haig left the administration, Kraemer supported Reagan, and over the years his estimate of the fortieth president increased. Reagan, he would later say, was one of the few politicians who possessed the "inner musicality" that Kraemer considered the most important character trait, one he himself sought to achieve. "Ronald Reagan was living proof of innate instinct's superiority over mere intellectual brilliance."

In 1982, ANTONIN Scalia, Robert Bork, and other conservative-minded professors at the Yale, Harvard, and University of Chicago law schools, with the encouragement of Reagan's counsel, Edwin Meese, founded the Federalist Society for Law and Public Policy Studies, pledged to the principle that "the separation of governmental powers is central to our Constitution." Their goal was to curb a judiciary they felt was making law rather than interpreting it. To do so, they trained legal scholars in the "strict construction" of the Constitution and identified candidates for the judiciary whom Reagan could appoint to replace judges they considered too liberal.

The Federalist Society's view of the powers of the presidency was derived from Alexander Hamilton's seventieth essay of *The Federalist Papers*, which described the characteristics of that office as "decision, activity, secrecy, and dispatch." Contending that the Executive Branch's authority had been sapped in recent years by the congressional assaults on the powers of Nixon, Ford, and Carter, the society said that it needed to be restored and augmented. Research in this area by the society's founders would eventually lead to the formulation of the "unitary executive" theory and to its use as rationale for many of the extraordinary actions of the George W. Bush administration.

One reason the Federalist Society became a force in legal circles was its inherent alliance with a strong executive, Ronald Reagan, who after two years in office finally felt confident enough to take actions he had refrained from pursuing in his early days. Two of these, he knew, would upset the

Kremlin. One was his approval of the military research projects that he hoped would pave the way for the Strategic Defense Initiative (SDI), and the second was his labeling of the Soviet Union as the "evil empire."

Reagan believed that a missile shield would be the ultimate defensive weapon. It would render nuclear missiles obsolete and thus make the world safer. Reagan announced SDI as a response to the increasingly large ABM systems with which the Soviets had surrounded Moscow and other important Soviet sites; out of public hearing, he also saw it as an answer to Soviet attempts (as reported by the CIA) to investigate the use of lasers, particle beams, kinetic energy, and microwaves to destroy missiles in midair.

According to Gates, Reagan's public announcement of SDI scared the Soviets, who realized that developing and deploying the system might take a decade or more, but believed that American economic force and technological know-how might very well eventually produce such a system—one that would inevitably skew the strategic balance of power back toward the United States.

At the moment when Reagan announced SDI, the administration was trying to negotiate with the Soviets on a new Strategic Arms Reduction Treaty (START). The announcement complicated that negotiation. So did a new report on the MX missile by a commission chaired by Brent Scowcroft that included Kissinger, Haig, Laird, Schlesinger, Harold Brown—and Donald Rumsfeld, who liked to claim that he had made possible the development of the MX. The Scowcroft report was a bastion of reasonableness to which even Haig and Kissinger were willing to sign on. The report took the view that the "window of vulnerability" Team B had touted in 1976 had simply never existed—in other words, that the Soviets did not possess nuclear superiority. If a new generation of "Peacekeeper" missiles were to be deployed, the commission recommended, a modest number—say one hundred—would suffice, not to respond to a serious Soviet missile strike but to demonstrate that the United States was still serious about missile defense. They saw the MX as a bargaining chip to pressure the Soviets into scrapping their ICBMs. As Frances FitzGerald writes in *Way Out There in the Blue*, her history of Reagan-era arms policy, "The deal the Scowcroft Commission brokered between Weinberger and the moderates on the Armed Services Committee was that the Administration could have its MX in unprotected silos so long as it made its START proposal more negotiable and less likely to confer a first-strike capability on either side."

Congress approved the missiles, but only fifty of them—a deployment even more likely to be used as a bargaining chip with the Soviets. Rumsfeld had refused to agree to the commission's recommendation and pointed out that Kissinger had wanted to use the original Sentinel ABM as a bargaining chip with the Soviets in 1969. Rumsfeld charged that Scowcroft—whom he identified as the current president of Kissinger Associates—was being too timid in his approach.

During the congressional debate on the MX, veteran reporter Mary Mc-Grory accompanied an anti-MX expert on a visit to Representative Dick Cheney, who also wanted a much-expanded MX fleet. She found Cheney very knowledgeable about the subject, but his dark belief that the world was populated by enemies persuaded her to call him "the most danger-ous [congressman] I've ever seen." Similarly, on a trip to Moscow in 1983, Cheney met a Soviet marshal, a deputy chief of the general staff, who suggested reopening discussions on arms limitations in Europe and a one-year ban on testing a very large new Soviet missile in exchange for a ban on testing the similar MX. Cheney would not even consider it. "Cheney did not want to allow the Russians to appear to be in any way reasonable," a congressman who had accompanied him recalled. "He doesn't believe in negotiations. He's completely rigid, states his position, and concedes nothing."

Inside the administration, Perle saw to it that the linkage the Scowcroft Commission agreed to on the START proposals was undermined. Scow-croft was "astonished" at this, FitzGerald reports, aghast that the Pentagon would misuse his report for its own anti-détente purposes. His objections were dismissed.

Reagan's second initiative, in that spring of 1983, was even more sym-bolic. As he was preparing to give a speech on foreign policy, Sven Kraemer, now the arms control director for the NSC, urged that the president identify the USSR as a "focus of evil" in the world, a phrase that would echo Sol-zhenitsyn's depiction of the USSR as "the concentration of world evil." The year before, when Haig was still at State, Reagan had come close to using the phrase in a well-regarded speech to the House of Commons, in which he declared that Communism would end up on "the ash heap of history," but under pressure from Haig the reference to evil was dropped. Now, with Haig gone, Reagan settled on a new phrase. In a speech to the National As-sociation of Evangelicals on March 8, 1983, he declared:

> In your discussions of the nuclear freeze proposals, I urge you to beware the temptation of pride, the temptation of blithely declaring yourselves above it all and label both sides equally at fault, to ignore the facts of history and the aggressive impulses of an evil empire, to simply call the arms race a giant misunderstanding and thereby remove yourself from the struggle between right and wrong and good and evil.

The phrase "evil empire" had a clarifying simplicity that resonated with the public. As historian John Lewis Gaddis argues in his history of the Cold War, it also announced a distinct break with the pursuit of détente. For a while, Reagan's rhetoric quieted critics such as Norman Podhoretz, who had recently accused the administration of "appeasement by any other name" in its dealings with the Soviets.

Reagan soon found, however, that the "evil empire" phrase constrained him in formulating foreign policy. The United States faced situations of increasing complexity that required almost continual negotiations with Moscow; as Reagan himself later said, such antagonistic rhetoric impeded his ability to negotiate with the Soviet Union. The phrase was soon dropped from his speeches. The "us versus them" formulation also made it difficult to find ways to resolve other world crises, such as that taking place in Lebanon.

Through the winter of 1982–83, the multinational force—composed of numerically equal contingents of American, French, and Italian troops—had managed to keep the peace in Lebanon. As the troops lingered indefinitely, however, local Lebanese and Islamic-militant opposition grew. In April 1983, suicide bombers armed with Iranian munitions hit the American embassy in West Beirut, an attack that killed sixty-three people. By August 1983 the situation had grown much worse. Local militias began to attack the multinational force, and in those battles killed several U.S. soldiers. When an American commander in Beirut learned that Reagan was considering a request to allow the U.S. Navy, stationed not far offshore, to shell the militia positions, he opined that the price for changing their mission from peace-keeping to offensive action would be paid in blood. Nonetheless, urged by the hard-liners, Reagan gave the go-ahead, and the navy shelled the militia positions. Conservatives in Congress and the media heralded the administration's willingness to confront both the embassy bombing and the local militias.

During the fighting in Lebanon, arms limitation talks continued in Geneva. While there, Paul Nitze and his Soviet counterpart took a "walk in the woods," where in privacy they devised a proposal to cut back nuclear missiles in Europe—the Soviets by destroying current ones and the United States by forgoing certain new ones. Nitze trumpeted the new idea to the press; it was welcomed at first by the Joint Chiefs, but Perle, Sven Kraemer, and Ken Adelman (the new head of ACDA) were appalled, as was Ed Rowny, who had previously defended Nitze. Rowny and Perle argued that the proposal didn't go far enough in disarming the Soviets. It was no matter: The proposal was dropped after the rest of the Soviet delegation disowned it, and the Geneva talks continued on a more cautious basis.

Then, between October 23 and November 23, 1983, a series of wrenching events in Lebanon, Europe, and the Caribbean called into question the appropriateness of the administration's fixation on the Communist enemy.

On October 23, a group of suicide truck-bombers blew themselves up at the MNF barracks at Beirut, killing 241 American and 58 French paratroopers and other soldiers. It was the most devastating military incident for the United States since the war in Vietnam. The attack also served to energize the young Islamic militant Osama bin Laden; he soon enlisted the bombing's mastermind, Imad Fayez Mughniyah, to guide him in planning his own attacks on American interests.

In the bombing's aftermath, there were calls for the multinational force to leave Lebanon, but Reagan insisted that the United States would not do so. Reagan's steadfastness cheered Kraemer and many other hard-liners, who saw it as an antidote to what they viewed as the U.S. decision to "cut and run" in Vietnam.

Two days after the Beirut bombing, U.S. forces invaded the tiny Caribbean nation of Grenada, accompanied by small military contingents from the neighboring states of Barbados, Jamaica, and a few others. The invasion was sparked by a recent coup in which a Communist-sponsored military leader had deposed and executed the country's former prime minister; since then, the new Communist government had threatened the safety of U.S. students attending the island's medical college. The administration feared that these students could be taken hostage just as American diplomats had been in Tehran in 1979. Also, satellites had observed Cuban military personnel building a nine-thousand-foot runway in the country, possibly preparing to make it a Soviet-Cuban air base.

In the successful action, U.S. troops captured more than six hundred Cuban military personnel in Grenada, most of them engineers. Reagan won praise for liberating Grenada, but he also received public and private rebukes from his ally and friend Margaret Thatcher, who insisted that Western democracies must use force only "to preserve our way of life—we do not use it to walk into other people's countries." Before the invasion, the prime minister had warned Reagan that if actions like the Grenada exercise should become the norm, and the United States was permitted to intervene whenever it disapproved of a foreign regime, "then we are going to have really terrible wars in the world." Thatcher's warning, noted with some interest at the time, would become increasingly relevant in years to come.

The administration followed the Grenada invasion with a ten-day NATO exercise, led by U.S. troops. Able Archer 83 was a simulated run-up to a war in Europe, complete with an elevated DEFCON level—also simulated, but so realistic that it reportedly scared the Soviets into putting their own nuclear forces and air units of the Warsaw Pact on very high alert. It was the closest the world had come to nuclear war since the Cuban Missile Crisis of 1962. No sooner did Able Archer 83 end than the Reagan administration made good on its most significant anti-Soviet move to date, fulfilling Jimmy Carter's promise by installing ground-based cruise missiles and Pershing II ballistic missiles in West Germany and Norway, over the protests of Soviet-backed "peace" and "antinuclear" movements, to counter the large missiles the USSR had placed in its satellite countries.

After these U.S. actions, the Soviet Union pulled out of the intermediate-range nuclear force (INF) talks and canceled the next round of START talks.

Weinberger, Perle, and the neocons celebrated the Soviets' reaction, taking it as evidence that the administration had made its point by introducing the missiles to Europe. "The stationing of the American mid-range nuclear weapons, cruise missiles and Pershing IIs in Europe in 1983 to balance out the SS-20 nuclear rockets the Russians had stationed against Western Europe was decisive," Fritz Kraemer later said.

The action also marked the height of the Reagan administration's aggressiveness toward the Soviet Union. Several months after the barracks bombing, the United States removed its armed forces from Lebanon. The other countries in the multinational force were withdrawing their contingents, so Reagan brought the marines home. The Pentagon brass had never been entirely comfortable with the prospect of leaving them there indefinitely, arguing that their mission was not specific and not related directly enough to their training and military purpose. Neither Shultz nor Weinberger saw this move as a retreat or defeat for the United States, and the neocons did not object to it either.

Elsewhere in the world, however, the decision to withdraw the marines was viewed differently. Osama bin Laden later pointed to the American withdrawal from Lebanon as an indication that the United States would not stand and fight when attacked on foreign soil.

Certainly in the years immediately after the Beirut barracks bombing and the departure of U.S. forces from Lebanon, terrorist attacks on American and European targets in the Middle East did escalate seriously. On December 12, 1983, the U.S. embassy and other buildings in Kuwait were bombed. On March 16, 1984, the CIA Beirut chief of station was kidnapped. In December 1984, a Kuwait airliner was hijacked and two American passengers executed. In 1985, in a similar hijacking, a navy diver was executed when the hijackers' demands went unmet. In that same year, the cruise ship *Achille Lauro* was seized and an American aboard was killed. In December 1985, airports in Vienna and Rome were bombed, with several Americans among the dead. In 1986 the target was a Berlin disco frequented by American servicemen.

Reagan did little to strike back at these attacks until his second term, when he finally decided to bomb Libya, which his administration believed was behind many of the attacks. When General Vernon Walters was dispatched to Paris to visit President François Mitterrand, through whose airspace American planes needed to fly to reach Libya, Mitterrand responded: "If you told me your president planned to remove Qaddafi from power and would commit your nation to do that, I would have three French divisions parachute into Tripoli. But if you are going to bomb him and leave him in power, we will have no part of it."

In later years, Walters would tell this story to conservative audiences to underline its Kraemerite point: that military action must be total, not half-hearted, or else it might backfire and provoke the enemy. Reagan found a way to bomb Libya without Mitterrand's cooperation, but Qaddafi remained in power and eventually emerged stronger than before. And days after the bombings, Islamic militants retaliated by executing three American employees of the American University in Beirut. The United States' lack of reaction to these executions only reinforced—in the eyes of a generation of terrorists—the impression that the United States did not have the stomach for a long and bloody fight.

DURING THE CARTER years, Donald Rumsfeld had moved into the private sector as chairman of Searle, the pharmaceutical giant. Partway through Reagan's first term, however, at George Shultz's request, he undertook a mission for the president, visiting Iraq's president, Saddam Hussein, in Baghdad in December 1983 and again in March 1984. Iraq was not faring well in its long war with Iran, and Rumsfeld was sent to help Iraq by arranging to build a pipeline to pipe Iraqi oil to the West in exchange for aid to help the Iraqis win the war against Iran. Rumsfeld was aware that Iraq had used poison gas against Iran—he mentioned it to the Iraqi foreign minister, but not to Hussein. After Rumsfeld's visits, the U.S. State Department normalized relations with Iraq, offered it monetary credits, and provided intelligence on Iran's battlefield positions.

Rumsfeld was also involved in a Reagan administration program, "Continuity of Government," designed to ensure that the federal government would remain in operation if a devastating nuclear strike against Washington should kill the president, the vice president, and other top leaders but leave some second-rank officials behind. The Pentagon's Andy Marshall was a leading proponent of these exercises, which were coordinated at the NSC by the ubiquitous Colonel Oliver North and featured Congressman Dick Cheney and Donald Rumsfeld. The members of Reagan's Cabinet participated on a rotating basis, but Rumsfeld was at every exercise and Cheney was at most. Participants were secretly whisked out of Washington for a weekend to play control-the-earth games. Some who took part noted how keenly Rumsfeld and Cheney appreciated the opportunity to give orders on which whole nations would depend.

The "Continuity" exercises were part of a plan put forth by Oliver North's NSC policy office and adopted at the highest levels of government—though not yet codified into law. It would suspend the Constitution in the event of a national emergency and give full and rather dictatorial power to the Federal Emergency Management Agency, which would appoint military commanders to run state and local governments. The exercises emerged in part from a belief that the United States was engaging the USSR on more and more fronts—conflicts that carried the possibility of escalation, especially with regard to the administration's efforts to halt Communist advances in Central America.

In the fight to support the Nicaraguan Contras and overthrow the Sandinistas, the U.S. embassy in Honduras and a nearby U.S. military base had become the logistics and jumping-off center. That embassy was then led by Ambassador John Negroponte; later, congressional critics would charge that in exchange for supporting this anti-Sandinista activity, Negroponte looked the other way when Honduran governmental and paramilitary "death squads" went after leftist partisans.

By early 1984, Reagan and Bill Casey had become dissatisfied with the pace of CIA actions in Nicaragua. To interdict incoming Soviet and Cuban arms supplies, the CIA now proposed to mine Nicaragua's harbors—a significant escalation. The White House agreed, brushing aside concerns about the mining's legality, its effects on other nations, or the need for congressional approval. As CIA boats laid the mines, CIA helicopters fired on Nicaraguan craft attempting to stop them. Soon, despite U.S. warnings to the international community, some foreign freighters entering Nicaraguan harbors hit mines and sustained damage.

In response, an action was filed against the United States in the World Court; outraged members of the U.S. Congress voted to condemn the mining, though in nonbinding resolutions. Forty-two Republican senators joined Democrats on the vote. The United States was forced to use its Security Council veto to defeat a UN resolution condemning the mining. Called to account by Congress, Casey equivocated, upsetting his longtime supporters Barry Goldwater and Pat Moynihan. When the New York senator threatened to resign from the CIA oversight committee in protest, Casey became more accommodating.

After the mining incident, Congress refused to approve further funding for the Contras. The administration agreed to stop the mining, and initially agreed to abide by the decision of the World Court—the first time the United States would ever have done so. Behind the scenes, however, Poindexter, North, and their allies at Defense and State were setting in place mechanisms to continue support of the Contras by illegally diverting money from the sale of arms to Iran, and the government soon reversed its decision to accept the judgment of the World Court.

Iran-Contra would be the first neocon foreign-policy operation. Conceived and conducted from an ideological basis, it was run by neocons Michael Ledeen and Elliott Abrams through Oliver North, John Poindexter, and their outside allies and contractors.

The path to the scandal seems almost inevitable in retrospect, given the contributing factors: Reagan's detachment, the concentration of power in the NSC, and the deep-seated anti-Communism and distrust of congressional oversight that was shared by Poindexter, North, former national security adviser Bud McFarlane, and every other member of the Contras' phalanx of American supporters. Reagan made his own contribution by expressing his desire to ransom the kidnapped CIA station chief from an Iran-backed group that had taken him hostage. When regular-channel efforts on this matter failed, Poindexter and North asked Israel for help. With the assistance of Ledeen and others, arm sales to Israel were sent on to Iran, which paid Israel in funds that were then returned to North; that gave him the cash he needed to support the Contras and the overthrow of the Sandinista government.

IN HIS 1984 bid for reelection, Ronald Reagan won easily over former vice president Walter Mondale. The results recalled Nixon's overwhelming victory in 1972 against the equally liberal George McGovern. Mondale carried only his home state, Minnesota, and the District of Columbia. Republicans retained the Senate, though their control narrowed. Democrats remained in control of the House. Reagan's overwhelming popular vote total, the largest in history, served to validate the administration's foreign policies and gave Reagan a stronger hand in raising defense budgets and in confronting the USSR and its outreach in various areas of the world.

As Reagan's second term began, the neocons were still within the fold of the administration. When *National Interest*, a new foreign policy journal founded by William Kristol, debuted in 1985, its first issue included contributions by Perle, Ledeen, Douglas Feith (then a deputy assistant secretary of defense), and others of similar intellectual stripe who had positions within the Reagan executive branch. Yet the journal's editor, Owen Harries, complained that Reagan had become a captive of the "old foreign policy establishment"—the Kissingerites—and "hasn't armed himself with people to provide him countervailing advice," since "none of the neoconservatives has been ideally placed."

In particular, the neocons were unable to prevent Secretary of Defense Weinberger from issuing what they considered a dangerously limiting edict about the prerequisites for the future deployment of American military forces. Weinberger waited until after the election (and until he had Reagan's approval) to make an important speech outlining six "tests" that should guide any future use of forces—tests that became known collectively as the Weinberger Doctrine. The main idea behind the doctrine was that the United States should not commit forces unless its "vital interests," or those of its allies, were involved. When U.S. forces did go in, they must have "clearly defined political and military objectives" and be deployed in sufficient strength to achieve them. Forces should be dispatched only as a last resort, and with clear support from Congress and from the public.

The Weinberger Doctrine was designed in part to counter the perception that Reagan was trigger-happy and might send troops anywhere at any time. It was also intended to help the United States avoid situations like the barracks bombing in Lebanon. (Before the bombing, the military hierarchy had argued that the mission there was not well defined, not achievable, and inadequately supported by the American public.) The professional military embraced the Weinberger Doctrine; Colin Powell, Weinberger's deputy, agreed with it wholeheartedly, and it would influence his later approach to similar challenges.

But the doctrine did not sit well with George Shultz, Weinberger's longtime rival. On this issue, Weinberger was the moderate and Shultz the more rabid militarist; the secretary of state felt that Weinberger's reluctance to commit U.S. forces except in cases of dire emergency gave the Soviets a free pass in Afghanistan, Nicaragua, and Africa. It was a surprising disjuncture: The professional military and a normally hard-line secretary of defense agreed that military action should only be conducted under certain circumstances, while the secretary of state and the armchair strategists wanted fewer restrictions on when and where military power could be used. Shultz's view would be echoed by Luttwak and Bill Buckley and adopted broadly by the neocons.

The hard-liners also found themselves in disagreement on another issue: the fostering of democracy as a way to influence foreign governments and rebel groups. In 1977, James Schlesinger had ridiculed democracy promotion as a foreign policy goal; so, more recently, had Jeane Kirkpatrick. But Reagan had spoken about spreading democracy for years before he became president, and for some time he had been looking for an opportunity to put the idea into practice. In his second term, he began to do so. Because supporting democracy abroad seemed a less belligerent way of pursuing America's interests than open militarism or CIA subversion of governments, moderate Republicans such as Senator Charles Percy of Illinois supported the idea, and it gained considerable political traction. Its main supporters inside the administration were Paul Wolfowitz and George Shultz.

Kirkpatrick continued to believe that the United States was better served by having dictators as friends in contentious parts of the world rather than democratically elected governments that might be swayed by leftist considerations. In the past Reagan had agreed with her—preferring Philippines dictator Ferdinand Marcos to the democratic forces that were pushing to elect Corazon Aquino, the widow of an opposition leader, to the presidency in 1985–86. Although the Aquino forces were pledged to a somewhat socialist agenda, Wolfowitz and Shultz considered Aquino and her lieutenants staunch enough proponents of U.S. involvement in the islands to warrant the administration's backing, and after Aquino's election Reagan yielded to State's entreaties and recognized her government. In his history of neoconservatism, Jacob Heilbrunn calls Aquino's ascension "a seismic event, showing that authoritarian dictatorships could be peacefully brought to an end, and it not only helped create the Reagan doctrine of promoting democracy but made it central to the neoconservative movement."

Although Reagan frequently referred to the leaders of the Contras as "the moral equivalent of our founding fathers," his administration's prodemocracy campaigns had little to do with the attempts to counter Soviet hegemony in the areas where there were active battles and blood being shed, in Nicaragua, Afghanistan, and Angola. In those clashes, the administration backed factions that were highly autocratic. Jeane Kirkpatrick offered the democracy proponents some philosophic balm, parsing the difference between *tyrannical* governments—which in her view were incapable of change—and *authoritarian* governments, which could be coaxed toward the light and might evolve into democracies. That rubric left the neocons room to support attempts to install either democratic governments or autocratic potential precursors.

The goal of thwarting Soviet expansion and influence spurred various attempts to evade legislative restrictions on executive actions. One such roadblock was the legislated restriction on the sale of U.S. advanced weaponry to insurgent groups. When Fred Iklé, at Defense, found that it would be illegal to have the Pentagon directly provide Stinger missiles to the mujahideen in Afghanistan—a transaction Andy Marshall was advocating—he arranged for the CIA to do so. (This was the situation later portrayed in the book and film *Charlie Wilson's War.*) Gates later wrote that the Stingers, by causing more Soviet plane and pilot losses and thereby raising the cost of the war to the USSR, turned the tide in Afghanistan, leading to a Soviet defeat.

Similarly, when Oliver North was advised that the 1982 Boland Amendment specifically forbade any "agency or entity of the United States involved in intelligence activities" from supplying the rebels in Nicaragua, he elicited an opinion that the restriction applied only to intelligence agencies such as the CIA and therefore not to the NSC. In 1984, when some of the activities in Central America were first revealed, Congressman Edward Boland of Massachusetts submitted a newer version of his amendment, reworded to exclude activities by *any* U.S. government agency in supply of the Contras. By then, however, North had already set up his pipeline to them through outside contractors. Elliott Abrams solicited additional money for this cause from some authoritarian, repressive countries, including South Africa, Brunei, Saudi Arabia, and South Korea. Israel also kicked in money, materiel, and expertise.

This first neocon-run foreign policy operation was conducted mostly in the shadows; paleocons such as Weinberger, Reagan, and Shultz were kept unaware of its details so they would not object. The most difficult aspects of the endeavor—and the matters that had to be buried the deepest—were outsourced to former general John Singlaub and friends. The use of outside contractors to do what the administration could not do legitimately also set a pattern that would be repeated in the 2003 war in Iraq. North's operation, investigators would later discover, was like a secret government that, in the words of a congressional report, operated "its own army, air force, diplomatic agents, intelligence operatives, and appropriations capacity." Though only a lieutenant colonel, North was able to command the targeting of satellites and the sending of spy planes on missions.

While Iran-Contra was in action, the administration pushed the military to take more direct action against Libya. In 1985, Bud McFarlane, John Poindexter, and Oliver North recommended a combined American-Egyptian strike against Qaddafi. Adamant opposition from the CIA and DoD killed the plan, but in March 1986 Libyan anti-aircraft missiles attacked U.S. warplanes. In retaliation the United States sank Libyan patrol boats and bombed SA-5 missile sites. On April 5 Libyan operatives detonated a bomb in a Berlin disco where American servicemen hung out. Reagan upped the ante by authorizing a strike on Qaddafi's military headquarters; the strike narrowly missed the Libyan leader, who had moved out only hours before, but killed his daughter.

IN NOVEMBER 1985, Reagan awarded Presidential Medals of Freedom to Paul Nitze and to Albert and Roberta Wohlstetter. As Perle and Wolfowitz looked on, beaming, Reagan praised the Wohlstetters for helping "to create a safer world." He did not mention that all three honorees had worked hard to capsize détente. Now there was a specific opportunity to do so. For years the neocons—Perle in particular—had been pushing Reagan to repudiate SALT II. Though Carter had withdrawn the treaty from the Senate as a protest against the invasion of Afghanistan, the United States and USSR had nevertheless been abiding by its terms ever since.

Perle was an undersecretary beneath Weinberger and Carlucci in the Department of Defense, but he was strong and vociferous enough to come to the notice of Shultz at State and other high administration officials, who took his phone calls and solicited his advice on Soviet matters. It was through such channels that Perle finally convinced Reagan to reject SALT II in June 1986.

Before the president could declare the treaty dead, however, Mikhail Gorbachev changed the calculus. The new Soviet leader, who replaced Konstantin Chernenko in 1985, named Eduard Shevardnadze to replace Andrei Gromyko, who had served as foreign secretary for twenty-eight years. Upon Gorbachev's elevation, Reagan sent him a message saying he hoped they could work together toward peace and a nonnuclear world. In January 1986, Gorbachev responded with a letter proposing that he and Reagan work out a schedule to eliminate all nuclear weapons in the world, in three stages, by the year 2000. Reagan did not immediately publicize the letter but sent copies to various departments and agencies, asking them to explore how to construct a positive response to Gorbachev's challenge.

"We must not discuss this as though it was serious. The worst thing in the world would be to eliminate nuclear weapons," Perle complained to Shultz. According to Shultz's autobiography, he laughed and said, "You've got a problem—the president thinks it's a good idea." Ed Rowny and many others on the right shared the view that complete elimination of nuclear weapons was bad for the United States, because the Soviets would find a way to cheat.

Reagan, no fool, had no intention of giving in to Gorbachev entirely; he would respond positively but add important conditions that would seriously modify the total-elimination proposal. He prepared a letter outlining those conditions and linking the drawdown of nuclear weapons to other issues such as moratoriums on testing and deployment of some missiles and the near-term elimination of intermediate-range nuclear forces (INF). Weinberger and Perle objected to nearly every such measure, but they were overruled. Before sending the letter to Gorbachev, Reagan solicited reactions from several key heads of state. The messengers bearing the letters were keenly chosen: men with impeccable anti-Soviet credentials who had worked hard to sabotage prior arms limitation treaties. Paul Nitze went to Europe, Ed Rowny to Asia, Sven Kraemer to a Geneva commission meeting with the Soviets. When no serious objections were returned, Reagan's letter to Gorbachev was sent in July. Reagan followed up with a speech at the United Nations in which he disclosed the big idea.

Now that the elimination of nuclear weapons idea was out in public, it could be debated. To prevent any substantial groundswell emerging against the idea, however, Gorbachev asked Reagan to meet him on short notice in Reykjavik, Iceland. There Gorbachev startled Reagan with the breadth of his proposals, which included a 50 percent reduction in offensive strategic arms and the immediate elimination of INF missiles from Europe. Shultz characterized the meeting as "the highest stakes poker game ever played." Reagan's counterproposal called for the complete elimination of all ballistic missiles (though not all nuclear weapons) within the next decade. Perle, in attendance at Reykjavik, was afraid Reagan would go further. According to nuclear historian Richard Rhodes, he managed to plant a seed of a doubt into Reagan's mind: that Gorbachev would insist on doing away with SDI along with other nuclear arms. Reagan loved SDI. He considered it the ultimate weapon, one that would render nuclear missiles "impotent and obsolete," and believed it would have to be retained even as the missiles were scrapped. He even assured Gorbachev that, once the technology of SDI was perfected, the United States would share it with the Russians.

Perle's scare tactics worked well. On the last day of the conference, despite substantial agreement on dramatically reducing nuclear weaponry in many categories, the superpowers walked away without agreeing on a treaty—because, as Reagan confided to Rowny after a session with Gorbachev, "I'm afraid he's going after SDI." Reagan refused to give in on that point, and the summit foundered.

Two weeks after the summit, the Soviet politburo ratified Gorbachev's suggestion to accept Reagan's desire to continue developing SDI while the two sides worked to eliminate other categories of missiles and nuclear weaponry. By then, however, it was too late for a deal: The Iran-Contra scandal had burst, and Reagan was fighting to save his presidency.

AFTER A SANDINISTA with a Stinger missile shot down a CIA plane bringing supplies to the Contras, the lone survivor confessed to being a CIA contract employee. The Nicaraguan government publicized the news, and soon the entire NSC-run Central American supply scheme and its Iranian connection began to unravel. Because the Iran-Contra affair did not topple a president or result in the conviction and jailing of high-ranking government officials, it has passed into history as a far less significant scandal than Watergate. But as Watergate had done, Iran-Contra did considerable damage to the foreign policy of the United States in the last several years of the Reagan presidency, at a moment when the Soviet Union, America's main enemy for more than forty years, had reached the brink of monumental changes.

Reagan's popularity began to drop in the fall of 1986, and in the mid-term elections that year Republicans lost control of the Senate. Not long afterward, Reagan relieved John Poindexter and Oliver North of their positions in the NSC. The firings appeased neither the public nor Congress. With both legislative chambers in Democratic control, the 100th Congress was determined to hold hearings on various aspects of Iran-Contra. These distracted public focus from the very positive continuing deliberations with the Soviets on arms control. Even the Kremlin recognized the problem, fretting in an internal 1987 memo that no agreements might be reached because "the Administration is weaker in terms of foreign policy" because of "Irangate."

The Iran-Contra hearings were just gearing up when Bill Casey resigned from his position as CIA director. Casey was dying—cancer had spread to his brain—and his illness and public silence enabled many witnesses (though not Oliver North) to pin the Iran-Contra matter on him. But plenty of blame stuck to North, Poindexter, and McFarlane, who attempted suicide over it. Also tarred were CIA operatives; Abrams, Secord, and Singlaub; and a broad range of right-wingers—neocons and fellow travelers who shared many of their ideological beliefs—whose machinations were exposed.

Iran-Contra also provided an occasion to clean house at the National Security Council. Frank Carlucci, who succeeded Poindexter as national security adviser, replaced twenty-four of the NSC's fifty-nine professional staffers and persuaded Colin Powell, then in Europe, to return as his deputy. Under Carlucci, the council pushed for MX deployment and SDI research while accelerating the schedule that would allow Reagan to reach agreement with Gorbachev on the Intermediate Nuclear Forces (INF) treaty and the START talks.

The possibility of new arms control agreements with the USSR alarmed some hard-liners, who left the administration while Iran-Contra was unraveling. Some were fired by Carlucci; others—including Perle, Sven Kraemer, and Fred Iklé—simply resigned. Iklé's departure, lamented an op-ed writer in the New York Times, left the administration without any "strategic thinkers." As a parting shot, he issued the report of a commission he chaired with Wohlstetter, whose members included Kissinger, Brzezinski, and Andy Marshall. The report recommended using new technology and nonnuclear deterrents while dialing down the construction of nuclear devices. Perle, when asked what his major accomplishment in the Reagan administration was, said it was that "we have passed through a difficult six years without concluding an arms control agreement that damaged our security." Perle formed a consulting group, International Advisors, Inc., with Turkey as his sole client; shortly thereafter, according to Perle biographer Alan Weisman, he brought in Douglas Feith as his business associate.

The prospect of Reagan signing an INF reduction pact with the Russians inspired one Republican congressman, Newt Gingrich, to make yet another comparison to Neville Chamberlain's appeasement of Hitler at Munich, the neocons' favorite historical reference point. Paul Weyrich and the Heritage Foundation told reporters they had been trying to meet with Reagan on the INF pact but had been rebuffed. Weyrich called Reagan a "weakened president [who was] not in a position to make judgments about Gorbachev." Weinberger intimated that he might resign over the INF matter.

The Reagan administration's willingness to sign the INF treaty startled even such former arms limitation champions as Bill Hyland, now the editor of *Foreign Affairs*, who dubbed the proposed treaty "a bad deal for the United States," and French president François Mitterrand, who called it a "nuclear Munich."

As the deal-making meeting approached, even Richard Nixon jumped into the fray. In an article he cowrote with Henry Kissinger for *Time*, Nixon opposed the INF treaty—but not for the reasons given by the hard-liners. When Ed Rowny came to brief the former president on the treaty, Nixon said he was pleased with seven of the eight points on which the agreement was to be based, but he had a problem with the last and major one. The proposed agreement would treat the provisions covering the INF and SDI separately; moreover, it would extract the INF from Europe first, in exchange for the Soviets then removing their SS-20 missiles. Nixon, who had begun his presidency by insisting on "linkage" on issues including Vietnam, the Middle East, and SALT talks as a condition for doing détente business, was not about to go back on that idea now. In their article, Nixon and Kissinger argued that removing an entire class of missiles would undermine America's ability to defend its NATO allies and render our overall defenses more vulnerable, since it relieved the USSR of any concern that Europe-based missiles might be triggered in response to a Soviet first strike at the U.S. homeland. In a rebuttal, Shultz dryly pointed out that even after removing its missiles the United States would have four thousand nuclear weapons in Europe available to be loaded onto bombers and dropped on the USSR at a moment's notice. "One must ask whether we wish to deny ourselves the success we have achieved in the negotiations and leave Europe in the shadow of the Soviet SS-20s," Shultz wrote.

On his way to Moscow, President Reagan kept the naysayers at bay, and his NATO allies on the line, when he stopped in Berlin, at the wall separating East and West, and told his opposite number, "Mr. Gorbachev, tear down this wall." This challenge allowed Reagan to negotiate more seriously in Moscow. Though the INF treaty was not signed on Reagan's trip, it was the following December—over the objections of Robert Gates, now the CIA's top Sovietologist and its deputy director of central intelligence. Even Rowny, who had worked so hard to defeat SALT II, thought INF was a good deal for the United States. Secretary of Defense Caspar Weinberger resigned in late November; many believed he did so to avoid having to acquiesce to INF. But the treaty was signed, and with it the neocons' influence on Ronald Reagan ended.

Richard Perle's assistant Frank Gaffney, whom Perle had been grooming to take over his job as assistant secretary of defense, was pushed out when the new secretary, Frank Carlucci, learned that Gaffney had sent a message from Moscow warning Weinberger that Reagan was about to do the wrong thing on INF and START. After he was fired, Gaffney wrote Reagan an open letter suggesting that the United States "take a 'time-out' on the INF treaty" and renegotiate the deal.

At a party for friends after Gaffney's ouster from the NSC, Perle and others joked that there were more neocons outside the administration now than in it. Frustrated at the idea that their voices were no longer being heard, they tried to figure out how to have more leverage. Perle thought the answer lay in being available to the media for quick responses to issues. "What we need," he quipped, "is a Domino's Pizza of the [foreign] policy business. If you don't get your analysis in thirty minutes, you get your money back." To answer the need, the group set up the Center for Security Policy, a think tank—led by Frank Gaffney—that became a new gathering point for anti-Soviet hard-liners and a fount of instant opinions for the media on foreign policy and national security issues. The institution's motto was "To promote world peace through American strength." Its first project was to oppose Reagan's apparent eagerness to accommodate the Soviets.

SOME REVERBERATIONS OF the Iran-Contra affair were overlooked by the public in 1987 but had important ramifications for the future.

In October 1987, as the Iran-Contra hearings were concluding, Bob Woodward's new book, *Veil*, was published. The book, which chronicled the "secret wars" of the CIA, contained a startling revelation in its last few pages. In May, Woodward wrote, he had sneaked in to see the dying Bill Casey. In a conversation about diverting money from the Iran arms sales to fund the Contras, Woodward said he asked Casey, "You knew, didn't you?"

Casey, Woodward claimed, answered by nodding "yes." Woodward then asked, "Why?" Casey's response, according to Woodward: "I believed."

The hospital-bedside scene caused public controversy. Casey's widow and many others said it could never have occurred; by then, they said, Casey was virtually brain-dead and could neither speak nor understand what was being said to him. But Woodward's version conformed with the testimony of Oliver North, who said (after Casey's death) that the former CIA director had approved the diversion of funds as "the ultimate covert operation." Woodward's major source for *Veil* was Inman, who had scores to settle. In this and other ways, *Veil* lauds the accomplishments of the military people in the intelligence community, treating them uncritically, while savaging the mistakes and excesses of the civilian political appointees at CIA, NSC, Defense, and State. This pattern would be repeated in books Woodward would later write about the George W. Bush administration.

Gates would go on to refute Woodward's version of Casey's involvement in Iran-Contra, contending that while Casey had known of and approved the armaments for Iran sale and was a prime mover in the anti-Sandinista campaigns, he did not know specifically about the diversion of funds. Gates cited an electronic message from Poindexter to North on May 15, 1986, instructing North not to inform Casey of the diversion. Gates also pointed out that by this point responsibility for the operation had shifted from the CIA to the NSC. Gates found several aspects of North's 1987 testimony less than credible, including North's dramatic account of being given a poison pill to take if he should be captured on a secret mission, in order to avoid divulging information. In his several decades in the CIA, Gates said, such a pill had been dispensed to an operative only once, and that after the supervisor and operative had filled out innumerable forms. No such paperwork supported North's tale.

Another, more potent, harbinger of future patterns came from the minority report of the joint House and Senate panel that investigated Iran-Contra, a report signed by Representative Dick Cheney and written largely by his protégé, David Addington, then at the American Enterprise Institute. Cheney had been the most pro-administration congressman on the panel, telling the hearings, "I personally do not believe the Boland Amendment applied to the president, nor to his immediate staff." This assertion held that Congress had no standing to constrain the executive branch on foreign policy.

The majority report on Iran-Contra concluded that the overreaching in Reagan's White House constituted an abuse of power. Cheney's minority report called this "hysterical" and blamed Congress for the mess because it had been inconsistent in providing aid to the Contras—thus, presumably, forcing the executive branch into extraordinary (though, in Cheney's view, not illegal) measures to provide that aid. It echoed North's charge to Congress, "You are to blame because of the fickle, vacillating, unpredictable, on-again, off-again policy toward the Nicaraguan democratic resistance—the Contras." North and Cheney were not alone in thinking this way; Brzezinski and Eagleburger, the latter now president of Kissinger Associates, shared the North-Cheney view that Congress was overly meddlesome.

The Cheney minority report was a brief—right out of the manifestos of the Federalist Society—championing the unitary executive theory. It argued for the need to rein in the legislative branch and allow the executive to conduct foreign policy. The Constitution "does not allow Congress to pass a law usurping presidential power," it stated, and cited Hamilton to support its case.

But the minority report did not cite Hamilton's warning that giving a president such control would be "utterly unsafe and improper," and later critics pointed out that in several other ways it misconstrued the conclusions and standard interpretations of Supreme Court rulings in cases involving the roles of the two branches in foreign policy. For example, the report cited Justice Louis Brandeis's statement about the doctrine of separation of powers being adopted "not to promote efficiency but to preclude the exercise of arbitrary power," and cited it as evidence that the "checks and balances" set into the Constitution by the framers were "used to guard against arbitrariness. But the principles underlying separation had to do with increasing the Government's power as much as with checking it." Most constitutional scholars saw the purpose of checks and balances as *restraining*, not augmenting, the powers of the executive branch.

Historian Theodore Draper, in articles at the time and later in a book, suggested that Iran-Contra was symptomatic of a deeper disorder—that "a very thin line" separated "the legitimate from the illegitimate exercise of power in our government." In Draper's view, the Reagan administration had collectively stepped over that line, as evidenced in activities that in other circumstances were deemed criminal: the sale of arms to an enemy nation; the employment of drug traffickers; the laundering of money to fund secret missions; and the use of CIA operatives inside the United States. He found evidence of a substantial "usurpation of power by a small, strategically-placed group within the government."

The Cheney minority report sloughed off these activities as minor excesses, in part because its main purpose was to stake out territory for future use by another president. It argued against the War Powers Act of 1973 and other attempts by Congress to assert its sway over military actions. It faulted

Reagan for signing the Boland Amendment in 1984 instead of vetoing it, and for his "less-than-robust defense of his office's constitutional powers, a mistake he repeated when he acceded too readily and too completely to waive executive privilege for our Committees' investigation." The report concluded that, with regard to foreign policy, "Congressional actions to limit the President in this area therefore should be reviewed with a considerable degree of skepticism. If they interfere with core presidential foreign policy functions, they should be struck down. Moreover, the lesson of our constitutional history is that doubtful cases should be decided in favor of the President." In later years, Vice President Cheney would recommend his old report to journalists as "very good in laying out a robust view of the president's prerogatives with respect to the conduct of especially foreign policy and national security matters."

By 1988, Reagan's last year in office, he had effectively come around to Draper's point of view—acknowledging Iran-Contra as a mistaken excess and agreeing to banish its perpetrators. His willingness to sign accords with the Soviets that involved removing weapons and troops, and to take other steps toward greater disarmament, earned him criticism in congressional hearings from Perle, Iklé, Gaffney, and other former officials of his administration. Only later, after the fall of the Soviet Union, would the neocons retroactively celebrate Reagan. "Some time after Reagan left office," Frances FitzGerald writes, "Republican right-wingers began to look back on the Reagan years . . . and enshrine the fortieth president as their patron saint. Conveniently forgotten at that stage was their own apostasy . . . during the last year of his presidency."

By the time Reagan's presidency was nearing its end, the neocons had lost confidence in him. The actions he had taken with their enthusiastic support, especially the military buildup, had not brought about the policy changes they desired. Given the opportunity during the Reagan years to make positive accomplishments, they had been able to prevent only ones that they thought of as presidential errors. They would now have to pin their hopes of further shaping American foreign policy on his likely successor— Vice President George Bush, a man whose approach to foreign affairs and the use of American military force was at once more moderate and more pragmatic than that of his predecessor.

24

Not Going to Baghdad

George H. W. Bush's tenure in the Oval Office saw two world-changing events: the fall of Communism and the first Gulf War, in both of which the United States triumphed over its enemies. Yet Bush served only one term and today his four years appear to have been a transitional time, especially when compared to the presidency of his son, George W. Bush. Most of the foreign policy difficulties of Bush 41's term can be traced to the magnitude of the task of charting a new direction for the United States after the collapse of the Soviet empire.

As THE LAST year of Ronald Reagan's presidency began, Gorbachev's *glasnost* and *perestroika* initiatives were producing far-reaching changes that roiled the Soviet Union. At the time, Gates later wrote, neither Gorbachev nor the "optimists in the West" fully grasped how deeply these attempts at reform "were sowing the seeds of destruction of the Soviet Union." Historian Roger Morris points out that most of the U.S. government's Soviet experts—Gates in particular—spent the period waging "a final battle against the Soviets, denying at every turn that the old enemy was actually dying."

In 1988, Americans were more concerned with whether George H. W. Bush could successfully step out from Ronald Reagan's shadow. As a campaigner, Bush embraced the positive aspects of Reagan's legacy, but he could not avoid the accompanying baggage of the Iran-Contra scandal. His combative responses to Dan Rather of CBS News in a rough interview helped solidify his standing with the Republican base. Bush was also helped by his challenger for the Republican nomination, Senator Bob Dole, who ran an unfocused primary campaign that rapidly squandered an early lead in the polls. For the Democrats, Massachusetts governor Michael Dukakis won a commanding lead for the nomination, taking primaries in five states in a single "Super Tuesday," and then five more from his most potent challenger, the Reverend Jesse Jackson. Long before the conventions, the contenders for the 1988 presidential race were set: Bush, a lifetime bureaucrat with solid international credentials, versus Dukakis, a northeastern liberal governor with little foreign policy experience.

While the primaries held the American public's attention, Mikhail Gorbachev announced that the Soviet Union would begin withdrawing its troops from Afghanistan on May 15, 1988, and that in mid-April he would join the United States, Pakistan, and the new Afghan government in signing an accord ending the war. U.S. conservatives considered the Soviet withdrawal a win for the United States. They gave a cooler reception to another peace accord then in formulation—one the Contras felt forced to sign with the Sandinista government.

As Reagan pushed Congress to ratify the INF treaty, Perle, Gaffney, and other neocons pointed out that the Soviets were violating existing accords. As an example, they cited the deployment, near the Siberian city of Krasnoyarsk, of a phased-array radar for tracking satellites, a radar Gorbachev had pledged to stop building. To buttress such treaty-violation charges, a sheaf of highly classified information from the State Department, the CIA, and the Defense Intelligence Agency (DIA) was given to Jesse Helms, who showed it to the Senate. Helms allegedly received these classified papers from the former CIA agent David Sullivan, then working for Helms, and from Michael Pillsbury, Senator Gordon Humphrey's aide for military and foreign affairs. Although Pillsbury and Sullivan denied being the sources for the papers, both men had been previously fired from government positions for leaking.

Opposition to INF also came from Democratic senators who were holding the treaty hostage in hopes of slowing down or killing SDI. With both right and left opposed, Reagan asked Rowny to lobby senators—this time not to kill a treaty, as he had with SALT II, but to rescue it. Rowny did so gladly; he agreed with the treaty's aim, to eliminate a whole class of missiles in Europe and Asia, and valued its provision to allow on-site inspection of Soviet missile assembly plants. Of the twenty-four recalcitrant senators Rowny called on, only five eventually cast votes against the treaty. The passage of INF, backed by Reagan, was a triumph for realism.

On his June 1988 trip to Moscow, Reagan won many Russian hearts and minds during a question-and-answer session with a thousand students at

Moscow University. Though he and Gorbachev signed the INF agreement during Reagan's visit, there was no progress on the parallel START talks. Further accords, it was believed, would have to wait until the next president took office.

During the campaign, George Bush's positions on foreign policy seemed deliberately opaque, far from the ringing denunciation of Communism that Reagan partisans hoped to hear. Bush said he supported "the freedom fighters of the world," but that he had opposed sending arms to the Contras. He agreed with Reagan's decision to work with Iran as the bulwark against the USSR in the Persian Gulf region, but not to send arms to Iran clandestinely. He wanted better relations with the USSR but not to sign treaties that he and his closest adviser, Brent Scowcroft, considered too weak. Although Bush and Scowcroft privately considered Reagan's SDI an impractical dream, Bush supported it in public. These have-it-both-ways stances worried the neocons. After sitting in on high-level policy meetings with Bush for four years, Jeane Kirkpatrick confessed, "I don't know what he feels about most issues in the world, and I don't know where he stands."

Polls of likely voters found that most felt Bush lacked Reagan's clarity and forcefulness of vision; Bush himself would later famously decry "the vision thing." It was fear of losing conservatives, as Ford had in 1976, that prompted Bush to choose conservative senator Dan Quayle as his running mate; the same concern led him to announce, in accepting his party's nomination, "Read my lips: no new taxes." Bush attacked Dukakis for being weak on defense and for championing a Massachusetts program that had let a murderer out of jail on furlough, after which the convict had committed armed robbery and rape.

Given the choice between Reagan's heir and a lackluster Democrat, the electorate chose Bush by a comfortable margin. Yet the voters hedged their bets, keeping the Senate and House of Representatives solidly in Democratic hands.

In his inaugural address, Bush vowed a "kinder, gentler" America that would use its strength as "a force for good" in the world—a pledge that sat well with the neocons. But of course the devil was in the details.

AS HIS SECRETARY of defense, Bush nominated John Tower. Although Tower was quite the militarist, and an economic and social conservative, he had earned the ire of moralistic conservatives by his womanizing and drinking, and that of liberals for his stewardship of the Tower Commission on the Iran-Contra affair, which had dismissed some significant evidence in concluding that neither Reagan nor Bush had any knowledge of wrongdoing.

After Tower's nomination was defeated in a floor vote, Bush needed a quick approval; he responded by nominating the most conservative member of the House, Dick Cheney. From their days in the Ford administration, Bush knew Cheney as a competent administrator; Cheney had also affirmed his loyalty to Bush by sitting out Donald Rumsfeld's brief challenge to Bush in the 1988 primaries. Bush still blamed Rumsfeld for pushing him into the CIA in 1975, which prevented him from becoming Ford's running mate the following year.

Immediately after his confirmation, Cheney agreed to retain the already-appointed Paul Wolfowitz as deputy secretary of defense. The two had not known each other well before, but they now grew close. "Intellectually, we're very much on similar wavelengths," Wolfowitz told a reporter about Cheney. Cheney, Wolfowitz, and Gates agreed on many of the key issues of the day—including the need for more missiles, for a continued aggressive posture toward the Soviet Union, and for controlling U.S. access to oil in the Persian Gulf—and the trio formed a hard-line front that was frequently at odds with Secretary of State James Baker and National Security Adviser Brent Scowcroft, the new president's more moderate advisers and close friends. The rival groups disagreed most significantly on how much support to give Gorbachev's regime and reforms: The younger hard-liners opposed giving too much help, being far more dogmatically anti-Soviet than the older advisers.

As Eastern European protests against Communist control rumbled east toward Moscow, they pushed Gorbachev toward ever-deeper reforms. Similar protests finally reached China. But the students and labor activists who marched for democracy in Beijing's Tiananmen Square were met by government resistance that culminated in a massacre of unarmed civilians in Tiananmen on June 4, 1989. The Chinese government declared martial law, hunted down democracy advocates, and purged Communist Party members who had sympathized with the students.

Although President Bush responded the next day by announcing the suspension of all arms sales to China, and the indefinite deferral of reciprocal visits by American and Chinese heads of state, he issued no severe punishment to the Beijing government for its bloody crackdown. This lack of official reprisal, coupled with the administration's refusal to take China off the list of Most Favored Nations, angered the American public. They were equally frustrated when Bush vetoed a bill that would have permitted Chinese students to remain in the United States after their visas ran out so they would not have to return home to a dubious future. The American public might have been even more annoyed had it known that Scowcroft made a secret visit to Beijing shortly thereafter to assure the Chinese leaders that the United States would continue to try to improve relations. (The visit was disclosed six months later, when Scowcroft returned to Beijing in full sight of the media.) According to Eagleburger, who accompanied Scowcroft on both missions, the "smarter" Chinese officials "absorbed the message that we can do a lot more for them when they aren't killing their own people."

As THE FABRIC of the Soviet bloc unraveled from the periphery toward the center, more quickly than almost anyone had imagined, Ed Rowny and Dick Walters, two old generals, negotiators, and longtime friends, sometimes met in odd places—including the Vatican, where each had been sent, separately, to brief the pope on various matters. In 1989, Walters—then serving as ambassador to West Germany—made one of the few gaffes of his career when he publicly predicted and celebrated the forthcoming reunification of Germany before the Bush administration had resolved to come out in support of it. Fritz Kraemer, who continued to tutor young policy scholars and military men from Europe, had long emphasized that they must convince their countries to maintain military readiness, not simply to appear belligerent but to create a protective deterrent and have more say in the affairs of the rest of the world. Now that the states of the Soviet Union were trying to break away, Kraemer, Rowny, and Walters—who since the 1940s had fought for the dissolution of the Soviet empire—were excited by the signs of its disintegration, and not in the slightest upset that the victory was not being won on the battlefield.

Bush, faced with this unprecedented situation and lacking a clear vision of what would be best for America in a post-USSR world, resisted pressure to accelerate the dissolution. The right wanted him to fan the flames of rebellion in Eastern Europe by using the Voice of America radio service; the administration rejected the idea. The left wanted him to insist on international monitors to ease the transitions to independence and to act as a check on last-ditch Soviet repression; the administration dismissed that, too. But by continuing to push forward arms control and mutual force reduction agreements with the USSR, the Bush administration aided Gorbachev's ability to carry out his reforms.

By mid-1989, Poland, Hungary, Bulgaria, East Germany, and the Baltic states had achieved some success in escaping rule by Moscow and in dissolving their countries' military ties to the USSR. That August, the first non-Communist government in modern Eastern European history took office in Poland. In September, the exodus from East Germany to neighboring states reached the hundreds of thousands. Events moved with breathtaking rapidity. In November, East and West Berliners tore down the Berlin Wall. "With the wall breached," historian John Lewis Gaddis writes, "everything was possible." The leaders of the Soviet satellite countries shredded the Warsaw

Pact, no longer willing to pledge their armies to maintain Communist control of any territory. Within the month, the Communist governments of Bulgaria, Czechoslovakia, and Romania were chased from power.

"The situation cries out for a President capable of imagining and describing the shape of a new world order and defining America's role in it. Bush has yet to show he can do that," David Broder wrote in the *Washington Post*. In the *Wall Street Journal*, Irving Kristol acknowledged that "a prudent posture of watchful waiting was the most natural—because most inertial—reaction," but he chastised Bush for lack of imagination in fashioning American responses to current events.

The old bipolar world had been easier to understand and respond to than the new multipolar one. Bush remained undecided about the most appropriate American response to the chaotic conditions in Eastern Europe. In December 1989, as he and Gorbachev met on a ship at Malta, Bush told the Soviet leader that the United States had been "shaken by the rapidity of the unfolding changes" and that he would "do nothing that would lead to undermining your position." Dick Cheney took a different, more pessimistic view of the evolving events. He insisted that the United States must not assume that the collapse of the Soviet Union was inevitable. Arguing that Gorbachev's survival in office was not ensured, and that the next Soviet leader might not be as willing to work with the United States and NATO countries to rid the European continent of missiles, Cheney saw the chaos in the Soviet Union as a reason to bolster, not cut back, U.S. defense plans. He charged that banning new ICBMs, which Bush had planned to agree to with Gorbachev, would kill the development of the next generation of MX missiles. Baker and Scowcroft argued that agreeing with Gorbachev to ban new multiple-warhead ICBMs and to remove existing short-range missiles would do more for U.S. security than building more missiles. But Cheney's fervent arguments convinced the president, and Bush did not push Gorbachev for further short-range missile talks.

The results of the Malta conference disappointed West Germany, Canada, and other U.S. allies, who were aghast at the Bush administration's unwillingness to seize the opportunity to build toward permanent peace that Gorbachev's revolutions presented.

Historian Garry Wills wrote at the time that the fall of the Soviet Union happened so quickly that it precluded analysis, but did expose a basic flaw in prior reasoning:

> Could anything come to pieces so fast if it had not been essentially
> hollow? Had we been scaring ourselves with bogeys? The evidence is
> very strong that the "window of vulnerability" that Reagan armed us

against was as false an alarm as the missile gap in Kennedy's day and the bomber gap in Eisenhower's. Had we outspent not only our enemy but also ourselves in battle with a phantom, becoming a debtor nation to accomplish a victory without spoils?

Cheney and the neocons thought the answer to Wills's questions was *no*. They argued that the victory over Communism did produce definite spoils—namely, the emergence of the United States as the world's sole super-power. Even though no obvious new enemy had emerged as a focus of U.S. foreign policy and military deterrence, Cheney felt sure one would surface, and that the United States must retain first-strike and second-strike nuclear capabilities—which meant building new nuclear-tipped weapons.

Although Bush yielded to Cheney's caution at Malta, as 1990 progressed he repeatedly beat back Cheney's efforts to enlarge the nuclear arsenal. Bush believed that the Cold War would not truly end until the two sides considerably downsized their nuclear forces. Gorbachev agreed eagerly, and together the two nations signed pacts that progressively reduced the number of missiles each could fire at the other. Bush also asked the Pentagon to prepare budgets that would reduce future expenditures by 25 percent— since America's main enemy had vanished from the field—and Cheney was obliged to comply. It seemed the reasonable thing to do, at a time when so many previously unimaginable events were now coming to pass. Germany was reuniting. The Warsaw Pact countries and the NATO countries were holding a joint meeting in Canada to agree to an "open skies" proposal and to discuss further reductions in forces. Even before the political dismantling of the Soviet Union, the Cold War was drawing to a close.

Throughout history, after seismic events, many groups yield to the impulse to rewrite the immediate past to show how their group or champion contributed to the inevitability of the change. In the wake of the fall of the Soviet Union, conservatives, especially the neocons, began to claim that— contrary to Garry Wills's assertion—it had been Reagan's staunch stand, and the attendant military buildup, that caused the collapse of Communism and ended the Cold War. Reagan, they said, had forced Yuri Andropov and then Gorbachev to spend the Soviet Union into poverty and collapse in an attempt to match U.S. defense expenditures.

The claim that Soviet overspending on defense caused the downfall of the Soviet Union was later belied by statistics obtained from Moscow showing that, although the Soviet military budget did expand at a rate of 4.3 percent from 1983 to 1987, Gorbachev thereafter cut it back toward the 1980 rate.

As Gaddis has noted, "The Soviet Union collapsed, after all, with its military forces, even its nuclear capabilities, fully intact." Most historians agree that the collapse owed more to the decline in the Soviet economy, which began seriously in the 1970s and had little to do with U.S. pressure. Frances FitzGerald writes that "the Soviet Union might have survived for many more years, for the system, though on the decline, was nowhere near collapse. It was Gorbachev's efforts to . . . modernize the country that knocked the props from under the system." Michael R. Beschloss and Strobe Talbott, in their book on the end of the Cold War, agree that Gorbachev was "an event-making" leader who "exhorted the rulers of Poland, East Germany, and other satellite countries to follow his lead, loosen the chains of totalitarianism, and emulate Soviet perestroika and democratization," until events overtook him and went beyond what he had foreseen or thought possible.

At Malta, Gorbachev had told Bush that "ordinary people" were creating the collapse, which had begun in satellite countries such as Hungary and Poland before it reached Russia. Underlying the entire revolt, Gaddis writes, was the "moral and spiritual critique" of Communism advanced by the future Pope John Paul II and by Aleksandr Solzhenitsyn, Andrei Sakharov, and other Russian dissidents. Another important factor, Gaddis adds, was "the information revolution" that spread the idea of democracy and the pursuit of material goods. These factors, more than Reagan's rhetoric or pressure, were responsible for the demise of the USSR and of its Communist satellite states. Gaddis, FitzGerald, and Beschloss and Talbot, among other historians, credit George H. W. Bush more than Ronald Reagan with assisting Gorbachev's reforms and reducing military pressure on the Warsaw Pact members, which in turn enabled the countries of Eastern Europe to transform their governance and economic systems.

Reagan had told Dick Allen in the mid-1970s that his goal was to "win" the Cold War, and after the breakup of the Soviet Union, Reagan and others concluded that the United States had won that war and the Soviet Union had lost it. The notion became a touchstone for the neocons, underscoring their emphasis on military power and moral rigor as the proper cutting edges of American foreign policy. Most historians now disagree that the Cold War was won. "This misreading of history," writes journalist Martin Walker, author of a recent book on the Cold War, "led, in turn, to the perception that American wealth and technology, along with the righteousness of its motives and the self-evident truths of the founding fathers, could cut through any strategic tangles and dilemmas."

Beyond the matter of whether the Cold War was won or lost, though, lies another, equally important question: Did the right's efforts to block détente and arms control treaties hasten the fall of the Soviet Union or hinder it? The argument that they accelerated the fall depends on the disproven theory that the U.S. arms buildup forced the Soviets into a competition that bankrupted their economy. An equally strong argument can be made for the obverse position: that by preventing the march of détente and of arms control from the 1970s on, the rightists actually *delayed* the inevitable collapse of the USSR. The Soviet leaders' need to continue the arms race—a product of the American right's blocking of détente and disarmament—allowed Brezhnev and Andropov to focus their people's attention and energies on continuing to counter the main enemy, the United States. Nuclear disarmament would likely have undercut the USSR's intense focus on nationalism and defense—and even earlier than it did when Bush was working with Gorbachev, allowing the nation's underlying economic and social turmoil to overwhelm the Soviet world more quickly, and likely hastening the collapse of the Soviet system several years earlier than 1989.

WHILE THE SOVIET Union unraveled, President Bush faced a more immediate foreign policy task: the need to deal with Panamanian dictator Manuel Noriega, who had been a thorn in the side of the United States for many years. Bush and Noriega had first met in 1976, when each was the head of his country's intelligence service; they met several more times during Bush's vice presidential years. Noriega had risen to power in Panama with the continued support of the Ford, Carter, and Reagan administrations, who viewed him as an anti-Communist ally. But then his drug-trafficking became too public to ignore. "Initially an instrument of convenience . . . the whole association [with Noriega] was a glaring contradiction," according to Herbert Parmet, Bush's biographer.

In February 1988, after the Iran-Contra connection was exposed, the Reagan administration decided to indict Noriega for his drug trade. Bush pronounced himself surprised at the news of Noriega's involvement with drugs, though Parmet writes that he had been briefed on it by a close aide in 1985. Bush's relationship to Noriega became a 1988 campaign issue even as Panamanians took to the streets in protest and the dictator evaded an attempted coup. In early 1989, a moderate candidate prevailed in a Panamanian election, but Noriega refused to allow him to be seated.

After Bush was criticized for failing to punish China for the Tiananmen Square massacre, plans were drawn up for a military action that would remove Noriega, bring him to the United States to stand trial, and seat his democratically elected successor. The United States already had quite a few troops stationed at a U.S. base in the Canal Zone. When the idea of removing Noriega by force first arose late in the Reagan administration, Admiral

William Crowe, chairman of the Joint Chiefs, had objected, arguing that the U.S. military should not be meddling in the affairs of a foreign country. Although neocon Elliott Abrams had called for a Grenada-style "liberation" of Panama to topple Noriega in 1988, no clear successor to Noriega had yet emerged, and Crowe was able to block the Abrams plan, partly by leaking its details. At a Reagan NSC meeting, Crowe argued, "We have military bases not just in Panama, but in Portugal, Spain, Turkey, and Greece. In all of those places there are sensitive political issues. How do you expect those governments would react to the specter of the U.S. using its military bases to overthrow a country's leadership?" By 1989, however, the presence of a duly elected alternative to Noriega trumped Crowe's objections. Bush had offered to reappoint Crowe to a third term as chairman of the JCS, but Crowe opted to retire rather than agree to use U.S. troops in Panama. He was replaced by General Colin Powell.

Three days after Powell took the reins, the United States backed a coup attempt against Noriega, but the dictator's forces blocked it. In response, Bush ordered an invasion of the Canal Zone by 28,000 U.S. servicemen, the largest use of force since the war in Vietnam. The invading troops quickly secured the territory and installed the new president, but they were unable to capture Noriega. Two weeks later, Noriega was coaxed out of sanctuary in the papal nunciature in Panama City and brought to the United States to stand trial for drug trafficking.

The capture of Noriega countered Bush's reputation as a "wimp," and before long his approval rating had shot up to 80 percent. But the neocons, despite their approval of the military action in Panama, were becoming as disenchanted with Bush as they had been with Reagan. Bush had not done enough to accelerate the collapsing Soviet empire; he was demanding a downsizing of the military; and on the domestic front he was reneging on what they saw as his most important promise: "no new taxes."

"Can the Right Survive Success?" asked *Time* magazine. Though the right was able to muster a forty-five-organization Conservative Political Action conference in Washington, the magazine noted, the affair seemed rudderless, with "a dearth of heroes and of crackling issues." David Keene, the onetime Agnew staffer and Reagan strategist who now led the American Conservative Union, acknowledged to a reporter that anti-Communism had been "the glue that holds the [conservative] movement together" and that its absence was troubling. At the conference, some neocons wanted to paint the Democratic-controlled Congress as the new enemy; paleocons such as Bill Buckley objected, defending Congress (and its check on executive power) as "the likeliest repository of conservative affinity." "New enemies and new issues are badly needed," *Time* concluded.

Shortly thereafter, Iraq's leader, Saddam Hussein, stepped into the role of chief enemy, bringing with him a new set of issues and allowing Bush to become a hero again.

IN THE SPRING of 1990, Saddam Hussein was feeling his oats. At fifty-three, he had been in sole power for more than a decade and had created a secular state that was a savvy marketer of Iraq's oil resources. Born relatively poor, without a father he knew, he had attended law school through the benevolence of an uncle, and supported himself by teaching school until joining the revolutionary Baath Party, composed mainly of Sunni Muslims. Saddam had helped to overthrow the country's leader, Faisal II, and his reputation grew when he escaped prison, took part in another coup, and emerged as a leading Baath figure.

In the eight-year war against Iran, Saddam had played both the United States and the Soviet Union to amass weaponry and consolidate power, while using the war as a cover to repress all dissent—especially that of the Kurds— and keep the majority Shiites in check. The end of the war, and the power vacuum in the Middle East created by the disarray of the Soviet Union and its withdrawal from Afghanistan, put him and Iraq in position to thrust for a larger share of the region's oil revenues. To neutralize Iran, Saddam completed an agreement with his former enemy to try to force Kuwait and other countries to raise the price of oil. Iraq's army, the fourth largest in the world, could easily overwhelm neighboring Kuwait if the Western powers did not interfere. Anti-Americanism was in the air, fueled by Palestinians and their allies who were angered by steadfast U.S. support for Israel during the prior two years of intifada. Other Arab states also resented Kuwait's wealth and its unwillingness to abide by OPEC oil-production quotas. There was a sense in the Islamic world that a coalition of Iraqis, Palestinians, and Iranians could profitably challenge the Arabic monarchies—Kuwait, Saudi Arabia, the United Arab Emirates, Syria, and Jordan—and their pro-American stances. Saddam Hussein also felt that if he could keep the challenge over the oil supply wholly within the Gulf States, the United States would not stop him from seizing Kuwait.

Saddam had reason to think this way. For a decade, the United States had been cultivating Iraq to help stave off Soviet influence and to counter Iran's anti-Americanism. In Donald Rumsfeld's two meetings with the Iraqi leader during the eight-year war with Iran, he had pledged the Reagan administration's support, which soon materialized in the form of an oil pipeline inside Iraq paid for by the United States. Bush had continued the close ties with Iraq, signing a directive in October 1989 that called for Iraq to receive millions of dollars in credits to buy grain and technology.

The Bush administration's belief in Iraq's utility to the United States— despite Saddam's attempts to create nuclear weapons, and his vocal threats to Israel and to Kuwait—continued through the first half of 1990. While the administration did bow to congressional pressure to stop some grain and technology shipments to Iraq, behind the scenes the U.S. ambassador to Iraq, April Glaspie, encouraged Saddam by eliding over the negative consequences he would face if he invaded Kuwait. Glaspie's messages to the Iraqi dictator conveyed that the United States would take no official position on Arab world border disputes, and that, as President Bush wrote to Saddam on July 28, 1990, "differences are best resolved by peaceful means."

Five days later, Saddam's troops crossed into Kuwait, taking over the small country. At that moment, Secretary of State James Baker was in the USSR meeting with his counterpart, Eduard Shevardnadze; after receiving news of the invasion, Baker asked his host to halt further arms deliveries to Iraq. Within a day this was done. This action by the USSR was a signal victory for détente, one that might presage an era of deeper cooperation beetween the superpowers.

Now the Carter Doctrine came into play. Carter's decade-old declaration committed the United States to ensure the integrity of the Gulf region and its oil flow; Saddam's attack on Kuwait was a clear assault on both. Bush's major concern was the integrity of Saudi Arabia; the president seemed willing to compromise with Hussein on Kuwait if there was no threat to the Saudis and if oil flow could be maintained.

Several factors, however, coaxed Bush toward war. Among them, the most potent may have been pressure from the Iron Lady, former British prime minister Margaret Thatcher, who pushed Bush to retaliate against Saddam with Great Britain as a partner, and to do so without waiting for international approval. Scowcroft agreed with Thatcher up to a point; he too made the moral argument for retaliation—appeasement would be another Munich—but he wanted the other nations of the world to fight alongside U.S. troops. So did Secretary of State Baker and JCS chairman Powell. When Saddam massed his armies on the border between Kuwait and Saudi Arabia, threatening the West's oil supply, Bush agreed with his advisers: Retaliation was imperative, and for the purpose of protecting Saudi Arabia. That particular objective was the reason for the name initially given to the military operation, "Desert Shield."

In what was his finest hour, President Bush drew upon his years as a diplomat to convince thirty-four other nations to join the effort to oust Saddam from Kuwait. His key ally, beyond the USSR, was Saudi Arabia, which needed to be convinced to allow American troops on its sand. Dick Cheney, the secretary of defense, served as the point man for the Saudis, leading an American delegation that negotiated a commitment to permit American troops and planes to use bases in Saudi Arabia—and to set up what amounted to a permanent garrison there. Years later, Osama bin Laden would cite the presence of an American military base in Saudi Arabia—in the country of the Muslim holy city of Mecca—as reason to declare a jihad against the United States, contending that Americans were "occupying" the Muslim holy land and pledging to oust them from it. The Saudis ostracized bin Laden for his stance and soon forced him to flee the country for the Sudan, but the United States did not take bin Laden's threat seriously.

Before Bush committed any troops to war, he and his foreign allies first wanted to try economic sanctions and complete a massive buildup of coalition troops in the region. Cheney argued that only military force would push out Saddam, but Baker, Scowcroft, and General Norman Schwarzkopf felt otherwise, and they prevailed.

In an attempt to slow things down and ensure complete victory in an eventual war, Colin Powell formulated a new doctrine, an extension of Weinberger's tenet that the United States should go to war only if its aims were clear and U.S. forces were present in substantial enough numbers to guarantee success. The first of the Weinberger-Powell conditions—a precise statement of war aims—was a major factor in Bush's declaration that his aims were limited to ousting Iraq from Kuwait. Another administration goal was alleviating Arab fears about undue American presence in the region; that explained why Bush did not cite "regime change" in Iraq as a war aim. There was a further reason to omit that notion: Gorbachev had agreed to support the coalition's plans on the condition that Bush would stop after ousting Saddam from Kuwait. "We are united in the belief that Iraq's aggression must not be tolerated," their joint communiqué read. "No peaceful international order is possible if larger states can devour their smaller neighbors."

Speaking to Congress, Bush heralded this joint communiqué and the plethora of international cooperation as the wave of the future:

> No longer can a dictator count on East-West confrontation to stymie concerted United Nations action against aggression. A new partnership of nations has begun. . . . The crisis . . . offers a rare opportunity to move toward an historic period of cooperation. Out of these troubled times . . . a new world order can emerge: a new era— freed from the threat of terror, stronger in the pursuit of justice. . . . Today that new world is struggling to be born, a world [in which] the rule of law supplants the rule of the jungle. A world in which nations recognize the shared responsibility for freedom and justice. A world where the strong respect the rights of the weak.

At the time, Bush's vision of a "new world order" was applauded. Only later would it become a point of neocon disagreement with Bush. The president was ready to go to war; he had the U.S. resolutions to enable him to do so; most Republicans were with him. But the Democratic-controlled Congress was not as convinced that war was necessary; usually hawkish Democratic senators such as Sam Nunn opposed using troops in the Gulf region because of the danger that they would become mired there after the initial mission was accomplished.

Secretary of Defense Cheney was sent to Congress to explain why the United States should go to war. "I was not enthusiastic about going to Congress to ask for an additional grant of authority," Cheney later recalled. In his view, he told Congress, Bush "didn't require any additional authority" from Congress "before attacking Iraq"; in Cheney's reading of the Constitution, the president already possessed it. To assuage critics in Congress, as well as in many foreign countries of the coalition, the administration had to agree to a very narrow definition of the military mission. Even so, when the authorization votes were taken in Congress on January 12, 1991, the margins for going to war were the narrowest since the war of 1812: 52–47 in the Senate, 250–183 in the House.

On January 15, a UN deadline for Iraq to leave Kuwait lapsed. Two days later, the United States and its allies began a massive bombing campaign. In response, Iraq fired Soviet Scud missiles at Israel and Saudi Arabia, hoping to widen the war and bring in other Arab states as allies. Just before the outbreak of hostilities, the Bush administration had sent Paul Wolfowitz, who had once lived in Israel, to that country to plead for forbearance of retaliation in the event of an attack by Iraq's missiles. Israel complied, which helped prevent the conflict from spreading. The provision of U.S. Patriot missiles to Israel to counter the Scuds also served, Jacob Heilbrunn writes, to keep Israel "on the sidelines" during the conflict.

In early February, the coalition began its ground attack on Iraqi forces in Kuwait, spurring their withdrawal almost immediately. As the Iraqis retreated north, they set fire to much of Kuwait. Coalition forces pursued and quickly overwhelmed Iraq's armies; one hundred hours after U.S. ground forces entered Iraq, President Bush declared Kuwait liberated and ordered a cease-fire. On February 27, 1991, U.S. forces were within 150 miles of Baghdad, and Iraq's decimated armies and defenses offered only feeble resistance. Taking Baghdad would have been easy.

The neocons wanted to do so. They hoped to establish there a "MacArthurian regency," an indigenous Iraqi government run by American rules, modeled on the regime Douglas MacArthur had set up in post–World War II Japan, which successfully steered that once-authoritarian country into the configuration of a functioning democracy.

But Bush ordered that coalition forces must turn around and not attack Baghdad.

At the time, the decision not to press on to Baghdad was mostly accepted. Before long, however, it became a neocon bone of contention. A month after hostilities ended, Vice President Dan Quayle said he thought that U.S. forces should have gone farther into Iraq, and the *Wall Street Journal* editorialized that General Schwarzkopf should have become the "viceroy" of Baghdad. This litany was sounded frequently through the next decade; by 2002, the need to finish the job left unfinished in 1991—"regime change," the toppling of Saddam Hussein—was one of the primary reasons given by the neocons for the George W. Bush administration's invasion of Iraq.

In 1992, when Secretary of Defense Cheney was asked about not having taken Baghdad, he was adamant: "If we had gone in there [in 1991], I would still have forces in Baghdad today. We'd be running the country. . . . The question in my mind is, how many additional American casualties is Saddam worth? And the answer is, not that damned many. So I think we got it right, both when we decided to expel him from Kuwait but also when Bush made the decision that we'd achieved our objectives and we were not going to go get bogged down in the problems of trying to take over and govern Iraq."

In his memoir, James Baker was more specific about why the administration had not pushed on to Baghdad:

> Even if Saddam were captured and his regime toppled, American forces would still be confronted with the specter of a military occupation of indefinite duration to pacify the country and sustain a new government in power. The ensuing urban warfare would surely result in more casualties to American GIs than the war itself, thus creating a political firestorm at home, criticism from many of our allies, and dissolution of the coalition.

In Bush's own memoir, which he wrote with Brent Scowcroft, he cited another reason for avoiding such an occupation: "The coalition would have instantly collapsed, the Arabs deserting it in anger, [and] the United States could conceivably still be an occupying power in a bitterly hostile land."

Wolfowitz was one of the few in the upper echelon who openly expressed the belief that U.S. armed forces should have seized Baghdad. In May 1991, according to General Wesley Clark, Wolfowitz told him that "we screwed up and left Saddam Hussein in power." Wolfowitz told the general that "the president believes [Saddam will] be overthrown by his own people, but I rather doubt it."

Not long after the fighting in Kuwait and Iraq ended, Bob Woodward published *The Commanders*, an account of the planning of the war. An uncritical paean to the professional military, its primary source was Colin Powell, who later admitted to Congress that he had given Woodward classified data and spent hundreds of hours with the reporter as he researched the book.

In *The Commanders*, Woodward detailed Powell's clashes with Cheney in the run-up to the war. But he also offered a description of a meeting between Cheney and King Fahd that could only have come from Cheney's files or memory. "How much trust between America and its allies has been injured" by that Cheney revelation? one military reviewer wondered. In the *New York Times*, Anthony Lewis suggested that the most important lesson in the Woodward book was Powell's assertion that economic sanctions and pressure short of all-out military force might well have pushed Iraq out of Kuwait. "The war option proved tremendously popular," Lewis wrote, sending Bush soaring in the polls, but the war had problematic results: "It has not produced new stability or security in the region. And it did not result in Saddam Hussein's fall."

AFTER THE GULF War, Bush was eager to resume negotiating treaties with the Soviet Union. He did sign the START treaty with Gorbachev on July 31, 1991, culminating nearly a decade of negotiating. It was unclear how long Gorbachev could remain in office. He narrowly survived a coup by a cabal of old-style military and KGB men but soon yielded peaceably to the prodemocracy mayor of Moscow, Boris Yeltsin. Five months after signing START, Gorbachev was out of power and the USSR had been replaced by a confederation of independent states. When START I came into force, both sides began destroying ICBMs and land-based and sub-based launchers. But four of the former Soviet states—Russia, Belarus, Ukraine, and Kazakhstan—all maintained nuclear missiles in their arsenals. The United States could not be certain whether the governments in those states would adhere to the arms control and other treaties Gorbachev and Bush had signed. Implementing START II, the next phase of arms reductions, had to wait.

The final collapse of the Soviet Union coincided with the end of the careers of many old Cold Warriors, including Dick Walters, who received the Presidential Medal of Freedom in November 1991. Walters then took to the lecture circuit, becoming a fixture on *National Review* cruises and similar forums, expressing openly the strong conservative opinions that had animated his fifty years of public service.

Ed Rowny also retired, in part because he was furious with Bush for not paying enough attention to the deterioration in the former Soviet republics, including Russia, after the fall of the Soviet Union. Rowny had been trying to tell his contacts in the administration that the United States had a lot of work to do in Eastern Europe if it wanted the new democracies to survive and not return to authoritarian ways. But Bush and his top advisers had no intention of putting America's resources to work to direct the action in Eastern Europe, so Rowny retired. At home in Washington, he was able to see more of Fritz Kraemer. While Andy Marshall, who was still in the Pentagon, saw China as the next major U.S. enemy, Kraemer focused his attention on how to help the newly independent countries of Eastern Europe create militaries and alliances that would ensure their survival.

THE DISSOLUTION OF the Soviet Union, and the Bush administration's refusal to allow the U.S. military to topple Saddam Hussein, restarted the battle among conservatives for supremacy in foreign affairs. The battle, which pitted "paleocons versus neocons" (as a *New Republic* article put it), was waged over several basic schisms. "In ideological terms," the article explained, "the neos are interventionist, the paleos isolationist. The neos are for free trade, the paleos for protectionism. The neos support immigration, the paleos are agin." In the early 1990s, the neocons collected money from "the four sisters"—the Scaife, Olin, Smith-Richardson, and Bradley foundations—while squeezing older conservatives out of their accustomed forums in newspaper op-ed pages and influential magazines. The neocons chastised Bush for being too close to Beijing, for not recognizing the new Baltic states governments quickly enough, for not pressing on to Baghdad when he had the chance, and for attempting to make loan guarantees to Israel (for resettlement of Soviet Jews) contingent on stopping the construction of settlements on the West Bank.

Although, as Jacob Heilbrunn notes, by then "the neocons had been shut out of the Bush Administration," a few remained within it, and after the Gulf War it fell to them to plan for future crises that might require military solutions. "With the end of the Cold War, we can now use our military with impunity," Wolfowitz told an associate. "The Soviets won't come in to block us. And we've got five, maybe ten years to clean up these old Soviet surrogate regimes like Iraq and Syria before the next superpower emerges to challenge us."

In 1991–92, after discussion with Cheney and under Wolfowitz's guidance, Zalmay Khalilzad (like Wolfowitz, a Wohlstetter protégé), I. Lewis "Scooter" Libby (a former Wolfowitz student at Yale), and old friends Wohlstetter, Andy Marshall, and Perle prepared a Defense Planning Guidance (DPG) report for fiscal 1994–99. The first draft was a blueprint for a neocon future. It contended that the United States must act to prevent the emergence of any "rival" that posed a threat "on the order of that formerly posed by the Soviet Union." As a corollary, it argued that "the U.S. must show the leadership necessary to establish and protect a new order that holds the promise of convincing potential competitors that they need not aspire to a greater role or pursue a more aggressive posture to protect their legitimate interests." Those potential competitors included "advanced industrial nations" as well as less industrialized ones. This contention, military historian Fred Kaplan writes, went beyond what Marshall advised; Marshall had written in a paper on revising the military, "We need to think through how to involve allies, what coalitions we want to form."

Wolfowitz and his associates recommended discouraging European military alliances that marginalized the United States, favoring Pakistan over "Indian hegemony," and blocking Japan from expanding its influence. Though their report agreed that the United States should not be the world's policeman, it nevertheless recommended that America should serve as the geopolitical arbiter of right and wrong. Only by doing so, it argued, could the United States "retain the preeminent responsibility for addressing selectively those wrongs which threaten not only our interests but those of our allies or friends, or which could seriously unsettle international relations." Going forward, the United States should make its alliances temporary, designed to help address crises while preserving for itself the right and ability to act unilaterally. Though the report did not mention the UN or NATO on this point, it implied that such groups could not and should not be relied on to ensure America's future.

By emphasizing military strength, dismissing the power of diplomacy, and identifying the squelching of potential rivals as the primary challenge to the United States in the coming years, the DPG adapted Fritz Kraemer's thinking to a post-Soviet environment. But it went beyond Kraemer's tenets in dismissing George H. W. Bush's coalition-building efforts in the Gulf War as a model for future efforts. Though Kraemer was no fan of the UN, he was a longtime admirer of NATO, a military-based organization, and often spoke in terms of the Western democracies acting in concert.

A draft of the DPG was leaked to the New York Times, which published some of its unclassified contents in February 1992. A hue and cry came from many quarters, from liberals but also from the capitals of Europe and Asia and from the White House, where the press was told that top officials had not seen the draft before it was leaked. Baker and Scowcroft distanced themselves from the document, which outside critics painted as suggesting that the goal of the United States was world domination, the imposition of a "pax Americana." A Cheney spokesman claimed that the report was a low-level draft the secretary had never reviewed, although one fifteen-page section of it claimed to have been generated from Cheney's "specific guidance."

The second draft was released in May 1992. Gone from its unclassified version was the explicit goal of preventing the emergence of specific rivals as superpowers. Also absent was any insistence on unilateral action; in its place was an emphasis on using the United Nations and other international bodies to resolve disputes. The "new language" of the second draft, the *Times* now reported, "represents a significant retrenchment and appears to have discredited the idea . . . that the United States should focus its energies on containing German and Japanese aspirations for regional leadership." The changes seemed to shift the document's emphasis away from ideology to a more pragmatic emphasis on diplomacy, humanitarian aid, the exchange of intelligence data, and the use of economic tools to augment and supplant military might as means for the United States to relate to other nations.

But looks were deceiving. As rewritten by Libby under Cheney's guidance, the document still said that the main business of the United States was "shaping the future security environment [to] preclude any hostile power from dominating a region critical to our interests." Documents like the Wolfowitz-Cheney DPG, which would continue to be the framework for considering defense-related matters in the early Clinton years, ensured that the old configuration—which involved viewing the goal of U.S. military power as the aggressive countering of one primary enemy—would continue. That philosophy was now broadened to encompass enemies beyond the defunct Soviet Union.

THE BUSH YEARS had produced a major foreign policy accomplishment, the international coalition that pushed Iraq out of Kuwait, and a promising start on the creation of a "new world order" dedicated to international cooperation between former enemies. George H. W. Bush, a pragmatist, had gone to war only when events forced his hand, and then only with a substantial number of allies. Whether those conditions could continue in the future would depend, in large measure, on eclipsing the attempts of Cheney, Wolfowitz, and neoconservatives outside the government to insist that, in any new world order, the United States must give the orders and be eager to enforce them.

25

The Post–Cold War Dilemma

Observers with long-term perspectives pointed out that for the previous hundred years the United States had faced centralized enemies: the Germans in World War I, the Axis powers in World War II, the Communist powers in Korea, Vietnam, and other hot spots. Now, with no identifiable country as a main enemy, the task of constructing a foreign policy was more difficult.

Although the domestic economy dominated the 1992 presidential race, after William Jefferson Clinton was elected the same geopolitical problems that had bedeviled President Bush troubled Clinton. At first he opted to continue Bush's policies; as time went on, he would conduct foreign affairs on an ad hoc, reactive basis. His partisans saw this as the ultimate in pragmatism; but to critics his foreign policy exuded a lack of vision or purpose. Clinton's lack of focus gave the neocons a unique opportunity to offer a credible alternative. Shaping that response would consume them throughout Clinton's first term.

IN JUNE 1992 President Bush traveled to Moscow to sign a preliminary START II agreement with Boris Yeltsin. It had taken Reagan eight years to make progress on START I, with its objective of banning the use of MIRVed warheads on ICBMs, and he had not been able to sign the treaty before he left office. Bush and Gorbachev signed it on July 31, 1991, and both sides complied by destroying parts of their nuclear arsenals. The neocons wanted to go no further. "The Bush Administration has gotten into a jam by emphasizing this arms control issue," Richard Perle told an American Enterprise Institute news conference. "Instead of endlessly negotiating about the number of warheads on ballistic missiles," Perle suggested, new summit negotiations should concentrate on pushing Russia's economy toward a free-market system.

Perle and his ideological soulmates were in a quandary over the 1992 election. Bush's only serious opponent in the 1992 Republican primaries was Pat Buchanan, who was known for his isolationism. As Jacob Heilbrunn notes, "some of the neoconservatives looked hopefully to Bill Clinton" as the candidate who would embrace their hawkish positions, and "Clinton himself did little to discourage that belief."

Clinton's in-house mantra, "It's the economy, stupid," reflected not only his understanding of what mattered to voters but also the public's lack of interest in foreign affairs, now that the Soviet Union had fallen and Saddam Hussein had been pushed back into Iraq. On the stump, Clinton faulted Bush for not articulating "a new American purpose" and for missteps on Iraq, the Balkans, and Africa—a stance that resonated with some neocons. His running mate, Senator Al Gore, charged, on one hand, that the Bush administration's poor treatment of Iraq before its Kuwait invasion had "struck the match" that ignited the war and then "poured gasoline on the flames"—a comment that annoyed neocons. On the other hand, Gore denounced Bush for not pursuing Saddam to Baghdad and deposing him; this was a complaint the neocons shared.

The neocons declined to flock around the strongest third-party candidate in decades, multimillionaire businessman H. Ross Perot. To them, Perot's positions on foreign and military policy were simplistic, vague, and insufficiently hawkish: He believed that large nations ought to do more for small ones—that the United States should pay its back dues to the UN—and that our military should remain sizable and strong but should not be used too often in regional conflicts.

Refusing to back Bush, and dismissive of Perot's naïveté, the neocons soon became uncomfortable with Clinton, labeling him antimilitary for decrying discrimination against gays in the armed forces and because he had assiduously avoided the draft so he would not have to fight during the Vietnam War. To counter rumblings that military personnel would refuse to serve under him, Clinton obtained the endorsement and vocal support of former JCS chairman William Crowe.

In the midst of the presidential campaign, in August 1992, a distinctly post–Cold War crisis arose. Horrific images of Serbian detention camps, televised around the world, called attention to the plight of Muslim civilians in the region. The Serbs, under the rubric of "ethnic cleansing," had already killed tens of thousands in Bosnia. NATO forces commanded by the British and French had been so inactive as to be complicit. The countering of "ethnic cleansing" was a purely moral issue, free of anti-Soviet purpose and the element of self-interest palpable in America's decision to oust Saddam from Kuwait and its control of the region's oil supplies. Would the United States act against this obvious new evil, even if it meant putting American servicemen in harm's way? Was Bush's "new world order" more than a rhetorical flourish? Sending U.S. troops to Kosovo would raise the possibility of similar involvement in comparable crises in Somalia, Ethiopia, Burundi, Burma, and Haiti.

Candidate Clinton called for President Bush to use American air and naval forces "against the Serbs to try to restore the basic conditions of humanity." Eventually Bush did send troops to Somalia, but he held off doing so for Kosovo; instead he let the Europeans take the lead, which they did so passively that the atrocities continued.

Such foreign affairs crises were unresolved in November when Clinton won the election, prevailing with only 37 percent of the votes cast in the three-way election. Democrats maintained control of both houses of Congress, though their margin of control slipped.

PRESIDENT BUSH, DEVASTATED by the electorate's rejection, had little inclination to take new action on any front before Clinton was inaugurated, but James Baker and other intimates argued that this was an opportunity for final actions in service of his objectives. Bush's first such action harked back, not forward. On Christmas Eve 1992, Bush pardoned Cap Weinberger, Bud McFarlane, Elliott Abrams, and three CIA officers; the six had either been indicted on charges or convicted of crimes connected to Iran-Contra. George Mitchell, Democratic leader of the Senate, scorned Bush for using the pardons to short-circuit the judicial system and wondered, "If members of the executive branch lie to the Congress, obstruct justice and otherwise break the law, how can policy differences be fairly and legally resolved in a democracy?" The pardons demonstrated to future administrations that lying to Congress and evading the legislative branch's oversight function could be done with relative impunity.

In Bush's last weeks as president he visited American troops in Somalia, signed START II in Moscow, and sent warning letters to Serbian president Slobodan Milosevic and to Saddam Hussein. "In the event of conflict in Kosovo caused by Serbian action," he wrote to Milosevic, "the United States will be prepared to employ military force . . . against the Serbians in Kosovo [and] in Serbia proper." The worry was that the Serbs would carry over their "ethnic cleansing" to Kosovo. Bush cautioned Saddam not to use the lame-duck period to test how far he could push the coalition-enforced "no-fly" zone over northern Iraq. Even with these actions, *Time* suggested, Bush was leaving for his successor "a frightening load of unfinished business." As columnist Henry Grunwald noted, he was also leaving behind a topsy-turvy political landscape: "Many liberals have suddenly turned hawkish, some, for instance, almost pushing to bomb Serbia back into the Stone Age, while many once hard-line conservatives now oppose intervention."

On the right, the neocons were distancing themselves further from their Kraemerite forebears. The split shone through an article in *Foreign Affairs* by James Schlesinger, which presented a distinctly Kraemerite view of post–Cold War geopolitics. Certainly the moment provided an important opening for a new foreign policy, Schlesinger said, but Bush had already pushed too many objectives: "We are urged to advance democracy and all its procedures, human rights, civil liberties, equality before the law, protection of minorities, self-determination, an orderly world, international law, economic growth, free markets, privatization, free trade, limits on environmental degradation, curtailment of the arms trade, prevention of the spread of advanced weapons, etc., etc." Absent a coherent, guiding philosophy, U.S. foreign policy would be shaped by "a capricious flow of events rather than defined guideposts and a careful plan." Schlesinger belittled the idea of making policy on the basis of do-gooder impulses or in reaction to televised images: "Starvation continues in the Sudan or Mozambique, suppression in East Timor or India, ethnic war in parts of the former Soviet Union, but it is Somalia or Bosnia that draw the attention, because the cameras are there." He disagreed with one particular ideological tenet that had been used as the basis for foreign policy: the attempt to instill democracy on unfamiliar turf—which had become, despite his and Jeane Kirkpatrick's best intentions, the centerpiece of neocon foreign policy:

> Do we seriously want to change the institutions of Saudi Arabia? The brief answer is no; over the years we have sought to preserve those institutions. . . . King Fahd has stated quite unequivocally that democratic institutions are not appropriate for his society. . . . In neighboring Kuwait, a nation whose renewal has depended on American power, we have been far more concerned with restoring legitimacy than with fostering democracy.

Schlesinger similarly believed the United States should not be in the business of "nation building" or of being the world's policeman. His remarks, though aimed at the neocons, also applied to the incoming administration, since Clinton had espoused a "pro-democracy foreign policy" whose "definition of security must include common threats to all people."

Irving Kristol, one of the intellectual creators of neocon philosophy, agreed with Schlesinger on democracy promotion: "The prospect of American military intervention and occupation to 'make democracy work' . . . something like an American empire with a purely ideological motive power . . . is not and cannot be a serious option for American foreign policy." But younger neocons, such as Kristol's son William, thought the old guard, including his father, were wrong. What good was a foreign policy without ideals? And championing democracy was as American an ideal as one could imagine.

Early in 1993, in a book called *Pandaemonium*, Pat Moynihan fulminated that none of the young neocons had ever served in combat, yet they embraced unending militarism as the route to empire and "wished for a military posture approaching mobilization; they would create or invent whatever crises were required to bring this about." Moynihan and Scoop Jackson had been close friends in the Senate, but after Jackson's death in 1983 Moynihan had become steadily less enamored of Jackson's protégés, accusing them of exaggerating the threat from the faltering Soviet Union and of spending America's resources on unnecessary armaments.

IN 1977, DONALD Rumsfeld had left incoming president Carter a roadblock in the form of a defiantly large defense budget. A similar and perhaps even more challenging obstacle awaited Clinton in 1993: a report from outgoing secretary of defense Dick Cheney titled "Defense Strategy for the 1990s." A restatement of neocon aims expressed in Paul Wolfowitz's Defense Planning Guidance document the previous year, the Cheney strategy report avowed that the United States must act to "preclude any hostile power from dominating a region critical to our interests." It cautioned that while the United States favored "collective action" by the UN or NATO, such a response would "not always be timely and, in the absence of U.S. leadership, may not gel" because "countries whose interests are very different from our own" might block tough actions. Therefore, the United States must reserve the right to act unilaterally.

Several twentieth-century presidents who entered office at a time of dramatic transition took pains to distance themselves from the faltering practices of previous administrations. After Franklin Roosevelt won election in 1932, he refused to do anything to halt the downward spiral of the Depression before he was inaugurated, so that when he took office he would not be bound by Hoover's unavailing remedies and could start completely fresh.

Similarly, President-elect Nixon refused to go along with the Johnson administration's attempts to formulate joint policy in the months before the inaugural, so as to be better positioned to wage his own revolution in foreign affairs. Bill Clinton, as the first post–Cold War president and the first Democratic president after twelve years of Republican rule, had an equal opportunity for revolutionary thinking, but when it came to foreign affairs he was slow to seize the moment.

Over the years, retroactive hostility toward Clinton has blurred the extent of his continuity with the prior Bush administration. At the time, though, it was recognized as substantial.

Before Clinton's inauguration, his associates and Bush's agreed to a continuation of previous, pragmatic American policy in four hot areas: no-fly zones in Iraq and Bosnia, and the missions in Somalia and off the shores of Haiti, where a worsening crisis threatened to increase a flood of refugees. Although during the campaign Clinton had advocated eased restrictions on Haitian refugees, as president-elect and as president he backed Bush's policy of returning to Haiti boatloads of those who had attempted to flee, and stationed U.S. vessels off the Haitian shore to enforce that rule. During the campaign Clinton had also urged that the Bosnia arms embargo be repealed; as president-elect and as president he embraced Bush's position that the embargo could not be lifted if European nations continued to enforce their own—despite evidence that the Serbs were mounting attacks on independent, democratic Croatia and Bosnia. In Iraq, during early January, Bush authorized the U.S. military, in collaboration with the governments of the USSR, France, and the United Kingdom, to destroy radar and SAM missile sites in southern Iraq that had been aimed at planes enforcing the no-fly zone. Clinton applauded.

By January 20, 1993, there were more flashpoints around the world approaching crisis proportions than at any time since October 1970. A month later, there was another—this time on American turf. On February 26, a car bomb exploded in the parking garage under the north tower of the World Trade Center in New York, killing six people and injuring more than a thousand, though the building remained structurally intact. Within ten days, the attack was traced to a gang of Muslim extremists in the United States tied to and funded by the terrorist group al-Qaeda and Osama bin Laden—a gang that owed its allegiance to a blind Muslim spiritual leader then in jail for ordering the murder of an American rabbi. Arrests and trials proceeded speedily.

Ten years later, the commission looking into the September 11, 2001, terrorist attacks concluded that the successful pursuit and convictions of the 1993 bombers "had the side effect of obscuring the need to examine the character and extent of the new threat facing the United States," causing the United States to "underestimate" the virulence and strength of bin Laden and al-Qaeda.

This 1993 precursor to the 2001 attacks offers a revealing window into the U.S. government's mind-set in the late twentieth century. Every president since Harry S. Truman had reacted to attacks on U.S. interests and allies as though they were controlled by one malevolent hand. That rationale faded with the end of the Cold War, and the Clinton administration responded to the 1993 World Trade Center bombing not by identifying the emerging radical Islamist tide as a new malevolent hand but by treating the attack as an isolated criminal act to be prosecuted. This was not a failing of Clinton or the Democrats alone; Reagan and Bush had repeatedly treated similar events in the Middle East and Africa the same way. Seeing Communists everywhere, Reagan and Bush had wrongly viewed such incidents as by-products of Soviet influence when they should have been ascribed to Muslim extremism and to deep anger at the Christianized West. The Clinton administration's too-narrow response to the 1993 World Trade Center bombing was a leftover result of this myopia.

Clinton's pragmatism was more evident, in a positive way, in the Oslo accords, a peace treaty between Israel and the Palestinians, signed at the White House in September 1993, that created limited Palestinian self-rule in the West Bank and Gaza. Republicans and Democrats applauded at the time, though many wondered how long peace would last in that volatile region. Clinton also displayed a pragmatic approach in bucking the trade-union portion of the Democratic Party to champion the North American Free Trade Agreement (NAFTA). Clinton acknowledged that NAFTA would likely accelerate the outsourcing of jobs and manufacturing capabilities from the United States to Mexico and Central and South America. But he argued that it would stabilize those countries' economies, which were vital to the economic health and safety of the United States.

Was NAFTA the product of a new pragmatism, one that recognized the interconnectedness of the world, or a function of Bill Clinton's desire to make deals to boost his own political stock? The neocons decided it was the latter. "The Clinton Administration has essentially repeated the pattern of [Bush's] inaction and obfuscation—only in a more obvious, embarrassing, and potentially destructive fashion," Patrick Glynn charged in the New Republic a year into Clinton's first term. "A sense of confusion about defining the national interest is the most troubling aspect of Bill Clinton's first year as president," Wolfowitz wrote in Foreign Affairs. Clinton—ostensibly liberal, seemingly more influenced by polls than by moral imperatives—was a much better foil for neocon anger than Bush had been.

The neocons' line on Clinton grew pointed as they decided that the common denominator of Clinton's policies was "international social work," and even more when they found a focus for their outrage in Clinton's refusal to take unilateral military action in Bosnia. A hundred rightists from three generations castigated the lack of action in Bosnia in an open letter to Clinton published in the *Wall Street Journal* on September 2, 1993. The letter, signed by Kirkpatrick, Wohlstetter, Perle, Wolfowitz, Gaffney, Muravchik, Thatcher, Shultz, Brzezinski, and columnist Charles Krauthammer, asserted that the West must "act now substantially to reduce Serbia's immediate and future power of aggression," because "if the West doesn't use force . . . 'the message' received will only bring American and Western resolve into contempt." The statement linked two of Fritz Kraemer's key theories: his warnings about provocative weakness and about the need to use military action in service of moral goals. Though Kraemer did not sign the letter—he never signed such public appeals—it represented the almost total adoption of his doctrine into mainstream conservative thought.

When war began in Bosnia in 1992, neocon historian Muravchik points out, Bush had "dismissed the violence there as a 'hiccup,' and James Baker, his Secretary of State, famously declared that 'we have no dog in that fight.' Once the new Clinton administration proved equally inert, and with the death toll mounting, a lobby developed for some form of American intervention." This, Muravchik says, gave the neocons a moment of definition, separating them from paleocons and the liberals. The need for intervention in Bosnia would spill over into later perceived needs for other interventions.

In October 1993, the price of America's reluctance to commit adequate military resources to an overseas fight was exposed in another hot spot: Somalia. When troops controlled by local warlords overwhelmed a small U.S. force, the UN sent a contingent in to rescue them. But the UN force was tardy and timid, and in the ensuing melee a U.S. Black Hawk helicopter was lost and the bodies of eighteen Americans were dragged through the streets before television cameras. After this debacle, it was clear that U.S. forces in Somalia must either be augmented and turned loose or be withdrawn. Clinton's response was immediate: He directed the Joint Chiefs to cease all U.S. military action in Somalia except for self-defense and soon after announced that all U.S. military would be out of Somalia by March 1994.

The conjunction of U.S. inaction in Bosnia, and the inadequate U.S. action in the Somalia fiasco, prompted such neocon writers as Muravchik, Glynn, Luttwak, and Wolfowitz to publish pieces in *The New Republic, Foreign Affairs*, and *Commentary* arguing that Clinton's vaunted pragmatism was nothing more than liberal naïveté.

Clinton gave these critics additional ammunition when he pushed for a ban on testing nuclear weapons, vowing that the United States would lead the way by continuing its moratorium. Russia and France expressed their willingness to go along, but China continued to set off underground tests—proof, to the neocons, that the United States had no business signing a Comprehensive Nuclear Test-Ban Treaty when it was meaningless without all nuclear powers on board. Soon the French, citing the Chinese tests, resumed their own.

In the spring of 1994 the situation in Bosnia worsened, with Milosevic's Serbia and the Serb majority in Bosnia attempting to eliminate or marginalize the Muslim minority. Many Americans, right and left, found Clinton's failure to act aggressively morally repugnant. Wohlstetter railed against "the weakness of the democracies," calling for concentrated air strikes and for lifting the embargo on sending arms to the Muslims. In *Foreign Affairs*, Wolfowitz argued that Clinton's "confusion about defining the national interest" had led to squandering the U.S. military's prestige in Haiti and Somalia and to confusion about using force in Bosnia. Wolfowitz thought the embargo of arms in Bosnia should not be lifted until our national interests there had been defined. And, he added, the United States was still ignoring the much larger problems that were sure to come from the "backlash states" of Iraq, Iran, and North Korea.

Clinton's inaction begat further inaction. His refusal to act unilaterally in Bosnia influenced the Western nations' refusal to come to the aid of moderate Hutu and Tutsi tribes in Rwanda, as militias massacred hundreds of thousands of them during a hundred-day period from April to July. The United States and most European countries did almost nothing to stop this genocide.

Clinton's vacillations and seemingly arbitrary uses of military power were grist for the mill of a July 1994 conference of Republican foreign policy experts Kissinger, Kirkpatrick, Cheney, and Baker—the latter two, Kissinger quipped, "half-declared" candidates to succeed Clinton in 1996. In statements that would later resonate uncomfortably with the neocon actions during the George W. Bush administration, Baker lambasted Clinton's "flip-flops [that] debase the currency of U.S. credibility," and said the United States should "never, never, never, never" threaten the use of military force without being willing to employ it. Cheney charged that Clinton had taken a molehill, Haiti, and made it a crisis mountain. "Why would we want to invade Haiti?" Cheney wondered. "And what are we going to do with it once we've got it?"

Clinton was able to laugh off such sniping, for just days before the conference he had brokered a peace accord between Israel and Jordan—a feat Nixon, Ford, Reagan, and Bush had all tried and failed to accomplish.

Moreover, Clinton's dispatch of troops to Haiti in September 1994 did produce a positive result: their presence offshore enabled Clinton's emissary, former president Carter, to talk the usurping military leaders into abdicating, clearing the way for the troops to help the elected leader, Jean-Bertrand Aristide, effect a bloodless change in government and begin steps toward restoring democracy. Carter also helped the administration convince North Korea to mothball its nuclear materials production plants. These were substantial accomplishments, but the neocons disparaged them—presumably because they were Clinton's.

In the 1994 midterm elections, dissatisfaction with Clinton's leadership on domestic issues—including the failure of his universal health-care initiative—carried more weight with voters than the triumphs or mistakes of his foreign policy. For the first time since the 1950s, Republicans, spearheaded by Representative Newt Gingrich, regained control of both the Senate and the House. The chorus of Republican complaints rose; it also moved toward the neocons' positions.

Clinton, too, followed that trend. To resolve the Balkan crisis, the Clinton administration brought the parties together in late 1994. When more outrages occurred in early 1995, Clinton finally took the military action the neocons had been demanding since 1993: The United States spearheaded a NATO bombing campaign to degrade Bosnian Serb forces and prevent them from attacking areas in Bosnia designated by the UN as "safe" for Muslim minorities. "Wolfowitz, Perle, Muravchik, [conservative columnist Charles] Krauthammer, Gaffney and others felt utterly vindicated when the Bosnian war was finally ended," historians Stefan Halper and Jonathan Clarke noted; these air strikes and concerted ground efforts followed exactly the strategy these neocons had argued for in their September 1993 open letter. The air strikes also proved the effectiveness of the technologically advanced weaponry long championed by Wohlstetter and Andy Marshall, pushing Milosevic to the bargaining table in three weeks. The Clinton-sponsored peace settlement gave the Republicans reason to pass a congressional resolution to lift the arms embargo in Bosnia with a veto-proof majority. Clinton had no choice but to sign it.

In June 1996, bombs crumpled the Khobar Towers, a residence for U.S. and other foreign servicemen in Saudi Arabia, killing nineteen Americans and injuring hundreds of other Americans and foreigners. FBI and Saudi investigations identified a Hezbollah faction, supported by Iran, as the culprits. Clinton tightened sanctions on Iran but took no further action, as his State Department believed that anything more consequential might hinder a growing reform movement inside Iran.

On the subject of Iraq, however, Clinton continued to be belligerent.

In September 1996, in response to Saddam's continued provocations—including shutting out weapons inspectors and stationing missile batteries on its borders—Clinton announced that he was expanding the no-fly zones in the northern and southern areas of Iraq. Some critics derided the expanded zones as a ploy to make Clinton look tough in an election year. In an op-ed piece, Paul Wolfowitz argued that now was the time to send in ground troops and push to Baghdad.

In the 1996 election, Clinton was opposed by Bob Dole, a relatively unattractive candidate who had run with Ford twenty years earlier and who now seemed to be going through the motions. But the neocons flocked to his side, helping him lash out at Clinton's foreign policy as "weak, indecisive, incoherent, inconsistent, vacillating, scattershot and self-contradictory," a product of "neglect, posturing, concessions and false triumphs . . . a string of failures dressed up for television as victories." Dole's running mate, Representative Jack Kemp, had long been a favorite of the neocons (Sven Kraemer had worked in Kemp's office). Donald Rumsfeld became Dole's campaign manager, Wolfowitz his deputy for foreign policy. Candidate Dole took many purely neocon stances: He advocated that the United States all but abandon working through the United Nations on military matters. He pledged not to send American troops into battle for any purpose other than victory—meaning for neither peacekeeping nor nation building. He called for more ballistic missiles, specifically to be stationed in Asia to deter China. And he called for an overt statement on defending Taiwan, and for the United States to cut off further contact with the dictators of North Korea and Iran.

These positions, which defined Bob Dole's foreign policy platform in 1996, became the foreign policy of the George W. Bush administration in 2001.

Dole ran a poor race, his momentum further sapped by a second Perot candidacy. Clinton won handily, carrying thirty-one states and 49.2 percent of the vote. But the president had no coattails: Republicans retained control of the House and Senate, increasing their majority in the Senate as conservative southern Republicans replaced retiring conservative southern Democrats. The neocons could now look forward happily to 2000, when Clinton would likely be replaced by a Republican whose foreign policy would mirror their own. They would have four years to prepare for that moment—years in which to plan and to kick Clinton around.

SECTION VI

Full Power

George W. Bush and Dick Cheney, July 24, 2007. *(Eric Draper, Reuters)*

26

Neocons Versus Clinton

L ike the TV-watching public, during his first term President Clinton had reacted to foreign events mostly out of humanitarian concern. Though his predecessor had been castigated for not having "the vision thing," the first President Bush had actually fashioned a vision—the new world order, with its promise of collaborative response to aggression. But as the debate about post–Cold War U.S. foreign policy widened in the 1990s, Clinton offered little beyond what his critics labeled "international social work."

Clinton's dearth of ideas allowed the neocons to frame that debate, through a series of position statements that began in the summer of 1996 but garnered little notice until after the election. The first of these was Sven Kraemer's testimony to a congressional committee in June:

> The Clinton Administration is grossly failing to deal with threatening global realities in its defense and arms control policies. The Administration is in denial, colors its official threat estimates and rejects both vigorous enforcement and advanced active defense programs in countering proliferation threats. The Administration is wedded to cornerstone myths about a benign new world order, about its ability to deal with dictators as if they were democrats . . . and about the efficacy of multilateral agreements. . . . Instead of working at home and abroad to block high-tech flows to rogue states and those who supply them, the flow of enabling technologies for advanced weapons continues virtually unchecked as the Clinton Administration too often seeks

short-term commercial gains over security and appeasement over enforcement. At the same time U.S. military forces and production as well as research and development levels have been drastically cut.

Sven Kraemer's statement was a complete rejection of current policy, and it cleared a path for the neocons to formulate their own, more active vision of future policy.

The need to make "A Clean Break" was made clear in a paper of that name, commissioned by the incoming Netanyahu government of Israel and issued in July 1996 by Richard Perle. It might as well have been prepared for the United States, since it encouraged Israel to pursue a militarily aggressive policy with U.S. assistance. Israel should made a clean break with the past, the brief paper argued, by not continuing to negotiate land for peace with the Palestinians, and by eschewing diplomacy in favor of an aggressive defense of its territorial integrity. The paper called for Israel to work with the United States, to set up regional missile defenses (encompassing Jordan and Turkey) to contain Syria—and to join with all of these countries, especially the United States, to rid Iraq of Saddam Hussein. Regime change in Iraq, the report stated, would not only remove a thorn in Israel's side but would also lead to the democratization of governments in other Muslim states.

Perle and many other neocons, including Wolfowitz, Douglas Feith, William Kristol, Elliott Abrams, and Norman Podhoretz, were Jewish and strong champions of Israel. With the publication of the "Clean Break" report, which attracted great media attention, the neocons became widely overidentified with unquestioning support for Israel. It was a notion that first bubbled up after the Gulf War, when the Bush administration was tough with Israel about its expansion of settlements in the West Bank, and the neocons had defended Israel's actions. Critics of the neocons leveled such charges frequently during the Clinton years, and during the presidency of George W. Bush they faulted the neocons for promoting a war against Iraq whose primary purpose, they insisted, was to protect Israel. Yet the charge was overstated on two counts: First, not all neocons were Jewish; indeed, the men who actually pulled the levers of power when the neocons finally took over—George W. Bush, Cheney, and Rumsfeld—were all Protestant. Second, the fact that a policy ostensibly helped Israel did not mean it was designed with that objective in mind: The neocons' overriding purpose was to further the aims of the United States.

Second-generation neocons William Kristol and Robert Kagan published a third neocon policy program broadside in the summer issue of *Foreign Affairs*. "Toward a Neo-Reaganite Foreign Policy" was a forthright attempt to wrap the authors and their ideas in the persona of a president beloved by all Republicans and not a few Democrats. The authors charged that the American public was currently "indifferent, if not hostile, to foreign policy and commitments abroad, more interested in balancing the budget than in leading the world, and more intent on cashing in the 'peace dividend' than on spending to deter and fight future wars." To the authors, this was an ostrich-in-the-sand attitude; as an alternative, they pointed fondly to the "bold challenge to the tepid consensus of the era" that Reagan had made in 1976, championing "American exceptionalism when it was deeply unfashionable." Trashing the Nixon-Kissinger-Ford foreign policies, as well as Carter and Clinton, Kristol and Kagan celebrated the accomplishments of Reagan-era policies—specifically the demise of the Soviet Union, which they felt entitled the United States to construct a "benevolent American hegemony." What did that mean? "Having defeated the 'evil empire,' the United States enjoys strategic and ideological predominance," they wrote. "The first objective of U.S. foreign policy should be to preserve and enhance that predominance by strengthening America's security, supporting its friends, advancing its interests, and standing up for its principles around the world." By enhancing military budgets—the authors suggested an increase of $60 to $80 billion a year on top of the $260 billion already budgeted—and stressing America's "moral clarity," the United States could extend a Pax Americana far into the future.

Even some who still credited Reagan with winning the Cold War disagreed with the Kristol-Kagan notion of a "benevolent American hegemony." One of them, Walter A. McDougall of the Foreign Policy Research Institute, wrote,

> Such a self-conscious, self-righteous bid for global hegemony is bound to drive foreign rivals into open hostility to the U.S. and make our allies resentful and nervous. . . . The authors' argument . . . ignores the historical record, which demonstrates that U.S. diplomacy has been most successful when it weighs in against would-be hegemons such as Germany and the Soviet Union for the purpose, as John F. Kennedy said, "to make the world safe for diversity." But Kristol and Kagan would have us arrogate to ourselves a hegemony for the purpose of making the world over in our image.

Kristol and Kagan took pains, in their seminal article, to refute John Quincy Adams's 1823 admonition that the United States should not go abroad "in search of monsters to destroy." "But why not?" they asked. "The alternative is to leave monsters on the loose, ravaging and pillaging to their heart's content, as Americans stand by and watch," a policy that was tantamount to "cowardice and dishonor." McDougall pointed out that Kristol and Kagan had deliberately failed to mention the reason Adams warned against going abroad to slay monsters: that such actions, in Adams's words, "would involve the United States beyond the power of extrication, in all the wars of interest and intrigue, avarice, envy, and ambition. . . . America might become the dictatress of the world, but she would no longer be the ruler of her own spirit."

Reagan had used the military abroad only four times in his eight years; Clinton, whose actions Kristol and Kagan disparaged, had used it eight times in four years. By advocating even more aggressive use of the military, Kristol and Kagan went beyond the "Reaganite" standards they claimed to espouse. Looking back in 2004, Halper and Clarke, who served in foreign policy posts under Reagan, wrote in their book *America Alone*:

> When we rallied to Ronald Reagan's clarion cry of the "Evil Empire," we did not imagine that a generation later we would see the nation embark on a perilous course of power projection and intimidation. . . . We never thought to see a small group of neoconservative policy makers appropriate Reagan's multilayered legacy, as though it were their exclusive property and, careless of history, boil it down to a few simplistic slogans.

In the wake of the 1996 election, a coterie who agreed with Kristol and Kagan, and that included most of Dole's foreign policy advisers, established a new group, the Project for a New American Century. The PNAC's military ideas were heavily influenced by Andrew Marshall, who remained at the Pentagon despite the efforts of Clinton's new secretary of defense, William Cohen, to remove him. But the PNAC's statement of principles went beyond military matters. As signed by "founding members" Cheney, Rumsfeld, Perle, Wolfowitz, Abrams, Gaffney, Iklé, Decter, Podhoretz, Quayle, Libby, Khalilzad, Kristol, Kagan, and Jeb Bush, a son of the former president, it read: "We seem to have forgotten the essential elements of the Reagan Administration's success: a military that is strong and ready to meet both present and future challenges; a foreign policy that boldly and purposefully promotes American principles abroad; and national leadership that accepts the United States' global responsibilities." The signers demanded hefty increases in defense spending "to challenge regimes hostile to our interests and values" and to "extend . . . an international order friendly to our security, our prosperity, and our principles."

With its simplistic reliance on military strength and moral clarity, the PNAC's "neo-Reaganite" program was reductionist Kraemerism—and as much a misunderstanding of Fritz Kraemer as it was of Ronald Reagan. While Kraemer often expressed his belief that "military might is indispensable," he just as often insisted he was "absolutely not a warmonger." Why? Because "anyone who has been a soldier in wartime, as I have, cherishes peace and knows what war means."

BILL CLINTON GAVE a boost to the neocons' moralistic posture when his own moral turpitude was aired in public during the Monica Lewinsky affair, which dominated the headlines throughout 1998. Though the Middle East and Africa were shaken by significant crises during that year, the American public shrugged them off, more interested in tales of sexual misconduct in the Oval Office.

The neocons increasingly focused their own attention on one overseas flashpoint: Iraq. They touted the need to bring about regime change in the country, to neutralize Iraq's purported weapons of mass destruction (WMDs), and to establish a democracy in Baghdad that would tilt the entire political alignment of the Middle East in America's favor. They argued that the dominoes would fall—not, as in the sixties, in a negative way, to the Communists—but in a positive way, fostering the democratization of autocratic regimes in the Muslim lands. Before that could happen, however, Saddam Hussein would have to be toppled, an action demanded in a January 1998 PNAC open letter to Clinton signed by Elliott Abrams, John Bolton, Robert Kagan, Zalmay Khalilzad, William Kristol, Richard Perle, Donald Rumsfeld, Paul Wolfowitz, and James Woolsey, a pupil of Wohlstetter and a Scoop Jackson Democrat who had led the CIA under Carter.

The PNAC letter insisted that because the sanctions and oil embargo had been undermined and ignored—Iraq had kicked out the UN inspectors—"the only acceptable strategy is one that eliminates the possibility that Iraq will be able to use or threaten to use weapons of mass destruction. In the near term, this means a willingness to undertake military action as diplomacy is clearly failing. In the long term, it means removing Saddam Hussein and his regime from power." Removing Hussein would entail "dangers and difficulties," but "we believe the dangers of failing to do so are far greater."

By stating that the United States should "eliminate the possibility" of Iraqi future weapons use, the PNAC issued the first clear call for a preemptive war, an action against a country that had not attacked the United States or its allies but that the PNAC construed as a threat to world stability. Fritz Kraemer and his old friends agreed with the neocons that Saddam Hussein threatened world peace and that the world would be better off with him gone, but they did not like preemptive war. By now, Kraemer, Rowny, and Walters were all suffering the traumas of age: Kraemer was going deaf, Rowny was going blind, and Walters was in a wheelchair. On the conservative lecture circuit, Walters asserted that refusing to attack another country unless first attacked by that country was a defining characteristic of a true democracy. Kraemer, Walters, and Rowny all believed that America's greatness derived both from its military strength and, equally, from the moral high ground it claimed by refusing to go to war unless and until attacked.

When Clinton did not immediately respond to the PNAC's call to topple Saddam, an ad hoc group including many of the same principals—as well as Dick Allen, Judge Clark, Douglas Feith, Sven Kraemer, Bud McFarlane, Hal Sonnenfeldt, and Cap Weinberger—sent Clinton a second letter outlining nine specific actions to take to remove Saddam.

Clinton agreed that Saddam was a danger. In a speech at the Pentagon he identified "an unholy axis of terrorists, drug traffickers and organized international criminals . . . predators of the twenty-first century [who] will be all the more lethal if we allow them to build arsenals of nuclear, chemical and biological weapons and missiles to deliver them. . . . There is no more clear example of this threat than Saddam Hussein's Iraq." But he took no new action against Iraq.

On May 29, 1998, the PNAC sent yet another public letter, this one addressed to House Speaker Newt Gingrich and Senate Majority Leader Trent Lott. By now Saddam had allowed in UN inspectors but had put even more obstacles in their way. The result, the PNAC said, was an "incalculable blow to American leadership and credibility." Congress must "take what steps it can to correct U.S. policy toward Iraq," since the administration was "pursuing a policy fundamentally at odds with vital American security interests." Congress must "do whatever is constitutionally appropriate" to make the "explicit goal" of U.S. foreign policy be "removing Saddam Hussein's regime from power and establishing a peaceful and democratic Iraq in its place."

The lawmakers liked the idea but had other matters on their plates, including the excitement over Clinton's sex life and the more urgent threats to world security then surfacing from Iran, India, Pakistan, and North Korea.

In early May, India set off an underground nuclear device. The move, which wasn't foreseen by the CIA, surprised the Clinton administration. When the international community issued no sanctions against India, Pakistan announced its intention to conduct its own, similar nuclear test. Clinton tried to bribe the Pakistanis into not doing so by promising jet fighters and also threatened to impose sanctions on both India and Pakistan that would hurt Pakistan more. Clinton acknowledged to Pakistani leader Nawaz Sharif that Sharif's government might fall if he did not proceed with the test, but Clinton kept pushing. Pakistan went ahead with the controlled explosion anyway. Clinton's critics pointed to Pakistan's defiance as a measure of Clinton's powerlessness to affect actions abroad, even in countries that depended on American assistance.

"We now have an Islamic bomb," said Pat Moynihan, expressing the fear that Pakistan would soon share its nuclear expertise with Middle East nations inimical to Israel. It did, through the notorious Abdul Qadeer Khan, who, without public notice, gave or sold the technology to other countries that disliked the United States.

Clinton now imposed the sanctions against India and Pakistan that had been mandated under a 1994 law. But he asked Congress for the power to lessen or lift them, contending that the all-or-nothing nature of the sanctions hampered his ability to induce such countries to end their tests. The sanctions helped push Pakistan into a severe economic crisis that hastened a bloodless coup that installed General Pervez Musharraf as Pakistan's ruler in October 1999. After it, the administration tacitly approved the coup by not challenging Musharraf—although, like his predecessor, the general refused to comply with U.S. requests to pursue terrorists near the Afghanistan border, back down on nuclear tests, move toward democratization, stop supporting the Taliban, or find Osama bin Laden and turn him over to American authorities.

In 1998, the dueling India-Pakistan nuclear tests coincided with a report to Congress by a commission led by Donald Rumsfeld. Set up by the Republican majority, the Commission to Assess the Ballistic Missile Threat to the United States was a new-generation Team B. The heavily stacked panel included Rumsfeld, Wolfowitz, Woolsey, and staff director Stephen Cambone, a former Bush administration defense official; the panel also resembled Team B in its mission to overturn a CIA finding and produce a predetermined recommendation. The commission's target was a 1995 CIA National Intelligence Estimate saying that Iran, Iraq, and North Korea would need ten to fifteen years in order to develop credible ICBMs. Clinton had cited this conclusion as a reason to cut military budgets; Sven Kraemer, testifying to a House committee in June 1996, called the NIE "tainted" because it rejected the conclusions of prior NIEs about the timelines on which smaller nations might be able to make nuclear bombs.

When Rumsfeld spoke about the commission's report to a sympathetic audience, the Center for Security Policy, his listeners included Fritz Kraemer, to whom Rumsfeld paid specific tribute from the dais as a "true keeper of the flame." (Kraemer was rarely singled out for public praise by government officials; this was one of few such acknowledgments.)

Rumsfeld's commission concluded that twenty-five to thirty countries either had ballistic missiles or were attempting to acquire them. Those "rogue countries," he charged, had adopted Al Capone's dictum, "You get more with a kind word and a gun than you do with a kind word alone." Their nuclear guns, Rumsfeld asserted, would be fully ready to fire in three to five years, not in ten to fifteen. Citing Roberta Wohlstetter's analysis of the causes of American inaction at Pearl Harbor, Rumsfeld said it was important not to underestimate the very real and immediate danger that these small states' missiles represented. What the Rumsfeld Commission wanted was for the United States to review—really to scrap—all sanctions, intelligence-collecting capabilities, and "U.S. offensive and defensive capabilities as well as strategies, plans, and procedures based on an assumption of extended warning" and to begin immediate plans to replace them with a missile defense system.

Three weeks after the report was issued, North Korea fired off a three-stage missile that flew over Japan before landing in the Pacific—an action that strengthened the neocon-led argument for a U.S. missile defense system.

Clinton refused to green-light such a system, citing his unwillingness to redefine the 1972 ABM treaty for fear of upsetting the Russians. This, New York Times columnist William Safire seethed, was forcing the United States "to remain forever naked to all our prospective enemies." Therefore, Safire insisted, one of the main achievements of Nixon's foreign policy, the 1972 ABM agreement, should finally be overturned—an action that had been demanded by the forebears of the 1998 neocons since the agreement was first proposed.

The argument dated back to 1969, when Jackson, Nitze, Wohlstetter, and the neophytes Perle and Wolfowitz had pushed for the American version of the ABM, called Safeguard, to be made into a real program, not just a bargaining chip for Kissinger. It had nonetheless become something of a bargaining chip, which had spurred Jackson to lead the opposition to the 1972 treaty, and then to champion modifications to make the treaty tougher on the Soviet Union before it was ratified. Safeguard did become a sham—underfunded, with very few silos, and therefore incapable of defending the United States in case of a nuclear missile attack. Ever since Reagan announced the Strategic Defense Initiative in 1983, neocons had warned that adherence to the 1972 ABM treaty would mean stopping development of SDI, the ultimate in antiballistic missile systems. The Russians, however, insisted the treaty must stay in force—which explained why the fate of the old Nixon-era ABM treaty resurfaced as a centerpiece of neocon foreign policy, twenty-five years after it was signed.

. . . .

A DEADLY ATTACK against U.S. interests occurred on August 7, 1998, but not from foreign missiles. Truck bombs destroyed U.S. embassies in Nairobi, Kenya, and Dar es Salaam, Tanzania. The Kenya blast killed 212 and injured more than four thousand, mostly local citizens but including among the dead twelve Americans; the Tanzania blast killed eleven and injured eighty-five, almost all Africans. The CIA quickly traced the attacks to al-Qaeda and Osama bin Laden, whose name then became widely known. Two weeks after the truck bombs, the United States executed retaliatory cruise missile strikes on al-Qaeda bases in Afghanistan and on a pharmaceutical plant in the Sudan believed to be manufacturing chemical weapons. In announcing these strikes, Clinton insisted that they had achieved their goals. But the strikes in Afghanistan missed bin Laden, and the strike in the Sudan raised outcries because many people said the plant had not been making chemicals for weapons, and the Clinton administration produced no proof that it was.

Clinton's ability to deal with such overseas crises was impeded by his need to fend off mounting calls for his impeachment. The distraction allowed Republicans to push foreign policy initiatives that in other circumstances Clinton might have squelched. In September, Congress used the language of the PNAC's January and May letters to fashion the "Iraq Liberation Act of 1998," declaring that "it should be the policy of the United States to seek to remove the Saddam Hussein regime from power in Iraq and to replace it with a democratic government." The bill, which was quickly passed by the House and Senate, was relatively toothless; it contained no provisions for militarily removing Saddam from power, just ways to encourage (and modestly fund) opposition to him. But signing it removed Iraq from the midterm election agenda, and Clinton did so.

Clinton concentrated on pursuing peace in the former Yugoslavia, particularly through the intense negotiations conducted by his envoy Richard Holbrooke, backed up by NATO's threat to renew air strikes if there was no settlement. An agreement to allow a peacekeeping force into Kosovo, completed in October 1998, brought peace to the region and removed another negative foreign policy item from the agenda of the 1998 elections.

Given the public outrage over Clinton's shoddy personal behavior, the other shortcomings of his administration, and the usual declines in public favor that accompany the sixth year of a presidency, Gingrich and the Republicans expected Congress to shift significantly toward their party in 1998. Those gains did not materialize, and Gingrich was forced to resign as Speaker. But Republicans insisted that nothing would stop them from impeaching the president and so began the process in December.

At that moment, Iraq was heating up again. Convinced that Clinton was distracted by the impeachment, and the NATO countries were similarly diverted by Kosovo, Saddam Hussein stopped the UN inspections entirely. In response, Clinton ordered four days of intensive bombing—he could not do more before the onset of the Muslim holy month of Ramadan—designed to degrade Iraq's capability of making WMDs. France, Russia, and China all continued to conduct significant business with Iraq. For several years these countries had argued in the UN to lift the sanctions. In reaction to the very damaging air strikes, France, Russia, and China petitioned the Security Council to lift the oil embargo and to fire the UN weapons inspectors.

On the last day of the Iraq bombing campaign, the House of Representatives passed the bill of impeachment against Clinton. A Senate trial on that bill then proceeded, even though there was little chance of a conviction, which required a two-thirds majority. The final votes, held on February 12, 1999, resulted in the predicted acquittal.

GEORGE W. BUSH, eldest son of the former president, had spent time in the family oil business and had been part owner of the Texas Rangers, a baseball team, before running for governor of Texas in 1994. He defeated the Democratic incumbent and four years later was reelected by a substantial majority. This brought him to national attention, and by December 1998, Republican power brokers had settled on him as their preferred presidential candidate for the year 2000.

Among his father's former intimates, George W. Bush preferred Dick Cheney, then CEO of Halliburton, a Texas-based company, to his father's closer friends Jim Baker and Brent Scowcroft. Cheney recognized that the governor needed an education on foreign affairs beyond Mexico; Condoleezza Rice, a former NSC Soviet expert, protégée of Scowcroft, and provost of Stanford University, was selected as the governor's tutor. Over the next year she brought Rumsfeld, Wolfowitz, Perle, and other neocons to the governor's mansion for seminars on foreign policy with an audience of one. All of these advisers agreed with the stances of the PNAC and of the Rumsfeld Commission on what the United States should be doing and what the Clinton administration should not.

In early 1999, the Holbrooke-brokered former Yugoslavia deal came apart, and Serbian forces moved to take complete control of Kosovo. Neocons flayed the "sham" deal and Clinton's inaction.

After his impeachment, however, Clinton grew more aggressive militarily. In March 1999, U.S. planes spearheaded a NATO assault consisting of a heavy bombing program against the Serbs that took out communications facilities and oil refineries as well as purely military targets. The UN protested; so did George W. Bush, but from the opposite end of the spectrum. Bush criticized Clinton for doing too little militarily in Kosovo, and for not planning how to get out of the country. "Victory," Bush told the press, "means exit strategy, and it's important for the president to explain to us what the exit strategy is." The governor did not want the U.S. military to stay in Kosovo too long as peacekeepers. Neither did former vice president Quayle, also vying for the 2000 nod, who called Kosovo a potential repeat of Vietnam: "Ambiguity, no stated, clear-cut mission, and then you are going to have to be there quite some time." "Clinton has never explained to the American people why he was involving the U.S. military in a civil war in a sovereign nation other than to say it was for humanitarian purposes," House Whip Tom DeLay charged. As the bombing continued, House Republicans defeated a resolution authorizing the campaign, and GOP members of the House Armed Services Committee voted against permitting the use of future defense funds for any NATO efforts in Kosovo. This attempt to use the congressional power of the purse to reverse a bombing campaign echoed the 1973 move to stay Nixon's hand. This time, however, it came from the Republicans.

By June 1999, after Serbian forces withdrew from Kosovo, all parties agreed to a peace plan and to a semipermanent NATO force to implement it. That force contained a high proportion of American troops, soon to be replaced by Europeans.

The neocons and the Republican Congress kept pushing Clinton on defense. He soon agreed to fund the first phase of the antimissile defense, $10 billion over six years. In October, the Senate rejected the Comprehensive Nuclear Test-Ban Treaty—the worst treaty defeat for a president since the Senate's refusal to accept the Treaty of Versailles in 1920. John Bolton, a former Bush administration assistant attorney general, foreign policy expert, and PNAC stalwart, welcomed the rejection. Fears that it would result in further proliferation or grave threats to international security, he wrote, were wrong:

> Contrary to this timid and neo-pacifist analysis, the Senate vote on the CTBT marks the beginning of a new realism on the issue of weapons of mass destruction [and] an unmistakable signal that America rejects the illusory protections of unenforceable treaties [that] may actually hobble our ability to maintain the most important international guarantee of peace—a credible U.S. nuclear capability.

In September 1999, Governor Bush gave his first foreign policy speech. He pledged to "renew the bond of trust between the American president and the American military," defend the U.S. against "missiles and terror," and create the "military of the twenty-first century."

As the election year began, Clinton was buffeted from the left for not moving quickly enough to prevent genocide in Rwanda and for waiting until too late to fix matters in Kosovo, and from the right for being too soft on Russia and China and too slow to use force in Iraq and Bosnia. But centrist Stephen M. Walt of Harvard offered "Two Cheers for Clinton's Foreign Policy" in *Foreign Affairs*, contending that Clinton had done reasonably well in tough circumstances—negotiating significant arms control agreements including one in which former Soviet satellites agreed to give up their nuclear arms; settlements of the Bosnian wars; peace settlements in Northern Ireland and the Middle East; and democracy in Haiti.

Neocons took issue with this benign assessment, arguing that Clinton had squandered the opportunities made available by the end of the Cold War. Michael Mandelbaum, a colleague of Wolfowitz's at the Nitze School of Advanced International Studies at Johns Hopkins, had advised Clinton during his campaign for the presidency but had not been given a post in the administration. After years of watching from the sidelines, Mandelbaum wrote in *Foreign Affairs*, he judged that "Clinton's foreign policy, rather than protecting American national interests, has pursued social work worldwide. Three failed interventions in 1993—in Bosnia, in Somalia, and the first try in Haiti—illustrate this dramatically. Preoccupied with 'helping the helpless,' the administration alienated vital allies, changed direction repeatedly to repair Clinton's sagging image, and let special interest groups harm U.S. policy toward Japan and Russia."

Neocons complained that Clinton's failure to resolve the situation in Iraq echoed his problems in other foreign arenas—all the product of a "profoundly misguided and potentially dangerous philosophy," according to John Bolton. Clinton made such wrong turns, neocons contended, because he lacked a moral context to steer his foreign policy decisions and determine U.S. reactions to fast-breaking events. This judgment echoed that of some Clinton champions and liberals. Robert E. Hunter had been Clinton's ambassador to NATO. While he was basically satisfied with Clinton's policies, he wrote in *Foreign Affairs*, Hunter nonetheless charged, "The measure of Clinton's tenure is less what he said and did than what he failed to say and do." Richard Haass, director of foreign policy at the Brookings Institution, worried that "Clinton may not leave a legacy in foreign affairs, but what he will leave is a void: no clear priorities, no consistency or thoroughness in the implementation of strategies, and no true commitment to building a domestic consensus in support of internationalism." "A fairer critique . . . might focus less on a lack of vision and more on a lack of attention," *Foreign Policy* magazine wrote, arguing that Clinton had basically continued George H. W. Bush's notion of a new world order, with strengthened Western democracies at its core. "As it did for Bush," the magazine editorialized, Clinton's "grand vision largely fell flat."

In foreign affairs, Clinton had been the ultimate pragmatist, exceeding Nixon in that direction. While Nixon was a realist, he had fashioned his policies from an underlying conviction that, in the future, the superpowers must cooperate rather than endlessly confront one another; Clinton appeared to have had no goal in mind for foreign affairs other than the maintenance of his own popularity.

In March 2000, the neocons, always on the lookout for instances of Clinton's alleged lack of moral grounding in foreign policy, found one when the president scheduled a stop in Pakistan during a trip to the Indian subcontinent. Clinton's agenda in Pakistan was twofold: He saw his stop there as a first step toward relieving tensions between India and Pakistan, and as a balance for his prior stop in India so that he would not be accused of favoring either nation. But neocons objected that for the American president to stop in Pakistan would certify as the country's leader Musharraf, a dictator who overthrew a democratically elected leader, dallied with terrorists, refused to give up his nuclear program, and allowed religious differences to create political tensions with India. And as the neocons predicted, during Clinton's brief visit, Musharraf refused to budge on any important issues.

BY THE TURN of the century, Clinton's pragmatic, reactive approach to foreign policy had run its course. Those who wished the United States would embrace a proactive foreign policy, informed by declared moral and philosophic principles, awaited the arrival of a new president—one whose main education in foreign affairs had come from his neocon tutors.

27

From Candidate to Bush 43

In theory, the new president, George W. Bush, aspired to be more like Reagan than like his own father. In practice, he was both bellicose and malleable, a combination that allowed the neocons to pursue a foreign policy based on Fritz Kraemer's defining concept, that military strength was the best way to prevent "provocative weakness."

Throughout Bush's campaign for the presidency, he had laid out the neocon program, so it should have been no surprise to the electorate when he began to implement it the moment he took office. The neocons' ability to put their tenets into practice did not reach full bloom, however, until nine months later, when the administration was faced with the task of responding to the terrorist attacks of September 11, 2001.

IN MARCH 2000, George W. Bush defeated his main challenger, Senator John McCain, in several primaries. Assured of the nomination, he asked Dick Cheney to lead the search committee for his running mate. To join him on the committee Cheney chose his daughter Liz and his protégé David Addington. One sympathetic biographer says that Cheney was reluctant to accept the position himself; other biographers assert that by this time Cheney had taken Bush's measure, found him easy to manipulate, and arranged matters so that Bush would naturally choose him for VP. Since the Twelfth Amendment forbids electors from voting for a president and a vice president from the same state, Cheney, who had become a Texan, moved his official residence back to Wyoming.

In choosing Cheney, Bush sealed the ideological, conservative direction of his administration's foreign policy. None of his other potential running mates, most of them governors, were as avidly neoconservative as Cheney, especially with regard to Iraq.

In Cheney's speeches on Iraq he employed the language the neocons had been using for the past nine years. He accused the Clinton administration of letting Hussein "slip off the hook" by avoiding weapons inspections, asserting that while there had been "a very robust inspection" program, Saddam had "kicked out all the inspectors and this Administration appears to be helpless to do anything about it."

At one point, early in the campaign, Bush was asked what he would do about Saddam Hussein and his weapons of mass destruction. Though normally guarded about such matters, this time he replied, "I'd take 'em out, take out the weapons of mass destruction. I'm surprised he's still there." But he then dialed down his belligerence as the race tightened. Cheney also took a softer line, telling a television interviewer that "we want to maintain our current posture vis-à-vis Iraq," and that the United States should not act as though "we were an imperialist power, willy-nilly moving into capitals in that part of the world, taking down governments." As events would later reveal, this was the opposite of what Cheney, Bush, and associates actually had in mind.

Had it been publicly known before the election that George W. Bush and Dick Cheney would go looking for an excuse to remove Saddam once in office, they might not have enticed onto their team the one prominent Republican who had not yet endorsed Bush by the spring of 2000: Colin Powell. The immensely popular former chairman of the Joint Chiefs, a hero of the 1991 Gulf War, had declined to run for president himself only out of concerns over his safety and that of his family. Bush, painted by rivals as inexperienced and somewhat of a radical, needed Powell to ensure his mainstream appeal. After meeting with Bush and Cheney in Texas, Powell agreed to become Bush's secretary of state and to endorse him at the Republican National Convention.

As the presidential campaign season wore on, a revolution of sorts was brewing inside the Defense bureaucracy. Leading it was Andy Marshall, who by now had been at the Pentagon with his Office of Net Assessment for almost a quarter century. A small, gnomic man who (unlike Kraemer) had fought to retain his post after the retirement age of seventy, Marshall's penchant for oracular pronouncements won him the nickname "Yoda," after a *Star Wars* character. Marshall was a longtime champion of new weapons systems, even during the Carter and Clinton administrations, when he touted new technology as less costly than older, large systems.

As the new century dawned, Marshall revived what he called the "revolution in military affairs," or RMA. The idea dated back decades, but Marshall had soft-pedaled it until the demise of the Soviet Union. In a post–Cold War environment, he now argued, high-tech weaponry and smaller but quicker forces transported by efficient delivery systems would be required in the local-scale military engagements of the future. These forces in turn would require significant alterations in military infrastructure and management to produce "effectiveness, efficiency, and flexibility."

Believing that President Clinton had only cautiously adopted the principles of RMA as they looked forward to 2000, the PNAC, the Republican Party, and candidate Bush embraced RMA—and the higher defense budgets that would be needed to achieve it—as a key distinction between their position and that of Democratic candidate Al Gore. Though a Vietnam veteran, Gore was more concerned with fighting nonmilitary enemies—the scourge of AIDS, global warming, and other environmental assaults—and Bush slammed such soft agenda items as the ultimate in social work. But Bush left himself vulnerable to counterattack through narrow-minded proclamations, declaring that "We should not send our troops to stop ethnic cleansing and genocide in nations outside our strategic interest." Bush speculated that future problems for the United States would come from China and Russia; the GOP platform charged that Clinton had "kowtowed" to Beijing and had ignored corruption in Russia and its massacres in the breakaway republic of Chechnya.

That Republican Party platform plank on foreign affairs, more than ten thousand words long—three times the size of the 1996 plank—repeated, verbatim at times, points drawn from the PNAC's reports: the need to expand defense budgets significantly, to challenge "regimes hostile to our interests and values," to defend Taiwan, to get rid of Saddam Hussein in Iraq, to support Israel, to take action in Bosnia, and to support Serbian opposition to Milosevic. The platform was highly specific about what a Bush administration would do and when—for instance in regard to the 1972 ABM treaty:

> We will seek a negotiated change in the Anti-Ballistic Missile (ABM) Treaty that will allow the United States to use all technologies and experiments required to deploy robust missile defenses. . . . If Russia refuses to make the necessary changes, a Republican president will give prompt notice that the United States will exercise the right guaranteed to us in the treaty to withdraw after six months. The president has a solemn obligation to protect the American people and our allies, not to protect arms control agreements signed almost 30 years ago.

The only item missing from the GOP's foreign policy plank was one that would be the highlight of the next PNAC report: a warning that the United States might not wake up to the dangers it was facing in the world "absent some catastrophic and catalyzing event—a new Pearl Harbor." Some critics suggested that the PNAC seemed to welcome the prospect of such a "new Pearl Harbor," if it offered an excuse to ramp up the military budget and the nation's defenses.

During the campaign, Bush said he would assist Taiwan militarily if it were attacked by China. In doing so, he not only went beyond his own party's platform but also overturned a deliberately ambiguous policy that every president since Nixon had followed. He further asserted that Africa was of no strategic interest to the United States, a contention many people found unsympathetic and possibly racist—especially when Bush rejected a U.S. plan to spend $300 million to prevent and treat AIDS in Africa. Asked during a debate whether he would have sent troops to Somalia, Bush said he would have withdrawn troops from Somalia rather than have them participate in "nation building," an exercise he deplored there and in the former Yugoslavia. Bush wanted American troops out of Kosovo entirely.

Bush's most memorable statement on foreign policy came in his televised debate with Gore on the subject. "If we're an arrogant nation," he predicted, foreign countries would "resent us; if we're a humble nation, but strong, they'll welcome us. And our nation stands alone right now in the world in terms of power, and that's why we've got to be humble, and yet project strength in a way that promotes freedom." He was equally adamant that the United States must not act as the world's policeman, stating, "I just don't think it's the role of the United States to walk into a country and say, 'we do it this way, so should you.'" Bush's foreign policy team explained that Bush's remarks were aimed at the Clinton administration's economic imperialism and arrogance; they chastised Secretary of State Madeleine Albright for labeling the United States "the indispensable nation," and Secretary of the Treasury Robert Rubin for lecturing the Japanese, in Tokyo, on how to run their economy.

Near Election Day, a poll showed that 54 percent of the electorate considered foreign policy a major issue, second in importance only to taxes. Bush had laid out his foreign policy in a fairly complete way, making definitive statements on all hot-button issues; whether or not the electorate liked his agenda, if the people chose Bush they would know what sort of foreign policy to expect.

Gore won the popular vote, but the outcome in the Electoral College was delayed and disputed by challenges to the counting of Florida's ballots. The Supreme Court eventually decided the election, with five Republican-appointed justices voting, in effect, to seat the Republican candidate as the nation's forty-third president. The election did diminish the Republican majority in the House, however, and when Senator Jim Jeffords of Vermont changed his affiliation from Republican to Independent and caucused with the Democrats, Democrats took control of the Senate.

"AS A MEASURE of Cheney's influence, the Cabinet was revealing," Cheney biographer Stephen F. Hayes has noted, citing the selection of Rums-feld, Powell, and treasury secretary Paul O'Neill, who had worked with Cheney during the Ford years. According to Hayes, Cheney worked closely with Bush on his Cabinet choices and oversaw the vetting pro-cess. Of the Cabinet choices, the most surprising was that of Rumsfeld, one of the few people Bush's father considered a rival. Many viewed the selection of Rumsfeld as the new president's attempt to reject his father's counsel.

"History shows that weakness is provocative," Rumsfeld said at his confirmation hearings. "Weakness invites people into doing things they would not otherwise think of. What we have to do is to better understand what will deter and what will defend against this new range of threats."

More than a dozen other PNAC members joined the administration in various slots at State, DoD, and in the vice president's office, which was expanded. John Bolton became undersecretary of state for arms control, a position that drew comment because Bolton was known to look askance at the very idea of arms control agreements. Paul Wolfowitz became the assistant secretary of defense. Passed over for secretary of defense, Perle declined the number-three slot, undersecretary of defense for policy, and became chairman of the defense advisory board. Douglas Feith took the policy slot and Sven Kraemer became a consultant to the department.

In one of his earliest decisions, Rumsfeld placed Andy Marshall, now seventy-nine, in charge of making a blueprint for the future, under a dead-line just weeks away. Marshall was expected to recommend budget cuts on conventional arms, thereby paving the way for greatly enhanced missile defense spending, which Rumsfeld (and the PNAC) wanted. Marshall's report was also expected to provide a rationale for countering the objec-tions to Rumsfeld's plans from those already known to oppose them—in-cluding General Eric Shinseki, the army's chief of staff and the former commander of the NATO troops in Bosnia, a firm believer in the absolute value of "boots on the ground."

. . . .

ON JANUARY 25, 2001, Richard Clarke, the counterterrorism chief of the NSC (and a Clinton administration holdover), petitioned Bush's new national security adviser, Condoleezza Rice: "We *urgently* need . . . a Principals level review on the al Qida network." Clarke wanted the administration to address several decisions that the Clinton White House had deliberately left to its successor: (1) how to aid an anti-Taliban force in Afghanistan, (2) how to aid a similar antiterrorist force in Uzbekistan, (3) "what the new Administration says to the Taliban and Pakistan about the importance we attach to ending the al Qaida sanctuary in Afghanistan," (4) whether to raise the CIA's antiterrorism budget, and (5) how to respond to the latest bombing, of the USS *Cole* in a Yemen harbor on October 12, 2000.

Rice later contended that the administration took all these points under consideration, and placed additional emphasis on countering terrorism by devoting more resources to it—but not a great deal more. Bush had announced that Rice would chair "principals" meetings that included the vice president and the secretaries of state and defense, Powell and Rumsfeld. Powell was shortly told that to see the president he would have to apply through Rice; at one Cabinet meeting, when Powell arrived late, Bush had the door closed and locked, ostensibly to tease him but surely also to teach Powell a lesson about his status. Before long, Cheney was undermining Rice's chairmanship of the principals meetings.

Most foreign leaders who met personally with Bush came away unimpressed. But British prime minister Tony Blair found the president quite well informed, and after a stay at Camp David called other European heads of state to say so. A French commentator expected out of the new Bush administration "more arrogance and more unilateralism," rather than the humility Bush had advocated during his debate with Gore. A Canadian analyst told the *New York Times*, "On the one hand, there's a disengagement from most of the issues and most of the international frameworks; on the other hand, a willingness to say to the Russians: 'You don't like it? That's too bad.' That's not a comforting view for close neighbors and friends."

Nor was it comforting for Democrats in Congress. Previous presidents who were elected by narrow margins and faced with a divided Congress had tried to govern from the center, seeking consensus for their actions. The Bush administration pushed a radical conservative agenda. For instance, though the American economy was on a downturn after the longest sustained expansion in history, the administration's plan to counter the downward trend featured a tax cut whose benefit would be reaped disproportionately by the very wealthiest Americans.

At an early NSC meeting, treasury secretary O'Neill was shocked to hear the administration making plans for invading Iraq. "It was about what we can do to change this regime," O'Neill later told journalist Ron Suskind. "The notion of pre-emption, that the U.S. has the unilateral right to do whatever we decide to do," horrified O'Neill, as did the fact that no one asked "Why Saddam? And why now?" Rather, according to O'Neill, Rumsfeld said, on January 30, 2001, "Imagine what the region would look like without Saddam and with a regime that's aligned with U.S. interests. It would change everything in the region and beyond. It would demonstrate what U.S. policy is all about." They discussed an occupation of Iraq, specific plans for a peacekeeping force, war crimes tribunals, and how Iraq's oil wealth would be divided. One March 5, 2006, Defense Intelligence Agency document obtained by Suskind was titled "Foreign Suitors for Iraq Oilfield Contracts."

By then the escalation against Iraq had already begun. In reaction to increased Iraqi firing at coalition fly-overs, on February 16 American and British planes targeted anti-aircraft radar sites at two dozen locations near Baghdad—the first time since 1998 that U.S. planes had struck targets outside the no-fly zones, despite many attacks on U.S. planes in the interim. In his memoir *War and Decision*, Douglas Feith explained:

> Saddam's attempts to shoot down U.S. and British patrol aircraft were a clever type of aggression. . . . They allowed Saddam to embarrass his enemies, impress Iraqis and the world with his defiance, and poke another hole in the tissue of measures that were supposed to keep him contained. Neither Britain nor the United States reacted strongly [and] another element of the containment strategy had been compromised.

In their most significant departure from Clinton administration practice, Rumsfeld, Cheney, and Bush signaled that the United States would abrogate the 1972 ABM treaty and would urge Russia to renounce it as well. The Constitution did give the president the right to abrogate a treaty, the White House pointed out to reporters. In Moscow, Rumsfeld told the Russians, "We need to get over . . . the whole network of treaties" on arms control, which he described as outdated. Despite such tough talk, the Russians declined to abandon the treaty and campaigned to have other nations support it and reject the U.S.'s proposed missile shield program. The abrogation date was put off, and John Bolton was dispatched to negotiate with the Russians about modifications.

Bush also made good on his campaign pledge to opt out of the Kyoto Protocol, the 1997 environmental pact signed by dozens of countries that was to go into effect in 2005; among the Western industrial nations, only the United States and Australia refused to sign it. Clinton had wanted to sign but did not, believing he lacked the sixty Senate votes necessary to ratify it. Bush now firmly refused to sign. Bush dismissed the notion of global warming, a key target of the protocol, as an unproven theory that required years of further study (a contention that had also appeared in the Republican platform in 2000).

Rejecting diplomacy far more completely than Kraemer ever had, the new president also indicated his intent to withdraw from or ignore a whole series of treaties, including one Clinton had signed just before leaving office that accepted International Criminal Court jurisdiction in war crimes. At the UN, the United States withdrew from a draft treaty on ways to enforce a biological weapons convention signed in 1995 and delayed a pact designed to stanch the illegal flow of handguns and shoulder-fired rockets until it excluded weapons sold to rebels by private firms. Bush also withdrew the United States from a treaty banning land mines, refused to resubmit the Comprehensive Nuclear Test-Ban Treaty to the Senate, and refused to ratify changes to START II.

"John Bolton, Doug Feith, Richard Perle, and Paul Wolfowitz . . . played important roles in defeating these agreements," former Reagan foreign policy officials Halper and Clarke wrote, asserting that "the neo-conservatives had significant influence in establishing the direction and priorities of U.S. foreign relations from the early months of the new Administration."

The Bush administration's decision to walk away from these treaties underscored a "unilateralist image" that would later be linked with the administration's many attempts to claim powers for the executive branch that were constitutionally shared with the legislative branch. Bush's position on executive prerogative with regard to treaties and foreign policy echoed that of the Cheney Minority Report on Iran-Contra, as well as the arguments of the Federalist Society.

The administration also ceased working on two other Clinton diplomatic initiatives: the Israeli-Palestinian peace process and talks intended to persuade North Korea to stop its nuclear bomb development. The only foreign affairs campaign promise Bush reversed was his threat to withdraw all U.S. ground troops from the Balkans. Rumsfeld favored the notion, but Powell convinced Bush that a withdrawal from Bosnia would unduly upset the NATO alliance when there was no urgent need to use the military resources elsewhere. But Bush declared that U.S. troops should not remain in the Balkans indefinitely, and Congress supported him.

Despite the absence of imminent, known threats to the country's security, in February 2001 the administration asked the largest telephone companies to give the National Security Agency access to records of Americans'

Internet connections and telephone calls. Later the administration would say that the phone companies' cooperation with NSA had begun only after September 11, 2001. But one ATT Solutions logbook cited in a trial confirmed that the interception program, dubbed "Pioneer-Groundbreaker," began on February 1. It was one of several programs the administration implemented to increase the volume and quality of its intelligence information. Since the 1960s, conservatives had been decrying the inadequacy of CIA information and estimates, and the critics' plaints in this regard had been ratified during the Clinton administration when the CIA failed to predict such things as the Indian underground nuclear test and North Korea's ICBM test firing. Bush did retain Clinton's CIA director, George Tenet; his FBI director, Robert Mueller; and his NSA director, General Michael Hayden; they made recommendations for stepping up intelligence-gathering and intelligence-analysis capacities, and he supported them.

Though they were little noticed at the time, the Bush White House also began appending "signing statements" to acts passed by Congress that the president signed into law. These statements often blunted or negated the intent of the legislation by reserving to the president the right not to enforce provisions with which he disagreed.

The signing statements often had as their philosophic basis the "unitary executive theory," the seeds for which had been sown by Cheney, Rumsfeld, and Antonin Scalia in the Nixon presidential papers case. Scalia, now on the Supreme Court, established precedent in his 1988 dissent in *Morrison v. Olson* questioning the legitimacy of the independent counsel statute and that counsel's right to extract documents from executive agencies. Such matters, Scalia argued, constituted a legislative infringement on the president's ability to carry out his duties.

THE GEORGE W. Bush administration's first foreign affairs crisis began on April 1, 2001, when a Chinese fighter jet clipped an American EP-3 Aries II reconnaissance aircraft over international waters near China; crippled by the impact, the American plane had to make an emergency landing on China's Hainan Island with its crew of twenty-four. The Chinese plane then crashed in the sea, and its pilot was not found. The U.S. ambassador to China warned the Chinese not to board the aircraft, whose equipment was described as among the most technologically advanced in the world. The Chinese accused the U.S. flyers of bumping the jet deliberately.

The incident recalled the moment in 1969 when North Korea downed an American aircraft, challenging the new Nixon administration. The Bush administration, having embraced a foreign policy very much at odds with

Nixon's, had repeatedly vowed not to let such provocations pass without appropriate military reaction. Nixon had thought the North Korean shootdown might be a deliberate test of his resolve; Bush could have no doubt that the 2001 incident was China's response to his administration's signals that it would sell advanced missile-detection radar and torpedo boats to Taiwan—an act that constituted a return to a pro-Taiwan policy, whether China liked it or not.

The Chinese held the American airmen on Hainan while the United States negotiated for their release. China demanded that the United States offer a written apology for the incident, which U.S. spokespeople called an accident. The Bush administration offered a statement expressing its "regrets," along with a letter of condolence to the widow of the lost pilot, and a number of mild threats. On the eleventh day after the incident, Bush's official letter to China was delivered, twice assuring the pilot's widow, and thus the Chinese government, that the United States was "very sorry" that the pilot had been killed. The Chinese released the crew and made arrangements for the plane to be retrieved, though they would not allow the plane to be repaired and flown back; rather, they insisted on having it disassembled on Hainan by its manufacturer, then brought back to the United States in the hold of a Russian cargo plane.

In the wake of this crisis, according to Powell's associate Colonel Lawrence B. Wilkerson, the neocons and their allies—Rumsfeld, Wolfowitz, Feith, Cambone (the new intelligence chief at DoD), and Bolton—"dispatch[ed] a person to Taiwan every week, essentially to tell the Taiwanese that the alliance [between the United States and Taiwan] was back on [and] that independence was a good thing." Then Powell would send his own envoy to "disabuse the entire Taiwanese national security apparatus of what they'd been told by the Defense Department." This went on, according to Wilkerson, until the president himself squelched Rumsfeld's attempt at overturning U.S. policy toward China.

Fritz Kraemer had been generally optimistic about the new Bush administration; he admired Rumsfeld and Wolfowitz, who shared—among other things—his deep distrust of official intelligence analyses. But at a luncheon after the resolution of the Hainan Island incident, Kraemer lamented the administration's handling of the episode: "When our president wrote to the widow of the Chinese pilot . . . saying 'we regret,' then 'we're sorry,' then 'we're very sorry,' the Chinese at that point said, 'All right, we've frightened them sufficiently. Now they'll think twice before helping Taiwan.'" It would have been far better to tell the Chinese we were definitely selling the radars and torpedo boats to Taiwan regardless of the EP-3 incident, he argued. Anything less would suggest that the incident had deterred the United States from its proper course.

Kristol and Kagan called the incident "a national humiliation." Another critic in the *Weekly Standard* added that Bush's response to the Chinese reflected a dangerous lack of "appropriate and palpable persistence, intensity, and determination at the highest levels of our government." Kristol and Kagan also chastised Bush for not increasing the defense budget, warning that he "may go down in history as the man who let American military power atrophy and America's post–Cold War prominence slip away."

On July 12, Wolfowitz testified to a Senate committee about the need for more missile defenses. Ten years after the Scud attacks on Israel, he said that "our capacity to shoot down a Scud missile is not much improved from 1991," and that we were "a year or two away" from deploying a countermeasure to such rockets. He noted that North Korea, Iran, Syria, and Libya either had long-range missiles or were developing them, and that these could carry nuclear, chemical, or biological payloads. In another speech around this time, Wolfowitz warned that "bad news" was flowing continually from Iraq, and that "there will be no peace in the region and no safety for our friends there—Arabs or Israelis, Kurds or Turkamen—as long as [Saddam Hussein] remains in power."

Through the spring and summer of 2001, news reports circulated of dissent within the administration on how to deal with Iraq. Douglas Feith would later assert that the pressure to do more on Iraq came from Wolfowitz and Cheney's chief of staff, Scooter Libby, and that State Department and CIA officials opposed it. "We were also concerned for the safety of our no-fly zone patrols, and for the Security Council's ability to enforce its containment measures," Feith writes, adding, "Unless we found ways to constrain him and undermine his regime . . . Saddam would become more threatening and influential in the coming years in his region and beyond. And as that happened, America would become less able to win cooperation from countries known to be subject, through intimidation or bribery, to Saddam's influence." According to Feith, Wolfowitz wanted the United States to recognize an alternative government for Iraq, and to support a semiautonomous Kurdish state and another separate entity near the Kuwait border. Rumsfeld was more cautious, but sent a memo advocating changing the current strategy on protecting the no-fly zone "from tit-for-tat responses to attacks on strategic targets that weaken Saddam's rule."

Most of the European countries that had joined the U.S.-led coalition in 1991 had little enthusiasm for doing more to counter the Iraqi regime a decade later. Rather, they moved toward lifting sanctions on Iraq and scrapping an odious and notoriously corrupt oil-for-food program that was eating up tens of millions of UN dollars while producing a public relations disaster that broadcast images of Iraqi misery and malnutrition around the world. Yet by the end of the summer of 2001, Feith asserts, "it was not clear that we had an effective alternative" to war with Saddam Hussein.

For three decades, since its beginnings as an insurgency in the Nixon White House, the neoconservatives had acted primarily as an opposition lobby, usually expressing their policy ideas as reactions to those of the current administration. Under Ronald Reagan, the neocons began generating more active ideas—especially as they joined Reagan's campaign to defeat the Soviet Union and spread democracy around the world—but they were brushed back by Reagan's pragmatic turn in his second term. Sidelined through most of the George H. W. Bush and Clinton years, they began to raise their collective voice by advocating positive action in Bosnia and, increasingly, in regard to Iraq.

In 1993, after the fall of the Soviet Union, Irving Kristol had pronounced the neocon movement dead. His pronouncement was entirely wrong. The George W. Bush administration gave neoconservatism a golden opportunity to pursue the full panoply of its active, militaristic, morality-based approach to American foreign policy. In the opening months of 2001, those actions began with brush clearing—removing what they saw as the detritus of the Clinton years' treaty-making mistakes. As the administration's first year continued, the neocons' plans for more significant action in Iraq, on missile defense, and on solidifying relations with the former Soviet satellites—who were now applying to join NATO—gathered speed, though they were hampered by Bush's slipping approval ratings. The threat of future terrorist attacks loomed somewhere in the middle distance. Actively combating terrorism was not high on the neocon agenda. One day in June 2001, terrorism advisor Clarke and CIA director Tenet both submitted reports to Rice on the same subject: a warning that incoming evidence of a forthcoming al-Qaeda attack had, as Clarke put it, "reached a crescendo." Clarke continued: "A series of new reports convinces me and analysts at State, CIA, DIA, and NSA that a major terrorist attack or series of attacks is likely in July." One report from an al-Qaeda source warned that something "very, very, very, very" big was about to happen, and that most of bin Laden's network was anticipating the attack. There was no such attack in July, but in early August the president's daily brief included a memo titled "Bin Laden Determined to Strike in the U.S."

Much of the information in that memo, the Bush administration later insisted, was historical, dealing with the ways al-Qaeda had been attempting to infiltrate the United States. Rice later called it "An explosive title on a non-explosive piece." But the details of the brief, and its accompanying documentation, buttressed the alarming reports Tenet and Clarke had received, and conveyed that the FBI had seventy open investigations into suspected al-Qaeda activities in the United States. The reports also warned about potential hijackings, and of the possibility that the terrorists might turn hijacked planes into flying suicide bombs, though these were described as likely to be aimed at U.S. embassies abroad.

In August, both Cheney and Bush took extended vacations, the president in Texas and the vice president in Wyoming. Their absence from Washington conveyed a sense that the government was not particularly concerned about an imminent attack.

On September 7, *New York Times* columnist Thomas Friedman gave Bush failing marks for "radical conservative policies on taxes and missile defense," and concluded that the Bush administration had the same "missionary zeal" as the Reaganites had—but without a context for their radicalism, and with no "Evil Empire" to combat.

ON SEPTEMBER 11, 2001, terrorists hijacked three planes loaded with fuel and captive passengers and flew them as suicide bombs into the World Trade Center towers in New York and the Pentagon near Washington, resulting in the loss of more than three thousand lives. A fourth hijacked plane, supposedly destined for the U.S. Capitol building, crash-landed in Pennsylvania after passengers rose up. The most devastating attacks on American soil since Pearl Harbor, they radically changed the direction of the United States of America and the future actions of the George W. Bush administration.

28

The Neocon Hour of Triumph

The fundamental and continual clash between ideology and pragmatism is a basic theme of human history. At certain times, however, it becomes possible to take actions that have both an ideological and a pragmatic basis. The September 11, 2001, attacks on the World Trace Center towers and the Pentagon provided such an occasion.

President Bush and his advisers construed those attacks, in the light of their neocon ideology, as the "new Pearl Harbor" the PNAC had predicted would be necessary to awaken the sleeping giant to the need to act aggressively in the world. So as they fashioned the response of the United States and its allies to the al-Qaeda terrorists who had planned and executed the attacks, they also conceived a new main enemy for America and the world, and the rationale for what President Bush called "a global war on terrorism."

As the victim of the vicious September 11 attacks, the United States had tremendous moral authority to undertake this mission, and utilized it as the Bush administration set out on its first action, to demolish the terrorists' base in Afghanistan, where Osama bin Laden was believed to be in hiding. But the administration's second action—which was under discussion within hours of the attacks—was not integrally connected to the attacks. Rather, it derived from a purely ideological objective that the neocons had been nurturing for a decade: an attempt to topple Saddam Hussein and turn Iraq into a democracy and an ally in the Middle East.

. . . .

PEOPLE FROM DOZENS of countries died in the attacks on the World Trade Center and the Pentagon. Sympathy and offers of assistance in pursuing the perpetrators poured into the United States from abroad; anti-Americanism receded as many nations and their people recognized the attacks as assaults on civilization, not just on America. NATO passed a resolution stating that the September 11 attack was an attack on all its member states. After investigators identified the suicide bombers as members of al-Qaeda, even longtime U.S. enemies such as Iran expressed a willingness to help find and punish the terrorists. The Bush administration pressured Pakistan's leader, Pervez Musharraf, to stop shoring up the Taliban in Afghanistan with military supplies, troop advisers, and money; Musharraf agreed and was promised new billions of dollars in support.

President Bush took mostly appropriate and uplifting public actions in the immediate aftermath of a very difficult time. In his widely lauded address to Congress on September 20, he gave an ultimatum to the Taliban: Turn over bin Laden and all terrorists and their supporters or face an American-led retaliatory invasion. When the Taliban refused, other Muslim countries withdrew recognition of the Afghan government. On October 7, American and British forces began a bombardment of Kabul and of suspected al-Qaeda strongholds. Ground forces soon followed, under a NATO banner.

The United States put other countries on notice that in this fight against terrorism there could be no neutrality: Either they were with us or we would consider them against us. This strong "us versus them" statement departed from recent policy. It harked back to the 1950s, when Secretary of State John Foster Dulles construed the world in Manichaean terms as aligned with either the United States and the Western democracies, or the USSR and Communist China. In 2001, Bush touted retaliation in Afghanistan as the opening action of a "global war on terror" in which the civilized nations would take military, economic, and social actions aimed at eliminating al-Qaeda and other international terrorist groups.

American governmental resources were redirected toward that war and away from less urgent concerns. But the president stopped far short of putting the United States on a war footing, which would have entailed restarting the draft, rationing resources, and other drastic measures. To do so, he argued, would only encourage the terrorists, whose fondest wish was to destroy the American way of life. In this national emergency, he urged Americans to continue shopping, to drive cars running on imported oil, and in other ways to maintain the health of the consumer-goods-based economy. Security was to be tightened, not belts.

Behind the scenes, within hours of the attacks, the hard-liners of Bush's inner circle started planning to put their standing neocon goals into practice. After the initial chaos, Richard Clarke recalled, he had expected to attend

> a round of meetings examining what the next attacks could be, what our vulnerabilities were, what we could do about them in the short term. Instead, I walked into a series of discussions about Iraq. . . . I realized with almost a sharp physical pain that Rumsfeld and Wolfowitz were going to try to take advantage of this national tragedy to promote their agenda about Iraq. . . . On September 12th, I left the video conferencing center and there, wandering alone around the situation room, was the president. He . . . grabbed a few of us and closed the door to the conference room. "Look," he told us, "I know you have a lot to do and all, but I want you, as soon as you can, to go back over everything, everything. See if Saddam did this. See if he's linked in any way."

Clarke insisted to Bush that the attacks were the work of al-Qaeda, but Bush persisted. "I know, I know, but see if Saddam was involved," Clarke recalls him saying.

On September 13, Paul Wolfowitz told the press corps assembled at the Pentagon that pursuit of the terrorists should go beyond Afghanistan, becoming a "broad and sustained campaign" that would include "removing" and "ending states." On September 15, at Camp David, Wolfowitz advocated going after Iraq.

By a week after the September 11 attacks, the Defense Policy Board, led by Richard Perle and including Woolsey, Kissinger, Schlesinger, Ken Adelman, and Harold Brown, trumpeted in the media the idea of a war against Iraq. The many neocon reports of the last ten years—the Wolfowitz DPG of 1992, the Cheney report of 1993, the PNAC statements and reports from 1997 through 2000—were all drawn upon to rationalize the need for taking out the Iraqi regime. The military was asked to make detailed plans to remove Saddam and install a friendly, protodemocratic government.

Why the road to "winning" the global war on terror must first lead through Iraq was unclear to the general public. Iran, Syria, Libya, Afghanistan, Somalia, and Sudan all harbored and financially backed terrorists. Pakistan's Abdul Qadeer Khan gave nuclear secrets to Iran, Libya, and North Korea. North Korea and China exported other weapons to Middle East Muslim countries. Iraq, by contrast, claimed to have rid itself of WMDs, a claim for the most part supported by the findings of Western intelligence organizations and the UN inspectors before the inspectors were kicked out in 1998. There was little if any evidence of links between the September 11 attacks and Iraq. Saddam Hussein and Osama bin Laden were not natural allies: The Iraqi dictator's regime was secular while bin Laden's stated aim was to overthrow all secular governments in Islamic countries such as Iraq and establish theocratic ones. Even Israel's chief of military intelligence saw no "direct link between Iraq and the hijackings and terror attacks on the United States." None of the nineteen hijackers had been Iraqis; most were Saudis.

But getting rid of Saddam Hussein had been a stated neocon objective for a decade, since the moment when Bush's father had refused to pursue Hussein to Baghdad. Now, under the banner of fighting terrorism and "radical Islam," fulfilling that goal would be possible.

HAVING DECIDED IN theory to go to war against Iraq, Cheney, Rumsfeld, Wolfowitz, and those who agreed with them now devoted their considerable energies to justifying the prospective invasion. The administration had clear objectives: toppling an awful dictator who threatened his own people and his neighbors, and replacing him with a democratic government. Though reasonable, these objectives might not be enough to convince the American public to support a preemptive war. For that, a more significant threat had to be invoked: Saddam's alleged possession and intent to augment a store of weapons of mass destruction, particularly nuclear weapons.

When Cheney received reports from the CIA and other intelligence agencies that Iraq had neither a firm connection to the September 11 attacks nor a verified stockpile of WMDs—and thus could not be considered an immediate threat to the United States—he and Rumsfeld set up a small intelligence analysis operation in the Pentagon under Doug Feith and reporting to Wolfowitz, which Feith christened the Policy Counter Terrorism Evaluation Group (PCTEG). A PCTEG report on the connections between Iraq and al-Qaeda was given to CIA director Tenet in August 2002. Cheney used it as a major source of information. It reported "cooperation in all categories" between Iraq and al-Qaeda, a "mature, symbiotic relationship" that included "some indications of possible Iraq coordination with Al Qaeda related to 9/11."

Tenet later testified that he questioned the PCTEG report's reliability, and Daniel Benjamin, a former counterterrorism director at the NSC under Clinton, wrote that rather than proving extensive ties between Saddam Hussein and Osama bin Laden, "the document lends substance to the frequently voiced criticism that some in the Bush administration have misused intelligence to advance their policy goals."

An investigation later concluded that certain items of intelligence had been selected and highlighted both by Feith's group and by the vice president's office—specifically, that they overemphasized connections between Saddam and al-Qaeda and information about supposed Iraqi WMDs to boost the case for war. Feith contends that his group did not "cherry-pick" the intelligence, as critics charged. Rather, he writes, he and Rumsfeld were scrupulous about forwarding both positive and negative facts and analyses to other agencies and to the White House, and that they would have failed had they "tried to keep the President in the dark about relevant facts and analyses. Our approach . . . was precisely the reverse of cherry-picking."

Secretary of State Powell continued to argue that an invasion of Iraq was not the best way to pursue the terrorists, which was still the public's priority. Powell's objections pushed back the hard-liners' timetable; before going to war against Iraq, the United States would have to exhaust less belligerent options against Iraq—economic sanctions, international pressure, UN inspections. The most propitious moment to invade Iraq was after Ramadan in the spring; that would not be possible in 2002, but the U.S. military could be prepared by the spring of 2003.

Meanwhile, the inner circle acted on several other long-held neocon tenets. In light of the September 11 attacks, the administration now argued, the United States must protect itself against the missiles of a rogue state by building an antimissile shield, and must not be hampered in doing so by the 1972 ABM treaty. The United States gave notice that it would unilaterally abrogate the treaty. Less publicly, Bush partially fulfilled a campaign promise to withdraw most American troops from their "nation-building" mission in the Balkans, bringing them home in anticipation of a posting to Iraq in the near future. Less than 15 percent of the troops remaining in the Balkans were Americans.

THE PRESIDENT'S HUGE new store of political capital resulted in the near-unanimous passage in October 2001 of the Uniting and Strengthening America by Providing Appropriate Tools Required to Intercept and Obstruct Terrorism Act, also known as the USA PATRIOT Act. Bush had laid the groundwork in a speech on September 14, telling the public that "a national emergency exists" because of "the continuing and immediate threat of further attacks on the United States." This declaration of national emergency, Addington and others would later argue, allowed the president to assume the extraordinary powers of a wartime chief executive, as Abraham Lincoln had at the outset of the Civil War. Lincoln argued that his oath to protect *and* defend the Constitution entitled him to take "measures, otherwise unconstitutional, [that] might become lawful, by becoming indispensable to the preservation of the Constitution, through the preservation of the nation." Bush made the same case.

In the days right after September 11, Attorney General John Ashcroft asked Congress for increased powers for the government, saying, "Unless Congressmakes these changes, we are fighting an unnecessary uphill battle . . . sending our troops into the modern field of battle with antique weapons." As some observers noted, Ashcroft's implication was that if Congress did not agree to such augmented powers—including monitoring Internet communications, indefinitely detaining people before trial or deportation, and extending court-ordered wiretaps across the nation—those who opposed the bill would be responsible for the inevitable next attack on the United States. The bill was passed. The 342-page USA PATRIOT Act was submitted a month later.

Among the most striking features of the PATRIOT Act was its resurrection of the long-discredited Huston Plan of 1970. The new bill permitted the FBI, CIA, and other agencies to engage in activities that had so horrified Attorney General John Mitchell that he convinced Nixon to rescind the plan four days after it was promulgated. Mitchell considered unconstitutional the Huston Plan's provisions for warrantless wiretapping, opening of mail, "black-bag" burglaries by U.S. agents, surveillance of various sorts, and preventive detention. The PATRIOT Act legalized these. It also enabled the government to detain noncitizens indefinitely without charging them and to intercept electronic and oral communications. The FBI could now examine medical, financial, student, and library records; the CIA could investigate citizens on U.S. soil, something previously forbidden by its charter. The government could designate any group as a terror-sponsoring organization and target it as such. Some of these provisions were later rescinded, suggesting they were unnecessary in the first place.

"Long before 9/11," writes Jack Goldsmith, an assistant counsel who sat in on discussions about executive power at the White House, "[David] Addington . . . and his boss [Cheney] had set out to reverse what they saw as Congress' illegitimate decades-long intrusions on 'unitary' executive power," particularly the 1973 War Powers Act and the 1978 FISA Act. The USA PATRIOT Act and the FISA revision fulfilled that new direction. According to Goldsmith, this 2001 power seizure was one of the goals of the Bush inner circle and was the product of a post-9/11 lawyers' "war council" composed of White House counsel Albert Gonzales, DoD counsel William J. Haynes, Jr., Addington from Cheney's office, and conservative scholar John Yoo of Justice.

Furthermore, as Pulitzer Prize–winning reporter Charlie Savage later charged, by ordering the NSA to institute surveillance of Americans without first seeking permission from the FISA court—known as "warrantless wire-tapping"—Bush "claimed the power to ignore a law," asserting, in effect, that "a president can set aside a statute or a treaty at will" if he chooses. The assertion echoed one of Richard Nixon's most famous lines, that "when the President does it, that means that it is not illegal." The administration's moves to take powers away from Congress and the courts also significantly constrained the rights granted to individuals by the Bill of Rights and other constitutional amendments. The White House justified this curtailment of civil liberties by insisting it needed to "take off the gloves" to fight a vicious, multinational, multifaceted terrorist enemy that had repeatedly targeted in-nocent civilians and whose members were willing to commit suicide for their cause. Not everyone agreed. The American Civil Liberties Union countered that the freedoms of Americans guaranteed in the Constitution could be upheld while fully protecting Americans' safety—indeed, that the American way of life, which Bush had pledged in the aftermath of Septem-ber 11 to protect, depended on being able to exercise those rights freely.

Under the new rules, federal authorities detained more than a thousand people; all but a few were eventually released without being charged. Such nonterror groups as Greenpeace and Operation Rescue were labeled as sus-picious and surveilled, generating nothing but records and embarrassment.

The new climate of fear and deference to authority that led to quick passage of the USA PATRIOT Act also led to self-censorship in the media. When video and photographs of casualties and hardships in Afghanistan were displayed on TV news programs and newspaper front pages, hundreds of telegrams poured into those news media complaining of their lack of patriotism. Feeling the pressure of what he labeled the "patriotism police," Walter Isaacson, then the CEO of CNN, pleaded with his staff to balance such images with others reminding viewers of the September 11 tragedy.

"TERRORISTS WHO ONCE occupied Afghanistan now occupy cells at Guan-tánamo Bay. And terrorist leaders who urged followers to sacrifice their lives are running for their own," President Bush stated triumphantly in his 2002 State of the Union speech. Claiming victory in Afghanistan—if not yet over al-Qaeda—he then quickly set new goals, naming Iran, Iraq, and North Korea as members of an "axis of evil." None had been involved with the September 11 attacks, but all had long been in neocon crosshairs. "By seeking weapons of mass destruction," Bush charged, "these regimes pose a grave and growing danger. They could provide these arms to terrorists, giving them the means to match their hatred. They could attack our allies or attempt to blackmail the United States. In any of these cases, the price

of indifference would be catastrophic." That, Bush said, was why he would
not "wait on events while dangers gather. I will not stand by as peril draws
closer and closer. The United States of America will not permit the world's
most dangerous regimes to threaten us with the world's most destructive
weapons." Bush left little doubt about which nation would be the first target:

> Iraq continues to flaunt its hostility toward America and to sup-
> port terror. The Iraqi regime has plotted to develop anthrax and nerve
> gas and nuclear weapons for over a decade. This is a regime that has
> already used poison gas to murder thousands of its own citizens. . . .
> This is a regime that agreed to international inspections then kicked
> out the inspectors. This is a regime that has something to hide from
> the civilized world.

Although the administration continued to say it would work through the
international community's programs to keep Iraq under control, the Pentagon continued to plan for a preemptive invasion. After General Shinseki
raised objections, the selection of his replacement was announced a year
ahead of schedule. Army secretary Thomas White also had problems with
a focus on Iraq, and was bureaucratically squeezed aside. Ken Adelman,
Rumsfeld's former assistant and friend, wrote in the *Washington Post* in February 2002 that a war against Iraq would be "a cakewalk," because Hussein's
regime was weaker than in 1991, the United States was stronger, and this
President Bush enjoyed more public support than even his father had.

Powell told a House committee there was "no doubt" that the Iraqis were
pursuing a nuclear program. According to later reports, information about
the Iraqis' purported nuclear program, some of which came from exile
group leader Ahmad Chalabi and other Iraqi exiles and defectors, was fun-
neled directly to Cheney's office rather than through the CIA. The vice
president visited the Middle East for ten days, during which he lobbied
Muslim countries for support in the event that the United States had to go
to war against Iraq. Many refused and backed Saddam Hussein's right to
rule his own country. On Cheney's return to Washington he told a Senate
Republican lunch group that the question was no longer whether the United
States would attack Iraq, but when. After meeting with Wolfowitz and Rice,
Sir David Manning reported to Prime Minister Tony Blair that "Condi's
enthusiasm for regime change is undimmed," although "there were some
signs [on the American side] of greater awareness of the practical difficulties
and political risks."

The challenge was to convince the public of the justice and the inevitability of invading Iraq. In a speech at West Point on June 1, 2002, Bush said,

"Our security will require all Americans [to] be ready for preemptive action when necessary to defend our lives." This was a novel, and neoconservative, argument. Previous presidents had studiously avoided going to war against an enemy that had not first attacked America, even when our allies would have welcomed the help, as in 1914 and in 1939. Woodrow Wilson and Franklin Roosevelt had found it imperative to endure direct attacks on U.S. interests before asking Congress to declare war. In 1964, Johnson had used a flimsy (and later discredited) casus belli to ask for a declaration allowing the United States to do more than advise the South Vietnamese on their battlefields. In 1991, over the objections of Secretary of Defense Cheney, the George H. W. Bush administration asked Congress for an enabling resolution before going to war against Iraq. In 2002, proponents of a preemptive war justified it on the grounds that the United States, as the world's dominant power, had the responsibility for keeping that world safe from rogue states and terrorists. This, the Bush Doctrine, was most lucidly stated in a National Security Strategy document that fall. "In an age where the enemies of civilization openly and actively seek the world's most destructive technologies, the United States cannot remain idle while dangers gather," it asserted.

> The greater the threat, the greater is the risk of inaction—and the more compelling the case for taking anticipatory action to defend ourselves, even if uncertainty remains as to the time and place of the enemy's attack. To forestall or prevent such hostile acts by our adversaries, the United States will, if necessary, act preemptively. . . . The purpose of our actions will always be to eliminate a specific threat to the United States or our allies and friends. The reasons for our actions will be clear, the force measured, and the cause just.

History had already shown, the document continued, that the American way of life was superior; it had vanquished Communism and provided "a single sustainable model for national success: freedom, democracy, and free enterprise." Spreading this model was not only America's responsibility; it also was, and should be, America's national security strategy. Bush reemphasized the basic goal in a speech later that year:

> Sixty years of Western nations excusing and accommodating the lack of freedom in the Middle East did nothing to make us safe—because in the long run, stability cannot be purchased at the expense of liberty. As long as the Middle East remains a place where freedom does not flourish, it will remain a place of stagnation, resentment, and violence ready for export.

Spreading democracy became the cutting edge of American policy.

The Bush Doctrine was wholly compatible with Fritz Kraemer's tenets in its emphasis on employing aggressive military action, at the behest of an elite, on what that elite considered a highly moral and Christian basis. That was made clear in the aftermath of September 11, when a reporter asked Kraemer to characterize the greatest threat to the world today. "Moral relativism," he replied. When Kissinger was apprised of this answer, he said he agreed. By using the phrase in this context, Kraemer—who had so often preached that good and evil existed in the world—implied that now was no time to delay action while weighing degrees of evil; rather, we had a moral obligation to answer the evil that was inherent in the September 11 attacks by punishing their perpetrators.

What "frightened" Kraemer about those attacks, he later said, was that they ratified what he had been warning about for decades: that the "bourgeoisie" in civilized nations did not "understand the dangers threatening from outside their own charmed, comfortable, soft environment." What "surprised" him about the attacks, he added, was the "unbelievably disproportionate damage" that the hijackers had produced, "a fearsome demonstration of the open, highly-technologized societies' vulnerability to very small groups of fanatic activists."

Still, though the Bush administration was drawing on Kraemerite thinking to build its case against Iraq, Fritz Kraemer himself was less comfortable with the prospect. He thoroughly supported the reprisals against the Taliban and al-Qaeda, finding the U.S. attacks on bin Laden's infrastructure in Afghanistan a proportional and appropriate response. But a preemptive war in Iraq, which the Bush Doctrine was preparing the ground for, Kraemer found problematic. He had been caustic about preemptive war tactics when the USSR employed them, for instance in Afghanistan in the 1980s. To Kraemer, to engage in preemptive war was to abandon the high moral ground that had previously characterized and even ennobled American actions.

Another Kraemer tenet also argued against invading Iraq—the need for the balance of powers. Contrary to the assertions of the neocons that defeating Iraq was needed to maintain stability in the region, this requirement suggested that the very opposite was needed to maintain the status quo in the Persian Gulf. Since Iran was the greater threat to peace in the region, and thus to the United States, the need for balance argued that Iraq should be left in place as a counterweight to Iran.

Iran had aided the United States in the early days after September 11, primarily because the terrorists had been identified as Sunni Muslims, and Iran's citizens were predominantly Shiites. Since then, however, the U.S.

government had resumed its posture of maintaining no formal diplomatic contact with Iran. Though Kraemer was fundamentally wary of diplomacy, he had never insisted on ignoring the enemy or potential enemy by refusing to talk to it. But the administration was doing just that, ignoring not only Iran and Syria, Iraq's neighbors, but also North Korea, even though there were potential challenges to world peace—including nuclear challenges—in all those countries. Adopting stances previously stated only by the armchair warriors of the *Weekly Standard*, the administration argued that dealing properly with Iran, Syria, and North Korea could wait. Those countries might well be cowed by the display of American might and will that would accompany Saddam's overthrow. But Iraq had to come first.

Bush administration hard-liners went into overdrive to identify and publicize the most persuasive justifications for an invasion. Most accounts suggest that Cheney, Rumsfeld, and other officials decided that the most easily understood reason for going to war against Iraq was its alleged amassing of weapons of mass destruction, which threatened the stability of the entire Middle East. Soon, an internal British intelligence memo to Blair, later known as the Downing Street Memo, reported after discussions with Bush's inner circle that the United States was set on going to war and that "the intelligence and facts were being fixed around the policy."

Earlier in 2002, President Bush, pushed by Cheney, had issued an edict about the prisoners at Guantánamo Bay: as terrorists rather than "lawful combatant" soldiers of a particular country, they were not covered by the protections of the Geneva Convention. That edict was the administration's rationale for keeping the prisoners in isolation and interrogating them aggressively. That had been done, and a great deal of information had been obtained. But by the middle of that year, some CIA men and Vice President Cheney came to believe that a few of the detainees had more information to divulge, and that it could only be obtained by even more aggressive techniques, some of which would later be deemed as torture. Around midyear, these interrogators sought and were granted permission to use the much more aggressive techniques. In 2009, information would surface suggesting that the vice president's office wanted the harsher methods used to try to extract from a detainee evidence of a direct connection between Osama bin Laden and Saddam Hussein's Iraq.

Permission, and the legal justification for these extreme methods, were the subjects of a memo from Alberto Gonzales on August 1, 2002, and of an accompanying DoJ memo redefining torture as a term applying only to pain "equivalent in intensity to the pain accompanying serious physical injury."

This definition permitted the use of highly coercive techniques such as waterboarding, putting prisoners in extremely hot or cold environments, and using dogs to scare them. Using these techniques, interrogators extracted from al-Qaeda prisoners some information judged at the time to be highly valuable, information the administration claimed had saved lives by preventing certain attacks that were already under way and by leading to the capture of terrorist attack planners.

Around the time of the interrogation memos, the White House established an "Iraq Group," under the direction of chief of staff Andrew Card and lead political strategist Karl Rove, whose purpose was to find ways to sell a war against Iraq. At a speechwriter's suggestion, the term "smoking gun/mushroom cloud" was to be used to convey Iraq's perceived nuclear weapons capability. The group made highly successful outreaches to the news media. A later Bill Moyers investigation compiled a list of 414 network TV news stories that were pro-invasion, and traced these stories' sources to information provided by the White House, the Pentagon, or the State Department. In the six months before the onset of the war in Iraq, the *Washington Post* published twenty-seven editorials in favor of going to war, and featured 140 front-page news stories that made the administration's case for the attack.

One very prominent reporter who published such pieces was Judith Miller of the *New York Times*. In half a dozen articles, her major source was Ahmad Chalabi or Iraqi defectors steered to her by Chalabi, who insisted that Saddam was producing WMDs and was training hijackers. On September 7, Miller uncritically reported the administration's contention that "in the last 14 months, Iraq has sought to buy thousands of specially designed aluminum tubes, which American officials believe were intended as components of centrifuges to enrich uranium." She did not report that many other government experts believed these tubes could not be used to refine uranium. *Times* columnists Safire and Friedman, whose political stripes differed widely, both echoed the administration's case for war with Iraq. MSNBC canceled a show hosted by the liberal Phil Donahue three weeks before the invasion of Iraq. An internal MSNBC memo, later given to Moyers, said, "Donohue presents a difficult public face for NBC in a time of war. At the same time our competitors are waving the flag at every opportunity." Executives and reporters at CNN and MSNBC also told Moyers they had muted challenges to the case for war.

"Is there an absolutely vital national interest that should lead us from containment to unilateral war and a long-term occupation of Iraq? And would such a war and its aftermath actually increase our ability to win the war against international terrorism?" In an op-ed in the *Washington Post*, Vietnam veteran and former Reagan navy secretary James Webb wrote that the U.S. professional military was "nearly unanimous" in asking these questions. Webb identified the central issue as "whether we as a nation are prepared to physically occupy territory in the Middle East for the next 30 to 50 years. Those who are pushing for a unilateral war in Iraq know full well that there is no exit strategy if we invade and stay."

The term *unilateral* came up with increasing frequency in these months, as it became clear that President Bush would not enjoy the same level of international cooperation his father had when he ousted Saddam from Kuwait in 1991. Webb, like others, noted that China and Russia, two permanent members of the UN Security Council, had been courting the "axis of evil" countries for years and were continuing to receive Iraqi emissaries. At the same time, Bush was needling the United Nations; in an address to that body in September 2002 he argued, "The conduct of the Iraqi regime is a threat to the authority of the United Nations. . . . Are Security Council resolutions to be honored and enforced, or cast aside without consequence? Will the United Nations serve the purpose of its founding, or will it be irrelevant?"

Germany, which had agonized in 1999 before deciding to send troops outside the country for the first time since 1945—to Kosovo, under the NATO banner—was one ally the United States wanted by its side in Iraq. Presented with "evidence" of Iraq's WMD and other dangers, however, the country's foreign minister, Joschka Fischer, told Rumsfeld, "Sorry, you haven't convinced me." Opposition by Germany and France made it impossible for the United States to act under a NATO banner.

On August 15, 2002, Brent Scowcroft published an op-ed in the *Wall Street Journal* titled "Don't Attack Saddam." The article surprised many readers, who assumed that any adviser to Bush's father would be eager to finish the job of ousting Saddam. But Scowcroft's piece was a quintessentially pragmatist response to the new administration's ideological drift, and specifically against ideologues such as Adelman who were so publicly predicting an easy victory in Iraq. Scowcroft warned that there was a "virtual consensus in the world" against an American attack on Iraq without the express cooperation of the United Nations. He added that such a war would be no "cakewalk," because in reaction Saddam might unleash his weapons against Israel; the result could escalate into a nuclear "Armageddon in the Middle East."

But the primary reason not to invade Iraq, Scowcroft insisted, was that it "would seriously jeopardize, if not destroy, the global counterterrorist campaign we have undertaken." Only one thing could possibly convince a reluctant United Nations to go along: "compelling evidence" that Saddam possessed a serious nuclear weapons capability. Scowcroft's warnings were picked up and celebrated by those opposed to the war, while those in sympathy with the administration derided his caution as outmoded in a post-9/11 world.

The potential fallout from an invasion of Iraq continued to raise concern. In an August memo called "The Perfect Storm: Planning for the Negative Consequences of Invading Iraq," the CIA cited the risks: anarchy in Iraq, a surge in terrorism around the world, deepening Islamic antipathy to the United States, and al-Qaeda exploiting the circumstances to find new safe havens. Ancillary results could include declining European confidence in U.S. leadership, Iran working to install an Iran-friendly regime in Baghdad, a Taliban resurgence in Afghanistan while the United States was occupied with Iraq, and chaos in Pakistan.

It was an extraordinarily prescient report: Virtually all of these negative consequences eventually came to pass. But the administration's top officials, Cheney and Rumsfeld, had a history of dismissing CIA reports with which they disagreed. Rice aide Stephen Hadley had requested this CIA memo, but according to George Tenet's memoir it was not presented to Bush immediately. Rather, it was tucked into the rear of a briefing book the president was shown at Camp David in September. The front sections of that book, according to Tenet, listed more positive potential results of Saddam's removal. According to Feith, Rumsfeld also prepared a "Parade of Horribles" memo outlining the negative consequences of an invasion. Initially prepared in August, it was revised by Rumsfeld, Feith, Wolfowitz, and top military personnel at the Pentagon. Sent out as a memo on October 15, 2002, it was also distributed and discussed at an NSC principals meeting.

By then, however, the principals had already been out in public for more than a month, hard-selling a potential invasion of Iraq. As the nation marked the first anniversary of the September 11 attacks, Cheney, Rumsfeld, Powell, and Rice appeared on the Sunday TV talk shows; they answered questions about Iraq in terms of being forced to invade and subdue a dangerous enemy. All four echoed Judith Miller's article in the *New York Times* about the tubes Iraq had supposedly purchased from Niger—an article based on information the administration had helped to furnish to Miller. The clinching line was Rice's: "We don't want the smoking gun to be a mushroom cloud."

White House Counsel Alberto Gonzales informed Bush, as Cheney had told Bush's father eleven years before, that the president already possessed all the authority needed to invade Iraq. But a group of moderate Republican and Democratic senators insisted that Bush ask Congress for authorization. Chuck Hagel, a Vietnam veteran, recalled that the resolution's first draft permitted the United States to go to war anywhere in the Middle East. At the moderates' insistence, that restriction was narrowed. The final resolution authorized "the use of United States armed forces against Iraq" in the event that all other options failed. Bush personally assured Hagel that he would try to work through the UN. Presented just before the 2002 midterm elections, the resolution was difficult to oppose, and Democrats who indicated they might do so were tarred as unpatriotic.

In this first national election since September 11, the majority of the electorate saw no reason to reject Bush's leadership. Republicans returned to a clear, though slim, majority in the House and gained control of the Senate. For the first time since the Eisenhower years, Republicans would be in control of Congress and of the presidency.

RIGHT AFTER THE election, Bob Woodward published *Bush at War,* his chronicle of the first years of the Bush presidency. Based on minutes of NSC meetings declassified for Woodward, and on Woodward's interviews—primarily with Powell but including several hours with Bush—the book featured the planning and execution of the Afghanistan operation. Thumping the cause for war, it painted Bush as heroic, favored Powell and Tenet over Rumsfeld and Cheney, and had little to say about the input of Perle and the other neocons. Though Woodward took a minor slap at the military for not having standing contingency plans to go into Afghanistan, the known lair of bin Laden, in all other ways his book, like *The Commanders* before it, celebrated the professional military and its valiant fight to fend off the absurdities of civilian supervision. Only Powell, the book showed, was preventing Cheney, Rumsfeld, and the neocons from convincing Bush to start a unilateral invasion of Iraq.

In late 2002, George Tenet presented Bush and Cheney with the best evidentiary reasons he could muster for war with Iraq. Bush said he was not terribly impressed with Tenet's tales of suspected WMDs, but Tenet insisted that they constituted a "slam-dunk." In any event, the case certainly echoed the conclusion of the October NIE: "We judge that Iraq has continued its weapons of mass destruction (WMD) programs in defiance of UN resolutions. . . . Baghdad has chemical and biological weapons as well as missiles with ranges in excess of UN restrictions; if left unchecked, it probably will have a nuclear weapon during this decade."

> Although . . . Saddam does not yet have nuclear weapons or sufficient material to make any, he remains intent on acquiring them. . . . How quickly Iraq will obtain its first nuclear weapon depends on when it acquires sufficient weapons-grade fissile material. If Baghdad acquires sufficient fissile material from abroad it could make a nuclear weapon within several months to a year.

With this rationale for action in hand, it became imperative for the administration to demonstrate that Baghdad was, indeed, acquiring "sufficient fissile material from abroad." The belief that Iraq had such materials depended on a British report that Iraq was buying "yellowcake" uranium from Niger, a report that former ambassador to Gabon (and envoy to Iraq in 1991) Joseph C. Wilson IV had been sent to West Africa to verify. When Wilson found no justification for the report, and told the CIA and the State Department as much upon his return, his information was ignored. So was a January 12, 2003, report from the State Department's Bureau of Intelligence and Research, which warned that the Italian memo on which the British had based their claim about the Niger-Iraq sale was a forgery. Nonetheless, in his 2003 State of the Union address Bush blithely told the world, "The British government has learned that Saddam Hussein recently sought significant quantities of uranium from Africa." Together with Tenet's statement to Congress that the CIA had evidence of Saddam's ties to Osama bin Laden, Bush's assertion convinced enough reluctant legislators to back the push for war.

The next obstacle was the United Nations. Bush asked Powell to make the case for war to the world body. Tenet and Powell collaborated on the presentation, and they had enough doubt about the uranium claim that Powell refused to include it. Powell also resisted pressure from Cheney to include an explicit connection between the September 11 hijackers and Saddam; a line to that effect, inserted by Cheney's office, was twice taken out of the draft. Powell did present other claims about WMDs that seemed quite convincing, saying of them, "These are facts, not allegations." But they *were* allegations, based on questionable premises, and some were outright fictions. An egregious example: A vehicle seen in a photograph that Powell described in his presentation as a mobile chemical warfare laboratory was nothing of the sort; that explanation was a lie concocted by an Iraqi defector to Germany, codenamed Curveball.

When the UN refused to put its official imprimatur on any future U.S. invasion of Iraq, Bush responded by announcing the members of a "coalition of the willing" that would go to war—a coalition that did not include Germany, France, or any large Muslim countries. Rumsfeld dismissed the former two countries as "old Europe" and embraced the willingness of "new Europe" countries Poland, Hungary, Lithuania, and Ukraine to send troops. Army Chief of Staff Shinseki, whose retirement had been announced a year earlier, told Congress that some 300,000 troops would be needed to control Iraq after an initial invasion. His numbers were lambasted by Rumsfeld, who had consistently argued that far fewer troops could do the job. Other high-ranking officers, who either disagreed with the push for war with Iraq or with the strategic and tactical planning for that war, were also forced to retire. When Wolfowitz was asked by Congress to estimate the cost of the war, he put it relatively low, considerably under the $95 billion figure of other experts, but refused to place a firm dollar figure on it. Hagel privately asked Rumsfeld and Wolfowitz, "How are you going to govern [postwar Iraq]? Who's going to govern? Where is the money coming from? What are you going to do with their army? How will you secure their borders? And I was assured every time I asked, 'Senator, don't worry, we've got task forces on that, they've been working, they're coordinated,' and so on."

On the eve of the war, in 2002, the ninety-four-year-old Fritz Kraemer was taken by a friend to an event at the Pentagon that Secretary of Defense Rumsfeld also attended. Kraemer embraced his old boss, advising him loudly, "No provocative weakness, please, Mr. Secretary." Everyone heard that. What most did not hear was the rest of the conversation, in which Kraemer pressed Rumsfeld about planning for the post-invasion of Iraq—posing, in effect, the same questions as Hagel. Without such planning, Kraemer insisted, there would be a disaster. He was not satisfied by the answers he received.

THE U.S.-LED MILITARY invasion of Iraq in March 2003 went well. The Iraqis did not welcome the troops with as much enthusiasm as the troops' grandfathers had received when they liberated France in 1944, but there was jubilation at the routing of Saddam's regime. Saddam fled and was believed to be in hiding. A new Iraqi government formed, pledged to move toward democratic governance and countrywide elections.

This was the high point of the crusade—the triumph of neocon foreign policy. They knew it and they celebrated it. On April 10, Adelman wrote a second op-ed for the *Washington Post*, patting himself on the back for his early 2002 prediction of a cakewalk, and marveling, "Even I could never have envisioned the [U.S.-led] coalition controlling the enemy capital within three weeks—less than half the time, with less than half the U.S. casualties, of the first Gulf War." He predicted that Germany and France would be angrier with us now because they would not forgive us our success. (Rumsfeld, too, belittled Germany and France in his post-invasion press briefings.) As Bob Woodward later reported, Cheney invited Adelman, Wolfowitz, and Libby to a private party at his Maryland shore retreat, where they gloated over the silencing of critics such as Scowcroft, whose prediction of an "Armageddon in the Middle East" now seemed ludicrous. Adelman confessed that he'd almost lost heart when so much time passed before the invasion. Now that they had won, he proposed a toast to the man who had made the decision for war: the president. They all drank to Bush.

. . . .

ON MAY 1, wearing a naval aviator's suit, President Bush landed in a jet fighter on the aircraft carrier USS *Abraham Lincoln*, off the coast of California. Standing in front of a banner that read MISSION ACCOMPLISHED, he congratulated the military on its work in Iraq and declared the end of major combat operations.

Shortly afterward, two actions were taken that would hamper the ability of the newly liberated Iraq to move beyond the fighting, and would have negative ramifications for the global war on terrorism: the dissolution of the Iraqi army and the outlawing of Saddam's Baath Party. Iraq, which was sharply divided into Shiite, Sunni, and Kurdish regions, had long been beset by ethnic and religious rivalries. The Sunnis and their Baath Party had previously suppressed the Shiite majority; now the Shiites became the American-backed leaders of the new Iraq. But once the Baathists and the former Iraq army members were out of work, al-Qaeda affiliates soon recruited them for antigovernment operations in Iraq.

The "de-Baathification" idea had floated for months through the State, Defense, NSC, and CIA bureaucracies. According to Feith, the impetus came from Condoleezza Rice's NSC staff; other reports say the idea originated with Wolfowitz, Feith, and other neocons. Feith writes, "we . . . recognized that if the coalition failed to take serious action against the Baath Party, Iraqis who detested the regime would feel betrayed." The bureaucracies agreed that some "de-Baathification" had to occur but disagreed on the extent to which Baathists should be purged from the new Iraqi state ranks.

L. Paul Bremer III, an expert on terrorism and a friend of Rumsfeld, was named to head the Coalition Provisional Authority in Iraq. A Reagan-era diplomat, he had worked for Kissinger Associates since 1992 and had most recently cochaired the Heritage Foundation's Homeland Security Task Force. As Bremer left Washington for Baghdad in early May 2003, Rumsfeld handed him a memo on "Principles for Iraq-Policy Guidelines." It specified that the coalition "will actively oppose Saddam Hussein's old enforcers—the Baath Party, Fedayeen Saddam, etc." and that "we will make clear that the coalition will eliminate the remnants of Saddam's regime." Upon arriving in Iraq, Bremer announced the outlawing of the Baath Party and the banishing of its top-tier men from eligibility for posts in the new government; Bremer also announced that Saddam's army, which had disbanded by itself during the invasion, would not be recalled to duty. He later wrote that he promulgated this order only after clearing it with Wolfowitz, Rumsfeld, military officials, and Bush, and cited a letter from Bush, in response to his report on de-Baathification, in which the president had assured Bremer of his "full support and confidence."

The U.S.-led troops found no caches of WMDs and no evidence of extensive al-Qaeda presence when they landed in Iraq. Their absence showed that the two main reasons given for invading Iraq were based not on fact but on unproven assumptions. Moreover, the extent of the looting, and the strength of the insurgency, quickly made it imperative that American troops remain in Iraq until the nation was truly pacified—thus disproving the notion that the military would not get bogged down as occupiers, another assumption that had been used to persuade Congress. When Bremer recommended to Rumsfeld that U.S. troops be increased to 500,000 to maintain control of the country, Rumsfeld said no. At the same time, the administration authorized the use of civilian contractors, including mercenaries, for police-type work in Iraq, a policy that effectively doubled the number of American-paid boots on the ground. Shinseki's prewar estimate, that it would take approximately 300,000 men to pacify Iraq, was reached, though only half that number were U.S. and coalition military troops.

Underlying all the mistakes of the post-invasion period, which stretched on for years, was the Bush inner circle's complex mix of cockiness, ideology, and ignorance of the ethnic and religious rivalries within Muslim countries. That deadly mix may also explain the administration's disregard of an astonishing offer it received from Iran in May 2003. In a two-page faxed letter, Iraq's longtime rival proposed a broad dialogue with the United States that would include Iran's potential recognition of the state of Israel and cooperation on nuclear safeguards and on the pursuit of terrorists—in exchange for the lifting of sanctions and for U.S. recognition of Iran's legitimate security aims. Rice later testified that she never saw the letter; one of her former deputies, Flynt Leverett, testified that he had received it and given it to Elliott Abrams, the neocon in charge of Middle East affairs, but that Abrams may have not given it to Rice or to Powell.

One possible reason for Iran to have made such an overture was that it had been scared by the invasion of Iraq, as the neocons had predicted and hoped. That much was certainly true of Libya's leader, Moammar Qaddafi, who agreed late in 2003 to give up all his WMD programs and cooperate with the United States in dismantling his nuclear machinery. The United States responded by restoring diplomatic relations with Libya.

The United States now began to talk to North Korea, but only as part of six-party talks. Just before the meetings, John Bolton, a member of the U.S. delegation, called North Korea's leader Kim Jong Il a "tyrant" who kept his people imprisoned in a "living hell"; Bolton warned against giving in to his "nuclear extortion." Another member of the U.S. delegation told *Time* that Bolton's speech "basically called for regime change" and reflected the neocons' view that any movement toward the North Korean position would only shore up Kim's regime. When State Department North Korea expert Charles "Jack" Pritchard tried to assure the North Koreans that Bolton was speaking only for himself, he was forced to resign; as *Time* reported, Pyongyang was told that "Bolton spoke for the Administration" on that issue. The North Koreans refused to go ahead with the talks unless Bolton was dropped from the delegation; having accomplished what he set out to do, Bolton left for home. The talks stalled for many months.

Stories were already emerging about the lack of planning for post-invasion Iraq, and about the possible falsity of the rationale for the invasion. Rumsfeld, Cheney, and Bush dismissed the critics. But on July 6, 2003, Joseph Wilson, the former ambassador to Gabon, wrote an op-ed in the *New York Times* bearing the provocative title "What I Didn't Find in Africa." It recounted, in telling detail, his unremunerated trip to Niger—at the behest of Cheney, paid for by the CIA—to try to verify that Iraq had indeed purchased yellowcake uranium from Niger. What Wilson found was a lot of evidence to the contrary, which he had reported to CIA and State. If his information had been disproved by other sources, he contended, he would have accepted it and moved on. But if his information was ignored "because it did not fit certain preconceptions about Iraq, then a legitimate argument can be made that we went to war under false pretenses. . . . Congress, which authorized the use of military force . . . should want to know if the assertions about Iraq were warranted."

Administration officials and friends were so upset by Wilson's article and media appearances that they attempted to undermine it, and him, by alleging that Wilson's wife, a CIA supervisor, had suggested the trip, and that it had an anti-administration agenda and a trumped-up conclusion. To buttress that claim they made public her name, Valerie Plame; it was first exposed in Robert Novak's syndicated column. Since the naming of a covert CIA operative is a felony, the Novak story triggered a federal investigation. Controversy over Plame's "outing" stayed in the headlines for months, diverting focus from the underlying issue—whether the administration had deliberately misled the American public into war.

IN SEPTEMBER 2003, at the age of ninety-five, Fritz G. A. Kraemer died. He was buried at Arlington National Cemetery in early October. His death came at a poignant moment, when some who had absorbed Kraemer's thoughts and principles were putting them into practice in the war in Iraq and running into the very difficulties about which Kraemer had warned Rumsfeld in their final meeting a year earlier.

Sven Kraemer could not decide whether to allow Kissinger to speak at the funeral, but Rowny convinced him. At the event, Kissinger, Haig, and Schlesinger were the most well known speakers; those in attendance included many neocons and hard-liners, such as former ACDA head Fred Iklé, and journalists such as Bill Beecher, all of whom had been touched by Kraemer's intellect and passion. Rumsfeld, still overwhelmed with day-to-day operations in Iraq, sent Sven a fulsome condolence note.

Kissinger's was the most poignant eulogy, a confession that Kraemer's "inspiration remained with me even during the last thirty years when he would not speak to me." Lauding Kraemer as "the prophet" and referring to himself as "the policymaker," Kissinger noted the inevitable differences between the two. "The prophet thinks in terms of crusades, the policymaker hedges against the possibility of human fallibility." That dichotomy, Kissinger told Rowny privately after the funeral, was the source of his estrangement from Kraemer, whose main weakness was his "lack of practicality."

The same split between ideological expectations and realities was becoming more apparent each day as American-led coalition forces continued to occupy Iraq. The Bush administration hoped that Iraq would soon be reconstructed and functioning, and that the country's newly independent and prosperous status would moot all questions about the legitimacy of the war and its true origins. But in the wake of the invasion, al-Qaeda affiliates in Iraq expanded their terrorist operations and alliances with the ousted Sunnis; their suicide bombings targeted the new government, especially the Shiite majority from which the ranking officers had been chosen. They destabilized the country, making all progress into a one-step-forward-two-steps-back endeavor. Iraq threatened to become the sort of unending trap for American forces and bottomless pit for American resources that Vietnam had once provided.

29

The Cheney Regency

P resident George W. Bush liked to call himself "the decider." He may have filled that role insofar as saying yes or no to various actions, but his ability to make real decisions and set policy was constrained by colleagues who severely limited his information and options and by a vice president who controlled his agenda and direction. From its earliest days, the Bush administration was a Cheney regency. As Barton Gellman of the *Washington Post*, Jane Mayer of the *New Yorker*, and others have documented, Cheney enforced conservative orthodoxy as well as controlled administration policy on Iraq, Iran, North Korea, the interrogation of prisoners, and the surveillance of Americans' communications.

The bad consequences of this decision-making system, and of the Cheney regency, surfaced increasingly as the war in Iraq wore on. The Iraqi occupation, with its demands for continual pacification, absorbed American resources. A side result: the occupation pointed up the inadequacies of the neoconservative ideas that had pushed the United States into the preemptive war. As Iraq became a sinkhole, it consumed and eventually destroyed the legitimacy of the neoconservative program for America's foreign policy.

IN THE SPRING of 2004, one year after the invasion of Iraq, the country's occupation by more than 100,000 U.S. troops continued; though a provisional, nonelected government was in place, hundreds of Iraqi civilians and U.S. and coalition servicemen died each month primarily because of IEDs— "improvised explosive devices" placed by insurgents and al-Qaeda adherents.

Al-Qaeda had used the Iraq War as a recruiting tool to lure young fighters into the country and into attempts to capsize the post-Saddam government. Suicide bombers regularly targeted police stations and Iraq army recruitment centers. Saboteurs routinely exploded Iraq's oil pipelines. Insurgents made continual attacks on the electricity and telephone services and water-providing facilities.

The American people were growing restive about the conduct of the war, but polls suggested that most were willing to wait for the results promised by the administration.

Those positive expectations received a great shock from the exposure, in early 2004, of the torture, humiliation, and abusive treatment of Iraqi prisoners by U.S. guard troops at the Abu Ghraib prison twenty miles west of Baghdad—abuse that was captured in photos taken by the guards for their own amusement and quickly disseminated via the Internet around the world, and then on a *60 Minutes* broadcast. To critics, Abu Ghraib became a symbol of American moral turpitude and decadent behavior. From what the public could discern, the excesses seemed to have been condoned if not explicitly permitted by higher officers; the torture and humiliation techniques and some of the instigators of the abuse were quickly traced back to the treatment of al-Qaeda prisoners at Guantánamo Bay.

War brings out the worst in human behavior: abusive treatment of prisoners occurs in all major conflicts, as does unnecessary killing of civilians by bands of soldiers bent on taking revenge for fallen comrades. But the Bush administration had claimed the high moral ground as reason for its aggressive terror-fighting tactics—and Abu Ghraib and stories of U.S. military units raping and executing Iraqi civilians demolished such claims. Voices around the world, including those of America's allies, condemned the Abu Ghraib excesses, and those condemnations combined with anger at what news investigations were now exposing about the casus belli. These investigative reports showed that the alleged prewar presence of WMDs, Iraq's nuclear program, and links between Saddam and al-Qaeda had been hyped at best and perhaps even deliberately falsified.

The excesses at Abu Ghraib, America's invasion and continued occupation of Iraq, the administration's refusal to deal diplomatically with Iran and North Korea, and its attempts to punish France and Germany for sitting out the war against Iraq dissipated virtually all the international goodwill and sympathy the United States had received after September 11, 2001. Nonetheless, Cheney, Rumsfeld, and Bush continued to push the neocon agenda, the president asserting in early April 2004 that the big lesson of 9/11 was that the United States "must go on the offense and stay on the offense."

In this atmosphere, Bob Woodward's *Plan of Attack*, published in April, helped the administration's public relations efforts. A second paean to Bush and the planners of the invasion of Iraq, it provided an antidote to the increasingly negative stories about the administration. The White House itself heavily promoted the book. By then the notion that Bush was not really in charge—that Cheney made all the significant decisions—was gathering force and specificity in reports in the *Washington Post*, the *New York Times*, and other leading venues. Woodward's account attempted to correct this, reporting that Bush had overruled Cheney on such matters as first presenting the U.S. case to the UN before invading Iraq.

Most reviewers faulted Woodward's narrative as lacking the balance it might have had if it covered the new information that was emerging about the questionable prewar claims of WMDs and al-Qaeda links. The existence of that contrary data underscored the appearance that Woodward was still, as in the past, a captive to his sources—a reporter too subject to what Joan Didion once identified as Woodward's fatal flaw, his "disinclination . . . to exert cognitive energy on what he is told." Woodward generally acted more as a stenographer than as a critical analyst of what his interviewees said, Didion charged. Roy McGovern, a CIA analyst for twenty-seven years before his retirement, predicted in a review that *Plan of Attack* "will provide useful yarn for White House spinners claiming the president was misled by faulty intelligence. And the slam-dunker [Tenet] can be left hanging on the rim of the basket . . . until he falls of his own weight."

As McGovern's review indicates, a blame game had begun. In reaction to the increasingly unsatisfying results in Iraq, the neocons and the administration pointed fingers at those who could be faulted for foiling the grandiose plans. In interviews, Richard Perle castigated the intelligence community and especially the CIA for giving the president bad information in the run-up to the war. Perle had recently been forced to resign as leader of the Defense Policy Board because of allegations of conflict of interest revealed in Seymour Hersh's articles in the *New Yorker*, but he nonetheless remained on that unpaid board. The idea of "Darth Vader" Perle faulting "Slam-Dunk" Tenet—the story of the CIA director's use of that phrase in Bush's office was one of the highlights of *Plan of Attack*—drew some derisive comment, as both Perle and Tenet had been integral to the push for war in Iraq. The intelligence community (and Tenet) fought back, accusing Cheney and the neocons of cherry-picking intelligence to justify an ideological war.

The Republican-controlled Congress refused to investigate any possible misdeeds by the administration in the run-up to the war, in the subsequent conduct of the war, or in the occupation of Iraq. Underlying these three problem areas—the run-up to the war, the military operation, and the occupation—were, in addition to neocon hubris, some ideas drawn from traditional conservative theory, for instance, the preference for giving more tasks to private industry and fewer to the government. Rumsfeld's decision to commit an inadequate number of troops to the fight led the government to hand off the reconstruction of Iraq to private contractors, such as Halliburton and Blackwater USA, who enjoyed the fruits of no-bid contracts. Massive fraud and waste were already being alleged in these programs, which had little U.S. government oversight. Critics charged that the contractors' relatively free rein stemmed from their having friends in high places.

But the problems went beyond ideology to blatant attempts by the administration to avoid inquiries into their conduct. Critics accused Gonzales and Cheney's office of blocking probes of wiretapping and other federal antiterror programs, which were coming under increasing fire for intruding into Americans' lives while producing nothing of use in the war on terrorism. When the general in charge of the investigation into the abuses at Abu Ghraib testified to Congress that the abuses might well be traceable to Department of Defense officials, Undersecretary of Defense for Intelligence Stephen Cambone insisted that only the military officers were to blame. The torture at Abu Ghraib was linked to techniques used in the treatment and interrogation of prisoners at Guantánamo. Accusations surfaced that Cheney and Addington had made the decision to interrogate some prisoners from the Afghanistan battlefields without affording them the protections of the Geneva Convention, which they contended did not apply to "unlawful combatants." As the *Washington Post*'s Gellman later wrote:

> The vice president's office played a central role in shattering limits on coercion of prisoners in U.S. custody, commissioning and defending legal opinions. . . . Cheney and his allies, according to more than two dozen current and former officials, pioneered a novel distinction between forbidden "torture" and permitted use of "cruel, inhuman or degrading" methods of questioning.

As more information surfaced about the intelligence problems in the run-up to the Iraq War, the clamor for a culprit rose, and George Tenet resigned as director of the CIA. Though his agency had raised alarms about al-Qaeda before September 11, and had tried to give proper warning of the absence of WMDs in Iraq, he had eventually caved in to pressure and delivered the "slam-dunk" message that helped to green-light the invasion of Iraq. Bush replaced him with Porter Goss, an undistinguished conservative politician whose major qualification was his previous service on the House's CIA oversight panel. At the direction of the White House, Goss quickly fired more than a dozen seasoned analysts, chief among them those who had leaked to the press about the CIA's prewar assessments about Iraq's WMDs.

. . . .

By July, with the 2004 election season well under way, President Bush had no real challengers for the Republican nomination, and Senator John Kerry of Massachusetts had won enough primary votes to become the Democratic nominee. A Vietnam veteran who had commanded riverine "swift boats" in the war and claimed responsibility for the innovative and aggressive tactic of turning the boats toward attackers on the shore when the boats were fired upon, Kerry had become famously antiwar after returning home, testifying to Congress as a leader of the Vietnam Veterans Against the War before becoming a public prosecutor and then a long-serving senator. When Kerry trumpeted the contrast between his military service in the Vietnam era and Bush's, he was countered by a group calling itself the "Swift Boat Veterans for Truth," which ran a series of misleading ads maligning Kerry as a liar and a traitor. But Iraq gave Kerry as much trouble as Vietnam: Having voted for the war authorization and for subsequent military appropriations bills, it was difficult for him to tap into Democratic anger over the war.

Ultimately, though, the election turned on a domestic issue: Eleven states had measures on the ballot that would mandate a ban on "gay marriage," a practice approved in some states—including Kerry's home state of Massachusetts—but which Christian conservatives deemed an abomination. The Christian right had helped propel Bush into office in 2000—some conservatives felt America's foreign policy needed to protect Israel so that biblical prophecies about the end-times could come to pass—and in 2004 that alliance was galvanized by the gay-marriage issue. In some states where a gay marriage ban was on the ballot, such as Ohio, Christian voters provided the margin of victory for Bush. After the results came in, however, Bush hailed his victory as a validation of his foreign policy and of the neocon agenda.

Several Bush advisers who had independent stature left the administration at the outset of his second term, replaced by people who owed their high positions to their loyalty to Bush. Condoleezza Rice succeeded Colin Powell as secretary of state, and Albert Gonzales replaced Ashcroft as attorney general. The relative weakness of the new secretaries, coupled with other, similar personnel changes, left Vice President Cheney and his allies—Rumsfeld, Wolfowitz, Libby, Feith, Addington—even more in control. In the second term, the vice president assumed more day-to-day control over the management of the government and the administration's legislative agenda. This triggered attempts to pursue more neocon ideas, such as the spreading of democracy as a way to create allies for the United States.

"The survival of liberty in our land increasingly depends on the success of liberty in other lands," Bush said in his second inaugural. "The best hope for peace in our world is the expansion of freedom in all the world." The task of the United States, Bush said, was therefore to instill democracy in places where it had not yet taken root. The first example was the "purple fingers" election in Iraq at the end of January 2005, during which citizens who voted had their fingers inked to ensure proper counting. *Newsweek* cited genuine exhilaration over this step toward democracy and similar pushes elsewhere in the Gulf region—in a story headlined "Where Bush Was Right."

This was the high point for the neocon agenda. From then on it would slide further and further into the abyss of Iraq.

Iraq's newly elected parliament, ostensibly democratic, was sharply divided along ethnic and religious lines and had very little real control over the country's destiny; power remained in the hands of the American and coalition forces. After the Iraq election, however, member nations of the "coalition of the willing" bowed to pressures at home and began withdrawing their small contingents from Iraq.

American troops, in contrast, were unable to go home except on a rotation schedule; the unstable country still needed policing. The administration made a series of predictions about the coming end of this phase of American involvement in Iraq: It would come in the fall of 2005, at the end of 2005, by the time of the 2006 U.S. midterm elections. The White House stopped talking about the idea that Iraq's oil would pay for the war, as it had done before the invasion, because insurgent attacks on the pipeline continued to seriously curtail oil production; the U.S. military had to import gas and oil to run its vehicles, at a high cost per gallon. The overall monetary cost of the war to the American taxpayer soared, while Iraqi citizens paid primarily in blood, with thousands of Iraqis dying each month in sectarian and al-Qaeda violence.

Meanwhile, in Washington, under Cheney's impetus the administration continued to aggrandize the powers of the presidency at the expense of the legislative and judicial branches. When Democrats accused the administration of hiding the influence of energy industry lobbyists on recent energy bills, Cheney refused to turn over to Congress any of his visitor records that might document such meetings with energy industry people. When a court challenge to such tactics resulted in a ruling the Cheney office did not like, contrary rulings were sought in more friendly courts. "We're one bomb away from getting rid of that obnoxious [FISA] court," Addington told Jack Goldsmith, and at Addington's lead the administration refused to use the FISA courts that were specifically empowered to review wiretap applications in secret, because it feared a negative ruling. Goldsmith added that Cheney,

Addington, "and other top officials in the administration dealt with FISA the way they dealt with other laws they didn't like: They blew through them in secret based on flimsy legal opinions that they guarded closely so no one could question the legal basis for the operations."

As Goldsmith suggests, that widespread pattern ran through almost every arena of the government. When experts on the federal payroll generated scientific reports that were at odds with administration positions, in agencies ranging from the National Institutes of Health to the Environmental Protection Agency to the National Aeronautics and Space Administration, political appointees in those agencies frequently bowdlerized the reports to eliminate negative findings and comments before publication, and levied penalties against government employees who endorsed the critical findings. At the request of the White House, the Justice Department forced out eight competent U.S. Attorneys and installed more politically accommodating replacements. Political appointees gave Republican campaign briefings on the premises of at least fifteen federal agencies, violating statutes forbidding partisan political activity on government grounds. The sum of these actions was governance by an elite that seemed to consider itself above most laws and believed it owed little to the public and nothing at all to congressional or judicial oversight.

A few reporters saw to it that some of these matters reached the public consciousness, but many ongoing problems did not. The administration's use of "signing statements," a by-product of Cheney's "unitary executive" principles, went largely unnoticed by the public; the Bush administration would eventually issue eleven hundred of them. As the war in Iraq dragged on, and legislators grew less inclined to yield to the administration's wishes, the number of signing statements increased. Not until 2006, when *Boston Globe* reporter Charlie Savage's articles about the statements won international attention (and eventually a Pulitzer Prize), did the administration cut back on issuing such statements.

THE ADMINISTRATION'S MAJOR claim about the war on terror and its extension in Iraq was that it had prevented further al-Qaeda attacks on American soil. But it was not able to prevent al-Qaeda-inspired and -modeled attacks in Spain in 2004, which killed hundreds and toppled a government that had joined the U.S.-led coalition that invaded Iraq. Nor could it prevent the July 7, 2005, suicide bomber attacks on the London underground, which produced dozens of casualties and chaos in the heart of America's most important ally. Two weeks after that, on July 21, terrorists made another attempt to explode four bombs in Great Britain, but the detonators were faulty and little damage was done. The bombings, traced to a bomb factory in Leeds, bore many of the characteristics of al-Qaeda suicide attacks; the dead bombers were either Muslims from Pakistan or had spent time in Pakistan in al-Qaeda circles, and organizations with ties to bin Laden claimed credit for the British bombings. Experts suggested that while bin Laden had been weakened, al-Qaeda had become like a Hydra; the destruction of one head or faction would not prevent others from pursuing the group's anti-American, anti-Western agenda.

Americans were sobered by these attacks in Spain and Great Britain, but by mid-2005, U.S. media attention was increasingly interested in how the United States had gotten into the Iraq War. Special Prosecutor Patrick Fitzgerald's investigation into the Valerie Plame–Joe Wilson matter took center stage, with its focus on the falsification of the run-up to war and the punishing of Ambassador Wilson by the publicizing of his wife's name and CIA affiliation. The two men suspected of leaking Plame's name and identity were White House political director Karl Rove and Cheney's chief of staff, Scooter Libby. The judge sent Judith Miller, the *New York Times* reporter, to jail for refusing to reveal her source. Matt Cooper of *Time* narrowly escaped jail when, under pressure, he testified that Rove had given him the information.

In the midst of all this, Bob Woodward created an odd spectacle when he offered on television to serve part of Miller's sentence, expressing solidarity with her for protecting her sources—while not revealing to his editors or to the public that he too had been told by administration sources of Plame's identity. After Miller emerged from jail, Woodward was finally forced to testify, and only then did he reveal that for two years he had concealed his knowledge about Plame's identity. He apologized to the *Post* management; they were forgiving, but he took intense criticism from other reporters and media analysts for withholding important information in a federal investigation. The incident only underscored Woodward's latter-day reputation as a mouthpiece for his sources in the administration rather than an unbiased reporter.

The White House continued to stymie the Fitzgerald investigation into the Plame leak and threw up similar obstacles in other arenas. It blocked the Senate testimony of retired senior military officers who wanted to call attention to the poor planning for the war in Iraq and the U.S. military's inability to pacify that country. It blocked an internal Department of Justice inquiry into whether Gonzales had acted improperly in overseeing the domestic surveillance program. It blocked internal attempts by Defense, State, and Justice to close Guantánamo and repatriate prisoners the government did not intend to try in court. When the Supreme Court forbade the administration from setting up military tribunals and rejected its interpretation of the Geneva Convention concerning abusive interrogations, Bush vowed to push Congress to grant him those powers explicitly. In 2006 they did just that, passing a bill severely limiting the right of defendants in military courts to the protection of habeas corpus that many scholars considered unconstitutional. As part of a defense appropriations bill, the administration also introduced amendments allowing the president to take control of any state's guard units without the consent of the governor, and to suspend the Posse Comitatus Act, a prohibition against the use of U.S. military forces within the United States. Few people paid attention, and the bill was passed.

The continuing occupation of Iraq swallowed ever-greater segments of the American treasury and consumed the administration's plans. "Commanders in the field had their discretionary financing for things like rebuilding hospitals and providing police uniforms randomly cut; money to pay Iraqi construction firms to build barracks was withheld; contracts we made for purchasing military equipment for the new Iraqi Army were rewritten back in Washington," according to the testimony of a recently retired general who had been in charge of training Iraqi troops. Groups of retired military officers agitated publicly for Rumsfeld to be replaced, calling him not just overbearing and dictatorial but incompetent. Senior active-duty military officials privately expressed their frustration that Rumsfeld had not provided enough troops to do the job in Iraq, or enough armor and armored vehicles to protect the troops from IEDs. Faced with such revolt, Bush convinced an ailing Gerald Ford to give Rumsfeld an endorsement that kept him at the Pentagon until the 2006 midterm election.

For the military officials, however, the problem went beyond Rumsfeld to the fundamental rationale for the war. In their view, the administration had not properly—professionally—taken into account the war's likely consequences (as Fritz Kraemer had demanded of Rumsfeld in their final meeting). Retired lieutenant general William Odom, a fellow of the right-leaning Hudson Institute as well as a professor at Yale, put the argument well in a widely reprinted article:

> First, invading Iraq was not in the interests of the U.S. It was in the interests of Iran and Al Qaeda. For Iran, it avenged a grudge against Hussein for his invasion of the country in 1980. For Al Qaeda, it made it easier to kill Americans. Second, the war has paralyzed the U.S. in the world. . . . Only with a rapid withdrawal from Iraq will Washington regain diplomatic and military mobility. Tied down like Gulliver in the sands of Mesopotamia, we simply cannot attract the diplomatic and military cooperation necessary to win the real battle against terror.

Staunch civilian conservatives now also publicly questioned the war in Iraq. Bill Buckley said in 2004 that if he had known in 2003 "that Saddam Hussein was not the kind of extra-territorial menace that was assumed by the Administration," and that the United States would become bogged down in Iraq, "I would have opposed the war." Rod Dreher, a former *National Review* editor who had initially supported the war and had dismissed pre-invasion critics as "unpatriotic," soon told a radio audience:

> In Iraq, this Republican President for whom I voted twice has shamed our country with weakness and incompetence, and the consequences of his failure will be far, far worse than anything Jimmy Carter did. The fraud, the mendacity, the utter haplessness of our government's conduct of the Iraq war have been shattering to me. It wasn't supposed to turn out like this.

WRESTING THE NATION'S attention from Iraq, Hurricane Katrina struck the American Gulf Coast with tremendous force at the end of August 2005, devastating New Orleans and wreaking havoc in smaller communities from Texas to Florida. Despite the widespread and debilitating destruction, the Bush administration's response to the disaster was slow, ineffectual, and shallow, partly because important resources, such as those of the Army Corps of Engineers and the National Guard, had been diverted to Iraq.

Katrina was a seminal event in modern U.S. history. Bush's apparent lack of distress over the disaster, and his administration's lackadaisical and inept response to it, seemed to validate the charges of incompetence, arrogance, and untruthfulness leveled against the administration over Iraq. After Katrina, Bush's poll ratings began a steady decline. Richard Viguerie, the conservative fund-raiser for Goldwater and Reagan, tied dismay about Iraq to the Katrina response and other administration failures:

> For all of conservatives' patience, we've been rewarded with the botched Hurricane Katrina response. . . . We've been rewarded with an amnesty plan for illegal immigrants. We've been rewarded with a war in Iraq that drags on because of the failure to provide adequate resources at the beginning, and with exactly the sort of "nation-building" that Candidate Bush said he opposed.

Theorist Francis Fukuyama, who had once hailed America's triumph over Marxism as "the end of history," now turned his thoughts to the relationship between the neoconservatism he had helped define and the reality its agenda had confronted in Iraq. "The problem with the neoconservative agenda lies not in its ends, which are as American as apple pie," Fukuyama wrote, "but rather in the overmilitarized means by which it has sought to accomplish them. . . . What is needed now are . . . new ideas that retain the neoconservative belief in the universality of human rights, but without its illusions about the efficacy of American power and hegemony."

Support for Fukuyama's charge about overmilitarization came in July 2006, when a war broke out in Lebanon between Israel and Iran-backed Hezbollah. Shiite militias fired rockets into Israeli territory, and Israel, backed by the Bush administration, retaliated and invaded the southern part of Lebanon. Soon Israel's military was bogged down and Israel was subjected to international denunciations and internal dissent as seldom before in its history. Whatever hope there had been that democracy would overcome the influence of Syria and Muslim extremists in Lebanon vanished in the war. A bad blow for Israel, it was also a setback for neocon backing of military aggression. As some critics noted, in both the Lebanon conflict and the U.S. war in Iraq the real beneficiary was Iran.

As the midterm congressional elections approached, and Bush's popularity sank to levels not seen since Nixon was enmeshed in Watergate, Cheney, Bush, Rumsfeld, and other leaders began to sound a drumbeat about the threat to civilization posed by Iran's nuclear program. Richard Perle even accused Bush of making an "ignominious retreat" on Iran by not answering the Iranian premier's boasts about nuclear development with firm military action.

Once again the CIA, as it had early in the run-up to the Iraq War, tried to douse the flames. It contended in secret reports that evidence from overheard telephone conversations between Iran's military commanders, among other things, convinced the intelligence community that Iran's nuclear program had been shut down, possibly in response to the invasion of Iraq, and had not been revived. In an August 2006 report, a congressional committee headed by an administration loyalist complained that the intelligence agencies were not sounding warnings about Iran loudly enough. The New York Times suggested that the report reflected "the views of some officials inside the White House and the Pentagon who advocated going to war with Iraq and now are pressing for confronting Iran directly over its nuclear program and ties to terrorism."

As the 2006 election approached, the neocons were joined by the Republican-controlled Congress in spoiling for war against Iran. It remained to be seen whether the results of that election, which were expected to challenge Republican control, would deter a second preemptive war.

30

Losing Power

It is a commonplace in American political life that a new election cycle begins immediately after the last one ends. This was never truer than in the period between the elections of 2006 and 2008. Since the invasion of Iraq in 2003, the Bush administration and outside supporters had rejected the comparison of Iraq to Vietnam, insisting that Iraq was no "quagmire." But as the Iraq occupation continued, until it was longer than the American participation in World War I, World War II, or Korea, the analogy acquired more force. After Congress had returned to Democratic hands in 2006, and the American populace had voted decisively against the war, it was clear that the administration would have to turn things around quickly in Iraq or risk losing the White House—and the chance to keep control of U.S. foreign policy in conservative hands. As the administration tried to ensure the succession, though, it incurred a series of moral and political losses that diminished its ability to control and influence events, even as it attempted to change course and abandon its once-treasured neocon positions.

RUMSFELD'S RESIGNATION IN November 2006 removed both a public relations problem and his heavy managerial hand at DoD. Secretary of Defense Robert Gates showed a new willingness to listen to the field commanders, especially General David Petraeus, now in charge of all forces in Iraq. This freed the military to try new tactics as the first of 30,000 additional troops reached Iraq, in a new gambit that had become known as "the surge." Several of these new tactics reversed decisions made early in the occupation on the basis of neocon tenets: The United States now solicited former members of the outlawed Baath Party to return to positions of responsibility and recruited some former veterans of Saddam's army as policemen. These measures fostered better alliances between U.S. troops and local Sunni chieftains against the members of al-Qaeda in Iraq.

Secretary of State Condoleezza Rice began taking steps the neocons had once blocked, diplomatically engaging North Korea and Iran on nuclear matters. She also worked to repair fences with European and Asian allies who had opposed unilateral U.S. operations in Iraq. State's diplomatic efforts made some progress toward getting North Korea to end its nuclear program, in exchange for badly needed supplies, food, and technical assistance from the United States—an approach the Clinton administration had pursued until conservative opposition stalled it, and that George W. Bush and John Bolton had both derided. Later in 2007, the United States participated in a UN climate change summit on Bali and agreed to take part in further talks to reverse global warming, a subject Bush had previously refused to consider. In the fall of 2007, Bush even hosted a summit designed to foster Israeli-Palestinian dialogue—another matter the administration had kept off its agenda for six years.

The administration also pledged to be tougher with the government of Iraq. In a speech on January 10, 2007, Bush described benchmarks Iraq would have to meet to merit continued American involvement:

> To establish its authority, the Iraqi government plans to take responsibility for security in all of Iraq's provinces by November. . . . Iraq will pass legislation to share oil revenues among all Iraqis. . . . The Iraqi government will spend $10 billion of its own money on reconstruction and infrastructure projects that will create new jobs. To empower local leaders, Iraqis plan to hold provincial elections later this year. And to allow more Iraqis to re-enter their nation's political life, the government will reform de-Baathification laws, and establish a fair process for considering amendments to Iraq's constitution.

Other conditions included drawing more Sunnis into the governmental process, working out an equitable distribution of expected oil revenues, and dismantling the Shiite militias. Bush said the United States would hold Iraq to these goals, but the Pentagon continued the surge even when it was clear the Iraqis had made little progress.

Meanwhile, the seamier aspects of the Bush presidency were emerging in the trial of the vice president's former chief of staff, Scooter Libby, for obstruction of justice and perjury. In early March the jury returned a verdict of guilty on four counts, making Libby the highest-ranked official convicted of a crime since Iran-Contra. Speculation immediately focused on whether Bush would pardon Libby, who many thought could possess considerable information involving the false pretenses for going to war in Iraq and other subjects, which he might try to use to bargain his way out of a jail sentence. Bush waited until Libby's appeals were exhausted and he was ordered to jail, then commuted his sentence; his fine and legal fees were paid for with donated funds.

Despite their new majorities in House and Senate, the Democrats seemed unable to do much about changing course in Iraq. Antiwar sentiment was nowhere near as strong as during Vietnam, when the draft affected tens of millions of draftees and their families; now, with all-volunteer forces, one or two million families were directly involved in the war. The Democrats failed to pass bills to force the president to set time limits on U.S. troops in Iraq or to enforce the benchmarks for the Iraqi government. But Congress was now able to investigate the administration's abuses of power, and did so with unusual allies—the bureaucracies of Defense, Justice, and State.

An investigation by the Defense Department's inspector general slammed Douglas Feith's Office of Special Plans and Policy Counter Terrorism Evaluation Group, saying that they "developed, produced, and then disseminated alternative intelligence assessments on the Iraq and al-Qaida relationship, which included some conclusions that were inconsistent with the consensus of the Intelligence Community, to senior decision makers." Though these assessments were not illegal, the report concluded, they were inappropriate, and Feith's office "did not provide 'the most accurate analysis of intelligence.'" Similar DoJ investigations sharply criticized Gonzales's approval of interrogation methods, extraordinary rendition, and his actions in approaching an ailing Attorney General John Ashcroft at his hospital bedside to secure an extension of what Ashcroft's deputy had called an illegal domestic wiretapping program. Justice also began to look into the firings of the eight U.S. attorneys for ostensibly political reasons—firings that were done in a manner that prevented the Senate from exercising its power to examine and confirm (or reject) their replacements. Attorney General Gonzales was forced to resign.

Rumsfeld was out, Libby convicted, Feith discredited, Perle silenced, Bolton pushed out of his acting UN ambassadorship when it became clear that the new Congress would reject his permanent appointment, and now Paul Wolfowitz was forced to resign for alleged improprieties as head of the World Bank. The neocon consortium that had led the United States into the preemptive war in Iraq was losing its hold on power. Cheney remained defiant, brazenly telling Congress that a presidential order governing the protection of classified documents, which required the routine submission of records for inspection by Congress, did not apply to him or his staff because his office was not part of the White House or the executive branch. Most scholars said this stance had no constitutional basis—it even contradicted the stance the vice president's office took in 2002 and 2003 when it submitted such reports—but Congress could do little about it.

After a long fight with the White House and the Department of Justice, Senator Sheldon Whitehouse, a Democrat from Rhode Island, managed to have three opinions from the Bush Office of Legal Counsel declassified, opinions that were at the heart of the administration's effort to expand executive authority. The opinions included the assertions that a president could alter any previous executive order issued by himself or his predecessors without reference to Congress; that Justice had to follow the law as the president interpreted it (rather than as written or in its own interpretation); and that the president alone could determine the scope of his powers under Article II of the Constitution. According to Whitehouse, a former U.S. Attorney, and most constitutional scholars, these assertions flew in the face of the 1803 Supreme Court decision in *Marbury v. Madison* that only the judicial branch "can say what the law is." The sum total of these Bush Office of Legal Counsel opinions, Whitehouse concluded, was to place the president above the law and outside the Constitution.

SENATOR BARACK OBAMA of Illinois, a first-term senator and an African American, announced for the Democratic nomination in 2007, touting, among other things, his early opposition to the war in Iraq. The early frontrunner, Senator Hillary Clinton of New York, and former senator John Edwards both said they now opposed the occupation of Iraq, but like Kerry in 2004 their position was hampered by their previous Senate votes for the invasion of Iraq and for later military funding bills. Republican candidates treated the war in Iraq as a responsibility the United States must continue. Senator John McCain of Arizona, a third-generation navy man who had been imprisoned in North Vietnam for five years, was the most militarily aggressive of the Republicans, an early proponent of increasing troop strength in Iraq and an adamant backer of the surge.

There was some progress in pacifying Iraq, attributable to the surge and to new efforts to increase community patrols and engage with Iraqi civilians—Petraeus initiatives that Rumsfeld had disparaged. Some of these developments were reported in the media, but they were largely drowned out by revelations about malfeasance in the early days of the war. The reliance on private military contractors, accepted originally as a way to keep down the total of U.S. military forces, became an embarrassment: Beyond the pre-dictable fraud and waste lay repeated instances of seemingly unwarranted killings of Iraqi civilians. And there were other problems: The State Depart-ment inspector general who was investigating Blackwater turned out to have a brother who was a consultant to the firm's board. Accusations of cronyism were buttressed by revelations of substantial procurement irregularities in contracts involving Cheney's former firm, Halliburton, its subsidiaries, and other U.S. firms operating in Iraq on no-bid contracts.

Comparable fraud and misuse of funds was discovered in Pakistan, to which the United States had given billions of dollars to pursue al-Qaeda and secure the Afghan border. President Musharraf, the man Bush liked to call "Mushy," had diverted the funds to shore up Pakistan's arsenals targeting India.

Members of the "coalition of the willing" accelerated their pullback from Iraq. When Prime Minister Tony Blair stepped aside, Gordon Brown, a man from Blair's own party, soon announced plans to draw down the British contingent of troops in Iraq and hand the key southern province of Basra back to the Iraqis. From an initial contingent of 45,000 British troops, the U.K. force in Iraq dwindled to less than one-tenth that size. The goal, Brown said, was "Iraqification" of the country's defense forces— a term the Bush administration had refused to use because of its obvious echoes of "Vietnamization." Australia's new prime minister, Kevin Rudd, announced the withdrawal of most of Australia's troops. By the end of 2007, besides the United States, only the former Soviet republic of Geor-gia had more than a thousand troops remaining in Iraq. Thirteen more nations, including longtime U.S. allies such as South Korea, planned to bring their troops home by the end of 2008.

Old mistakes returned to haunt the administration. In preparation to invade Iraq, the Pentagon had pulled troops out of Afghanistan prematurely. In 2007, resurgent violence from the Taliban and tribal chieftains threatened to capsize the Hamid Karzai government's fragile hold on the sprawling country. The U.S. Marine Corps formally asked to have its 25,000 troops in Iraq transferred from policing work there to Afghanistan, where they could do more militarily. Gates rejected the transfer and pressured NATO coun-tries to step up to the plate in Afghanistan. Their reluctance stemmed in part from their disapproval of America's actions in Iraq, and in part because they were unprepared for such detail, having relied on the United States to shoulder their defense responsibilities for generations.

In late 2007, Russian president Vladimir Putin announced that his country was opting out of the 1990 treaty that reduced conventional forces in Europe, one of the glories of the George H. W. Bush–Gorbachev cooperation. Withdrawing would free Russia from the whims of NATO and the United States and allow it to move its forces wherever it thought best—precisely what the neocons had once been so keen to prevent. *Time* honored Putin as its Man of the Year. China also flexed its muscles, denying American aircraft carriers and attendant vessels temporary berths in Hong Kong, destroying a satellite in midair, test-firing long-range missiles, hacking the Pentagon's security system, and becoming a major player dispensing aid and investment in Africa. The neocons had insisted that the war in Iraq would increase U.S. power in the world. Instead China and Russia seemed intent on exercising theirs, in ways that flew in the face of U.S. interests.

"NOTHING WORKS WITHOUT power," Fritz Kraemer was fond of saying. In October 2007, Kraemer's devoted pupil Hubertus Hoffmann quoted the line in a speech that was heavily influenced by Kraemer's thinking. Hoffmann, a German industrialist, media baron, and former arms control expert, had worked in the United States when young and taped his conversations with Kraemer. Before the world's oldest debating society, the University Philosophical at Trinity College in Dublin, Ireland, he said that "as a friend of the United States of America who wants to strengthen the most important democracy on earth and the leader of the Free World," he felt compelled to call attention to the many errors in America's foreign policy during the Bush administration.

Hoffmann described recent U.S. foreign policy as "mismanaged . . . and dominated by U.S.-centric provincialism." The U.S. actions in Iraq and Afghanistan had been "unsuccessful," he charged, because the United States had focused on military conquest without adequate analysis of the international context, or for the need for regional forces, and had failed to understand the ethnic, religious, and economic divisions in Iraq and Afghanistan. The United States, Hoffmann asserted, must commit to an intelligent "grand strategy" entailing not only the use of military power but also diplomacy and the need for reconciliation. Hoffman insisted—as he implied Kraemer would have—that U.S. foreign affairs could not be conducted solely by scaring enemies; there must also be "charm, kindness, greatness, principles of human rights and law and openness," qualities that Hoffmann maintained had underlain all prior American victories. Henceforth, Hoffmann said, the United States must "believe and fight for" the true Kraemer creed—not a simplistic emphasis on military might but rather a soldierly code of honor that relied on "absolute values."

. . . .

Fritz Kraemer was a man of his times, and his tenets were grounded in—some might say unduly tethered to—the realities of twentieth-century totalitarianism as embodied by Hitler's Germany and Stalin's USSR. To survive beyond the era of its founder, any philosophy, political, economic, or religious, must be adaptable to new circumstances and realities. Kraemer himself largely understood the difference between the need to confront the Soviet empire at every turn and the need to confront international terrorists who attacked the United States. But his neocon disciples did not make that shift without rejecting some of his principles. Kraemer's sense of America's mission in the world did not include the urge to expand American hegemony or to enforce America's values on peoples that did not willingly embrace them. His view of America's role as the world's only superpower put more emphasis on the moral responsibilities of leadership than on the possibility of using that status to aggrandize American power.

The neocons, some of whom had learned Kraemer's ideas from him directly, embraced his tenets of aggressiveness, elitism, military strength and readiness, the centrality of power in the formulation of foreign policy, and the need for moral clarity in taking military action. Despite the neocons' frequent claims to be acting on moral ground, they often unduly conflated their moral imperatives with their dreams of exercising power. In the first years of the twenty-first century, the results of this conflation included the negation of hard-won treaties, a refusal to engage with sovereign states they disagreed with, a trampling on civil liberties in the name of safety, a push to aggrandize the executive branch at the expense of the democratic process, and a preemptive war with untold costs in blood and treasure. In the process, the moral authority and economic stability of the United States were seriously diminished.

The situation in Iraq improved in the fall of 2007. Oil production finally reached prewar levels. General Petraeus reported to Congress a considerable reduction of violence in the battle zones, though it was unclear to him whether the peace in Baghdad was permanent or merely a temporary result of increased troop levels. Without Iraqi political progress, however, Petraeus and others testified that the strides being made by the augmented U.S. military presence would not continue. That month, a Government Accountability Office report showed that Iraq's government had met only one of the eight core "legislative, security, and economic benchmarks" the U.S. government had set for it to meet by November.

In the first week of December 2007, the Bush foreign policy suffered three telling blows.

The first and most important came from the CIA's new National Intelligence Estimate on Iran, which reported that Iran had shut down its nuclear program in 2003 and was still dormant in 2007, though it could resume at any moment. A defector from Iran had brought out confirming evidence of the shutdown in March 2007, but it had not been made public. According to some reports, it took a threat of resignation from some intelligence officials to overcome Cheney's yearlong attempt to keep this information secret. An immediate uproar followed: Just weeks earlier Bush and Cheney had been warning that the United States might need to bomb Iran to avert a possible World War III if the country refused to stop its nuclear program—yet even as they made these apocalyptic pronouncements Bush and Cheney evidently already knew of the NIE's conclusions. Bush now said he'd only been told of the NIE's new conclusions very recently. This raised echoes of questions surrounding Ronald Reagan's knowledge of Iran-Contra: Had the president lied? Or had he been deliberately kept in the dark?

The second matter also involved the need for diplomacy. Early in the Bush administration, the president and John Bolton of the State Department had said unkind things about the North Korean leader, Kim Jong Il, and had refused to conduct direct negotiations with North Korea. Now, in December 2007, Bush wrote what the White House described as a cordial letter to Kim, to encourage progress in the multiparty talks aimed at eliminating North Korea's nuclear program and bringing the country closer to South Korea and the West. The letter marked an explicit break with the neocons' obstinate refusals to engage in dialogue with those perceived as enemies.

The third matter was the unexpected revelation by the CIA that it had destroyed tapes of its interrogations with imprisoned al-Qaeda leaders, despite instructions from Congress and the courts. The CIA said it had destroyed the tapes because if they became public their harshness would have aided al-Qaeda recruitment. The implication was that the interrogations had been so rough that they may either have qualified as torture or come perilously close to it. The tapes, made in 2003, were destroyed in 2005 after discussions at the White House among Gonzales, Addington, Bush confidante Harriet Miers, and lawyers from the CIA and DoD. The notion of lawyers sitting in the White House weighing whether to destroy tapes that could be evidence of a crime was an unsettling echo of the Nixon White House.

To the astonishment of the press, President Bush insisted that he had been apprised of matters such as the destruction of the CIA's interrogation tapes and the reversal of the NIE on Iran's nuclear program only in broad outline, and only weeks before the knowledge became public. This tactic took "plausible deniability" to a new and much higher level, insulating the president from charges of destruction of evidence by contending that decisions on highly important matters had been made without him.

ON DECEMBER 12, 2007, *USA Today* published an article hailing the positive signs of progress in Iraq. Yet it observed that "there is no clear picture of the endgame in Iraq. . . . Exactly what do we expect success to look like? Will we leave behind a permanent presence? None of the answers are any clearer than they were when the news began improving." The White House had "lowered the benchmarks for [Iraqi political] success to the level of irrelevance," the paper charged, making for "an open-ended commitment."

The newspaper also pointed out that antiwar Democrats had missed the point of the surge by continuing to insist on withdrawing the troops very soon—an action that could "squander the progress of recent months."

The *Economist* took a harsher view, succinctly expressed in the title of its cover story, "Iraq and Afghanistan: Must They Be Wars Without End?"

> The hope (once shared, we admit, by this newspaper) that the West's armies could return swiftly home and leave good order behind them was naïve. Saddam Hussein and the Taliban ran cruel dictatorships. But in uprooting them the West exposed deep tribal and sectarian schisms, unleashing violent forces that the dictators had kept in check.

The neocons had used their power to plunge the United States into war in Iraq, but by the end of 2007 even once-fervent proponents of the war no longer believed it could be won on the ground. The Iraq venture had damaged their arguments, perhaps beyond repair. The Forty Years War was now all but over, to be sealed by one final battle: the presidential campaign of 2008.

President Barack Obama with his secretary of state, Hillary Clinton, at a NATO summit in Strasbourg, France, April 4, 2009. *(U.S. Army)*

Epilogue: Foreign Affairs
and the Election of 2008

I n the final year of the George W. Bush administration, the foreign policy battle between the pragmatists and the ideologues was reignited by the presidential campaign clash between Democrat Barack Obama and Republican John McCain. If the general election had involved different candidates on either side, foreign policy issues such as the continuation of the war in Iraq and whether or not to make diplomatic overtures to Iran, Syria, and North Korea might have been lost in the candidates' shuffle to distance themselves from President Bush. McCain's total embrace of Bush's foreign policy, and Obama's promise of a new day in America's relations with the rest of the world, defined their battle.

A MORE AGGRESSIVE militarist than any major party candidate in the previous century, Senator McCain counted among his foreign policy advisers a who's who of the neocon movement, including William Kristol, Robert Kagan, James Woolsey, Peter Rodman, and Randy Scheunemann, a project director for the PNAC. Although endorsed by Kissinger, Haig, Eagleburger, and other Republican former secretaries of state, McCain was clearly a man of force, not diplomacy: If elected, he made clear, he would not only continue the wars in Iraq and Afghanistan, but might very well take military action against Iran and confront Russia and China as well. McCain called for ousting Russia from the Group of Eight industrialized nations. When the Iraqi government floated the idea of sending home American forces after another year or so—a timetable resembling that suggested by Obama—McCain said he wouldn't allow it to happen, and ventured that the United States, not Iraq, would decide how long to stay there—a hundred years if need be. Frustrated with the UN's unwillingness to back U.S. actions automatically, McCain endorsed a proposal for a "League of Democracies" that would supersede the UN and take action around the globe whenever and wherever it felt appropriate. "The nations of the NATO alliance and the European Union," he wrote in the *Financial Times* of March 18, 2008, "must have the ability and the will to act in defense of freedom and economic prosperity. They must spend the money necessary to build effective military and civilian capabilities that can be deployed around the world, from the Balkans to Afghanistan, from Chad to East Timor." McCain's League of Democracies echoed an old neocon fear, expressed in Cheney's "Defense Strategy for the 1990s," that "countries whose interests are very different from our own"—even members of NATO—might block U.S. military action abroad. If McCain won the presidency, it was evident that neocon ideology would dominate U.S. policy for another decade or more.

Those moderate Republicans and independents who wanted an end to the war in Iraq had an increasingly difficult time justifying their potential vote for McCain. In 1976, the refusal of ultraconservatives to vote in the election ensured the defeat of Gerald Ford; in 2008, the Republican moderates might be the ones sitting on their hands.

Senator Obama made it clear that he would remove almost all American troops from Iraq within sixteen months of his taking office, but he also said that the war in Afghanistan demanded more American and NATO troops. He advocated direct, high-level talks with Iran, Syria, and North Korea, more diplomatic engagement with Russia and China, and new overtures to states in the European Union, such as Germany and France, that had kept their distance since the invasion of Iraq. It was a pragmatic approach, one that included both military action and diplomacy.

The events of the post–Cold War era, and the period of the global war on terrorism, had made it quite apparent to most Americans that the United States required a set of core principles to guide its foreign policy, not just a willingness to react to events and pressures as they occurred. During the Cold War Nixon had confronted the similar problem of the need for principles through fashioning pragmatic policies that expressed his preference for engagement over confrontation, for using more carrots than sticks, and for relying on regional alliances rather than superpower intervention. Such preferences now seemed more relevant than they had in decades, yet they were not sufficient to provide principles to deal with the complex realities of an increasingly multipolar world—one that faced the linked evils of poverty and radicalism, one in which small nations as well as large might possess weapons capable of launching warheads at targets thousands of miles away. How should America frame its foreign policy to deal with these complex and interrelated problems?

The question devolved more to the candidacy of Obama, who promised hope and change, than to that of McCain, who was largely pledged to continue prior policies. With a Muslim middle name and a background that included a Kenyan father, a Kansas mother, and an early childhood spent in Indonesia, Obama was accustomed to accommodating disparate influences. Most people understood that his message of change meant not substituting one ideology for another, but something quite different.

Precisely what that new posture would be, Obama left deliberately unclear. That was one reason that some voters, including both Democrats and independents, did not respond to him at first: His speeches sounded reasonable, they agreed, but did not express the sort of coherent underlying philosophy for which they hungered. The danger for Obama was that Democratic moderates might not vote in large enough numbers in November, thereby giving the Republicans and the neocons another four years.

Some neocons, including Ken Adelman and Richard Perle, deserted the Bush administration, declaring that it had botched the occupation of Iraq so badly that it had undercut all the potential good that should have come of the toppling of Saddam. Adelman told journalist David Rose,

> I am extremely disappointed by the outcome in Iraq, because I just presumed that what I considered to be the most competent national-security team since Truman was indeed going to be competent. They turned out to be among the most incompetent teams in the postwar era. Not only did each of them, individually, have enormous flaws, but together they were deadly, dysfunctional.

Adelman believed that "a tough foreign policy on behalf of morality" was still a good idea, but that after the debacle in Iraq, "it's not going to sell." Perle did not blame the president for any military or diplomatic failures; rather, as he put it in a later article, the fault lay with the "sprawling bureaucracies charged with carrying out the president's policies," particularly the Powell-led State Department, and with Paul Bremer, who in Perle's view had contravened all of the Defense Department's good ideas on Iraq.

Moderate Republicans such as Baker, Scowcroft, and Powell, who held back from endorsing McCain, recognized that the Reagan Revolution was rapidly coming to a close, and with it the period of neocon ascendancy. For the past quarter century, the neocons had acted as the glue holding together social conservatives, fiscal conservatives, and foreign policy conservatives, fashioning electoral victories for the Republicans and the continuance of Reagan's vision for America. Based on a belief in American exceptionalism and on a willingness to use military power to expand U.S. influence abroad, the neocons' foreign policies had drawn cheers and votes from several generations of American voters; since George W. Bush had become president, their policies had been America's policies. The neocons' adventure in Iraq, and their willingness to ignore or punish countries that disagreed with the United States' decision, had far-reaching consequences, only a few of which had redounded badly on them and their party since 2001. But that seemed about to change.

The end of the neocon era was approaching, for two reasons. Voter discontent was one. The neocons had overlooked a basic aspect of human nature—that in a democracy most voters have little interest in sacrificing a comfortable way of life on the altar of a political ideology, especially one that involves continual confrontation with the rest of the world. Fritz Kraemer had understood this, but the neocons had lost sight of it in their push to act out their bellicose visions in the name of protecting the United States from another September 11 attack. They launched a preemptive war, among other reasons, to prevent the United States from displaying provocative weakness but overlooked the possibility that a badly managed display of American strength could be equally provocative and produce a severe backlash. The second reason was economics: Worsening financial conditions were hastening the demise of neocon rule. Throughout 2008, the world's economies all contracted at once and entered the deepest recession since the Great Depression in the 1930s. It became clear that when this recession ended, the United States would no longer be the sole driver of economic growth or stability in the world; the economic power of China, India, the Russian sphere of influence, and a more united Europe would become increasingly dominant. That in itself would deter a future return to the promotion of American hegemony that the neocons had pursued so aggressively.

It became clearer that economic strength was now at least on a par with military might as a determinant of power in the world. Eighty years earlier, Peter Drucker had argued to Fritz Kraemer that economic strength should be considered along with military and political strength in weighing the power of nations. Back then Kraemer thought he had the evidence with which to reject his argument. A hundred years after Kraemer's birth, however, the world had changed enough that his emphasis on military might above all had finally become obsolete.

. . . .

A key moment in the 2008 presidential campaign, not long before Election Day, came when former chairman of the Joint Chiefs and former secretary of state Colin Powell endorsed Barack Obama for president. John McCain had called Powell the man in public life he most admired, and their admiration was mutual. But Powell revealed that his endorsement was largely a matter of principle. Contending that the next president would have to "show the world that there is a new administration that will reach out," Powell essentially ratified Obama's rejection of the neocon refusal to engage other countries diplomatically and Obama's willingness to pursue results through dialogue rather than relying on threats and bullying in dealing with America's enemies and friends.

Powell was the last in a long line of Republican moderates to endorse Obama or his intended foreign policies—a line that had already included James Baker, Brent Scowcroft, Republican senators Richard Lugar and Chuck Hagel, and even Henry Kissinger, who was listed among McCain's supporters but told reporters that he agreed with Obama on the necessity of talks with Iran and a more moderate approach to the resurgent Russia than McCain advocated. As Bush's first secretary of state, Powell had been active in getting the United States into the war in Iraq. Now he was backing a man who pledged to get us out quickly. On several grounds, Powell viewed Obama as "a transformational figure."

At around the time of the Powell endorsement, the Bush administration extended the doctrine of preemptive war by launching a raid inside Syrian territory aimed at taking out an Iraqi insurgent leader who had been wreaking havoc inside Iraq. Secretary of Defense Gates said the United States was justified in pursuing terrorists anywhere, and that we would pursue anyone—a state or an individual—who aided them "whether by facilitating, financing or providing expertise or safe haven for such efforts." And Paul Wolfowitz, reappointed by Condoleezza Rice as head of an advisory board, warned that the United States needed to build more missiles to keep up with those China was now constructing— a notion that at least one critic viewed as a potential opening bell in a new Cold War between the United States and China. McCain applauded these stances.

Two weeks later, Obama won the presidency by a comfortable margin. His victory sent waves of jubilation around the world, not only at the prospect of Obama's presidency but also at the certainty that Bush's legacy would not be carried over into a McCain administration.

. . . .

During the campaign, Barack Obama—like Richard Nixon before him—had published an article in *Foreign Affairs* that laid out his foreign policy goals: "After thousands of lives lost and billions of dollars spent, many Americans may be tempted to turn inward and cede our leadership in world affairs. But this is a mistake we must not make. America cannot meet the threats of this century alone, and the world cannot meet them without America."

President-elect Obama's choices for foreign policy positions confirmed his centrist, pragmatic outlook. He chose his rival in the primaries, Senator Hillary Clinton, as secretary of state; retained Gates as secretary of defense; brought back from retirement Marine Corps general and former NATO commander James L. Jones, Jr., as national security adviser; and tapped Susan E. Rice, a Brookings scholar and advocate for international coopera- tion, as ambassador to the United Nations. During Senator Clinton's confir- mation hearings, she echoed Obama's *Foreign Affairs* article in contending, "America cannot solve the most pressing problems on our own, and the world cannot solve them without America. The best way to advance Amer- ica's interest in reducing global threats and seizing global opportunities is to design and implement global solutions. This isn't a philosophical point. This is our reality."

In his inaugural address, Obama addressed both the foreign policies of the previous administration and the sources of strength for the country's future direction:

> As for our common defense, we reject as false the choice between our safety and our ideals. . . . Those ideals still light the world, and we will not give them up for expedience's sake. . . . Earlier generations faced down fascism and communism not just with missiles and tanks, but with sturdy alliances and enduring convictions. They understood that our power alone cannot protect us, nor does it entitle us to do as we please. . . . Our security emanates from the justness of our cause; the force of our example; the tempering qualities of humility and re- straint. . . . Guided by these principles once more, we can meet those new threats that demand even greater effort, even greater cooperation and understanding between nations. . . . We will not apologize for our way of life nor will we waver in its defense.

With Obama's first week in office, the new administration's intentions in foreign policy became clearer. In Secretary Clinton's first address to State

Department employees, she proclaimed a "new era" for American foreign policy; there were, she said, "three legs to the stool" of foreign policy—defense, diplomacy, and development—and State was responsible for two of the three. The president joined her in announcing the appointment of two senior diplomats for special assignments, former senator George Mitchell as an envoy to the Middle East, and former ambassador Richard Holbrooke as an adviser on Afghanistan and Pakistan. Mitchell was immediately dispatched to help make peace after a three-week battle between Israel and the Palestinians in the Gaza Strip; Holbrooke flew farther east to attempt to bring stability to Afghanistan and to work closely with Pakistan on al-Qaeda and Taliban problems in the Afghanistan–Pakistan border region.

In one of his first actions as president, Obama announced that the United States would work toward closing the prison facilities at Guantánamo Bay, a move greeted with approval from around the world. He followed it on January 22 with an executive order directing that U.S. government agencies follow the Geneva Conventions and the Army Field Manual rules regarding treatment of prisoners, meaning that the United States would renounce torture. He also ordered the CIA to close its prisons abroad.

President Obama gave an early interview to al-Arabiya, a Dubai-based television network, in which he told Muslims explicitly that "the U.S. is not your enemy" and pledged to work more closely with the Muslim world—for instance to have his administration talk directly with Iran. The interview aired in the Middle East as Mitchell arrived in Egypt on the first stop of an eight-nation peacemaking tour through the Middle East, France, and Great Britain. The White House soon let reporters know that the president and the State Department were preparing a letter to Iran giving assurances that the United States was not seeking regime change in Tehran.

When some critics charged that for the United States to directly communicate with Iran was a show of weakness on our part, Obama justified the opening by saying that this issue had been settled by his election: "The whole notion that somehow if we showed courtesy or opened up dialogue with a government that had previously been hostile to the U.S., that somehow that would be a sign of weakness—the American people didn't buy it."

Vice President Joseph Biden led a high-level U.S. delegation to an annual European security conference in Munich that in the past had been the province of the secretary of defense—another signal that the new administration would favor diplomacy over military force. "We will engage. We will listen. We will consult. America needs the world just as I believe the world needs America," the vice president said. Biden's diplomatic overture was matched with a warning that Iran must be prevented from accumulating nuclear weapons; he also said that the United States, "in cooperation with our NATO allies and Russia," would continue to develop a missile shield to be placed in Europe that was designed to counter Iranian nuclear weapons. He welcomed Russia's participation in areas such as Afghanistan while rejecting the idea of a Russian sphere of influence there.

THE OBAMA ADMINISTRATION inherited daunting foreign policy challenges, but they were not without precedent. Forty years earlier, on entering the White House, Richard Nixon had to deal with a quagmire of a war begun by his predecessor, with the need to extract the United States from that war in a way that enhanced the country's world position, and with the need to forge new relationships with the other great powers.

Obama's approach toward his similar problems and challenges was thoroughly pragmatic, as Nixon's had been, but it was also based on Obama's frequently articulated belief in the need for a moral basis to foreign policy— which recalled Fritz Kraemer's insistence on "absolute values" as the basis for action, whether by individuals or by the United States of America.

The possibilities of Obama's "transformative" presidency also represented a fitting end to the Forty Years War—the beginning of a way forward in foreign affairs that could combine the morally grounded position of the United States that is the positive legacy of Fritz Kraemer with the realism that underlay Richard Nixon's pragmatic breakthroughs in foreign policy. Such a formula might finally transcend those two philosophies' excesses and baggage, blending our highest ideals with the best practical approaches toward solving what are now, and will increasingly be, worldwide problems.

Acknowledgments

The Forty Years War has been in formation since Len Colodny and Tom Shachtman began discussing the subject in the 1990s; the authors would like to thank Monica Crowley, Robert Estabrook, Robert Gettlin, Fred Graboske, Joan Hoff, Hubertus Hoffmann, Peter Klingman, Ray Locker, Roger Morris, Herb Parmet, and James Rosen for many years of encouragement and advice on this project. Rosen kindly shared his archives for *The Strong Man* and was helpful in other research, for instance, allowing us to use his long interview with Alexander Haig from the year 2000. Rick Moss assisted in locating some materials on Kissinger and Kraemer, and Luke Nichter provided new transcriptions of some Nixon White House tapes.

Portions of the manuscript were read and critiqued for us by Charlie Carlson, John Colodny, Larry DeNardis, Fred Graboske, Ray Locker, Edward Nickerson, James Rosen, John G. Ryden, Noah Shachtman, and Chuck Shanberg; their suggestions and counsel helped the final product.

Editor Calvert Morgan of HarperCollins, by his sharp queries and demands for added information and word sense, also guided and improved this book in ways that went beyond the usual editor's shepherding tasks, and for this we thank him. We also thank our agent, Mel Berger, for his diligence and continued support for the project.

The authors are indebted to the National Archives II Library in Maryland, the New York Public Library, the Nixon Library, the Scoville Library of Salisbury and the Connecticut interlibrary loan system, and the University of Iowa Library for assisting us in various research endeavors and for providing research homes for us at various times during the long haul.

3333333

Sandy Colodny and Tom's wife, Harriet Shelare, our families and friends, our colleagues on various civic boards and neighborhood associations were all helpful to us in so many ways that it is impossible to enumerate them all, but for which we are grateful.

Despite the efforts of all these people, any errors that remain in the manuscript are ours alone.

—Len Colodny and Tom Shachtman

A PERSONAL NOTE BY LEN COLODNY

The Forty Years War is being published during the fiftieth year of our marriage. Sandy Colodny has been the rock of my life during all those years; a great friend, wife, and mother. Without her love and support I would never have been able to write this book. I love her and respect her. Happy fiftieth anniversary, Sandy, and I hope for many more.

Notes and Bibliography

MAJOR DOCUMENTARY SOURCES

The notes and bibliography have been constructed to provide interested readers with the most widely available sources. Where possible, we have included Web addresses for citations. The "Nixon Presidential Materials" (NPM) files are at the College Park depot of the National Archives, and at http://nixon.archives.gov, and www.nara.gov/Nixon/. Also there are the Henry A. Kissinger (HAK) papers and tape transcripts. Papers and memoranda from the Ford years are at the Ford Presidential Library, and some are online at www.fordlibrarymuseum.gov/library/docs.asp. The largest collection of Nixon White House tapes and matched transcripts are at http://nixontapes.org/. The most important nongovernmental collection of documents from the entire era is that assembled by the National Security Archive, under the auspices of George Washington University, at www.gwu.edu/~nsarchiv/NSAEBB. Oral history interviews of the Nixon, Ford, Carter, and Reagan years, conducted for the Miller Center in Virginia, are also online, at http://millercenter.virginia.edu. Information on Fritz Kraemer, Alexander Haig, James Schlesinger, and other individuals profiled by journalist Nick Thimmesch are in the Nick Thimmesch Papers, University of Iowa, Iowa City. Index at http://www.lib.uiowa.edu/spec-coll/MSC/ToMsC750/MsC709/thimmesch.html. Interviews conducted by Colodny or Shachtman are indicated by date and interviewer. Some excerpts from Colodny interviews of Mitchell, Haldeman, Ehrlichman, Laird, Ford, Woodward, and others are also online at www.watergate.com.

IN THE INTEREST OF BREVITY

Full citations for most printed book and magazine sources will be found in the selected bibliography rather than in the notes. Regular news articles from the *New York Times*, *Washington Post*, *Time*, *Newsweek*, and other general-circulation periodicals are not usually referenced, nor are short quotations by individuals that come from such articles. Readily available Nixon White House tapes and authorized transcripts are also not individually referenced. We do note where we have transcribed previously untranscribed tapes or added sections of previously available tapes. Generally, books or articles cited only once are not part of the selected bibliography.

Notes

PROLOGUE: IS THIS THE BEGINNING OF THE END OF THE NEOCONS?

2   *"as long as Donald Rumsfeld"*: Thomas E. Ricks, *The Gamble: General David Petraeus and the American Military Adventure in Iraq, 2006–2008* (New York: Penguin, 2009).

2   *"Clearly, what U.S. forces are currently doing"*: Rumsfeld to Bush, November 6, 2006. Quoted in Michael R. Gordon and David S. Cloud, "Rumsfeld Memo Proposed 'Major Adjustment' in Iraq," *New York Times*, December 3, 2006.

2   *Bush had determined to fire*: Bradley Graham, *By His Own Rules: The Ambitions, Successes, and Ultimate Failures of Donald Rumsfeld* (New York: Public Affairs Press, 2009).

3   *he had influenced generals*: Kraemer's tenets are quoted in Hubertus Hoffmann, *Fritz Kraemer on Excellence* (New York: World Security Network, 2004).

4   *"Fortunately, we do have a president"*: Wolfowitz, remarks at Hoffmann/Kraemer book party, www.worldsecuritynetwork.com/showArticle3.cfm?article_id=10650&topicID=46.

6   *Iraq Study Group*: Report of the Iraq Study Group, http://www.usip.org/isg/iraq_study_group_report/report/1206/index.html.

1. NIXON'S FOREIGN POLICY DREAMS

13   *"has lived during the last decade"*: Hans J. Morgenthau, *A New Foreign Policy for the United States* (New York: Praeger, 1969).

14   *speech to the Bohemian Club*: reprinted in *Foreign Relations of the United States, 1969–1976* (hereinafter *FRUS*), vol. 1, *Foundations of Foreign Policy, 1969–1972* (Washington, D.C.: U.S. Government Printing Office, 1999–2005).

14   *"Asia after Vietnam"*: Richard M. Nixon, *Foreign Affairs*, October 1967, in *FRUS, 1969–1976*, vol. 1., op. cit.

16   *"My role was not discovering Kissinger"*: Kraemer, quoted in Nick Thimmesch, "The Iron Mentor of the Pentagon," syndicated column, March 2, 1975.

16   *"I was in awe of Kraemer"*: Kissinger eulogy, reprinted in Hoffman, op. cit., and at www.henryakissinger.com/eulogies/100803.html.

17   *"treason"*: Johnson to Everett Dirksen, October 30, 1968, Johnson Library tapes, http://www.lbjlib.utexas.edu.

17   *conservative voters actually provided*: See also Mary C. Brennan, *Turning Right in the Sixties* (Chapel Hill: University of North Carolina Press, 1995).

18 *the so-called secret plan*: Richard Whalen, "Revolt of the Generals," *Nation*, October 16, 2006, http://www.thenation.com/doc/20061016/whalen.

19 *"We need you in there"*: Richard V. Allen in Miller Center interview, May 8, 2002, Miller Center, Ronald Reagan Oral History Project, http://millercenter.org/scripps/archive/oralhistories/detail/3205.

19 *"You are not going to be able to make foreign policy"*: Kraemer, quoted in Bernard Collier, "The Road to Peking," *New York Times Magazine*, November 14, 1971.

19 *"damage to his soul"*: Kraemer, interview notes in Thimmesch Papers, University of Iowa.

19 *"important to move promptly"*: Memorandum from President Johnson to President-elect Nixon, November 25, 1968, Johnson Library, National Security File, Rostow Files, Nixon & Transition.

20 *"the President-elect meant it when he said"*: Memorandum, Kissinger to Nixon, December 18, 1968, NPM, HAK Files.

20 *Goodpaster was perturbed*: Nixon Administration National Security Council Roundtable, October 8. 1998. Transcript at www.brookings.edu/projects/archive/nsc/19981209.aspx.

20 *"If the State Department has had a new idea"*: Nixon, quoted by Lee Holdridge in Nixon NSC Roundtable on China Policy, 1999. Transcript at www.cissm.umd.edu/papers/display/php?id=84.

20 *"I refuse to be confronted"*: Nixon, quoted in Peter W. Rodman, *Presidential Command: Power, Leadership, and the Making of Foreign Policy from Richard Nixon to George W. Bush* (New York: Knopf, 2009).

20 *"recreate the illusion"*: Ellsberg, quoted in Larry Berman, *No Peace, No Honor: Nixon, Kissinger, and Betrayal in Vietnam* (New York: Free Press, 2001).

21 *His first choice for Defense*: Robert G. Kaufman, *Henry M. Jackson: A Life in Politics* (Seattle: University of Washington Press, 2000).

21 *"Rogers felt that Kissinger was Machiavellian"*: Richard Nixon, *RN: The Memoirs of Richard Nixon* (New York: Grosset & Dunlap, 1978).

22 *came with a personal note*: Kraemer, quoted in Hoffman, op. cit. Henry A. Kissinger, in *Years of Renewal* (New York: Simon & Schuster, 1999), confirms that Kraemer recommended Haig to him.

2. THE ANTI-NIXON

23 *"a cadaverous man, naked except for"*: Peter Drucker, "The Man Who Invented Kissinger," in Drucker, *Adventures of a Bystander* (New York: Harper & Row, 1979).

23 *"destroyed all foundations"*: Sven F. Kraemer, "My Father's Pilgrimage," in Hoffman, op. cit.

25 *"Somewhat incongruously, a few miles"*: Kissinger, *Years of Renewal*, op. cit.

26 *"history is not really made"*: Kraemer to Kissinger, November 1, 1956, letter in Rockefeller Brothers Fund collection, quoted in Jeremi Suri, *Henry Kissinger and the American Century* (Cambridge, Mass.: Harvard University Press, 2007).

26 *a trio of fervent anti-Communists*: Kraemer, telephone conversation with Kissinger, in Kissinger telephone conversation transcripts (telcons), National Archives; and Edward Rowny, interview with Shachtman, October 12, 2007. The National Archives recently released about two dozen transcripts of telephone conversations between Kissinger and Kraemer, dating from 1969 to 1973, and a few others, including a Nixon tape, that reference Kissinger-Kraemer conversations.

27 *"strong convictions and his great love"*: Haig to Thimmesch, February 11, 1975, Thimmesch Papers, op. cit.

27 *"too long," "too bourgeois"*: Rowny interview, op. cit. See also Rowny, *It Takes One to Tango* (Washington, D.C.: Brassey's, 1992).

28 *"ability to look above the horizon"*: Walters interview with Thimmesch, notes for "Iron Mentor" article, Thimmesch Papers, op. cit.

28 *could successfully deter aggression*: F. G. A. Kraemer, "The Modern World, a Single 'Strategic Theater,'" occasional paper for Henry Kissinger, September 22, 1969, NARA, Nixon NSC Files, Box 822.

28   *"We [the United States of America] are a rich country"*: Kraemer, in Wes Vernon, "U.S. Posi-
     tion on China: 'Provocative Weakness,'" Newsmax, April 28, 2001, http://archive.newsmax.
     com/archives/articles/2001/4/27/205658.shtml.
29   *"The statesman is suspicious of those"*: Kissinger, *The Troubled Partnership: A Re-appraisal of
     the Atlantic Alliance* (Garden City, N.Y.: Doubleday, 1966).
30   *"spellbinder"*: Haig to Thimmesch, February 11, 1975, op. cit.
30   *"close, both personally and professionally"*: Ibid.
30   *Years later, when Rowny found out*: Rowny interview, op. cit.
31   *"Kraemer's values were absolute"*: This, and quotations from Rowny, Sonnenfeldt, Haig, and
     Rumsfeld, are in Hoffman; Schlesinger quoted in Thimmesch, "Iron Mentor," op. cit.

3. SENDING SIGNALS

33   *"Without secrecy there would have been"*: Memorandum for the President's Files, "Briefing
     of the White House Staff on the July 15 Announcement of the President's Trip to Peking,"
     July 19, 1971, NSC Files, Box 1136, China—General, July–October 1971, document 41 at
     http://www.gwu.edu/~nsarchiv/NSAEBB/NSAEBB66/.
34   *believed they were finally in position*: Lewis A. Sorley, *A Better War: The Unexamined Victo-
     ries and Final Tragedy of America's Last Years in Vietnam* (San Diego: Harcourt, 1999).
34   *Johnson's rules of engagement had seriously hampered*: H. R. McMaster, *Dereliction of Duty:
     Lyndon Johnson, Robert McNamara, the Joint Chiefs of Staff, and the Lies That Led to Viet-
     nam* (New York: HarperCollins, 1997).
34   *Laird was an astute politician*: Dale Van Atta, *With Honor: Melvin Laird in War, Peace, and
     Politics* (Madison: University of Wisconsin Press, 2008).
34   *"Laird would think nothing"*: Henry A. Kissinger, *White House Years* (Boston: Little, Brown,
     1979).
35   *"potential military actions which might jar"*: Memo, Laird to Kissinger, February 21, 1969,
     contained in memo, Haig to Kissinger, March 2, 1969, NPM, HAK files, document 2 at
     http://www.gwu.edu/~nsarchiv/NSAEBB/NSAEBB81/index2.htm.
35   *"actual or feigned"*: Haig to Kissinger, ibid. In February–March 1953, Eisenhower directed
     similar feigned actions to pressure North Korea and the People's Republic of China to end
     the Korean war. Cf. Stephen E. Ambrose, *Eisenhower: The President* (New York: Simon &
     Schuster, 1984).
35   *kept Fritz Kraemer updated*: Rowny interview, op. cit.
35   *They would phone each other's office*: Kissinger telephone conversation transcripts.
36   *Dobrynin tried to raise the topic*: Anatoly Dobrynin, *In Confidence* (New York: Times Books,
     1995).
36   *At the first back-channel meeting*: Dobrynin–Kissinger exchanges, culled from American
     and recently released Russian sources, at www.gwu.edu/~nsarchiv/NSAEBB/NSAEBB233/
     index.htm.
37   *"Our Leader has taken leave"*: Kissinger, quoted by Haig in Alexander M. Haig, Jr., with
     Charles McCarry, *Inner Circles: How America Changed the World, A Memoir* (New York:
     Warner, 1992). Cf. similar wording, Haig interview in *Nixon's China Game*, PBS, *The
     American Experience*.
38   *"without any notice to people"*: Nixon, quoted in John Prados, *Keepers of the Keys: The
     National Security Council from Truman to Bush* (New York: Morrow, 1991).
38   *an ABM system known as Galosh*: John Newhouse, *Cold Dawn: The Story of SALT* (Wash-
     ington, D.C.: Pergamon-Brassey's, 1989).
38   *no ABM system could adequately protect*: Minutes of NSC meeting, February 19, 1969, NSC
     files, NPM.
39   *"ignorant of the ways of Washington"*: Kissinger, *White House Years*, op. cit.
40   *recommended to the national security adviser*: Memo, Haig to Kissinger, March 2, 1969,
     op. cit.
40   *"subsequent indications of serious US intent"*: Memo, JCS to Laird, no date, appended to
     Haig to Kissinger, idem.

40 *"less elaborate actions"*: Memo, Kissinger to Laird, March 3, 1969, bundled with Haig to Kissinger, idem.

40 *"before the time given the new Administration"*: Goodpaster, quoted in James F. Wilbanks, *Abandoning Vietnam: How America Left and South Vietnam Lost Its War* (Lawrence: University Press of Kansas, 2004).

40 *"certainly had not come to Saigon"*: Abrams, quoted in Sorley, op. cit.

40 *When he returned, Laird reported*: "Trip to Vietnam," memo, Laird to Nixon, April 13, 1969, NPM.

41 de-Americanization: Kissinger, *White House Years*, op. cit.

41 *in an April 14 memo*: Nixon to Rogers, Laird et al., April 14, 1969, NSC Files, NPM.

41 *"The great fundamental issue"*: Ibid. There is some evidence that the conception and wording were Kissinger's.

41 *on "Vietnamizing of the war"*: National Security Study Memorandum 36, NSC Files, NPM.

42 *"the brooding melancholy of a man"*: Stanley Hoffmann, "The Task of Henry Kissinger," *Chicago Tribune*, April 27, 1969.

43 *The EC-121 incident*: Richard A. Mobley, *Flash Point North Korea: The Pueblo and EC-121 Crises* (Annapolis, Md.: Naval Institute Press, 2003).

43 *"We were being tested"*: Nixon, *RN*, op. cit.

43 *he also consulted Fritz Kraemer*: Collier, op. cit.

44 *"a strong reaction"*: Nixon, *RN*, loc. cit.

44 *"when [North Korean] radar picked"*: U. Alexis Johnson with J. O. McAllister, *The Right Hand of Power* (Englewood Cliffs, N.J.: Prentice-Hall,1984).

45 *"generally unresponsive"*: Kissinger memo, quoted in Mobley, op. cit.

45 *"We set the crisis machinery"*: Kissinger, *White House Years*, op. cit.

45 *Kraemer was so upset*: Kraemer to Kissinger, "View of the Future," June 13, 1969, NPM, NSC Files, Box 822.

46 *In an article on the front page*: William Beecher, "Raids in Cambodia by U.S. Unprotested," *New York Times*, May 9, 1969. Beecher broke silence about this in a 2005 speech, transcribed at http://athome.harvard.edu/programs/fym/fym_video/fym3.html. He claimed that he had figured out the target from bombing statistics and asked sources to confirm or deny it. One said, "I've never lied to you, Bill, so let's change the subject." But cf. the CIA "Family Jewels" for a contention that Beecher's article contained verbatim phrases from classified reports: www.gwu.edu/~nsarchiv/NSAEBB/NSAEBB22/index/html.

46 *One candidate was Morton Halperin*: Martin Tolchin, "Kissinger Issues Wiretap Apology," *New York Times*, November 13, 1992; "The Week the Cloud Burst," *Time*, June 24, 1974, includes Hoover memorandum of 1973 discussing events of 1969. See also memo, J. Edgar Hoover to senior FBI officials, May 9, 1969, 11:05 A.M., NARA, Record Group 460, Plumbers Task Force, Gray/Wiretap Investigations, Box 8, FBI Wiretap Correspondence with White House.

46 *"destroy whoever did this"*: Memo, Hoover to senior FBI officials, May 9, 1969, 5:05 P.M., Gray/Wiretap Investigations, op. cit.

46 *"It is clear I don't have anybody"*: Quoted in memo, Sullivan to Hoover, May 20, 1969, Gray/Wiretap Investigations, op. cit., Box 27, Witness Statements—Sullivan.

47 *"make decisions privately, with K"*: H. R. Haldeman, *The Haldeman Diaries: Inside the Nixon White House*, electronic edition (Santa Monica, Calif.: Sony Imagesoft, 1994). Notes of June 4, 1969.

47 *The North Vietnamese already knew*: William Shawcross, *Sideshow: Kissinger, Nixon, and the Destruction of Cambodia* (New York: Simon & Schuster, 1979).

4. YOUNG MEN IN A HURRY

49 *Nitze had been asked to tutor Nixon*: Paul H. Nitze, Ann M. Smith, and Steven L. Bearden, *From Hiroshima to Glasnost: At the Center of Decision* (New York: Grove & Weidenfeld, 1989).

49 *"the desire of many to wish away"*: Ibid.

50 *"probably would have ended up a very unhappy"*: Wolfowitz, quoted in Bill Keller, "The Sunshine Warrior," *New York Times Magazine*, September 22, 2002.

50 *"enormously impressed with Jackson"*: Perle, in *Neocons and America's Foreign Policy*, America Abroad radio, June 23, 2005, www.allamericanpatriots.com/node/11496.

51 *on her deathbed*: Mrs. Thurmond, quoted in Jack Bass and Marilyn W. Thompson, *Strom: The Complicated Personal and Political Life of Strom Thurmond* (New York: PublicAffairs, 2005).

51 *collectively lobbied CIA director*: Fred Kaplan, *The Wizards of Armageddon* (New York: Simon & Schuster, 1983).

51 *"would counsel me"*: Perle, in *Neocons and America's Foreign Policy*, op. cit.

51 *do more to further Lyndon Johnson's*: Joan Hoff, *Nixon Reconsidered* (New York: Basic Books, 1994).

52 *"That is exactly why we want you"*: Nixon, quoted by Rumsfeld in Midge Decter, *Rumsfeld: A Personal Portrait* (New York: ReganBooks, 2003).

53 *flunked the interview*: Stephen F. Hayes, *Cheney: The Untold Story of America's Most Powerful and Controversial Vice President* (New York: HarperCollins, 2007).

53 *"valiant cold warriors"*: Westerfield, quoted in John Nichols, *The Rise and Rise of Richard B. Cheney* (New York: New Press, 2004).

53 *"had other priorities"*: Cheney, quoted in James Mann, *Rise of the Vulcans: The History of Bush's War Cabinet* (New York: Viking, 2004).

53 *"Dick said what [his colleagues] all thought"*: Unidentified congressman, quoted in Nichols, op. cit.

54 *among the tasks assigned*: This section draws on interviews with Moorer, Laird, Friedheim, and Morris; transcripts at www.watergate.com. Cf. Len Colodny and Robert Gettlin, *Silent Coup: The Removal of a President* (New York: St. Martin's, 1990) and Jim Hougan, *Secret Agenda: Watergate, Deep Throat, and the CIA* (New York: Random House, 1984). Woodward, in *The Secret Man* (New York: Simon & Schuster, 2005), denies that he was a briefer, that he was in the Naval Reserves, and that he knew Alexander Haig in 1969–70.

54 *"kind of a high-ranking position"*: Eugene Carroll, interview with Colodny, November 4, 1986.

55 *"we'd have to ask certain people"*: Edmond D. Pope, in Pope and Tom Shachtman, *Torpedoed* (New York: Little, Brown, 2001).

55 *"Officers can resign about any time"*: Gene LaRocque, interviews with Colodny, 1985–86.

55 *"that [the resignation] I don't understand"*: Carroll interview, op. cit. Carroll contends that a resignation could be accepted only if Woodward went from active duty into either the reserves or another category of service, off the books. "BUPERS order 066226" to Woodward, dated January 29, 1969, references Woodward's resignation. The U.S. Navy has refused to certify Woodward's date of release from active duty, though it has confirmed his "date of discharge," August 1, 1970.

55 *"come to us on a very high recommendation"*: Harry Rosenfeld, quoted in Brendan McGarry, "Uncovering History: Editor Looks Back at Breaking Watergate Story," *Saratogian*, August 1, 2004.

56 *Roger Farquhar, who hired*: Farquhar, interview with Colodny, 1987.

56 *"to 'go out and ask'"*: Donald Stewart, interview with Colodny, 1986.

56 *"I created a dummy audit board"*: Buzhardt, quoted in Bill Gulley with Mary Ellen Reese, *Breaking Cover* (New York: Simon & Schuster, 1980).

57 *"exploded" when the content*: Roger Morris, interview with Colodny, 1987.

57 *"little, intimate bits of gossip"*: Gulley, op. cit.

58 *"Did a little editing here"*: Ibid.

58 *"He's selling us out on Vietnam!"*: Charles Colson, interview with Colodny, 1987.

5. "ACTUAL OR FEIGNED"

59 *"military solution to the Vietnam problem"*: Dobrynin-Kissinger exchanges, op. cit.

60 *"a political triumph"*: Kissinger, *White House Years*, op. cit.

60 *"as phony as a two-dollar bill"*: Haig, James Rosen interview, 2000.

60 *"drained of virtually any plausibility"*: Kissinger, *White House Years*, op. cit.

60 *"we must avoid that kind of policy"*: Nixon, quoted in Jeffrey Kimball, "The Nixon Doctrine: A Saga of Misunderstanding," *Presidential Studies Quarterly* 36, no. 1 (March 2006).

61 *"will participate in the defense of allies and friends"*: Report by President Nixon to Congress, February 18, 1970, Public Papers of the Presidents: Nixon, 1970.

61 *Kissinger reported that Buchanan had overstated*: Memo, Kissinger to Nixon, August 29, 1969; Haldeman File 1969, San Clemente [Part I], Box 52, White House Special Files/Staff Member and Office Files (WHSF/SMOF): Haldeman, NPM.

62 *Soviet-Chinese border tensions: The Sino-Soviet Border Conflict, 1969*, National Security Archive electronic briefing book, ed. William Burr, June 17, 2001, www.gwu.edu/~nsarchiv/NSAEBB/NSAEBB49/.

62 *Sinologist Allen Whiting*: Letter, Whiting to Kissinger, August 16, 1969, "Sino-Soviet Hostilities and Implications for U.S. Policy." NPM, Box 839, China, document 9 at http://www.gwu.edu/~nsarchiv/NSAEBB/NSAEBB49/#docs.

62 *"go for broke"*: Nixon, RN, op. cit.

62 *"I [Nixon] would regretfully find myself obliged"*: Ibid.

63 *tactical use of nuclear weapons*: Berman, op. cit., and Burr, ed., "Nuclear Weapons, the Vietnam War, and 'Nuclear Taboo,'" NSAEBB #195, July 31, 2006, www.gwu.edu/~nsarchiv/NSAEBB/NSAEBB195/.

63 *rejected Robinson's first draft*: Memo, Lake and Morris to Robinson, September 29, 1969, NPM, Folder 4: VIETNAM (General Files), Sep 69–Nov 69, box 74, NSC Files, document 1 at http://www.gwu.edu/~nsarchiv/NSAEBB/NSAEBB195/index.htm.

63 *"Withdrawal of American troops will become"*: Memo, Kissinger to Nixon, September 10, 1969, www.state.gov/documents/organization/64647.pdf.

63 No *"bridge to neutralist figures"*: Ibid. The Kissinger memo echoes one by Sven Kraemer, quoted in William Bundy, *A Tangled Web: The Making of Foreign Policy in the Nixon Presidency* (New York: Hill & Wang, 1998).

63 *"to achieve maximum political, military"*: September 16 plan, in Berman, op. cit., and Bundy, op. cit.

63 *"The train had just left the station"*: Memo of Kissinger-Dobrynin Conversation, September 27, 1969, NPM, Box 489, Dobrynin/Kissinger 1969, Part I.

63 *Just a few days earlier*: "Meeting Between Zhou Enlai and Kosygin At the Beijing Airport," PRC Foreign Ministry, www.fmprc.gov.cn/eng/zilliao/3602/3604/t18005.htm. This discussion also draws from Burr and Kimball, "Nixon's Nuclear Ploy," *Bulletin of the Atomic Scientists* 59, no. 1 (January–February 2003); Burr and Kimball, "New Evidence on the Secret Nuclear Alert of October 1969: The Kissinger Telcons," *Passport* 36, no. 1 (April 2005); Kissinger telephone conversations, NPM; and Burr, ed., "Nuclear Weapons, the Vietnam War, and 'Nuclear Taboo,'" op. cit.

64 *"bug out or accelerate"*: Haldeman diaries, op. cit. Entry for October 3, 1969.

64 *"It was important that the Communists"*: Nixon, RN, op. cit.

64 *"shouting matches"*: Haig, *Inner Circles*, op. cit.; Pursley, interview with Colodny, 1986.

64 *An internal army memo*: Referred to in Kraemer-Kissinger conversation of September 3, 1969, Kissinger telephone conversations.

65 *fear he was slightly mad*: H. R. Haldeman and Joseph DiMona, *The Ends of Power* (New York: Times Books, 1978).

65 *"Don't get rattled"*: Quoted in Jonathan Aitken, *Nixon: A Life* (Washington, D.C.: Regnery, 1993).

65 *"K has all sorts of signal-type activity"*: Haldeman diary, op. cit.

66 *"Your basic purpose will be"*: Memo, Kissinger to Nixon, October 18, 1969, quoted in Scott D. Sagan and Jeremy Suri, "The Madman Nuclear Alert," *International Security* 27, no. 4 (Spring 2003). See also Burr and Kimball, "New Evidence on the Secret Nuclear Alert of 1969," op. cit.

66 *Dobrynin never mentioned*: Dobrynin, op. cit., depicts this meeting as solely about SALT.

66 *"The Soviet Union is going to be stuck with me"*: Nixon, *RN*, op. cit.

66 *Kissinger told Kraemer*: October 20, 1969, telephone conversations, Rockefeller, 11:20 A.M., Kraemer, 12:30 P.M., HAK telcons, op. cit.

66 *"The reaction in the Kremlin"*: Dobrynin, quoted in Burr and Kimball, "Nixon's Nuclear Ploy," op. cit.

66 *"no longer remain silent"*: Kraemer, occasional paper for Kissinger, "The Modern World, A Single 'Strategic Theater,'" September 22, 1969, op. cit. Also printed in FRUS, 1969–76, vol. 1, op. cit. An editorial note (92) cites Nixon's margin comments and quotes Kissinger's cover memo. See: http://history.state.gov/historicaldocuments/frus1969-76v12/d92.

70 *"hopeful signs"*: Haig, *Inner Circles*, op. cit.

6. CAMBODIA AND ECHO

72 *"I read each and every cable"*: Memo, Haig to Kraemer, January 9, 1970, NPM, NSC Files, Box 822.

73 *Walters had also been keeping Fritz Kraemer*: Thimmesch interview with Walters, 1975, notes for "Iron Mentor" article, Thimmesch Papers, op. cit.

73 *"A general commands troops"*: Walters, quoted in Haldeman and DiMona, op. cit.

74 *the team was disturbed*: Raymond Garthoff, *Détente and Confrontation* (Washington, D.C.: Brookings Institution, 1994).

74 *"leading lost opportunity"*: Gerard C. Smith, *Doubletalk: The Story of the First Strategic Arms Limitation Talks* (Garden City, N.Y.: Doubleday, 1980).

74 *North Vietnamese "sanctuaries"*: Shawcross, op. cit.

75 *National Security Council divided*: Isaacson, Walter. *Kissinger: A Biography* (New York: Simon & Schuster, 1990).

75 *"100 percent successful"*: Laird, March 26, 1997, interview, www.gwu.edu/~nsarchiv/coldwar/interviews/episode-16/laird1.html.

75 *Haig demanded that the Pentagon*: Shawcross, op. cit.

76 *painted the whole mission as unrealistic*: Johnson, *The Right Hand of Power*, op. cit.

76 *"Kissinger's really having fun today"*: Haldeman diary, April 20, 1970, op. cit.

76 *"Suharto and the Indonesians"*: Notes of Washington Special Actions Group meeting of June 15, 1970, NPM.

76 *"Your views represent the cowardice"*: Kissinger, quoted by Watts, in Seymour Hersh, *The Price of Power: Kissinger in the Nixon White House* (New York: Summit, 1983).

76 *"You've just had an order"*: Haig, quoted by Watts in Roger Morris, *Haig: The General's Progress* (Chicago: Playboy, 1982).

76 *"We have often heard courage equated"*: Morris, Lake, and Lynn letter of April 29, 1970, quoted in Berman, op. cit.

78 *"actually ran much deeper"*: John F. Lehman, Jr., *The Executive, Congress, and Foreign Policy: Studies of the Nixon Administration* (New York: Praeger, 1974).

78 *"combination of demonic ceremony"*: Haig, *Inner Circles*, op. cit.

78 *Haig on his first solo mission*: Shawcross, op. cit.

78 *the formation of a high-level*: James Bamford, *The Puzzle Palace: Inside the National Security Agency, America's Most Secret Intelligence Agency* (New York: Penguin, 1983). For comment on FBI involvement, see William C. Sullivan and Bill Brown, *The Bureau: My Thirty Years in Hoover's FBI* (New York: Norton, 1979).

79 *Mitchell found out about it*: Mitchell, interviews with Colodny, 1985–88. See also James Rosen, *The Strong Man: John Mitchell and the Secrets of Watergate* (Garden City, N.Y.: Doubleday, 2008).

79 *to keep him from undue influence*: Elmo R. Zumwalt, *On Watch: A Memoir* (New York: Quadrangle, 1976).

79 *"we may already be at a condition"*: Moorer, quoted in Zumwalt, loc. cit.

80 *four new proposals*: Anne Campbell, "The Road to SALT," in *Milestones in Strategic Arms Control, 1945–2000*, www.usafa.af.mil/df/inss/books/mile/front.htm.

80 *"Having already made substantial"*: Nitze et al., op. cit.

80 *"fateful decision"*: Garthoff, op. cit.

80 *"the weapons then available"*: Zumwalt, op. cit.

80 *"I see him once a week"*: Kissinger-Kraemer conversation, June 2, 1970, Kissinger telephone conversations, op. cit.

81 to spy on Kissinger, the NSC, and the president: This section draws on interviews with Radford, Welander, Moorer, and others; on the "Welander confession" tape, transcript in Colodny and Gettlin, op. cit.; and in congressional testimony.

81 *"people in the reproduction center"*: Radford interview with Gettlin, 1986.

81 *"The Chiefs' viewpoint was being disregarded"*: Welander, interview with Colodny, 1989.

82 *"deliberate, systematic, and unfortunately"*: Zumwalt, op. cit.

82 *"As the possibility emerges"*: Murrey Marder, "Selling the Nixon Doctrine to the GOP Right Wing," *Washington Post*, September 1, 1970.

7. CRISES EXPOSE FISSURES

85 *"Those soccer fields could mean war, Bob"*: Kissinger, in Haldeman and DiMona, op. cit.

85 *"I want a report on a crash basis"*: Nixon to Kissinger, September 24, 1970, NPM, HAK Office Files.

85 *"some clown senator demanding"*: Nixon, quoted in Kissinger, *White House Years*, op. cit.

85 *"horsing around in Cuba"*: Kissinger to Sulzberger, quoted in Isaacson, op. cit.

86 *"Either you take those weapons"*: Haig, *Inner Circles*, op. cit.

86 By 1972 the base had been: "Reaching for Supremacy at Sea," *Time*, January 31, 1972.

86 *"We are engaged in a mortal struggle"*: Walters to Kissinger, September 1970, NPM.

88 *"I want you to push through"*: Nixon-Kissinger telephone conversations, September 17, 1970, op. cit.

88 so the Soviets would be sure: Haig, *Inner Circles*, op. cit.

88 *"I had no authority to encourage"*: Haig, loc. cit.

89 as the JCS did at the time: Cf. Lawrence J. Korb, *The Joint Chiefs of Staff* (Bloomington: Indiana University Press, 1976).

89 *"so that if any bad results follow"*: Quoted in Robert Dallek, *Nixon and Kissinger: Partners in Power* (New York: HarperCollins, 2007).

89 *"a certain period of time"*: Dobrynin papers, op. cit.

90 *"K does not agree with the P"*: Zumwalt, *On Watch*, op. cit. In 1978, when Zumwalt published this exchange, Kissinger denied having said any such thing; but interviews of NSC staffers and Kissinger long-term associates Peter Rodman and Helmut Sonnenfeldt (for Kaufman, op. cit.) confirmed that Kissinger made similar statements on many occasions.

91 *"Get ahold of Moorer"*: Transcript, Nixon-Kissinger telephone conversation, December 9, 1970, 8:45 P.M., NPM, HAK telephone conversation transcripts, Home File, Box 29, File 2.

91 *"every goddamn thing that can fly"*: Transcript, Kissinger-Haig telephone conversation, December 9, 1970, 8:50 P.M., HAK telephone conversation transcripts, Home File, Box 29, File 2.

91 dolchstosslegende: Kraemer occasional paper, September 22, 1969, op. cit.

92 *"prodded remorselessly"*: Haig, *Inner Circles*, op. cit.

92 impetus came principally from Haig: See Sorley and Bundy, op. cit.

92 *"Those of us involved in the planning"*: Haig, loc. cit.

93 *"That a senior military officer"*: Bundy, op. cit.

93 *"Incredibly, [Haig's] military assessments"*: General Bruce Palmer, Jr., *The 25-Year War: America's Military Role in Vietnam* (Lexington: University Press of Kentucky, 1984).

93 *"I thought that [Haig] was placing"*: Radford interview, op. cit.

93 *"Were I in the same case"*: Welander interview by Ehrlichman and Young, December 22, 1971, transcript in Colodny and Gettlin, op. cit.

94 *"Haig knew that Radford was observing"*: Welander interview, op. cit.

94 The youngsters informed the graybeards: Gregory L. Schneider, *Cadres for Conservatism: Young Americans for Freedom and the Rise of the Contemporary Right* (New York: New York University Press, 1999).

8. APPROACHING THE ZENITH

97 *"Soviet doctrinal and strategic writings"*: Memo, Kissinger to Nixon, February 16, 1971, NPM. Cf. James Rosen, "CIA Shortcomings Infuriated Nixon, Newly-Released Documents Show," Fox News, December 2, 2007, and Michael Tanji, "How Our Intel Analysts Were Lobotomized," *Danger Room*, December 2, 2007.

97 *forced to tell his protégé*: Thimmesch, "Iron Mentor," op. cit.

97 *"a freeze on offensive deployments"*: Kissinger, memorandum to files after meeting with Dobrynin, January 28, 1971, NSC Files, HAK Office Files, Box 79.

99 *"when you have two Bolshevik regimes"*: Kraemer, quoted in Vernon, op. cit.

99 *"so many members of Congress"*: Eisenhower, quoted in Nancy Bernkopf Tucker, "Taiwan Expendable? Nixon and Kissinger Go to China," *Journal of American History* 92, no. 1 (June 2005).

100 *"We should just stay out"*: Nixon, White House tape, cited in *FRUS*, vol. 11, "The South Asia Crisis, 1971." Cf. Claude Arpi, "1971 War: How the U.S. Tried to Corner India," Reuters, December 26, 2006.

100 *"Don't squeeze Yahya"*: Nixon to Kissinger, handwritten note on memo of April 28, 1971, in *FRUS*, vol. 11, op. cit.

100 *"Goddamn New York Times exposé"*: Haig to Nixon, transcript of June 13, 1971, conversation, 12:18 P.M.

101 *"that you're a weakling, Mr. President"*: Haldeman, quoting Kissinger, from Haldeman diary notes.

101 *"People've gotta be put to the torch"*: Nixon to Kissinger, White House tape, June 13, 1971, 3:09 P.M.

101 *"ran the Ellsberg case for politics"*: Stewart interview, op. cit.

102 *"Be careful and don't get caught"*: Welander, quoted by Radford, interview, op. cit.

102 *revealed to the Chiefs their systematic exclusion*: Welander-Ehrlichman confession transcript, op. cit.; interviews with Welander, Radford, and Moorer, op. cit.; and congressional testimony by Radford and Moorer.

102 *had not realized how thoroughly*: Welander and Radford interviews, op. cit.

102 *"ranks with DeGaulle as the most impressive"*: "My Talks with Chou En-Lai," July 14, 1971, memo, Kissinger to President, Box 1033, NSC Files, Miscellaneous Memoranda Relating to HAK Trip to PRC, July 1971, NPM, document 40 at http://www.gwu.edu/~nsarchiv/NSAEBB/NSAEBB66/#docs.

103 *Perino's: Haldeman Diaries*, op. cit. *Time* gave the price of the wine as forty dollars; Haldeman's diary suggests the higher price.

9. MAKING ALLIES INTO ENEMIES

108 *"After this 'Nixon shokku'"*: Johnson et al., op. cit.

108 *India and the USSR*: Cf. Robert Jackson, *South Asian Crisis*, op. cit., and Vidya Subrahmaniam, "A War Won Against the 'Tilt,'" *Hindu*, July 3, 2005.

108 *"No one was more surprised and confused"*: Dobrynin, op. cit.

108 *"had no bearing whatsoever"*: Kissinger, in ibid.

108 *"their whole tone"*: Kissinger-Nixon telephone conversation, July 26, 1971.

108 *"I could tell from his style"*: Ibid. Cf. Kraemer-Kissinger telephone conversation of August 3, 1971. Kissinger: "Your memo has been read with approbation. . . . I didn't put your name on it and he said 'That's the same man as the author of the memo I read last year.'" "My God," Kraemer responded.

108 *the phone rang in the California*: John B. Judis, *William F. Buckley Jr.: Patron Saint of the Conservatives* (New York: Simon & Schuster, 1988).

109 *"the strategic intentions of the President"*: Kissinger to Buckley, quoted in Judis, op. cit.

109 *"taken in by the other side's"*: William F. Buckley, Jr., "Say It Isn't So, Mr. President," *New York Times Magazine*, August 1, 1971.

109 *a dozen conservative leaders*: Judis, op. cit.

110 *"Kissinger sat there and told us"*: Jeffrey Bell, quoted in ibid.

110 *six-page list of demands*: Ibid.

111 *"high-level Presidential aide"*: Memo, Rumsfeld to Nixon, February 27, 1971, National Security Name Files (Rumsfeld), NPM.

111 *"Let's dump him right after this"*: and other quotes, White House Tape 246-7, April 7, 1971.

111 "When we get down to it": Nixon, White House tape, summer 1971, www.pbs.org/wgbh/pages/frontline/shows/pentagon/paths/audio.html.

112 *"not a warm and cordial one"*: Perle, March 1997 interview, www.gwu.edu/~nsarchiv/coldwar/interviews/episode-19/perle1.html.

112 *"Why does it hurt to say"*: Nixon, Comments to Staff, July 19, 1971, op. cit.

113 *the Beecher leak*: Interviews, Mitchell and Stewart, op. cit.

113 *demanded that "polygraphs"*: Tapes and transcription notes, President's office, July 24, 1971.

113 *"Little people do not leak"*: Ibid.

114 *Haig reported to Nixon*: Hersh, *The Price of Power*, op. cit.

115 *Hunt sent regular reports and packages*: Hougan, and Colodny and Gettlin, op. cit.

115 *"The intensity of the national security concern"*: Krogh, in defendant's statement, accepting guilt as charged in 1973, court papers, cases of Ehrlichman, Colson, and Krogh. Cf. Krogh's statement at sentencing, www.budkrogh.com/sentencing.pdf. Also cf. Egil Krogh, "The Break-In That History Forgot," *New York Times*, June 30, 2007.

115 *ordered the logs and summaries*: Nixon to Ehrlichman, White House tape of July 12, 1971.

115 *"basically sold Young and me on the idea"*: Krogh, interview with Colodny, July 26, 1989.

116 *"If done under [the] assurance"*: Memo, Young and Krogh to Ehrlichman, with handwritten notes, in 1973 court papers, op. cit.

116 *Liddy was puzzled*: G. Gordon Liddy, *Will* (New York: St. Martin's, 1980).

116 *Black-bag professionals*: Cf. Sullivan, op. cit., and Frank J. Donner, *The Age of Surveillance* (New York: Vintage, 1981).

116 *"not to a foreign power"*: Memo, Krogh and Young to Ehrlichman, November 1, 1971, in Book VII, Impeachment Hearings, NARA.

117 *"We tried"*: Kraemer-Kissinger telephone conversation, October 28, 1971.

117 *"The agreement now is"*: Kissinger, White House conversation, 576–6, September 18, 1971.

118 *"write serious books on power"*: Kraemer, quoted in Collier, op. cit.

119 *Furious, Jackson responded*: Kaufman, op. cit.

10. "A FEDERAL OFFENSE OF THE HIGHEST ORDER"

120 *"ruthless, uncompromising"*: Jackson, *South Asian Crisis*, op. cit. See also Subrahmaniam, op. cit.

121 *"Threaten to move forces or move them"*: Nixon tape, quoted in Jackson, op. cit.

121 *"We were always behind events"*: Zumwalt, op. cit.

122 *"The President very definitely wants to tilt"*: WSAG meeting minutes, December 4, 1971, quoted in Zumwalt, loc. cit.

122 *"it would help the Soviets cement"*: Zumwalt, ibid.

123 *"salute and 'click his heels' type"*: Jack Anderson, interview with Colodny, 1986.

124 *"one place in the federal government"*: White House Tape 639-30, December 21, 1971. This tape was transcribed by James Rosen and Len Colodny, with technical help from Mountain States University; parts were first published in Rosen, "Nixon and the Chiefs," *Atlantic*, April 2002. Cf. also, David Young memorandum of record, December 15, 1971, "Description of Unique Character of Welander Memorandum dated December 10, 1971," in Buzhardt files, NPM.

127 *"a full recount of our involvement"*: Welander "confession" tape, op. cit.

127 *"heard what Welander was saying"*: Ehrlichman, interview with Colodny, op. cit.

128 *"Haig was drawn in"*: Laird, interview with Colodny, op. cit.

128 *"the worst thing we could do now"*: Nixon to Haig, White House tape, December 24, 1971, quoted in FRUS, *Organization and Management of U.S. Foreign Policy, 1969–1972*.

128 *Years later, Moorer would make*: Moorer, interview with Colodny, op. cit.

129 *"Don't let K blame Haig"*: Ehrlichman notes, *FRUS*, op. cit.

129 *Buzhardt told Stewart*: Stewart, interview with Colodny, op. cit.

130 *Welander absolves Haig*: Stewart summary of Welander re-interview in Colodny and Gettlin, op. cit. This re-interview was not taped, but Stewart summarized it from his notes
immediately after it was done.

131 *"I know that your protégé sometimes"*: Kraemer-Kissinger telephone conversation, February
15, 1972.

11. "THREE OUT OF THREE, MR. PRESIDENT"

133 *"acid, amnesty, and abortion"*: Jackson, quoted in Kaufman, op. cit.

134 *"that Communism was the deadly enemy"*: Ashbrook speech, www.4president.org/speeches/
johnashbrook1972announcement.htm.

134 *"Nobody in our government"*: Kissinger memo, February 23, 1972, www.gwu.edu/~nsarchiv/
NSAEBB/NSAEBB106/index.htm.

134 *"are selling us out to the Communists"*: Haig, quoted by Chapin, interview with Colodny,
2007.

136 *"I am the commander in chief"*: Nixon to Moorer, quoted in Stephen R. Randolph, *Powerful
and Brutal Weapons: Nixon, Kissinger, and the Easter Offensive* (Cambridge, Mass.: Harvard University Press, 2007).

136 *Nixon and Kissinger had specifically promised*: Kissinger-Nixon telephone conversation,
April 15, 1972, 11:30 A.M.

137 *"ruined North Vietnam's economy"*: Allan R. Millet and Peter Maslowski, *For the Common
Defense* (New York: Free Press, 1984).

137 *"not been outclassed"*: Haig, *Inner Circles*, op. cit.

138 *"open revolt"*: Campbell, op. cit.

138 *roused Nixon and Kissinger "out of bed"*: Haig, interview with Rosen, op. cit.

138 *"It is no comfort that the liberals"*: Nixon to Haig, quoted in Randolph, op. cit.

138 *"a lot of pressure . . . from Scoop Jackson"*: Odeen, in Oral History Roundtables, "Arms Control Policy and the National Security Council," March 23, 2000.

139 *"What the issues and goals"*: Ibid.

139 *instances of such poor planning*: Hougan, op. cit.

140 *"Holy shit! The CIA"*: Woodward, quoted in Woodward and Carl Bernstein, *All the President's Men* (New York: Simon & Schuster, 1975).

140 *described Bennett as boasting*: CIA memo, Agent Martin Lukoskie, quoted in Nedzi, Minority Report, Watergate Committee, NARA, Group 46. Cf. Hougan, op. cit.

141 *According to Gray's memoir, Dean learned*: L. Patrick Gray III and Ed Gray, *In Nixon's Web:
A Year in the Crosshairs of Watergate* (New York: Henry Holt, 2008).

141 *"There is no CIA involvement"*: Note, reprinted in Gray, op. cit.

142 *"out of control"*: Dean, quoted in Haldeman and DiMona, op. cit., and *Haldeman Diaries*,
op. cit.

142 *"Our problem now is to stop the FBI"*: Dean, quoted in Haldeman and DiMona, op. cit.

142 *no conversations between Mitchell and Dean*: Colodny and Gettlin. op. cit., viewed Mitchell
phone logs and diaries for June 22–23, 1972.

142 *"the whole Bay of Pigs thing"*: White House tapes, June 23, 1972.

142 *"If the investigation gets pushed"*: Walters, quoted in Gray, loc.cit.

143 *another, uncredited contributor*: Kaufman, op. cit.

144 *"helped make Jackson more effective"*: Douglas Feith, quoted in Alan Weisman, *Prince of
Darkness: Richard Perle* (New York: Union Square, 2007).

144 *a stroll in the Rose Garden*: Kaufman, op. cit.

144 *"three out of three"*: Kissinger, White House tapes, October 12, 1972.

145 *they weren't lifting a finger*: Kissinger telephone conversations, October 1972.

12. A MEETING OF MIND-SETS

147 *"raised our eyebrows (and blood pressure)"*: Palmer, op. cit.

147 *Laird reminded Nixon*: Lewis Sorley, *Thunderbolt: From the Battle of the Bulge to Vietnam and
Beyond: General Creighton Abrams and the Army of His Times* (Herndon, Va.: Brassey's, 1992).

148 *"Many wars have been lost"*: Cable, Kissinger to Haig, October 23, 1972, quoted in Kissinger, *White House Years*, op. cit.

148 *"was often immersed in a state"*: Palmer, op. cit.

148 *"Henry would send"*: Nixon to Thimmesch, November 6, 1975, Thimmesch Papers, op. cit.

148 *"You will find Dr. Kraemer"*: Memo, Kissinger to Nixon, October 24, 1972, NPM, NSC Files, Box 822.

149 *"my father and Dr. Kissinger would agree"*: Memo, Sven Kraemer to Haig, October 23, 1972, NPM, NSC Files, Box 822.

149 *the three began to chat*: White House tape, October 24, 1972, 11:15–11:45 A.M., excerpted transcription by Shachtman and Colodny, 2007.

153 *"You've just ruined all my policies"*: Kissinger to Kraemer, quoted by Kraemer to friends, anonymous interview with Shachtman, 2007.

153 *"He's against any settlement"*: White House tape 372-11, October 25, 1972.

153 *"If you sign that treaty,"* Kraemer friend, anonymous interview, 2007, op. cit.

154 *"react very strongly and rapidly"*: Letter, Nixon to Thieu, printed in "Letters Made Public by Saigon Official," *New York Times*, May 1, 1975.

154 *"If Russia invaded the U.S."*: Thieu to Haig, quoted in Berman, op. cit.

154 *"I wanted to discuss two things"*: Kraemer-Kissinger telephone conversation, November 27, 1972.

155 *"Should Hanoi violate the agreement"*: Haig, *Inner Circles*, op. cit.

155 *"The Christmas bombing extracted"*: Bundy, *A Tangled Web*, op. cit.

156 *"Should you decide"*: Nixon to Thieu, "Letters Made Public," op. cit.

156 *"If Kissinger had the power to bomb"*: Thieu, quoted in Berman, loc. cit.

156 *"I can't of course say"*: Kraemer-Kissinger telephone conversation, January 18, 1973.

13. ACTIONS AND REACTIONS

158 *"in the nature of a family quarrel"*: Kissinger, *Years of Renewal*, op. cit.

159 *"The belief that the security"*: Coalition for a Democratic Majority manifesto, 1972.

160 *"Over my dead body"*: Moorer to Rowny, quoted in Rowny, op. cit.

160 *To Kraemer, Kissinger was Machiavelli*: Rowny, loc. cit.

161 *"I'm here to make sure you don't"*: Schlesinger, quoted by Ray McGovern, in Alexander Cockburn, "Politicize the CIA? You've Got to Be Kidding," *Nation*, December 20, 2004.

161 *Dick Walters*: Walters, *Silent Missions*, op. cit.

161 *"political operatives in the White House"*: Decter, op. cit.

163 *historians have taken their road map*: This section draws on White House tapes from the period March 13–21, some not yet officially transcribed. Stanley I. Kutler's book of edited and excerpted transcripts, *Abuse of Power* (New York: Free Press, 1997), does not print a transcript or summary of the March 13 tape, though the transcript had been printed in a *New York Times* book of the tapes in 1974. Kutler's editing also conflates two tapes of March 16, an Oval Office conversation and a telephone conversation, and omits Dean's line about "not a scintilla of evidence." The March 20 "typing" tape does not appear in the Kutler compilation. The two March 16 tapes and the March 20 tape are now online at http://www.nixontapes.org/watergate/037-134.mp3; http://www.nixontapes.org/watergate/881-003.mp3; and http://www.nixontapes.org/watergate/884-017.mp3. Following publication of Patricia Cohen, "John Dean at Issue in Nixon Tapes Feud," *New York Times*, January 31, 2009, nixontapes.org posted comparison transcripts and audio at http://www.nytimes.com/2009/02/01/washington/01kutler.html?partner=permalink&exprod=permalink.

165 *"I felt queasy"*: John W. Dean III, *Blind Ambition: The White House Years* (New York: Simon & Schuster, 1976).

165 *"I didn't feel that it was my job"*: Deposition for *Dean v. St. Martin's*, September 12–15, 1995, and January 22–25, 1996.

169 *"These demonstrations of a much more assertive"*: Bundy, op. cit.

171 *"For those few who knew the inner workings"*: Roger Morris, *Haig: The General's Progress*, op. cit.

172 *"Don't you know we have this guy?"*: Califano, quoted by Haig, interview with Rosen, op.

cit. Califano, in his autobiography, says only that he told Haig that Nixon was certain to be impeached or forced to resign. He writes of not learning of Agnew's pending indictment until some weeks later. Cf. Joseph A. Califano, Jr., *Inside: A Public and Private Life* (New York: PublicAffairs, 2005).

14. THREE QUICK STRIKES

176 *allotted doses*: Higby, interview with Colodny, 1987, and Bull, interview with Colodny, 2007.
176 *"Al controlled everything"*: Higby and Brennan interviews with Colodny, 1987–88.
176 *"a more rigid administrator"*: Nixon, *RN*, op. cit.
177 *"without enthusiasm"*: Haig, *Inner Circles*, op. cit.
177 *Haig's learning of the White House taping system*: Bull interview, op. cit.,and Walter Isaacson interview with Kissinger, in Isaacson, op. cit.
178 *"Haig trusted Buzhardt and not me"*: Garment interviews with Colodny, 1985–88.
179 *"instructions which in any way"*: Memo printed in CIA "Family Jewels" collection, op. cit.
179 *sent a helicopter to meet Walters*: Walters, op. cit.
179 *On May 11, at Haig's request*: This discussion of the events of May 11–14, 1973, derives from the transcripts of White House tapes as printed in Kutler, op. cit., from Walters, op. cit., and from interviews with Haldeman, op. cit.
183 *"Do you honestly believe that Henry"*: Haig to Hersh, in Hersh, op. cit.
184 *the source Woodward called "Deep Throat"*: In *The Secret Man* (New York: Simon & Schuster, 2006), Woodward identified Deep Throat as FBI man Mark Felt. In mid-May 1973, Felt retired from the FBI. If Felt met with Woodward on May 16, it is curious that Woodward does not report asking this top FBI executive about the Walters testimony and memcons, which were leading the news just then and involved the FBI being blocked by the CIA.
185 *"Wouldn't it be better just to check out?"*: Nixon to Haig, May 25, 1973, transcript in Kutler, op. cit.
186 *"waves of uneasiness"*: Bob Woodward and Carl Bernstein, *The Final Days* (New York: Simon & Schuster, 1976).
186 *"the only thing he [Dean] has in there"*: Nixon to Haldeman, June 4, 1973, transcript in Kutler, op. cit.
187 *"one of the ablest geopolitical minds"*: Kissinger, *Years of Renewal*, op. cit.
187 *Dean began his Senate testimony*: The testimony and transcripts of question-and-answer sessions are in Ervin Committee, Select Committee on Presidential Campaign Activities, NARA, Record Group 46, 18.175.
188 *"I was wrong"*: Buzhardt to Laird, Laird interview, op. cit.
189 *Higby told Haig about the committee's questions:* Higby interview, op. cit.
190 *Thompson phoned Buzhardt*: Fred D. Thompson, *At That Point in Time* (New York: Quadrangle, 1975).
190 *"When the prosecutor discovers the smoking gun"*: Armstrong, quoted in Michael Kranish, "Not All Would Put a Heroic Sheen on Thompson's Role," *Boston Globe*, July 4, 2007.
190 *Concerned "about a White House set-up"*: Woodward and Bernstein, *All the President's Men*, op. cit.
190 *Nixon had been well enough to see visitors*: Logs of the president's activities, including his time in the hospital, are in NPM.
191 *Garment gave Butterfield no instructions*: Interviews with Garment and with Butterfield, op. cit.
191 *"I thought that at least executive privilege"*: Nixon, *RN*, op. cit.
191 *According to Haig's autobiography, Buzhardt was concerned*: This section draws on Haig, op. cit.; on Woodward interviews with Buzhardt, op. cit.; Nixon, op. cit.; and Haig interview with Rosen, op. cit.

15. NULLIFYING NIXON

193 *General Walters helped organize*: Notes for "Iron Mentor" article, Thimmesch Papers, op. cit.

193 *"Your integrity and selflessness have inspired"*: Kissinger to Kraemer, July 3, 1973, in NPM, NSC Files, Box 822.

193 *"stood for the good and true"*: Tribute by Herman Kahn, reprinted in Hoffman, op. cit.

193 *"When it came time"*: Palmer, op. cit.

194 *"where the country is in foreign policy"*: Kraemer-Kissinger telephone conversation, July 10, 1973.

194 *"cash in on our present weakness"*: Kraemer-Kissinger telephone conversation, July 19, 1973.

194 *there was another who did*: Nick Thimmesch, "Professor in the Pentagon," *Washington Post*, October 6, 1974.

194 *"Schlesinger persuaded Kraemer"*: Kissinger, *Years of Renewal*, op. cit.

195 *"Kraemer's values were absolute"*: Kissinger eulogy in Hoffman, op. cit., and at www.henryakissinger.com/eulogies/100803.html.

195 *"We began to see less"*: Kissinger, *Years of Renewal*, op. cit.

197 *"In the supercharged atmosphere"*: Ibid.

197 *"White House staff had been set up"*: Bork, interview, "Legends in the Law," www.dcbar.org/for_lawyers/resources/legends_in_the_law/bork.cfm.

198 *"all kinds of crazy things"*: Bork, interview with Gettlin, 1988.

198 *"I am the president"*: Former PFIAB member, interview with Shachtman, 2005.

199 *"Stewart clearly is in a position"*: Tufaro to Garment, memo, May 14, 1973, "Investigation of National Security Leaks Re: Donald Stewart."

199 *"Fred believed that it would be calamitous"*: Garment interview, op. cit.

199 *"warrant a criminal investigation"*: Peterson to Richardson, July 10, 1973, "Letter from Leonard Garment Recommending Prosecution of W. Donald Stewart."

201 *Kraemer later told reporter Nick Thimmesch*: Thimmesch Papers, op. cit.

202 *"The best thing that could happen"*: Kissinger to Schlesinger, cited in Isaacson, op. cit. See also Kissinger, memcon of conversation with Ambassador Huang Zhen, PRC Liaison Office, October 6, 1973. This and other important documents on the Yom Kippur War can be found at www.jewishvirtuallibrary.org/jsource/History/73wardocs.html.

202 *overheard what he characterized as Kissinger lying*: Perle, cited in Kaufman, op. cit.

202 *"I would not have done if I had been"*: Zumwalt, op. cit.

204 *"Richardson's assurance that if Cox"*: Nixon, RN, op. cit.

205 *"If you find it impossible"*: Letter, Brezhnev to Nixon, October 24, 1973, NMP, HAK, Box 69, Dobrynin/Kissinger, vol. 20 (October 12–November 27, 1973), document 71 at http://www.gwu.edu/~nsarchiv/NSAEBB/NSAEBB98/index.htm.

205 *"very much overdrawn"*: Telephone conversation, Haig and Dobrynin, 8:04 P.M., October 26, 1973, HAK telephone conversations, Box 28. Dobrynin later reached Kissinger and made the same arguments to him. Cf. notes to document 73 at http://www.gwu.edu/~nsarchiv/NSAEBB/NSAEBB98/index.htm.

207 *"Now we're going to get a real professional"*: Bork, Legends interview, op. cit.

207 *implications of a Bud Krogh petition*: Papers in acceptance of guilty plea, 1973, op. cit.

208 *"a new low point for me"*: Nixon, RN, op. cit.

208 *"of a suspicious nature"*: Woodward and Bernstein, *All the President's Men*, op. cit.

209 *Haig would later say he knew*: Christopher Ruddy, "Gen. Haig: Deep Throat Not Lone Source," Newsmax, May 31, 2005, http://archive.newsmax.com/archives/ie/2005/5/31/211941.shtml.

209 *consultant Sam Powers*: Powers, interview with Colodny, January 21, 1988.

16. PROTECTING THE FLANKS

211 *"I think that you should get the finest"*: Jaworski to Haig, in Haig, *Inner Circles*, op. cit. Slightly different wording in Jaworski, *The Right and the Power: The Prosecution of Watergate* (New York: Reader's Digest, 1976).

211 *Woodward asked Welander for more*: Welander interview, op. cit.

212 *"Had Moorer been blackmailed"*: Garthoff, op. cit.

212 *When hearings began on February 6*: "Transmittal of Documents from the National

Security Council to the Chairman of the Joint Chiefs of Staff," Hearing before the Committee on Armed Services, U.S. Senate, Parts I, II, and III, U.S. Government Printing Office, 1974.

213 *"would serve no useful purpose"*: Laird interview, op. cit.

213 *In a call to Don Stewart*: Stewart interview, op. cit. Stewart also showed Colodny his contemporaneous notes of the phone call.

214 *he went to the White House to review*: Ehrlichman interview, op. cit.

215 *The original memo, from Butterfield to Magruder*: The real and doctored memos are printed in Colodny and Gettlin, op. cit.

17. ENDGAME

216 *"men who know too much to believe"*: Daniel Patrick Moynihan, "Was Woodrow Wilson Right? Morality and American Foreign Policy," *Commentary*, May 1974.

217 *he chose not to include his bedrock opposition*: James Buckley, *Gleanings from an Unplanned Life* (Wilmington, Del.: Intercollegiate Studies Institute, 2006).

218 *Haig had allowed Jaworski to hear*: Jaworski, *The Right and the Power*, op. cit.

218 *"good strategy to the extent"*: Nixon, *RN*, op. cit.

218 *"there was no doubt now"*: Nixon, *RN*, loc. cit.

219 *"The President has no friends in the White House"*: Connally to Nixon, quoted in Nixon, *RN*, op. cit.

219 *Using information from Rowny, Nitze, and Iklé*: Kaufman, op. cit.

219 *"serious prospects for SALT"*: Kissinger, *White House Years*, op. cit.

219 *"strategic thinkers and worriers"*: Cited in Anne Hessing Cahn, *Killing Détente: The Right Attacks the CIA* (State College: Pennsylvania State University Press, 1997).

220 *"But, Mr. President"*: NSC Minutes, June 20, 1974, www.lib.umich.edu/govdocs/pdf/nsc meet5.pdf.

220 *"Defense people don't want agreement"*: Notes quoted in Nixon, *RN*, op. cit.

220 *"If détente unravels in America"*: Nixon, *RN*, loc. cit.

221 *"understood the depth of the neoconservative"*: Kissinger, *Years of Renewal*, op. cit.

222 *Haig also raised the possibility*: Ford testimony, October 17, 1974.

224 *Both Haldeman and his lawyer*: Colodny interviews with Haldeman, September 3, 1987, and Strickler, August 24, 1987.

224 *Haig secretly went to Leon Jaworski's*: Richard Ben-Veniste and George Frampton, *Stonewall: The Real Story of the Watergate Prosecution* (New York: Simon & Schuster, 1977).

224 *"was always loyal to the commander"*: Nixon, *RN*, loc. cit.

18. A SHORT HONEYMOON

229 *the tumultuous period*: Cf. Shachtman, *Decade of Shocks: Dallas to Watergate* (New York: Simon & Schuster, 1983).

230 *"At this time, do not commit"*: Memo quoted in Colodny and Gettlin, op. cit.

230 *When attorney Benton Becker*: Colodny and Gettlin, op. cit., and Becker interview with Colodny, March 5, 1987.

231 *Ford did something Nixon had never*: Kaufman, op. cit.

232 *among ten men around the table*: Cf. minutes of various Ford years NSC meetings, http://www.ford.utexas.edu/library/document/nscmin/minlist.htm.

232 *aloof and arrogant manner*: Gerald R. Ford, *A Time to Heal* (New York: Harper & Row, 1979).

232 *"Over the next seven years"*: Ford NSC meeting, September 14, 1974.

233 *he consulted Fritz Kraemer*: Thimmesch Papers, op. cit.

233 *"a worthy opponent"*: Thimmesch, "Professor in the Pentagon," op. cit.

233 *"Not just any [SALT II] agreement"*: Ford, in NSC meeting, October 18, 1974.

234 *"I've lost the battle"*: Haig, quoted by Jones, interview with Colodny, December 10, 1987.

234 *"making an agreement"*: Ford, op. cit.

234 *"if he allowed the papers"*: Becker interview, op. cit.

235 *"spending an inordinate amount of time"*: "terHorst Says Ford Spent 'Inordinate' Amount of Time on Haig," Associated Press, September 14, 1974.

236 *"three Haig appearances"*: Walter Pincus, "Questioning Haig's Role," *Washington Post*, October 1, 1974.

236 *"These boys have prepared sworn"*: Buzhardt to Haig, in Haig, *Inner Circles*, op. cit.

238 *"The understanding when I took the job"*: Cheney, in Hayes, op. cit.

238 *"we have restrained presidential authority"*: Cheney, Minority Report on Iran-Contra Hearings, 1987. See also Tim Harper, "Cheney Argues for Nixon-Era Powers," *Toronto Star*, December 21, 2005. Excerpts from the report are available at www.pbs.org/wgbh/pages/frontline/darkside/themes/ownwords.html.

239 *While CIA estimates*: William G. Hyland, *Mortal Rivals: Superpower Relations from Nixon to Reagan* (New York: Random House, 1987).

240 *"provide an increase"*: Ford NSC meeting, October 18, 1974.

240 *"I think we came away with a good agreement"*: Ford NSC meeting, December 2, 1974.

241 *"should have been a turning point"*: Hyland, op. cit.

241 *"There is no doubt that what Jackson did"*: Kissinger to Hyland, Kissinger telephone conversation, February 22, 1975.

241 *Soviet expert Robert Gates*: Robert M. Gates, *From the Shadows* (New York: Simon & Schuster, 1996).

241 *"It was an absurd situation"*: Hyland, op. cit.

242 *"breakdown of America's Soviet policy"*: Peter W. Rodman, *More Precious Than Peace: The Cold War and the Struggle for the Third World* (New York: Scribner's, 1994).

245 *"Kraemer is a seminal influence"*: Schlesinger, quoted in Nick Thimmesch, "The Iron Mentor," op. cit., syndicated article, March 1975, and notes for same, Thimmesch Papers, op. cit.

246 *"roll up his sleeves"*: Haig, Rosen interview, op. cit.

247 *"What are our options"*: Ford NSC meeting, May 12, 1975. See also meetings of May 13, 14, and 15, 1975.

248 *"Virtually everything that could go wrong"*: John F. Guilmartin, Jr., *The Mayaguez Incident, 12–15 May 1975, A Thirty Year Retrospective*, adapted from Guilmartin, *A Very Short War* (College Station: Texas A&M Press, 2005).

19. YIELDING TO THE RIGHT

249 *"we not contribute any more"*: Cheney memo, cited in Nichols, op. cit.

250 *"The Moral Foundations of Foreign Policy"*: Kissinger speech, July 15, 1975, reprinted in Kissinger, *American Foreign Policy*, 3rd ed. (New York: Norton, 1977).

251 *"a lot of conservatives are screaming"*: Kissinger to Buckley, transcript, July 21, 1975, Kissinger telephone conversations, NARA.

251 *"oblivious to the context"*: Kissinger, *Years of Renewal*, op. cit.

252 *"détente was playing into Soviet hands"*: Rowny, op. cit.

253 *"The Soviets have forged ahead"*: Joseph Alsop, "Challenge America Must Meet," *Reader's Digest*, August 1975.

253 *"various strategies were tried"*: Nessen, quoted in Craig Shirley, *Reagan's Revolution: The Untold Story of the Campaign That Started It All* (Nashville, Tenn.: Nelson Current, 2005).

254 *Rumsfeld consulted Paul Nitze*: Bradley Graham, *By His Own Rules*, op. cit.

254 *"for showing cowardice"*: Ford, op. cit.

255 *"I hope you know it wasn't my idea"*: Kissinger to Schlesinger, November 5, 1975, transcript, Kissinger telephone conversations, op. cit.

255 *"extremely ruthless and irritating"*: Kissinger telephone conversation, James Reston, November 3, 1975.

255 *"The guy that cut me up"*: Kissinger telephone conversation, Secretary Simon, November 3, 1975.

255 *Kissinger asked Kraemer to come*: Kraemer friend interview with Shachtman, 2007.

256 *"As a human being, you have to stand"*: Kraemer, quoted in Isaacson, op. cit.

256 *"Kraemer took Schlesinger's dismissal"*: Kissinger, *Years of Renewal*, op. cit.

256 *"The next time you see Dr. Fritz Kraemer"*: Nixon to Thimmesch, Nov. 6, 1975, op. cit.

258 *"a marked change in congressional"*: *Aviation Week*, January 1976.

258 *"I don't understand how the Arms Control"*: Kissinger telephone conversation, Iklé, February 6, 1976.

20. PRIMARY BATTLES

260 *"götterdammerung for the GOP"*: Shirley, op. cit.

261 *"We are in for a real battle"*: Memo, Jones to Cheney, cited in Shirley, loc. cit.

262 *"Well, Governor, you can go out there"*: Keene, interview quoted in Shirley, loc. cit.

264 *sent Cherne a congratulatory note*: Cahn, op. cit.

265 *"with results that could only resurrect"*: Paul Nitze, "Assuring Strategic Stability in an Era of Détente," *Foreign Affairs*, January 1976.

265 *"I am advised that the composition"*: George H. W. Bush, letter, quoted in Cahn, op. cit.

266 *"dedicated to proving that the Russians"*: Quoted in Cahn, loc. cit.

266 *"Now either there is a conscious effort"*: Rockefeller to Ford, quoted in Robert T. Hartmann, *Palace Politics: An Inside Account of the Ford Years* (New York: McGraw-Hill, 1980).

267 *"truly frightening suspicion"*: Kraemer, "The Modern World, A Single 'Strategic Theater,'" op. cit.

268 *"the bill unnecessarily derogates"*: Documents from 1976, in "Wiretap Debate Déjà Vu," www.gwu.edu/~nsarchiv/NSAEBB/NSAEBB178/index.htm.

269 *"did everything but strip Henry bare"*: Cheney, quoted in Shirley, op. cit.

21. THE CARTER INTERREGNUM

272 *"out of the recognition that America"*: Joshua Muravchik, "The Past, Present, and Future of Neoconservatism," *Commentary*, October 2007, www.commentarymagazine.com/view-article.cfm/The-Past-Present-and-Future-of-Neoconservatism-10935.

273 *"domino effect*: Rumsfeld, quoted in Bob Weidrich, "The 'Domino' Effect of Military Cutbacks," *Chicago Tribune*, January 16, 1977.

274 *"drained of manpower, morale"*: Haig, *Inner Circles*, op. cit.

275 *assailed the integrity and acumen*: Cf. Cahn, op. cit., and Richard Pipes, *Vixi: Memoirs of a Non-Belonger* (New Haven, Conn.: Yale University Press, 2003).

277 *"believed that America was stronger"*: Allen interview, Miller Center, op. cit.

278 *Kraemer enjoyed regular visits*: Rowny interview, op. cit.

279 *"one of the most effective pork-seeking"*: Silverstein, quoted in Jason Vest, "The Dubious Genius of Andrew Marshall," *American Prospect*, January 2001, www.prospect.org/cs/articles?article=the_dubious_genius_of_andrew_marshall. Cf. Silverstein and Daniel Burton-Rose, *Private Warriors* (New York: Verso, 2000).

280 *"options for nuclear war-fighting"*: Kaplan, op. cit.

283 *eldest member of the Madison Group*: Rowny, op. cit., and interview, op. cit. Cf. William Safire, "The Madison Group," *New York Times*, December 4, 1980.

285 *"Since [Carter's] inauguration"*: Jeane Kirkpatrick, "Dictatorships and Double Standards," *Commentary*, November 1979, http://www.commentarymagazine.com/viewarticle.cfm/dictatorships—double-standards-6189.

286 *"Contrary to Carter"*: Muravchik, op. cit.

289 *"a seismic impact"*: Andrew Bacevich, *The New American Militarism: How Americans Are Seduced by War* (New York: Oxford University Press, 2005).

290 *"Who better than Bush"*: Herbert S. Parmet, *George Bush: The Life of a Lone Star Yankee* (New Brunswick, N.J.: Transaction, 2001).

22. FITS AND STARTS

294 *"Team B became, in essence"*: Cahn, op. cit.

295 *Haig presented the plan*: Lou Cannon, *President Reagan: The Role of a Lifetime* (New York: Simon & Schuster, 2001).

296 *"contribute[d] mightily to lifting the armed"*: Bacevich, op. cit.

296 *a "rollback" of this empire*: Thomas Bodenheimer and Robert Gould, *Rollback! Right-Wing Power in U.S. Foreign Policy* (Boston: South End, 1989).

296 *Casey was "obsessed"*: Gates, op. cit.

297 *"I mean every once in a while"*: Moorer interview with Colodny, October 4, 1989. See also Moorer interview with Jim Hougan, 1982, in *Secret Agenda*, op. cit.

297 *"William Tavoulareas and his son Peter"*: Summary in U.S. Court of Appeals for the District of Columbia Circuit, 817 F.2d, March 13, 1987, *Tavoulareas v. Washington Post Co.*, http://www.altlaw.org/v1/cases/417683.

298 *"The downside of holy shit stories"*: Jack Shafer, "The Changelings," *Slate*, July 4, 1998, www.slate.com/id/2075.

298 *"In for a dime, in for a dollar"*: Woodward, quoted in William Green, "Janet's World: The Story of a Child Who Never Existed—How and Why It Came to Be Published," *Washington Post*, April 19, 1981.

298 *"I believed it, we published it"*: Woodward, quoted in David A. Maraniss, "Post Reporter's Pulitzer Prize Is Withdrawn," *Washington Post*, April 16, 1981.

299 *Wolfowitz and his associates*: James Mann, *About Face: A Story of America's Cautious Relationship with China, From Nixon to Clinton* (New York: Knopf, 1998).

300 *"organize, propagandize, or practice terrorism"*: Casey memo, quoted in Gates, op. cit.

301 *Woodward was given the notes*: Woodward, "Meetings' Notes Show the Unvarnished Haig," *Washington Post*, February 19, 1982, and William Safire, "The Leaker Speaks," *New York Times*, March 22, 1982.

23. THE HIGH TIDE OF ANTI-COMMUNISM, AND AFTER

306 *"is so weak of will"*: Kraemer, quoted in Hoffman, op. cit.

306 *Two of these, he knew, would upset the Kremlin*: Cf. Gates, op. cit.; Rowny, op. cit.

307 *"The deal the Scowcroft Commission"*: Frances FitzGerald, *Way Out There in the Blue: Reagan, Star Wars, and the End of the Cold War* (New York: Simon & Schuster, 2000).

308 *"the most dangerous [congressman]"*: McGrory, quoted in Lou DuBose and Jake Bernstein, *Vice: Dick Cheney and the Hijacking of the American Presidency* (New York: Random House, 2006).

308 *"Cheney did not want to allow"*: unidentified congressman, quoted in DuBose and Bernstein, op. cit.

308 *Sven Kraemer, now the arms*: Frank Warner, "The Evil Empire Speech," www.nae.net/index.cfm?FUSEACTION=editor.page&pageID=37.

309 *announced a distinct break*: John Lewis Gaddis, *The Cold War: A New History* (New York: Penguin, 2005).

309 *American commander in Beirut learned*: Timothy J. Geraghty, "25 Years Later: We Came in Peace," *Naval Institute Proceedings*, October 2008, www.usni.org/magazines/proceedings/story.asp?STORY_ID=1616.

309 *Rowny and Perle argued that the proposal*: Rowny, op. cit.

310 *"to preserve our way of life"*: Thatcher, quoted in Geoffrey Wheatcroft, "Our Imaginary Friend," *New York Times*, September 19, 2007.

311 *"The stationing of the American mid-range"*: Kraemer, in Hoffman, op. cit.

312 *"If you told me your president"*: Mitterrand, quoted by Walters, in Christopher Ruddy, "General Vernon Walters, RIP," Newsmax, February 13, http://archive.newsmax.com/archives/articles/2002/2/12/222236.shtml.

312 *featured Congressman Dick Cheney and Donald Rumsfeld*: James Mann, *Rise of the Vulcans: The History of Bush's War Cabinet* (New York: Viking, 2004).

313 *part of a plan put forth by Oliver North's*: Bodenheimer and Gould, op. cit.

314 *arms sales to Israel were sent on to Iran*: Cf. Jonathan Marshall, Peter Dale Scott, and Jane Hunter, *The Iran Contra Connection* (Boston: South End, 1987), inter alia.

315 *Weinberger Doctrine*: Weinberger, "The Uses of Military Power," speech at National Press Club, Washington, D.C., November 28, 1984. Transcript: www.pbs.org/wgbh/pages/frontline/shows/military/force/weinberger.html.

317 *that the restriction applied only*: Theodore Draper, *A Very Thin Line: The Iran-Contra Affairs* (New York: Hill & Wang, 1991).

317 *"to create a safer world"*: Reagan, quoted in Alex Abella, *Soldiers of Reason: The RAND Corporation and the Rise of the American Empire* (New York: Harcourt, 2008).

318 *"We must not discuss this"*: Perle, quoted in George P. Shultz, *Turmoil and Triumph: My Years as Secretary of State* (New York: Scribner's, 1993).

318 *Ed Rowny and many others*: Rowny interview, op. cit.

319 *Perle, in attendance at Reykjavik, was afraid*: Richard Rhodes, *Arsenal of Folly: The Making of the Nuclear Arms Race* (New York: Knopf, 2007).

319 *"I'm afraid he's going after SDI"*: Rowny interview, op. cit.

320 *"the Administration is weaker in terms of foreign policy"*: Document in Reykjavik File, www .gwu.edu/~nsarchiv/NSAEBB/NSAEBB203/index.htm.

321 *Perle formed a consulting group*: Weisman, *Prince of Darkness*, op. cit.

321 *Nixon said he was pleased*: Rowny interview, op. cit.

322 *"What we need is a Domino's Pizza"*: Perle, quoted in http://rightweb.irc-online.org/ profile/1183/.

322 *"You knew, didn't you?"*: Casey, quoted in Bob Woodward, *Veil* (New York: Simon & Schuster, 1987).

323 *Gates would go on to refute Woodward's*: Gates, op. cit.

323 *"I personally do not believe"*: Cheney, statement made during Iran-Contra hearings, 1987.

323 *Cheney's minority report*: Cheney Minority Report, excerpted at www.pbs.org/wgbh/pages/ frontline/darkside/themes/ownwords.html.

324 *later critics pointed out*: Sean Wilentz, "Mr. Cheney's Minority Report," *New York Times*, July 9, 2007.

324 *"very thin line"*: Draper, op. cit.

325 *"less-than-robust defense"*: Cheney Minority Report, op. cit.

325 *"Some time after Reagan left office"*: FitzGerald, op. cit.

24. NOT GOING TO BAGHDAD

326 *"optimists in the West"*: Gates, op. cit.

326 *"a final battle against the Soviets"*: Roger Morris, "The Rise and Rise of Robert Gates, part 3," Tomdispatch, June 25, 2007, http://www.tomdispatch.com/post/174814/ roger_morris_the_cia_and_the_gates_legacy.

327 *allegedly received these classified papers from*: Lawrence Zuckerman, "Washington's Master Leakers," *Time*, May 23, 1988.

328 *considered Reagan's SDI*: FitzGerald, op. cit.

329 *Bush needed a quick approval*: Parmet, op. cit.

330 *"absorbed the message"*: Eagleburger, quoted in Parmet, loc. cit.

330 *who continued to tutor*: Hubertus Hoffman, interview with Shachtman, 2007.

330 *"With the wall breached"*: Gaddis, *The Cold War*, op. cit.

331 *"shaken by the rapidity"*: Quoted in Michael R. Beschloss and Strobe Talbott, *At the Highest Levels: The Inside Story of the End of the Cold War* (Boston: Back Bay, 1994).

331 *Arguing that Gorbachev's survival*: Hayes, op. cit., and Gates, op. cit.

331 *"Could anything come to pieces so fast"*: Garry Wills, "The End of Reaganism," *Time*, November 16, 1992.

333 *"The Soviet Union collapsed"*: Gaddis, op. cit.

333 *"might have survived for many more"*: FitzGerald, op. cit.

333 *"exhorted the rulers"*: Beschloss and Talbott, op. cit.

333 *"This misreading of history"*: Martin Walker, "Smoking Guns and Mushroom Clouds," *New York Times*, November 25, 2007, and Walker, *The Cold War: A History* (New York: Henry Holt, 1994).

334 *"Initially an instrument of convenience"*: Parmet, op. cit.

334 *Admiral William Crowe*: Bruce Anderson, "An Admiral at the Court of St. James's," *Stanford Alumni Magazine*, 1997, www.stanfordalumni.org/news/magazine/1997/sepoct/articles/ crowe.html.

335 *"We have military bases not just"*: Crowe, in NSC meeting, March 1988, quoted in Fred-
     erick Kempe, *Divorcing the Dictator: America's Bungled Affair with Noriega* (New York:
     Putnam, 1990).

338 *did not cite "regime change"*: Cf. Parmet, op. cit.

338 *"No longer can a dictator count"*: George H. W. Bush address to Joint Session of Congress,
     September 11, 1990, www.sweetliberty.org/issues/war/bushsr.htm.

339 *"I was not enthusiastic"*: Cheney, quoted in Hayes, op. cit.

339 *"on the sidelines"*: Jacob Heilbrunn, *They Knew They Were Right: The Rise of the Neocons*
     (New York: Doubleday, 2008).

340 *"I would still have forces in Baghdad"*: Cheney, interview with C-SPAN, 1992. Cheney made
     similar statements in interviews elsewhere and through 1994.

340 *"Even if Saddam were captured"*: James A. Baker III, with Thomas N. DeFrank, *The Politics
     of Diplomacy: Revolution, War, and Peace, 1989–1992* (New York: Putnam, 1995).

340 *"The coalition would have instantly"*: George Bush and Brent Scowcroft, *A World Trans-
     formed* (New York: Vintage, 1998).

340 *"we screwed up and left Saddam"*: Wolfowitz, quoted in Wesley K. Clark, *A Time to Lead:
     For Duty, Honor, and Country* (London: Palgrave Macmillan, 2007).

341 *had given Woodward classified data*: Powell testimony to Senate Armed Services Commit-
     tee, July 1991.

342 *"neos are interventionist, the paleos isolationist"*: Jacob Weisberg, "The Hunter Gatherers,"
     New Republic, September 2, 1991.

342 *"neocons had been shut out"*: Heilbrunn, op. cit.

342 *"on the order of that formerly posed"*: Wolfowitz, Defense Planning Guidance document,
     quoted in Patrick E. Tyler, "Pentagon Imagines New Enemies to Fight in a Post-Cold-War
     Era," *New York Times*, February 17, 1992.

343 *"We need to think through"*: Andrew Marshall, quoted in Fred Kaplan, *Daydream Believers:
     How a Few Grand Ideas Wrecked American Power* (New York: Wiley, 2008).

344 *"shaping the future security environment"*: Secretary of Defense Dick Cheney, "Defense
     Strategy for the 1990s: The Regional Defense Strategy," Department of Defense, January
     1993, www.informationclearinghouse.info/pdf/naarpr_Defense.pdf.

25. THE POST–COLD WAR DILEMMA

346 *"some of the neoconservatives looked hopefully"*: Heilbrunn, op. cit.

348 *"We are urged to advance democracy"*: James Schlesinger, "Quest for a Post-Cold War For-
     eign Policy," *Foreign Affairs* 72, no. 1 (January 1993).

349 *"wished for a military posture"*: Daniel P. Moynihan, *Pandaemonium: Ethnicity in Interna-
     tional Politics* (New York: Oxford University Press, 1993).

349 *"preclude any hostile power"*: Secretary of Defense Dick Cheney, Defense Strategy for the
     1990s, op. cit.

350 *"had the side effect of obscuring"*: Report of the National Commission on Terrorist Attacks
     on the United States, www.9-11commission.gov/.

351 *"essentially repeated the pattern"*: Patrick Glynn, "See No Evil," *New Republic*, October 25,
     1993.

351 *"A sense of confusion"*: Wolfowitz, "Clinton's First Year," *Foreign Affairs*, January–February
     1994.

352 *"act now substantially to reduce"*: Wohlstetter et al., "Open Letter to President Clinton,"
     Wall Street Journal, September 2, 1993.

352 *"dismissed the violence there"*: Muravchik, op. cit.

353 *"confusion about defining"*: Wolfowitz, "Clinton's First Year," op. cit.

354 *"Wolfowitz, Perle, Muravchik"*: Stefan Halper and Jonathan Clarke, *America Alone: The
     Neo-conservatives and the Global Order* (New York: Cambridge University Press, 2004).

355 *that the United States all but abandon*: Dole 1996 foreign policy document, www.4president
     .us/issues/dole1996/dole1996foreign.htm.

26. NEOCONS VERSUS CLINTON

359 *"The Clinton Administration is grossly"*: Sven Kraemer, testimony, June 19, 1996, House Committee on International Relations, www.globalsecurity.org/wmd/library/congress/1996_h/h960619a.htm.
360 *"A Clean Break"*: Perle et al., "A Clean Break: A New Strategy for Securing the Realm," 1996, www.iasps.org/strat1.htm. Authorship of this document is in question. Douglas J. Feith's name was appended as one of a group of authors, but he denies authorship and attributes it to David Wurmser. Cf. Feith, op. cit.
361 *"benevolent American hegemony"*: William Kristol and Robert Kagan, "Toward a Neo-Reaganite Foreign Policy," *Foreign Affairs*, July 1996, http://www.carnegieendowment.org/publications/index.cfm?fa=view&id=276.
361 *"Such a self-conscious, self-righteous"*: Walter A. McDougall, "Why Some Neo-Cons Are Wrong About U.S. Foreign Policy," Foreign Policy Research Institute, December 1997, www.fpri.org/pubs/nightthoughts.199712.mcdougall.neoconswrong.html.
362 *"When we rallied to Ronald Reagan's"*: Halper and Clarke, *America Alone*, 2004.
362 *Andrew Marshall, who remained*: Kaplan, *Daydream Believers*, op. cit.
362 *"We seem to have forgotten"*: PNAC Statement of Principles, 1997, www.newamericancentury.org/statementofprinciples.htm.
363 *"military might is indispensable"*: Kraemer, in Hoffman, op. cit.
363 *"the only acceptable strategy"*: PNAC letter to President Clinton, January 26, 1998, www.newamericancentury.org/iraqclintonletter.htm.
364 *"an incalculable blow"*: PNAC to Gingrich and Lott, May 29, 1998, www.newamericancentury.org/iraqletter1998.htm.
365 *called the NIE "tainted"*: Sven Kraemer, testimony, June 19, 1996, op. cit.
365 *"true keeper of the flame"*: Rumsfeld, remarks at Center for Security Policy, October 7, 1998, *Congressional Record*, October 14, 1998, www.fas.org/irp/congress/1998_cr/s981014-rummy.htm.
367 *"Iraq Liberation Act of 1998"*: http://www.iraqwatch.org/government/US/Legislation/ILA.htm.
369 *"Contrary to this timid"*: John Bolton, "Test Ban Defeat Marks New Realism," *New York Times*, October 20, 1999.
370 *"Two Cheers for Clinton's Foreign Policy"*: Stephen M. Walt, *Foreign Affairs*, March–April 2000.
370 *"Clinton's foreign policy"*: Michael Mandelbaum, "Foreign Policy as Social Work," *Foreign Affairs*, January–February 1996.
370 *"profoundly misguided"*: Bolton, op. cit.
370 *"The measure of Clinton's tenure"*: Robert E. Hunter, "East Is West," *Foreign Affairs*, September–October 2000.
370 *"Clinton may not leave a legacy"*: Richard N. Haass, "The Squandered Presidency: Demanding More from the Commander in Chief," *Foreign Affairs*, May–June 2000.
371 *"A fairer critique"*: "Clinton's Foreign Policy," *Foreign Policy*, November–December 2000.

27. FROM CANDIDATE TO BUSH 43

372 *to join him on the committee*: Lou DuBose and Jake Bernstein, *Vice: Dick Cheney and the Hijacking of the American Presidency* (New York: Random House, 2006).
373 *A small, gnomic man*: Jason Vest, "The Dubious Genius," op. cit.
374 *"revolution in military affairs"*: Cf. collection of articles, "The RMA Debate," www.comw.org/rma/.
374 *"regimes hostile to our interests"*: Republican Party Platform, 2000, www.cnn.com/ELECTION/2000/conventions/republican/features/platform.00/.
375 *"absent some catastrophic"*: Project for a New American Century, "Rebuilding America's Defenses: Strategy, Forces, and Resources for a New Century," September 2000, http://www.newamericancentury.org/publicationsreports.htm.

375 *"If we're an arrogant nation"*: George W. Bush, in Bush-Gore debate, October 3, 2000, transcript at www.debates.org/pages/trans2000a.html.

376 *"As a measure of Cheney's influence"*: Hayes, op. cit.

377 *"We urgently need"*: Clarke memo, in Richard A. Clarke, *Against All Enemies: Inside America's War on Terror* (New York: Free Press, 2004).

377 *Bush had the door closed and locked*: Bob Woodward, *Bush at War* (New York: Simon & Schuster, 2002).

378 *"It was about what we can do"*: Paul O'Neill, quoted in Ron Suskind, *The Price of Loyalty: George W. Bush, the White House, and the Education of Paul O'Neill* (New York: Simon & Schuster, 2004).

378 *"Saddam's attempts to shoot down"*: Feith, *War and Decision*, op. cit.

379 *"John Bolton, Dougls Feith"*: Halper and Clarke, op. cit.

379 *asked the largest telephone companies*: Ryan Singel, "NSA Domestic Surveillance Began 7 Months Before 9/11, Qwest CEO Claims," http://blog.wired.com/27bstroke6/2007/10/nsa-asked-for-p.html; "Threat Level," October 11, 2007; and Singel, interview with Shachtman, 2007.

380 *These statements often blunted*: Cf. Charlie Savage, *Takeover: The Return of the Imperial Presidency and the Subversion of American Democracy* (Boston: Little, Brown, 2007).

380 *Chinese fighter jet clipped*: "China-U.S.: Aircraft Collision Incident of April 2001: Assessment and Policy Implications," congressional report, October 10, 2001, www.fas.org/sgp/crs/row/RL30946.pdf.

381 *"dispatch[ed] a person to Taiwan"*: Wilkerson, quoted in Jeff Stein, "Defense Officials Tried to Reverse China Policy, Powell Aide Says," *Congressional Quarterly*, June 1, 2007, http://public.cq.com/docs/hs/hsnews110-000002523531.html.

381 *"When our president wrote"*: Fritz Kraemer, quoted in Wes Vernon, "U.S. Position on China: 'Provocative Weakness,'" Newsmax, April 28, 2001, www.newsmax.com/archives/articles/2001/4/27/205658.shtml.

382 *"may go down in history"*: Kristol and Kagan, "No Defense," *Weekly Standard*, July 23, 2001.

382 *"our capacity to shoot down"*: Wolfowitz testimony and speech, reprinted in Les Crane, ed., *Wolfowitz on Point* (Philadelphia: Pavilion, 2004).

382 *"We were also concerned"*: Feith, op. cit.

382 *"from tit-for-tat responses"*: Rumsfeld "snowflake" memo, quoted in Feith, loc. cit.

383 *"reached a crescendo"*: Richard Clarke, op. cit.

383 *"Bin Laden Determined"*: Reprinted in "Report of National Commission on Terrorist Attacks," http://www.9-11commission.gov/.

28. THE NEOCON HOUR OF TRIUMPH

387 *"a round of meetings examining"*: Richard Clarke, op. cit.

388 *Policy Counter Terrorism Evaluation Group*: Feith, op. cit.

388 *"cooperation in all categories"*: Quoted in DoD Inspector General, Report on Review of the Pre-Iraqi War Activities of the Office of the Under Secretary of Defense for Policy (Report No. 07-INTEL-04), February 9, 2007, www.dodig.osd.mil/IGInformation/archives/OUSDP-OSP percent20Brief.pdf.

388 *"the document lends substance"*: Daniel Benjamin, "The Case of the Misunderstood Memo," *Slate*, December 9, 2003, http://www.slate.com/id/2092180/.

389 *"tried to keep the President"*: Feith, op. cit.

390 *"Long before 9/11"*: Cf. Jack L. Goldsmith, *The Terror Presidency: Laws and Judgment Inside the Bush Administration* (New York: Norton, 2007).

391 *"claimed the power to ignore a law"*: Savage, op. cit.

391 *hundreds of telegrams*: "Buying the War," *Bill Moyers Journal*, PBS, April 25, 2007, transcript at www.pbs.org/moyers/journal/btw/transcript1.html.

391 *"Terrorists who once occupied"*: President George W. Bush, State of the Union address, 2002, www.whitehouse.gov/news/releases/2002/01/20020129-11.html.

392 *"a cakewalk"*: Adelman, "Cakewalk in Iraq," *Washington Post*, February 13, 2002.

392 *"Condi's enthusiasm for regime change"*: Memo, David Manning to Prime Minister Blair, March 14, 2002; see John Daniszewski, "New Memos Detail Early Plans for Invading Iraq," *Los Angeles Times*, June 15, 2005.

393 *"In an age where the enemies"*: National Security Strategy, September 2002, www.white house.gov/nsc/nss/2002/index.html.

393 *"Sixty years of Western nations"*: Bush used variations of these lines in several speeches. The fullest version, November 2003, to National Endowment for Democracy, is at www .whitehouse.gov/news/releases/2003/11/20031106-2.html.

394 *"understand the dangers threatening"*: Fritz Kraemer, in Hoffman, op. cit.

395 *Cheney, Rumsfeld, and other officials*: Thomas R. Ricks, *Fiasco: The American Military Adventure in Iraq* (New York: Penguin, 2006).

395 *Downing Street Memo*: Memo of July 23, 2002, meeting, in "The Secret Downing Street Memo," *Sunday Times* (London), May 1, 2005; memo available at http://downingstreet-memo.com/docs/memotext.pdf.

395 *"equivalent in intensity"*: Various DoJ and Office of White House Counsel memos and letters of August 1, 2002, http://news.findlaw.com/wp/docs/doj/bybee80102ltr.html.

396 *published twenty-seven editorials*: Moyers, "Buying the War," op. cit., made the calculation and also cites Miller and Friedman articles, broadcast magazine pieces, and internal MSNBC memo.

396 *"Is there an absolutely vital"*: James Webb, "Heading for Trouble," *Washington Post*, September 4, 2002.

397 *"The conduct of the Iraqi regime"*: Bush, speech at United Nations, September 12, 2002, www.whitehouse.gov/news/releases/2002/09/20020912-1.html.

397 *"Sorry, you haven't convinced me"*: Fischer, quoted in "Local Hero," *Economist*, December 1, 2007.

397 *"virtual consensus in the world"*: Scowcroft, "Don't Attack Saddam," *Wall Street Journal*, August 15, 2002.

398 *In an August memo*: Cited in Walter Pincus, "Before War, CIA Warned of Negative Outcomes," *Washington Post*, June 3, 2007.

398 *tucked into the rear of a briefing book*: Tenet, cited in ibid.

398 *"Parade of Horribles"*: Feith, op. cit.

398 *recalled that the resolution's first draft*: Hagel, quoted in Wil S. Hyton, "The Angry One," *Gentlemen's Quarterly*, January 2007.

399 *"We judge that Iraq has continued"*: Unclassified version of NIE published July 18, 2003, www.fas.org/irp/cia/product/iraq-wmd.html.

400 *When Wilson found no justification*: Joseph C. Wilson IV, "What I Didn't Find in Africa," *New York Times*, July 6, 2003.

401 *Hagel privately asked*: Hagel, quoted in Hyton, "The Angry One," op. cit.

401 *Kraemer pressed Rumsfeld*: Kraemer friend, interview with Shachtman, 2007.

401 *"Even I could never have envisioned"*: Adelman, '"Cakewalk' Revisited," *Washington Post*, April 10, 2003.

401 *Cheney invited Adelman, Wolfowitz, and Libby*: Bob Woodward, *Plan of Attack* (New York: Simon & Schuster, 2004).

402 *"recognized that if the coalition"*: Feith, op. cit.

402 *"Principles for Iraq-Policy Guidelines"*: L. Paul Bremer III, "How I Didn't Dismantle Iraq's Army," *New York Times*, September 6, 2007.

403 *"full support and confidence"*: Bush, quoted in Bremer, op. cit.

404 *"because it did not fit certain"*: Wilson, op. cit.

405 *"The prophet thinks"*: Kissinger, quoted in Hoffman, op. cit.

405 *"lack of practicality"*: Kissinger, quoted by Rowny, interview, op. cit.

29. THE CHENEY REGENCY

408 *"disinclination . . . to exert cognitive"*: Joan Didion, "The Deferential Spirit," *New York Review of Books*, September 19, 1996.

408 *"will provide useful yarn"*: Ray McGovern, "Court Historian Woodward Disguises Bush Aims in Invading Iraq," Commondreams.org, April 23, 2004, www.commondreams.org/views04/0430-04.htm.

411 *"The survival of liberty in our land"*: George W. Bush, second inaugural address, January 20, 2005, www.whitehouse.gov/news/releases/2005/01/20050120-1.html.

411 *"We're one bomb away"*: Addington, quoted in Goldsmith, op. cit.

412 *The administration's use of "signing statements"*: Cf. Savage, op. cit.

414 *"Commanders in the field had their"*: Cited in Noah Shachtman, "China Tops Osama, Iraq in QDR," Defensetech blog, February 3, 2006, http://www.noahshachtman.com/archives/002110.html.

414 *"First, invading Iraq was not in the interests"*: William E. Odom, "Iraq: Get Out Now," *Los Angeles Times*, May 4, 2006.

415 *"In Iraq, this Republican president"*: Rod Dreher, "Bush, Iraq, Lead a Conservative to Question," NPR essay, January 11, 2007, www.npr.org/templates/story/story.php?storyid=6817201.

415 *"For all of conservatives' patience"*: Richard Viguerie, "Bush's Base Betrayal," *Washington Post*, May 21, 2006.

416 *"The problem with the neoconservative agenda"*: Francis Fukuyama, *America at the Crossroads: Democracy, Power, and the Neoconservative Legacy* (New Haven, Conn.: Yale University Press, 2006).

30. LOSING POWER

418 *"To establish its authority"*: George W. Bush, January 10, 2007, http://www.cnn.com/2007/POLITICS/01/10/bush.transcript/index.html.

419 *"developed, produced, and then disseminated"*: DoD Inspector General Report on Review of the Pre-Iraqi War Activities of the Undersecretary of Defense for Policy, No. 07-INTEL-04, www.dodig.osd.mil/IGInformation/archives/OUSDP-OSP percent20Brief.pdf.

420 *three opinions*: Sheldon Whitehouse, FISA speech to Senate, December 7, 2007, http://whitehouse.senate.gov/newsroom/speeches/speech/?id=aa332b8e-d7fc-401b8459-4f3f849a3d58.

422 *a speech that was heavily influenced*: Hubertus Hoffman, speech at Trinity College, October 2007, www.worldsecuritynetwork.com.

424 *new National Intelligence Estimate on Iran:* "Iran: Nuclear Intentions and Capabilities," National Intelligence Estimate, December 3, 2007, Office of the Director of National Intelligence, www.dni.gov/press_releases/20071203_release.pdf.

425 *"little seems to have changed"*: "Our view of the war in Iraq," editorial, *USA Today*, December 12, 2007.

425 *"The hope"*: "Iraq and Afghanistan, Must They Be Wars Without End?," *Economist*, December 15–21, 2007.

EPILOGUE: FOREIGN AFFAIRS AND THE ELECTION OF 2008

428 *"The nations of the NATO alliance"*: John McCain, "America Must Be a Good Role Model," *Financial Times*, March 18, 2008.

429 *"I am extremely disappointed"*: Adelman, quoted by David Rose, "Neo Culpa," *Vanity Fair*, November 3, 2006, http://www.vanityfair.com/politics/features/2006/12/neocons200612.

429 *"sprawling bureaucracies charged with"*: Richard Perle, "Ambushed on the Potomac," *National Interest*, January 21, 2009, http://www.nationalinterest.org/Article.aspx?id=20486.

432 *"After thousands of lives lost"*: Barack Obama, "Renewing American Leadership," *Foreign Affairs*, July–August 2007.

432 *"As for our common defense"*: President Barack Obama, inaugural address, January 20, 2009, http://www.nytimes.com/2009/01/20/us/politics/20text-obama.html.

Selected Bibliography

Abella, Alex. *Soldiers of Reason: The RAND Corporation and the Rise of the American Empire.* New York: Harcourt, 2008.

Aitken, Jonathan. *Nixon: A Life.* Washington, D.C.: Regnery, 1993.

Arquilla, John. *The Reagan Imprint: Ideas in American Foreign Policy from the Collapse of Communism to the War on Terror.* Chicago: Ivan R. Dee, 2006.

Bacevich, Andrew J. *The New American Militarism: How Americans Are Seduced By War.* New York: Oxford University Press, 2005.

Bamford, James. *Pretext for War: 9/11, Iraq, and the Abuse of America's Intelligence Services.* Garden City, N.Y.: Doubleday, 2004.

Berman, Larry. *No Peace, No Honor: Nixon, Kissinger, and Betrayal in Vietnam.* New York: Free Press, 2001.

Bodenheimer, Thomas, and Robert Gould. *Rollback! Right-Wing Power in U.S. Foreign Policy.* Boston: South End, 1989.

Brennan, Mary C. *Turning Right in the Sixties.* Chapel Hill: University of North Carolina Press, 1995.

Brinkley, Douglas. *Gerald R. Ford.* New York: Holt, 2007.

Bundy, William. *A Tangled Web: The Making of Foreign Policy in the Nixon Presidency.* New York: Hill & Wang, 1998.

Burr, William, and Jeffrey Kimball. "Nixon's Nuclear Ploy." *Bulletin of the Atomic Scientists* 59, no. 1 (January–February 2003).

Bush, George [H. W.], and Brent Scowcroft. *A World Transformed.* New York: Vintage, 1998.

Cahn, Anne Hessing. *Killing Détente: The Right Attacks the CIA.* State College: Pennsylvania State University Press, 1997.

Cannon, James. *Time and Chance: Gerald Ford's Appointment with History.* New York: HarperCollins, 1994.

Cannon, Lou. *President Reagan: The Role of a Lifetime.* New York: Simon & Schuster, 2001.

Clarke. Richard A. *Against All Enemies: Inside America's War on Terror.* New York: Free Press, 2004.

Cockburn, Andrew. *Rumsfeld: His Rise, Fall, and Catastrophic Legacy.* New York: Scribner, 2007.

Colodny, Len, and Robert Gettlin. *Silent Coup: The Removal of a President.* New York: St. Martin's, 1991.

Crane, Les, ed. *Wolfowitz on Point.* Philadelphia: Pavilion, 2004.

Dallek, Robert. *Nixon and Kissinger: Partners in Power.* New York: HarperCollins, 2007.

Dean, John W., III. *Blind Ambition: The White House Years.* New York: Simon & Schuster, 1976.

Decter, Midge. *Rumsfeld: A Personal Portrait.* New York: ReganBooks, 2003.

Dobrynin, Anatoly. *In Confidence.* New York: Times Books, 1995.

Draper, Theodore. *A Very Thin Line: The Iran-Contra Affairs.* New York: Hill & Wang, 1991.

Drucker, Peter. "The Man Who Invented Kissinger." In Peter Drucker, *Adventures of a Bystander.* New York: Harper & Row, 1979.

DuBose, Lou, and Jake Bernstein. *Vice: Dick Cheney and the Hijacking of the American Presidency.* New York: Random House, 2006.

Feith, Douglas J. *War and Decision: Inside the Pentagon at the Dawn of the War on Terrorism.* New York: HarperCollins, 2008.

FitzGerald, Frances. *Way out There in the Blue: Reagan, Star Wars, and the End of the Cold War.* New York: Simon & Schuster, 2000.

Ford, Gerald R. *A Time to Heal.* New York: Harper & Row, 1979.

Foreign Relations of the United States, 1969–1976, Vols. 1–6. U.S. Government Printing Office, 2003–2006.

Fukuyama, Francis. *America at the Crossroads: Democracy, Power, and the Neoconservative Legacy.* New Haven, Conn.: Yale University Press, 2006.

Gaddis, John Lewis. *The Cold War: A New History.* New York: Penguin, 2005.

Garthoff, Raymond. *Détente and Confrontation.* Washington, D.C.: Brookings Institution, 1994.

Gates, Robert M. *From the Shadows.* New York: Simon & Schuster, 1996.

Gellman, Barton. *Angler: The Cheney Vice-Presidency.* New York: Penguin, 2008.

Goldsmith, Jack L. *The Terror Presidency: Law and Judgment Inside the Bush Administration.* New York: Norton, 2007.

Graham, Bradley. *By His Own Rules: The Ambitions, Successes, and Ultimate Failures of Donald Rumsfeld.* New York: PublicAffairs Press, 2009.

Gray, L. Patrick, III, and Ed Gray. *In Nixon's Web: A Year in the Crosshairs of Watergate.* New York: Henry Holt, 2008.

Gulley, Bill, with Mary Ellen Reese. *Breaking Cover.* New York: Simon & Schuster, 1980.

Haig, Alexander M., Jr., with Charles McCarry. *Inner Circles: How America Changed the World: A Memoir.* New York: Warner, 1992.

Haldeman, H. R. *The Haldeman Diaries: Inside the Nixon White House,* Electronic edition. Santa Monica, Calif.: Sony Imagesoft, 1994.

Haldeman, H. R., and Joseph DiMona. *The Ends of Power.* New York: Times Books, 1978.

Halper, Stefan, and Jonathan Clarke. *America Alone: The Neo-conservatives and the Global Order.* New York: Cambridge University Press, 2004.

Hayes, Stephen F. *Cheney: The Untold Story of America's Most Powerful and Controversial Vice President.* New York: HarperCollins, 2007.

Hayward, Stephen F. *The Age of Reagan: The Fall of the Old Liberal Order, 1964–1980.* Roseville, Calif.: Prima, 2001.

Helgerson, John L. "Briefings of Presidential Candidates: A CIA History." https://www.cia.gov/library/center-for-the-study-of-intelligence/csi-publications/books-and-monographs/cia-briefings-of-presidential-candidates/cia-2.htm.

Helms, Richard, and William Hood. *A Look over My Shoulder.* New York: Random House, 2003.

Hersh, Seymour. *Chain of Command: The Road from 9/11 to Abu Ghraib.* New York: HarperCollins, 2004.

———. *The Price of Power: Kissinger in the Nixon White House.* New York: Summit, 1983.

Hoff, Joan. *A Faustian Foreign Policy from Woodrow Wilson to George W. Bush: Dreams of Perfectibility.* Cambridge, U.K.: Cambridge University Press, 2008.

———. *Nixon Reconsidered.* New York: Basic Books, 1994.

Hoffman, Hubertus. *Fritz Kraemer on Excellence*. New York: World Security Network Foundation, 2004.

Hougan, Jim. *Secret Agenda: Watergate, Deep Throat, and the CIA*. New York: Random House, 1984.

Hyland, William G. *Mortal Rivals: Superpower Relations from Nixon to Reagan*. New York: Random House, 1987.

Isaacson, Walter. *Kissinger: A Biography*. New York: Simon & Schuster, 1992.

Jackson, Robert. *South Asian Crisis: India, Pakistan, and Bangla Desh*. New York: Praeger, 1975.

Jaworski, Leon. *The Right and the Power: The Prosecution of Watergate*. New York: Reader's Digest, 1976.

Johnson, U. Alexis, with J. O. McAllister. *The Right Hand of Power*. Englewood Cliffs, N.J.: Prentice-Hall, 1984.

Judis, John B. *William F. Buckley Jr.: Patron Saint of the Conservatives*. New York: Simon & Schuster, 1988.

Kaplan, Fred. *Daydream Believers: How a Few Grand Ideas Wrecked American Power*. New York: Wiley, 2008.

———. *The Wizards of Armageddon*. New York: Simon & Schuster, 1983.

Kaufman, Robert G. *Henry M. Jackson: A Life in Politics*. Seattle: University of Washington Press, 2000.

Kimball, Jeffrey. "The Nixon Doctrine: A Saga of Misunderstanding." *Presidential Studies Quarterly* 36, no. 1 (March 2006).

———. *Nixon's Vietnam War*. Lawrence: University Press of Kansas, 1998.

Kirkpatrick, Jeane. "Dictatorships and Double Standards." *Commentary*, November 1979. http://www.commentarymagazine.com/viewarticle.cfm/dictatorships—double-standards-6189.

Kissinger, Henry A. *White House Years*. Boston: Little, Brown, 1979.

———. *Years of Renewal*. New York: Simon & Schuster, 1999.

———. *Years of Upheaval*. Boston: Little, Brown, 1982.

Korb, Lawrence J. *The Joint Chiefs of Staff*. Bloomington: Indiana University Press, 1976.

Kristol, William, and Robert Kagan. "Toward a Neo-Reaganite Foreign Policy." *Foreign Affairs*, July 1996. http://www.carnegieendowment.org/publications/index.cfm?fa=view&id=276.

Kutler, Stanley I. *Abuse of Power*. New York: Free Press, 1997.

Lehman, John F., Jr. *Command of the Seas*. New York: Scribner's, 1988.

Mann, James. *About Face: A Story of America's Cautious Relationship with China, from Nixon to Clinton*. New York: Knopf, 1998.

———. *Rise of the Vulcans: The History of Bush's War Cabinet*. New York: Viking, 2004.

Marshall, Jonathan, Peter Dale Scott, and Jane Hunter. *The Iran-Contra Connection*. Boston: South End, 1987.

Mayer, Jane. *The Dark Side: The Inside Story of How the War on Terror Turned into a War on American Ideals*. Garden City, N.Y.: Doubleday, 2008.

Mobley. Richard A. *Flash Point North Korea: The Pueblo and EC-121 Crises*. Annapolis, Md.: Naval Institute Press, 2003.

Morris, Roger. "The CIA and the Gates Legacy." Tomgram, June 25, 2007. ttp://www.tomdispatch.com/post/174814/roger_morris_the_cia_and_the_gates_legacy.

———. "The Gates Inheritance." Tomgram, June 19, 2007. http://www.tomdispatch.com/post/174812/roger_morris_the_gates_inheritance.

———. *Haig: The General's Progress*. Chicago: Playboy Press, 1982.

———. "The World That Made Bob," Tomgram, June 21, 2007. http://tomdispatch.com/post/174813/roger_morris_the_world_that_made_bob.

Muravchik, Joshua. "The Past, Present, and Future of Neoconservatism." *Commentary*, October 2007. www.commentarymagazine.com/viewarticle.cfm/The-Past-Present-and-Future-of-Neoconservatism-10935.

Newhouse, John. *Cold Dawn: The Story of SALT*. Washington, D.C.: Pergamon-Brassey's, 1989.

Nichols, John. *The Rise and Rise of Richard B. Cheney*. New York: New Press, 2004.

Nitze, Paul H., Ann M. Smith, and Steven L. Bearden. *From Hiroshima to Glasnost: At the Center of Decision.* New York: Grove Weidenfeld, 1989.

Nixon, Richard M. "Asia After Vietnam." *Foreign Affairs,* October 1967, in *Foreign Relations of the United States, 1969–1976,* vol. 1. Washington, D.C.: U.S. Government Printing Office, 2003.

———. *RN: The Memoirs of Richard Nixon.* New York: Grosset & Dunlap, 1978.

Nixon Administration Roundtables. National Security System Project. Washington, D.C.: Brookings Institution, various dates.

Olmsted, Kathryn S. *Challenging the Secret Government.* Chapel Hill: University of North Carolina Press, 1996.

Packer, George. *The Assassins' Gate: America in Iraq.* New York: Farrar, Straus & Giroux, 2005.

Palmer, Bruce, Jr. *The 25-Year War: America's Military Role in Vietnam.* Lexington: University Press of Kentucky, 1984.

Parmet, Herbert S. *George Bush: The Life of a Lone Star Yankee.* New Brunswick, N.J.: Transaction, 2001.

Pipes, Richard. *Vixi: Memoirs of a Non-Belonger.* New Haven, Conn.: Yale University Press, 2003.

Powers, Thomas. *The Man Who Kept the Secrets: Richard Helms and the CIA.* New York: Knopf, 1979.

Prados, John. *Keepers of the Keys: The National Security Council from Truman to Bush.* New York: Morrow, 1991.

Rhodes, Richard. *Arsenals of Folly: The Making of the Nuclear Arms Race.* New York: Knopf, 2007.

Ricks, Thomas E. *Fiasco: The American Military Adventure in Iraq.* New York: Penguin, 2006.

———. *The Gamble: General David Petraeus and the American Military Adventure in Iraq, 2006–2008.* New York: Penguin, 2009.

Rodman, Peter W. *More Precious Than Peace: The Cold War and the Struggle for the Third World.* New York: Scribner's, 1994.

———. *Presidential Command: Power, Leadership, and the Making of Foreign Policy from Richard Nixon to George W. Bush.* New York: Knopf, 2009.

Rose, David. "Neo Culpa." *Vanity Fair,* January 2007.

Rosen, James. "Nixon and the Chiefs." *Atlantic,* April, 2002.

———. *The Strong Man: John Mitchell and the Secrets of Watergate.* Garden City, N.Y.: Doubleday, 2008.

Rothkopf, David. *Running the World: The Inside Story of the National Security Council and the Architects of American Power.* New York: PublicAffairs, 2005.

Rowny, Edward L. *It Takes One to Tango.* Washington, D.C.: Brassey's, 1992.

Sagan, Scott D., and Jeremi Suri. "The Madman Nuclear Alert." *International Security* 27, no. 4 (Spring 2003).

Savage, Charlie. *Takeover: The Return of the Imperial Presidency and the Subversion of American Democracy.* Boston: Little, Brown, 2007.

Schlesinger, James. "Quest for a Post-Cold War Foreign Policy." *Foreign Affairs* 72, no. 1 (January 1993).

Schneider, Gregory L. *Cadres for Conservatism: Young Americans for Freedom and the Rise of the Contemporary Right.* New York: New York University Press, 1999.

Shachtman, Tom. *Decade of Shocks, 1963–1974.* New York: Simon & Schuster, 1993.

Shawcross, William. *Sideshow: Kissinger, Nixon and the Destruction of Cambodia.* New York: Simon & Schuster, 1979.

Shirley, Craig. *Reagan's Revolution: The Untold Story of the Campaign That Started It All.* Nashville, Tenn.: Nelson Current, 2005.

Shultz, George P. *Turmoil and Triumph: My Years as Secretary of State.* New York: Scribner's, 1993.

Smith, Gerard C. *Doubletalk: The Story of the First Strategic Arms Limitation Talks.* Garden City, N.Y.: Doubleday, 1980.

Sorley, Lewis. *A Better War: The Unexamined Victories and Final Tragedy of America's Last Years in Vietnam.* San Diego: Harcourt, 1999.

———. *Thunderbolt: From the Battle of the Bulge to Vietnam and Beyond: General Creighton Abrams and the Army of His Times.* Herndon, Va.: Brassey's, 1992.

Steinfels, Peter. *The Neoconservatives: The Men Who Are Changing America's Politics.* New York: Simon & Schuster, 1979.

Suskind, Ron. *The Price of Loyalty: George W. Bush, the White House, and the Education of Paul O'Neill.* New York: Simon & Schuster, 2004.

Thimmesch, Nick. Notes and drafts of article "The Iron Mentor of the Pentagon," 1975, in Thimmesch Papers, University of Iowa, Iowa City.

Tucker, Nancy Bernkopf. "Taiwan Expendable? Nixon and Kissinger Go to China." *Journal of American History* 92, no. 1 (June 2005).

Van Atta, Dale. *With Honor: Melvin Laird in War, Peace, and Politics.* Madison: University of Wisconsin Press, 2008.

Vest, Jason. "Darth Rumsfeld." *American Prospect,* February 26, 2001. http://www.prospect.org/cs/articles?article=darth_rumsfeld.

———. "The Dubious Genius of Andrew Marshall." *American Prospect,* January 2001. http://www.prospect.org/cs/articles?article=the_dubious_genius_of_andrew_marshall.

———. "The Men from JINSA and CSP." *Nation,* September 2, 2002. http://www.thenation.com/doc/20020902/vest.

Walker, Martin. *The Cold War: A History.* New York: Henry Holt, 1994.

Walters, Vernon A. *Silent Missions.* Garden City, N.Y.: Doubleday, 1978.

Weisman, Alan. *Prince of Darkness: Richard Perle.* New York: Union Square, 2007.

Werth, Barry. *31 Days: Gerald Ford, the Nixon Pardon, and a Government in Crisis.* Garden City, N.Y.: Doubleday, 2006.

Whalen, Richard. "Revolt of the Generals." *Nation,* October 16, 2006. http://www.thenation.com/doc/20061016/whalen.

Wilbanks, James F. *Abandoning Vietnam: How America Left and South Vietnam Lost Its War.* Lawrence: University Press of Kansas, 2004.

Wolfowitz, Paul. "Clinton's First Year." *Foreign Affairs,* January–February, 1994.

Woodward, Bob. *Bush at War.* New York: Simon & Schuster, 2002.

———. *The Commanders.* New York: Simon & Schuster, 1991.

———. *Plan of Attack.* New York: Simon & Schuster, 2004.

———. *The Secret Man: The Story of Watergate's Deep Throat.* New York: Simon & Schuster, 2005.

———. *State of Denial.* New York: Simon & Schuster, 2006.

———. *Veil.* New York: Simon & Schuster, 1987.

Woodward, Bob, and Carl Bernstein. *All the President's Men.* New York: Simon & Schuster, 1975.

———. *The Final Days.* New York: Simon & Schuster, 1976.

Zumwalt, Elmo R., Jr. *On Watch: A Memoir.* New York: Quadrangle, 1976.

Index

Abington Corporation, 274, 279
Abrams, Creighton, 4, 33–34, 75, 92–94, 136, 147, 235
Abrams, Elliott, 196, 304, 314, 317, 320, 335, 347, 360–63, 403
absolute values. *See* moral absolutism
Abu Ghraib prison scandal, 407, 409. *See also* prisoner torture issue
Acheson, Dean, 49
Achille Lauro hijacking, 311
Addington, David, 323, 372, 389–90, 412–13, 424
Adelman, Ken, 53–54, 293–94, 309, 392, 401, 429
Afghanistan
 George W. Bush and NATO invasion and occupation of, 385–86, 391, 399, 421
 George W. Bush's lack of exit strategy for, 425–26
 Jimmy Carter and, 281
 Bill Clinton's missile strikes on al-Qaeda in, 367
 intelligence warnings about al-Qaeda in, 377
 Barack Obama and, 428, 433
 Donald Rumsfeld vs. professional military on, 1
 sale of weapons to, by CIA, 316
 Soviet invasion of, 287
 Soviet withdrawal from, 327

Agnew, Spiro, 51, 76–77, 134, 172, 197, 201, 203
Albert, Carl, 196
Albright, Madeleine, 375
Allen, Richard V., 15–19, 101, 264, 277, 286–89, 293–94, 301, 333, 364
Allende, Salvador, 86–87
all-volunteer military, 61
al-Qaeda, 350–51, 367, 377, 383–84, 387–89, 405–7, 412–13, 424–25. *See also* bin Laden, Osama; September 11, 2001, terrorist attack
Alsop, Joseph, 253
alternative fuels issue, 243
American Civil Liberties Union (ACLU), 391
American Conservative Union, 110, 217, 233, 266, 335
American Enterprise Institute, 19, 323
Anderson, Jack, 122–23, 129, 199–200, 207, 213, 233
Anderson, Martin, 15
Andropov, Yuri, 332, 334
Angleton, James Jesus, 26
Angola, 244, 250, 262
Anti-Ballistic Missile (ABM) treaty, 38, 48–51, 97, 137–39, 143–44, 366, 374–75, 378. *See also* arms control
anti-communism. *See* Communism
antiwar movement (Vietnam War), 47–48, 59–60, 63–65, 68–69, 77–78, 100–101, 243–44. *See also* Vietnam War

appropriations, congressional
  for bombing of Yugoslavia, 369
  for Vietnam War, 90–92, 196
Aquino, Corazon, 316
Aristide, Jean-Bertrand, 354
arms control. *See also* Anti-Ballistic Missile
    (ABM) treaty; nuclear weapons;
    Strategic Arms Limitation Talks
    (SALT I and SALT II); Strategic Arms
    Reduction Treaties (START I and
    Start II)
  George W. Bush and, 376–79
  Comprehensive Nuclear Test-Ban Treaty,
    353, 369–70, 379
  fall of the Soviet Union and, 334
  fight over Paul Warnke and, 276–77
  Intermediate Nuclear Forces (INF) treaty,
    311, 318–22, 327–28
  neoconservatives and, 73–74, 219–21,
    345–46 (*see also* Bolton, John; Feith,
    Douglas J.; Iklé, Fred; Jackson, Henry
    M. "Scoop"; Nitze, Paul; Perle, Richard;
    Rowny, Edward L.; Wolfowitz, Paul D.;
    Zumwalt, Elmo "Bud")
  Nuclear Non-Proliferation Treaty, 19–20
  Ronald Reagan and, 300–301, 305–6
  Schlesinger Doctrine and, 206–7
Arms Control and Disarmament Agency
    (ACDA), 38, 143–44, 196, 258, 294
Armstrong, Scott, 184, 189–90, 297
Ash, Roy, 198
Ashbrook, John, 118, 133–34
Ashcroft, John, 390, 410, 419
Asia, 13–15, 67. *See also* China; Japan
Atomic Energy Commission, 161
authoritarian governments, 316
"axis of evil" speech, George W. Bush's,
    391–92

Bacevich, Andrew, 289, 296
Backfire bombers, Soviet, 241–43, 259,
    275–76
Baker, Howard, 116, 140, 190–91, 200, 212
Baker, James, 295, 329, 331, 337, 340, 343, 347,
    352–53, 368, 431
Baroody, Bill, 199–200
Bartley, Robert, 219
Becker, Benton, 230, 234–35
Beecher, William, 27, 46, 78, 113–14, 405
Begin, Menachem, 281
Bell, Jeffrey, 110
Benjamin, Daniel, 388
Bennett, Bob, 140
Bennett, John, 208–9

Berlin Wall, 330
Bernstein, Carl, 161–62, 184–86, 190, 208,
    211–12, 217, 267
Beschloss, Michael R., 333
Biden, Joseph, 433
bin Laden, Osama, 310–11, 338, 350–51, 367,
    383–88. *See also* al-Qaeda
Blackwater USA, 409, 421
Blair, Tony, 377, 392, 395, 421
Boland, Edward, 317
Boland Amendment, 317, 323, 325
Bolton, John, 363, 369–70, 376, 378, 403–4,
    419, 424
Bork, Robert, 197–98, 204, 207, 306
Bosnia. *See* Serbian ethnic-cleansing
    campaign
Bradlee, Ben, 140, 190, 297
Brady, Jim, 295
Brandeis, Louis, 324
Bremer, Arthur, 139
Bremer, L. Paul, III, 402–3
Brennan, Jack, 176
Brezhnev, Leonid, 97–98, 138, 149, 187,
    205–6, 219–20, 240–42, 249–51, 283
Brezhnev Doctrine, 98, 138
Broder, David, 331
Brookings Institution, 370
Brown, Gordon, 421
Brown, Harold, 274, 277–78
Brzezinski, Zbigniew, 275, 281–83, 324
Buchanan, Patrick, 61, 101, 223, 260, 346
Buchen, Phil, 230, 234–37
Buckley, James, 108–9, 117–18, 217, 263
Buckley, William F., Jr., 28, 108–10, 114, 118,
    251, 315, 335, 415
Bulgaria, 330–31
Bull, Steve, 177, 208–9
Bundy, William, 92–93, 155, 169
Bunker, Ellsworth, 92
Burnham, James, 109–10
Bush, George H. W., 326–44
  Cabinet of, 328–30, 341–42
  Clinton administration continuation of
    policies of, 349–50, 371
  fall of the Soviet Union and, 330–34,
    341–42
  as Ford administration CIA director, 254,
    264–65
  Gulf War of, 336–41
  neoconservatives and, 6, 342–44
  Richard Nixon and, 15
  Panama invasion of, 334–36
  political campaigns of, 289, 326–28,
    345–49

as Reagan administration vice president,
   290
as United Nations ambassador, 122
Bush, George W., 372–433
   Bush Doctrine of, 393–94
   Cabinet of, 376, 410
   Dick Cheney's power during administration
      of, 406–16
   criticisms of Bill Clinton by, 368–71
   Foreign Intelligence Surveillance Act
      (FISA) and, 268
   foreign policies of, 5, 377–83, 423–25
   invasion and occupation of Iraq by, 340,
      401–4, 406–7 (see also Iraq War)
   Fritz Kraemer's death and, 404–5
   lack of exit strategy by, for Afghanistan and
      Iraq, 425–26
   lack of response of, to Hurricane Katrina,
      415
   loss of power by, 417–26
   malfeasance investigations of Iraq War,
      408–9
   neoconservatives and, 5–7, 383–84,
      414–16
   Valerie Plame case and, 412–13
   political campaigns of, 372–76, 410
   preparations of, to invade Iraq, 387–89,
      391–401
   presidential power issue and, 410–12
   prisoner torture issue and, 395–96, 407,
      413–14
   Donald Rumsfeld's removal by, 1–7, 417
   September 11, 2001, terrorist attack and,
      384–88
   USA PATRIOT act and, 389–91
   War Powers Act and, 200
   Bob Woodward and, 323, 407–8
Bush, Jeb, 362
Bush Doctrine, 393–94
Butterfield, Alexander, 177, 184, 189–91, 215,
   221
Buzhardt, J. Fred
   Spiro Agnew and, 197
   at Defense Department, 51
   executive privilege issue and, 179–83
   Gerald Ford's removal of, for taking Rich-
      ard Nixon's papers, 234
   Alexander Haig, Gerald Ford's pardon of
      Richard Nixon, and, 236–37
   Alexander Haig and, 50
   Moorer-Radford spy ring and, 125, 129–30,
      199–200, 210–15, 235
   as Richard Nixon's lawyer and Alexander
      Haig's advisor, 176–92

Richard Nixon's resignation and, 208,
      222–23
   Pentagon Papers and, 101, 170
   Saturday Night Massacre and, 203–4
   Don Stewart, PX scandal, and, 56
   Strom Thurmond, Safeguard ABM, and,
      50–51
   Watergate affair and, 179–83, 197–200
   White House taping system and, 185–92,
      208–9, 218–19
   Bob Woodward and, 297
Byrne, Matthew, 170–71, 179

Cabinet officials
   George H. W. Bush's, 328–30, 341–42
   George W. Bush's, 376, 410
   Gerald Ford's, 253–56
   Richard Nixon's, 19–22, 177–78, 201–4
Cahn, Anne Hessing, 219, 265, 275–76,
   294
Califano, Joseph, 22, 30, 172, 176, 191
Callaway, Hollis "Bo," 253
Cambodia, 35, 46–47, 71–79, 90–92, 151, 169,
   194, 222, 244–48
Cambone, Stephen, 365, 409
Canal Zone. See Panama
Carbaugh, John, 278, 283
Card, Andrew, 396
Carlisle, Margo, 283–84, 294
Carlucci, Frank, 293–94, 320, 322
Carrington, Lord, 301–2
Carroll, Eugene, 54–55
Carter, Jimmy, 270–90
   Carter Doctrine of, 287–90, 337
   as Bill Clinton's emissary to Haiti, 354
   foreign policies of, 275–78, 280–82
   Fritz Kraemer's influence during adminis-
      tration of, 278–80
   neoconservatives and, 5, 272–75, 285–87
   presidential campaign of, 260
Casey, William, 50, 284, 294–97, 300, 304,
   313–14, 320–23
Castro, Fidel, 85. See also Cuba
Center for Security Policy, 322, 365–66
Central America, 296, 300, 351. See also
   Nicaragua; Panama
Central Intelligence Agency (CIA)
   James Angleton and, 26
   antiwar movement and, 243–44
   George W. Bush and, 380
   Chile and, 86–87
   William Colby and, 178
   covert actions of, in Central America, 296,
      300

Central Intelligence Agency (*continued*)
  destruction of prisoner interrogation tapes
    by, 424–25
  intelligence estimates of, 97, 264–65,
    365–66, 424 (*see also* intelligence
    estimates)
  Iran-Contra operation and, 319–25
  on Iraq War, 388–89, 398, 409
  Bud Krogh and, 113
  Nicaraguan Contras and, 313–14
  Richard Nixon and, 19–21
  outing of Valerie Plame as agent for, 404
  PATRIOT Act and, 390
  Plumbers group and, 114–17, 177
  Ronald Reagan and, 296–97
  sale of weapons to Afghanistan by, 316
  Team B report on, 275–76
  warnings about al-Qaeda from, 383–84
  Watergate affair and, 139–43, 179–83
  wiretaps and, 79
Chalabi, Ahmad, 392, 396
Chapin, Dwight, 134, 164
Cheney, Richard B. "Dick"
  anti-Soviet Republican Party plank and, 269
  in George H. W. Bush administration and,
    329
  in George W. Bush administration and,
    368, 372–73, 376
  "Continuity of Government" program and,
    312–13
  criticism of Bill Clinton by, 353
  Defense Planning Guidance (DPG) report
    and, 342–44
  defense strategy document by, 349
  fall of the Soviet Union and, 331–32
  in Ford administration and, 231, 237–42,
    254
  Foreign Intelligence Surveillance Act
    (FISA) and, 280
  Gulf War and, 337–41
  Iran-Contra minority report by, 323–25
  Iran's nuclear capacity and, 424
  Iraq War and, 388–89, 392, 401
  Henry Kissinger and, 63
  MX missiles and, 308
  neoconservative movement and, 5, 231,
    419–20
  obstruction by, of investigations, 409
  PATRIOT Act and, 390
  political campaigns of, 274, 282, 372–73
  on presidential power, 339
  prisoner interrogation and, 409
  Project for a New American Century and,
    362

Condoleezza Rice and, 377
  Donald Rumsfeld and, 1–3, 53–54, 112
  William Simon and, 242
  undermining of Ford administration for-
    eign policies by, 238–42
  War Powers Act and, 200
Cherne, Leo, 264
Chernenko, Konstantin, 318
Chile, 86–87
China
  George H. W. Bush and, 290, 329–30
  George W. Bush and, 374
  Jimmy Carter and, 281–82
  Bob Dole and, 355
  EP-3 Aries II reconnaissance plane incident
    and, 380–82
  Alexander Haig and, 299–300
  Iraq and, 368
  Henry Kissinger and, 37–38
  Fritz Kraemer on, 67, 149–50
  Richard Nixon's opening of, 5, 13–15,
    98–103, 134–35, 144–45
  nuclear tests of, 353
  Pakistan and, 121
  power of, 422
  Ronald Reagan and, 299
  relations of, with Soviet Union, 18, 62, 83,
    99, 134–35, 282
  United Nations dual recognition of Taiwan
    and, 99, 117–18
Christianity, 4, 24, 30, 410
Church, Frank, 77–78, 244
Cienfuegos submarine base crisis, 84–86
Clark, Wesley, 340
Clark, William, 301
Clarke, Jonathan, 354, 362, 379
Clarke, Richard, 377, 383–84, 387
"Clean Break" paper, 360
Clements, William, 232
Clifford, Clark, 60, 215
climate change, 378–79, 418
Clines, Thomas, 304
Clinton, Hillary, 7, 420, 432–33
Clinton, William Jefferson "Bill," 345–71
  George W. Bush's criticism of, 368–71
  foreign policy of, 349–55, 370
  Iraq, terrorism, and, 367–68
  neoconservatives and, 6, 346–47,
    359–63
  nuclear weapons and, 363–66
  political campaign of, 345–49
Coalition for a Democratic Majority, 159,
    221, 264
Coalition Provisional Authority, 402–3

coalition warfare, George H. W. Bush's, 337–41, 344

Cohen, William, 362

Colby, William, 178, 247–48, 254

Cold War, 4–6, 50, 331–34. *See also* arms control; communism; Soviet Union

Collier, Bernard, 118

Colson, Chuck, 58, 110, 115, 140, 166, 168, 172, 211

Commission to Assess the Ballistic Missile Threat to the United States, 365–68

Committee on the Present Danger (CPD), 264–65, 275–77, 283, 294. *See also* Team B

Committee to Maintain a Prudent Defense Policy, 49

Committee to Re-Elect the President, 136, 139–43

communism
    Leonid Brezhnev and, 97–98
    Chinese (*see* China)
    conservatives and, 108–12, 231–33
    containment policy for, 13–14, 31
    Henry Kissinger and, 80, 250
    Fritz Kraemer and, 26, 28, 31, 194
    neoconservatives and, 272–73, 286
    Richard Nixon and, 14–15, 31, 61–62, 69–71, 83–90, 108–12
    Ronald Reagan and, 296
    Donald Rumsfeld and, 5
    James Schlesinger and, 194
    Soviet (*see* Soviet Union)
    Vietnam War and, 13–14, 244–47

Comprehensive Nuclear Test-Ban Treaty, 353, 369–70, 379

Congress
    appropriations limitations of, for bombing of Yugoslavia, 369
    appropriations limitations of, for Vietnam War, 90–92, 196
    Comprehensive Nuclear Test-Ban Treaty and, 369–70
    Democratic control of, during Ford administration and, 239
    impeachment of Bill Clinton by, 367–68
    impeachment of Richard Nixon by, 197, 204, 217, 221–22
    investigation of CIA by, 243–44
    Iran-Contra reports of, 323–25
    Iraq Liberation Act of 1998 by, 367
    Iraq War resolution of, 398–99
    slush-fund investigation of, 162
    Strategic Arms Limitation Talks (SALT) treaty and, 143–44

Watergate affair investigations of, 140, 163–68, 200, 218–23

Connally, John, 178, 219

Conservative Political Action conference, 335

conservatives. *See also* Republican Party
    arms control and, 82–83, 137–39
    Jimmy Carter and, 282–85
    Gerald Ford and, 231–33, 243–44, 249–59
    Sven Kraemer and, 278
    Manhattan Twelve, 108–12, 133–34
    neoconservatives vs., 158–59, 342–44, 352, 429–30 (*see also* neoconservative movement)
    Richard Nixon and, 15–17, 94–95, 107–19, 216, 221–22
    Vietnamization and, 60

containment policy, 13–14, 31. *See also* communism

"Continuity of Government" program, 312–13

Contras, Nicaraguan, 300, 313–14, 317–29. *See also* Iran-Contra operation

Cooke, Janet, 298

Cooper, John Sherman, 77–78

Cooper, Matt, 413

Coors, Joseph, 260

counterforce missile doctrine, 206–7, 217, 219

cover-ups, Richard Nixon's, 131, 141–43, 165, 168. *See also* Moorer-Radford spy ring; Watergate affair

Cox, Archibald, 192, 197, 203–4

Croatia. *See* Serbian ethnic-cleansing campaign

Crommelin, Quentin, 278, 283

Crowe, William, 335, 346

Cuba, 28, 84–86, 244, 300, 310

Cushman, Robert, 114–16, 177, 181–82

Dean, John Wesley, III, 141–43, 161–72, 175, 183–89, 218

Deaver, Mike, 295

Decter, Midge, 159, 161, 362

"Deep Throat" informant, 55, 184, 208–9

DEFCON alerts, 40, 64–66, 205–6, 310–11

Defense Department. *See also* military; Pentagon
    arms control and, 219–21
    Dick Cheney at, 329
    Richard Nixon and, 19–21
    Pentagon Papers and, 101
    Donald Rumsfeld at, 1–7 (*see also* Rumsfeld, Donald H.)

Defense Department. (*continued*)
   James Schlesinger at, 178 (*see also*
      Schlesinger, James)
   Vietnam War and, 37–38
Defense Intelligence Agency, 240, 257, 378
Defense Planning Guidance (DPG) report,
   342–44
Defense Policy Board, 387
DeLay, Tom, 369
democracy
   fall of the Soviet Union and, 333–34
   fostering of, 315–16, 348–49, 393–94,
      410–11
   in Iraq, 363–64
   Fritz Kraemer on, 4, 29, 62
   neoconservatives and, 273
Democratic Party
   control of Congress by, 239, 376
   Scoop Jackson and, 21
   neoconservative movement and, 158–59
   Ronald Reagan and, 290
   Watergate burglary attempt and, 139–43
Department of Defense. *See* Defense
   Department
Department of State. *See* State Department
Desert Shield operation, 337–41
détente, Soviet, 5, 13–15, 96–98, 144–45,
   216–17, 252–53, 334. *See also* arms con-
   trol; Soviet Union
"Dictatorships and Double Standards" article,
   285–87
Didion, Joan, 408
diplomacy
   George W. Bush and, 379
   Fritz Kraemer on, 3–5, 28–29
   John McCain and, 427
   Richard Nixon and, 31
   Barack Obama and, 428, 432–34
   Richard Perle on, 360
Dirksen, Everett, 17
Dixiecrats, 159
Dobrynin, Anatoly, 33, 36–37, 59, 63–66,
   86, 89–90, 97, 102–3, 108, 196, 204–6,
   231–32
Dole, Bob, 111, 270, 327, 355
domestic policy, Fritz Kraemer on foreign
   policy vs., 24
domestic surveillance, 280, 380, 390–91
Downing Street Memo, 395
draft-dodger amnesty issue, 224, 233,
   277–78
Draper, Theodore, 324–25
Dreher, Rod, 415
Drucker, Peter, 23–26, 30, 430

dual recognition of China and Taiwan, United
   Nations, 99, 117–18
Duck Hook offensive, 62–64
Dukakis, Michael, 327–28
Dulles, John Foster, 134–35

Eagleburger, Lawrence, 43, 205, 300, 324,
   330
East Germany. *See* Germany
East Pakistan. *See* Pakistan
EC-121 incident, 42–45
economic strength, 24, 29, 430
Edwards, John, 420
Egypt, 87, 202–7, 281, 300
Ehrlichman, John
   China rapprochement and, 103
   Ellsberg trial and, 179
   Moorer-Radford spy ring and, 123–30, 200,
      212–15, 224, 235
   Plumbers group and, 113–16, 211
   Watergate affair and, 141–42, 161, 165–72,
      179–82, 185
Eisenhower, Dwight, 18, 65, 99
elections. *See* political campaigns
electronic surveillance, 79. *See also* wiretaps
elite rule, Fritz Kraemer on, 4, 28, 30–31,
   394
Ellsberg, Daniel, 20, 100–101, 114–17, 170–72,
   179, 214
England, 412–13, 421
EP-3 Aries II reconnaissance plane incident,
   380–82
Ervin, Sam, 162–64, 170, 191–92
espionage ring. *See* Moorer-Radford spy ring
Evans, Rowland, 233, 258, 261–63, 268, 279
"evil empire" speech, 307–9, 361–62
exceptionalism, American, 361, 430
executive power. *See* presidential power issue
executive privilege issue, 175–85, 189–92,
   214
exit strategy issue, 369, 397, 425

Fannin, Paul, 111
Farquhar, Roger, 56
Federal Bureau of Investigation (FBI)
   al-Qaeda and, 384
   L. Patrick Gray III at, 139
   Robert Mueller at, 380
   PATRIOT Act and, 390
   Watergate affair and, 141–43, 161–63,
      179–83, 208–9
   wiretaps and, 46–47, 79, 115
Federal Emergency Management Agency
   (FEMA), 312–13

Federalist Society for Law and Public Policy
    Studies, 238, 306–7
Feith, Douglas J.
    George W. Bush administration and, 376
    on de-Baathification idea, 402
    discrediting of alternative intelligence as-
        sessments by, 419
    Iraq invasion consequences and, 398
    Iraq regime change and, 364, 378, 382
    Israel and, 360
    Scoop Jackson and, 196
    National Interest contributions, 314
    Richard Perle and, 144, 321
    Policy Counter Terrorism Evaluation
        Group (PCTEG) of, 388–89
    Donald Rumsfeld and, 3
Felt, W. Mark, 55, 208–9
Fielding, Lewis J., 115–16, 166, 170–71, 177,
    183, 211
Finch, Robert, 111
Fischer, Joschka, 397
Fitzgerald, Frances, 307, 325, 333
Fitzgerald, Patrick, 413
Fitzpatrick, Francis J., 54
Ford, Gerald R., 229–71
    Cabinet of, 229–31, 253–56
    continuation of policies of, by Jimmy
        Carter, 280–82
    fall of South Vietnam and, 244–47
    Alexander Haig's removal by, 235–37
    intelligence estimates and, 264–65
    Henry Kissinger and, 289–90
    Melvin Laird and, 34
    Mayaguez incident and, 247–48
    neoconservatives and, 5, 231–33, 243–44,
        249–59
    as Richard Nixon's vice president, 203, 217,
        222–24
    pardon of Richard Nixon by, 234–37
    political campaigns of, 260–71
    Donald Rumsfeld and, 1, 52, 237–38,
        242–43, 256–59
Foreign Intelligence Surveillance Act (FISA),
    267–68, 280, 390, 412–13
foreign policy
    George H. W. Bush's, 328
    George W. Bush's, 2, 355
    George W. Bush's instruction in, 368
    Jimmy Carter's, 270–71, 275–82
    Bill Clinton's, 345–55
    Bob Dole's, 355
    Alexander Haig's opposition to Richard
        Nixon's, 175
    Fritz Kraemer on, 3–5, 24

neoconservative intelligence estimates and,
    264–65
Richard Nixon's, 13–22, 32–47, 61, 69–71
paleocons vs. neocons on, 342–44
Ronald Reagan's attacks on Gerald Ford's,
    261–64
remilitarization of, 206–7, 219
Republican Party plank on, 269
Donald Rumsfeld's neoconservative, 2, 231,
    237–38, 273–74
undermining of Gerald Ford's, 238–42
undermining of Richard Nixon's, 193–209
Foreign Policy Research Institute, 361
France, 368, 397
Friedman, Thomas, 384, 396
Froehlke, Robert, 147
Fukuyama, Francis, 415–16
Fulbright, J. William, 201
funding, congressional. See appropriations,
    congressional

Gaddis, John Lewis, 309, 330, 333
Gaffney, Frank, 322, 362
Gandhi, Indira, 121
Garment, Leonard, 178, 188, 191, 199–200,
    208
Garthoff, Ray, 74, 212
Gates, Robert M., 1, 241, 251, 296, 307, 316,
    322–23, 326, 329, 417, 421, 431–32
gay marriage issue, 410
Gellman, Barton, 406, 409
Geneva Convention
    George W. Bush and, 395–96, 409,
        413–14
    Barack Obama and, 433
geostrategy, 4, 279
Germany, 23–25, 330–32, 397
Gesell, Gerhard, 214
Gingrich, Newt, 321, 354, 364, 367–68
glasnost initiative, 326
Glaspie, April, 337
global hegemony concept, 360–62
global warming, 378–79, 418
global war on terror, 5, 385–86, 391–92,
    412–13. See also terrorism
Glynn, Patrick, 351–52
Goldsmith, Jack, 390, 412–13
Goldwater, Barry, 217, 224, 253, 313
Gonzales, Albert, 390, 395–98, 409–10, 419,
    424
Goodpaster, Andrew, 20–22, 34, 40–41, 131,
    161, 236–37
Gorbachev, Mikhail, 318–19, 326–28, 331–34,
    338, 341

Gore, Al, 346, 374–76
Goss, Porter, 409
Graham, Bradley, 2
Graham, Daniel, 240, 257, 265, 275, 296, 304
Graham, Kay, 162
Gray, L. Patrick, III, 139, 141, 162–64
Great Britain, 412–13, 421
Green, William, 298
Grenada invasion, 310
Gromyko, Andrei, 299, 318
Grunwald, Henry, 348
Guantánamo Bay prison, 395–96, 407, 409, 413–14, 433
Gulf War, 336–41. See also Iraq
Gulley, Bill, 56–58, 130

Haass, Richard, 370–71
Hadley, Stephen, 398
Hagel, Chuck, 398–400, 431
Haig, Alexander M. Haig, Jr.
    Spiro Agnew and, 197
    as Army vice chief of staff, 161
    Cambodian incursion and, 76
    China rapprochement and, 134–35
    Cienfuegos submarine base crisis and, 85–86
    cover-ups by (see Buzhardt, J. Fred)
    EC-121 incident and, 43–44
    executive privilege issue and, 179–83
    feigned DEFCON alert and, 62–66
    Gerald Ford and, 230, 234
    Leon Jaworski and, 207, 210–11
    Henry Kissinger and, 30, 39–40, 56–58, 70, 78, 146–48, 200–201, 236
    Fritz Kraemer and, 4, 27, 30–31, 36, 72–73, 152–53, 193–95, 405
    Laos incursion and, 92–95
    Manhattan Twelve and, 110
    Moorer-Radford spy ring and, 101–2, 123–31, 175, 192, 199–200, 210–15
    as NATO Supreme Allied Commander–Europe (SACEUR), 235–37, 274–75, 282–83
    Richard Nixon and, 22, 146–49, 172, 201–4, 224
    Richard Nixon's pardon and, 236–37
    Richard Nixon's resignation and, 222–24
    Pentagon Papers and, 100, 171
    presidential ambition of, 289
    Ronald Reagan and, 294–303
    Syrian invasion of Jordan and, 87–89
    Vietnam War and, 60, 70–71, 136–38, 154–57, 169–70

Watergate affair and, 197–98
White House taping system and, 177, 189–92, 208–9, 218–19
wiretaps and, 46–47, 78–79, 183–85, 215, 221
Bob Woodward as Pentagon briefer for, 55
Yom Kippur War and, 205–6
Hainan Island incident, 380–82
Haiti, 350, 353–54, 370
Haldeman, H. R. "Bob"
    on Cambodian incursion, 76
    campaign slush fund and, 162
    China rapprochement and, 103
    Cienfuegos submarine base crisis and, 84–85
    Ervin Committee and, 164
    on feigned DEFCON alert, 65–66
    Alexander Haig and, 57–58
    leaks and, 47
    Moorer-Radford spy ring and, 124–26, 200
    Richard Nixon and, 21, 111
    pardon request of, 223–24
    Pentagon Papers and, 101
    Vernon Walters and, 73
    Watergate affair and, 141–42, 161, 165–72, 179–82, 185–86, 189
    White House taping system and, 218–19
Halliburton, 409, 421
Halloween Massacre, 253–56
Halper, Stefan, 354, 362, 379
Halperin, Morton, 20, 22, 39, 43, 46–47, 100, 171, 215
Harries, Owen, 314–15
Hartmann, Robert, 222–23
Hayden, Michael, 380
Hayes, Stephen, 238, 376
Haynes, William J., Jr., 390
Heilbrunn, Jacob, 316, 339, 342, 346
Helms, Jesse, 153, 239, 266, 278, 290, 327
Helms, Richard, 20–21, 51, 79, 114, 140–41, 161
Heritage Foundation, 284, 296, 321, 402
Hersh, Seymour, 183, 212, 243–44, 408
Hickel, Walter, 77
Higby, Larry, 176, 189
Ho Chi Minh, 62–64
Hoffmann, Hubertus, 422
Hoffmann, Stanley, 42
Holbrooke, Richard, 367, 433
Hoover, J. Edgar, 46, 79, 101, 139, 201
Hoover Institution, 16, 19
House of Representatives. See Congress
Hudson Institute, 414–15

Hugel, Max, 296–97
human rights, 250–51
Humphrey, Gordon, 279, 327
Humphrey, Hubert H., 15–18, 159
Hungary, 28, 330
Hunt, E. Howard, 114–16, 136, 139–42, 162, 166–68, 177
Hunter, Robert E., 370
Hurricane Katrina, 415
Hussein, King, 87–88
Hussein, Saddam, 312, 336, 347–48, 355, 360, 363–64, 368, 373–74, 378, 385, 387–88, 401. *See also* Gulf War; Iraq; Iraq War
Huston, Tom Charles, 78–79
Huston Plan, 79, 183, 390
Hyland, William, 239–41, 321

ideologues vs. pragmatists, 4–7, 84, 385, 427
Iklé, Fred
    at Arms Control and Disarmament Agency (ACDA), 143–44, 160, 196, 221, 232, 258
    on Jimmy Carter, 284, 288
    Fritz Kraemer and, 4, 405
    Project for a New American Century and, 362
    provision of Stinger missiles to mujahideen by, 316
    Reagan administration and, 294, 304
    resignation of, 320
impeachments
    of Bill Clinton, 367–68
    of Richard Nixon, 197, 204, 217, 221–22
India, 99–103, 108, 120–23, 343, 364–65, 371
Inman, Bobby Ray, 54, 294–97, 301, 323
intelligence estimates, 38–39, 51, 97, 195, 220, 232, 238–39, 264–65, 275–76, 365–66, 419, 424. *See also* Office of Net Assessment (ONA)
intercontinental ballistic missiles (ICBMs), 41, 240, 341
Intermediate Nuclear Forces (INF) treaty, 311, 318–22, 327–28
International Advisors, Inc., 321
International Criminal Court, 379
internationalism, 32, 272
interrogation. *See* prisoner torture issue
Iran
    George H. W. Bush and, 328
    George W. Bush and, 391, 394–95
    Jimmy Carter and, 281, 285
    Hezbollah and, 354, 416

hostage crisis in, 289
    intelligence estimates of, 365–66, 424
    Iraq and, 6, 256, 312, 336
    military sales to, 61
    Barack Obama and nuclear weapons of, 433–34
    offer to George W. Bush from, 403
    Reagan administration and (*see* Iran-Contra operation)
Iran-Contra operation, 314, 317–29, 347
Iraq
    George W. Bush and, 373, 378, 382–83
    Bill Clinton and, 354–55, 368
    Gulf War with (*see* Gulf War)
    intelligence estimates of, 365–66
    invasion and occupation of (*see* Iraq War)
    Iraq Liberation Act of 1998 and, 367
    leaked Paul Wolfowitz report on, 284–85
    neoconservatives and, 360, 363
    no-fly zone of, 350
    Barack Obama and, 428, 433
    Donald Rumsfeld and, 312
    stopping assistance to Kurds in, 256
    weapons inspections of, 368
Iraq Liberation Act of 1998, 367
Iraq War
    arguments against, 396–98
    congressional resolution supporting, 398–99
    invasion and occupation of Iraq, 401–5
    lack of exit strategy for, 425–26
    malfeasance investigations of, 420–21
    John McCain on, 427–28
    Niger uranium story and, 396, 400, 404
    Barack Obama's opposition to, 420
    occupation issues after, 6, 411, 414, 418–24
    preemptive war issue and, 391–95
    regime change issue, 338–40, 360, 363–64, 367, 373–74
    Republican Party platform on, 374
    Donald Rumsfeld vs. professional military on, 1–2
    September 11, 2001, terrorist attack and, 387–88
    weapons of mass destruction (WMDs) issue and, 388–89, 395, 399–401
Isaacson, Walter, 256, 391
Islamist militants, 5, 365. *See also* al-Qaeda; Muslims; terrorism
Israel
    Jimmy Carter and, 281
    Gulf War and, 339
    Iran-Contra operation and, 314

Israel (*continued*)
  neoconservatives and, 360
  peace accord between Jordan and,
    353–54
  peace process of, with Palestinians, 351,
    379, 433
  Richard Perle's "Clean Break" paper for,
    360
  Syrian invasion of Jordan and, 87–89
  war of, with Lebanon, 302, 416
  Yom Kippur War and, 202–6

Jackson, Henry M. "Scoop"
  arms control and, 49–51, 97–98, 138–39,
    143–44, 219–21, 239–40, 276–77
  Leonid Brezhnev and, 187
  on George H. W. Bush, 254–55
  China rapprochement and, 112
  Democratic Party and, 153
  Gerald Ford and, 231–33
  Jackson-Vanik Amendment of, 144, 159–60,
    219
  Fritz Kraemer and, 4
  leak by, 113–14
  Patrick Moynihan and, 349
  neoconservative movement and, 159–60,
    196
  Richard Nixon and, 21
  Richard Perle and, 278–79 (*see also* Perle,
    Richard)
  presidential candidacy of, 133–35, 242
  Vietnam War and, 82, 118–19
  Yom Kippur War and, 202–3
Jackson, Jesse, 327
Japan, 96, 102, 107–8, 134, 300, 343–44
Javits, Jacob, 232
Jaworski, Leon, 207, 210–11, 218–19, 223–24,
    234
Jeffords, Jim, 376
Jews
  arms control and Soviet Union, 144, 160,
    219, 231–32, 241–42
  Fritz Kraemer and, 24–25
Johnson, Alex, 44, 76, 107–8, 232
Johnson, Lyndon B., 15–20, 28, 51–52, 99
Joint Chiefs of Staff (JCS). *See also* military;
    Pentagon
  arms control and, 73–74, 137–39, 160,
    219–20
  Jimmy Carter and, 283
  draft-dodger amnesty issue and, 277–78
  feigned DEFCON alert and, 65
  Lyndon Johnson and, 34

Moorer-Radford spy ring and (*see* Moorer-
    Radford spy ring)
  Richard Nixon and, 21, 70, 91
  Syrian invasion of Jordan and, 87–88
  War Powers Act and, 200
Jones, James L., Jr., 432
Jones, Jerry, 234, 261
Jordan, 87–89, 353–54

Kagan, Robert, 360–63, 382, 427
Kahn, Herman, 193
Kalmbach, Herbert, 167–68
Kampelman, Max, 159, 294
Kaplan, Fred, 279–80, 343
Karzai, Hamid, 421
Kauffman, William W., 206–7
Keene, David, 262, 266, 335
Kemp, Jack, 355
Kennedy, Edward, 289
Kennedy, John F., 20, 28, 61, 85, 99
Kerry, John, 410
Khalilzad, Zalmay, 342–44, 362–63
Khan, Abdul Qadeer, 365, 387
Khan, Daoud, 281
Khan, Yahya, 99–100, 120–22
Khobar Towers bombing, 354
Khomeini, Ayatollah, 281, 285
Kim Jong Il, 403–4, 424
Kirkpatrick, Jeane, 159, 264–65, 285–87, 294,
    302, 315–16, 328, 348, 352–53
Kissinger, Henry A.
  arms control and, 138, 220
  on birth of neoconservative movement,
    158–59
  Cambodian incursion and, 75–76, 91
  China and Taiwan dual recognition issue
    and, 117
  China rapprochement and, 99–103, 134–35
  Cienfuegos submarine base crisis and,
    84–86
  Daniel Patrick Moynihan on, 216
  EC-121 incident and, 42–45
  endorsement of Barack Obama by, 431
  feigned DEFCON alert and, 62–66
  Gerald Ford and, 230–32, 254–56
  on foreign policy, 29–30
  Alexander Haig and, 30, 39–40, 56–58, 70,
    78, 146–48, 200–201, 236
  India-Pakistan war and, 121
  Kissinger Associates firm of, 308, 324, 402
  Fritz Kraemer and, 4, 16, 25–26, 31, 35–36,
    72–73, 97, 118, 148–49, 154–57, 160,
    193–96, 244, 255–56, 405

on Melvin Laird, 34
Laos incursion and, 92
Manhattan Twelve and, 108–12
Mayaguez incident and, 247–48
Moorer-Radford spy ring and (*see* Moorer-Radford spy ring)
neoconservatives and, 221, 251–52
Richard Nixon and, 18–22, 54, 144–45, 201–4
Nixon Doctrine and, 59–62
Richard Nixon's resignation and, 223
Nobel Peace Prize of, 146, 206
Pentagon Papers and, 100–101
pragmatism of, 70, 97
Ronald Reagan and, 261–64, 321
Richard Nixon's meeting with Fritz Kraemer and, 149–53
William Rogers and, 21
Donald Rumsfeld's undermining of, 238–43, 257–59
Schlesinger Doctrine and, 206–7
Single Strategic Theater memo and, 66–68
Aleksandr Solzhenitsyn and, 249–50
Soviet détente and, 252–53
Syrian invasion of Jordan and, 87–89
Vietnam War and, 34–35, 41–42, 108, 147–48, 244–47
White House taping system and, 177
wiretaps and, 46–47, 78–79, 183–85
Yom Kippur War and, 204–7
Kleindienst, Richard, 171–72
Kosovo. *See* Serbian ethnic cleansing campaign
Kosygin, Alexei, 63–64, 77, 82–83
Kraemer, Fritz G. A.
on arms control, 138, 311
article about, 244
George W. Bush, Hainan Island incident, and, 381
on China rapprochement, 99
death of, 404–5
EC-121 incident and, 43–45
fall of the Soviet Union and, 342
Alexander Haig and, 22, 30–31, 36, 58, 64, 72–73, 130–31, 152–53, 236
on history, 158
influence of, during Carter administration, 273
influence of, during Ford administration, 229–33
influence of, during Nixon administration, 193–96

intelligence estimates and, 97–98, 365–66
Scoop Jackson and, 49
Henry Kissinger and, 16, 19, 35–36, 72–73, 80, 97, 118, 130–31, 148–49, 154–57, 160, 193–96, 201, 244, 255–56
life and philosophy of, 23–31
John McCain and, 7
neoconservative movement and, 423, 430
neo-Reaganite program vs., 362–63
Richard Nixon and, 117–18, 256
Nixon Doctrine and, 61–62
Richard Nixon's meeting with, 4, 146–57
on Pentagon Papers, 100
on power, 422–23
preemptive war and, 363–64, 394
on provocative weakness, 3–5
Ronald Reagan and, 306
retirement of, 278–80
Donald Rumsfeld and, 258, 401
Single Strategic Theater memo of, 66–68
on Taiwan, 117
on troop deployment to Lebanon, 306
on Vietnam War, 91, 108, 156–57
Vernon Walters and, 73
Kraemer, Sven
arms control and, 309, 318–19
George W. Bush and, 376
on Clinton administration, 359–60
congressional staffers and, 278
death of Fritz Kraemer and, 405
evil empire phrase and, 308
on Alexander Haig and Henry Kissinger, 183
as hard-line conservative, 39–40
intelligence estimates and, 365
on Fritz Kraemer, 148–49, 244
as Fritz Kraemer's son, 23–27
Madison Group and, 283–84
neoconservative movement and, 196
on Paul Nitze, 301
Richard Nixon and, 22
Ronald Reagan and, 293–94, 304
regime change and, 364
resignation of, 320
Vietnam War and, 63, 70, 169–70
Kraft, Joseph, 219, 233, 236
Krauthammer, Charles, 354
Kristol, Irving, 159, 331, 349, 383
Kristol, William, 314, 349, 360–63, 382, 427
Krogh, Egil "Bud," 101, 112–17, 207–8, 211
Kupperman, Charles, 284

Kurds, 336
Kuwait, 284–85, 311, 336–41. *See also* Gulf
    War
Kyoto Protocol, 378–79

Laird, Melvin
    Creighton Abrams and, 136–37
    Cambodian incursion and, 75–77
    Duck Hook offensive and, 64
    on Alexander Haig and Moorer-Radford spy
        ring, 128–29
    Moorer-Radford spy ring investigation and,
        213
    Nixon administration and, 21, 34–41, 178
    Pentagon Papers and, 101
    Soviet arms control agreements and, 138,
        253
    Task Force 74 and, 122
    on Watergate affair, 188
    on Bob Woodward and Alexander Haig, 55
Lake, Tony, 57, 63, 75–76, 274, 278
Lam Son 719 campaign, 92–95
Laos, 75, 92–95, 151, 169
LaRocque, Eugene, 55
Latvia, 251
Laxalt, Paul, 266
leaks
    to Jack Anderson, 122–23
    of Defense Planning Guidance (DPG)
        report, 343
    Gerald Ford and, 233
    by foreign policy bureaucracy, 37–38
    by Alexander Haig, 57
    Richard Nixon's wiretaps in response to,
        46–47, 78–79
    Pentagon Papers and, 100–101
    by Richard Perle (*see* Perle, Richard)
    Valerie Plame case and, 413
    Plumbers group and, 112–17
    by David Sullivan and Michael Pillsbury,
        327
    by Paul Wolfowitz, 284–85
Lebanon, 302, 305–6, 309–11, 416
Ledeen, Michael, 293–94, 304, 314
Le Duc Tho, 35, 206
Lehman, John, 78, 241, 258, 274, 279,
    293–95
Leverett, Flynt, 403
Levi, Edward, 267
Lewinsky, Monica, 363
Lewis, Anthony, 277, 341
Libby, I. Lewis "Scooter," 342–44, 362, 382,
    413, 418–19
Libya, 299, 312, 317, 403

Liddy, G. Gordon, 115–16, 136, 165–67
"Limited Contingency Report" leak,
    284–85
Lithuania, 251
Lord, Winston, 75
Lott, Trent, 364
Lovestone, Jay, 26, 80
Lugar, Richard, 54, 431
Luttwak, Edward, 293–96, 315, 352
Lynn, Larry, 75–76

Madison Group, 283–85
Magruder, Jeb, 165, 168, 215
Mahon, George, 254
Mandelbaum, Michael, 370
Manhattan Twelve, 108–12, 118, 133–34
Manning, Sir David, 392
Mansfield, Mike, 98, 178, 187, 196
Maraniss, David, 298
Marcos, Ferdinand, 316
Marshall, Andrew
    Clinton administration and, 362
    "Continuity of Government" program and,
        312
    Defense Planning Guidance (DPG) report
        and, 342–43
    new weapons technology and, 279, 354,
        373–76
    Office of Net Assessment (ONA) of, 97,
        195, 239
    provision of Stinger missiles to mujahideen
        and, 316
    Donald Rumsfeld and, 258
    Team B and, 265, 275
Martinez, Eugenio, 116
Mayaguez incident, 247–48
Mayer, Jane, 406
McCain, John, 7, 372, 420, 427
McCarthy, Eugene, 145
McCloskey, Pete, 134
McClure, James, 283–84
McCord, James, 115–16, 136, 139–40, 162,
    170
McDougall, Walter A., 361–62
McFarlane, Bud, 314, 317, 320, 347, 364
McGovern, George, 133, 139–41, 145, 153
McGovern, Roy, 408
McGrory, Mary, 308
McNamara, Robert, 22, 30
media. *See* news media
Meese, Edwin, 290, 295, 306
Meir, Golda, 87, 121, 202
Mexico, 351
Meyer, Cord, 140

Middle East. *See also* Egypt; Iran; Israel
    Jimmy Carter and, 281
    Fritz Kraemer on, 67–68
    leaked Paul Wolfowitz report on, 284–85
    Richard Nixon and, 87–89
    Ronald Reagan and, 300–302, 305–6,
        309–12
    Yom Kippur War in, 197, 201–7
Middleton, Drew, 274–75
Miers, Harriet, 424
military. *See also* Defense Department; Joint
        Chiefs of Staff (JCS); Pentagon
    all-volunteer, 61
    George W. Bush and, 372
    Fritz Kraemer on, 24, 28–29, 364
    John McCain and, 427
    neoconservative movement and, 3–7, 272,
        342–44, 430
    Richard Perle on, 360
    Ronald Reagan and, 288–89, 295–96
    Soviet spending on, 332–33
    White House spy ring of (*see* Moorer-Rad-
        ford spy ring)
    Bob Woodward's sources in, 296–97
Miller, Judith, 396, 413
Milosevic, Slobodan, 347, 353–54
MIRVs (Multiple Independently Targetable
        Reentry Vehicles), 49–51, 74, 80, 143–44,
        206–7, 240
missile defense systems, 38, 366, 369. *See also*
        Safeguard anti-missile system; Strategic
        Defense Initiative (SDI)
Mitchell, George, 347, 433
Mitchell, John, 21, 46, 79, 101, 124–28, 142,
        166–68, 178, 201
Mitterrand, François, 312, 321
Mondale, Walter, 314
Moore, Robert A., 166–67
Moorer, Thomas, 54–55, 70, 73, 76, 79–82, 87,
        97, 136–39, 144, 160, 211–13, 297
Moorer-Radford spy ring
    articles about, 210–15
    creation of, by Thomas Moorer and Elmo
        Zumwalt, 79–82
    John Dean and, 170
    Alexander Haig and, 92–93, 101–2, 175,
        192, 199–200, 207
    leak to Jack Anderson and Nixon adminis-
        tration discovery of, 120–31
    Richard Nixon's tapes and, 224, 235
    Rembrandt Robinson, Robert Welander,
        and, 57
moral absolutism, 24, 29, 31, 195, 221, 244,
        272–73, 352

moral relativism, 29, 61–62, 138–39, 394
Morgenthau, Hans, 13
Morris, Roger, 63, 75–76, 171, 326
Most Favored Nation (MFN) trade status, 98,
        159–60, 187, 231–32, 241–42, 329
Moyers, Bill, 396
Moynihan, Daniel Patrick, 216–17, 249–50,
        313, 349, 365
MRVs (Multiple Reentry Vehicles), 49–51,
        143–44
Mueller, Robert, 380
Mughniyah, Imad Fayez, 310
mujahideen guerrillas, 296, 316
Muravchik, Johsua, 272–73, 286, 352–54
Musharraf, Pervez, 365, 371, 386, 421
Muskie, Edmund, 118, 133, 289
Muslims
    Bosnian, 346–47, 353–54
    Iraqi, 336
    Islamist militants, 5, 365 (*see also* al-Qaeda;
        terrorism)
    Barack Obama and, 433
mutual assured destruction (MAD), 206
MX cruise missiles, 278, 307, 331

National Interest, 314–15
National Security Agency (NSA), 379–80
National Security Council (NSC)
    George W. Bush and, 377–78
    Cambodian incursion and, 74–78
    Alexander Haig and, 294–95
    Iran-Contra operation and, 319–25
    leaks and, 46–47
    Moorer-Radford spy ring and (*see* Moorer-
        Radford spy ring)
    Richard Nixon and, 18–20, 22
    Oliver North and, 312–13, 317
    Ronald Reagan and, 301
    Donald Rumsfeld and, 258–59
    Vietnam War and, 70–71
    warnings about al-Qaeda from, 383–84
national security issue, 166, 182–84,
        211–14
NATO (North Atlantic Treaty Organization),
        235–37, 282–83, 369, 385–86, 391, 397,
        399, 421
Negroponte, John, 313
neoconservative movement
    birth of, 158–61
    birthplaces of, 196
    George H. W. Bush administration and (*see*
        Bush, George H. W.)
    George W. Bush administration and (*see*
        Bush, George W.)

neoconservative movement (*continued*)
Carter administration and, 272–90 (*see also* Carter, Jimmy)
Center for Security Policy of, 322
Clinton administration and, 359–71 (*see also* Clinton, William Jefferson "Bill")
Committee on the Present Danger (CPD) of, 264–65
conservatives vs., 158–59, 342–44, 352, 429–30 (*see also* conservatives; Republican Party)
core beliefs of, 272–73
discrediting of, 417–20
fall of the Soviet Union and, 331–34
Ford administration and (*see* Ford, Gerald R.)
foreign policy overmilitarization by, 415–16
Iran-Contra operation as first foreign-policy operation, 314, 317
Fritz Kraemer and, 23–31 (*see also* Kraemer, Fritz G. A.)
Madison Group of, 283–84
National Interest journal of, 314–15
Nixon administration and (*see* Nixon, Richard M.)
Barack Obama's election and decline of, 427–34
Reagan administration and, 293–325 (*see also* Reagan, Ronald)
Donald Rumfeld's retirement as fall of, 1–7 (*see also* Rumsfeld, Donald H.)
Nessen, Ron, 253
New Orleans, George W. Bush and, 415
news media, 27, 391, 396. *See also* leaks
Nicaragua, 300, 313–14, 319–25
Niger uranium story, 396, 399–401, 404
Nitze, Paul
Arms Control and Disarmament Agency (ACDA) and, 144, 160–61, 196
arms control negotiations of, 73–74, 301, 309
Committee on the Present Danger (CPD) and, 264–65
fight over Paul Warnke by, 276–77
Scoop Jackson and, 49–50
Richard Nixon and, 135, 217
Reagan administration and, 294, 317–19
resignation of, 219
Donald Rumsfeld and, 243
Nixon, Richard M., 13–224
abandonment of, by conservatives, 216–17
Spiro Agnew and, 197–98

alienation of allies by, 107–19
alteration of files of, 215
arms control negotiations of, with Soviet Union, 36–37 (*see also* arms control)
Cabinet of, 201–4
Cambodian incursion and SALT negotiations by, 72–83
China rapprochement by, 98–103, 134–35
conservatives and, 48–58
continuation of policies of, by Jimmy Carter, 280–82
domestic policy of, 51–54
executive privilege issue and, 185
foreign policies of, 13–22, 69–71, 132–45
Alexander Haig and, 146–49, 172, 294
intelligence estimates and, 38–39
international communism and, 84–90
Scoop Jackson and, 118–19
Joint Chiefs of Staff and, 70
Henry Kissinger/Alexander Haig interplay and, 38–40, 57–58 (*see also* Haig, Alexander M., Jr.; Kissinger, Henry A.)
Fritz Kraemer and, 4–5, 66–68, 117–18, 146–57, 193–96, 256
Laos incursion and, 92–95
lawyer for (*see* Buzhardt, J. Fred)
leaks, wiretaps, and, 46–47
malfeasance investigations of, 420–21
Moorer-Radford spy ring and (*see* Moorer-Radford spy ring)
neoconservative movement and, 5, 158–61, 193–209
Nixon Doctrine of, 59–62, 67, 96–98
North Korea, EC-121 incident, and, 42–45
opposition of, to Ronald Reagan's INF treaty, 321
pardon of, by Gerald Ford, 234–37
political campaigns of, 133–34, 139
resignation of, 216–24
Donald Rumsfeld and, 2–5
Safeguard anti-missile system and, 48–51
secrecy and deception of, 32–47
Silent Majority speech of, 68–69
Vietnam War and, 59–71, 90–92, 168–70
Watergate affair and, 139–43, 161–72
wiretaps of, 200–201
Nobel Peace Prize, Henry Kissinger's, 146, 206
no-bid contracts, 409, 421
no-fly zone, Iraqi, 348, 350, 355
Nol, Lon, 74–75, 78, 155
Noriega, Manuel, 334–35

North, Oliver, 304, 312–14, 317, 320, 323–24
North American Free Trade Agreement (NAFTA), 351
North Korea, 42–45, 354, 391–92, 395, 403–4, 424
North Vietnam, 47, 60, 89–90, 108, 136–37, 144–45, 155, 162–63, 168–69, 196, 244–47, 365–66, 379. *See also* Vietnam War
Novak, Robert, 233, 258, 261–63, 268, 279, 404
nuclear weapons. *See also* arms control; weapons of mass destruction (WMDs) issue
  Cienfuegos submarine base crisis and, 84–86
  DEFCON alerts and, 40, 64–66, 205–6, 310–11
  Alexander Haig on using, 300
  Henry Kissinger on using, 44
  India, Pakistan, and, 364–65
  Iran and, 416, 424, 433–34
  Iraq and, 392
  new technology and, 279–80
  Safeguard anti-ballistic missile system, 41, 48–51
  Vietnam War and tactical, 63
Nunn, Sam, 339

Obama, Barack
  election of, 7, 431
  foreign policy goals of, 432
  as foreign policy pragmatist, 428, 434
  presidential campaign of, 420, 427
O'Brien, Larry, 140
Odeen, Philip, 138–39
Odom, William, 414–15
Office of Economic Opportunity (OEO), 52–54, 111
Office of Net Assessment (ONA), 97, 195, 239, 258, 279, 373–74
oil-for-food program, 382–83
O'Neill, Paul, 376–78
Option E controversy, 79–82

Packard, David, 38, 121, 178, 264
Pahlavi, Shah Reza, 61, 281, 285
Pakistan, 99–103, 108, 120–23, 343, 364–65, 371, 377, 386, 421
paleocons vs. neocons, 352
Palestine Liberation Organization (PLO), 87, 281

Palestinians, 336, 351, 379
Palmer, Bruce, 92–93, 147
Panama
  invasion of, 334–35
  Panama Canal issue, 252, 262–63, 280, 298–99, 334–35
pardons
  of Iran-Contra operatives, 347
  of Richard Nixon, 222–23, 234–37
Paris Peace Accord of 1973, 16–17, 35, 73, 77, 89–90, 102, 108, 144–48, 154–58, 162, 196
Parmet, Herbert, 290, 334
PATRIOT Act, 389–91
Pentagon. *See also* Defense Department; Joint Chiefs of Staff (JCS); military
  J. Fred Buzhardt at, 56
  Cambodian incursion and, 75
  Daniel Ellsberg and, 20
  Fritz Kraemer at, 26, 30, 278–80
  Andrew Marshall at, 362
  Moorer-Radford spy ring and (*see* Moorer-Radford spy ring)
  Office of Net Assessment (ONA) (*see* Office of Net Assessment (ONA))
  Pentagon Papers and, 100–101
  Reagan administration budget for, 295–96
  Donald Rumsfeld and, 256–59
  September 11, 2001, terrorist attack on, 384–88
  Bob Woodward at, 54–56
Pentagon Papers, 100–101, 170–71, 214
People's Republic of China. *See* China
Percy, Charles, 316
perestroika initiative, 326
"Perfect Storm" memo, 398
Perle, Richard
  arms control and, 143–44, 187, 221, 258, 276–77, 301, 309, 317–18, 345–46
  George W. Bush and, 368, 376, 429
  "Clean Break" paper by, for Israel, 360
  Defense Planning Guidance (DPG) report and, 342
  Alexander Haig and, 300
  Iraq War and, 387, 408
  on Scoop Jackson, 112
  Henry Kissinger and, 202
  Fritz Kraemer and, 4
  leaks by, 113–14, 278–79, 290
  Madison Group and, 283–84
  National Interest and, 314
  neoconservative movement and, 159, 196, 231

Perle, Richard (*continued*)
    Nixon administration and, 5, 48–51
    Project for a New American Century and,
        362–63
    Reagan administration and, 293–94, 304
    resignation of, 320–22
    Scowcroft Commission report and, 308
Perot, H. Ross, 346, 355
Pershing II missiles, 283, 311
Persian Gulf, Carter Doctrine and, 287–90.
    See also Gulf War
Peterson, Henry, 199–200
Petraeus, David, 417, 420, 423
Philippines, 96, 316
Phillips, Howard, 217, 260
Phillips, Kevin, 260
Phouma, Souvanna, 151
Pillsbury, Michael, 278, 283, 294, 327
Pincus, Walter, 236
Pipes, Richard, 265, 293–94
Plame, Valerie, 404, 413
Plumbers group, 112–17, 184–85, 208,
    214–15
Podhoretz, Norman, 159, 285, 299, 309,
    360–62
Poindexter, John, 304, 314, 317, 320, 323
Policy Counter Terrorism Evaluation Group
    (PCTEG), 388–89
political campaigns
    George H. W. Bush's, 326–28, 345–49
    Bill Clinton's, 355
    Gerald Ford's, 260–71
    Richard Nixon's, 133–34, 139, 153–54
    Ronald Reagan's, 314
Powell, Colin, 315, 320, 335–38, 341, 373,
    376–81, 389, 392, 399–400, 410, 431
Powers, Sam, 209
pragmatism
    George H. W. Bush's, 344
    Bill Clinton's, 345, 351–52, 371
    idealism vs., 4–7, 84, 385, 427
    Henry Kissinger's, 42, 70, 90, 97, 250
    Richard Nixon's, 32, 61, 84, 169
    Barack Obama's, 428, 432, 434
preemptive war issue, 363–64, 378, 388,
    392–94, 430–31. *See also* unilateral
    action
presidential power issue, 200, 231, 238, 268,
    274, 306, 323–25, 339, 379, 390–91,
    411–12, 420
prisoners-of-war (POWs) issue, 162, 168–69
prisoner torture issue, 395–96, 407–9, 413–14,
    424–25, 433
Pritchard, Charles "Jack," 404

Project for a New American Century, 362–64,
    368, 374–76
provocative weakness, 3–5, 26, 28, 43–47,
    68–69, 152, 352, 372, 376, 401
Pursley, Robert, 46, 64
Putin, Vladimir, 421–22

Qaddafi, Moammar, 299, 312, 317, 403. *See
    also* Libya
Quayle, Dan, 328, 340, 362, 369

Radford, Charles, 81–82, 92–93, 101–2,
    123–29, 213. *See also* Moorer-Radford
    spy ring
RAND Corporation, 20, 38–39, 100–101,
    160
Rather, Dan, 326
Reagan, Ronald, 293–325
    Dick Allen and foreign policy discussions
        with, 277
    anti-Soviet policies of, 304–12
    attacks of, on Gerald Ford, 253, 257
    Cabinet of, 293–98
    campaign to draft, 203, 233, 239
    continuation of previous administration
        foreign policies by, 298–303
    fall of the Soviet Union and, 326–28,
        331–34
    fostering of democracy by, 315–17
    Grenada invasion by, 310
    Iran-Contra operation and, 313–14,
        319–25
    Madison Group and, 284
    negotiations of, with Soviet Union, 317–19
    neoconservatives and, 5–6, 252, 285–90,
        325, 360–63
    Richard Nixon's China rapprochement and,
        108–9
    political campaigns of, 260–70
    Donald Rumsfeld and, 312–13
    sending of troops into Lebanon by, 305–6
    on Taiwan, 118
    Weinberger Doctrine and, 314–15
realism. *See* pragmatism
regime change issue, 338–40, 360, 363–64,
    367, 373–74. *See also* Iraq War
Republican Party. *See also* conservatives;
    neoconservative movement
    George H. W. Bush and, 346
    George W. Bush and, 368, 374–75
    Jimmy Carter and, 283
    Christian right and, 410
    control of Congress by, 354, 399
    endorsements of Barack Obama from, 431

losses of, during Clinton Administration, 367–68
Richard Nixon and, 15, 223
Ronald Reagan and, 260–70, 320
Nelson Rockefeller and, 233
Donald Rumsfeld's retirement and, 1–2
Vietnamization policy and, 60
Reston, James, 242, 255, 276–77
Rhodes, John, 223–24
Rhodes, Richard, 319
Ribicoff, Abraham, 232
Rice, Condoleezza, 368, 377, 383–84, 392, 398, 410, 418
Rice, Susan E., 432
Richardson, Elliot, 172, 199–200, 203–4
Ricks, Thomas, 2
Robinson, Rembrandt, 57, 62, 81, 101, 125
Rockefeller, Nelson, 16, 66, 233, 243, 247, 253–54, 266, 269
Rodman, Peter, 242, 427
Rogers, William P., 21, 37–38, 44, 64, 75–77, 88
Romney, George, 77
Romney, Mitt, 7
Rose, David, 429
Rosenfeld, Harry, 55–56
Ross, Dennis, 284–85
Rostow, Eugene, 294
Rove, Karl, 396, 413
Rowny, Edward L.
    arms control and, 144, 160, 196, 221, 241, 258, 309, 318–22, 327
    on détente, 252
    fall of the Soviet Union and, 330
    Scoop Jackson and, 49
    Fritz Kraemer and, 4, 27–28, 30, 193, 405
    Madison Group and, 283–84
    neoconservative movement and, 196
    preemptive war and, 364
    Ronald Reagan and, 294
    retirement of, 341–42
Rubin, Robert, 375
Ruckleshaus, William, 204
Rudd, Kevin, 421
Rumsfeld, Donald H.
    ambition of, 242–43
    arms control and, 307–8, 365–66
    George H. W. Bush and, 329
    George W. Bush and, 368, 376, 381
    defense budget of, 273–74, 349
    Bob Dole and, 355
    Gerald Ford and, 230–31, 237–38, 254–59
    Foreign Intelligence Surveillance Act (FISA) and, 280

Saddam Hussein and, 336
Iraq War and, 382, 387–89
Fritz Kraemer and, 4, 258, 401
Mayaguez incident and, 247–48
on negative consequences of Iraq War, 398
neoconservative movement and, 231
Richard Nixon and, 5, 52–54, 111–12
Project for a New American Century and, 362–63
Ronald Reagan and, 312–13
retirement of, as end of neoconservative power, 1–7, 414, 417
Nelson Rockefeller and, 266, 269
undermining of Gerald Ford's foreign policies by, 238–42, 263–64
War Powers Act and, 200
Watergate affair and, 161
Russia, 341–42, 368, 374, 378, 421–22. See also Soviet Union
Rwanda, 353, 370

Sadat, Anwar, 281, 300
Safeguard anti-missile system, 41, 48–49, 259, 366
Safire, William, 56, 113, 288, 293, 366, 396
St. Claire, James, 211, 222–23
Sakharov, Andrei, 138, 333
Sanders, Don, 189
Sandinistas, 300, 313–14. See also Iran-Contra operation
Saturday Night Massacre, 197, 201–4
Saudi Arabia, 281, 337–39, 348, 354
Savage, Charlie, 390–91, 413
Scalia, Antonin, 238, 306, 380
Scheunemann, Randy, 427
Schlesinger, James
    arms control and, 219–21, 241
    CIA and, 160–61, 179–80
    at Defense Department, 178, 224
    on détente, 252–53
    at Energy Department, 277
    Gerald Ford and, 217, 230, 232, 254–57
    on fostering democracy, 315
    Fritz Kraemer and, 4, 194–95, 244, 405
    Mayaguez freighter incident and, 247–48
    Moorer-Radford spy ring and, 212
    Office of Net Assessment (ONA) and, 97
    on Panama Canal issue, 252
    on post–Cold War geopolitics, 348–49
    Donald Rumsfeld and, 238–39, 243
    Schlesinger Doctrine of, 206–7, 280
    Aleksandr Solzhenitsyn and, 249–50
Schwarzkopf, Norman, 338

Schweiker, Richard, 269
science, George W. Bush and, 413
Scott, Hugh, 224
Scowcroft, Brent, 201, 254, 258–59, 307–8, 328–31, 337, 340, 343, 368, 397–98, 431
Sears, John, 252
Secord, Richard, 304, 320
secrecy, Richard Nixon's, 32–47, 54, 134–35
Secret Service, 191
Segretti, Donald, 135, 164–67
Senate. *See* Congress
Sentinel antiballistic missile, 38, 307–8
September 11, 2001, terrorist attack, 5–6, 383–88
Serbian ethnic-cleansing campaign, 346–54, 367–70, 375, 379
sexual issues, 129, 135
Shackley, Theodore, 304
Shafer, Jack, 298
Shanghai Communiqué, 134–35
Sharif, Nawaz, 364–65
Shevardnadze, Eduard, 318, 337
Shiite Muslims, 336, 405, 416–18
Shinseki, Eric, 376, 392, 400
Shirley, Craig, 260
Shultz, George P., 77, 191, 264, 300–302, 305, 315–21
signing statements, George W. Bush's, 380, 413
Sihanouk, Norodom, 74
Silent Majority speech, Richard Nixon's, 68–69
Silverstein, Ken, 279
Simon, William, 242–43, 255
Singlaub, John, 304, 317, 320
Single Strategic Theater memo, 66–68
Sirica, John, 162, 170, 199, 208, 211, 219
slush fund investigation, 161–62
Smith, Gerard, 38, 74, 97, 144
smoking gun/mushroom cloud terminology, 396–98
Solzhenitsyn, Aleksandr, 138, 249–50, 262, 286, 333
Somalia, 347, 350–52, 370
Sonnenfeldt, Helmut "Hal," 22, 57, 263, 364
Sorley, Lewis, 92
South America, 67, 296, 351
South Korea, 96
South Vietnam. *See* Vietnam War
Soviet Union
  Afghanistan invasion by, 287
  Afghanistan withdrawal by, 327
  arms control negotiations with (*see* arms control)

Jimmy Carter and, 275–78, 283
Cienfuegos submarine base crisis and, 85–86
Bill Clinton and, 366
détente with, 5, 13–15, 96–98, 144–45, 216–17, 252–53
fall of, 326, 330–34, 341–42
feigned DEFCON alert and, 63–66
Alexander Haig and, 299–300
India and, 108, 121
intelligence estimates of (*see* intelligence estimates)
Lyndon Johnson on, 19–20
Jeane Kirkpatrick on, 285–86
Henry Kissinger and, 252–53, 274–75
Fritz Kraemer on, 28–29, 149
military spending of, 332–33
Most Favored Nation (MFN) trade status and, 98, 159–60, 231–32, 241–42
neoconservatives and, 286
Richard Nixon and, 5, 13–15, 33, 144–45
Ronald Reagan and, 261–64, 269, 296, 305–6, 318–19, 326–28
relations of China and, 18, 62, 83, 99, 108, 134–35, 282
Donald Rumsfeld and, 258–59, 273–74
Syrian invasion of Jordan and, 87–88
Vietnam War negotiations with, 59–71, 89–90
Yom Kippur War and, 202–7
Speakes, Larry, 295
spy ring. *See* Moorer-Radford spy ring
Squires, James, 210
Stans, Maurice, 142, 178
Star Wars. *See* Strategic Defense Initiative (SDI)
State Department
  Cambodian incursion and, 75–77
  China and, 37–38
  Hillary Clinton at, 432–33
  Alexander Haig at, 294–96
  Henry Kissinger at, 194–95, 200–201
  Richard Nixon and, 19–21
  Vietnam War and, 37–38
Steiger, Bill, 53
Stennis, John, 50–51, 97, 178–79, 203–4, 212–14
Stewart, Don, 56, 101, 113–14, 123–30, 199–200, 211–13
Stinger missiles, 316
Strachan, Gordon, 164–67, 186
Strategic Arms Limitation Talks (SALT I and SALT II), 36–37, 70, 73–74, 77–83, 108, 113–14, 137–39, 143–44, 160, 187, 207,

219–21, 241, 258–59, 263–64, 277–78, 283–84, 287, 305–6, 318
Strategic Arms Reduction Treaties (START I and Start II), 307–8, 311, 320, 341, 345–47, 379
Strategic Defense Initiative (SDI), 296, 307, 319, 366
Strauss, Leo, 26
Strickler, Frank, 224
submarine base crisis, 84–86
submarine-launched ballistic missiles (SLBMs), 97, 113–14, 138
Sudan, 338, 367
Sullivan, David S., 279, 290, 327
Sullivan, William, 79
Sulzberger, C. L., 85
Sunni Muslims, 336, 394–95, 405, 418
Supreme Court, 221, 376, 413–14
surveillance, 280, 379–80, 390–91
Suskind, Ron, 378
Syria, 6, 87–89, 202–7, 431

Taiwan, 96, 99, 108–10, 117–18, 134–35, 282, 299, 355, 374–75, 381
Talbott, Strobe, 333
Taliban, 377, 386, 421
tapes, prisoner interrogation, 424–25
taping system, Richard Nixon's, 177–92, 198–99, 203, 207–8, 211, 218–24, 230, 234–35, 294–95
Tavoulareas, William and Peter, 297–98
tax cuts, George W. Bush's, 377
Team B, 265, 275–77, 288–89, 293–94. See also Committee on the Present Danger (CPD)
Tehran embassy hostage crisis, 285, 289
Tenet, George, 380, 383–84, 388–89, 398–400, 409
terHorst, Jerry, 235
terrorism
    al-Qaeda and (see al-Qaeda; Islamist militants)
    bombing of embassies in Kenya and Tanzania, 367
    global war on, 5, 385–86, 391–92, 412–13
    Iraq War and, 397–98
    Islamic, 311–12
    Khobar Towers bombing, 354
    in Lebanon, 309–10
    neoconservatives and, 383–84
    September 11, 2001, terrorist attack, 5–6, 383–88
    Tehran embassy hostage crisis, 285, 289
    USS Cole bombing, 377
    World Trade Center bombing, 350–51

testing, nuclear, 353, 364–65
Thailand, 75, 96
Thatcher, Margaret, 301–2, 310, 337
Thieu, Nguyen Van, 17, 92–94, 118–19, 147–48, 153–57
Thimmesch, Nick, 27, 30, 148, 201, 233, 244, 256
Thomasson, Dan, 210
Thompson, Fred, 186–90
Thompson, W. Scott, 287
Thurmond, Strom, 18, 50–51, 278
Tomahawk missiles, 241
torture issue. See prisoner torture issue
totalitarian dictatorships, 28–29, 62, 80, 149–50
"Toward a Neo-Reaganite Foreign Policy" article, 360–62
Tower, John, 18, 111, 278, 328–29
Truman Doctrine, 13
Tufaro, Richard, 199
Tyler, Patrick E., 296–98
tyrannical governments, 316

Ulasewicz, Tony, 168
unilateral action, 343–44, 349, 352–53, 378, 397. See also preemptive war issue
Union of Soviet Socialist Republics (USSR). See Soviet Union
unitary executive theory, 238, 306, 380, 390, 413. See also presidential power issue
United Nations
    George H. W. Bush at, 122
    CIA operations in Nicaragua and, 313–14
    dual recognition of Taiwan and China by, 99, 117–18
    Iraq War and, 397
    Fritz Kraemer on, 4
    Colin Powell's argument to, for Iraq War, 400
United States
    Central Intelligence Agency (see Central Intelligence Agency [CIA])
    Congress (see Congress)
    Defense Department (see Defense Department; military; Pentagon)
    Federal Bureau of Investigation (FBI) (see Federal Bureau of Investigation [FBI])
    September 11, 2001, terrorist attack on, 5–6, 383–88
    State Department (see State Department)
Uniting and Strengthening America by Providing Appropriate Tools Required to Intercept and Obstruct Terrorism Act (USA PATRIOT Act), 389–91
USS Cole bombing, 377

Vance, Cyrus, 277, 280–83
Van Cleave, William, 113–14, 265, 275, 288, 293–96
Vietnam War
  antiwar movement, 47–48, 59–60, 63–65, 68–69, 77–78, 100–101, 243–44
  China rapprochement and, 103
  Congressional limitation of appropriations for, 90–92
  draft-dodger amnesty issue, 224, 233, 277–78
  Duck Hook offensive, 62–64
  fall of South Vietnam, 244–47
  Alexander Haig and, 70–71
  Scoop Jackson and, 118–19
  Fritz Kraemer on, 28, 31, 108, 149–53, 156–57
  Lam Son 719 campaign, 92–95
  Linebacker bombing operations, 136–37, 155–56
  Richard Nixon and, 4–5, 13–18, 32–36, 40, 68–69, 72–79, 132–33
  Nixon Doctrine and, 59–62
  North Vietnam's violation of peace accords, 162–63, 168–69
  Paris Peace Accord for (see Paris Peace Accord of 1973)
  Pentagon Papers and, 100–101
  Donald Rumsfeld on, 111–12
  Soviet Union negotiations on, 36–37, 89–90
  troop withdrawals from, 82, 89–92
  Vietnamization policy, 40–42, 60, 71–73, 94
Viguerie, Richard, 233, 260, 415

Walker, Martin, 333
Wallace, George, 17–18, 133, 135, 139
Walt, Stephen M., 370
Walters, Vernon A. "Dick"
  at Central Intelligence Agency, 4, 178
  Chile and, 86
  fall of the Soviet Union and, 330
  Gerald Ford and, 232
  Fritz Kraemer and, 4, 28, 35, 193, 244
  on military action and Libya, 312
  Richard Nixon and, 73
  preemptive war issue and, 364
  retirement of, 341
  Watergate affair and, 142, 161, 179–82, 218–19
Warnke, Paul, 276–78
War Powers Act, 200, 247, 324, 390

Washington Special Actions Group (WSAG), 121–22, 205
Watergate affair, 139–43, 161–68, 170–72, 218–19
Wattenberg, Ben, 159
Watts, William, 75–76
weakness. See provocative weakness
weapons of mass destruction (WMDs) issue, 363–64, 369–70, 373, 387–89, 395, 399–401, 403. See also nuclear weapons
Webb, James, 396–97
Weinberger, Caspar, 294–95, 300, 304, 315, 322, 338, 347, 364
Weinberger Doctrine, 315
Weinberger-Powell Doctrine, 338
Weinraub, Bernard, 280–81
Weisman, Alan, 321
Weiss, Seymour, 265, 294
Welander, Robert, 54, 57, 81–82, 92–93, 101–2, 200, 211–13. See also Moorer-Radford spy ring
Westerfield, H. Bradford, 53
West Germany. See Germany
Westmoreland, William, 34, 147
West Pakistan. See Pakistan
Weyrich, Paul, 260, 321
Whalen, Richard, 15
Wheeler, Earle "Bus," 34–35, 40, 65, 73
White, Thomas, 392
Whitehouse, Sheldon, 420
White House taping system. See taping system, Richard Nixon's
Whiting, Allen, 62, 171
Wilkerson, Lawrence B., 381
Williams, Edward Bennett, 176
Wills, Garry, 331–32
Wilson, Joseph C., IV, 400, 404
Wilson, Peter, 50
wiretaps
  Federal Bureau of Investigation (FBI) and, 163
  Foreign Intelligence Surveillance Act (FISA) and, 267–68, 280
  Alexander Haig and, 183–85, 200–201, 215, 221, 236, 294–95
  Henry Kissinger and, 183–85, 200–201
  Richard Nixon and, 46–47, 78–79, 115
  PATRIOT Act and, 390–91
  Watergate affair and, 170–72, 179
Wohlstetter, Albert, 26, 49–50, 97, 160, 219–20, 232, 265, 317–18, 342, 353–54
Wohlstetter, Roberta, 317–18, 366

Wolfowitz, Paul D.
  arms control and, 144, 221, 241, 258, 431
  George W. Bush and, 368, 376
  Dick Cheney and, 329
  on Bill Clinton, 351–55
  on end of Cold War, 342–44
  on fostering democracy, 316
  Gulf War and, 339–40
  intelligence estimates and, 365
  Iraq War and, 382, 387, 398, 401
  Israel and, 360
  Henry Kissinger and, 202
  Fritz Kraemer and, 4
  leaked report by, 284–85, 288
  neoconservative movement and, 196, 231
  Nixon administration and, 5, 50–51
  at Pentagon, 274
  Project for a New American Century and,
    362–63
  Ronald Reagan and, 294, 304
  Donald Rumsfeld's retirement and, 3–4
  Team B and, 265, 275–76
  triangular relationship report of, 299–300
  World Bank improprieties of, 419
Woods, Rose Mary, 175–76, 208–9, 218
Woodward, Robert "Bob"
  books by, 208, 267, 297, 322–23, 341, 399,
    407–8

  embarrassment of, 297–98
  Alexander Haig and, 294–95, 301–2
  Max Hugel story and military sources of,
    296–97
  Moorer-Radford spy ring and, 211–13
  as Pentagon briefer, 54–56
  Valerie Plame case and, 413
  Watergate affair and, 140, 161–62, 184,
    190, 217
Woolsey, James, 363–65, 427
World Court, 313–14
World Trade Center, 5–6, 350–51,
  385–88

Yeltsin, Boris, 341, 345
Yom Kippur War, 201–7
Yoo, John, 390
Young, David, 101, 112–17, 123–29, 199–200,
  212, 235
Young Americans for Freedom (YAF), 69,
  94–95, 252
Yugoslavia, former. See Serbian ethnic
  cleansing campaign

Zhou En-Lai, 63–64, 98–103, 134–35
Ziegler, Ron, 167–69, 183, 234–35
Zumwalt, Elmo "Bud," 4, 73–74, 79–82, 90,
  93, 121–22, 144, 202–3, 264